Northwestern University
STUDIES IN *Phenomenology &*
Existential Philosophy

Genesis and Structure
of Hegel's *Phenomenology of Spirit*

Jean Hyppolite

Translated by

Genesis and Structure of Hegel's *Phenomenology of Spirit*

SAMUEL CHERNIAK
and JOHN HECKMAN

NORTHWESTERN UNIVERSITY PRESS

EVANSTON   1974

Originally published in French under the title *Genèse et structure de la Phénoménologie de l'esprit de Hegel* by Aubier, Editions Montaigne, Paris, copyright 1946 by Editions Montaigne.

John Heckman teaches at the New School for Social Research; Samuel Cherniak is Assistant Professor of Comparative Literature at Queen's College, CUNY.

Contents

[ix]

x / CONTENTS

Translators' Preface

THE PROBLEM of any translation arises from the divergence between the most common signification of the semantic and other linguistic elements of a given text and the author's specific use of these elements. This problem takes on a particular twist in the case of translations of Hegel. As Alexandre Koyré pointed out more than forty years ago in his excellent essay on Hegel's terminology (and the possibility of translating it), Hegel revolted against the overly technical and abstract terminology that prevailed in contemporary German philosophical writing.[1] He often used words taken from ordinary language, attempting to restrict them to more specific, technical signification. Thus the signification of ordinary words as Hegel uses them does not fully coincide with the ordinary signification of these words. Consequently—and ironically—Hegel has been thought to have not only a highly technical but also a highly abstract vocabulary. For the most part translations of Hegel have compounded this irony, for in dealing with the divergence between the ordinary signification of Hegel's words and what is understood to be Hegel's meaning, translators have often been led to preserve the specificity of Hegel's meaning by using special terms. For example, *Wirklichkeit*, which ordinarily means simply "reality," is translated by Hyppolite as *actualité* and by Baillie as "actual reality"; *Einsicht*, which ordinarily means "insight," is translated by Hyppolite as *intellection*. Hence, too, neologisms such as Hyppolite's *extranéation* and archaisms

1. "Note sur la langue et la terminologie hégéliennes," *Revue philosophique* (1931), reprinted in *Etudes d'histoire de la pensée philosophique* (Paris, 1961), pp. 175–204.

[xi]

like Baillie's "diremption." The danger arises of a text cut off from the ordinary language that Hegel, in fact, deliberately used.

Since Hyppolite's book is a close commentary on Hegel, the semantic problems involved in translating the *Phenomenology* are also the problems of translating Hyppolite. An additional difficulty arises from the fact that Hyppolite's commentary is in French and is thus throughout—and not merely in its quotations from Hegel—a translation as well as a commentary. We have sought to present a readable text which adequately reproduces Hyppolite's meaning and the terminology of which is consonant both with accepted translations of Hegel and with the rigor of Hegel's work. In particular, the reader should note that "is" frequently appears in a strong usage. We have also tried to reserve the expressions "in-itself" and "for-itself" for technical usage; hence occasional awkwardness. We have provided a glossary giving the major terms used by Hyppolite, the German words of which these are the translation, and our translations.

Hyppolite quotes Hegel in the standard French translations, which in the case of the *Phenomenology* is his own published translation. Thus, when he quotes from the *Phenomenology*, he is able to maintain a unified vocabulary. But Hyppolite's translation (and his method of quoting) is in places interpretive or tendentious; and Baillie's English translation (the only one available at present) is poor and almost impossible to read. We have, therefore, checked quotations from the *Phenomenology* against the original German text. In the case of significant omissions or changes on Hyppolite's part we have translated Hegel's text in brackets; Hyppolite's interpolations have been placed in parentheses. Quotations from the *Phenomenology* are followed by references to Hyppolite's translation, to Hegel's original, and to the page of Baillie's translation on which the passage is translated. We have followed a similar procedure in translating quotations from the *Philosophy of History*. For all other quotations from Hegel we have cited an English translation when available and otherwise translated directly from the German original. A list of Hegel's works cited is on p. xiii.

We wish publicly to thank Mary O'Connell, formerly of Northwestern University Press, for her excellent editorial help, her patience, and her unfailing good humor.

S. C., Queens College, CUNY
J. H., The New School

List of Hegel's Works Cited

Except where indicated, all works by Hegel are taken from the edition by Georg Lasson and Johannes Hoffmeister, *Sämtliche Werke (SW)* (Leipzig and Hamburg: Meiner Verlag, 1905–   ). The titles are followed, where appropriate, by the short references by which they are abbreviated in the text.

"Differenz des Fichteschen und Schellingschen Systems der Philosophie," in *Erste Druckschriften,* SW, I, 1–113 ("Differenz").

Encyclopädie der philosophischen Wissenschaften, SW, V, VI. English translation by Gustav E. Müller, *The Encyclopaedia of Philosophical Sciences* (New York, 1959) (*Encyclopaedia*).

"Geistesphilosophie" (1805–6), in *Jenenser Realphilosophie* 177–253 ("Philosophy of Spirit," no. 2).

Geschichte der Philosophie, SW, XV, XVI, XVII. English translation by E. S. Haldane and Frances H. Simson, *Lectures on the History of Philosophy,* 3 vols. (New York, 1963).

"Glauben und Wissen oder die Reflexionsphilosophie der Subjektivität," in *Erste Druckschriften,* SW, I, 221–346 ("Glauben und Wissen").

Grundlinien der Philosophie des Rechts, SW, VI. English translation by T. M. Knox, *The Philosophy of Right* (Oxford, 1952).

Jenenser Logik, Metaphysik, und Naturphilosophie, SW, XVIIIa (Jena *Logic*).

Jenenser Realphilosophie, SW, XX, no. 2 (Jena *Realphilosophie*).

Phänomenologie des Geistes, SW, II (*PG*). French translation by Jean Hyppolite, *Phénoménologie de l'esprit* (Paris: vol. I,

[xiii]

1939; vol. II, 1941) (*PE*). English translation by J. Baillie, *Phenomenology of Mind* (London, 1909) (*PM*).

"Philosophie des Geistes" (1803–4), in *SW*, XX, no. 1, 193–241 ("Philosophy of Spirit," no. 1).

Propaedeutic, *SW*, XXI.

Realphilosophie, *SW*, XIX.

"System der Sittlichkeit," in *Schriften zur Politik und Rechtsphilosophie*, *SW*, VII, 1–154.

"Systemfragment," in *Theologische Jugendschriften*.

Theologische Jugendschriften, ed. Herman Nohl (Tübingen, 1907). English translation by T. M. Knox, *Early Theological Writings* (Chicago, 1948). Note: Not all texts in the German edition are contained in the translation; references to the German title indicate works found only in that edition.

"Über die wissenschaftliche Behandlungsarten des Naturrechts," in *Schriften zur Politik und Rechtsphilosophie*, *SW*, VII, 327–411 ("Naturrecht").

"Die Verfassung Deutschlands," in *Schriften zur Politik und Rechtsphilosophie*, *SW*, VII, 1–154.

"Verhältnis des Skeptizismus zur Philosophie," in *Erste Druckschriften*, *SW*, I, 161–211 ("Skeptizismus").

Vorlesungen über die Aesthetik, *SW*, X, XI. English translation by F. P. B. Omaston, *The Philosophy of Fine Art*, 4 vols. (London, 1920).

Vorlesungen über die Philosophie der Weltgeschichte, *SW*, VIII, IX. English translation by J. Sibree, *The Philosophy of History* (New York, 1956).

Vorlesungen über die Philosophie der Religion, *SW*, XII, XIII, XIV. English translation by E. B. Speirs and J. Burdon Sanderson, *Lectures on the Philosophy of Religion*, 3 vols. (New York, 1962).

Wissenschaft der Logik, *SW*, III, IV. English translation by W. H. Johnston and L. G. Struthers, *The Science of Logic*, 2 vols. (New York, London, 1929) (*Logic*).

Introduction

THE UPSURGE OF INTEREST in Hegel in France in the years immediately following World War II was linked with the question of Marxism, a link which was reinforced by the participation of the Communist party in de Gaulle's government. Far from being a matter of historical or intellectual curiosity, the problem of Hegel was one of actuality. At stake was not so much Hegel himself, as the use to which his work was to be put; whether Hegel was to be seen as leading toward Marxism or as the last line of defense against Marxism. Typical of this problem is a statement by Alexandre Kojève, written in 1946:

> Thus we can say that for the moment, any interpretation of Hegel, if it is more than idle chatter, is but a program of struggle and of work (one of these "programs" being called *Marxism*). And that means that the work of an interpreter of Hegel is equivalent to a work of political propaganda.[1]

Recent work on Hegel, especially in France, bears witness to a similar concern. Jean Hyppolite, in the last article he wrote before his death in 1968, remarked, "the current state of our planet leads to new questions about Marxism, to a return to the works and fundamental texts of Marx, which cannot be separated from Lenin's interpretations."[2]

The central question with which we must concern ourselves is not whether Hyppolite's work is an "objective" commentary on

1. Kojève, "Hegel, Marx et le christianisme," *Critique*, no. 7 (December, 1946), p. 366.
2. J. Hyppolite, "Le 'Scientifique' et l'idéologique' dans une perspective marxiste," in *Figures de la pensée philosophique* (Paris, 1971), p. 360.

Hegel's *Phenomenology* (which in fact is an impossibility), but the extent to which Hyppolite's reading (among others) is historically determined. To a certain degree, every generation, every tendency has found in Hegel what it sought: a "phenomenological" Hegel, an "existential" Hegel, a "Marxist" Hegel. The question is whether a given reading of Hegel is arbitrary, or whether it both conforms to the text and is a projection through time of a certain tendency or aspect of Hegel's work which is illuminated by the current situation.

Many of the questions which will be raised by the publication in English of Hyppolite's *Genesis and Structure of Hegel's Phenomenology of Spirit* will doubtless bear a certain resemblance to questions which were discussed in the period after World War II, when it was first published. Any discussion of it, and of Hyppolite's translation, must therefore take these historical questions into account if it is not to be condemned to a farcical repetition of history.

Hyppolite's translation of Hegel's *Phenomenology* rendered not only this book, but, given the almost total lack of French translations of his works, Hegel in general (as viewed, of course, through the *Phenomenology*) accessible to the French. Published from 1939 to 1941, its effect was felt immediately after the war. Hyppolite's thesis-commentary appeared in 1946, followed in 1947 by the publication of the lectures Alexandre Kojève had given at the Sorbonne from 1933 to 1939, *Introduction to the Reading of Hegel*. And although the postwar period is usually associated with the triumph of "existentialism" in the persons of Jean-Paul Sartre and Maurice Merleau-Ponty, the moment of existentialism's triumph was also, in proper Hegelian form, the moment of its death. For the famous manifesto of the first number of *Les Temps modernes* in October, 1945, signaled a turn by Sartre and Merleau-Ponty away from Edmund Husserl and Martin Heidegger and toward Hegel and Marx.

To understand fully Hyppolite's position in the history of this period, the role of his written works, and even more that of his courses on Hegel and Marx at the Sorbonne from 1949 to 1954 and on the *Phenomenology* at the *lycées* Henri IV and Louis-le-Grand during the war, we must go back to the developments which prepared and made possible the expansion of interest in Hegel after the war.[3]

3. Hyppolite's personal version (written in 1957) is contained in "*La Phénoménologie* de Hegel et la pensée française contemporaine" in his collected writings, *Figures*, pp. 230–41.

The development in France in the 1930s of various philosophical currents, especially phenomenology, must be seen against the double background of academic philosophy and the rise of, and response to, fascism. The mainstream of academic philosophy and sociology since Marx and Engels (and through them since Hegel) constitutes, even if sometimes unconsciously (e.g., in Nietzsche) an effort to construct an alternative to Marx and Hegel: Max Weber, Georg Simmel, Emile Durkheim, Karl Mannheim, Henri Bergson, among others, can be included in this tradition. And although, as Jean Wahl has pointed out, there has always been a slim Hegelian tradition in France, his influence was relatively minor.[4] One can point to a few essays of Emile Meyerson, to courses of Charles Andler or Alain (whose influence on Hyppolite perhaps even lies at the origin of his translation of Hegel).[5] But the line is slim indeed. The most important opposition to French academic philosophy at that time, represented by the twin poles of Bergson and Léon Brunschvicg, was phenomenology. Not insignificantly, the relation of phenomenology—of Husserl, Max Scheler, Nicolai Hartmann, and Heidegger—to Hegel and Marx is more complex than that of other academic philosophy. T. W. Adorno, for example, has said that after Hegel, Husserl "discovered the north pole for the second time." This is not the place to enter into the relation of phenomenology to Hegel and Marx as far as the German originators were concerned, however; we will restrict ourself to this relation insofar as it affected the French.[6]

Beginning roughly with the publication of Heidegger's *Being and Time* in 1927, interest in phenomenology and the "philosophy of existence," especially Husserl and Heidegger, grew rapidly. In 1929, Jean Cavaillès and Maurice de Gandillac organized a Franco-German philosophical encounter at Davos,

4. Interview, May 11, 1972. M. Wahl, who died recently, was most generous in giving his time for what may have seemed like minor details, but which in fact were important elements in arriving at an over-all picture of Hyppolite and the place he occupied. I also wish to thank Mme Dina Dreyfus, MM. Emmanuel Levinas, Jacques D'Hondt, and especially Mme Jean Hyppolite and M. Jacques Derrida.

5. Emile Meyerson, *De l'explication dans les sciences*, 2 vols. (Paris, 1921), I, 9–180. Charles Andler taught courses at the Sorbonne in the 1920s and at the Collège de France in 1928–29. Alain taught Hegel in his famous courses of *première préparatoire* (*khâgne*) in the 1920s.

6. For an orientation, see the little book of Jean-François Lyotard, *La Phénoménologie*, Series Que Sais-je? (Paris, 1954).

which brought together Ernst Cassirer and Heidegger on the German side, and on the French side Léon Brunschvicg, the leading representative of French academic rationalism, and Albert Spaier, later a founder of the influential *Recherches philosophiques*.[7] With Cavaillès and Gandillac came a number of students from the Ecole Normale Supérieure, which was to become one of the centers for both phenomenology and Marxism. Shortly thereafter, a small but steady stream of French students began to go to Germany to study with Husserl and Heidegger (and to a lesser extent Karl Jaspers): Gandillac, Emmanuel Levinas, Sartre, and Merleau-Ponty among the best known.

In 1930, Alexandre Koyré published the first translation of Heidegger in the review *Bifur* and Emmanuel Levinas published his important little book *The Theory of Intuition in Husserl's Phenomenology*. The first issue of *Recherches philosophiques* (1931) published a text of Heidegger, and Husserl's *Cartesian Meditations* were published in French translation by Levinas and Gabrielle Peiffer in 1931.

Many of the students or young philosophers who, like Levinas, turned toward phenomenology and the "philosophy of existence" did so because of the glaring insufficiencies of French academic philosophy, which appeared irrelevant, bourgeois, and part of the establishment. It was, as Levinas has suggested, like a fine lace network: fragile, possessing a certain attractiveness on the surface, but useless—and in fact more like a cobweb than lace.[8] French philosophy represented moribund idealism which had to be fought. Phenomenology, on the other hand, appeared serious, down to earth. The famous call for a "return to the things themselves" appeared like a call to relevancy. It offered "something to believe in" (Levinas), and that was both its strength and its weakness. It was the fight against subjectivist idealism which Marxism and the otherwise extremely diverse forms of phenomenology had in common, and which accounts for apparently incongruous alliances. Thus, for example, Georges Politzer, one of the leading intellectuals of the French Communist party, shows a certain sympathy for phenomenology in his early book on Bergson when he says that in a systematic confrontation of Husserl with Bergson, "even though Husserl is no God, the comparison would not be to the advantage of Mr. Bergson: then we would see what tricks he uses to pass from

7. Interview with Emmanuel Levinas, May 10, 1972.
8. Interview with E. Levinas.

psychology to the theory of knowledge and to metaphysics." [9]
For most of those who became interested in phenomenology
(with the notable exception of Hyppolite[10]), the question of
breaking from Bergson was important, since it represented a
break from idealism.

The turn away from university scholasticism toward phenomenology was crystallized in the *Recherches philosophiques*,
which was founded by Koyré, H.-Ch. Puech, and Spaier in 1931
and appeared yearly in some five hundred or more pages until
1936, when the last (sixth) number appeared. A simple list of
those who wrote regularly for it, or were published in it, is in-
dicative of its importance: Henri Gouhier, Gaston Bachelard,
Gabriel Marcel, Wahl, Kojève, Aron Gurwitsch, Eric Weil, Karl
Löwith, Pierre Klossowski, Bernhard Groethuysen, Levinas,
Koyré, Gandillac, Etienne Souriau, Georges Bataille, Heidegger,
even the omnivalent Raymond Aron. It included reviews of
Sartre's first book, *Imagination*, of Jacques Lacan's thesis on
paranoia, of Scheler, Hartmann, Groethuysen's *Dialektik der
Demokratie*, Ernst Bloch, Jaspers. In particular, it included influential articles by Groethuysen, "De quelques aspects du
temps" (no. 5), E. Weil, "De l'intérêt que l'on prend à l'histoire"
and Löwith, "L'Achèvement de la philosophie classique par
Hegel et sa dissolution chez Marx et Kierkegaard" (no. 4).

Underlying the phenomenological orientation of the *Recherches* was an interest in, and "existential" reading of, Hegel.
Jean Wahl's study of Hegel, *Le Malheur de la conscience dans
la philosophie de Hegel,* appeared in 1929, and exercised a significant influence on Sartre. In addition, Koyré published two
major articles on Hegel: "Note sur la langue et la terminologie
hégéliennes," in the 1931 Hegel issue of the *Revue philosophique,* and "Hegel à Iéna," in the *Revue d'histoire et de
philosophie religieuses* (1934)[11] which translated for the first
time many of Hegel's texts from the period 1803–6, which lead
to the *Phenomenology.* The importance of these works was no
doubt as great for others as it was for Hyppolite, who later said:

> I should say that the first real shock came from Jean Wahl, and
> that reading *La Conscience malheureuse dans la philosophie de*

9. Georges Politzer, *La Fin d'une parade philosophique: Le
Bergsonisme* (Paris, 1929, reprint ed. 1968), p. 13.

10. See Hyppolite, "Du Bergsonisme à l'existentialisme" in
Figures, pp. 443–58.

11. Republished in *Etudes d'histoire de la pensée philosophique*
(Paris, 1961), pp. 175–204, 135–173.

Hegel was a sort of revelation . . . reading "Hegel à Iéna" was for me (with the translation of texts on time) as basic as *La Conscience malheureuse*.[12]

The "phenomenological" reading of Hegel is unmistakable; witness Koyré's statement that "the Hegelian 'dialectic' is a phenomenology." To which he immediately adds in a note: "We can see from the above analyses that the famous triad: thesis, antithesis, synthesis, in which interpreters have, quite wrongly, tried to see the basis of the Hegelian method, does not at all play a preponderant role in his phenomenological labors."[13]

During this period of the mid-1930s, it was impossible to ignore either surrealism or the rise of fascism. The presence and influence of the surrealists was still great. Breton especially was interested in Hegel, seeing in him a powerful force for liberation as well as the grand master of the dialectic, the greatest game of all. This interest was no less real for being mainly formal, since most important texts of Hegel were unavailable in French. In particular for Jean Wahl and Georges Bataille (who was associated with them for a certain period), the surrealists occupied an important place. While teaching in the provinces, Hyppolite became well acquainted with surrealist positions and knew Roger Vitrac, whose works have recently been rediscovered.

At that time, the surrealists were still maintaining their valiant effort at assimilating their literary activity with political activism, combining Rimbaud and Marx. "'Transformer le monde' a dit Marx; 'changer la vie' a dit Rimbaud: ces deux mots d'ordre pour nous n'en font qu'un."[14] This effort lasted until Breton's exclusion from the Writers' Congress in June, 1935, for treating Ilya Ehrenburg as he deserved.

Beginning with Hitler's takeover, the interest in social questions among philosophers began to be more explicit. The question of the brief active period of Heidegger's membership in the Nazi party (1933–34) no doubt contributed then, as it has re-

---

12. *Hegel-Studien*, Special issue 3: *Hegel-Tage* (Royaumont, 1964), p. 11. The replacement of the actual title of Jean Wahl's book by "La Conscience malheureuse" deserves a commentary all its own, since it replaces what Wahl sees as a general problematic of consciousness by a specific figure of consciousness.

13. Koyré, *Etudes*, p. 164.

14. Cf. Maurice Nadeau, *History of Surrealism*, (New York, 1965), pp. 193–95.

peatedly since then, to obliging the phenomenologists to deal explicitly not only with political questions, but even more with the possible political implications of philosophical positions.[15] Although the interest was latent from the beginning, and was accentuated by the presence of a certain number of German-Jewish refugees such as E. Weil or Groethuysen, it was substantially augmented by an influx of refugees from Nazism, in particular by the presence in Paris of Walter Benjamin and the "Frankfurt school"—Adorno, Herbert Marcuse, Max Horkheimer.

Benjamin was the key figure of the group, not only because he was the most brilliant and had the closest relations with people around the *Recherches* (who experienced Adorno, for example, as Benjamin's "omnipresent watchdog"), but mainly because Benjamin himself combined the Marxism of the Frankfurt school with a substantial interest in mysticism which was shared by many members of the *Recherches*—Levinas and Gandillac in particular. Benjamin (and Raymond Aron, who was then "on the left") reviewed issues of the *Recherches* for the journal of the Frankfurt school, the *Zeitschrift für Sozialforschung*;[16] and regular contributors to the *Recherches* such as Koyré, E. Weil, C. Bouglé, and R. Aron also wrote occasionally for the *Zeitschrift*. Although there was little intellectual sympathy, and even overt hostility (Adorno, for example, strongly attacked Wahl's *Etudes kierkegaardiennes*[17]), both groups shared a (somewhat proprietary) interest in the same figures: Husserl, Kierkegaard, and Hegel.

Surrealism, the Frankfurt school, the problem of an appropriate response to fascism: all raised the question of Marxism and with it that of the French Communist party. Henri Lefebvre's translations of selections from Hegel, his *Dialectical Materialism* (1936), and especially his edition, with Norman Gutermann, of Lenin's *Notebooks on Hegel's Dialectic* (1935), along with Cornu's thesis on the left Hegelians, were universally recognized. The fact that Lenin had spent six months in the

15. See the articles by Alfred de Towarnick and Maurice de Gandillac in *Les Temps modernes* (January, 1946), and by Alphonse de Waehlens and Eric Weil in *Les Temps modernes* (July, 1947); also articles by Jean-Pierre Faye, François Fedier, and François Bondy in *Critique*, nos. 234 (November, 1966), 237 (February, 1967), 242 (July, 1967), and 251 (March, 1968).

16. VI (1937), 41 and 173.

17. In *Zeitschrift für Sozialforschung*, VIII (1939), 232–35.

midst of World War I reading Hegel could not but modify the Stalinist image of him then being put forward. In addition, the obvious importance Lenin accorded Hegel not only went against the Stalinist image, but was also in tune with the philosophical preoccupations of many non-Marxists. To cite only two of the more notorious passages: "It is impossible completely to understand Marx's *Capital*, and especially its first chapter, without having thoroughly studied and understood the *whole* of Hegel's *Logic*. Consequently, a half-century later none of the Marxists understood Marx!!" and "Intelligent idealism is closer to intelligent materialism than stupid materialism. Dialectical idealism instead of intelligent; metaphysical, undeveloped, dead, crude, rigid instead of stupid." [18]

Although there was a certain respect on the part of left intellectuals for some of the CP intellectuals, such as Politzer, Lefebvre, and Auguste Cornu, any serious development toward the French Communist party was probably effectively stifled by the crude form of Stalinized Marxism that was *de rigueur* in the party. While the phenomenologists were attacking nationalism and its relation to fascism, leading CP intellectuals like Politzer were churning out attacks on the phenomenologists and "philosophers of existence" as being "obscurantists," "mystics," and reactionaries (which some of them doubtless were); these attacks were written in the name of French nationalism, of *la pensée française* which (as opposed to that of *les sales Boches*) had always been that of "reason." [19] To any serious Marxist, it makes no sense to privilege, as did Politzer, Descartes over Husserl or even over Heidegger. One has only to compare some texts of Politzer with, for example, the texts of Contre-attaque, a group of intellectuals and surrealists:

> 1. Violently hostile to any tendency, whatever form it may take, which cuts short the Revolution to the profit of the ideas of nation or fatherland, we address ourselves to all those who, by any means and without reservations, are determined to bring down capitalist authority and its political institutions. . . .
>
> 5. We say that the current program of the Popular Front, whose leaders will doubtless gain power within the framework of bourgeois institutions, is doomed to failure. The constitution of a government of the people, of a leadership of public safety, re-

18. Lenin, *Complete Works*, XXXVIII (Moscow, 1963), 180, 276.

19. Cf. Georges Politzer, "La Philosophie et les mythes," in *Ecrits* (Paris, 1969), I, 178–79 (originally published in 1939).

quires A RELENTLESS DICTATORSHIP OF THE ARMED POPU-
LACE.[20]

This declaration was signed by Breton, Georges Ambrosino, Georges Bataille, Roger Blin, Paul Eluard, Pierre Klossowski, and Benjamin Peret, among others.

As crystallizations of a mood, written forms such as journals, however important, lag somewhat behind the prevailing intellectual atmosphere. Much harder to seize and define, this atmosphere is nonetheless crucial. Two of the most important focal points of interest in both Hegel and the philosophy of existence were the courses on Hegel's *Phenomenology* given by Kojève and the social meetings at Gabriel Marcel's.

Kojève's legendary courses were taught on the margin of the Sorbonne since he had only a part-time and not a regular appointment. Further, the presence of Alexander Kojevnikoff, Russian *émigré* and sympathizer with the Soviet Russia of Stalin, "the most powerful man in the world," [21] must have been rather disconcerting to proper French university professors such as, for example, the then influential Léon Brunschvicg. Kojève-Kojevnikoff's courses were attended by Raymond Queneau, who later published them, by Merleau-Ponty, E. Weil, Lacan, Levinas, Koyré, and Sartre, among others. These were the people who formed the center of the group with which Kojève continued discussion over coffee and beer in a local café after formally adjourning the class.

Kojève's course consisted essentially of a translation and running commentary on the *Phenomenology*. Since at that time there was no French translation, students were forced to rely on notes and impressions. Even with complete notes, like Queneau's, it was impossible for most students to check Kojève's reading against Hegel's text. Despite this limitation, the course served as an indispensable preparation for the renewal of serious interest in Hegel after World War II. In large part, it is fair to say that Kojève created the reading public for Hyppolite's translation and commentary.

Kojève shared with many others what was then considered an "existential" reading of Hegel. Jean Wahl's 1929 book, as well as important articles by Koyré, had emphasized the early Hegel, the Hegel of Jena. Whereas received university opinion

20. Contre-attaque, in *La Position politique du surréalisme* (Paris, 1971).
21. Interview with E. Levinas.

had stressed almost exclusively the late Hegel of the *Logic* and the *Encyclopaedia* (one of the few works then available in French), those interested in phenomenology and the "philosophy of existence" tended to privilege the *Phenomenology* as opposed to the *Logic*. In retrospect, however, one is struck not so much by the common effort of those interested in "existentialism" to break from previous interpretations of Hegel dominant in France, but by the wide differences among them. At one pole, Kojève's Hegel is shorn of the absolute (or equates the absolute with mankind). His reading insists on an atheistic, anthropological interpretation with the master-slave dialectic at its center. I shall return to the question of different interpretations later; for the moment it is enough to say that Kojève can be taken as representing a distinct pole pointing in the direction of Marx.

The opposite pole of interpretation, which stresses Hegel's religion, or at least the absolute at which his philosophy arrives, has always tended toward using Hegel in opposition to Marx. This view is defended by people as different as Jean Wahl, who sees *le malheur de la conscience* as the key to an interpretation of Hegel, the Jesuits in charge of the official Hegel Congresses (such as Gaston Fessard and André Régnier), and a variety of mystics of one sort or another. Initially, at any rate, it was in this direction that many of the phenomenologists and "existentialist philosophers" developed, which was the reason for the numerous attacks against them from the left.

At that time, the "mystical" (not to say religious) pole was represented by the soirées at Gabriel Marcel's. These were a curious mixture in that they brought together atheists such as Sartre and Groethuysen, explicitly religious men such as Marcel, even neo-Thomists like Jacques Maritain, and were mediated by writers who occupied complex positions somewhere in between the two poles, such as Bataille, Vladimir Jankélévitch, Klossowski, and Minkowski.

By viewing these historical data as symptomatic, we can say that the curious discussion which took place just before the end of the war, in March, 1944, represents the intellectual culmination of these meetings.[22] The topic for discussion was a lecture by Georges Bataille on *le péché*, sin, which he wanted to give before a mixed Christian and non-Christian audience. Among those present were Gabriel Marcel, Marcel Moré, Jean Daniélou, Dominique Dubarle, and Augustin Maydieu on the Christian side;

22. Published in *Dieu vivant*, no. 4 (1945), pp. 83–133.

Sartre, Merleau-Ponty, Maurice Blanchot, Gandillac, Hyppolite, Klossowski, Michel Leiris, and Jean Paulhan on the non-Christian side. Bataille viewed *le péché* paradoxically both as negativity, decline, the search for *le néant,* and, positively, as necessary and liberating, the drive on which the highest morality is based.[23] Bataille played on different meanings of the term because he wants—and as Hyppolite pointed out in the discussion, needs—to maintain a position which is neither Christian nor totally atheist. Hyppolite and Sartre joined forces in their critique of Bataille (with which Bataille later said he agreed). They saw not a play on multiple meanings but an equivocation in Bataille's choice of vocabulary and his "non-Christian mysticism." Hyppolite accused him of misusing terms. Sartre formulated the problem as follows: "Either we are plenitudes and what we seek is nothingness or we are vacuums (*vides*) and what we seek is being." Bataille took the first position and Sartre and Hyppolite the second, which sees sin not as an effort toward transcendence or, as Bataille ambiguously puts it, toward *l'Autre* and communication, but simply as negation. Bataille was concerned with the final resolution in the absolute, whereas Sartre and Hyppolite were concerned with a phenomenological analysis of the negativity of actual conditions. Thus Bataille's Hegelian interpretation of sin, which stresses the *conscience malheureuse* and yet through it, the final (although humanly impossible) reconciliation in the absolute, poses an opposite pole to Kojève, or in a slightly different way, to Sartre or Hyppolite.

In looking back over the period leading to the publication of Hyppolite's translation of Hegel's *Phenomenology* and to the outbreak of World War II, it is clear that a number of thinkers reacted to the stultification of the French university and the chauvinism which dominated French intellectual life by attempting to return to serious philosophical roots, whether these appeared in the German phenomenologists or elsewhere. They shared in some vague way the sense of "crisis" which Husserl expressed in his *Crisis of European Sciences.* On the one hand, political events forced them to the left and toward Marxism; on the other hand they were repelled by the narrow patriotic chauvinism of the French CP.

It was therefore natural and inevitable that they should

23. Bataille's text is reprinted as an appendix to his *Sur Nietzsche* (Paris, 1967).

come to grips with the greatest of all bourgeois philosophers, the philosopher of the French Revolution, Georg Wilhelm Friedrich Hegel.

IN THE MIDST of the intellectual ferment (not to say confusion) of this period, Jean Hyppolite occupied a position which was distinct from that of any of the major groupings and at the same time typical; as his obituary in *Le Monde* put it, he served as "la conscience de notre temps." [24]

Born in 1907, Hyppolite combined his ability in mathematics and in philosophy to succeed in entering the Ecole Normale Supérieure.[25] Although, like so many others, he had heard Alain lecture on Hegel in his year in *khâgne*, it was not until leaving the Ecole Normale in 1929 that he became seriously interested in Hegel. When Hyppolite began his round of teaching in provincial *lycées* which was then the path of all aspiring French academics, he began seriously to read Hegel in Limoges in 1929.

At that time, however, there were almost no translations of Hegel, none of the *Phenomenology* in particular, and Hyppolite knew no German: he therefore began to teach himself German by reading the *Phenomenology* in the original! He continued laboring over the German text during the "spare moments" of his military service (1930–31) and indeed for the next half-dozen years.

By the late 1930s Hyppolite had climbed the academic ladder to a post in a Paris *lycée*. In Paris, he scrupulously avoided attending Kojève's lectures, as he put it, "for fear of being influenced." [26] Spurred on by what he himself later referred to as the twin stimuli of Jean Wahl and the essays of Koyré, about 1936 Hyppolite decided to translate the *Phenomenology*, even though he had no publisher, no assurances. He had learned German by reading Hegel in isolation; he began his translation, a "travail de Bénédictin," [27] in isolation.

Hyppolite worked rapidly, arguing terminology with friends who knew German well, such as Maurice de Gandillac, and the

24. *Le Monde*, October 31, 1968.
25. This, and most of the other biographical information, I owe to the generosity and cordiality of Mme Hyppolite. Hyppolite did not have Greek, which was then a requisite for philosophy, and he replaced it with mathematics.
26. Mme Hyppolite.
27. Interview with Mme Dina Dreyfus, literary executor of Hyppolite's estate, May 19, 1972.

first volume appeared at the beginning of World War II, in 1939, with the second in 1941. Beginning in 1941, Hyppolite taught the *khâgne* at the Paris *lycées* Henri IV and Louis-le-Grand. He elaborated his commentary on the *Phenomenology*, which was to become *Genesis and Structure*, in common with his students in *khâgne* during the war and the Nazi occupation. His antifascist readings of Hegel, and statements such as that for Hegel, "insofar as we seek the universal, we are all Jews," impressed many of the students. Immediately after the war, Hyppolite received a position at the University of Strasbourg. In 1949 he was appointed to a chair at the Sorbonne, where he taught until 1954, when he became director of the Ecole Normale Supérieure. He headed the Ecole Normale for ten years, until being appointed to the Collège de France in 1963.

Hyppolite's immediate influence was as much due to his role as a teacher as it was to his publication of the *Phenomenology* in French or his commentary on it. Some of the most important figures in the current alignment of the ever-changing constellation of French intellectual stars were students of Hyppolite at one level or another. Thus Michel Foucault and Gilles Deleuze were introduced to Hegel by Hyppolite's classes in *khâgne*, and Jacques Derrida studied under him at the Ecole Normale.

Hyppolite's major works—the translation, his commentary, and *Logique et existence*—coincided with the apogee of interest in Hegel. The major works on Hegel by Hyppolite, Kojève, H. Niel, and E. Weil were all written or published in the period from 1945 to 1950 or slightly thereafter. Both Hyppolite's *Logique et existence* (1953) and his *Studies on Marx and Hegel* (1955) represent continuations of this period; in the case of the latter, all the essays were written before 1952. It thus seems correct to say that this was the period of the main spurt in interest in Hegel. Furthermore, there was a clear change in atmosphere after about 1950; concomitant with the temporary cessation of publication of *Critique* between September, 1949, and October, 1950, the strength of the wave of Hegel studies was broken. After about 1950, *Les Temps modernes* also turned entirely away from directly philosophical subjects. Further, it was in the first years of the 1950s that the first articles by what would be the next generation begin to appear in *Les Temps modernes* and *Critique*: Claude Lévi-Strauss, Georges Poulet, Jean Starobinski, as well as the novels of Alain Robbe-Grillet and Michel Butor. Roland Barthes's *Writing Degree Zero* appeared in 1953. By the time Hyppolite went to the Ecole Normale, the first wave of Hegel studies was over. This is not to say that interest in Hegel disappeared—for at the Ecole Normale Hyppolite came into contact with the next generation—but merely that it reemerged in the 1960s in a different form, to which I shall return.

WHAT, THEN, WERE THE MAJOR LINES of interpretation at the height of interest in Hegel, between the end of World War II and the outbreak of the Korean War or slightly thereafter?

The first point that should be stressed is the broad range of interests. We have already noted the undercurrent of interest in the thirties which prepared the way for the postwar upsurge. Koyré's comment on the *Phenomenology* (above, p. xx) was typical. Sartre's debt to Hegel in the process of developing his ontology has been sufficiently commented on to make superfluous a further presentation here. Finally, if Husserl was largely unaware of Hegel, the same is not true for Heidegger, who devoted a crucial (if somewhat obscure) section at the end of *Being and Time* to Hegel's conception of the relation of time and *Geist* (§ 82). Heidegger's other major essay on Hegel, "Hegel's Begriff der Erfahrung," though somewhat later, is also important.

After the war, there was a unanimity among intellectuals who occupied otherwise widely divergent positions. Kojève continues the passage which we quoted at the head of this essay by saying: "It is possible that in reality the future of the world, and thus the meaning of the present and that of the past, depend, in the last analysis, on the way in which the Hegelian writings are interpreted today." [28] Georges Bataille, the founder and driving force behind *Critique* in the period immediately after the war, wrote: "The economic interpretation of history in the precise meaning of class struggle is already given in Hegel." [29] And, in an attempt to reconcile Marx and Kierkegaard, Bataille states:

> The primacy of life over thought takes these two forms: Marx affirms the primacy of need; the primacy of a desire which goes beyond the satisfaction of needs is given in Kierkegaard's position. I will first speak of the primacy of desire (before also showing

28. Kojève, "Hegel, Marx et le christianisme," pp. 339–66.
29. "De l'existentialisme au primat de l'économie," *Critique,* no. 21 (February, 1948), p. 139.

that it, like the primacy of need, can be reduced to economic givens).[30]

In a much different vein, Brice Parain, who attempts to equate communism with "the religion of the future"—and on that ground consider it "progressive"—concludes that "Marx is but a left Hegelian." [31] In *Les Temps modernes*, Merleau-Ponty, summarizing a lecture by Hyppolite (a summary which is more Merleau-Ponty than Hyppolite), wrote: "Hegel is at the origin of everything great in philosophy for the last century." [32] Finally, Koyré, looking back over this period in 1961, concluded that among the multiple reasons for the renaissance in Hegel studies, was *"last but not least*—the emergence of Soviet Russia as a world power and the victories of the communist armies and ideology . . . Hegel *genuit* Marx; Marx *genuit* Lenin; Lenin *genuit* Stalin." [33]

There seemed to be a common agreement on what has been traditionally termed a left Hegelian position. But this unity was primarily a negative one: it was a unity against both idealism *and* anticommunism. Even Eric Weil, who by all accounts is far from being "on the left," wrote a number of articles in *Critique* devastating anticommunist books and tracts.

It is generally accepted that the main intellectual characteristic of the period after the war is that of existentialism, even if lip service is sometimes paid to the divergences between, say, Sartre and Gabriel Marcel as representatives of "atheistic" and "religious" existentialism. This characterization is also frequently applied to Hegel studies, including, for example, Hyppolite's "attraction" to existentialism. On closer examination, however, this characterization does not stand up. At least as important as the fragile negative unity against idealism and anticommunism were the differences among Hegel interpretations. It is possible to distinguish at least three major interpretative trends.

First, there were those who stressed in Hegel the philosopher of the absolute, the mystic, the religious: traditionally, the "right Hegelians." Although it is somewhat surprising in view of

30. "De l'existentialisme au primat de l'économie," *Critique*, no. 19 (December, 1947), p. 517.
31. Brice Parain, "Critique de la dialectique matérialiste," *Dieu vivant*, no. 5 (1946), p. 11.
32. *Les Temps modernes* (April, 1946), p. 1311.
33. Koyré, *Etudes*, p. 228.

his personal attitudes, Jean Wahl's *Le Malheur de la conscience dans la philosophie de Hegel* revitalized this position both through his presentation and through his stress on the texts of the young Hegel. Wahl's work was extremely important in renewing interest in Hegel, but it did so within a basically religious context. His "existential" reading is one which goes from Hegel to Kierkegaard: Wahl's next major work after *Le Malheur de la conscience* was his *Etudes kierkegaardiennes*.

Thus, for Wahl, "the motif of division, sin, torment . . . little by little is transformed into that of reconciliation and beatitude." [34] And if Hegel goes beyond traditional Christianity, it is toward a new religion of man—but a religion just the same, in which "the depth of Christian reconciliation would be united with the beauty of the Greek vision." [35] Finally, Wahl presents the unhappy consciousness and the "enormous power of the negative" in such a way as to effectively neutralize them:

> So that what is negative in him [Hegel] is something absolutely positive. . . . Not only does the torment of the soul bear witness to the spirit; not only is it the affirmation through belief of the divine apparition . . . not only does the unhappy consciousness find its place in the happy consciousness . . . but even more, we can say that the unhappy consciousness is but the darkened image of the happy consciousness. [36]

More explicitly religious interpretations could therefore find support in Wahl's work. Grouped around Emmanuel Mounier and *Esprit*, around the review *Dieu vivant* after the war, and, of course, around the Jesuits, there were many efforts at salvaging Hegel for religion. Henri Niel's *De la médiation dans la philosophie de Hegel*, published in 1945, was perhaps one of the most important works. In the same vein were numerous articles in *Dieu vivant*. Maurice de Gandillac, in his review of Kojève, concludes that "it is certain that [Hegel's] effort to *go beyond* what he considered Christianity can furnish the Christians themselves with an enrichment, or at least a valuable *prise de conscience* of their patrimony." [37] This line of reasoning is carried to its logical conclusion by Brice Parain in an article in *Dieu vivant*, "Critique de la dialectique matérialiste." Parain

34. Jean Wahl, *Le Malheur de la conscience dans la philosophie de Hegel* (Paris, 1929), p. 29.
35. *Ibid.*, p. 149.
36. *Ibid.*, pp. 147–48.
37. "Ambiguité hégélienne," *Dieu vivant*, no. 11 (1948), p. 144.

argues (correctly) that *any* system which is indeed a *system,* which culminates in a synthesis, is fundamentally religious, and that the synthesis, being absolute, is in reality a metaphor for God.[38] Misunderstanding Marxism as a "system" in the traditional metaphysical sense, Parain concludes with his extraordinary statement that "Marx is a left Hegelian."

Second, basing themselves primarily on the *Phenomenology* —and thus again indirectly showing the importance of Hyppolite's translation—were those who stressed an anthropological, atheistic, even materialistic Hegel who led to Marx. Thus Merleau-Ponty's somewhat tendentious summary of Hyppolite: "If the Hegel of 1827 can be reproached with idealism, one cannot say the same of the Hegel of 1807." [39] First among these was of course Kojève, who insisted at length on Hegel's atheism: "In fact, the theology was always an unconscious anthropology; man projected into the beyond, without realizing it, the idea he had of himself." [40]

If Jean Wahl made *le malheur de la conscience* the center of his interpretation of Hegel, Kojève privileges in a similar way the master-slave dialectic. Kojève's courses were frankly tendentious, taking what could be used from Hegel and minimizing the rest. Thus Kojève reads the end point of the system, absolute knowledge, as an anthropology, rather than a theology: "The only, the single *reality* of the Christian notion of God is, for this philosophy, Mankind taken in the totality of its historical evolution within nature." [41] Or again, concerning the master-slave relation (and such quotations could be multiplied):

The complete, absolutely free man . . . will be the Slave who has "overcome" his Slavery. If idle Mastery is an impasse, laborious Slavery, in contrast, is the source of all human, social, historical progress. History is the history of the working Slave. . . . In the raw, natural, given World, the Slave is slave of the Master. In the technical world transformed by his work, he rules —or, at least, will one day rule—as absolute Master. And this Mastery that arises from work, from the progressive transformation of the given World and of man given in this World, will be an entirely different thing from the "immediate" mastery of the Master. The future and History hence belong not to the warlike

38. Brice Parain, "Critique de la dialectique matérialiste," pp. 81–98, 11.
39. *Les Temps modernes* (April, 1946), pp. 1312–13.
40. Kojève, "Hegel, Marx et la christianisme," p. 345.
41. *Ibid.,* p. 340.

Master, . . . but to the working Slave. . . . If the fear of death, incarnated for the Slave in the person of the warlike Master, is the *sine qua non* of historical progress, it is solely the Slave's work that realizes and perfects it.[42]

Finally, a third major trend, which existed mainly in the intellectual atmosphere and has left few traces, is what might be termed phenomenologico-Marxism. Although this remains a significant tendency in Italy, and is currently represented in the United States by the review *Telos,* in France the major work is undoubtedly that of Tran Duc Thao, *Phénoménologie et matérialisme dialectique.* In his introduction, Thao states categorically: "Marxism imposed itself on us as the only conceivable solution to the problems posed by phenomenology itself." Or again—a statement with which many would have been in agreement—"the principal merit of phenomenology was to have liquidated definitively formalism within the very horizon of idealism and to have posed the problems of value in the field of the concrete." [43]

Jean-François Lyotard has attempted to define the relation between phenomenology and Marxism as follows:

[Phenomenology's] ahistoricism, its intuitionism, its intent of being radical, its phenomenalism, are so many ideological factors destined to mask the real meaning of the crisis, to avoid drawing the unavoidable conclusions. The "third path," neither idealist nor materialist (neither "objectivist" nor "psychological," as Husserl said), is the reflection of this equivocal situation. The "philosophy of ambiguity" translates in its way an ambiguity of philosophy in this state of bourgeois history, and that is why intellectuals grant it a certain truth, insofar as they live this ambiguity and insofar as this philosophy, hiding its real meaning, fulfills its ideological function satisfactorily. It is thus clear that no reconciliation can seriously be attempted between these two philosophies.[44]

One must undoubtedly see much of the work of Sartre and Merleau-Ponty as being shaped by this tendency which, without ever directly taking on Hegel, attempted to go from Husserl and Heidegger to Marx directly. Though neither Sartre nor Merleau-

42. A. Kojève, *Introduction to the Reading of Hegel,* ed. Allan Bloom, trans. James H. Nichols, Jr. (New York: Basic Books, 1969), pp. 20, 23. Note that this section of Kojève's commentary had also appeared in *Mesures,* no. 1 (January, 1939).

43. Tran Duc Thao, *Phénoménologie et matérialisme dialectique,* reprint ed. (Paris, 1971), pp. 5, 19.

44. Jean-François Lyotard, *La Phénoménologie,* pp. 114–15.

Ponty wrote direct commentaries on Hegel in the way that most of those we have been concerned with did, their works are nonetheless informed by the presence of Hegel. It is well known that many of Sartre's analyses presupposed Hegel. If we leave aside the question of the relation of Sartre and Merleau-Ponty to Hegel, it is both because it would require a far too lengthy exposition and because it has so often been dealt with.

Hyppolite accurately portrays the attitude of the phenomenologico-Marxists toward Hegel when, in speaking of the *Phenomenology*, he writes, "no doubt the work ends with an absolute knowledge which seems to close off existence, but it is worthy of consideration because of the concrete details and the complexity of the itinerary of consciousness." [45]

Interpreters of Hegel who stressed the links between Hegel and Marx, the way in which Hegel leads to Marx, were faced with a dilemma. For if Hegel leads to Marx, why restrict oneself to Hegel, why not become a Marxist? Some, such as Kojève and Hyppolite, ultimately refused to become Marxists; others, such as Sartre, nominally claimed to be Marxists; and a very few, such as Louis Althusser or Tran Duc Thao, joined the Communist party.

Any consideration of the relation between philosophy (especially Hegel) and Marxism in the immediate postwar period must take into account the question of Stalinism. Stalinist Russia emerged from the war with considerable military and political prestige, and the French CP wore the laurels of the Resistance. Despite Stalin's deals with the West and the opportunism of the French CP (its initiative in disarming the Resistance and reestablishing the bourgeois state, its behavior in the government), the Stalinists seemed a powerful political force. On the other hand, the question of Stalinism was posed sharply in Arthur Koestler's anticommunist diatribes, the beginning of the cold war, and Merleau-Ponty's defense of the Moscow trials in his articles in *Les Temps modernes* in 1946, which were published as *Humanism and Terror* in 1947. Merleau-Ponty's articles were an effort to pose the problem of political power, which had always disturbed the liberals, from a philosophical as well as a political point of view. In the political sphere, de Gaulle could successfully oust the CP from the government in 1947 only because the policies of the CP allowed, and even encouraged, him to do so.

45. *Figures*, p. 264.

Over and over, one finds pro-Marxist articles whose authors feel obliged to separate themselves from the actual practices of Stalinist Russia. Roland Caillois's review of Merleau-Ponty's *Humanism and Terror* in *Critique* is a good example. In speaking of the influence of the French CP he says: "What has become of proletarian consciousness? It has become the consciousness of a schoolboy who does his homework but no longer tries to understand." [46] And he continues:

> Of course the critique of the capitalist world remains valid, and any "humanism" which criticizes Marxism in the name of an individualistic and liberal spiritualism is on the near side of proletarian humanism, but on the condition that one does not make of Marxism a science of the future and that one does not justify anything at all in the name of the end of history.[47]

Similar quotations abound.

The casuistry to which Marxism was reduced by the Stalinist bureaucracy was all too evident: witness the cases of Henri Lefebvre, who was still struggling to remain in the CP, and Georges Politzer before he was shot by the Nazis. The repeated criticism that Marxism had become a theology, if self-serving for those who made the charge, had all too much foundation in the practice and theory of "socialism in one country." Stalin's uncritical assertion in 1936 that "socialism was definitively established in Russia," the attitude toward "socialist realism," the assertion that the party of the working class could not be mistaken because it "embodied" an "inevitable" historical force—these and other positions had strongly fatalistic, and hence ultimately theological overtones. When they are combined with the social patriotism of the CP, which on the day the Allies entered Paris (August 25, 1944), headlined *L'Humanité* with "Vive la France immortelle," it is small wonder that the policies of the CP repelled serious leftist intellectuals.[48]

Given the situation in France, the hungry intellectual welcome given a relatively accomplished and sophisticated Stalinist like Georg Lukács can easily be understood. Merleau-Ponty's glowing description of Lukács' participation in a congress of

46. Roland P. Caillois, "Destin de l'humanisme marxiste," *Critique*, no. 22 (1948), p. 249.
47. *Ibid.*
48. That many intellectuals found the failings of the CP a convenient excuse for their own inaction and would not in any case have become communists does not change the value of the critique.

intellectuals from East and West, the International Encounters in Geneva in 1947, is typical. Although never actually proclaiming himself a Marxist, Merleau-Ponty positively gloats over Lukács' ability to defeat resoundingly his bourgeois and anticommunist opponents in any debate.[49] Similarly, the reviews of Lukács' *Der junge Hegel* (published in Zurich and Vienna in 1948) are generally complimentary if somewhat reserved.[50]

Given the hopeless state of the intellectuals of the French CP, Lukács' work no doubt did a great deal to rehabilitate the intellectual reputation of Stalinism. For with the halfhearted exception of Merleau-Ponty and of a few articles in *Les Temps modernes* by Claude Lefort (of the *Socialisme ou barbarie* group), there was no turn to the only Marxist alternative to Stalin: Trotsky and the heritage of the Lenin of the *Notebooks on Hegel's Dialectic*.[51]

Attracted to Marxism and to the real achievement of Soviet Russia; repelled by the Stalinized party; having neither a political nor a philosophical alternative to the practice of the CP, the only solution appeared to be that of an "intellectual Marxism" à la Sartre, which agitated in intellectual reviews (*Les Temps modernes, Critique, Socialisme ou barbarie*) but which had no politically organized force other than the individual prestige of the writers.

Like so many others, Hyppolite was also fascinated by Marx and the question of Marxism without being willing or able to enter a communist movement. Indeed, since he voluntarily restricted himself to the role of commentator, the tension between Hegel and Marx is perhaps greater in his work than in that of others who claimed to have found a purely intellectual solution. In rejecting Marx, he never claimed to have achieved a reconciliation between Marx and Hegel. On the contrary, he saw clearly the necessary relation between them. At the beginning of his 1951 review of Lukács' *Der junge Hegel*, Hyppolite wrote: "The understanding of Hegel, and the variety of interpretations of his philosophy, force upon us a confrontation with Marxism.

49. See Merleau-Ponty, "Pour les rencontres internationales," *Les Temps modernes* (April, 1947), pp. 1340–44.

50. Cf. Pierre Bonnel, "Lukács contre Sartre," in *Critique*, no. 27 (August, 1948), pp. 698–707; Eric Weil, "Lukács: *Der junge Hegel*," *Critique*, no. 41 (October, 1950), pp. 91–93; and of course Hyppolite's review.

51. The question of why there was no turn to Trotskyism is too complex to be gone into here.

It has to be recognized that Marx is one of the best commentators upon Hegel." [52] And in an article he wrote shortly before his death in 1968, he said: "The current state of our planet leads to new questions about Marxism, to a return to the works and fundamental texts of Marx, which cannot be separated from Lenin's interpretations." [53]

After being named to the Sorbonne in 1949, Hyppolite introduced Marx to the sacred halls of French academia and also taught Heidegger and Hegel. Both his students and his contemporaries agree that one of his prime qualities was his openness and ability to pursue various possibilities of the relation between Marx and Hegel, a relationship analogous, as Hyppolite himself remarks in *Logique et existence,* to the relation between the *Phenomenology* and the *Logic.* "The key difficulty of Hegelianism is the relation between the *Phenomenology* and the *Logic,* or, as we would say today, between anthropology and ontology." [54] Throughout his writings, Hyppolite refuses to adopt unequivocally either an interpretation that privileges the *Logic* and the absolute, and hence leads toward a religious interpretation of Hegel, or one that privileges the *Phenomenology,* the master-slave dialectic of recognition, and hence leads toward Marxism.

However, when forced to choose, there can be no doubt that Hyppolite leans to the latter approach. The very fact that he translated and commented on the *Phenomenology* and not the *Logic* is significant. Although Hyppolite himself was not necessarily conscious of the significance of his decision to translate the *Phenomenology,* the fact itself bears witness to the force of the events outlined here. Further, although he ostensibly restricts himself to the role of commentator, there are repeated instances in which his commentary leans toward an anthropological reading of Hegel. This was clear to everyone at the time, and Hyppolite was alternately reproached for sneaking in an interpretation while pretending not to (H. Niel) [55] and for not developing his interpretation sufficiently (Roger Caillois). [56]

52. Reprinted in *Figures,* pp. 122–45, 123; English translation in *Studies on Marx and Hegel* (New York, 1969), p. 70.
53. "Le 'Scientifique,'" *Figures,* p. 360.
54. *Logique et existence* (Paris, 1953), p. 247.
55. H. Niel, "L'Interprétation de Hegel," *Critique,* no. 18 (November, 1947), pp. 426–37.
56. Roger Caillois, review of Hyppolite's *Genèse et structure,* *Les Temps modernes* (April, 1948), pp. 1898–904.

In a more explicit way, in his review of Lukács' *Der junge Hegel,* Hyppolite speaks of "Hegel's remarkable description of the rise of capitalist society . . . Hegel's prophetic vision of the contradictions in this society . . . the impossibility . . . of resolving the contradictions in capitalist society which he perceived in such a profound manner." [57] It is also in this light that we should view the discussion of Bataille's presentation of sin in 1944, where Hyppolite joined forces with Sartre to oppose a Hegelian reading of sin culminating in a final resolution, albeit a resolution, for Bataille, in a far from Christian manner.

In fact, Hyppolite's openness and his choice of becoming a "commentator" rather than an "interpreter" already implies an interpretation. Apparently standing somewhat outside the traditional categories, Hyppolite places the process of negativity at the center of Hegel: "Hegel's philosophy is a philosophy of negation and of negativity." [58] Over and over, Hyppolite quotes and stresses Hegel's reference to "the enormous power of the negative," and "the seriousness, the torment, the patience, and the labor of the negative." In addition, and here Hyppolite clearly draws the line which, for all his sympathy, separates him from Marx, he privileges a universal "alienation" over and above Marx's "objectification."

To the extent that his insistence on negativity as a key concept in Hegel places Hyppolite in firm opposition to any form of spiritualism, he can follow and ally himself with a materialist analysis. It is this orientation which explains his generally favorable review of Lukács' book on Hegel, and his ability to grasp Marx's method in *Capital:*

> It is obvious that this work [*Capital*] is not comprehensible for anyone who does not know Hegel's *Phenomenology,* for it is the living response to it. Whereas in the *Phenomenology,* it is absolute spirit become its own object which raises itself to self-consciousness, in *Capital,* it is alienated social man, this total product or this *common labor of man,* namely Capital, which *phenomenonalizes itself,* if we may invent the term, and *presents itself* to the *consciousness of the proletariat.*[59]

Here again we find the link between Marx, Hegel, and phenomenology: the desire to combat idealism.

But Hyppolite's stress on "negativity" has certain limitations.

57. *Figures,* p. 130; *Studies on Marx and Hegel,* p. 76.
58. *Logique et existence,* p. 135.
59. *Studies on Marx and Hegel,* p. 103.

He is able to analyze acutely the partiality of both a Kojève and a Jean Wahl; he can analyze the "crisis" of philosophy; but when it is a practical matter, he turns to the Popular Front or to Mendès-France, as he did during the late 1930s or toward the end of the French war on Indochina, for salvation! When Jean Wahl asks somewhat rhetorically: "Is this interest in negation a sign of the crisis of our time? The question is at least worth asking," [60] he captures unconsciously what is at stake. Hyppolite's approach is precisely a *sign* of the period: neither more nor less. He can ask the appropriate questions, but (not surprisingly) has no answer for them.

Hyppolite's self-limitation to the role of commentator, what one reviewer termed his "modesty," also dictates that he remain a Hegelian and not become a Marxist. If Hyppolite was uncomfortable in his position, a "Hegelian against his will," he would have been even more uncomfortable as a Marxist. His position comes out clearly at the end of the review of Lukács, where he privileges Hegel over Marx. Besides negativity, the other central point of Hyppolite's interpretation is the problem of alienation. Whereas for Marx, alienation is only the specific form in which objectification (reification) appears under capitalism, and is therefore historically determined rather than inevitable, for Hegel it is more than that. Marx accused Hegel of identifying alienation and objectification. But Hegel, Hyppolite says,

> cannot have confused the historical alienation of the human spirit with objectification without some valid reasons, other than those one might find in the economic structure of the period and the stage reached by the capitalist system. By objectifying himself in culture, the State, and human labor in general, man at the same time alienates himself, becomes other than himself, and discovers in this objectification an insurmountable degeneration which he must nevertheless try to overcome. This is a *tension inseparable from existence,* and it is Hegel's merit to have drawn attention to it and to have preserved it in the very center of human self-consciousness. On the other hand, one of the great difficulties of Marxism is its claim to overcome this tension in the more or less near future and hastily to attribute it to a particular phase of history.[61]

60. Jean Wahl, "La Situation présente de la philosophie française," in *L'Activité philosophique contemporaine en France et aux Etats-Unis* (Paris, 1950), II, 55.
61. *Figures,* pp. 141–42; *Studies on Marx and Hegel,* p. 87.

Clearly, this is the point at which Hyppolite firmly sides with Hegel against Marx. His choice, however, seems to be more personal than philosophical, for in choosing Hegel he does not claim a philosophical resolution which would dissolve the tension between Hegel and Marx.

Ultimately, then, the position in which Hyppolite finds himself is one traditionally identified as that of the left Hegelians. By insisting on the one hand on a nonidealist, almost materialist Hegel, he opposes the bourgeoisie; by refusing to advance to the position of Marx he inevitably becomes susceptible to the pressures of the bourgeoisie: witness his support for the Popular Front, for Sartre's RAR after World War II, and for Mendès-France in the early 1950s. It is to Hyppolite's credit that he drew the greatest possible philosophical benefit from this ultimately untenable position. Whether one views his dilemma as that of a tortured Hegelian who wanted to escape from the dilemma and who could not bring himself to write on Marx between 1952 and 1965, or as that of a man who had for his *projet* the reconciliation of *logique* and *existence,* is a matter of sympathy: the dilemma is the same.

By 1953, the date of the publication of Hyppolite's *Logique et existence,* the historical problematic entered into and explored by the generation that took up phenomenology and turned to Hegel had produced its major works. Yet the first chapters of *Logique et existence* on language mark the beginning of the *dépassement* of that problematic. If the triumph of existentialism was also the moment of its death, that moment— when Sartre proclaimed himself a Marxist—also marked the beginnings of rebirth. It is precisely the fact of choosing Hegel over Marx without claiming a false philosophical resolution which no doubt accounts for Hyppolite's ability to indicate developments that go beyond the range of Hegel interpretations prevailing in the period 1945–50, of which he himself was one of the best illustrations.

Reacting against these interpretations as too individualistic or humanistic, the late 1950s and early 1960s saw the rise of "structuralism" and with it a rejection of Hegel. Beginning with Lévi-Strauss's articles collected in *Structural Anthropology,* structuralism rapidly infected other areas as well. In particular, the articles of Althusser and his disciples collected in *For Marx* and *Reading Capital* marked a sharp break from Hegel. For Althusser, Marx is not the dialectical continuation of Hegel, but represents a sharp break—so much so that it simply does not make sense to place the two in relation or to examine Hegel closely. Althusser's antihumanistic reading of Marx presupposes a humanistic reading of Hegel which is to be rejected in the name of science. Most often, however, this "science" disguises a retreat to formalism. François Châtelet's *Logos et praxis* and Michel Foucault's *History of Madness* and even more *Les Mots et les choses* continued the trend that proclaimed: "Hegel is dead."

Recently, however, there has been a marked renewal of interest in Hegel and the Hegel-Marx relation which coincides with a reaction against structuralism. An important sign of this tendency has been the republication of Lefebvre's edition of Lenin's *Notebooks on Hegel's Dialectic* and the increasing importance being accorded to Lenin as an interpreter of Hegel. Recent attempts to develop a reinterpretation of Hegel tend to use Saussure and methods inherited from structural linguistics. This is by no means an attempt to return to a "humanistic" reading of Hegel or Marx, but rather to develop a materialist theory of language.

Whereas both the phenomenologists of the 1930s and Hegel center on the question of consciousness, recent work has centered on the question of language. Hegel begins from consciousness and ultimately reaches absolute knowledge; recent work begins and ends with language, eliminating the subject. Thus, for example, an article by J.-J. Goux in *Théorie d'ensemble* tries to read language as alienation, parallel to Marx's development of money as alienation in *Capital*. Bearing more directly on Hegel, Jacques Derrida's "Le Puits et la pyramide: Introduction à la sémiologie de Hegel" is also an important article.[62] It should be stressed that this is a direction which is only now beginning to be explored. None of the more traditional academic work on Hegel has ceased, nor have the religiously oriented given up hope. But in light of these developments, it is easy to see why Hyppolite's *Logique et existence* again becomes attractive.

Hyppolite stresses that for Hegel, "language is the Dasein of spirit."[63] Further, language is not a replacement for, or reflection or derivation of, anything *else*: "Language unfolds and determines itself without being previously given in an ineffable form." "Language refers only to itself." "Meaning as it appears

62. In *Hegel et la pensée moderne* (Paris, 1970), pp. 27–84.
63. *Logique et existence*, p. 23.

in language, meaning as the becoming of the concept in speech, are prior in relation to the movement which seems to engender them. There is no meaning without language." [64]

It is as if the end point of major work on Hegel after the war has become a starting point for a rebirth of work on Hegel. This has also been true in the past: while talking with various people who knew Hyppolite and the atmosphere in which he worked, I was struck to discover that each generation—represented by Jean Wahl, Emmanuel Levinas, Jacques Derrida—felt that it had discovered or rediscovered Hegel. Hyppolite's *Genesis and Structure*, which represents an effort at a commentary on the entire *Phenomenology*, should not only help make Hegel more available, but should, in the continuing process of rereading Hegel, serve as a guide against which to measure and evaluate the adequacy of successive "rediscoveries" of the *Phenomenology*.

JOHN HECKMAN

64. *Ibid.*, pp. 26, 38, 28.

PART I

Generalities on
the *Phenomenology*

1 / Meaning and Method
of the *Phenomenology*

WE KNOW THAT HEGEL wrote the preface[1] to the *Phenomenology* after he had finished the book, when he was able to take stock of his "voyage of discovery." It was meant primarily to establish the connection between the *Phenomenology*, which, by itself, appears as the "first part of science," and the *Wissenschaft der Logik* [*The Science of Logic*, hereafter *Logic*—trans.], which, from a different perspective, is to constitute the first moment of an encyclopedia. We can understand that in a text linking the *Phenomenology* and the *Logic*, Hegel should be particularly concerned to give a general idea of his entire system. In an earlier essay, "Differenz des Fichteschen und Schellingschen Systems der Philosophie" ["The Difference between the Systems of Fichte and Schelling," hereafter "Differenz—trans.], he had risen above his predecessors, appearing to adopt Schelling's view but in fact moving beyond it; in the preface, but this time in full consciousness, he locates himself among the philosophers of his time and shows his philosophic originality. Also, referring back to many of the obscure points in the *Phenomenology*, he gives valuable indications of the pedagogical significance of the work, of its general relation to the history of the world, and of his own concept of negativity.

The introduction[2] to the *Phenomenology*, however, was conceived at the same time as the book itself, and written first. It seems to contain the original thought from which the whole

1. *Vorrede*. We shall discuss the history of the composition of the *Phenomenology* in part I, chapter 3.
2. *Einleitung*.

[3]

work emerged. It is literally an introduction only to the first three moments of the book, that is, consciousness, self-consciousness, and reason. The content of the last part of the book, which contains the especially important arguments on spirit and on religion, exceeds the *Phenomenology* as the latter is defined *stricto sensu* in the introduction. Hegel seems to have inserted something into the framework of the phenomenological development which he had not at first meant to include. For the moment, we shall be content with this observation, without which we could not understand the precise scope of the introduction. But we shall return to this question when we study the structure of the book. We mean to analyze the introduction as closely as possible. Moreso than the preface, it allows us to determine both the meaning of the work that Hegel wished to write and what the technique of phenomenological development was for him. The preface is an hors d'oeuvre; it contains general information on the goal that Hegel set for himself and on the relation between his work and other philosophic treatises on the same subject. The introduction, on the contrary, is an integral part of the book: it poses and locates the problem, and it determines the means to resolve it. First, Hegel defines how the problem of knowledge is posed for him. In some respects he returns to the point of view of Kant and Fichte. The *Phenomenology* is not a noumenology or an ontology, but it remains, nonetheless, a knowledge of the absolute. For what else is there to be known if "only the absolute is true, or only the true is absolute" (*PE*, I, 67; *PG*, 65; *PM*, 133)?[3] But instead of presenting knowledge of the absolute in-and-for-itself, Hegel considers knowledge as it is present in consciousness, and it is from considering the self-criticism of this phenomenal knowledge that he rises to absolute knowledge. Second, Hegel defines the *Phenomenology* as the development and the formation of natural consciousness and its progression to science, that is to say, to philosophic knowledge, to knowledge of the absolute. He indicates the necessity of an evolution of consciousness and, at the same time, the end point of this evolution. Finally, he specifies the technique of phenomenological development, showing how this development is the work of consciousness engaged in experience and how the [internal] necessity of this development can be thought out retrospectively by philosophy.

3. See Translators' Preface, p. xi, for a discussion of editions of the *Phenomenology*.

I. THE PROBLEM OF KNOWLEDGE: IDEA OF A PHENOMENOLOGY

IN THE PHILOSOPHIC WORKS that Hegel wrote in Jena before the *Phenomenology*, he criticized all propaedeutics to philosophy. One cannot, he argued, remain like Reinhold, forever in the square before the temple. Philosophy is not a logic, an organon, which, before knowledge, deals with the instrument of knowledge. Nor is it a love of truth that is not the possession of truth. It is science and, as Schelling claimed, science of the absolute. Beginning with his essays on the philosophy of nature, Schelling had contraposed an ontological conception to the philosophy of reflection of Kant and Fichte. He argued that instead of halting at the point of reflection, at the knowledge of knowledge, it is necessary to immerse oneself in the object to be known, whether it be called nature, the universe, or absolute reason. Such, too, was Hegel's view, in "Differenz," as well as in the article "Glauben und Wissen oder die Reflexionsphilosophie der Subjectivität" ["Faith and Knowledge, or the Reflective Philosophy of Subjectivity," hereafter "Glauben und Wissen"— trans.] in the *Kritische Journal der Philosophie*. In the latter, Hegel reproached Kant's transcendental idealism with having remained a subjectivism despite its deduction of the categories. The basis of Kant's merely critical philosophy had not, according to Hegel, progressed beyond Locke: "Kantian thought is true to its principle of subjectivism and of formal thought in that its essence consists in critical idealism." [4] By intending to be "a critical examination of human understanding," it condemns itself to being unable to move beyond its starting point. The final subjectivism is only a consequence of the point of departure. It is necessary to pass beyond the critical point of view and, as with Schelling, to start straight off with the absolute identity of the subjective and the objective in knowledge. The knowledge of this identity is primary and it constitutes the basis of all true philosophic knowledge.

In his introduction to the *Phenomenology*, Hegel again takes up his criticism of any philosophy that is only a theory of knowledge. And yet, as all commentators have noted, in some respects the *Phenomenology* clearly marks a return to the point

4. Hegel, *Erste Druckschriften*, p. 235; for fuller information on Hegel's works, see "List of Hegel's Works Cited," p. xiii.

of view of Kant and Fichte.[5] In what new sense, then, is this point of view to be understood? Hegel's criticism of Reinhold remains valid. It is a mistake to imagine that, before we can truly know, we must examine knowledge as an instrument or a medium. When we begin to reflect, it is indeed natural to compare knowledge to an instrument or a medium through which the truth reaches us. But these conceptions lead straight to relativism. For if knowledge is an instrument, it modifies the object to be known and fails to present it to us in its purity. And if it is a medium, it does not transmit the truth to us without altering it according to its own nature as an intermediary. But perhaps this natural conception is fallacious; in any case, it constitutes a series of presuppositions which we would do well to mistrust. If knowledge is an instrument, then that implies that the subject and the object of knowledge are separate. The absolute would then be distinct from knowledge. The absolute could not be self-knowledge, nor could knowledge be knowledge of the absolute (*PE*, I, 67–68; *PG*, 65–66; *PM*, 131–33). The very existence of philosophic science, which actually knows, is a refutation of such presuppositions. It is precisely this duality that Schelling recognized when, in *Bruno oder über das göttliche und natürliche Prinzip der Dinge* [*Bruno, or on the Divine and Natural Principles of Things*], he contraposed phenomenal knowledge to knowledge of the absolute. But Schelling failed to show how the two are linked. It is not clear how, according to Schelling, phenomenal knowledge is possible once absolute knowledge is posited. Likewise, phenomenal knowledge remains cut off from absolute knowledge.[6] Hegel, by contrast, returns to phenomenal knowledge, that is, to the knowledge of common consciousness, and claims to show how it necessarily leads to absolute knowledge, or, even, how it is an

5. Cf., for example, R. Kroner, *Von Kant bis Hegel* (Tübingen, 1921, 1924), II, 362: "The *Phenomenology* is both an introduction to the system and, in a certain sense, 'the whole of the system.' How is such a contradiction possible?" Kroner has shown very well how the *Phenomenology* is the *whole of the system* from the point of view of *knowledge*.

6. Friedrich Schelling, *Sämtliche Werke* (we shall refer to K. F. A. Schelling's edition of the *Works* [Stuttgart, 1856]). Schelling's absolute surpasses all knowledge and all consciousness; it is the *Weder-Noch aller Gegensätze* (IV, 246). On *absolute knowledge*, see IV, 326. The difficult problem is that of the possibility of a separation, the *Heraustreten aus dem Ewigen*, the emergence from the eternal, on which consciousness is based.

absolute knowledge which does not yet know itself as such. But this implies a return to the point of view of consciousness, the point of view that was Kant's and Fichte's. Having formerly criticized all propaedeutics, Hegel now insists on the need to place oneself at the point of view of natural consciousness and to lead it gradually to philosophic knowledge: one cannot begin with absolute knowledge. In the preface, Hegel will again return to this point: "For natural consciousness to entrust itself immediately to science is a new attempt on its part to walk on its head, not knowing what moves it to do so" (*PE*, I, 24; *PG*, 25; *PM*, 87). An unnecessary violence is thus imposed on natural consciousness, while science appears to be placed beyond self-consciousness. There is no doubt that Hegel's criticism here is aimed at Schelling. We cannot begin abruptly with absolute knowledge, rejecting different positions and declaring that we wish to know nothing about them.

It is therefore necessary to adopt the point of view of consciousness, as Kant and Fichte had, to study the knowledge peculiar to the consciousness which assumes the distinction between subject and object. Absolute knowledge is not abandoned; it will be the end point of a development specific to the consciousness which here takes the place of critical philosophy. But in returning to the point of view of consciousness, to a kind of epistemology, Hegel does not limit himself to adding a propaedeutic to Schelling's absolute knowledge; he modifies the very conceptions of knowledge and of the absolute. In Hegel's philosophy, the absolute is no longer only *substance;* it is *subject* as well. Schelling's Spinozism can be superseded only by a return to the subjectivism of Kant and Fichte. Then the absolute will not be beyond all knowledge; it will be self-knowledge in the knowledge of consciousness. Phenomenal knowledge will be the knowledge which the absolute gradually has of itself. Manifestation, or the phenomenon which is for consciousness, will thus not be irrelevant to essence but will reveal it. Reciprocally, consciousness of the phenomenon will rise to consciousness of absolute knowledge. The absolute and reflection will no longer be separated; reflection will be a moment of the absolute. Such appears to us the general meaning of the reintegration of the point of view of the I or of consciousness within Schelling's philosophy of the absolute. Hegel wanted to prove that Schelling's absolute idealism was still possible if one started, not with nature, but with consciousness, with the I, if one deepened Fichte's subjectivism.

Hegel himself indicates that the point of view of the *Phenomenology* corresponds to the point of view of a philosophy of consciousness prior to the knowledge of identity. In the *Encyclopaedia of Philosophical Sciences* [hereafter *Encyclopaedia* —trans.] he notes that the *Phenomenology* represents precisely the position of Kant and even that of Fichte: "The Kantian philosophy is a phenomenology," [7] a knowledge of the knowledge of consciousness insofar as this knowledge is only for consciousness. But phenomenology constitutes an essential moment in the life of the absolute, a moment in which the absolute is subject, or self-consciousness. The phenomenology of consciousness is not external to absolute knowledge. It is itself a "first part of science," for the essence of the absolute is to manifest itself to consciousness, to be self-consciousness.

Yet if, in certain respects, Hegel adopts the point of view of Kant and Fichte here, we can already see from the above remarks that his study of phenomenal knowledge and its subjective conditions will differ from theirs. On the one hand, he envisages in an original way consciousness' critique of its own knowledge; on the other hand, he enlarges considerably the notion of experience, so that for him the critique of experience is extended from theoretical experience alone to ethical, juridical, and religious experience as well.

For Kant, the critique of knowledge was a critique that the philosopher exercised on common consciousness and on scientific consciousness (in the sense that science was still only a phenomenal science—that of Newton—and differed from metaphysics). Common consciousness did not criticize itself; the philosopher's reflection was added to it. Phenomenal understanding, as opposed to nature, was then led by philosophic reflection to the transcendental understanding that founds all (theoretical) experience as original synthetic unity. This understanding thus became objective understanding, and the philosopher discovered his identity with the objectivity of objects. In this way experience was demonstrated to be possible. In that part of Fichte's *Wissenschaftslehre* [*Science of Knowledge*] which he wished to make a "pragmatic history of the human spirit" and which is called "Deduction of Representation," there was an early model of what Hegel's *Phenomenology* would be. In the deduction of representation, Fichte means indeed to lead common consciousness from immediate sensuous knowledge

7. Hegel, *Encyclopaedia*, p. 370.

to philosophic self-knowledge. That which the philosopher reached through reflection in the first part of the doctrine of science, he intends to have consciousness rediscover in its own development. As Martial Guéroult wrote,

> the philosopher no longer reflects on the I from the outside; the intelligent I actually reflects on itself. The "pragmatic history" of the human spirit begins here. When the intelligent I will have grasped itself through an action in which it determines itself as being determined by the not-I (that is, when it rejoins the philosophic point of view on it), it will be for itself a theoretical I.[8]

Schelling, following the epochs of the formation of self-consciousness, had taken the same step in his transcendental idealism.[9] Philosophical self-consciousness, being presupposed, was to be rediscovered by the empirical I. But, precisely, philosophic self-consciousness is already presupposed in these two works, and, despite their intention (which is quite close to that of Hegel's *Phenomenology*), the history of the empirical I which they present remains rather artificial. It is not the experience of common consciousness that is considered here, but the necessary reflections through which the latter is to rise from what it is in-itself to what it is for-itself. Hegel, on the contrary, describes common consciousness much more than he constructs it. The philosopher disappears in the face of the experience he apprehends, and naïve consciousness enters into its own experience and thus sees both itself and its object change. Reflection is not added to it from without (as for Kant), nor posited in it in a manner still more or less artificial (as by Fichte and even by Schelling); rather, it is literally a history of this consciousness. At most, the history of naïve consciousness will be internalized (*Erinnerung*) by being recollected in the milieu of philosophic thought. We shall see how it is possible that philosophic thought not intervene in its description of the experience of consciousness. Hegel emphatically insists on this: "We need not bring our standards with us, or use our personal ideas and thoughts in the course of research; it is, to the contrary, by setting them aside that we will succeed in considering

8. M. Guéroult, *L'Evolution et la structure de la doctrine de la science chez Fichte*, in *Publications de la Faculté de Strasbourg* (1930), I, 225.
9. Schelling, *SW*, III.

the thing as it is in-and-for-itself" (*PE*, I, 74; *PG*, 72; *PM*, 141).

Commentators have been struck by this characteristic tack of Hegel's phenomenology: to describe rather than to construct, to present the spontaneous development of an experience as it offers itself to consciousness and in the way that it offers itself.[10] This characteristic could lead us to compare Hegel's phenomenology to the phenomenology of Husserl if the differences between the two were not much deeper than their similarities. It is truly by going "to the things themselves," by considering consciousness as it presents itself directly, that Hegel wishes to lead us from empirical to philosophic knowledge, from sensuous certainty to absolute knowledge. In this way, the *Phenomenology*, which truly presents itself as a history of the soul, differs from Fichte's "Deduction of Representation" and from Schelling's *System des transzendentalen Idealismus* [*The System of Transcendental Idealism*, hereafter *Idealismus*—trans.].

It also differs from them on another, no less important, score. The experience that consciousness works through here is not only theoretical experience, knowledge of the object; it is the whole of experience. The point is to consider the life of consciousness both when it knows the world as object of science and when it knows itself as life or intends a goal. Since it is the experience of consciousness in general that is to be considered, all the forms of experience, ethical, juridical, and religious, will be included. Kant's problem, "how is experience possible?" is here considered in the most general way. A moment ago, we thought of comparing Hegel's phenomenology with that of Husserl; now we can see a similarity to contemporary existentialist philosophies. In many cases, when he discovers the experience worked through by consciousness, Hegel describes a mode of existing, a particular world view. But in contradistinction to existentialist philosophy, he does not stop with that existence itself; he sees it as a moment which, in being superseded, makes possible the attainment of an absolute knowledge. It is precisely on this point that Kierkegaard attacked Hegel.

Considering in all its breadth the experience that consciousness enters into, letting this consciousness test itself and pro-

10. See, in particular, N. Hartmann, *Die Philosophie des deutschen Idealismus* (Berlin and Leipzig, 1929), II, 80, 81, and Hartmann's article in the special Hegel issue of the *Revue de métaphysique et de morale*, XXXVIII, no. 3 (July–Sept., 1931), 285.

mote its knowledge of itself and of the world, Hegel can say of the *Phenomenology*, understood in this way, that

> this presentation can be considered the route of natural consciousness, which undergoes an impulse pushing it toward true knowledge, or the path of the soul traversing the series of its formations as the way-stations prescribed to it by its own nature; the soul moves through these way-stations, purifies itself, and thereby raises itself to the level of spirit when, through the complete experience of itself, it reaches the knowledge of what it is within itself (*PE*, I, 69; *PG*, 67; *PM*, 135).

II. The Formation of Natural Consciousness, Its Development, and the End Point of This Development

The *Phenomenology*, then, is the itinerary of the *soul* which rises to *spirit* through the intermediary of *consciousness*. The idea of such an itinerary was undoubtedly suggested to Hegel by the philosophic works mentioned above, but the influence of the *Bildungsromanen* of the time seems to us to have been just as important. Hegel had read Rousseau's *Emile* at Tübingen and had found in it a preliminary history of natural consciousness rising to liberty through particularly educative experiences which were specific to it. The preface to the *Phenomenology* emphasizes the pedagogical nature of Hegel's book, as well as the relation between the evolution of the individual and that of the species, a relation also considered in Rousseau's book. Royce, in his study of German idealism, emphasizes Goethe's *Wilhelm Meister*, which the Romantic circles of Jena considered one of the essential events of the time, and Novalis' answer to it, *Heinrich von Ofterdingen*.[11] In each book, the hero completely gives himself up to his conviction. Wilhelm Meister believes in his theatrical vocation; Heinrich von Ofterdingen allows himself to be trapped in the prosaic milieu in which he still lives. Through a series of experiences, each comes to abandon his first conviction: what had been a truth becomes an illusion. But whereas Wilhelm Meister leaves, so to say, the poetic world for the prosaic world, Heinrich von Ofterdingen progressively

11. Royce, *Lectures on Modern Idealism* (New Haven, Conn., 1919).

discovers that the poetic world alone is absolute truth. Hegel's *Phenomenology,* for its part, is the novel of philosophic formation; it follows the development of consciousness, which, renouncing its first beliefs, reaches through its experiences the properly philosophic point of view, that of absolute knowledge.

But according to Hegel, such a history of consciousness is not a novel but a work of science. The very development of consciousness presents an [internal] necessity. The end point of this development is not arbitrary, although neither is it presupposed by the philosopher: it results from the very nature of consciousness.

a. *The development and its necessity*

Since the *Phenomenology* is a study of the experiences of consciousness, it continually comes upon negative consequences. What consciousness takes to be truth is revealed to be illusory; consciousness must abandon its first belief and move on to another. "Thus, this route is the way of doubt or, more properly, of despair" (*PE,* I, 69; *PG,* 67; *PM,* 135). Schelling had already said that transcendental idealism necessarily began with universal doubt, a doubt extending to all objective reality: "If for transcendental philosophy the subjective is the first and the only foundation of reality, the sole principle by which one can explain everything, then transcendental philosophy necessarily begins with a universal doubt as to the reality of the objective." [12] Schelling considers this doubt, with which Descartes inaugurated modern philosophy, to be the necessary means by which to prevent any mingling of the objective with the pure subjective principle of knowledge. Whereas the philosophy of nature, by contrast, seeks to eliminate the subjective, transcendental philosophy seeks absolutely to elucidate it. But Hegel, who starts with common consciousness, cannot pose systematic universal doubt as a first principle, for such a doubt is specific to philosophic reflection. He contraposes to it the concrete evolution of a consciousness which progressively learns to doubt what it previously took to be true. The road which consciousness follows is the detailed history of its education (*PE,* I, 70; *PG,* 68; *PM,* 136). The road of doubt is the actual route that consciousness follows. It is its own itinerary, not that of the phi-

12. Schelling, SW, III, 343.

losopher who resolves to doubt. In contrast to such a resolve, by means of which consciousness instantly purifies itself of all its prejudices—in particular, of the fundamental prejudice that things exist outside us, independent of knowledge—the *Phenomenology* is a concrete history of consciousness, of its departure from the cave and its ascent to science. This route is not only the way of doubt; it is, Hegel adds, the way of despairing doubt (*Verzweiflung*) (*PE*, I, 69; *PG*, 67; *PM*, 135). Natural consciousness loses its truth; what it took to be authentic real knowledge is revealed to it as a nonreal knowledge. We have already emphasized the extension Hegel gives to the word "experience." In the course of its development, consciousness loses not only what it held to be true from a theoretical point of view, but also its own view of life and of being, its intuition of the world. Experience bears not only on knowledge, in the narrow meaning of the word, but also on conceptions of existence. The journey of consciousness, therefore, entails not only doubt but actual despair.

Hegel had already reflected on the *ascesis* that is necessary if consciousness is to reach genuine philosophic knowledge when, in Jena, he studied the nature of ancient skepticism. In an article on Schultz in the *Kritische Journal der Philosophie*, he contraposed ancient to modern skepticism. Modern skepticism—a kind of positivism, we would say today—attacks only metaphysics and leaves the unshakable certainties of common sense untouched. But it is precisely these certainties that ancient skepticism meant to shake. As with Plato, skepticism served as something of an introduction to metaphysics, and every philosophy at the time included a moment of skepticism by means of which it purified naïve consciousness. In the article on Schultz, Hegel envisaged for the first time the route of doubt which at the same time is an *ascesis* of the soul, and he reflected on the power of negativity in the dialectic.[13]

What is most striking for the consciousness engaged in experience is indeed the negative character of its result: it initially posited a certain truth which had absolute value for it, but in the course of its journey that truth is lost. It entrusted itself absolutely to "immediate sensuous certainty," then to the "thing" of perception, and to the "strength" of understanding; but it discovers that what it thus took to be the truth is not, and it loses its truth. The double meaning of the word *aufheben*,

13. Hegel, "Skeptizismus," p. 161; in particular, on Plato, p. 174.

which Hegel uses continually, shows us nonetheless that this exclusively negative perception of the result contains only half the truth. The [double] meaning of negativity allows Hegel to affirm that "the complete system of the forms of nonreal consciousness will result from the necessity of the process and from the interconnection of these forms" (*PE*, I, 70; *PG*, 68; *PM*, 137). The result of an experience of consciousness is absolutely negative only for that consciousness; in point of fact, however, negation is always *determinate* negation. Now if it is true that every determinate position is a negation (*omnis affirmatio est negatio*), it is no less true that every determinate negation is a particular position. When consciousness has tested its sensuous knowledge and discovered that the "here-and-now" which it thought it could grasp in an immediate way has escaped, this negation of the immediateness of its knowledge is a new knowledge. It can be put this way: "The presentation of untrue consciousness in its untruth is not simply a negative movement, as it is considered to be by the one-sided view of natural consciousness" (*PE*, I, 70; *PG*, 68; *PM*, 137). It has often been noted—particularly by Lambert in his *Phenomenology*, which was a kind of transcendental optics—that the presentation of an untruth as untruth is already a movement beyond the error.[14] To be cognizant of one's error is to be cognizant of another truth; the perceived error implies a new truth. In the preface, Hegel emphasizes this characteristic of error by showing that error transcended is a moment of the truth. The double meaning of *aufheben* is thus essential to the whole *Phenomenology*. But it remains the case that the consciousness engaged in experience does not know the positivity of negation. As we shall see, only the philosopher perceives the genesis of a new truth in the negation of an error. Every nothingness, Hegel says, is the nothingness of that of which it is the result. On the other hand, skepticism, which is itself one of the forms of imperfect consciousness and which as such will appear in the course of the journey, isolates negativity from all content: "It abstracts

14. J.-H. Lambert, in his book *Neues Organon oder Gedanken über die Enforschung und Bezeichnung des Wahren und dessen Unterscheidung von Irrtum und Schein*, 2 vols. (Leipzig, 1764), seems to have been the first to use the term "phenomenology." He speaks of a "phenomenology or doctrine of appearance" (*Phenomenologie oder Lehre von dem Schein*), which he calls a "transcendental optic." Cf. "Phenomenology" in Kant's *Metaphysical Foundations of Natural Science*, trans. James Ellington (Indianapolis, 1970).

from the fact that nothingness is in a determinate manner the nothingness of that from which it results" (*PE*, I, 70; *PG*, 68; *PM*, 137). Thus, skepticism is empty of content; it ends up with the abstraction of nothingness, with the void, and for that reason it can go no further. Negativity, then, is not a form opposed to all content; it is immanent in content, and it allows an understanding of the latter's necessary development. From its beginning, naïve consciousness aims at the entire content of knowledge in all its richness. But it fails to reach it. It must experience its own negativity, which alone allows content to develop in successive affirmations, in particular positions, interconnected by the movement of negation.

> If, on the contrary, the result is apprehended as it is in truth, that is, as determinate negation, then a new form is immediately born and through negation the transition is made, a transition which results in the spontaneous process realizing itself through the complete series of the forms of consciousness (*PE*, I, 71; *PG*, 69; *PM*, 137).

This role of negation, which as determinate negation engenders a new content, is not apparent at first. If we assume a term *A*, can its negation, not-*A*, engender a truly new term, *B*? It seems not. In our opinion, if we are to understand Hegel's argument here we must assume that the whole is always immanent in the development of consciousness.[15] Negation is creative because the posited term had been isolated and thus was itself a kind of negation. From this it follows that the negation of that term allows the whole to be recaptured in each of its parts. Were it not for the immanence of the whole in consciousness, we should be unable to understand how negation can truly engender a content.

b. *The end point of the development*

We have evidence of the immanence of the whole in consciousness in the teleological nature of the latter's development: "The goal of knowledge is fixed as necessarily as the series of progressions" (*PE*, I, 71; *PG*, 69; *PM*, 137). Consciousness, indeed, is concept of knowledge, and that is why it is not actually real knowledge. But to say that consciousness is concept of

15. That is, the *self*, which in posing itself in a determinate manner contraposes itself to itself and thus negates and transcends itself.

knowledge is to say that it transcends itself, that it is *in-itself* what it must become *for-itself*. "Consciousness is for itself its own concept; it is therefore immediately the act of exceeding the limited, and, when the limited pertains to it, the act of going beyond itself" (*PE,* I, 71; *PG,* 69; *PM,* 138). The positive and the negative meanings of *aufheben* merge in a third meaning: transcending. Consciousness is not a thing, a determinate Dasein; it is always beyond itself; it goes beyond, or transcends, itself. This transcendental requirement constitutes the nature of consciousness as such. Was this not the case in some respects for Kantian philosophy? If truth is defined as an accord between subject and object, it is not clear how this accord is ascertainable, since representation cannot step out of itself to give proof of its conformity or nonconformity to its object. Yet if the object is not posited beyond representation, truth loses its transcendental signification for consciousness, while, if this transcendence is absolutely maintained, representation is radically cut off from its object. The immanence of the object in common consciousness on the one hand and radical transcendence on the other equally make it impossible to pose the problem of truth. But for Kant, that which made the objectivity of the object was immanent not, to be sure, in common consciousness but in transcendental consciousness. Thus, the object was transcendent to common, or finite, consciousness but immanent in transcendental consciousness. The problem of truth was shifted away from the relation between consciousness and its object to the relation between common consciousness and that within common consciousness that goes beyond it—transcendental consciousness. Now every common consciousness is also a transcendental consciousness, and every transcendental consciousness is also necessarily a common consciousness; the first is realized only in the second. This is to say that common consciousness goes beyond itself; it transcends itself and becomes transcendental consciousness. But the movement of transcending itself, of going beyond itself, is typical of consciousness as such. Every consciousness is properly more than it thinks it is, and because of this its knowledge divides: it is certainty (subjective) and as such is contraposed to [itself as] truth (objective). Thus, since it must continually go beyond itself knowledge is disquieted. And this disquiet, which Hegel describes in existential terms, is unassuaged so long as the end point of the process is not reached, an end point set necessarily by the "given" of the problem: "The goal is the point at which knowledge need not go beyond itself, the point at which it discovers itself, and at which concept corresponds to object and object to concept. Hence, the progression toward this goal also has no possible resting place and is not satisfied with stopping prior to the goal" (*PE*, I, 71; *PG*, 69; *PM*, 137–38). Consciousness' knowledge is always knowledge of an object; and if by concept we mean the subjective side of knowledge and by object its objective side, its truth, then knowledge is the movement of self-transcendence which goes from concept to object. But the whole of the *Phenomenology* shows, precisely, that this opposition is reversible. The object is the object *for consciousness*, and the concept is the knowledge of itself, the self-consciousness of knowledge. But this consciousness is deeper than it thinks; it finds the object insufficient, inadequate to it; and we can also say, even more properly, that it is the object which must be identical to the concept. In either case, this discrepancy, present in common consciousness itself, is the heart of the phenomenological development and directs it inexorably toward its goal. Thus, this whole development is characterized by an immanent finality, which the philosopher glimpses. Phenomenology is characterized in relation to ontology (the science of the absolute in-and-for-itself which will first be presented by the *Logic*) precisely by this discrepancy between consciousness and its concept, a discrepancy that is but the requirement of a perpetual transcendence.[16]

That this requirement is the very characteristic of consciousness, by virtue of which consciousness is not a determinate Dasein, a natural being, as it were, seems to us to be clearly indicated by the following text: "What is limited to a natural life is not able on its own to go beyond its immediate Dasein but is pushed beyond that Dasein by an other; this being-torn-from its position is its death. But consciousness is for itself its own concept" (*PE*, I, 71; *PG*, 69; *PM*, 138). Dasein is only what it is; its concept, to use Hegel's terminology, is entirely outside it. Dasein thus belongs to nature. The translation *être-là* [being-there], which corresponds to the etymological meaning of Dasein, seems to us to have the merit of translating this position of the natural being, which is only a here and a now and which

16. There are differences within the logos too, and there is a movement immanent in it, a dialectic different from the phenomenological dialectic. But the differences within the logos are differences "in content itself." (For a discussion of this particularly thorny problem see part VII, below.)

has other heres and nows outside itself. The negation of Dasein, which on account of its finitude must necessarily come about, is a negation alien to it, a negation it does not include for itself. But this is not the case with consciousness, which is its own concept for itself, which, that is to say, is for its own self the negation of its limited forms or, we may say, of its own death. Whereas in nature death is an external negation, spirit carries death within itself and gives it positive meaning. The whole *Phenomenology* is a meditation on this death which is carried by consciousness and which, far from being exclusively negative, an end point in an abstract nothingness, is, on the contrary, an *Aufhebung*, an ascent. Hegel says this explicitly in a passage of the *Phenomenology* about the fight between self-consciousnesses which clash in natural life: "Their act is abstract negation, not the negation [characteristic] of consciousness, which abolishes [*aufhebt*] in such a way as to preserve and keep what is abolished [*das Aufgehobene*]; in precisely this way consciousness survives the fact of being abolished" (*PE*, I, 160; *PG*, 145; *PM*, 234).[17] With regard to ethical spirit, Hegel will say that the goal of the cult of the dead in the polis is to remove death from nature in order to make it what it really is for man: an action of self-consciousness.

The death of the natural Dasein thus is merely the abstract negation of a term, *A*, which is only what it is. But in consciousness death is a necessary moment by means of which consciousness survives itself and rises to a new form. That death is the beginning of a new life of consciousness.[18] In this manner, consciousness, being for its own self its own concept, incessantly transcends itself, and the death of what it held as its truth is the appearance of a new truth. "Consciousness undergoes this violence which it inflicts on itself, a violence by which it spoils for itself all limited satisfactions" (*PE*, I, 71; *PG*, 69; *PM*, 138). As we have already noted, the whole *Phenomenology* tends to prove that this anguish which possesses human consciousness and ever drives it before itself until it is no longer a human consciousness and a human understanding (as it is for Kant) but reaches absolute knowledge, which is at once knowledge of the object and self-knowledge, is an existential anguish and not merely anguish in the cognitive sphere.

17. Cf. the preface (*PE*, I, 29; *PG*, 29; *PM*, 92).
18. Royce, *Modern Idealism*, speaks of "metempsychosis" with reference to the sequence of figures in the *Phenomenology*.

But this anguish cannot be assuaged. In vain it seeks to settle down in a thoughtless inertia—thought comes to trouble the absence of thought and its disquiet disturbs the inertia; in vain it hangs on to a sentimentality which assures that all is good in its kind—this assurance suffers as much violence from reason, which finds something to be not good precisely insofar as it is a kind (*PE*, I, 71; *PG*, 69; *PM*, 138).

As has often been noted, the *Phenomenology* is less a reduction of the experience of the life of consciousness to logical terms than a description of that life, a description which takes a certain logical form.[19] We see how negation is interpreted in the introduction and how it is assimilated to what death is in human life. Moreover, the dialectic is defined in the introduction as being the very experience of consciousness.

III. THE TECHNIQUE OF PHENOMENOLOGICAL DEVELOPMENT

IT NOW REMAINS for us to examine this last point. What is the method of the development? Fichte, in his "Deduction of Representation," and Schelling, in his *Idealismus,* had already indicated one step which consciousness takes that leads to philosophic knowledge, that is, to self-knowledge. Schelling, following Fichte here, defines transcendental idealism as follows:

If only the subjective has a primary reality for the transcendental philosopher, he will concern himself directly only with the subjective in the knowledge he will make his object. The objective will become an object for him only indirectly; and whereas, in common knowledge, knowledge itself (the act of knowing) disappears in the face of its object, in transcendental knowledge the object disappears qua object and only the act by which knowledge proceeds remains. Thus, transcendental knowledge is a knowledge of knowledge insofar as the latter is purely subjective.[20]

At the end of its development, common consciousness will rediscover the knowledge of knowledge (self-consciousness), initially presupposed by the philosopher. The case is the same

19. For example, Royce, *Modern Idealism;* Hermann Glockner, *Hegel,* 2 vols. (Stuttgart, 1929, 1940), contraposing Hegel's "pantragedism to his panlogism"; Hartmann, *Die Philosophie des deutschen Idealismus,* II, 155, with his theory of Hegel's dialectic of the real; etc.
20. Schelling, *SW*, III, 345.

for Fichte (and this is characteristic of his subjective idealism):
the I always remains occupied with itself. If common consciousness loses itself in its object, it must feel that it feels; it feels
itself, it intuits itself in intuition, it knows itself in its conceptualization. In this manner it comes to be for-itself what it is
in-itself, i.e., what it is for the philosopher. Indeed the end point
of the evolution of common consciousness is the knowledge of
knowledge insofar as the latter is purely subjective. Consciousness always reflects on itself. It discovers itself in the object
which it thought it had discovered, but in this way the object—
nature, the world, or whatever one names this other term of consciousness—disappears. Reflection is always a reflection on itself; it can find only the I in its barrenness.[21] Hegel's idealism is
of a different order; it takes seriously the theory of identity which
Schelling himself did not see how to use: "Scientific knowledge
requires that one surrender oneself to the life of the object or, in
other words, that one keep in mind and express the internal
necessity of that object" (PE, I, 47; PG, 45; PM, 112). The object of the philosopher here is indeed the knowledge of common consciousness, but he must take this knowledge as it comes
and not interfere with it. The subjective idealism which Schelling
still admitted as the second science of his philosophy, the one
that begins with the subjective, is superseded by this requirement and thereby also becomes an objective idealism. This is
not a play on words. The difference is profound, and it is important that it be emphasized. Despite his theory of the identity
of the subjective and the objective in knowledge, for Schelling
as for Fichte transcendental idealism is a "knowledge of knowledge insofar as the latter is purely subjective." The return to
identity will be effected later in a more or less artificial manner.
Such is not the case for Hegel. Consciousness is taken as it
offers itself, and it offers itself as a relation to the other—object,
world, or nature. It is quite true that this knowledge of the other
is a self-knowledge. But it is no less true that this self-knowledge
is a knowledge of the other, a knowledge of the world. Thus, we
discover in the various objects of consciousness what consciousness is itself: "The world is the mirror in which we rediscover
ourselves." The point is not to contrapose knowledge of knowledge to knowledge of the other but to discover their identity. As
Hartmann properly notes, this is a new way of studying consciousness and its metamorphoses: "This new tack is Hegel's

21. The word is Hegel's (PE, I, 72; PG, 70; PM, 139).

discovery, a *novum* in philosophy, a trajectory of the self-conception of consciousness in its transformations on the basis of its conception of its objects in their transformations." [22] If we wish to conceive consciousness, we must ask what the world is for it, what it gives out as its truth. We shall objectively discover consciousness itself in its object, and we shall read its own history in the history of its objects. Inversely, and here subjective idealism is rejoined, consciousness must discover that that history is its own and that in conceiving its object it conceives itself. At the end of this phenomenology, knowledge of knowledge will not be contraposed to anything else; according to the very evolution of consciousness it will be in effect self-knowledge and knowledge of the object. Since this object, Hegel's absolute, is spirit in its full richness, we can say that it is spirit that knows itself in consciousness, and that consciousness knows itself as spirit. As self-knowledge, it will be not the absolute that is beyond all reflection but the absolute that reflects back on itself. It will thus be subject and no longer merely substance. [23]

It is on this point that Hegel's philosophy, as a phenomenology, differs from Kantian reflection and even from Schelling's transcendental idealism. We have already quoted a text of Schelling's which defines the point of view of transcendental idealism as knowledge of knowledge insofar as it is purely subjective. Schelling begins, indeed, by assuming philosophical self-consciousness (what Hegel calls science), and he shows how common consciousness is to reach this presupposed science by reflecting back on itself. Empirical knowledge is to be measured against philosophic truth, "but where science arises first, neither it nor anything else justifies itself as essence or as the in-itself; and without something of that kind no test seems possible" (*PE*, I, 72; *PG*, 70; *PM*, 139).

In fact, consciousness must be taken as it presents itself without yet being interpreted. Now there are two moments in it, for to be conscious is to distinguish what one is conscious of from oneself, to distinguish it and at the same time to relate to it: "Consciousness *distinguishes* something from itself to which,

22. Hartmann, *Die Philosophie des deutschen Idealismus*, II, 80.
23. Cf. the preface (*PE*, I, 17; *PG*, 19; *PM*, 80): "According to my point of view, which will be justified only through the presentation of the system, everything depends on this point: to apprehend and express the true not only as substance but also as subject." Cf. also *PE*, I, 21; *PG*, 22; *PM*, 83: "the need to represent the absolute as subject."

precisely, it *relates*" (*PE*, I, 72; *PG*, 70; *PM*, 139). For conscious-ness, being is *for*-it; at the same time, consciousness posits being as in-itself, as external to that relation. "The aspect of in-itself is called truth" (*PE*, I, 73; *PG*, 70; *PM*, 139). Thus conscious-ness knows something: it has certainty, and it lays claim to a truth independent of its certainty. Now if we, that is, philoso-phers, consider knowledge as our object, then its in-itself is its being-for-us. The truth of knowledge, then, lies in the knowledge of knowledge, in philosophic consciousness. The measure against which common consciousness' knowledge is compared is that knowledge of knowledge which Fichte and Schelling presuppose at the start. But in that case this measure is part of philosophic consciousness and not of common consciousness. It is externally imposed on the latter, and we do not see why common con-sciousness is bound to accept it: "The essence, or the criterion, would lie in us, and that which should be compared to it, that about which, through this comparison, a decision should be made would not necessarily be bound to recognize [i.e., accept] it" (*PE*, I, 73; *PG*, 71; *PM*, 140). For this reason, phenomenal knowledge must test itself; the philosopher need only observe its experience.

Indeed, the measure that consciousness uses lies within itself, not outside in a philosophic knowledge that remains alien to it: "Consciousness carries its own measure within itself; research here will be a comparison of consciousness with itself" (*PE*, I, 73; *PG*, 71; *PM*, 140). It is indeed consciousness that poses a moment of truth and a moment of knowledge and distinguishes the one from the other. By designating what for it is the truth, it gives the criterion of its own knowledge. Thenceforth we need but attend to its experience, an experience that is a comparison of what for it is the truth, the in-itself, with the knowledge that it takes of it: "In what consciousness designates within itself as the in-itself, or as the true, we have the measure that it sets up for gauging its own knowledge" (*PE*, I, 73; *PG*, 71; *PM*, 140). A particular consciousness, like one of those we shall encounter in the course of the phe-nomenological development, is characterized by a certain struc-ture. It is a shape or, better, a figure (*Gestalt*) of consciousness. This figure is objective as well as subjective. For it, the true is a certain world posited as existing in-itself. This world may be sensuous immediateness, or the thing of perception, or force, or life; but to this true is linked a certain knowledge which is the knowledge of this true, or this object posited as existing in-itself.

We can call knowledge the concept and the true the object just as well as we can call the true the concept and knowledge the object, i.e., the object as it is for an other. There is nonetheless always a difference, which is the heart of the development of the figure: "The examination consists, in fact, in seeing whether the concept corresponds to the object (or whether the object corresponds to its concept)" (*PE*, I, 73–74; *PG*, 71; *PM*, 141). The theory of knowledge is at the same time a theory of the object of knowledge. Consciousness cannot be separated from what for it is its object, from that which it takes to be the true. But if consciousness is consciousness of the object, it is also consciousness of itself. These two moments lie in it and are different: "[Consciousness] is consciousness both of what for it is the true and of its knowledge of that truth." But these two moments are related, and this relation, precisely, is what is called "experience," Consciousness tests its knowledge in that which it takes to be true; and insofar as it is still finite consciousness, a particular figure, it is constrained to go beyond itself. Its knowledge of the true is changed when it discovers the inadequateness present in that true. In its object it experiences itself, and in its knowledge it experiences its object. In this manner, it progresses of its own accord from one particular figure to another without the philosopher having to be anything but a spectator who recollects the process.

> Not only would our intervention be superfluous from the point of view that concept and object, the measure and the matter to be examined, are present in consciousness itself, but we are also spared the trouble of comparing the two, of an examination in the strict sense of the word; so that, from this point of view, when consciousness examines itself there remains for us only to be mere spectators (*PE*, I, 74; *PG*, 72; *PM*, 141).

We have already indicated that experience bears not only on knowledge but also on the object, for this particular knowledge is knowledge of an object. Consciousness tests its knowledge in order to render it adequate to that which it holds to be true—a certain world posited as existing in-itself—but, when its knowledge changes, its object also changes. The latter had been the object of a certain knowledge; this knowledge having become other, the object also becomes other. In testing out its knowledge of what it took as the in-itself, what it posited as being the absolutely true, consciousness discovers the latter to have been *in-itself* only for it. This, precisely, is the *result* of experience:

the *negation* of the preceding object and the *appearance* of a new object, which in turn engenders a new knowledge. For "the measure of examination changes if that for which it was to be the measure does not stand up through the examination; and the examination is an examination not only of knowledge but also of its unit of measure" (*PE*, I, 75; *PG*, 72–73; *PM*, 142). Clearly, epistemology is also a theory of the object of knowledge.

"This *dialectical* movement which consciousness exercises within itself, in its knowledge as well as in its object, is, *insofar as the new true object rises up from this movement,* what is properly called *experience*" (*PE*, I, 75; *PG*, 73; *PM*, 142). In this definition Hegel assimilates the experience which consciousness enters into to a dialectic, but, conversely, he makes us understand how the dialectic, especially in the *Phenomenology*, is properly speaking an experience. There is, however, a difference between the dialectic and the experience consciousness enters into. To reflect on this difference will lead us to understand why phenomenology can also be a science and why it can present a necessity which has meaning only for philosophic consciousness, and not for the consciousness which is itself engaged in experience.

In experience, in the usual sense of the word, consciousness sees what it held to be the true and the in-itself disappear, and at the same time it sees a different object *appear* as though it were a new thing, something *discovered*.[24] "This new object contains the annihilation of the first; it is the experience based on it" (*PE*, I, 75; *PG*, 73; *PM*, 143). But the matter appears otherwise to consciousness. It believes that after having disowned its first truth, it discovers a second one, which is completely different. That is why consciousness posits the new truth as contraposed to it, as an object (*Gegenstand*), and not as that which results from the prior movement and is engendered by it (*Entstandenes*, no longer *Gegenstand*). Experience thus seems to consciousness to be a discovery of new worlds. And this is so because consciousness forgets the course of the development of those worlds. Like skepticism, it sees only the negative result of

24. This is, moreover, the usual meaning of the word "experience." In experience, consciousness sees something new *appear,* something contraposed to it, an object. But for philosophic consciousness this object (*Gegenstand*) is engendered; it sees it *born* out of the prior development (*Entstandenes*). Phenomenal consciousness, on the other hand, forgets this past and begins anew with each new experience as though it were reborn each time.

its past experience. Facing its future and not its past, it is unable to understand how its past experience was a genesis of what for it is a new object.

That is why the necessity of the experience which consciousness enters into presents itself in two lights. Or, rather, there are two necessities: the necessity of the negation of the object, effected by consciousness itself in its experience, in the testing of its knowledge, and the necessity of the appearance of the new object which takes shape through the prior experience.[25] The latter necessity pertains only to the philosopher who rethinks the phenomenological development. There is in this a moment of the in-itself or the "for-us" which is not found in consciousness:

> This circumstance accompanies the whole succession of the figures of consciousness in its necessity. But this very necessity, the birth of the new object which appears to consciousness without consciousness knowing how it came to it, is what for us goes on behind the latter's back. In this movement, a moment of being-in-itself, or being-for-us, that is, for the philosopher, is thus produced which is not present for the consciousness that is itself in the grip of experience (*PE*, I, 76–77; *PG*, 74; *PM*, 144).

The content is, indeed, for-it, but the origin of the content is not. It is as though consciousness forgot its own development, which has made it what it is at every particular moment. "What is born exists for [consciousness] only as an object (*Gegenstand*); for us it exists at the same time as movement and as becoming" (*PE*, I, 77; *PG*, 74; *PM*, 144).[26]

It is enough to take several chapters of the *Phenomenology* to see that each moment is indeed the result of a development of which consciousness itself is unaware. Only the philosopher sees in force (the object of understanding) the result of the movement of perceiving consciousness, or in life, which seems a new object, the result of the understanding's dialectic of the infinite. Thus the various particular consciousnesses which meet in the *Phenomenology* are bound to one another, not by a contingent development, which is what is ordinarily meant by experience,

25. We may call this necessity "retrospective."
26. The *Phenomenology* is simultaneously a *theory of knowledge* and a *speculative philosophy*, a *description* of phenomenal consciousness and the *comprehension* of that consciousness by philosophy. But it is a speculative philosophy only for us. (On this point, see part VII, below.)

but by an immanent necessity which is only for the philosopher. "It is by virtue of this necessity that such a route toward science as this, is already *itself* science and, on account of its content, is the science of the *experience of consciousness*" (*PE*, I, 77; *PG*, 74; *PM*, 144).[27]

27. Thus, in the *Phenomenology*, the sequence of the experiences of consciousness is contingent only for phenomenal consciousness. We who recollect these experiences in so doing discover the necessity of the progression from the one to the next. What the *Phenomenology* demonstrates is the immanence in consciousness of every experience. But we must recognize that this (synthetic) necessity is not always easy to grasp and that to the modern reader the transitions appear arbitrary. Moreover, these transitions pose the problem of the relation of the *Phenomenology* to history.

2 / History and Phenomenology

I. THE SPIRIT IS HISTORY

BEFORE STUDYING the structure of the *Phenomenology,* it is impossible to avoid asking whether the *Phenomenology* is a history of humanity, or whether, at least, it claims to be a philosophy of that history. In *Idealismus,* Schelling had posed the general problem that a philosophy of history must resolve. It will be useful to recall here the clues, and they are only clues, which Schelling's system contains in order better to note the similarities and differences between such a philosophy of history and the *Phenomenology.*

Schelling posed the question of a "transcendental possibility of history,"[1] a question that would lead him to a philosophy of history which would be for practical philosophy what nature is for theoretical philosophy. The categories of intelligence are made real, or realized, in nature; those of the will are expressed in history. The practical ideal, the ideal of an order of cosmopolitan law, is only a far-off ideal for a particular individual, an ideal whose realization depends not only on his free will but on the free will of other rational beings as well. History thus bears on the species and not on the individual: "All my actions, indeed, finally lead to a result the realization of which cannot be attained by the individual alone but only by the whole species."[2] Thus, the only history is a history of humanity. Now this history of humanity is possible only on the condition that

1. Schelling, *SW,* III, 590.
2. *Ibid.,* p. 596.

[27]

in it necessity is reconciled with liberty, the objective with the subjective, and the unconscious with the conscious. In other words, "freedom must be guaranteed by an order that is as manifest and unchanging as that of nature." [3] History must have a meaning. Freedom must necessarily be realized in it, and the individually arbitrary must play only an episodic and fragmentary role. In order that there really be a history of humanity which is for practical philosophy what nature is for theoretical philosophy, it is necessary that unconscious actions be combined with the conscious actions of individualities. This identity of free will and necessity allows Schelling to recognize his absolute in history and to see in history not simply a work of men with no guarantee of lasting effect, but also a manifestation or a revelation of the absolute itself:

> Necessity must be in liberty, which means through my liberty, and while I think I am acting freely something which I do not foresee must come about unconsciously, that is, without my participation. In other words, an unconscious activity must be contraposed to conscious activity, to that activity, already deduced, which freely determines; an unconscious activity by which a result is added to the most unlimited external manifestation of freedom without the author of the action taking notice of it, without his wishing it, and perhaps even against his will, a result that he could never have brought about by his will. [4]

We can easily grasp here the difference between Fichte's point of view, which stops with a moral order of the world that ought to exist but does not exist necessarily, and Schelling's point of view, which sees in history an actual and necessary realization of freedom, through destiny or providence. Hegel follows Schelling on this point. He sees in human passions and in the individual goals which men believe they pursue only the tricks of reason, which in this way comes to make itself actually real. The phrase "history is a theodicy" was Schelling's before it was Hegel's.

But though Schelling indicates the possibility of a philosophy of history, he fails to fulfill this possibility. He limits himself to

3. *Ibid.*, p. 593. For a discussion of the antecedents of this kind of historical thought in Germany and of the Leibnizian origin of this teleology in history, see M. Guéroult, *L'Evolution et la structure de la doctrine de la science chez Fichte*, in *Publications de la Faculté de Strasbourg* (1930), I, 8 ff.
4. Schelling, *SW*, III, 594.

ascribing to history that identity of the subjective and the objective which for him is the absolute, without showing us how this absolute is brought to reflect itself or to manifest itself in the particular form of a history. How, in fact, is this synthesis of conscious and unconscious activity possible? Schelling poses, or presupposes, it: "Such a preestablished harmony between the objective (that which conforms to law) and the determining (that which is free) can be conceived only by means of a higher term, raised above both, which therefore is neither intelligence nor freedom but the common source of that which is intelligent and that which is free." [5] The very manner in which Schelling puts the problem leads him radically to separate the absolute from its reflected image in consciousness, and essence from its manifestation. The following quotation demonstrates this perhaps even more clearly:

> If this higher term is only the principle of the identity of the absolutely subjective and the absolutely objective, of the conscious and the unconscious, which separate in free action in order to manifest themselves, then this higher term cannot itself be either subject or object or both at once: it is only the absolute identity, in which there is no duality and which can never reach consciousness precisely because duality is the condition of all consciousness. [6]

Schelling's absolute, which is the condition of history, is thus raised above history itself. To be sure, Schelling writes, in a phrase similar to Hegel's, that, "considered in its entirety, history is a continual and progressive revelation of the absolute," but he does not manage to take this assertion seriously and to draw from it a genuine philosophy of the spirit in history. He sees history as a manifestation of the absolute, like nature, but this absolute does not know the reflection back on itself which would make it what Hegel calls a subject: "In my view, which will be justified only in the presentation of the system, everything depends on this essential point: to apprehend and express the true not only as substance but also precisely as subject" (*PE*, I, 17; *PG*, 19; *PM*, 80). [7] In Hegel's view, Schelling remains a Spinozist:

5. *Ibid.*, p. 600.
6. *Ibid.*
7. On the idea of a progressive revelation, see Lessing (whose influence on the young Hegel was important), especially *Das Christentum der Vernunft* and *Die Erziehung des Menschengeschlechts*.

he successfully grasped the identity of the absolute, but he was unable to move from that to reflection, which remains for him alien to the life of the absolute. For this reason, Hegel, in the preface to the *Phenomenology,* judges Schelling's view of identity severely: "to consider a given Dasein as it is in the absolute is to say that, although one is indeed speaking now as if about some thing, there are certainly no such things in the absolute, in the A = A, because there all is one" (*PE,* I, 16; *PG,* 19; *PM,* 79). "This absolute is the night in which all cows are black."

It is on the subject of history that we can best understand the differences between Schelling's philosophy and Hegel's. In spite of the texts quoted above which seem to indicate that Schelling already had developed a philosophy of history similar to Hegel's, we must not be fooled by the apparent similarities. Schelling began with an intuition of the absolute that led him primarily to a philosophy of nature. Knowledge should become identified with life. Insofar as it is an unconscious product of intelligence, organic life, like artistic production in which consciousness joins unconsciousness, is a manifestation of the absolute. From these differences between knowledge and life, which are only quantitative, mere differences of power, knowledge must go back to the first source, the absolute. To coincide with the source is what Schelling calls "intellectual intuition." After the point of coincidence, the intuition of pure life is either beyond or this side of any reflection. Reflection is external to it. One can indeed find in Hegel's early works, especially in the "Systemfragment" ["Fragment of a System" (in *Early Theological Writings*)], expressions similar to Schelling's e.g., "to think pure life, that is the task." [8] But despite this it seems to us that Hegel's early works indicate a different perspective. Hegel was interested neither in organic life nor in the life of nature in general but in the life of spirit insofar as that life is history. Thus, from its first elaboration, Hegelian thought is a thought of human history, while Schelling's is a thought of nature or of life in general. And Hegel's view of history is a tragic view. The ruse of reason presents itself in history not simply as a means of conjoining unconsciousness and consciousness, but as a tragic conflict between man and his destiny, a conflict perpetually overcome and

8. Cf. Hegel, *Theologische Jugendschriften,* pp. 302 and 345 ff. Also see our article "Les Travaux de jeunesse de Hegel d'après des ouvrages récents," *Revue de métaphysique et de morale,* XLII, (July, Oct., 1935).

perpetually renewed. It is this conflict that Hegel seeks to think through, and to think through in the very heart of the absolute: "The life of God and divine knowledge can indeed be expressed, if one likes, as the play of love with itself, but this idea is reduced to mere edification and even to insipidity if the seriousness, the torment, the patience, and the labor of the negative are lacking" (*PE*, I, 18; *PG*, 20; *PM*, 81). The pantragedism of history and the panlogism of logic are one and the same, as this sentence in which Hegel speaks at the same time of the pain and the labor of the negative shows.

The duality which is the foundation of history and which Schelling eliminates from the absolute is an essential moment in the *Phenomenology*. It characterizes consciousness, but consciousness is not therefore alien to the absolute. On the contrary, the historical development of consciousness is the reflection back on itself of the absolute—of spirit. Before asking ourselves in what way this reflection of consciousness is a history, and what kind of history it is, we must define more closely Hegel's view of the relation between spirit and history. *The spirit is history for Hegel*—this is a fundamental thesis identical to the thesis that *the absolute is subject*—"but organic nature has no history" (*PE*, I, 247; *PG*, 220; *PM*, 326). For in organic nature universality is only an interior without actual development in the world. There are indeed living individuals, but life comes to express itself in them only as an abstract universal, only as the *negation* of all particular determinations. In other words, the meaning of organic life is death, the annihilation of everything that claims a separate subsistence. The intuition of life as universal either is lost in the contingency of separate individuals or is present in them as the power which annihilates them and which alone makes them actually alive. To try to reach this intuition of life as creative of ever-new individualities or as destructive of these individualities (the two are one, since the double process is but a single one: reproduction and death) is to submerge oneself "in the night in which all cows are black."

The passage we are now commenting on, which is part of one of the most obscure sections of the *Phenomenology*, "The Observation of Nature as an Organic Whole" (*PE*, I, 238–48; *PG*, 216–21; *PM*, 318–27), is devoted to a philosophy of nature which is possible for the consciousness that here appears as reason. In the *Idealismus*, Schelling worked out the "ages" of self-consciousness and the categories of nature or of history in a parallel way. In the second age, the self raises itself from productive intuition to reflection; it becomes aware of this production, which was an unconscious one in the first age. In these conditions, the producing I, the intelligence, must be aware not only of a product which is external to it and which is presented to it as though coming from elsewhere, but also of the activity of producing. Now, since it can be conscious only of a finite product, a product which is at once finite and infinite must be presented to it, a product about some aspects of which it can have the intuition of its own producing activity in an objective mode. For Schelling, the organic world, the living universe, is such a product: "Every plant, for example, is a symbol of intelligence."[9] In this universe of life intelligence contemplates, as it were, itself. Just as intelligence is an infinite effort to organize itself, so too life as a whole manifests itself in a series of stages, as a kind of "history" in which organization becomes progressively more autonomous. It is in this life that intelligence can first contemplate itself: "Is not nature the odyssey of the spirit?"

The book Hegel writes is a *Phenomenology of Spirit* and not of nature, but the thought of nature has a place in it. But whereas Schelling, almost forgetting his starting point in the *Idealismus*, viz., "the study of subjective knowledge," latches onto categories which are specific only to nature and deals with them for themselves, Hegel asks whether nature, considered in its entirety as an organic whole, can provide reason with an adequate expression of itself. This seems to be the meaning of the passage of the *Phenomenology* we are considering here. The answer is negative. What reason contemplates in nature as a whole is a syllogism the outer terms of which are universal life as universal, on the one hand, and the earth, the environment in the midst of which all living beings develop, on the other. The middle term, then, is constituted by particular living beings who are but representatives of universal life and who are subjected to disrupting influences from the external environment on which they depend. Between the organization of the genus into species and the ceaseless influences of the environment, the living individual represents for reason only a contingent expression of itself. In the eighteenth century, Lamarck at first held that all living species were related in a way that resulted from a development intrinsic to life. But he was then led to attribute increasing importance to the enormous influence of the en-

9. Schelling, *SW*, III, 489.

vironment. These two distinct principles of explanation came to be confused in his natural philosophy, and thus make interpretation of it particularly difficult. Hegel has something similar in view:

> The genus (that is, universal life) divides itself into species according to the [universal] determination of number; the basis of its subdivision can also be the particular determination of its Dasein, for example, shape, color, etc. But in this calm occupation, it is subjected to violence by the universal individual, the earth, which, as universal negation, asserts against the systematization of the genus differences such as the earth has within itself. The nature of these differences, by virtue of the substance to which they pertain, is different from living nature. The actions of the genus become a completely limited undertaking which can be carried out only within the powerful elements of the earth and which, interrupted on all sides by their unbridled violence, is full of lacunae and of failures (*PE*, I, 246; *PG*, 219; *PM*, 325).

Reason, thus, cannot discover itself in the spectacle of life. No doubt, universal life as life is indeed what Hegel calls the concept (*Begriff*), the universal which always is at once itself and its other; but this life, like Schelling's absolute, cannot manage to develop while keeping its universal character in all its particular forms. Life is indeed entirely present in each particular living being—it is what makes it be born, reproduce itself, and die—but it does not express itself as such in each of its particular differences. The death of one living being is intimately related to the birth of another, but in this way life repeats itself without really developing itself. Unlike the genus, it does not express itself in its history: "This life is not a self-sufficient system of figures" (*PE*, I, 247; *PG*, 219; *PM*, 326).

We return, then, to the starting point of our analysis of the text "organic life has no history." Only spirit has a history, that is, a development of itself by itself such that it retains its identity in each of its particularizations, and when it negates them, which is the very movement of the concept, it simultaneously preserves them in order to raise them to a higher form. Only spirit has a past which it internalizes (*Erinnerung*) and a future which it projects ahead of itself because it must become for-itself what it is in-itself. There is a conception of time and temporality implied in the *Phenomenology*. What interests us here is the definition of spirit as history and the importance of this definition for the *Phenomenology*.

Hegel tells us that, as opposed to universal life, which rushes immediately from its universal, viz., life, to its sensuous singularity without expressing itself in a development that is at once universal and particular (the "concrete universal"), consciousness presents the possibility of such a development. "Thus consciousness has as its middle term, between its universal spirit and its singularity as sensuous consciousness, the system of figurations of consciousness which we understood as the life of spirit ordering itself until it becomes the whole. This system is considered in this book and has its own objective Dasein as world history" (*PE*, I, 247; *PG*, 219; *PM*, 326). Sensuous consciousness is, properly speaking, the particular, but only abstractly particular, consciousness, limited to a here and a now as these are presented in the chapter on sensuous certainty at the beginning of the *Phenomenology* (*PE*, I, 81; *PG*, 79; *PM*, 151). But the universal spirit is itself abstractly universal consciousness. The two terms stand by virtue of each other, and any actual consciousness is at once particular and universal and is able to discover through its particularity the universality essential to it. This movement, by means of which every particular consciousness becomes at the same time universal consciousness, constitutes authentic specificity; the course of this specificity through all the phases of its development is precisely the *Phenomenology*.[10]

II. THE *Phenomenology* IS NOT THE HISTORY OF THE WORLD

BUT, ON THE OTHER HAND, the *Phenomenology* is not the history of the world, although in certain respects it is a history and is related to the history of the world. There is a special problem here which we must now consider. Hegel says explicitly that the *Phenomenology* is distinct from the history of the world and from a philosophy of that history. He says this both in the preface and in the text we have just commented on ("system [which] is considered in this book and [which] has its

10. The final reconciliation—redemption and the remission of sins—is precisely this double movement of universal consciousness becoming particular and particular consciousness becoming universal. It is in this relative movement that spirit still knows spirit in its "other." See *PE*, II, 190; *PG*, 463; *PM*, 667 and our commentary on that passage, part VI, chapter 2, below.

own objective Dasein as world history"), and also in the passage at the end of the book where he contraposes, in a more ambiguous way, the free temporal development of history to the conceptual history that the *Phenomenology* is (*PE*, II, 313; *PG*, 564; *PM*, 808).[11] In many other passages, he speaks of a "world spirit," the development of which is distinct from the phenomenological development.[12] Besides, we need but look at the content of the *Phenomenology* to rule out the hypothesis that the *Phenomenology* is properly speaking the philosophy of world history in its entirety.

The role of history in the *Phenomenology* is so great that Haym could define the book as "a transcendental psychology vitiated by history and a history vitiated by transcendental psychology."[13] But history does not play the same role throughout the book. In what we will call the first part of the *Phenomenology*, including the major sections, "Consciousness," "Self-consciousness," and "Reason," the only ones which remain in the *Propaedeutic* and in the *Encyclopaedia*, history plays little more than the role of example. It allows concrete illustration of what, according to Hegel, is a novel and a necessary development of consciousness. These historical illustrations occur especially in the most concrete chapters, on self-consciousness and on reason. Self-consciousness is formed in the relations of the struggle between opposed self-consciousnesses and that between master and slave, struggles which, properly speaking, are not temporal, although they can be found at the origin of all human civilizations and reproduce themselves in different forms throughout the history of humanity. The developments that follow evoke more precisely particular moments of human history: stoicism, skepticism, and unhappy consciousness. Though generally stingy with historical detail and proceeding always by allusions, Hegel does not hesitate to say, after having described in abstract terms the self-consciousness that has raised itself to autonomy, that "when this liberty of self-consciousness enters the history of the

11. More precisely, Hegel appears to distinguish a temporal development some of whose manifestations are contingent, a science of phenomenal knowledge (the *Phenomenology*), and a philosophy of history which will be part of the system proper and will genuinely be history conceptualized in-and-for-itself.

12. See especially *PE*, I, 169, 198, etc.; *PG*, 152, 175; *PM*, 243, 272, as well as the passages from the preface on which we comment below.

13. R. Haym, *Hegel und seine Zeit* (Berlin, 1927), p. 243 (originally published in 1857).

spirit as the conscious appearance of self-consciousness, it is, as is well known, called stoicism" (*PE*, I, 169; *PG*, 152; *PM*, 243–44). And at the end of this paragraph on stoicism, he adds, "Stoicism could arise as the universal form of the world spirit only in a time of universal fear and slavery, but also only at a time of a universal culture [*Bildung*] that had raised education and culture [*das Bilden*] to the level of thought" (*PE*, I, 170; *PG*, 152; *PM*, 245).[14] As we see, the phenomenological development, necessarily encountering a moment of the abstract freedom of self-consciousness, uses the corresponding phase of world history to illustrate its description and make it more precise.

We know from Hegel's early works that unhappy consciousness is intermingled at its origin with Judaism and then carries over to the Christianity of the Middle Ages. But the passage of the *Phenomenology* which discusses unhappy consciousness includes no explicit mention of Judaism. It is thus always a matter of historical illustrations in the service of a necessary development of self-consciousness. The case is the same in the section on reason, in which we find allusions to the Renaissance, and in the precise use of works contemporary with Hegel—Schiller's "The Robbers," Goethe's *Faust*—or works such as *Don Quixote* which were particularly appreciated by the Romantics (*PE*, I, 297 ff.; *PG*, 262; *PM*, 384).[15]

Are these examples, these concrete illustrations of moments of the development of consciousness, chosen arbitrarily or do they absolutely impose themselves? A commentary on the *Phenomenology* can try to resolve this problem by taking cognizance of the precise task that Hegel set himself, but it is certain that there is no complete philosophy of human history in the book. Besides, Hegel clearly insists that the three moments, consciousness, self-consciousness, and reason, are not to be considered as a succession. They are not in time; they are abstractions contrived from within the whole of spirit and studied in their separate development. Only the specific forms of these moments —sensuous certainty, perception, understanding, etc., which

14. Thus, in his conversation with M. de Sacy, Pascal, wishing to contrapose two necessary attitudes of spirit, used stoicism and Montaigne.

15. See also the preceding page, in which Hegel explains his choice of contemporary examples to illustrate the necessary moments of the development (pleasure and necessity, the law of the heart, etc.).

represent a concrete totality—can be considered to be successive within the moment of which they are a part. But this temporal succession is the sign of a novel development of the moment under consideration. The movement from sensuous certainty to perception can be thought of as a temporal movement. Similarly, it must be admitted that the movement from the master-slave relation to stoicism, the relationships between stoicism and skepticism, between Greek skepticism and the Old Testament feeling of the vanity of all things, and between all this and Christianity present a certain historical interpretation. The phenomenological development within a single moment, that of consciousness or that of self-consciousness, indeed coincides with a passage of time or is at least susceptible to being represented temporally.

In what we will call the second part of the *Phenomenology*, which includes the chapters "Spirit," "Religion," and "Absolute Knowledge," the problem is much more complex. We sometimes seem to have before us a veritable philosophy of history; we shall try to explain why this is so when we study the structure of the *Phenomenology*. What is certain is that starting with the *Propaedeutic* and the *Encyclopaedia* Hegel suppressed the chapters "Spirit" and "Religion" from the phenomenology *stricto sensu*. This is because in these two chapters the development of individual consciousness is only formally at issue. In the chapter on spirit, for example, concrete totalities, particular spirits, are considered: that of the Greek city, that of the Roman Empire and Roman law, that of Western culture, that of the French Revolution, and that of the Germanic world. Hegel says so himself at the beginning of the chapter on spirit. After indicating that the spirit alone is "existence," the reason which became a living world, the individual who is a world (*PE*, II, 12; *PG*, 315; *PM*, 460), he notes that the prior moments, self-consciousness and reason, were only abstractions of the spirit: "all the earlier figures of consciousness are abstractions of this spirit; they are by virtue of the spirit analyzing itself, distinguishing its own moments and dwelling on the specific moments" (*PE*, II, 11; *PG*, 314; *PM*, 459). Hegel adds that this action of isolating such moments presupposes the spirit and can take place only in it. Only the spirit, in the meaning Hegel gives the word, is thus a concrete whole which, consequently, has a novel development and a real history. This is why the figures of the spirit differ from the preceding figures: "these figures are distinguished, however, from the preceding figures in that they are themselves real spirits, authentic real entities, and in that instead of being merely the figures of consciousness they are the figures of a world" (*PE*, II, 12; *PG*, 315; *PM*, 460).

From that moment on, the development of the spirit seems to coincide with a real historical development. This is the history of the formation of a consciousness of the spirit, understood as a supraindividual reality, from the ancient polis to the French Revolution. But with reference to actual history there are many gaps in this development. There is nothing on the Renaissance, for example, only questionable allusions to the Reformation, and, on the other hand, long passages on the Enlightenment (*Aufklärung*) and on the French Revolution. How are these choices and these omissions justified, and what was Hegel's method here? If the *Phenomenology* were an attempt to present a complete philosophy of history, we should have to judge it a failure. Yet Hegel insists on the scientific nature of his book and on the necessity of the development he traces. The justification of this necessity must lie elsewhere than in a general history of the world.

The chapter on religion poses no fewer problems. Hegel clearly says that with regard to religion nothing that precedes it is to be considered as a historical development. Religion, in its turn, presupposes the whole of the spirit, and a phenomenological study of religion must consider all previous moments as gathering up and constituting the substance of absolute spirit which rises to consciousness of its own self. "Besides, the course of these moments with reference to religion cannot be temporally represented" (*PE*, II, 207; *PG*, 476; *PM*, 689). There is, on the other hand, a development of religion (from natural to aesthetic to revealed religion) which does appear to have a historical meaning per se.

From these very general remarks, we can at least conclude that the *Phenomenology* is not exactly a philosophy of world history. Only in the second part of the book can a closer connection between the phenomenological development and the development of history in the proper sense of the word be made. Yet spirit does not precede religion in time; it precedes it only *for us*, who need to have completed the development of spirit as existence and reached the thought of reconciliation in order to understand the meaning of religion. Finally, the various moments chosen in these two chapters do not encompass universal history but only coincide with those historical phenomena which Hegel considers especially important for his task. The question is not resolved. We must try to ascertain more closely the significance of the phenomenological development with regard to the development of history.

III. THE *Phenomenology*: A HISTORY OF INDIVIDUAL CONSCIOUSNESS

THE *Phenomenology* raises empirical consciousness to absolute knowledge. This was the book's first intention, as the introduction shows, and it remained the way that Hegel considered it later, in the preface. "The task of leading the individual from his unformed state to knowledge is to be understood in its most general sense. It consists in considering the universal individual—self-conscious spirit—in the process of its formation" (*PE,* I, 25; *PG,* 26; *PM,* 89). But the rise of empirical consciousness to absolute knowledge is possible only if the necessary stages of its ascent are discovered within it. These stages are still within it; all that is needed is that it descend into the interiority of memory by an action comparable to Platonic recollection. Indeed, the individual, child of his time, possesses within himself the whole substance of the spirit of that time. He needs only appropriate it to himself, make it present to himself again "in the same way that one who begins the study of a higher science reviews the preparatory knowledge he has known implicitly for a long time in order to bring that content fully to mind again" (*PE,* I, 26; *PG,* 27; *PM,* 89).

Thus, the problem which the *Phenomenology* poses is not that of world history but that of the education of the specific individual who must, necessarily, be formed to knowledge by becoming aware of what Hegel calls his substance. This is a specifically pedagogical task not unrelated to the task Rousseau set for himself in *Emile.* The "primary idea" of Rousseau's book has been described as "rigorously scientific; if the individual's development summarily repeats the evolution of the species, then the child's education must largely reproduce the general movement of humanity." [16] But while Rousseau concluded from this that the age of sensation had to precede that of reflection, Hegel took the immanence of human history in general in the individual consciousness seriously.

16. Gustave Lanson, *Littérature française,* 22d edition, p. 796.

Since not only the substance of the individual but also the world spirit had the patience to pass through these forms over a long stretch of time and to undertake the prodigious labor of universal history in which it incarnated its own total content into each form to the extent that that form allowed it, and since the world spirit could not reach its self-consciousness with less labor, so, in the very nature of things the individual cannot grasp his substance by a shorter road. Yet the pain is less, for in-itself all this is already finished, the content is the actual reality already annihilated in possibility, the immediateness already forced, the configuration already reduced to outline, to the simple determination of thought (*PE*, I, 27; *PG*, 27–28; *PM*, 91).

The history of the world is finished; all that is needed is for the specific individual to rediscover it in himself.

The specific individual must pass through the content of the stages of the formation of universal spirit, but as figures already unseated by spirit, as stages of a way already traced and flattened out. Thus, we see that in the sphere of knowledge what absorbed adult minds in earlier ages is now reduced to something familiar, to school exercises, even to children's games. In pedagogical progress we see projected a sketch of the history of universal culture (*PE*, I, 26; *PG*, 27; *PM*, 89–90).

It is this history of universal culture, to the extent that it contributes to the preparation of what Hegel calls absolute knowledge, that must be called forth in individual consciousness. Individual consciousness must become aware within itself of its substance, which at first—when this consciousness is still at the beginning of its philosophical and human itinerary—appears to it as external. Schelling had already insisted on this immanence of history in the individual's present: "We assert that no individual consciousness could be posed with all the determinations with which it is posed and which necessarily belong to it, if the whole of history had not preceded it—as could easily be demonstrated by examples if we were discussing works of art." [17] Schelling concludes from this that history can be thought out retrospectively, simply by trying to understand the present state of the world and of the individuality that is under consideration in it.

Thus there is a certain relation between phenomenology and the philosophy of history. Phenomenology is the concrete, ex-

17. Schelling, *SW*, III, 590.

plicit development and formation of the individual, the rise of his finite self to absolute self. But that elevation is possible only through the use of the moments of world history, moments which are immanent in that individual consciousness. Instead of being satisfied with well-known representations which, precisely because they are familiar, are in fact not known (*PE*, I, 28; *PG*, 28; *PM*, 92), individual consciousness must analyze and develop them within itself. Thus it will rediscover within itself earlier phases of history and, instead of traversing them without seeing what is at stake, it will, on the contrary, have to dwell in them and reconstitute its past experience in order that the meaning of that experience appear to it. "Impatience attempts the impossible: to obtain the goal in the absence of the means" (*PE*, I, 27; *PG*, 27; *PM*, 90); the length of the road must be borne, and each particular moment must be sojourned in. The history of the world, which is immanent in the individual but of which he has not become aware, then becomes conceptualized and internalized history, the meaning of which he is progressively able to elaborate.

In conceiving the *Phenomenology* this way, Hegel seems to set a double task for himself. On the one hand, he wishes to introduce empirical consciousness to absolute knowledge, to "philosophy" which for him is the system of absolute idealism, the system in which self-consciousness and consciousness of being are identified; on the other hand, he wishes to raise the *individual I* to the *human I*. When we consider the precise meaning of this second task, Fichte's and Schelling's problem of the transition of finite I to absolute I becomes the problem of the transition from individual I to human I, from the abstractly specific I to the I that encompasses within it the whole spirit of its time. In his *Science of Knowledge* of 1794, Fichte spoke of the finite or empirical I as the individual I, but he did not pose the problem of the relation between the specific I and the human I in all its implications. Only Hegel could pose this problem, because he greatly enlarged the concept of the experience of consciousness, from theoretical or moral experience (in the narrow sense of the word) to everything that is actually experienced by consciousness—not only the object thought or the final goal, but also all manner of living, as well as aesthetic and religious world views which constitute experience in the larger sense of the word. In thus posing the problem of all experience, of everything that is susceptible to being actually experienced by consciousness, Hegel was necessarily led to the relation between the individual I and the I of humanity. The empirical consciousness considered was specific consciousness, which must progressively become aware once again of the experience of the species and, in forming itself to knowledge, form itself to a human wisdom [*sagesse*]; it must learn its relation to other consciousnesses and grasp the necessity of a mediation through universal history so that it can itself become spiritual consciousness.

Thus defined, the second task—raising the specific I to the I of humanity—is in its deepest significance what Hegel calls "culture" (*Bildung*). But this culture is not only the individual's, it does not involve him alone; it is also an essential moment of the whole, of the absolute. If indeed the absolute is subject and not only substance, then it is its own reflection back on itself; it is the course of its becoming conscious of itself as consciousness of spirit. Thus when consciousness progresses from one experience to the next and enlarges its horizons, the individual rises to humanity and at the same time humanity becomes self-conscious.[18] Spirit becomes the self-consciousness of spirit:

> In this respect, culture, seen from the individual's point of view, consists in the individual acquiring the present, consuming his inorganic nature and appropriating it; with respect to universal spirit, insofar as that spirit is substance, culture consists uniquely in that substance giving itself its own self-consciousness and producing by itself its own development and its own reflection (*PE*, I, 26; *PG*, 27; *PM*, 90).[19]

Thus the *Phenomenology* is indeed a part of philosophic science. From the point of view of the individual, it is an introduction to science; from the point of view of the philosopher, it is that science becoming aware of itself. And, as reflection is not alien to absolute knowledge, as the absolute is subject, the *Phenomenology* itself enters into the absolute life of the spirit.

The desire to fulfill this task undoubtedly led Hegel to expand his initial project of introducing nonscientific consciousness to science. Before arriving at absolute knowledge, Hegel

18. Cf. Kroner, *Von Kant bis Hegel* (Tübingen, 1921, 1924), II, 377.
19. It is only in the preface, written after the completed text of the *Phenomenology*, that Hegel specified the general implication of his work, its signification for the individual and for substance becoming subject. In the introduction, which was written before the book, the relation between the *Phenomenology* as a whole and the history of the world spirit was not envisaged.

integrates into his work all the more specifically historical arguments on objective spirit and on religion. Since the problem is to raise the individual to the consciousness of spirit, to make spirit become self-consciousness in the individual, how can the individual understand his substance without rediscovering within himself the development of the spirit that is still a part of his present world?

We can wonder nonetheless how the two tasks which we have just defined can coincide: on the one hand, the passage of empirical consciousness to science, and on the other, the elevation of the specific individual to the consciousness of the spirit of his time, to the consciousness of humanity within himself. Hegel gradually abandoned his early ambition to influence his age directly through pedagogical and practical works, an ambition generated by the French reformers and the French Revolution. Beginning with his arrival in Jena, he reflected on the philosophic systems of Fichte and Schelling and tried to define philosophy as the expression of the culture of an epoch in world history. His speculative interest was engaged by philosophy's attempt to resolve the oppositions in which that culture was crystallized. Much later, in the *Philosophy of Right,* he wrote:

> One word more about giving instructions as to what the world ought to be. Philosophy in any case always comes on the scene too late to give it. As the thought of the world, it appears only when actuality is already there cut and dried after its process of formation has been completed. The teaching of the concept, which is also history's inescapable lesson, is that it is only when actuality is mature that the ideal first appears over against the real and that the ideal apprehends this same real world in its substance and builds it up for itself into the shape of an intellectual realm.[20]

The same idea is expressed in the famous phrase "The owl of Minerva flies only at dusk." But although these passages, written in 1820, are clearly more conservative in tone than the *Phenomenology,* Hegel already knew in 1807 that philosophy, absolute knowledge, is a result that coincides with the thought of the spirit of a certain age. Can we not conclude from this, as Hegel himself suggests in the preface, that the road that leads to absolute idealism coincides with a particular moment of world history? Absolute knowledge has historical presuppositions. To rise to absolute knowledge empirical consciousness

20. *Philosophy of Right,* pp. 12–13.

must become aware of these historical presuppositions; it must raise its specific I to the I of the humanity of the time at which alone absolute knowledge can appear. In the *Phenomenology,* Hegel writes of Kant's and Fichte's idealism that, "instead of presenting this road [of the historical presuppositions of idealism], this idealism starts off with the assertion [I = I] and therefore is no more than a pure assertion which neither conceives itself nor can make itself conceivable to others" (*PE,* I, 198; *PG,* 177; *PM,* 275). The same argument is made in a more general way: "The immediate manifestation of truth is the abstraction of its being-present, of which the essence and the being-in-itself are the absolute concept, that is, the process of its having-become" (*PE,* I, 198; *PG,* 178; *PM,* 275).[21] When Kant's and Fichte's idealism appeared in world history as a particular philosophic system, it was not justified but remained a gratuitous assertion. Its genuine justification could only be the history of the formation of human consciousness. One of the innovations of the *Phenomenology* was to justify idealism through history, to view it as the result of prior experiences. And the result is nothing without the course of its development (*PE,* I, 7; *PG,* 11; *PM,* 69).

Thus for Hegel the two tasks which we distinguished are not separate. When empirical consciousness rises to absolute knowledge, it must simultaneously become aware of a certain history of the spirit, without which that absolute knowledge would be inconceivable. This act of becoming aware is not a pure and simple return to the past; in its retrospective apprehension it justifies the past and determines its meaning.

> Thus science (that is, absolute knowledge), the crown of a world of spirit, is not yet full-fledged at its beginning. The beginning of the new spirit is the result of a vast upheaval of many and varied forms of culture, the reward of a complex, sinuous itinerary and a no less arduous and painful effort. This beginning is the whole which, outside of its succession and its extension, has returned into itself and has become the simple concept of that whole. But the actual reality of that simple whole is the process through which the prior formations, which have now become moments, develop anew and take on new configurations, develop into new elements which however are in accordance with the development they have already undergone (*PE,* I, 13; *PG,* 16; *PM,* 76).

21. On idealism, a phenomenon of the history of spirit, see Hartmann, *Die Philosophie des deutschen Idealismus* (Berlin and Leipzig, 1929), II, 112 ff.

Thus absolute knowledge is not accessible to individual consciousness unless that consciousness becomes consciousness of the spirit of its times. But conversely Hegel does not conceive of this absolute knowledge only as what is usually meant by knowledge. It corresponds to a new stage in world history. And we cannot understand certain passages in the last chapter of the *Phenomenology*[22] if we do not see that for Hegel humanity, having just undergone profound upheavals, has entered a new stage of its history. Absolute knowledge corresponds to this stage of history and is its expression. "Moreover, it is not difficult to see that ours is a time of gestation, a time of transition to a new age. Spirit has broken with the world of its Dasein and of the representation that has lasted until now; it is on the point of burying this world in the past; it is engaged in the labor of its own transformation" (*PE*, I, 12; *PG*, 15; *PM*, 75).

IV. INDIVIDUAL COUNSCIOUSNESS AND UNIVERSAL CONSCIOUSNESS

WE CAN NOW SEE the full scope of the task the *Phenomenology* set for itself, and the obstacles, perhaps insurmountable, that stand in its way. As we have seen, the task is to lead individual consciousness to become aware of the spirit of its times, to become aware of its own substance, its inorganic nature, and simultaneously to rise thereby to an absolute knowledge which claims to transcend all temporal development, to surmount time itself. "This is why spirit necessarily manifests itself in time. And it does so until it grasps its pure concept, that is, until it eliminates time" (*PE*, II, 305; *PG*, 558; *PM*, 800). Is there not a contradiction here? How can consciousness on the one hand surmount the continuous call to transcend itself, which is essential to it, and coincide absolutely with its truth while that truth becomes self-certainty—truth and life—and on the other hand be the consciousness of a particular stage in the history of spirit? Are we to think that this stage is precisely the end of time and that Hegel naïvely thought that history came to an end with his system? Although this accusation has often been made, it seems unjust in certain respects. The difficulty

22. The section on absolute knowledge, which concludes the *Phenomenology*.

of the last chapter of the *Phenomenology* ("Absolute Knowledge") is not merely due to Hegel's terminology and the manner of his exposition; it is inherent in the very nature of the problem. To surmount all transcendence and yet to preserve the life of spirit presupposes a dialectical relation between the temporal and the supratemporal which cannot easily be thought. But this is not precisely the problem that we wish to discuss here. We are less concerned here with the future that appears to consciousness that has reached absolute knowledge than we are with the past that that consciousness has used in the course of its development. Our question is to what extent that past—which coincides only in part with world history and which, properly speaking, is not a philosophy of history but the recollection of world history in an individual consciousness that is rising to knowledge—is determined abstractly and to what extent it evinces a necessity. Perhaps the problem of the past of absolute knowledge is not entirely different from the problem of its future. There too, the solution must be dialectical. In each case, individual consciousness gathers up within itself the two extremes, universal consciousness and particular consciousness, and must find universality in its particularity, while remaining unable completely to avoid that particularity. We know that for Hegel consciousness is always universal and particular at the same time; the dialectical synthesis is genuine specificity, universal individuality which rises from its particularity to universality. With regard to the future, Hegel writes in the *Philosophy of Right* (contradicting the thesis that he claimed to stop time at his time): "To comprehend what is, this is the task of philosophy, because what is, is reason. Whatever happens, every individual is a child of his time; so philosophy too is its time apprehended in thoughts. It is just as absurd to fancy that a philosophy can transcend its contemporary world as it is to fancy that an individual can overleap his own age."[23] This does not mean that the conception of what exists is merely the conception of a contingent, transitory element; on the contrary, in the cross of present suffering we must recognize the rose and rejoice in it.

Let us return to the problem of the past. It is important to note that the individuality whose formation is considered in this way is not merely a random individuality, submerged in a too-narrowly defined particularity. "The particular individual is in-

23. *Philosophy of Right*, p. 11.

complete spirit, a concrete figure in the total Dasein of which one single determination predominates while the others are present only as effaced traits" (*PE*, I, 26; *PG*, 26; *PM*, 89). Only *universal individuality*, individuality that has raised itself to absolute knowledge, can rediscover within itself, and develop by itself, the moments entailed by the course of its development. The same consciousness, when it reaches philosophic knowledge, turns back on itself and, qua empirical consciousness, begins the phenomenological itinerary. One must find the way to absolute knowledge in oneself before one can point it out to others. "For this reason, it was necessary to consider the *universal individual*, self-conscious spirit, in the process of its formation" (*PE*, I, 25; *PG*, 25; *PM*, 89).[24] What for that individual is recollection and internalization is the route by which others ascend. But qua individuality, that individuality necessarily includes elements of particularity. It is tied to its times; the French Revolution and the Enlightenment are more important to it than other historical events. But is this not evidence of an irreducible contingency? Hegel's entire youthful itinerary reappears in the *Phenomenology* in a rethought and organized form. Everything that Dilthey and Nohl found in the notebooks of Hegel's youth, everything Hegel wrote in Stuttgart, in Bern, and in Frankfurt about the ancient world and about Christianity and its destiny, everything he elaborated in Jena about the life of a people and its organization: all these developments which led him to his philosophic thought and to the thought of his times reappear in the *Phenomenology*. We can ask whether the *Phenomenology* does not portray Hegel's own philosophic itinerary, in the way that the *Discourse on Method* is an abridged and reconstructed history of the formation of Descartes's thought. As Valéry has written, "Descartes's intention was that we hear and understand himself, that is, that his necessary monologue be inspired in us and that we pronounce his own vows. *We were to find in us what he found in himself.*" [25] Similarly, we may say that Hegel presents his own philosophic itinerary so that we, or rather his contemporaries, may find in

24. "The individual," Hegel writes, "can legitimately demand that science furnish him at least the ladder by which he might rise to this viewpoint, and that it indicate that ladder in him" (*PE*, I, 24; *PG*, 25; *PM*, 87).

25. P. Valéry, "Fragment d'un Descartes," *Variété* (Paris, 1929), II, 13.

it a pathway that is not only Hegel's but that carries in the particularity of its history a universal significance. Much more ponderously than Descartes, and in a far different spirit (instead of rejecting prior history we must integrate it within ourselves and rethink it in order to supersede it), Hegel sets forth what is universally valid in his particular journey. The road, like Descartes's, is a road of doubt, even of desperate doubt, but that doubt is not the result of a resolution taken once and for all. On the contrary, it is the "detailed history of the formation of consciousness itself to science." Perhaps when Hegel wrote this phrase, which occurs in the introduction, he was specifically thinking of Descartes and comparing their two journeys.

But by what right can this route, which is tied to particular contingencies, be called a science? How can it present a genuine necessity? Of course the necessity is seen only at the end of the voyage, when the philosopher rethinks what appeared to be offered to him as contingency. And, as we know, Hegel later suppressed the subtitle, "First Part of Science." [26] But the introduction, and the preface as well, insist on the scientific nature of the whole development. Subsequently, Hegel preserves under the name "phenomenology" only the first moments, and only in their most abstract and most general form. The problem is no longer posed then, but by the same token the *Phenomenology* no longer has the character of a concrete philosophical journey, a character which makes it one of the most beautiful works of philosophic literature.

Without claiming completely to resolve the problem of the necessity of the phenomenological development, as that development is presented in 1807, we can quote something Hegel wrote several years earlier: "Man can and must connect the imperishable and the sacred to the contingent." In his thought of the eternal, man binds the eternal to the contingency of his thought:

> The *Phenomenology* appears as a science because from the route of the formation of individually and historically conditioned consciousness it extracts the moments by means of which that path is simultaneously the path of the formation of consciousness

26. In the new edition of the *Phenomenology* which he was working on before his death.

to science, that is, the path through which consciousness becomes universal and rises above every conditioned situation.[27]

The abstractly individual consciousness is a consciousness only because it opposes itself and is thus simultaneously universal consciousness. But universal consciousness is not merely abstractly universal; it is absolute consciousness only insofar as it opposes itself and is individual. Beginning with his earliest writings, Hegel tried to think through the unity of particular consciousness and universal consciousness. He struggled—as Sophocles had in *Antigone* and Shakespeare in *Hamlet*—to bring to life characters who embody a moment of human history. He wrote several "lives of Jesus," but unlike Kant, for instance, for whom Jesus was the sensuous outline of morality, Hegel tried to grasp the irreducible individuality of Christ and at the same time, by deepening his particularity, to discover the universal in him. For Hegel philosophic doctrines are not abstract doctrines, they are ways of life. Skepticism, stoicism, unhappy consciousness, the moral world view: these are expositions not of philosophic thought but of experiences of life. Their human universality is fulfilled only in the actual experience of a particular consciousness. But, conversely, the meaning of that actual experience lies only in a thought that is universal. Thus the pre-Revolutionary period in France is embodied for Hegel in the lacerated consciousness of culture, and the Terror is interpreted as a certain "metaphysics."[28] This attempt to gather up the universal and the particular into spiritual individuality is what makes Hegelianism, and especially the *Phenomenology*, interesting. Hegel refuses to choose between an existentialism (like Kierkegaard's) which, according to him, would be abstract —an existentialism in which individuality is unique and resists transcribing its life situation in the code of universality—and a universalism that would exclude actual experience. The truth lies in their unity: that truth which also is life, as the life of spirit is truth. To understand the meaning of the phenomenological development and its relation to world history it

27. Kroner, *Von Kant bis Hegel*, II, 379. The passage from Hegel is in *Early Theological Writings*, p. 172.

28. PE, II, 79; PG, 372; PM, 543–44, where Rameau's nephew embodies the laceration of consciousness, and PE, II, 136; PG, 419; PM, 605, where the Terror, Robespierre, and the Law of Suspects are interpreted in the light of a certain metaphysics.

is therefore necessary to think through this dialectic of universal individuality: to think universality through particularity and particularity through universality. Is not consciousness the unity of these two moments?[29]

29. The problem of individuality is the central problem of Hegelianism. Spirit is not the *abstract universal;* it is *individual* (the spirit of a great man, or of a people, or of a religion, etc.). But Hegel strives to grasp individuality as the *negation of negation,* as a movement to surmount its particularity. Thus, the *pantragedism* of his youth (positivity—destiny) gave way to a *panlogism.*

3 / The Structure
of the *Phenomenology*

We intend first to study the general structure of the *Phenomenology*, to view its organization as a whole. We are aware that an attempt of this sort must necessarily be superficial and that it cannot reach what is essential in a work, especially if that work is the *Phenomenology of Spirit*. For the *Phenomenology* is the work of Hegel's whose development seems the most organic. The same concepts return at various stages of the book and grow richer in meaning. Yet, although we can hope to glimpse the movement of the *Phenomenology* only if we closely analyze the development of the work, its substantive content as well as its dialectical steps, it is indispensable before undertaking such a study to view the whole of the development and to point out its guiding articulations.

I. The History of the Birth of the *Phenomenology*

It is also important to specify the external circumstances in which the book appeared. Beginning with the "System der Sittlichkeit" ["The System of Morality"] and the article "Uber die wissenschaftliche Behandlungsarten des Naturrechts" ["On the Scientific Treatment of Natural Law," hereafter "Naturrecht" —trans.], both dating from the early Jena period, Hegel drew away from Schelling and nearer to Kant and to Fichte. The *prise de conscience* indeed, appears to play a decisive role in the course of the development of Hegel's final philosophy of spirit.[1] Subjective knowledge prevails over any intuition which does not reflect on itself, and thus it rises above substance. Viewed from the inside, within the context of the development of Hegel's thought, the *Phenomenology* appears to meet a true requirement. Viewed from without, however, this does not seem to be the case. T. Haering, one of Hegel's commentators, was of the opinion that "the *Phenomenology* was born not organically, according to a carefully deliberated and well thought-out plan, but in an almost unbelievably short time as the result of a sudden decision taken under external and internal pressure and in the form of a manuscript delivered to the publisher bit by bit while the author's intention with regard to the work was changing."[2] If, on the whole, we must accept Haering's conclusions, at least with regard to the circumstances in which the book was published, this in no way changes our argument that the *Phenomenology* fulfilled a need within the development of Hegel's philosophy. Often apparently external circumstances best allow us to reveal ourselves. Whether Hegel was conscious of it or not, the *Phenomenology* was his way of conveying to the public not a completed system but the history of his own philosophical development. We have become better able to understand the significance of the *Phenomenology* since Hegel's early works (those written in Stuttgart, in Bern, and in Frankfurt) have become known. The later *Logic* and the *Encyclopaedia* have their origin in the Jena period, but in the *Phenomenology* Hegel recapitulated his own philosophical journey. And if indeed Hegel's philosophy is primarily a philosophy of spirit and is based on human history, then we must say that—as the Jena courses on the philosophy of spirit had already foreshadowed—Hegel gave an authentic expression of his thought in the *Phenomenology,* his first major work.

Let us briefly summarize Haering's argument, which Hoffmeister restates in the introduction to his edition of the *Phenomenology.*[3] From the time he arrived at Jena, Hegel was

1. Cf. the Jena *Realphilosophie.*
2. "Entstehungsgeschichte der *Phänomenologie des Geistes,*" in *Congrès hégélien de Rome* (Tübingen and Haarlem, 1934), III, 119.
3. Hoffmeister's introduction includes a clear exposition of Haering's thesis and an excellent discussion of the circumstances in which the *Phenomenology* was published. We refer the reader to this introduction and to Haering's own work, *Hegel: Sein Wollen und sein Werk,* 2 vols. (Leipzig, 1929).

anxious to publish the whole of his philosophic system in a single work. In 1802, and then in 1803, he spoke of a book that was to be called "Logik und Metaphysik oder Systema reflexionis et rationis." His intentions did not become more specific until 1805 when he announced that he would present "totam philosophiae scientam, id est (a) philosophiam speculativam (logicam et metaphysicam), naturae et mentis ex libro per aestatem prodituro, et (b) jus naturae ex eodem." This division indeed corresponds to the manuscripts of the first system which were published by H. Ehrenburg, G. Lasson, and Hoffmeister. Remarkably, there was as yet no thought of an introduction to this system, much less of an introduction to be called the *Phenomenology of Spirit*. But apparently Hegel dropped the idea of publishing his entire system in a single book and made up his mind to publish only a first part of that system, a part that was to include his logic and his metaphysics, preceded by an introduction. It was only during the winter semester of 1806–7 that that introduction came to be called *Phenomenology of Spirit*.[4] What followed is known. In the course of its composition, the introduction itself came to be the first part of the system of science, and the *Phenomenology* originated at the very time that Hegel's contract with his publisher, Göbhart, in Bamberg, called for a logic and a metaphysics as the first part of the system, to be preceded by an introduction called *Phenomenology*. The introduction became a self-sufficient work the range and the importance of which were only gradually discovered by its author.

What was to have been only an introduction to the system grew on its own and, despite Hegel's own assertions that there can be no introduction to philosophy, became a self-sufficient whole, an exposition of the entire Hegelian philosophy from a phenomenological point of view. We know from a letter to Niethammer, probably written in September, 1806, that Hegel had at that time delivered part of his manuscript. That part did

4. There is, of course, the 1805 letter to Voss, but see Haering's apt discussion on this point in the article quoted above. See also Hoffmeister's introduction (p. xxxi). His reference to *The Phenomenology of Spirit* as a System of Philosophy does not stand up. For the winter semester of 1805–6, Hegel announced "(a) Logicam et metaphysicam sive philosophiam speculativam, praemissa Phaenomenologica mentis ex libri sui: *System der Wissenschaft* proxime proditura parte prima . . . (b) Philosophiam naturae et mentis ex dictatis. . . .'"

not include the preface, which was sent at the very end, but included the whole of the phenomenology of consciousness, of self-consciousness, and of reason. The considerable portion of the book that constitutes a genuine philosophy of spirit, including the chapters on spirit proper, on religion, and on absolute knowledge, was still missing. These chapters were only delivered to the publisher, bit by bit, in October, 1806. The manuscript of the preface followed in January, 1807, and the first copies of the *Phenomenology* were circulating in April of that year.[5] The break in the manuscript of the *Phenomenology*, a break which corresponds to the chapter on spirit, probably explains something that has bothered all editors of the book. Whereas Hegel himself indicated that the first part of the book is divided into three sections, A) "Consciousness," B) "Self-consciousness," and C) "Reason," there is no corresponding division in the second part. In order to establish a correspondence with the "Phenomenology" presented in the *Encyclopaedia*, editors have generally gone on to subdivide the section on reason into (AA) "Reason," (BB) "Spirit," (CC) "Religion," and (DD) "Absolute Knowledge." But in addition to his tripartite division, Hegel also ordered spiritual phenomena as follows: (1) sensuous certainty, (2) perception, (3) understanding (these three moments are grouped under the general heading A, "Consciousness"), (4) self-consciousness (B), (5) reason (C), (6) spirit, (7) religion, (8) absolute knowledge. The last phenomena, reason, spirit, religion, and absolute knowledge, do not actually correspond to a third unique moment that can be contraposed to the first two.[6]

There has always been a question as to whether the *Phenomenology* is an introduction to Hegel's system or a part of it.

5. As we know, and as he wrote in a letter to Schelling on May 1, 1807, Hegel finished the *Phenomenology* on the eve of the battle of Jena.
6. It is rather silly to try at all costs to find a tripartite division everywhere in Hegel's thought. The schema of thesis, antithesis, and synthesis was at first a living dialectic, but by the time Hegel wrote the *Encyclopaedia* it had become a pedagogical device. And in Hegel's first essays, side by side with the dialectical movement necessarily organized in three stages, we find a sequence of phenomena which cannot readily be integrated into that schema. The *Phenomenology* presents itself simultaneously as thesis (consciousness), antithesis (self-consciousness), and synthesis (reason) and as a sequence of spiritual "phenomena" numbered from one to eight.

According to Haering, the answer is clear: at the beginning it was meant to be an introduction; in the course of its elaboration it became part of the system. But what led Hegel, who had always commented ironically about the possibility of an introduction to a system with a life of its own, to publish one himself? He had pedagogical reasons, no doubt, for he had realized that one could not begin abruptly with absolute knowledge; that, necessarily, common consciousness had to be led to science.[7] Also, this introduction had to be a phenomenology of spirit, recapitulating in its broad outlines Hegel's own youthful journey. In opposition to Schelling, who began with a philosophy of nature, Hegel had clearly to note his originality by starting from spiritual phenomena.

In the final system, the *Phenomenology*, as an introduction to the system and as the first part of science, disappears; it shrinks and becomes only a specific moment in the development of the philosophy of spirit. It was not without some embarrassment that Hegel spoke of his work, which to us, on the contrary, seems his most brilliant.[8] In the letter accompanying the copy that he sent to Schelling, Hegel wrote, "My book is finally finished, but even in sending copies to friends the same baleful embarrassment that dominated the publication and the printing and even in part the writing appears." [9] Commentators have been struck by the fact that the chapters on spirit and on religion, which made up that second half of Hegel's Jena work which, according to Haering, was delivered to the editor later, disappeared in that part of his system that Hegel called the "phenomenology." Is there in fact a break in the 1807 *Phenomenology*, and are the chapters on spirit and religion a development which does not, strictly speaking, belong to this introduction? It is quite possible that Hegel's intention changed in the very course of completing his book, but the stress he laid on certain chapters of the first part (observation of the organic, physiognomy, phrenology) left him no opportunity to turn back. He was led, almost despite himself, to write not only a phenome-

7. In the preface, Hegel explained and justified himself at some length on this score (*PE*, I, 25; *PG*, 26; *PM*, 89).

8. As we have already noted, in the revision of the *Phenomenology* that Hegel was working on before his death, he deleted the phrase "first part of science" from the title (*PE*, I, 25; *PG*, 26; *PM*, 89).

9. From a letter to Schelling, May 1, 1807.

nology of consciousness but a phenomenology of spirit, in which all spiritual phenomena would be studied from a phenomenological point of view. As Hoffmeister correctly noted, "With the chapter on the 'self-actualization of rational self-consciousness,' the tendency toward objective spirit is already so strong that there can be no pause in the flow of the presentation before reaching the 'figures of the world' through which alone self-consciousness can reach its truth." [10] Individual reason is pushed, as though by an internal requirement, to become a world for itself as spirit, and spirit is similarly pushed to discover itself as spirit for-itself in religion. The method of *prise de conscience*, which dominated the whole development of consciousness, extends to all the phenomena of spirit, and the "phenomenology of individual consciousness" necessarily becomes the "phenomenology of spirit in general."

Does it follow that this transformation poses no problems? That Hegel could present his whole system in the form of a *Phenomenology of Spirit*—dealing with the development of individual consciousness as well as with knowledge of nature, with the development of objective spirit as well as with religion —before he had reached absolute knowledge seems to point to a certain ambiguity in the interpretation of Hegelianism. How is the *Phenomenology of Spirit* connected to the later *Logic*? We shall try to broach this problem in the conclusion of our study, taking off from the chapter on absolute knowledge, but it is a problem which fundamentally will remain almost insoluble because it will lead us to ask whether Hegel's philosophy is itself a phenomenology or an ontology. It is both, no doubt, but which is the authentic proceeding, which is the source of Hegelianism? Is Hegel's logic independent of all phenomenology? [11]

10. Hoffmeister, in his introduction to his edition of the *Phenomenology*, p. xxxiv.

11. As Hegel himself wrote (*PE*, II, 310; *PG*, 562; *PM*, 806), in one aspect the 1807 *Phenomenology* presents the whole of Hegelianism: "To each abstract moment of science there corresponds a figure of phenomenal spirit in general." In the *Phenomenology*, *all* the moments of knowledge are presented "according to the inner opposition" of *for-itself* and *in-itself*, of certainty and truth. The *Phenomenology* is truth inasmuch as the latter appears to itself, or inasmuch as the concept splits and "represents itself according to the inner opposition." See our last chapter, below; and cf. David Strauss's phrase, quoted by Hoffmeister (p. xvi): "Hegel's posthumous works are merely extracts from the *Phenomenology*."

II. THE *Phenomenology* IN THE LATER WORKS

IN ORDER TO FIT into the system of the *Encyclopaedia,* the only three moments of which are logic, nature, and spirit, the *Phenomenology* of 1807 had to be limited. It lost precisely the chapters on spirit and religion. This change appears in the Nuremberg *Philosophische Propädeutik* [hereafter *Propaedeutic* —trans.] and then in the *Encyclopaedia.* Let us look at this change in detail and try to specify the reasons for it.

a. *In the* Propaedeutic

As rector of the Gymnasium of Nuremberg, Hegel faced a particularly difficult pedagogical task. He had to adapt his thought to instruction that properly speaking was preparatory to, rather than at, university level. As he told Niethammer, he had to give his thought a more accessible and more popular form.[12] These pedagogical considerations always influenced the formulation and the development of Hegel's system. Hegel thought first for himself; he was a "visionary of the spirit" rather than a teacher. The first *Logic,* the one written at Jena, is the history of a thought that seeks itself, doubles back, and follows its own path without worrying about how it might be communicated and without sticking to a form appropriate to teaching—rather than a didactic exposition of what Hegel calls "logic." At Nuremberg he had to present his logic to fifteen-year-olds, and it was impossible to teach them directly what for him was speculative logic, a logic of spirit that is alive and dialectical. He had to take up the "calcified matter" of previous logic, to attach himself to it in an attempt to give it life again and to transform it into a dialectical logic, and he had to find a mediation between the previous logic and his own new logic. Aware of the need for this change of logic, he had already written in the preface to the *Phenomenology:*

In modern times, on the contrary, the individual finds abstract form ready made. . . . Hence, the task now is no longer to purify

12. In a letter to Niethammer, October 10, 1811.

the individual from the mode of sensuous immediateness in order to make of him a substance that thinks and is thought, so much as the opposite of this: to make the universal actually present and to infuse spirit into it as a result of the suppression of determinate and solidified thoughts. But it is much more difficult to render solidified thoughts fluid than it is to render sensuous Dasein fluid (*PE*, I, 30; *PG*, 30; *PM*, 94).

Later, in 1812, Hegel presented this spiritual logic, which is not formal logic and which does not accept abstract determinations of thought as they are but grasps them in their movement and their becoming, in a much more accessible form than that of the preparatory works of Jena. Pedagogical needs led him to seek and to find this mediation: the "splinter in the flesh" was to teach "abstract thought without speculative thought." [13]

Logic, thus, owes much to Hegel's teaching in Nuremberg. As for the *Phenomenology*, it was a work Hegel left behind him. In the *Doctrine of Spirit as Introduction to Philosophy* there is still mention of an "introduction to knowledge" which has the same purpose as the *Phenomenology* of 1807. The name "phenomenology" does not occur, but the task Hegel sets for himself in this doctrine of spirit is the same as that planned in the *Phenomenology:* "In philosophy, an introduction must especially consider the different properties and activities of spirit, by which it rises to science. Since these properties and spiritual activities present themselves in a necessary connection, this self-knowledge also constitutes a science." [14] We can see in this sentence the idea of the *Phenomenology* that would be simultaneously an introduction to science and a particular science, but we may wonder how this science differs from psychology, in the general sense of the term, a science which is to have a place within the whole of the philosophical system.

As for the content of the *Propaedeutic*, Hegel takes up again in a very schematic way the first three moments of the 1807 *Phenomenology*, consciousness, self-consciousness, and reason. But the development of self-consciousness as it is worked out in the *Phenomenology* (stoicism, skepticism, unhappy consciousness) and the development of reason into observing reason and acting reason are absent. Also gone are the sections on spirit and religion. Hegel says, nevertheless, that consciousness is

13. Cf. the Nuremberg *Propaedeutic*, and Hoffmeister's introduction to the *Phenomenology*, p. xvii.
14. *Propaedeutic*, p. 14.

divided into three principal stages: (a) consciousness of incomplete, abstract objects, (b) consciousness of the world of
finite spirit, and (c) consciousness of absolute spirit. But this
indication, which, apparently, would lead us to spirit as presented in the *Phenomenology* and to religion, is not pursued.
Only the consciousness of abstract or incomplete objects—that
is to say, consciousness properly speaking, self-consciousness,
and reason—is developed.

The problem Hegel seems to face at this point is that of the
relation of his *Phenomenology* to psychology. In the prospectus
to the *Phenomenology* which he wrote in October, 1807, he had
already said of that book that "it considers preparation for
science from a point of view that makes it a new science. The
Phenomenology of spirit must replace psychological explanations and more abstract discussions of the foundation of knowledge." [15] In the short chapter on the laws of logic and of
psychology there is a brief critique of empirical psychology,
that is, of the psychology of faculties. But is the *Phenomenology*
an introduction to the philosophy of spirit, or is it this philosophy
itself?

"I divide the exposition of psychology in two parts," Hegel
wrote in a letter to Niethammer, "(1) spirit manifesting itself,
(2) spirit being in-and-for-itself. In the first, I deal with consciousness from the standpoint of my *Phenomenology of Spirit*,
but only in the first three stages of that *Phenomenology*, consciousness, self-consciousness, and reason." [16] This text clearly
shows Hegel's effort to constitute a philosophy of spirit which,
no longer merely phenomenological, would be integrated into
his system. Consciousness of spirit is distinguished from spirit
itself, in-and-for-itself, which is to constitute the subject of
psychology, *stricto sensu*. Thus, the *Phenomenology* plays the
role of an introduction. But with the developments that follow
the chapter on reason lopped off, it becomes only a particular
moment in the systematic concatenation of knowledge offered
by the *Encyclopaedia*.[17]

15. Quoted by Hoffmeister, introduction, p. xxxvii.
16. The letter is quoted by Hoffmeister in his introduction to the
Propaedeutic, p. xix.
17. While the 1807 *Phenomenology* presents all the figures
(*Gestalten*) of spirit, including reason (*Vernunft*), in the aspect of
the for-itself, in later works the phenomenological sections present
only the transition from consciousness to reason. Reason in these
works is truth in-and-for-itself which develops as such.

b. *The* Phenomenology *in the* Encyclopaedia

This introduction to philosophy completely disappeared as of the first *Encyclopaedia,* written in Heidelberg in 1817. The name "phenomenology" was retained, but it was applied to a specific part of the philosophy of subjective spirit. As a theory of consciousness, phenomenology is located between anthropology, the subject of which is soul, and psychology, the subject of which is spirit. Let us briefly study the final place that Hegel accords to phenomenology in the *Encyclopaedia* of 1817. The three large moments of the system are logic, nature, and spirit. But subjective spirit itself is at first nature; it is the soul which does not yet distinguish anything about itself and which for us is only the reflection of events in the world, events which it carries within itself.

This soul is spirit *in-itself;* it is not yet spirit *for-itself.* In order to become for-itself it must become consciousness. The movement of the soul to consciousness is the truth of a dialectic that is still a dialectic of nature, a dialectic of awakening. The soul sunk into itself is the slumbering spirit, but the truth of the awakening of the soul is consciousness of its content, consciousness of a world that has become external to it: "the soul separates itself from its content which for it is the world," the other. The soul is then no longer merely self-certainty; its truth has become for it an other than itself, an object.[18]

Thus, consciousness is the subject of a specific science, phenomenology, which stands contraposed to anthropology and which prepares the way for psychology *stricto sensu.* In this phenomenology, the I has the abstract certainty of itself; it is for-itself, but this certainty is contraposed to the presence of an object, of an other than the I. It is, Hegel says, reflection being for-itself, the ideal identity of the soul rather than its immediate identity: "the I is the light that manifests itself and the other." In this form, however, spirit is not in-and-for-itself; it is merely spirit which appears, which manifests itself to itself: "As consciousness, spirit is only the appearing of spirit."[19]

For the I thus reflected back on itself, it is the object that changes; hence the dialectical progression is a progression within the object itself. The phenomenological dialectic is a dialectic of experience. But for us, consciousness changes along with

18. Hegel, *Encyclopaedia,* p. 369.
19. *Ibid.,* p. 370.

its object. The function of spirit as consciousness is to make its manifestation identical to its essence. The I must raise its certainty to truth. The stages of this ascent are consciousness that is consciousness of an object (the object is a general other), self-consciousness (in which the object is the I), and, finally, reason (the unity of consciousness and self-consciousness in which the object is I as well as object): "Spirit sees the content of the object as itself and sees itself as determinate in-and-for-itself." [20] Reason is the concept of spirit; truth which knows itself, which is no longer separated from self-certainty, is spirit in-and-for-itself.

This spirit, this unity of soul and consciousness, is in turn the subject of a psychology that leads to objective spirit, to spirit that is no longer merely internal but that has become a spiritual world existing in the shape of moral and political institutions, of peoples and states, of world history. Finally, the unity of subjective spirit and objective spirit is absolute spirit, revealing itself as art, religion, and philosophy.

We have given a schematic account of the movement of Hegel's system. We see that phenomenology is no longer an introduction to it but is a part of the philosophy of spirit, that part which corresponds to the moment in which consciousness of spirit manifests itself to itself as object. Yet Hegel himself indicates that this part is of particular importance to the history of philosophy when he describes the phenomenology as the philosophy of Kant and Fichte, philosophers who, unable to rise above consciousness, proved incapable of overcoming the duality inherent in consciousness, that between subject and object, certainty and truth, concept and being: "Kantian philosophy can be described most precisely as envisaging spirit as consciousness; it contains essentially the determinations of phenomenology and not of the philosophy of spirit." [21] It considers the I as being in touch with a beyond which in its abstract determinateness is called the thing-in-itself, and it grasps intelligence as well as will only according to this finitude. In the *Critique of Judgement*, no doubt, Kant rises to an idea of nature and of spirit, but this idea has only subjective significance and is hence only a manifestation, and not truth that knows itself in-and-for-itself.

Phenomenology, the general introduction to the whole sys-

20. *Ibid.*, p. 371.
21. *Ibid.*, p. 370.

tem of absolute knowledge, becomes a specific moment of the system, the moment of consciousness, while at the same time it loses part of its content. Consciousness pertains to subjective spirit, but there are also objective spirit, which rises above consciousness, and absolute spirit (in art, religion, and philosophy) which is not only the manifestation of the true, but the true itself.

Yet, in our opinion, it is not by chance that Hegel presented his whole philosophy of spirit—subjective, objective, and absolute—in the form of a *Phenomenology of Spirit*. In objective spirit, spirit still appears to itself in the form of a history, and in absolute spirit it appears to itself as spirit in-and-for-itself. This self-manifestation, which is essential to spirit, makes the *Phenomenology* more than a specific moment of the system. We can understand that a philosophy of spirit, in the broadest sense of the term, would be a philosophy of the life and development of consciousness and that in certain respects consciousness manifests the entire content of spirit. Consciousness must become consciousness of spirit; it must become aware that its object is spirit, that is, itself. In absolute knowledge, truth cannot be such that it leaves certainty out of account (just as certainty without its truth is only abstract), but is the truth that knows itself; it is self-certainty, that is, consciousness. To present spirit in phenomenological form, as the self-manifestation of spirit in the development of consciousness, must have seemed all the more important to Hegel in 1806 because of his determination to maintain against Schelling that the true is not only substance but also subject. It is clear to us that there is an opposition between the *Phenomenology of Spirit*, which is the becoming of spirit for consciousness, and which is in fact unfinished since the movement of transcending is essential to consciousness, and a finished system of truth, an absolute knowledge, in which consciousness is actually transcended. It seems to us that this opposition could be shown within Hegel's system itself, in his philosophy of history, and in his philosophy of absolute spirit. If it is true that spirit is history and that the act of becoming aware is essential to the development of spirit, then it seems impossible completely to eliminate phenomenology. The latter, in fact, is a moment that threatens to absorb all the rest.

III. The Organization of the *Phenomenology* in 1807

Before we study in detail the phenomenology of spirit as it is presented in the 1807 work, we shall attempt a general view of the book which will show its unity despite the apparent large break between the first part, which corresponds to a phenomenology of consciousness in the narrow sense of the word and which alone will be retained in the later system, and the second part, which corresponds to a phenomenology of spirit in Hegel's sense of the word; on the one hand, finite spirit as objective spirit, and on the other, absolute spirit as religion (also as art in certain respects, but art is included in religion) and as philosophy (absolute knowledge).

We can say that the first three moments of the *Phenomenology,* consciousness, self-consciousness, and reason, are the basis of all subsequent developments. The dialectic of their development will recur in more concrete form in the very midst of reason, in the opposition between observing reason and acting reason. What Hegel calls "the actualization of rational self-consciousness by its own activity" is nothing else than the development of self-consciousness repeated in the element of reason. "Just as, in the element of category, observing reason repeats the movement of consciousness, that is, sensuous certainty, perception, and understanding, so reason will again traverse the double movement of self-consciousness, and move on from independence to the freedom of self-consciousness" (*PE,* I, 289; *PG,* 254–55; *PM,* 374–75). The organic synthesis of consciousness and self-consciousness is accomplished once again and in a more concrete form in this new element; this occurs in chapter 4c, "Individuality That Knows Itself to Be Real In-and-for-itself" (*PE,* I, 322 ff.; *PG,* 283 ff.; *PM,* 413 ff.). At that point spirit will correspond to consciousness while religion will be a self-consciousness of spirit still opposing itself to real spirit (*PE,* II, 206; *PG,* 475–76; *PM,* 688). This is why in the chapter on absolute knowledge, where Hegel summarizes and reorganizes all prior developments in order to lead them to their conclusions, the problem he poses is in actuality* that of the dialectical reconciliation of consciousness and self-consciousness: "This reconciliation of consciousness and self-consciousness reveals itself as the product of a double development, first in religious spirit and then in consciousness itself, as such" (*PE*, II, 298; *PG*, 553; *PM*, 793–94).

We see that the first moments of the *Phenomenology* are the very terms with which Hegel works: consciousness, in the limited sense, is spirit insofar as spirit in analyzing itself retains and fixes on the moment by which it is with regard to itself an objective entity in the element of being; spirit leaves out of account that this entity is its own being-for-itself. "If, on the contrary, spirit fixes on the other moment of the analysis, according to which its own being-for-itself is its object, then it is self-consciousness" (*PE*, II, 11; *PG*, 315; *PM*, 459).

Consciousness, self-consciousness, and reason are thus abstractions of spirit, which is the only concrete reality; they exist "due to the fact that spirit analyzes itself." "This action of isolating such moments presupposes spirit and subsists within it; or, it exists only in spirit, which is existence" (*PE*, II, 11; *PG*, 314; *PM*, 459). This text clearly shows that consciousness, self-consciousness, and reason are not to be thought of as temporally successive in an ordinary way. They are rather *components* of spirit which can be isolated and which then develop temporally, each by itself, in such a way as to lead to the other moments. What we have just discovered is a method of Hegel's which it is essential to note. The *Phenomenology* moves from the abstract to the concrete; it rises to ever-richer developments which however always reproduce within themselves the prior developments and give them new meaning. Each concept that Hegel uses is taken up again, recast, and, so to speak, rethought at a higher level of the development. This reworking of abstract moments which gradually enrich themselves characterizes Hegel's very mode of thought; so much so that he himself finds it necessary continually to retrace his argument and to summarize the stages already crossed in order to show them reappearing with new meaning. We quoted above both the passage from the chapter on reason in which Hegel shows the development of consciousness and of self-consciousness reappearing in the element of reason and the passage from the chapter on spirit in which these moments have become mere abstractions, elements that are disintegrating. "At the point that spirit, the reflection of these moments in themselves, has been posed, our reflection can recollect them from this point of view [i.e., that the essence of the figures of spirit consists in the movement and disintegration of their moments—trans.]" (*PE*, II, 11; *PG*, 315; *PM*, 459).[22]

Hegel's method makes the *Phenomenology* a truly organic system. As one development ends, a new element is born, but in this new element the prior development is represented and acquires richer and more concrete meaning. This goes on until the end of the work which is to present the whole *Phenomenology* in its concrete richness. This richness in turn becomes a simple element in the midst of which science once again begins its development. The element of absolute knowledge becomes the element of speculative philosophy, especially of logic, and the moments of logic correspond in certain respects to the moments of phenomenology. But here, difference is no longer presented as difference between consciousness and self-consciousness; it has become a difference immanent in the content, and no longer a difference in the apprehension of content. From this point of view, the three terms of the phenomenological dialectic, consciousness, self-consciousness, and reason, are specific to the *Phenomenology*. But in this case we may ask what is left of the distinction between an "objective logic" and a "subjective logic."[23]

Let us consider the first three moments, consciousness, self-consciousness, and reason, as abstractions, that is, before they become what they already are in-themselves, moments of concrete spirit. It is easy to see why they constitute the framework of the whole *Phenomenology*. What does consciousness mean if one leaves self-consciousness out of account? The *Phenomenology* starts with the opposition that is expressed by various pairs of terms all of which set forth the opposition specific to the problem of knowledge: subject and object, self and world, consciousness and its objective correlative, certainty and truth. Insofar as it is only consciousness, spirit approaches a world that is alien to it, hence a world which can be sensed and which spirit merely receives passively into itself. It senses this world; it perceives it; it conceives it according to its understanding (*Verstand*). These three subdivisions of consciousness can be considered the three concrete stages of its development. Every

22. The progressive enrichment in the meaning of each concept can be followed in the analytical index at the end of our translation of the *Phenomenology*.

23. The *Logic* is divided into "objective logic" (being and essence) and "subjective logic" (concept).

sensuous consciousness necessarily becomes a perceiving consciousness; every perceiving consciousness becomes an understanding. No doubt, consciousness is also self-consciousness; while it believes that it knows its object as its truth, it also knows its own knowledge. But it is not yet aware of this, and hence it is self-consciousness only for us and not yet for itself. It aims only at the object; it wishes to reach certainty about knowledge of the object and not certainty about its own knowledge. This orientation toward the object characterizes consciousness as such and is the starting point of phenomenological consciousness.

To be sure, for phenomenological consciousness the object is not what it is for the philosopher who has reached absolute knowledge, nor what it is for reason, that is, for science seeking itself in its own object; it is posited as being completely external to consciousness which has but to receive it passively. The certainty of immediately possessing the truth in receiving it characterizes that phase of consciousness which Hegel calls "sensuous certainty." The object, truth, is there before me; I need only apprehend it. My certainty is immediately truth, and this truth has no internal reflection. The correlative of consciousness is not beyond knowledge, and yet it is alien to all knowledge. This naïve position of consciousness with respect to the world must be superseded, yet insofar as consciousness is a moment of spirit we return to it continually.[24] Consciousness cannot stop at this certainty but must discover its truth, and in order to do this it must turn toward itself rather than toward the object. It must seek the truth of its certainty, that is, it must become self-consciousness, consciousness of its own knowledge rather than consciousness of the object. The truth of consciousness of the object is self-consciousness, as will be established by understanding, the last subdivision of consciousness.

We shall study the movement from consciousness to self-consciousness in greater detail in the chapter on understanding.[25] It is important to note here that self-consciousness—the moment contraposed to consciousness—is not itself aware that it is the result of the previous movement. It appears in a concrete form, as though it had forgotten the transition from consciousness to self-consciousness. When we develop all the

24. It is even "consciously" returned to in the sensualist philosophy of the eighteenth century. Cf. PE, II, 110; PG, 397–98; PM, 577.
25. Part II, chapter 3.

moments of consciousness according to the phenomenological itinerary, we reach the point of view of transcendental idealism with which Fichte started in his *Science of Knowledge.* We believe that we know an object outside us (certainty), but we know only ourselves (truth of this certainty). The realism of naïve consciousness leads to transcendental idealism. In figurative language, Hegel writes: "It is clear then that there is nothing to be seen behind the [so-called] curtain that covers the interior (of things) unless *we* step behind it—as much that there be someone to see as that there be something to be seen" (*PE,* I, 140–41; *PG,* 129; *PM,* 212). As Charles Andler put it, "The inside of things is a construction of spirit. If we try to lift the veil covering reality we will see only ourselves, only the universalizing activity of the spirit which we call understanding." [26] In a similar way, empirical science thinks that it deals with real forces, with electricity, gravity, etc.; in fact, it deals with, and discovers, itself. Knowledge of the world is self-knowledge. Certainty about the other becomes self-certainty. The I takes itself as object by moving beyond the other.

But this self-certainty—self-consciousness in the narrow sense of the term—is an abstraction all over again; it condenses within itself, in the concrete form of desire and satisfaction, the previous dialectic of which it is unaware. The object is there, before me; I do not contemplate it; I grasp and assimilate it. Hegel's originality was to see this self-consciousness as a second moment contraposed to consciousness and to follow through in it its own specific dialectic. This consciousness is not experienced as the I in the reflection of scientific thought, but in its impulses and their actualization, in the movement of its desires. Consciousness aimed at the other; self-consciousness aims at itself through the other: it is *desire.* It can be an I only insofar as it contraposes itself to another I and discovers itself in him, and it is in this still elementary form that consciousness develops as self-consciousness in the three relations of primitive social life (struggle for recognition, domination, and servitude). In a higher form, self-consciousness becomes consciousness of its independence and its freedom. As stoic consciousness, it must nonetheless test the truth of this certainty in skepticism and in unhappy consciousness.

26. Charles Andler, "Le fondement du savoir dans la *Phénoménologie de l'esprit* de Hegel," in the special Hegel issue of the *Revue de métaphysique et de morale,* XXXVIII, no. 3 (July–Sept., 1931), 317.

What is the immediate meaning of these dialectics if not that the truth of self-consciousness considered abstractly, as certainty, negates self-consciousness? Thus, in a certain way, consciousness, which is consciousness of the other, is reintroduced. Consciousness, when developed for itself, led us to self-consciousness; self-consciousness, similarly developed for itself, brings us back to consciousness. In the first case, consciousness by itself is abstract and universal; only its content is concrete. But for it this content is "the other." In the second case, consciousness has indeed become concrete; it is its own content. But it is limited to individuality, to the I that aspires to freedom but does not really reach it. The world, the universe, remains external to it. The unity of the universal and the specific is made real only in the figure of the immutable, in unhappy consciousness. But this unity is beyond consciousness; as a matter of fact, it is the unity of consciousness and self-consciousness, a unity that is made real in a third moment, that of reason.

"Reason is consciousness' certainty that it is all of reality" (*PE*, I, 196; *PG*, 176; *PM*, 273); it is the dialectical synthesis of consciousness and self-consciousness. Like consciousness, it is consciousness of the universe, of the object, but, like self-consciousness, it is consciousness of the I, of the subject. It is hence universal like the first and specific like the second. For consciousness the reality of things was only objective and in-itself; for self-consciousness that reality was only a means for the satisfaction of its desires: the world was for-it and not in-itself. Reason gathers these two moments into an original unity. In being-in-itself, it discovers its own truth; in the world of things, it experiences itself. Reason is idealism. But before expressing itself in philosophy, with Kant and then with Fichte, idealism was a historical reality. It, too, is a concrete given, just as much as consciousness and self-consciousness were when they were considered in isolation, that is, when the transition from one to the other was forgotten and the result alone was treated as a new experience—which is what phenomenological consciousness, that consciousness which experiences and not that which repeats the experience so as to rethink it, always does.

Idealism posited this result, that "the I is all of reality," without considering how this result came about; but its development is essential to this affirmation. The Renaissance, as well as the entire development of modern science, is this idealism as a historical phenomenon. Yet in the element of reason, consciousness and self-consciousness will again oppose each other in a more concrete and a more profound form.

In the element of reason, consciousness becomes observing reason, which considers nature and itself from a scientific point of view. It still believes that it is looking for the other, but at this level, a higher level than that of sensuous certainty, what it seeks is itself. "Reason seeks its other knowing full well that in it it will find only itself; it seeks only its own infinity" (*PE*, I, 204; *PG*, 183; *PM*, 281). At the end of this search, reason will find itself as a being, as a *thing;* it will observe inorganic and organic nature, universal life; it will observe itself as self-consciousness and as the realization of self-consciousness in the human body, as expression (physiognomy) and as dead thing (phrenology). The strange result at which it will arrive—which was, however, implicit in the dictates of its search—is a kind of materialism. *Reason is a thing;* it is being. But self-consciousness will appear in the selfsame element of reason as the negation of being. Reason is not; it creates itself, negating objective being so as to pose itself. From this point on, the immediate opposition of consciousness and self-consciousness becomes an opposition between theoretical reason and practical reason, between knowledge and action.

Knowledge is knowledge of the universe; it is the [presence of the] universal in consciousness, but action presents itself as the action of an individual self-consciousness. As with self-consciousness, the problem is that of the relation between the subjective I and the world. But the meaning of I and of world changes somewhat when they are both posed in what Hegel calls "the element of category." They become more concrete: the I is penetrated by reason, becoming an I which *has* reason though it is not yet itself reason; the world is the entirety of individuals living in a community (*PE*, II, 11; *PG*, 314–15; *PM*, 459–60). Spirit that is the truth of reason is already foreshadowed here, and it would have been impossible for Hegel to have ended the phenomenological development after individual reason because the whole movement of individual consciousness—which has reason—has been directed toward a world that is both subjective and objective, toward the spiritual community, "the I that is a we and the we that is an I" (*PE*, I, 154; *PG*, 140; *PM*, 227). The phenomenology of consciousness had to be enlarged into a phenomenology of spirit in order that consciousness might become consciousness of spirit. It is, indeed, only by being self-consciousness of spirit that it can be absolute knowledge.

Active reason is the reason of specific self-consciousness which confronts the world (a world made up of other individualities), but which also knows that this opposition is only apparent—is merely the opposition necessary for action—and that through the mediation of this action, it must discover itself in being. This individualism abandons the point of view of knowledge, and consciousness therefore ceases to be universal. Hegel quotes from Goethe's *Faust,* part I: "It scorns understanding and science, / The supreme gifts granted to men." Consciousness abandons the universality of knowledge to give itself over to the spirit of the earth (*PE,* I, 298; *PG,* 262; *PM,* 384).

What the individual consciousness, contraposed to universal consciousness, seeks thereby is to discover itself in being—a definition of happiness not as platitudinous as that of the Enlightenment or of Kant but which at first is only the aspiration of the specific consciousness. But individual consciousness is also (although it does not know it) universal consciousness, and in its quest for individual happiness it must therefore undergo a fate which reveals it to itself. The world appears alien to it; it stumbles against harsh necessity; it fails to recognize itself in that which happens to it. This, precisely, is the notion of fate. And yet this fate is individual consciousness itself, unaware of itself. Renouncing its individual happiness, it wishes to transform the world and to strive for the well-being of humanity— like Karl Moor in Schiller's play, who expresses the claims of the heart against established institutions. But Schiller's hero is a bandit chief. Consciousness, thus, experiences in the real world the contradiction that is within itself. It then claims to reform itself, to surrender its individual aims and to establish the reign of virtue in and around itself. But this quixotism comes up against the order of the world, and consciousness must finally learn that "the course of the world is not as bad as it seemed" (*PE,* I, 320; *PG,* 281; *PM,* 411).

From here on, active reason must join with observing reason. Hegel presents the synthesis of being and action, which reproduces at this new level the first synthesis of consciousness and self-consciousness—reason—in the chapter on "Individuality that Knows Itself to Be Real In-and-for-itself." This individuality no longer opposes the universal so as to negate it, nor is it merely contemplative reason, the inactive consciousness of the universal; it is "the copenetration of being-in-itself and being-for-itself, of the universal and individuality. This action is its own truth and actual reality, and for it the presentation (*Darstellung*) and expression of individuality is a goal in-and-for-itself" (*PE*, I, 323; *PG*, 284; *PM*, 415). The synthesis of certainty and truth is accomplished once again, but once again it proves illusory; and the dialectic begins anew within this synthesis. The "thing itself" (*die Sache selbst*) is the honesty of this reason. But the "thing itself" is abstract because it is the reason of individuality and not the reason that is realized in a spiritual world as such. The thing itself, as *objective rationality,* links the individual to other individuals and to humanity. But it is also the thing of passion and of interest. The division between I and world becomes immanent in the I. As of the beginning of chapter 5B, "The Actualization of Self-Consciousness through Its Own Activity," Hegel tends toward spirit which is not merely individual reason but the truth of reason, that is, actual reason achieved in a world that is its authentic manifestation. We can see this if we refer to several passages in the introduction to this part of the chapter and compare them to passages at the beginning of the chapter on spirit. "Thus, in a free people, reason has already been made real; this reason is the presence of the living spirit" (*PE*, I, 292; *PG*, 258; *PM*, 378). "Yet self-consciousness, which at first is spirit only *immediately* and *according to the concept,* is no longer in the happy condition of having reached its destination [determination] and of living within it; or, and this comes to the same thing, self-consciousness has not yet reached this felicity" (*PE*, I, 292; *PG*, 258; *PM*, 378).

All the preceding dialectical developments thus lead to ethical substance, that is, to real spirit, or, if we hold that this ethical spirit has dissolved in individual consciousnesses, to a consciousness of this substance, a moment which appears in the modern world as morality, in opposition to ethos (ἔθος), the immediate state of life of a people. Insofar as it is individual, the "thing itself," consciousness of morality, is only an abstraction. Truth is the world in which this "thing itself" is the concrete subject: spirit.

The second half of the *Phenomenology* differs from the first half in that it coincides, as we have noted, with a certain historical development and does not expound moments which in themselves and without their reflection in unity would be merely abstractions. Hegel says this clearly at the beginning of the chapter on spirit: "These figures are differentiated, however, from the preceding ones in that they are themselves the real spirits, authentic actualities, and are figures of the world instead of being only figures of consciousness" (*PE*, II, 12; *PG*, 315; *PM*, 460). The individual is no longer the abstractly singular individual, but rather the individual who is a world.

The development of spirit is achieved in three stages which coincide with moments of world history. Spirit—reason that has been realized—is at first only immediate substance; it merely is and has not yet raised itself to self-consciousness. The first stage that Hegel calls "true" spirit corresponds to the Greek city. There, truth—objectivity—overcomes certainty. Spirit does not yet know itself; it *is* in the element of being. At the heart of this ethical organism—which was the ideal of Hegel's youth and which he had described several years earlier in Jena in the "System der Sittlichkeit"—the oppositions of consciousness and self-consciousness reappear, but always with new meaning. Self-consciousness is tied to the individual's self, but the individual does not yet exist as universal self; he can incarnate only one of the two laws into which substance is divided according to the duality of consciousness: human law, the law of the state, which openly manifests itself, or divine law, the law of the family, which, still unconscious, links the individual to the maternal substance. In action, this duality becomes a tragic opposition. But action is necessary, and through it the self of self-consciousness emerges from its obscurity and becomes actual.

Simultaneously, the conflict of ethical communities leads to an empire, for the communities are still at one with nature, a oneness in which individuals lose connection with their substance. Substance passes into them completely; they become *persons*:

> The universal unity to which the immediate living unity of individuality and substance returns is the spiritless community which has ceased to be the unself-conscious substance of individuals and in which they now have a value according to their specific being-for-itself as autonomous essences and as substances. The universal, fragmented into atoms which make up the absolute multiplicity of individuals—this dead spirit—is an equality in which everyone equally has worth as a person (*PE*, II, 44; *PG*, 342; *PM*, 501).

This moment corresponds in history to the Roman Empire.

The person's self-consciousness opposes itself to consciousness of essence, and thenceforth immediate spirit splits into two worlds, the world of culture and the world of faith. In the world of culture, the abstract person itself must mold itself in order to become a concrete person. This formative experience [*Bildung*] is the world of alienation: spirit realizes itself through the renunciation of the person, and, conversely, the person obtains concrete and actual reality through this self-alienation. This formation in the element of alienation corresponds to the modern world and culminates in the French Revolution.

The world of essence, the world of faith, opposes the world of alienation, but insofar as it does so, faith is not free of alienation. The world of faith is a flight from reality: "Spirit that has become alien to itself in the actual world takes refuge in an object which reconciles everything that is in opposition in the real world, but which is itself in opposition to the real world." This moment of the development of spirit is characterized by the division between a here-below and a beyond; it culminates in a clash between faith and pure intellection. Faith is the self-consciousness of spirit as essence, as positive repose; intellection is the self-consciousness of spirit as only self-consciousness, as the negation of everything other—especially of essence. The clash between faith and intellection, which corresponds to the Enlightenment, also ends with the French Revolution. For in that experience of world history "the two worlds are reconciled; heaven comes down to earth."

After the failure of this new experience, spirit becomes conscious of itself as spirit. It is spirit certain of itself and no longer the true, merely objective, spirit of the beginning.[27] This is Kant's and Fichte's moral world view, and it characterizes the romanticism of German philosophy in Hegel's time. Spirit is no longer substance; it is subject. We move to a new realm, religion.

To be sure, the forms of religion do not sequentially follow those of spirit. Religion, too, has a history in history. It is no longer immediate spirit but the self-consciousness of spirit, absolute spirit, and this self-consciousness must present itself as an object without losing itself. This is the meaning of the dialectical development of religions from religions of nature—in which the self-consciousness of spirit knows itself only as substance in the objects of nature or in the still unconscious works of man—through the religion of art, to absolute religion, which

27. As we shall see, it does not follow from this that, as certain commentators, Rosenzweig in particular, thought, Hegel renounced his theory of the state. On this point see the introduction to part V, below.

is Christianity. Once again in this development, the dialectical movement is from substance to subject, from (objective) truth to (subjective) certainty. This is the general direction of the whole *Phenomenology* which proceeds through a continuous *prise de conscience*.

But religion is self-consciousness of spirit which, as consciousness of true spirit, still opposes actual spirit. Self-consciousness and consciousness are once again contraposed in this new form. Their unity, the signification of which it will be important to elucidate, constitutes absolute knowledge, the philosophy of the new era which itself has a history in history. What is the meaning of this new figure, not only with respect to the individual consciousness which accedes to knowledge, but also with respect to spirit and its historical development, and to religion? This is without doubt one of the most obscure problems of the *Phenomenology,* and we must admit that the very dense and abstract passages on absolute knowledge are hardly enlightening.

PART II

Consciousness,
or the Phenomenological Genesis
of the Concept

Introduction

THE DIALECTIC THAT HEGEL PRESENTS in the first part of his book on consciousness is not very different from Fichte's or Schelling's. One must begin with naïve consciousness, which knows its object immediately or, rather, thinks that it knows it, and show that in the knowledge of its object it is in fact self-consciousness, knowledge of itself. The movement specific to this dialectic, a dialectic effected in three stages (sensuous consciousness, perception, understanding), is hence that movement which goes from consciousness to self-consciousness. Yet the object of this consciousness becomes for us the concept (*Begriff*).[1] Hegel differs from Fichte and Schelling in that he does not start with self-consciousness, with the equation I = I, but reaches it while claiming to follow the very steps of non-philosophical consciousness.

Self-consciousness will thus appear as a result and not as a presupposition. On the whole, the general movement of eighteenth- and nineteenth-century philosophy—a philosophy which founded a science of nature but culminated with Kant's critical reflection—corresponds to this development. Indeed, Kant himself began with a theory of the heavens, with a knowledge of

1. Hence the title of this part of our work: "The Phenomenological Genesis of the Concept" (*Begriff*). Just as the first part of the *Logic* (objective logic) presents an ontological genesis of the concept, the *Phenomenology* shows us how in the course of the experiences of consciousness the object of consciousness becomes the concept, that is, "life" or "self-consciousness." This genesis is only *for-us* who recall the experiences of consciousness.

nature, before he reflected on this knowledge and showed that it was fundamentally a kind of self-knowledge. Yet this development from a philosophy of nature, or of the world, to a philosophy of the I is at a higher level than the development which Hegel follows through in his chapter on consciousness. The part of the *Phenomenology* that corresponds more closely to this historical movement is the development of reason seeking itself in being. If, in a general way, the dialectic of consciousness—especially in the final chapter on understanding—already prefigures the movement from a philosophy of the world to a philosophy of the I, it must be said that for Hegel this dialectic requires a more rudimentary study. The object of consciousness is not yet the object that reason considers; it is not yet defined as a *world*. It is the object at its simplest stage, the object which is alien to all reason. At the start, it is only what is given and nothing but what is given. The first development, that of sensuous certainty, therefore, rather brings to mind the themes of Greek philosophy, of Platonic philosophy or of the ancient skepticism which Hegel had studied in his article on "Verhältnis des Skeptizismus zur Philosophie" [hereafter "Skeptizimus"—trans.], an article which had appeared in Schelling's journal.[2] The second chapter, on perception, corresponds to the notion of "thing," distinct from its properties and yet defined by them. We are still dealing with common perception, and Hegel's study of perceiving consciousness often seems inspired by a philosophy like Locke's, for example, which, though remaining at the level of common perception, begins to criticize it. Finally, in the chapter on understanding, which takes us from consciousness to self-consciousness, the object is no longer given immediately; it is no longer the thing of perception; it is force, or law. Leibniz' dynamism or Newton's philosophy of nature might come to mind here, but in our opinion Hegel was less concerned to rediscover a philosophy of nature than to find its presentiment in common consciousness—beneath science (of nature). We wish to emphasize this point. Hegel's study is the study of common consciousness, not of philosophical consciousness, and yet, though Hegel names no philosopher, he uses the history of philosophy to develop his analysis and make it specific. The goal always is to lead consciousness to self-consciousness, or, better, to show that consciousness is led there by itself, by a kind of

2. "Skeptizismus," p. 161.

internal logic of which it is not aware and which the philosopher discovers by following its experiences.[3]

3. Hegel does not doubt that there is a connection between these experiences of consciousness and philosophic systems. The history of philosophy is a part of philosophy itself, and, as Novalis said (*Werke,* ed. Paul Kluckhohn [Leipzig, n.d.], III, 183), "The genuine philosophic system must contain the pure history of philosophy."

1 / Sensuous Certainty

WE COULD ALSO SUMMARIZE the three chapters on consciousness—sensuous certainty, perception, understanding—by saying that for us, but only for us, the object of consciousness comes to be what Hegel calls the "concept" (*Begriff*), which is nothing other than the subject, that which is only by virtue of self-development, opposing itself to itself and rediscovering itself in that opposition. The three moments of the concept—universality, particularity, and specificity—should not be thought of as juxtaposed; the universal, which Hegel compares in the *Logic*[1] to omnipotence and to love, is itself only by being its other. As separated universal, it is the particular; it is determinateness. The indeterminate, in fact, is a kind of determinateness, the determination of indeterminateness—just as in aesthetics the spatial isolation of sculptures which are meant naïvely to symbolize the sublime whole is an abstraction, an opposition to determinate situation. The universal, then, is the particular, or rather it is itself and its other, the one that is in the many.[2] The particular, in turn (that is, the determinate), is *absolutely* determinate only insofar as it negates and overcomes its particularity; as absolute negativity, it is the negation of the negation. It is specificity, the return to immediateness, but this immediateness contains mediation because it is the negation of the

1. That is, the *Science of Logic*, 1812. This is usually referred to as the "Major *Logic*," in opposition to the "Logic" of the *Encyclopaedia* which is called the "Minor *Logic*." The comparison of the "concept" with "omnipotence" or "love" is in the second volume of the Major *Logic* (SW, IV, 242).
2. *The Philosophy of Fine Art*.

negation, an internal movement of the immediate which opposes itself to itself, which becomes what it is. If we are to grasp the whole of Hegel's thought, we must understand this starting point of his philosophy: the intuition of life or of the I which develops by opposing itself and rediscovering itself. The logical form that this starting point took during Hegel's Jena period merely hides this initial seed and lends it progressively greater intellectual consistency.[3] The true is subject, or concept, which is to say that it is itself this movement of coming to be what it is, of positing itself. The true, therefore, is not the immediate but the "immediateness that has come about" (*PE*, I, 19–20; *PG*, 21–22; *PM*, 84). In the preface to the *Phenomenology*, Hegel strives to explain this basis of his entire philosophical system and to contrapose his conception of the true which includes mediation within it to any system that posits truth or the true as an immediate, a being, a substance beyond mediation. For Hegel, mediation is not alien to the true but within it. In other words, the true is subject and not substance. The true is not the immediate as such, that which is and remains equal to itself; "it is its own self-becoming, the circle which presupposes and has at the beginning its own end as its goal and which is actually real only by means of its developed actualization and of its end" (*PE*, I, 18; *PG*, 20; *PM*, 81).

It has not been superfluous to recall these texts before beginning our study of the starting point of the whole phenomenological development, sensuous consciousness or immediate knowledge, that is, knowledge *of* the immediate. In fact, in this part of the book Hegel shows how consciousness begins with an equality that will later be its end, the goal that it will strive to reach, to reconquer reflectively. This equality is that between (subjective) certainty and (objective) truth. The entire phenomenological development issues from this origin and tends to reconstruct it, for it has "at the beginning its own end as its goal." In this sense, we shall have to compare absolute knowledge—the last chapter of the *Phenomenology*—with sensuous certainty—the first chapter. Whereas in sensuous certainty the immediate is, in the last chapter it has come to be what it is:

3. See our article "Vie et prise de conscience de la vie dans la philosophie hégélienne d'Iéna," in *Revue de métaphysique et de morale*, vol. XLIII (1936), reprinted in *Studies on Marx and Hegel* (New York, 1969), pp. 3–21, in which we showed how Hegel strove to give a logical form to his intuition of an infinity that is "as anxious as the finite."

it has actualized itself through an internal mediation. In the first chapter, truth and certainty are immediately equal; in the last chapter, certainty, i.e., subjectivity, has posed itself in being, posed itself as truth, and truth, i.e., objectivity, has shown itself to be certainty, self-consciousness. Identity is no longer immediate; it comes to be by means of the whole prior development. The true is then posed for consciousness as subject, and consciousness itself is this true, which is what Hegel expresses in a different way when he says that the absolute is spirit that knows itself as spirit.[4]

Thus we can consider the sensuous certainty with which consciousness starts as at once its highest truth and its greatest error. This consciousness thinks that it has the richest, the truest, the most determinate knowledge, but its knowledge is the poorest where it imagines itself the richest, the most false where it imagines itself the truest, and, above all, the least determinate where it imagines itself the most determinate. Yet that wealth, that truth, that complete determinateness, are not purely illusory: they are only intended, only a δόξα. The testing of this intending will reveal the dialectical reversal, but the moment of intending will subsist and, through the calvary of mediation, consciousness will rediscover that identity with which it had started as truth that is certain of itself. Writing at the end of the *Phenomenology* about the incarnation of God according to Christianity, Hegel says that "what is called sensuous consciousness is precisely the pure abstraction, the thought for which being, the immediate, *is*. The lowliest is hence at the same time the supreme; the revealed, completely emerging to the surface, is by that very fact the most profound" (*PE*, II, 267–68; *PG*, 529; *PM*, 760).

For us, philosophers who follow the experience of consciousness, what must result from its movement through sensuous certainty, perception, and understanding is first the concept in a still immediate form, then life, and then spirit. Hegel says this

4. Christianity revealed the subjectivity of the absolute, and all of philosophy since has tried to understand that "the absolute is subject." In the preface to the *Phenomenology*, Hegel wrote: "That substance is essentially subject is expressed in the portrayal of the absolute as spirit; this is the most elevated concept and it belongs to the modern age and its religion." Descartes wrote that God is "his own cause" (*cause de soi*), but Böhme, albeit still in a naïve and barbarous manner, glimpsed the subjectivity and the life of God that is "Mysterium magnum revelans seipsum."

explicitly in the chapter on revealed religion from which we have just quoted: "Thus spirit that knows itself arose for us through the movement of the knowledge of immediate consciousness, or of consciousness of the existing object" (*PE*, II, 264; *PG*, 526; *PM*, 757). Indeed, the object considered by sensuous certainty is the immediate, the true as immediate, i.e., being, or the universal opposed to determinateness or to specificity. But in perception the object becomes the thing, tied to its properties, the universal combined with the particular. And in understanding, finally, this thing is no longer an inert substratum separate from its determinations, but becomes force that expresses itself in its externalization, or law that unites separate terms. Finally, the object itself becomes self-consciousness in-itself, the concept which no longer juxtaposes the universal and the particular but is their movement, their development. At the level of self-consciousness, the second chapter of the *Phenomenology*, this immediate concept is life; it must then become spirit. We can say that for us the three chapters we have mentioned constitute a genesis, through the experiences of consciousness, of what Hegel calls the concept. At the same time, as we have noted, for itself this consciousness becomes self-consciousness.

I. Sensuous Certainty: General Considerations

HENCE IT IS IMPORTANT to analyze the first chapter of Hegel's dialectic in detail. It is at once a critique of all immediate knowledge and a movement from sensuous certainty to perception. Moreover, Hegel's critique of sensuous certainty is largely inspired by Greek philosophy. Several years earlier, Hegel had taught a first course in the history of philosophy at Jena and had meditated on the meaning of the ancient σχέψις as opposed to modern empiricism, as we know from the article on "Skeptizismus." Without exaggerating, as Purpus does,[5] the specificity of all the allusions to Greek philosophy in this chapter, we cannot but notice similarities between this first dialectic of the *Phenomenology* and that of such ancient Greek philosophers as Parmenides and Zeno—and, especially, Plato.

5. W. Purpus, *Die Dialectik der sinnlichen Gewissheit bei Hegel* (Nuremberg, 1905) and *Zur Dialectik des Bewusstseins nach Hegel* (Berlin, 1908).

Hegel's starting point is the situation of the most naïve consciousness. In the part of the *Encyclopaedia* called "Philosophy of Spirit," he will show how sensuous consciousness, the lowest form of consciousness, develops from the way in which the soul appears in anthropology. In the *Encyclopaedia*, in fact, anthropology precedes phenomenology.[6] The sensuous soul does not yet distinguish itself from its object. It experiences within itself the whole universe of which it is the reflection, but it is not aware of the universe: it does not contrapose it to itself. But the moment of consciousness appears as the moment of separation, as the moment of the distinction between subject and object, between certainty and truth. The soul no longer senses but is consciousness: it has a sensuous *intuition*. This distinction is present in its simplest form at the beginning of the *Phenomenology*. Consciousness knows its object immediately—an immediate relation as close as possible to unity: "the immediate relation in fact means only unity" (*PE*, II, 188; *PG*, 461; *PM*, 664). Hegel could not avoid this first distinction since he started the *Phenomenology* with consciousness itself. But the two terms are posed in their equality. There is indeed knowledge, i.e., there is a distinction between certainty and truth, but this knowledge is immediate, which is to say that here certainty equals truth. Otherwise, knowledge would surpass its object or its object would surpass it, either of which alternatives would introduce a reflection, a difference that would be a mediation. That is why, Hegel says, this knowledge appears immediately as the richest, without limits in space or time since it unfolds itself in them indefinitely: it is as if space and time were the very symbol of that inexhaustible richness. It appears also as the truest and the most precise, as the most determinate, "for it has not yet separated anything from the object but has it before it in all its fullness" (*PE*, I, 81; *PG*, 79; *PM*, 179). Is this richness merely illusory? The answer will be revealed by the internal dialectic of sensuous certainty.

Let us begin by noting that by virtue of being immediate this immediate knowledge is a knowledge *of* the immediate: "The knowledge that is our object at the beginning, or immediately, can only be the knowledge that is itself immediate knowledge, that is, knowledge *of* the immediate, knowledge *of* the existing" (*PE*, I, 81; *PG*, 79; *PM*, 179). At the end of the *Phenomenology*, Hegel shows how absolute knowledge returns to consciousness by presenting itself in its immediateness:

6. *Encyclopaedia*, p. 369.

Indeed, precisely because it grasps its concept, spirit that knows itself is immediate equality with itself (which we call immediate knowledge), and in its difference this equality is certainty *of* the immediate, or sensuous consciousness, which is what we started with. This movement of detaching itself from the form of its self is the greatest freedom and the security of its self-knowledge (*PE*, II, 311; *PG*, 563; *PM*, 806).

Immediate knowledge, with the difference entailed by consciousness, is hence indeed knowledge *of* the immediate, or *of* the existing. Such is sensuous certainty. Since it rejects any mediation or any abstraction that might alter its object, it knows being and only being; it does not develop as consciousness which represents objects to itself diversely or compares them among themselves, for that would be to introduce reflection and thus substitute mediate knowledge for immediate knowledge. If I say that it is night or that this table is black, I am using words which designate *qualities* and which presuppose comparisons, words, that is, which introduce mediation into knowledge. The words "night" and "black" stand not only for what I experience immediately but also for other nights and other black objects. This is a working of abstraction (for Hegel, of negation), for night is what is not this or that particular night. Still less could we speak of a thing like the table, an object which would be known only by its qualities and inferred from these. If we are to describe the situation of this naïve consciousness which knows its object immediately, we must revert, according to a phrase in the *Logic*, to the state of mind of natives who, faced with the novelty of an object, can only cry out "here is."

This is why from the start Hegel contraposes the actual truth of this consciousness to its pretended richness: "In point of fact, nevertheless, this certainty explicitly acknowledges that it is the most abstract truth and the poorest. It only says 'it is' about what it knows, and its truth contains only the being of the thing" (*PE*, I, 81; *PG*, 79; *PM*, 149). This certainty is ineffable; it seizes the ἄλογον. And for Hegel this suffices to show its impotence. That which is ineffable, the ἄλογον, is only aimed at but never reached. What I experience but am unable to express in any way has no truth. Language is truer.

Assuredly we do not portray the universal this, or being in general, but we voice the universal. In other words, we do not at all speak in the same way that we intend [*meinen*] in sensuous certainty. But, as we see, language is truer. It allows us to go so far as immediately to refute our *intention,* and since the universal is the true of sensuous certainty and language expresses only the true, it is certainly impossible for us to name [*sagen*] a sensuous being that we intend [*meinen*] (*PE,* I, 84; *PG,* 82; *PM,* 152).

Somewhat later, Hegel writes of speech as having the divine nature of immediately reversing my opinion and immediately transforming it into something else, without letting it really express itself in words (*PE,* I, 92; *PG,* 89; *PM,* 160). This philosophy of language, which already appears in Hegel's first chapter, reminds us of Plato's dialectics. For Plato, too, there was a question of the possible expression of knowledge, of the λόγος and the resistance it put up to us.[7]

Whatever the case, sensuous certainty, the certainty of the immediate, cannot name its object lest it introduce a mediation. Hence, it experiences the object in its ineffable uniqueness. This object and the I that grasps it are, in effect, purely specific: "In this certainty, consciousness is only qua pure I, where I am qua pure this one and the object is qua pure this. . . . The specific knows a pure this; it knows the specific" (*PE,* I, 82; *PG,* 79–80; *PM,* 149–50). This ineffable specificity is not the specificity that includes negation, or mediation, and hence encloses determinateness so as to negate it; a long development will be necessary before we reach authentic specificity, which is the concept and which is expressed in living beings or in spirit. The specificity we are discussing is immediate, or positive, specificity, which opposes the universal but is in fact identical to it:

> By saying about something only that it is an actually real thing, an external object, we say only what is most universal and we thereby state the object's equality with everything much more than its difference. If I say "a specific thing," I express it rather as completely universal, for every thing is a specific thing (*PE,* I, 91; *PG,* 88; *PM,* 160).

Clearly, to say "here" or "now," which seems most determinate, is in fact to say any moment in time, any point in space. The

7. One of the profound defects in Hegel's thought is revealed perhaps in his philosophy of language and his conception of specificity, which banished "specific souls" because they are ineffable. For Hegel, specificity is a *negation* rather than an irreducible *originality;* it either manifests itself through a determination which is a negation or, qua genuine specificity, it is the *negation of negation,* an internal negation—which may indeed lead us to a *universal subject* but which tends to eliminate *specific existents.*

most precise is also the most vague. But generally, the being that is the immediate—the essential truth of sensuous certainty—is itself every being and none. It is therefore negation and not merely positing, as was affirmed at the beginning. Thus sensuous certainty illustrates the first theorem of Hegel's logic, the theorem which, positing the immediate, positing being, discovers it to be identical to nothingness; the positing of being refutes itself.

Let us remember this essential point: the specific aimed at by sensuous certainty, which is itself specific, is in fact its own contrary: it is the most abstract universal. To be sure, consciousness aims at something else, but it cannot say what it aims at, and it therefore fails to reach it. Language withholds itself. According to Aristotle, it is impossible to define the sensuous individual: "If, for example, you were being defined and you were told that you are a lean animal or a white one, or an animal with some other attribute, that would be a characteristic that could belong to another being as well." [8]

In criticizing the claims of sensuous certainty here, Hegel criticizes all immediate knowledge, any philosophical intuition of the ἄλογον, any philosophy that foregoes thinking so as to bring us back to the ineffable, that is, to pure being. The feeling of the ineffable can appear infinitely profound and infinitely rich to itself, but it can give no proofs and it cannot even test itself lest it give up its immediateness. This intuition in which "all cows are black," this depth, is always what is most superficial. [9]

But in describing the situation of sensuous consciousness, we have substituted ourselves for it; it is essential that this consciousness itself discover the poverty beneath its apparent richness. The dialectic of sensuous consciousness must be its own, not ours. But how can sensuous consciousness experience its immediate knowledge and discover its negative character, that is, introduce within it mediation, the universal? If we were content

8. *Metaphysics* Z.15.
9. The complete unity of being and the knowledge of being will lead us either not to reach or to go beyond consciousness, which is characterized by the *distinction* between certainty and truth, between knowledge and essence. Beyond it lies *absolute knowledge*, in which *being* is simultaneously a *knowledge of being*. But that speculative thought (ontological logic) is of such a nature that its starting point (being that is identical to nothingness) contains the cleavage *in another form*. For if *being* is not only *being*, if it contains the possibility of the *knowledge* of being and of the *question* of being, then it must be its own negation. The beginning of the *Logic* corresponds to that of the *Phenomenology*. Cf. part VII, below.

with the pure and simple identity of certainty and truth, sensuous consciousness would be unable to progress, but it would by the same token no longer be consciousness or knowledge. There is, in fact, a distinction within it, between its knowledge and its object, and a requirement: to determine the *essence* of its knowledge. In fact, a multitude of actual specific certainties is at play in the pure being which constitutes the essence of this certainty: "An actual sensuous certainty not only is this pure immediateness but also is an example of it." [10] Hegel uses the terms *Beispiel* and *Beiherspielen* ("example" and "bypass"). The specific sensuous certainty is in juxtaposition with the absolute immediateness; at the first stage of the development there is no interpenetration of universal and specific, of essence and accident. Now the distinction between the essential and the nonessential is the very work of consciousness. It is consciousness that distinguishes what is in-itself from what is for-it. If the immediate is its truth, it therefore differentiates itself within itself as sensuous certainty of its essence. If we reflect on this distinction, we see that the difference between subject and object already implies a certain mediation. "I have certainty but I have it through the mediation of an other, the thing, and this thing also is in certainty through the mediation of an other, the I."

Thus, consciousness directs itself sometimes toward the object, which it then considers essential, and sometimes toward its subjective certainty, which it then posits as essential while the object is nonessential. Driven away from these two positions in which it fails to find the immediateness which is its essence, it returns to the immediate relation from which it started, posing the whole of that relation as essential. The progression of sensuous certainty from object to subject and from subject to whole is a concrete progression. The mediation that is external at the beginning completely penetrates sensuous certainty at the end, after which that certainty is no longer immediate knowledge but the knowledge of perception. We shall distinguish and examine these three moments: (1) that at which the object is posed as essential; this dialectic leads to Parmenides' being, as opposed to opinion, δόξα, but this being reveals itself as the con-

---

10. In order to understand this distinction we must recall what accompanies consciousness: the distinction between a truth (the essence, the in-itself) and a certainty. At this stage, truth for consciousness is the *immediate*, but its certainty is distinct from that truth: "This other is not only for-it; it is simultaneously truth outside that relation, in-itself" (*PE*, I, 73; *PG*, 71; *PM*, 141).

trary of an immediate being, as abstraction, or as negation (the terms are equivalent for Hegel); (2) that at which opinion, subjective knowledge, is posed as essential in opposition to the empty being of the preceding stage; this dialectic leads to Protagoras' "man," the measure of all things, but the I that is thus reached is itself only an abstraction—as much this unique I as the I in general, all I's. Nonetheless, the relation between the universal and the specific is more profound in this second stage than in the first;(3) that at which sensuous certainty is posed in its concrete unity, with the whole of the relation defined as "unity of that which feels and that which is felt." But this unity reveals itself as including an ineluctable multiplicity and as being a mediation of various "heres" and "nows." The *thing*, the unity of various properties and the negation of their separation, is born *for-us*. The object and the I are no longer immediate but have become the former an *extended thing* and the latter a *thinking thing*.

II. WITH RESPECT TO THE OBJECT: PARMENIDES' THINKING AND OPINION

KNOWLEDGE MUST JUDGE ITSELF by its norm, by what for it is its essence. But in the case of sensuous certainty, its norm is its immediateness. The first experience is that in which being is posed as the essence; it is immediate, while knowledge, on the contrary, is inessential and mediated, a knowledge which can be but which needs not be: "But the object *is;* it is the true and the essence; it is indifferent to being known or not known; it subsists even if it is not known; but without the object there is no knowledge" (*PE*, I, 83; *PG*, 81; *PM*, 151). The privilege that being has over knowledge is due to its permanence. But in what does this permanence consist? And what experience does consciousness have of its object here, an object that subsists despite the vicissitudes of subjective certainty, which is only an example, only an aside in comparison to the immediateness of its object? We need not consider what this object truly is but only how sensuous certainty contains it.[11]

11. Whereas for us the two terms exist through each other, for sensuous certainty *being* at the start *is the immediate:* it is valid in-itself, independently of our knowledge of it. Indeed this realism of

What thus is *independent* of all knowledge is being, in Parmenides' sense. Although sensuous consciousness does not reach such a philosophic thought, this moment of logic expresses its truth. Indeed, sensuous consciousness can say only "this is," thus posing the absolute nature of an existent independently of all mediation. This being is the necessary being, and the necessity is but the immediate reflection of this being back on itself: "It is because it is" (*PE*, I, 82; *PG*, 80; *PM*, 150). Yet just as Parmenides had to distinguish opinion (δόξα) from being (τὸ ὄν), so sensuous consciousness must distinguish its aim (*Meinung*) from being. Sensuous knowledge experiences its own inconstancy with respect to being, which is its truth and its essence. In considering this experience of inconstancy, we shall see sensuous certainty discover that being, which is its essential truth, is so only by the artifice of negation. The object of sensuous certainty, far from being immediate existence, is an abstraction, the universal as the negation of every particular this; it is the first negative manifestation of the universal in consciousness.

The crucial question is this: what in sensuous certainty subsists? "If we consider the this in the double aspect of its being, as the now and as the here, its internal dialectic will take a form as intelligible as the this itself" (*PE*, I, 83; *PG*, 81; *PM*, 151). Sensuous certainty, indeed, does not have the right to rise above the notions of the this, the here, the now. In saying "the now is daytime" or "the this is a tree," it introduces qualitative determinations into its knowledge which are opposed to the immediateness that it requires for its object. "These notions of night and of day, of tree and of house, are generic terms which we cannot yet use and which belong to a more highly evolved consciousness. Nouns presuppose a classification by genus and species which cannot be present in immediate sensuous consciousness, the most formless of all knowledge." [12] Classification, indeed, requires a comparison, a movement by consciousness above what is given to it immediately; with specific particularity,

___

being is characteristic of naïve consciousness. "In this certainty a moment is posed as what simply and immediately *is*, or as the essence; this is the object. The other moment, on the contrary, is posed as the inessential and as the mediated; that which is not in-itself but only exists through the mediation of an other is the I, a knowledge that knows only the object because the *object* exists whereas the knowledge can either be or not be" (*PE*, I, 83; *PG*, 80; *PM*, 151).

12. Andler, "Le fondement du savoir dans la *Phénoménologie de l'esprit* de Hegel," p. 322.

consciousness introduces mediation into the object. But sensuous certainty must reject this mediation lest what constitutes its own essence vanish before its eyes.

If Hegel uses these notions (night, day, tree, house), he does so because it is impossible not to use them in a judgment that must be able to express itself one way or another. Yet sensuous certainty does not take these notions for what they are, specific determinations which presuppose an entire system of mediations in knowledge; it takes them rather as the pure essence of the ineffable quality of the this. Thus, if we ask, "What is the now?" and answer, "the now is nighttime," this in no way signifies an understanding of what the generic term "night" designates; it is simply a qualification of this now, the specificity of which can by right not be said but only aimed at. The continuation of this dialectic bears this out. The now must indeed maintain its being lest it lose its characteristic of truth and immediateness; it is, but what is it if, reviewing this written truth (*PE*, I, 83; *PG*, 81; *PM*, 151) at noon, for example, I must state the new judgment that the now is noon? The now is different from itself. What is preserved when certainty experiences the inconstancy of the now? Being subsists when knowledge changes. Xenophon and, later, the Greek skeptics called this perpetual alteration of the now "appearance," that which is not. Thus, the now does not appear as an existent; it changes continually, or, even better, it is always other. Yet we still say "now," this now. But the now, which maintains itself and whose permanence is the truth of sensuous consciousness, is not an immediate term as it claimed to be: it is something *mediated*. It is, because night and day pass through it without changing it at all; it is their negation (which, for Hegel, characterizes abstraction itself; every abstraction is a negation). It is neither night nor day, and yet it can be night as well as day. "It is in no way affected by its being-other." This, precisely, is the first definition of the universal. "We call a simple entity of this kind, which *is* through the mediation of negation, which is neither this nor that but can be equally this or that, a universal" (*PE*, I, 84; *PG*, 82; *PM*, 152).[13] In point of fact then, the universal is the true of sensuous certainty.

The dialectic we have just developed for the now is repro-

13. What we have reached through this dialectic is a first definition of the universal, but as the being of "pure abstraction" and as the precondition of every other abstraction; what has been shown to be essential in this universal is negation.

duced with regard to the here. "The here is a tree," but if I turn around it is a house. These differences are rejected as being merely opinions which do not yet have the consistency that mediation will confer on them. The here is hence neither tree nor house; it can be the one or the other. It is not affected by its being-other. It is the universal here, which is indifferent to what goes on within it. Similarly, the this is indifferent to everything it can be; it is the universal this as the now is the universal now and the here the universal here. The result of this experience is indeed what we have indicated: the truth of sensuous certainty is being, universal space, and universal time, but this being, this space, and this time are not, as they claim to be, immediate givens. They are because something else is not. "Thus what subsists is no longer that which we intended as being, but is a determinate being—abstraction or the purely universal—and our intention, according to which the true of sensuous certainty is not the universal, is what alone remains vis-à-vis this empty and indifferent now and here" (*PE*, I, 85; *PG*, 82; *PM*, 153).

Our starting point was the ineffable, but positive, here and now; we have discovered the negation that lies within them. They are only by virtue of negating their being-other. Specificity transforms itself into its opposite, universality. But this universality is not a positive one; it appears as pure abstraction and yet as the simple element, which is such by the mediation of the other. What subsists, indifferent to all that is not it, is a universal "this" which is the basis of all "thises," a universal now which is the time in which the now repeats itself indefinitely, remaining equal to itself despite its becoming-other, and a space in which all particular points are located. What has been gained by this experience is the first notion of the universal contraposed to, but mediated by, the specific. But the particularity of determinateness, the particularity which expresses mediation and which will appear in perception, has not yet been fixed upon. Rather, quality, which was no doubt in the ineffableness of the sensuous this, has been negated, and what remains in view is not day or night, and the universal, but abstract here as specificity and universality and the now as specificity and universality. The dialectic corresponding to this stage is that of pure quantity in the field of space and time as it is expressed in the arguments of Zeno the Eleatic. In the movement from the specific this to being in general, to the universal this, the dialectic has abandoned quality, but there remains a dialectic of the one and the many. Like the heres, all the nows are indeed identical, and the identity that constitutes their community is the continuity of space and of time. But on the other hand, they are all different, and this difference is what constitutes the discontinuity of numbers. But this difference is an intended difference; it is a random difference: each point in space is identical to any other, as any moment in time is identical to any other. If we begin with their identity, or with their continuity, we necessarily reach their difference and come upon discontinuity; if we begin with discontinuity, that is, with their difference, we necessarily come back to their equality and their continuity. All "ones" are simultaneously different and identical. Such, in the field of quantity, is the opposition between specificity, *the one that is different from the others* (though this difference is only aimed at and there is no question here of being-for-itself or of genuine specificity which contains negation within itself), and the *one that is absolutely identical to all the others* (the universal, though this universal is not contraposed to itself and is not the genuine universal).

III. With Regard to the Subject

At first, sensuous certainty posited its truth in the object. The object was, it was essence; knowledge, on the contrary, was the inessential. Now, sensuous certainty must reverse its first hypothesis. The object does not reveal itself to sensuous consciousness as the immediate; rather, its being appears as posed by negation. The object is because another thing, to wit, knowledge, is not. Hence, it is necessary to return to knowledge and to make being the inessential. This last is the position of the Greek Sophists. Sensuous consciousness expects to preserve its immediateness by abandoning the dogmatism of being for a subjective phenomenalism: "Hence, the strength of [sensuous certainty's] truth is now found in the I, in the immediateness of my sight, my hearing, etc." (*PE*, I, 85; *PG*, 83; *PM*, 153–54). The "now is night" no longer means the immediate being-in-itself of night but its being-for-me. Truth is what I experience immediately, insofar as I experience it. This is Protagoras' thesis, which is taken up again in Plato's *Theaetetus:* "Man is the measure of all things: of those that are, the measure of their being; of those that are not, the measure of their nonbeing." Theaetetus concluded from this that science was nothing but sensation.[14] On this point, Hegel says that "truth lies in the object insofar as it is my object or is in my view; it is because I have knowledge of it" (*PE*, I, 85; *PG*, 83; *PM*, 153). The now is night or day because I see it as such and not because it is such in-itself. Truth is *my* truth, which then is immediate. (Hegel puns here on the analogy of *mein* ["my"] and *meinen* ["intend"].) This subjective idealism now knows only what the I experiences. It always poses the I, or Protagoras' "man," as truth.

Yet we find the same dialectic in this position as in the preceding one. Truth lies in the I. But in which I? "I, a this one, see the tree and affirm it as the here, but another I sees the house and affirms that the here is a house and not a tree" (*PE*, I, 86; *PG*, 83; *PM*, 154). These affirmations have the same authenticity and the same immediateness. What I know immediately is the antithesis of what another I knows no less immediately. Each one of these truths is swallowed up in turn by the other; what remains is no longer this I, unique and ineffable, but the universal I which with regard to the subject matches the universal this, now, and here. The same refutation [of subjective phenomenalism] appears in Socrates' argument in the *Theaetetus:* "Doesn't he say something like this: things are for me as they appear to me, one by one; things are for you as they appear to you; but you are a man and so am I?"[15] The dialectic which Hegel follows is a naïve refutation—as naïve as the idealism it refutes—of solipsism. Nonetheless, the interaction of specific I's at this stage of consciousness (an interaction of attraction and repulsion because they are characterized by identity and difference, as spatial entities are) prefigures a higher dialectic, that of the unity of specific I's in the universal I.

> What in fact is not swallowed up in this experience is the I insofar as it is universal, whose sight is neither the seeing of the tree nor the seeing of the house but simple sight, mediated by the negation of this house and yet remaining simple and indifferent with regard to what is still at stake [*beiher spielt*]: the house, the tree etc. (*PE*, I, 86; *PG*, 83; *PM*, 154).

There is another possible refutation of this immediate knowledge, one that has no recourse to the plurality of I's: I need but compare my knowledge at two different points in time. The now is day because I see it, but later it is night for the same reason. The I persists through this difference and remains equal to

14. *Theaetetus* 152.a.
15. *Ibid.*

itself. Thus the truth of my aim, as my aim, is the I as universal
I. But it is symptomatic that Hegel chose the refutation which
presupposes the plurality of I's. It leads in fact to the common I,
which is one of the essential presuppositions of his philosophy:
"The I that is a we, the we that is an I" (*PE*, I, 154; *PG*, 140;
PM, 227). Andler appropriately quotes the following passage
from the *Logic* concerning this dialectic:

> One of the most profound and correct insights in the *Critique of
> Pure Reason* is that unity, which constitutes the essence of the
> concept, must be recognized as the primitive synthetic unity of
> apperception, as the unity of the "I think" or of self-consciousness.
> We must thus recognize in us two I's which cannot be separated.
> The sensuous I that I am in a specific sensuous certainty is thus
> situated in a universal I which posits it, but without the specific
> I's there would be no universal I.[16]

The argument with regard to the object, which led us to
being in general, to space, and to time, here, with regard to the
subject, leads us to the universal I. "I indeed intend a specific I,
but I can no more say what I intend about this I than I can say
what I mean about the now and the here. . . . Similarly, when
I say I, this specific I, I say all those I's in general; each of them
is precisely what I say, this particular I" (*PE*, I, 86; *PG*, 83–84;
PM, 154). We do not reach a positive specificity on this last
point either. We fancy that we are unique and that we have an
unmediated I with no comparison to others, with no mediation,
the only one. But each I says the same. Its specificity falls into
universality. The movement from the specific to the universal is
the same as the one that was effected in space and in time. Each
I is alone and unique, but every I says this. The dialectic with
regard to the I does not seem to take us further than that with
regard to the object. Yet there is an advance. Between the individual I and the universal I there is a deeper tie than in the
case of the spatiotemporal object. There is not so much a juxtaposition between the universal and the specific as a more intimate interpenetration, and this interpenetration is the concrete
truth toward which we are aiming.

Purpus has noted that the dialectic of I's is important from
the very first chapter of the *Phenomenology*. "The essence and
experience of subjective idealism," he wrote, "are here noted in

16. Andler, "Le fondement du savoir dans la *Phénoménologie
de l'esprit* de Hegel," p. 324.

an incomparable way." [17] This idealism, the consequences of which should be to determine as pure appearance the I that opposes it, fails before the solidity of the other I, which claims the same right for itself and attributes the same value to its determinations. The two I's are indeed transcended, each in the ideality of the other, and stand thus in the relation of identity and of attraction. But they are also in this relation as different from each other (repulsion). Now the I sees and limits itself in the other, and this self-limitation of the I implies in itself an essential step forward. There is a dynamic relation here, a mediation between the universal and the specific that is already vital and is therefore of another order than the mediation that presented itself in the object, in the this. The fact is that there is a cleavage between a dogmatic philosophy of being and an idealistic philosophy of the I. This cleavage will disappear only when the I discovers itself in being, when consciousness becomes self-consciousness.

Before moving on to the third experience, which will lead us to particularity, we can note that seductive though it is, Hegel's argument here can be understood only if we already know where it is leading. As we have emphasized, Hegel undoubtedly does not presuppose self-consciousness, the equation "I = I" as Fichte did; rather, he uncovers it in the development of consciousness. But in order to follow him, we must admit the movement from the specific to the universal, which at the level of the I is the original identity of this I and the universal I, of an "I think" that transcends any specific "I think" and of the "specific I think" itself. The self-transcendence of consciousness discovering this is significant only at the level of a transcendental philosophy. In other words, to determine the meaning of this experience of sensuous certainty we must already know that the universal and the specific must interpenetrate, or better, that there is a universal that exists through negation.

IV. THE THIRD EXPERIENCE: THE CONCRETE UNITY OF SENSUOUS CERTAINTY

THE THIRD EXPERIENCE gets us out of this oscillation between specific and universal. In posing the whole of sensuous

17. Purpus, *Zur Dialectik des Bewusstseins nach Hegel*, p. 45.

certainty (as the act common to the sensing and the sensed) as the essence of sensuous certainty, we reach a more concrete sphere. And mediation is no longer outside the specific sensuous certainty which is taken as an example (*Beispiel*), but is discovered within it.

In the first experience, the object was posited as the essential and knowledge as the inessential. But the object showed itself to be different from what it had been seen as: it was being, that is, a universal abstract. In the second experience, the ineffable I was aimed at and was the essential in relation to an inessential being. But this idealism experienced within itself the same dialectic: aiming at immediateness, it reached only an abstract universal, the I in general, which is neither this I nor that one.

What remains is to return to the starting point, that is, to pose the immediate relation of knowledge and its object without trying to distinguish which of them is the essential and which the inessential term. The essence is only the unity of this simple relation: "The now is day (and I know it as day)" (*PE*, I, 87; *PG*, 85; *PM*, 155). I refuse to leave this specific certainty and to consider another now or another self. Like the Heracliteans, according to Plato, I refuse to argue for the object or for the subject:

> Let us not posit anything [Socrates says] as being in-and-for-itself. We shall then see that black or white or any other color is the meeting of the eyes with the specific transmission which, manifestly, engenders the color and that any color whose specific being we affirm is neither what meets nor what is met but something intermediate, a product that is original for each individual.[18]

Since this certainty does not emerge from itself, we shall go to it and we shall have indicated the unique now that is aimed at. This movement, which is not yet the act of naming a quality, is nonetheless an act of mediation. It constitutes the claimed immediate: "We are shown the now, this specific now. But now, when it is shown, it has already ceased to be; the now which is, is immediately other than the now that was shown, and we see that the now is precisely what no longer is when it is" (*PE*, I, 88; *PG*, 85; *PM*, 156). It has been, but what has been is not. And it is being that we sought. Thus, in the midst of a sensuous certainty, and without privileging either object or

18. *Theaetetus* 153.d.

knowledge as essence, there is already a mediation. What is posed no longer is as soon as it is posed, yet in its very disappearance it still is—which Hegel expresses in the first elementary dialectic that constitutes the present (richer and more concrete than the now):

1. I pose the now as truth, and I negate it; it no longer is;
2. I pose as truth that it is not, that it has been;
3. In a negation of the negation, I negate this second truth, which apparently brings me back to the first truth.[19]

Yet this is not the case. For the term I reach is the first to have passed through negation, to have negated its negation, and to be only through the negation of its being-other. "The first term reflected back on itself is no longer quite the same as it was, viz., an immediate. It is something reflected back on itself, something simple which remains what it is in being-other, a now which is many nows" (PE, I, 89; PG, 86; PM, 157), the day that is many hours, these hours which are many minutes. What remains is a certain unity in the multiple, a quantum; and a particular sensuous certainty is the experience of this mediation that constitutes what it claims to be immediate. From this point on, we are dealing not with a unique and ineffable now or here but with a now or here that includes mediation within itself, that is a thing including both the unity of universality and the multiplicity of specific terms. A thing will be for us an ensemble of coexisting properties and a unity of these properties—as a determinate place in space is a high or a low, a right or a left. We reach a simple complex of many heres. "The intended here would be the point, but the point does not exist." On the contrary, when we indicate it as existing, the act of indicating is shown to be not an immediate knowledge but a movement which from the aimed-at here reaches, through many heres, the universal here, which is a simple multiplicity of here, just as day

19. We note a first dialectic of temporality here: in this movement negation arises from the surge toward the *future*, which negates the now. This negation culminates in the *past* which has been (*gewesen*) and which, therefore, becomes essence. But in this manner a concrete unity which includes mediation within itself is constituted by the negation of this negation. In the preface, Hegel states that temporality is mediation itself (PE, I, 19; PG, 21; PM, 82).

is a simple multiplicity of now (*PE*, I, 89; *PG*, 86; *PM*, 157–58).[20]

We thus experience a certain interpenetration of the universal and the specific, a certain unity of the diverse and unity. This is what perception, our new object of experience, will reveal to us in "the thing endowed with multiple properties." But in the movement of indicating, sensuous consciousness emerges from itself, and the object as well as knowledge become other for it: it genuinely *perceives,* and its object is a *thing* with *multiple* properties. In sensuous consciousness, negation and mediation are indeed external to being and to knowledge. "The richness of sensuous knowledge pertains to perception and not to immediate certainty, in which that richness was only what was bypassed; for only perception includes negation, difference, or diverse multiplicity in its essence" (*PE*, I, 94; *PG*, 90; *PM*, 163). We can also say that the essence of sensuous certainty was being or the I, separated from this unique being or from this unique I. But what is henceforth posed is multiplicity in the unity of being, or being that has negation within it; it is multiplicity in the I, or the I that includes negation. Such is particularity, the second moment of the concept.

20. These passages can be compared with Kant's distinction between the form of intuition (pure variety) and formal intuition (the unity of the synopsis).

2 / Perception

General Characteristics of Perception

THE POINT OF VIEW of perception is that of common consciousness and, more or less, of the various empirical sciences which raise the sensuous to the universal and mingle sensuous determinations with determinations of thought, while remaining unaware of the contradictions which thus arise.[1] For the essence of the sensuous is known only through these determinations of thought: "They alone constitute the sensuous as essence for consciousness; they alone determine the relation between consciousness and the sensuous, and only in them does the movement of perception and its perceived truth run its course" (*PE*, I, 107; *PG*, 101; *PM*, 177). We think that the piece of wax of which Descartes speaks in the second meditation, or the salt crystal of which Hegel speaks in this chapter of the *Phenomenology*, is perceived exclusively with our senses, or even with our imagination. But in fact our understanding intervenes. We perceive an extended thing, but the thing qua thing is never seen or touched. What do we know of it if not that it is not exhausted by this or that sensuous determination? "Perhaps," says Descartes, "it was as I now think, that the wax was neither that softness of honey, nor that pleasant scent of flowers, nor that whiteness, nor that shape, nor that sound." The introduction of negation is significant here, and if we quote this text of Descartes, whose purposes in this analysis are quite different

1. Hegel, *Encyclopaedia*, p. 573.

from those of Hegel in the latter's contemplation of a salt crystal, it is because, besides the parallel between the two examples, we can grasp in Descartes's text a movement of thought analogous to Hegel's. This thing before me is neither this nor that, though it can be this or that and can even take on shapes which the imagination cannot exhaust. Though the thing is *understood*, it expresses itself in its properties; it subsists in the properties we perceive in it.[2] To perceive is no longer to remain content with the ineffable of sensuous certainty but to move beyond this sensuousness and to reach what Hegel calls the universal—which he has defined in the preceding chapter of the *Phenomenology:* "We call a simple entity of this kind, which *is* through the mediation of negation, which is neither this nor that but can be equally this or that, a universal." This universal, which we have seen arise in the course of the dialectic of sensuous certainty and which is henceforth the new object of phenomenal consciousness, is the principle of perception. All is *one thing,* the extended thing and the thinking thing, the spirit, the God himself: precritical dogmatism merely formulates a metaphysics from the attitude of perceiving consciousness, as Hegel shows in his preface to the "Logic" of the *Encyclopaedia* under the title "First Position of Thought with Respect to Objectivity."[3]

Yet the universal, as we have seen it appear, "thingness" as such, is not without mediation, abstraction, or negation—three terms which here are synonymous for Hegel. It exists because something else does not exist, and hence by virtue of a reflection which at first is external to it but which the development of its dialectic will show can be conceived as internal. The thing of perception will then have dissolved itself qua thing. The determinations of thought which are successively attributed to the thing in order to rule out any contradiction and to preserve its identity with itself will come together in a universal that will include difference within it rather than being conditioned by it. The object will be force, law, or the necessity of law, and no longer

2. Cf. Berkeley's die: "[Philosophers] will have it that the word 'die' denotes a subject or substance distinct from the hardness, extension, and figure which are predicated of it, and in which they exist. This I cannot comprehend; to me a die seems to be nothing distinct from those things which are termed its modes or accidents" (Berkeley, *A Treatise concerning the Principles of Human Knowledge,* § 49).

3. *Encyclopaedia,* p. 59.

the naked thing; it will be the concept in-itself while consciousness, moving beyond the stage of perception, will genuinely have become understanding. The critique of the thing in this chapter of the *Phenomenology* is as much a critique of substance (which is not subject) as of the "thing-in-itself" [*Ding an sich*] a notion that haunts more or less every perceiving consciousness. In the *Encyclopaedia*, Hegel tells us that Kant's philosophy grasped spirit mainly at the level of perception; we might say that it analyzed perceiving consciousness without discovering the dialectic at the heart of that very analysis. The thing is a web of contradictions. As for the "thing-in-itself," it is but the absolute abstraction of pure thought made real as object, the final end point of every "thingism."

> The thing-in-itself—and by thing we also mean the spirit, God— expresses the object insofar as it is abstracted from all that it is for consciousness, from all its sensuous determinations as well as from all its determinations of thought. It is easy to see what remains: the absolute abstract, the total void, still determined only as a beyond, the negative of representation and of sensuousness, the negative of determinate thought.[4]

This "thing-in-itself" also presents itself as the pure matter of materialism, as Berkeley saw it, and as the supreme being of the Enlightenment, which is identical to it.

> Here it is essential to consider that pure matter is merely what remains when we abstract from sight, touch, taste, etc., that is, that pure matter is not what is seen, tasted, touched, etc. It is not matter that is seen, touched, and tasted, but color, a stone, a salt crystal. Matter, rather, is pure abstraction, and thus the pure essence of thought, or pure thought itself, is present as the absolute with no distinctions in itself, not determinate and without predicates (*PE*, II, 124; *PG*, 409; *PM*, 592).

We can plainly see the importance of a critique of the perceptive attitude, an attitude which thinks that it feels but which in fact makes abstractions real, an attitude which is the dupe of an unconscious metaphysics and yet accuses philosophy of dealing only with "beings conjured up by reason." But it is precisely the *not-I* as thing that is the creature of reason. Once again, the thought that calls itself "concrete" is fundamentally an abstract thought which does not master its determinations but grasps

4. *Ibid.*, p. 69.

them in their isolation; it is a nondialectical thought which, consequently, is prey to a dialectic that transcends it. Hegel dwells on this point at the end of the chapter on perception. Only philosophy can master the concrete because it succeeds in dominating and transcending the abstractions of the perceiving human understanding: "The latter is always poorest where it is richest. . . . Taking itself to be real and solid consciousness, it is in perception merely the interplay of these abstractions." Its opinion of philosophy is that the latter deals only with things of thought. Philosophy does indeed deal with them; it recognizes them as pure essences, as the absolute elements and powers. But it also knows them in their determinateness, and hence it masters them. "Perceiving understanding takes them to be the true and is sent on by them from one error to the next" (*PE*, I, 106; *PG*, 101; *PM*, 177). The dialectic, by contrast, as Hegel defined it some years later in the *Propaedeutic*, grasps the insufficiency of each determinateness isolated by understanding and shows that it is not in-itself what it is in its determinateness and that it changes into its contrary.[5] Philosophy grasps precisely this movement and thereby, like genuine empiricism, it rejoins the concrete whole. It does so better than does philosophical empiricism or common consciousness, since common consciousness stops at abstraction while unaware that it is an abstraction.[6] The two fundamental abstractions are the *universality of thingness* and the *exclusive unity of the thing*.

It is rather difficult to follow in detail the steps of the chapter which Hegel devotes to perceiving consciousness, a chapter which constitutes one of the moments of the genesis of the concept, which we have undertaken to reconstitute. Both the *Propaedeutic* and the *Encyclopaedia* briefly summarize the contradiction inherent in the object of perception in order to show how this contradiction makes the thing a mere phenomenon which reveals on the outside (for-an-other) what it is inside (for-itself): the object of perception is simultaneously the site of properties or rather of independent free matters and the unity in which these matters dissolve. (How can they coexist in one and the same place? How can the unique thing be an ensemble

5. *Propaedutic*, p. 32.
6. In his article "Naturrecht" Hegel contraposed the genuine empiricism of the man of action, who dominates all determinations instead of congealing them in their particularity, to the empiricism of the understanding.

of independent properties?) The *Phenomenology*, on the other hand, develops the various aspects of this contradiction at greater length. First, the notion of substance expressing itself through its attributes, but expressing itself for some reflection external to it, is transcended. The notion of monad—the negative unity of the properties of the monad—which is next reached is judged to be equally inadequate because the intrinsic determinateness of any monad, which makes it distinguishable from every other monad, also places it in relation to other monads, and this relation to the other is the negation of its being-for-itself. Finally, this unity of being-for-itself and being-for-another, of negative entity and passive universality, appears as the end point of this development. At the same time, reflection, which at first is in consciousness as opposed to its object, appears as inherent in the object. The object itself becomes the whole of the movement, having first split itself into object and consciousness, so that at the end phenomenal consciousness contemplates its own reflection in the thing. In summary, the whole movement of perception is from substance (positive unity) to monad (negative unity), from thingness to force, from mechanism to dynamism, from thing to relation, from a reflection external to the object to an internal reflection. The object becomes concept, but only in-itself. For as yet, consciousness is not its own concept, "which is why it does not know itself in this reflected object" (*PE*, I, 110; *PG*, 103; *PM*, 180).

We shall try to recapitulate this detail of Hegel's dialectic, especially emphasizing its starting point, what perception is for us, that is, for the philosopher who witnesses the development of phenomenal consciousness, or what it is in-itself for this consciousness. This starting point contains all the contradictory elements of the thing, elements which will show themselves as such in the course of the experience and allow us to follow the original development of that experience.

I. THE PERCEPTIVE ATTITUDE, THE CONCEPT OF THE THING

IN WHAT SENSE has the universal appeared to us as the general principle of perception? In the experience of sensuous certainty we saw the ineffable, or the immediate, transcended by that movement thanks to which, it was claimed, it could be seen or pointed out.

The now and the act of indicating the now are so constituted that neither is an immediate simple but each is a movement which contains various moments [. . .]. Similarly, when we indicate the here as being, this indication reveals itself not as an immediate knowledge but as a movement which starts from the here that is aimed at and through many heres reaches the universal here which is a simple multiplicity of here as day is a simple multiplicity of now (*PE*, I, 88, 89; *PG*, 85, 86; *PM*, 156–57).

This act of indicating—this synthesis of apprehension in intuition, as Kant would say, which in turn presupposes reproduction and recognition—effects a mediation; it culminates in a *simple* term which, however, encloses a *multiplicity*. The intended here was the point, but it does not exist. What exists is a here that is affected by its being-other; it includes a high and a low, a right and a left, etc. It is this that Hegel calls a "universal," and that is the sensuous transcended (*aufgehoben*). This universal, in turn, is conditioned by the sensuous; it exists by means of the mediation of the sensuous through which it is posited. Moreover, each of these moments itself becomes a universal, but a determinate universal (the particular). That is why Hegel says that

> even in its simplest form, the principle of the object, the universal, is a mediate principle; the object must express this within itself as its nature. Thus the object shows itself as the thing with multiple properties. The richness of sensuous knowledge pertains to perception and not to immediate certainty, in which richness was only what was bypassed [*das Beiherspielende*]. For only perception includes negation, difference, and diverse multiplicity in its essence (*PE*, I, 94; *PG*, 90; *PM*, 163).

The universal is nothing but thingness (*Dingheit*), a milieu which is a simple ensemble of multiple terms, just as extension is composed of a right and a left, a high and a low, etc. This salt is a simple here, and at the same time it is a manifold: it is white; it is *also* cubical, *also* savory, *also* of a determinate weight. All these properties coexist in it with ease. They neither penetrate nor affect each other but they participate in universality because they express, in a term that Hegel deliberately borrows from Spinoza, thingness. The sensuous quality lodged in a being can be named; the whiteness or the savoriness of this salt is itself a determinate universal, a not-this, without losing its immediateness. The sensuous, which perception has transcended but not suppressed, is still present precisely in the form of a determinateness. "Nothingness, as nothingness of the this, preserves immediateness and is itself sensuous, but it is a universal immediateness" (*PE*, I, 94; *PG*, 90; *PM*, 164). Every sensuous determination is universal when it is thus caught in thingness; physics tends to make of it a "free matter" diffused in the universe, only some part of which is localized in a specific body.[7] The whiteness and the savoriness of this salt resemble the whiteness and savoriness of another mineral; they extend beyond this salt crystal which I contemplate, just as spatial extension always exceeds the uniqueness of the point.

Yet thingness, the universal, which expresses itself in the various determinations that are its attributes, is a determination of thought that is never felt. It is, we may say, the substance, the "also" which gathers up all these determinations, the medium in which they coexist. "This 'also' is hence the pure universal itself, or the medium; it is thingness gathering all these properties" (*PE*, I, 96; *PG*, 91; *PM*, 165). But we do not perceive only thingness, the simple medium of the properties; we also claim to perceive a determinate thing in-and-for-itself, *this* crystal of salt. At this point, another characteristic of perception, another determination of thought, appears. This determination is that of pure uniqueness, of the exclusive entity, which is genuinely manifested neither by substance in general nor by attributes, but rather by its mode insofar as it is the negation of negation. According to Hegel, Spinoza correctly saw the three moments of the concept—the universal as substance, the particular as attribute, and the specific as mode—but he failed to see that if every determination is a negation, that negation is genuinely expressed (for-itself and no longer only in-itself) only in the mode, insofar as the latter is the negation of negation, negation bearing on itself and thus expressing the activity of the substance as an internal activity, as subject. Thingness is determinate in-and-for-itself only as thing—a unique thing—this salt crystal, which excludes from itself everything else, which ends indeed by excluding itself insofar as for-itself it is merely a being-other. We have not yet reached that movement which transforms substance to subject and thing to force, the movement that Leibniz was able to perceive in the monad. But we can note one characteristic of the perceived thing: it is a unique thing. Moreover, each property is determined absolutely, and as

7. A usual term in the natural science of Hegel's time. Heat, savoriness, etc., would be called "free matters."

such it excludes another property—white excludes black, sweet-
ness excludes bitterness, etc. Things then are not only universal
but also specific, and these two characteristics, the "also" of the
free matters and the negative entity, constitute the thing that is
the object of perceiving consciousness. These two determinations
of thought, the also and the entity—abstract universality and
abstract specificity—are already present in the sensuous but universal property which seems to present itself immediately to
consciousness. "In the property, negation as determinateness is
immediately one with the immediateness of being, and this
immediateness, in turn, is universality through its unity with
negation. But negation is like an entity when negation is freed
from this unity with the contrary and exists in and for itself."
"Sensuous universality, or the immediate unity of being and the
negative," Hegel continues, "is thus a property only when the
entity and universality are developed from it and distinguished
from each other, and when this sensuous universality combines
them; only this relation of sensuous universality to the pure essential moments completes the thing" (*PE,* I, 96, 97; *PG,* 92;
PM, 166).

What we have said about the perceived thing can also be
said about the perceiving thing; at this level, the *res extensa* and
the *res cogitans* are parallel. Hence the soul is sometimes perceived as an ensemble of faculties—memory, imagination, and
so on—just as the thing is made up of its whiteness, its savor,
and so on. When perceiving consciousness wishes to explain this
coexistence of various qualities in one place, it has recourse to
a fiction of the understanding which it offers as a physical
reality: it speaks of the pores of one kind of matter through
which another kind of matter enters. But since the reverse is
also true, a vicious circle results. With regard to the thinking
thing, we are led in a parallel way to speak of "the influence of
memory on imagination and of imagination on memory, of their
interpenetration." This parallelism between consciousness and
its object is characteristic of the *Phenomenology.* When the object changes, consciousness changes, and conversely. But here
it is especially important to note the common birth of perceiving consciousness and of the thing perceived. We (philosophers) have seen them take shape together in the earlier
experience of sensuous certainty. They diverge only in their manifestation; their common principle is the universal. They are
both inessential in relation to this principle, which is their essence. We think of Spinoza's substance which expresses itself

through the order and connection of things as well as through the order and connection of ideas. But let us consider these two moments as they appear in their common genesis.

> One is the movement of indicating; the other, this same movement but as something simple. The first is the act of perceiving; the second is the object. In its essence, the object is the same thing as the movement. The movement is the unfolding and the differentiation of the moments; the object is their assembling and their unification (*PE*, I, 93; *PG*, 89; *PM*, 162).

This synthesis of a diversity, effected by consciousness, is the act of perceiving; the same synthesis, but as though congealed, is the thing perceived. The importance of this distinction becomes apparent when we consider that from the point of view of perceiving consciousness essence is attributed to the object and nonessence to consciousness itself. Later, Hegel will make the same apportionment with regard to the opposition between unhappy consciousness and unchanging consciousness. "Because it is itself the consciousness of this contradiction, consciousness places itself on the side of changing consciousness and appears to itself as the inessential" (*PE*, I, 177; *PG*, 159; *PM*, 252). Consciousness begins by attributing the inessential reflection to itself while making the object in its self-identity the essence. For this consciousness, truth—and truth is conformity with the object—is independent of the reflection that reaches the object. "The object, determined as the simple, is the essence, indifferent to whether it is perceived or not. But perceiving as movement is something inconstant, which may or may not be, and it is the inessential" (*PE*, I, 94; *PG*, 90; *PM*, 163). This is why perceiving consciousness knows that it can err in its apprehension of the true. In its principle, which is the universal (the self-identity of the true), the being-other is contained, but as a moment that has been transcended, as a nothingness which can have a place only within itself but not in truth. For perceiving consciousness, the criterion of truth will then be the search for the equality of the object with itself and the exclusion from it of any otherness. If there is a contradiction it can only be in consciousness; the object, the true, is noncontradictory. Thus proceed common consciousness and the dogmatic thought which is its extension; they see in contradiction the sign of our reflection within ourselves, external to the true.

> Since, at the same time, diversity is for the perceiving consciousness, the latter's behavior is the act of relating the various

moments of its apprehension to each other. But if in this comparison an inequality is produced, that is an untruth not of the object, for the object is that which is equal to itself, but only of the perceiving activity (*PE*, I, 97; *PG*, 93; *PM*, 167).

We can now understand the title of Hegel's chapter: "Perception, or Thing and Illusion." The object side, the thing, is truth; the subject side, reflection, is illusion. But we also understand the inevitable reversal. Consciousness will discover that its naïve position is untenable. For according to that position, it would suffice to take the object as it is without changing it in any way. Truth, then, would be given to us; we would merely have to reproduce it. In fact, however, the discovery of contradictions in the pure determinateness of the thing leads us to a critical position (closer, by the way, to Locke's than to Kant's), and we then try to distinguish what comes from the thing itself, i.e., from the true, and what comes from our reflection and changes the true. But this reflection, which is external to truth, manifests itself in various forms, so that the true is sometimes this when reflection is that, sometimes that when reflection is this. Thus in the end, the true itself appears as reflecting itself outside itself at the same time as in-itself, as having its being-other within itself. From that moment on, the movement of the object and of perceiving consciousness relative to each other becomes the integral movement of the object. And consciousness, as we have already noted, sees itself, without knowing it, in its object which in-itself is concept. "For us, the development of this object by means of the movement of consciousness has become such that consciousness itself is implicated in the development and that reflection is the same on both sides—or is one single reflection" (*PE*, I, 110; *PG*, 103; *PM*, 180). "*From one and the same point of view*," Hegel says at the end of the chapter on perception, "*the object is the opposite of itself, for-itself insofar as it is for-an-other, and for-an-other insofar as it is for-itself*" (*PE*, I, 104; *PG*, 99; *PM*, 175).

We can now see the relevance of this whole chapter to the study of the development of phenomenal consciousness. It is a matter of moving definitively beyond thingism, a thingism which at first characterizes common consciousness and then promotes itself to the metaphysics of a substance which is not absolute negativity, to a metaphysics of the doorless and windowless monad. This dogmatic metaphysics is not, incidentally, corrected by a critical philosophy which tries to define the part played by our reflection in the apprehension of the true. The true is not a thing, a substance, or even a monad; it is subject, that is, identity of identity and nonidentity; it is its own becoming. It manifests itself outside—it is external to itself—in order to posit itself and to reflect back on itself in its being-other. Starting with a universal which keeps mediation and reflection external to it, we reach a universal which posits itself, that is, which, contains its mediation within it. This universal is precisely what at the end of this chapter Hegel calls the "unconditioned universal," which in-itself is concept. It still needs to know itself, to be self-consciousness, in order to be concept for-itself.

II. THE EXPERIENCE OF CONSCIOUSNESS

LET US CONSIDER now what perceiving consciousness experiences. The seeds of these experiences are contained in what has already occurred. Consciousness wishes to apprehend the thing, but it experiences the contradictions of the thing. It becomes aware, then, of its reflection as being outside the true and distinguishes it from its pure apprehension of the true. But this reflection also reveals itself to be constitutive of the thing itself, which includes "a truth opposed to itself" (*PE*, I, 102; *PG*, 97; *PM*, 172). The multiplicity of things cannot prevent the dissolution of the thing, either by excluding the being-other both from consciousness and from the specific thing or by discovering in each particular thing both a determinate essence which makes it distinguishable from every other particular thing (the principle of individuation of the monad) and an inessential variety of properties which is nonetheless necessary to it. All these means, which a recalcitrant consciousness uses in order to preserve its dogmatism, prove futile, and the thing, or things in their mutual intercourse, become merely *phenomena* through which the unconditioned universal which understanding is striving to conceive manifests itself. "In the continuous change, this something transcends itself and changes into an other, but the other changes too. Now the other of the other, or the changing of the changeable, is the development of the permanent, of the subsisting in-and-for-itself, and of the internal." [8] One must no longer say *esse est percipi*, but *esse est intelligi*.

8. *Logic, SW*, III, 104 ff.

The contradiction of the thing is simple. It first appears to us as one and then as infinitely divisible—*partes extra partes.* Such is the antinomy presented by Kant in his transcendental dialectic. On the one hand, we must stop dividing, and reach the simple; on the other hand, this simple, in turn, shows itself to be a composite, and the division is endless. As Hegel says, objective essence appears sometimes as the entity, the atom, and sometimes as a community or a continuity, the "Cartesian extension." So far, we have reached only objective essence in general and not the thing endowed with multiple properties. In the 1812 *Logic,* in which he wishes to show that existence, that is, the thing or things, is merely phenomenon, Hegel again takes up this dialectic with regard to the category "existence," and notes more directly, "The 'also' is what appears in external representation as spatial extension while the 'this,' the negative unity, is the thing taken as a point." [9] But it would be wrong to think that this antinomy holds only for extension. The object of perception is the mingling of abstraction and the sensuous which we call a "property." Now this property is abstract and general; it is the result of a negation, and it extends beyond the unique thing that we are contemplating. This crystal of salt is white, but its whiteness is a universal sensuous determination; we go beyond this crystal when we perceive it as white.

But the property is determinate as well as universal. When we look at it as determinate and not merely as universal, we say that it excludes other properties from itself. This salt crystal is white and therefore not black; it has one particular shape and therefore not another. We are again led to the thing as being an entity, but this time it is a question no longer of an abstract unity but of a concrete unity. This crystal excludes other things but it encloses a multiplicity of properties which we perceive to be coexistent. In the isolated entity we rediscover a medium for properties each of which is for-itself and which, only insofar as they are determinate, exclude the others. Do they exclude them from the salt crystal, or do they mutually exclude each other? In order to save the thing from contradiction, common understanding tries to expel the opposition from the particular medium that this salt crystal is. But it cannot succeed. How can those properties, which have become whiteness, alkalinity, weight, etc., coexist in a specific unit? Either the thing is one

9. *Ibid.*, SW, IV, 116–17. Thus, Kant's pure variety would be the support and, as it were, the pure symbol of empirical variety.

and properties merge in it, or it is multiple: white, and also savory, and also cubical. In the first case, the properties are no longer each for-itself in their indifferent universality but are interpenetrable, and they reciprocally negate each other; in the second case, we would be dealing with a composite. A number of "matters"—caloric, chemical, electrical—are grouped in this particular enclosure and are there juxtaposed. Yet how can they be next to each other? They must occupy each other's interstices. This whole web is a fiction created by understanding, which does not forego imagining and which hides contradiction from itself in the fog of the infinitely small. If these matters interpenetrate, their independence disappears, and there remains only one unique thing without determinations; if they are juxtaposed, their independence is saved, but the unique thing is lost and we return to objective essence, a dust cloud made up of parts that are not the parts of anything and that are themselves infinitely divisible into parts. It is impossible to avoid this contradiction because the sensuous property with which we start, e.g., the alkalinity of salt, is simultaneously universal and determinate. Insofar as it is universal, it is firmly anchored in thingness, it is independent, and it is substance; insofar as it is determinate, it is specific, and excludes otherness. For this reason the two contradictory moments of the thing, on the one hand its universality, its substantiveness—which makes it indifferent to all its parts (the universal is that which can be this or that and is indifferent to being this or that)—and on the other hand its specificity, which makes it exclusive, the negative entity: both of these develop from some sensuous property. In point of fact, taken in their purity, these two moments, universality and specificity—between which the particular, the determinate universal, oscillates—meet absolutely. Pure specificity, or exclusive unity, has no determinations; it is the very universal. Every thing is a unique thing, and in that respect all things are equal. But this dialectic is a logical one, and perception is unaware of it. Hence it returns to sensuous properties and considers them in the medium of the entity without bringing itself either to merge them or to distinguish them absolutely. It is left, then, with properties taken each for itself—the whiteness, the alkalinity, the cubical shape of the salt. But considered without their medium of thingness and without the unity of the thing, these properties are no longer properties since they are no longer inherent in a medium, and they are not determinate since they do not exclude each other. Perceiving consciousness again aims at the this; it returns to a subjectivism of the second degree. This crystal is alkaline only on my tongue and is white only to my eyes. Am I then to begin again the movement from aiming at the this to perception without ever being able to get out of it? No. Because this subjectivism will allow me to become aware in myself of my reflection in coming to know the thing; it will lead me to a critical position—which Locke had already formulated and which Kant sometimes developed under the name "transcendental idealism" when he distinguished the thing-in-itself from the thing-for-us. The thing will always be the real thing, equal to itself, but the knowledge I gain of it will be disturbed by my reflection within myself. My perception will be considered no longer as a pure and simple apprehension but as an apprehension mixed with a reflection which alters the thing and makes it different *for me* from what it is *in-itself*. In this manner, the thing will remain unchanged and illusion will arise only in consciousness. But consciousness is mistaken if it imagines that truth thus simply falls outside it. Since consciousness itself discerns the respective proportions of its reflection and of objectivity, it unknowingly becomes the very *measure* of truth. Our starting point, according to which the perceived object was the essence and perceiving consciousness the inessential, is already transcended, if not for consciousness which effects this critical discernment, then at least for us who philosophize. Do we not already know that the universal, the principle of all perceiving consciousness, is as much the I as it is being, and that the rigidity of the thing that sets itself up over against consciousness is merely the projection of the I outside of itself?

Consciousness now undergoes a double experience: at times it appears to itself as the indifferent milieu, the passive universal in which the properties are but do not mingle; at other times it appears as an entity. In the first case, the "thing-in-itself" is an entity, and pure variety is only for consciousness. This variety, of which Kant speaks, pertains not to the thing but to the multifaceted sensuousness which refracts within itself the unity of the thing. This crystal is white to my eyes, cubical to my touch, savory to my tongue. Here we have a kind of psychological idealism which is not alien to common consciousness if it is cornered: the green of this tree leaf and the moisture in it are only mine; taken alone, the thing is one. It brings about this diversity in me because I have a variety of senses by which to apprehend it. As Hegel notes somewhere, this psychological idealism has no depth because it attributes to me a passivity that seems most alien to my activity as consciousness. But the coherence of the thing is saved in this way, and its truth of being an entity is preserved. Yet it is impossible to stop here, for there seems no way to distinguish one thing from another. If the thing is an entity it is because it is distinguishable from every other thing, and it is distinguishable not because it is an entity as such, but because it has particular properties which completely determine it. This complete determinateness of the thing is what Leibniz had in mind in his principle of indistinguishables; in Kant's philosophy, moreover, sometimes matter appears as that which determines form and sometimes form as that which determines matter, the ideal being the complete determinateness of the object which, according to Maimon, is only an idea called up by reason.

In the second case, to which the first refers us, we must take responsibility for the unity of the thing and necessarily attribute diversity to it. If the thing is indeed determinate it is because it is determinate *within itself* and this complete determinateness is not possible without an intrinsic variety. The thing could not have one single property because in that case it would not be different. In his polemic against Locke, Leibniz saw better than his adversary that relation is intrinsic and not extrinsic, that the unique thing has diversity at its heart in order in-itself to be distinguishable from every other. "But the truth is that every body is changeable and in fact is always altered so that it differs within itself from every other." [10] But if variety is thus in the thing, it is there in terms of an indifferent multiplicity, and it is we who introduce the unity, which hypothesis, as we see, is the reverse of the preceding one. The "thing-in-itself" is white, cubical, savory, etc.; its unity is created by us; what unites the properties is an act of the spirit, uniform in all its perceptions. "The act of positing this multiplicity of terms in an entity is performed only by consciousness, which must therefore avoid letting these terms coincide in the thing itself" (*PE*, I, 101; *PG*, 96; *PM*, 171). For this reason we say that the thing is white insofar as it is not cubical and is not savory insofar as it is white. By saying "insofar as" we avoid contradiction in the object, and we reserve the act of positing these properties, or rather these free matters, in an entity. "In this manner, the thing is raised to a genuine 'also,' and instead of being an entity is a

10. Leibniz, *New Essays concerning Human Understanding,* book II, chapter xxvii.

collection of matters; it becomes merely the surface that envelops them."

Reflecting on this double experience, that is, on our first reflection in apprehending the thing, we discover that we alternatively make both of ourselves and of the thing at times the pure entity, without multiplicity, and at other times the "also," divided up into matters that are independent of each other. As a consequence, this first reflection of ours becomes the object of our second reflection and appears to us as inherent in the thing itself. It is the thing that reflects itself back on itself and is different for-itself from what it is for-an-other (specifically, for our consciousness). It is at times single when it appears multiple, at times multiple when it appears single. It includes within itself a truth opposed to itself; it is a contradiction, that of being simultaneously for-itself and for-an-other. This new opposition of form (being-for-itself, being-for-an-other) replaces the opposition of content (single being, multiple being). But can we not still avoid it and keep truth pure of any contradiction by saving the *coherence* of the thing? The thing, as we have said, is at once for-itself and for-an-other—two diverse beings—and it is different for-itself from what it is for-an-other. That is, the thing becomes thinkable as a multitude of things or of monads which exclude contradiction from themselves by assigning it to the intercourse among them. In this manner, monism becomes pluralism. We can foresee in this Hegelian dialectic, presented in so condensed and obscure a manner in the chapter on perception, a step that will appear at every stage of the *Phenomenology*. Force will split itself into two forces, self-consciousness into two self-consciousnesses, etc. But this pluralism, in turn, is merely an appearance, and the contradiction which has been expelled from the thing that is different not from itself but from other things in fact returns to dwell within the thing as a difference of itself to itself, an internal reflection within external reflection.

Let us consider the thing, or the monad, different from all others. It is for-itself as unity within itself in its own determinations, a determinateness which is suitable only to it and which constitutes its essence. No doubt, there is also a diversity in it, for how could it be determinate without that diversity which is its being-for-an-other? But this diversity is inessential to it and is its exteriority. Contradiction is indeed avoided by this distinction between *essential* and *inessential*, an inessential that is always necessary (which is a new, concealed contradiction). But contradiction reappears in its definitive form, for this thing which is equal to itself and is for-itself is such only in its absolute difference from every other. And this difference implies a relation with other things, a relation which is the cessation of its being-for-itself: "It is precisely by means of its absolute character and its opposition that the thing relates to others and is essentially only this process of relating. But this relation is the negation of its independence, and the thing indeed collapses due to its own essential property" (*PE*, I, 104; *PG*, 99; *PM*, 174).

Thanks to this dialectic we proceed from *thing* to *relation*, from the thingism of perception to the relativity of understanding. This movement is a familiar one in the history of science and of philosophy. What disappear in this movement are the artifices that common consciousness uses to preserve the single and independent thing: the distinction between essential and inessential, the separation of being-for-itself and being-for-an-other. "From one and the same point of view," Hegel writes, "the object is the opposite of itself, for-itself insofar as it is for-an-other, for-an-other insofar as it is for-itself." (*PE*, I, 104; *PG*, 99; *PM*, 175). What appears, and this is specific to Hegel, is a notion of relation which manifests the life of relation. Relation is both the separateness and the unity of these terms; correctly understood, it is that unity of unity and multiplicity, that identity of identity and nonidentity, which Hegel had planned since his early writing to think through as the life of the absolute. Undoubtedly, it often seems that his dialectic is better suited to living or conscious beings than to material beings. When we wish to understand Hegel's dialectic of being-for-itself which is for-itself only in its being-for-an-other, examples taken from human life or human relations seem more appropriate than the example of the salt crystal. For a dynamism must be introduced into being—which is relation—which we can attribute to living beings, or to consciousness, but which it seems difficult to introduce into what we generally call "inert matter." But Hegel's thought seeks to grasp universal being as concept, that is, as subject, and it sees in nature merely one specific moment of this dialectic.

But these considerations have taken us away from our subject. Perceiving consciousness has been transcended. Since the thing is contradiction, it dissolves as thing equal to itself and becomes phenomenon. The mingling of the sensuous and thought, which the sensuous property constitutes, has decomposed into its extremes, the "also" and the "entity," being-for-another and being-for-itself. And these extremes have become identified with each other in a universal that is unconditioned (by the sensuous). This universal is the new object of consciousness, which has become understanding. We must now follow this *esse* which *est intelligi,* for though it is the concept in-itself, it is not yet the concept for-itself. At first, for consciousness, it is force and its manifestation, then law and its necessity, and, finally, infinite life in which the self discovers itself in its other. At that moment, consciousness of the other becomes self-consciousness, and the concept in-itself becomes the concept for-itself.

3 / Understanding

General Development of This Chapter

For perceiving consciousness, everything was "a thing."[1] The category of substance, as the substratum of sensuous qualities—a category Berkeley had criticized in his *Three Dialogues of Hylas and Philonaus*—gives way to a new category. Understanding rises from substance to cause, from thing to force. For understanding, everything is at first a *force*. But force is nothing but the concept, the thought of the sensuous world; it is the reflection of this world back on itself—or its reflection in consciousness, which, for us, comes to the same thing. This thought of the sensuous world, which at first manifests itself to consciousness as the empty beyond of this world, as the extra-sensuous as such, becomes, as a system of *laws*, the interior of this world. These laws, laws of experience, are beyond the phenomenon, yet they constitute its framework. Consciousness experiences the contingency of the laws of nature; in seeking their necessity, it returns from the world to itself. At first, its explanation of these laws is tautological, and consciousness reaches a merely analytic necessity. But that necessity becomes synthetic when it appears to consciousness in its object. Sensuous world and extrasensuous world, phenomenon and law, identify with each other in the genuine concept—the thought of infinity which, after expressing Leibniz' dynamism, the legal-

1. Not *Sache* but *Ding*. See part IV, chapter 5, below, for a discussion of this difference.

[118]

ism of Newton and Kant, and Schelling's polarity, expresses Hegel's own point of view. Infinity, or absolute concept, is relation come alive, the universal life of the absolute which remains itself in its other and reconciles analytic and synthetic identity, the one and the many. At that moment, consciousness of the other has become a consciousness of itself in the other, the thought of a difference that is no longer a difference. In its object, consciousness reaches itself; in its truth, it is self-certainty, self-consciousness.

Such is the general development of this chapter, the implications of which we shall try to specify. We shall pay special attention to the important movement from consciousness to self-consciousness. At first, consciousness is universal consciousness, the medium of being, while its object, inaccessible in its concrete richness, is the sensuous this. Self-consciousness, on the contrary, is first a unique consciousness, a negation of all otherness in its pure relation to itself. But from this negative uniqueness it must rise to universality and return to the moment of consciousness qua universal self-consciousness. The unity of the universality of consciousness and the uniqueness of self-consciousness will then arise as reason (*Vernunft*).[2]

I. Force

UNDERSTANDING now has as its object the unconditioned (*unbedingt*) universal, which, according to its German etymology, is not a thing. For us,[3] this universal is the concept which combines in it the contradictory moments that perceiving consciousness posited alternately in the subject and in the object: the moment of indifferent thingness *expressing* itself in a multitude of subsisting differences, i.e., the matters of physics or sensuous properties materialized, and the moment of the unique thing *excluding* all multiplicity from itself. These moments appeared as being-for-an-other and being-for-itself. The failure of perception lies in the impossibility of thinking these

2. "Understanding," on the contrary, the title of this chapter, corresponds to the German term *Verstand*.
3. In order to avoid any ambiguity let us recall once again that this "for us" denotes the point of view of the philosopher as opposed to the point of view of phenomenal consciousness.

two together. But the result of the previous dialectic, though negative for the consciousness engaged in experience, appears positive to us. "The result has within it the positive signification that in it the unity of being-for-itself and being-for-an-other, the absolute opposition, is immediately posited as one and the same essence" (*PE*, I, 110; *PG*, 104; *PM*, 181). This result applies to the content as well as the form. Expansion into the realm of differences and contraction into the unity of being-for-itself constitute all the contents which can henceforth appear to consciousness. But this expansion and contraction can no longer be isolated and posited separately; it is their unity which makes up the unconditionality of the universal. "First, it is clear that because they exist only in this universality these moments can no longer remain apart from each other but are in themselves essentially aspects which suppress [*aufheben*] themselves; only their transition into each other is posed" (*PE*, I, 111; *PG*, 104; *PM*, 182). This transition was the very movement of perceiving consciousness, which at times attributed exclusive unity to the thing in order to reserve for itself the diversity of its coexisting aspects and at times attributed this diversity to its object while reserving exclusive unity to itself. But whereas this movement was not an object for perceiving consciousness itself, now it *is* its object, and consciousness knows the *transition,* which only we knew when we retraced the experience of perceiving consciousness. It is crucial to note that what is now given to consciousness, which has become understanding, is the transition itself—the connection—which previously occurred in it without its knowledge and which was, therefore, external to its moments. Nonetheless, this transition first appears to understanding as having an objective form; for understanding, the transition will be *force.* In contradistinction to the thing, which has no link to its many properties, force makes sense only insofar as it manifests itself and poses what is inside itself outside itself. Thus, by itself, force expresses the *necessity of the transition* from one moment to the other, but for understanding it is still an object.

> But in this movement the content of consciousness is only objective essence and not consciousness as such; therefore, the result must be posed for it in an objective signification, and consciousness must once again be posed as withdrawing from the having-become [*von dem Gewordenen; du devenu*] in such a way

that this having-become is, qua objective, its essence (*PE*, I, 110; *PG*, 103; *PM*, 180–81).[4]

> A reality appears among the things that are tangible, visible, and in other ways perceptible, and all of a sudden disappears, hides, becomes imperceptible. We believe that its effects can be known but not its nature. We then invent a creature of reason [*un être de raison*] which is called force and which alternately manifests itself in spending itself and then, spent, becomes invisible in order to spend itself.[5]

Such is force, the unity of itself and its externalization. In positing force, we posit this very unity, already, that is, the *concept*. "In other words, the differences posed in their independence immediately pass over into their unity, their unity into their unfolding, and this unfolding, in turn, into reduction to unity. It is precisely this movement that we call force" (*PE*, I, 112; *PG*, 105; *PM*, 183). The universal being of sensuous certainty became the medium of properties or of distinct matters, and this medium, in turn, has become their reduction to unity inasmuch as it is the means of their expansion. Thus, for Leibniz, the essence of matter resides neither in extension, which is merely an indefinite multitude, nor in the atom, which is a sensuous image, but in force, the only true unity:

> I realized that it is impossible to find the principles of a genuine unity in mere matter, or in that which is merely passive, since everything is but an infinite collection, or heap, of parts. Now since the multitude could have its reality only in the genuine unities which come from elsewhere . . . I had to have recourse to a formal atom. . . . Thus I discovered that their nature consists in force, that from this follows something analogous to sentiment and appetite, and hence that they had to be conceived in imitation of our notion of souls!"[6]

4. It is quite remarkable that what understanding takes to be being is the very reflection of the previous consciousness (perceiving consciousness). But since phenomenal consciousness always forgets its development, it is not aware that this object is itself. It does not yet know itself in the *transition* from one term to the next.

5. Andler, "Le fondement du savoir dans la *Phénoménologie de l'esprit* de Hegel," in *Revue de métaphysique et de morale*, XXXVIII, no. 3 (July–Sept., 1931), 328.

6. Leibniz, "A New System of Nature and the Communication of Substances," *Philosophical Papers and Letters*, trans. Leroy Loemker, 2 vols. (Chicago, 1956), I, 739.

II. THE CONCEPT OF FORCE AND THE REALITY OF FORCE

THE TWO MOMENTS OF FORCE—force as externalization or expansion of itself into the realm of differences, and force "driven back on itself," or force proper—are not distinct to begin with. In the first *Logic*, that of Jena, Hegel deals with force while discussing the category of modality. Force driven back on itself, or concentrated on itself, is force as possibility; its externalization is its reality.[7] When we envisage the fall of a body in space, we posit the same being twice: as reality, the motion is a juxtaposition that can be broken down into parts (or, at least, this decomposition is present in the spatial trajectory), but we can also consider the "whole of the motion," the integral of which it is the realization. We then have force, the content of which is identical to its manifestation, but which *formally* differs from that manifestation. As the reflection back on itself of sensuous externality, force is identical to that externality. There is a *doubling* here, which Hegel emphasizes in the Jena *Logic*: we conceive the unity of reality as force; consequently, our explanations of this reality in terms of force are tautological.[8] Nevertheless, force allows us to think causality and relation without positing reciprocally external substances. Two bodies attract each other in space, the magnet attracts iron; for perceiving consciousness, this signifies an external relation between two substantialized things. To conceive gravitation or magnetism is to conceive relation itself, to conceive the transition from one moment to another as transition. But force, as we have just defined it, is absolutely identical to its manifestations —so much so that the differences (force driven back on itself and force externalized) are differences only for consciousness. When we grasp the two moments in their immediate unity, the fact is that understanding, to which the concept of force belongs, is, properly speaking, the concept that maintains the distinct moments as distinct. For in force itself they are surely not distinct. The difference is only in thought. In other words, what we have posed above is only the concept of force, and not yet its reality (*PE*, I, 112; *PG*, 105; *PM*, 183).

That force manifests itself to consciousness as reality and

7. Jena *Logic*, pp. 41 ff.
8. *Ibid.*, pp. 44 ff.

no longer as concept signifies that its moments take on a certain independence. But since, on the other hand, this independence is contrary to the essence of force, it also signifies that these moments suppress (*aufheben*) themselves as independent and return into the unity of the concept, or of the unconditioned universal which is the permanent object of understanding throughout the whole of this dialectic. But the concept thus reached is no longer the immediate concept with which we began; it is

> determined as the negative of that force which has a sensuous objectivity. The concept is force as the latter is in its true essence, that is, only as object of understanding. The first universal, then, is force driven back on itself, or force as substance, but the second universal is the inside of things qua inside, which is identical to the concept qua concept (*PE*, I, 118; *PG*, 110; *PM*, 189).

The experience of consciousness here is quite remarkable. In making force real, it discovers that "the realization of force is at the same time the loss of reality" (*PE*, I, 118; *PG*, 110; *PM*, 189). In the sensuous world, force first opposes an other without which it seems unable to exist. Then that other appears as another force, and what is then posed is the duality of forces —as Boscovitch and Kant had already noticed. But these two forces, in turn, are only apparently independent. They presuppose each other. "To every attraction corresponds a repulsion; otherwise, the matter of the whole universe would coagulate at one point." Each force, then, presupposes another force and is presupposed by it. The play of forces (*Spiel der Kräfte*), which we will later come upon as the relation between self-consciousnesses, is hence a reciprocal relation such that only the thought of this play, only the concept of phenomenal reality, or the inside of things, subsists in the perpetual interplay of determinations. Force has become what it already was for us, the thought of the phenomenal world which, as an interplay of forces, is now no more than an incessant exchange of determinations, a perpetual instability whose unity and consistency lie only in thought.

The realization of force expresses itself in three dialectics which Hegel subtly distinguishes: (1) force and the other, (2) the two independent forces, and (3) the reciprocal action of forces, the interplay of forces. To begin with, force is posed as the infinite expansion of itself in the medium of differences. But in order to exist as force driven back on itself, reflected back on itself, an other must approach and call for it to turn in upon itself. Fichte's "I," for instance, reflects itself only through a shock (*Anstoss*) which seems alien to it. Similarly, if force is already posited as driven back on itself, as pure possibility, then in order for it to exist as externality it must be called forth by an other. When we compare these two roles of the other, we are led to define this other itself as force. What is then posed is no longer force and an other-than-force but two real forces which act on each other: "Thus force has not in general exceeded the bounds of its concept by the fact that an other exists for it and that it exists for an other. Two forces are present simultaneously. To be sure, the concept of the two is the same but the concept has left its unity to pass over into duality" (*PE*, I, 115; *PG*, 107; *PM*, 186). This whole dialectic concerning the being of things for consciousness prefigures a dialectic of spirit, a dialectic which seems to be more profound in the world of spirit than in nature. Here, Hegel's subtlety strikes us as somewhat empty and forced. What is essential is to understand the direction of his whole argument: to lead us to see the dialectic of intelligence in the dialectic of the real. "The spirit of nature is a hidden spirit; it does not appear in the form of spirit; it is spirit only for cognizant spirit. Or, in other words, it is spirit in-itself and not for-itself." It is a matter of finding in the dynamism and the interplay of forces, in the polarity of opposing forces, a dialectic whose meaning is for-itself only in the cognizant spirit. When the two forces are posed in their independence, their interplay reveals their interdependence. "They are not like extremes, each keeping something solid for itself and each transmitting merely an external property to the other through their common term and their contact. What these forces are, they are only in this common term and in this contact" (*PE*, I, 117; *PG*, 109; *PM*, 188). Each vanishes in the other, and this movement of vanishing is the only reality of forces that has sensuous objectivity. There then remains only manifestation, the phenomenon (*Erscheinung*), which no longer has consistency and stability within itself but refers back to an internal truth that at first appears beyond it. Here we may recall the following passage of the preface to the *Phenomenology* on the nature of phenomena: "Manifestation (the phenomenon) is the movement of being born and of perishing, a movement which itself neither is born nor perishes but which is in-itself, and which constitutes the actuality and the movement of the life of truth" (*PE*, I, 40; *PG*, 39; *PM*, 105).

III. The Interior, or the Bottom of Things

UNDERSTANDING HAS DISCOVERED the element of truth: it is the interior, or the bottom of things, which stands contraposed to phenomenal manifestation. This opposition, which reproduces at a new level the opposition between force and its externalization, is at first empty of meaning. As the negation of the phenomenon, the interior is beyond it. But Hegel's whole dialectic here will tend to bring these two terms closer until they are identified, an identification already set forth in the passage from the preface that we have just quoted. The phenomenon, qua phenomenon, is the extrasensuous, that is, the phenomenon seen as something in the process of vanishing. The great joke, Hegel wrote in a personal note, is that things are what they are. There is no reason to go beyond them; they are simply to be taken in their phenomenality instead of being posed as things-in-themselves. The essence of essence is to manifest itself; manifestation is the manifestation of essence. The end point of our dialectic, therefore, will be to gather anew the sensuous and the extrasensuous into the infinity of absolute concept.

Summarizing the prior moments with regard to religion, Hegel writes: "Insofar as it is understanding, consciousness already becomes consciousness of the extrasensuous, or of the interior of objective Dasein. Yet the extrasensuous, the external, or whatever we may wish to call it, has no self; it is at first merely the universal which is still far from being spirit that knows itself as spirit" (*PE*, II, 203; *PG*, 473; *PM*, 685). This universal is at first posed outside consciousness and outside the phenomenon as a possibly intelligible world of which we can well have some notion but no knowledge. In the last chapter of his "Transcendental Analytic," which deals with the distinction between phenomena and noumena, Kant insists that we cannot take this world, the world of the here-below, as a thing-in-itself, but that, on the other hand, as soon as we move beyond it, using our categories transcendentally and no longer empirically, we reach an empty place, a noumenon in the negative sense. But for Hegel, this beyond of the phenomenon is a kind of optical illusion. Understanding hypostatizes its own reflection, it does not reflect it back on itself, and it fails to see in nature the self-knowledge that is implicit in it. Knowledge of the phenomenon is a self-knowledge and, as such, it has a truth that is no longer located in the beyond. But in order to reach such an idealism, reflection, which Kant uses in his critical philosophy, must reflect itself. In objectifying this "interior as the universal without the self," understanding does not know that "there is nothing to be seen" behind the curtain which is thought to cover the inside of things "unless *we* step behind it—as much that there be someone to see as that there be something to be seen" (*PE*, I, 140–41; *PG*, 129; *PM*, 212–13). The noumenon (in the negative sense) is criticized here, just as the "thing-in-itself" of "transcendental aesthetics" was criticized in the dialectic of perception. Starting from this movement, consciousness reflects itself back on itself as it does in the true; but, as consciousness, it again makes an objectified interior of this true and distinguishes this reflection of things from its reflection back on itself. Similarly, for this consciousness the movement that carries out the mediation remains an objective movement (*PE*, I, 119; *PG*, 110; *PM*, 190). Thus, the three terms of this fundamental syllogism—*understanding*, the *movement of the phenomenal world*, and the *interior or the bottom of things*—are posed in their mutual externality. But there can be no knowledge of this interior, as it is immediately—not, as Kant claimed, because reason is limited, but because of the simple nature of the thing, for in the void nothing is known, or, more precisely, because this interior is posed as the beyond of consciousness.

Yet, in fact, this interior has been born for us. It has been posed only through the mediation of the phenomenon, which is why Hegel expresses the nature of the interior in the following remarkable way: "It derives from the phenomenon, and the phenomenon is its mediation, or, the phenomenon is its essence and, indeed, its fulfillment. The extrasensuous is the sensuous and the perceived posed as they truly are. But the truth of the sensuous and the perceived is to be phenomenon. Hence the extrasensuous is the phenomenon qua phenomenon" (*PE*, I, 121; *PG*, 113; *PM*, 193). We do not thereby return to the prior sensuous world, to perception, for example, or to objective force, but we see this world as it genuinely is—as the movement by which it continuously disappears and negates itself. What subsists throughout this instability of the phenomenon, throughout the continuous exchange of its moments, is indeed difference, but difference taken up into thought and become universal, that is, the *law* of the phenomenon. In this way, the universal is no longer the nothingness beyond the phenomenon; it carries difference, or mediation, within itself, and this difference at the heart of this universal is difference become equal to itself, the simple image of the phenomenon. This difference is expressed in law as the "invariable image of the ever-unstable phenomenon." The extrasensuous world is thus a calm realm of laws. "These laws are, no doubt, beyond the perceived world—for this world presents law only through continuous change—but they are also present in it and are its immediate and immobile copy" (*PE*, I, 123–24; *PG*, 115; *PM*, 195).

At the end of the "Transcendental Analytic," Kant wrote that nature is the collection of phenomena ruled by laws. In their universality, at least, these laws are the forms of phenomena; in their stability they reflect the uninterrupted development of that which appears. Just as force was the reflection back on itself of its externalization, so law is the unity of the sensuous world. But it is a unity which includes difference and which through this constant difference translates phenomenal movement. In the free fall of a body, space and time vary continuously, but their relation remains the same and the well-known mathematical formula, $d = \frac{1}{2} gt^2$, is the invariable expression of the perpetual variance of these two terms. The law that is the interior of phenomenal nature finds its content in this nature and, in exchange, imparts its form to it.

But form and content remain inadequate. According to Maimon's early interpretation of Kantianism, a form that completely determined content or a content that was completely taken up into form would be the idea.[9] But this perfect adequation is never realized. Content, the matter of understanding, is infinitely diverse and varying; form, taken to its highest power, is the abstract unity of abstract difference. We can say, in more picturesque language, that the "Transcendental Analytic" gives us the law of laws, the skeleton of a nature in general. But between this skeleton and concrete nature lies an abyss. To be sure, this abyss is partly filled by empirical induction which rises from particular laws to progressively more general ones. But this induction can never reach the idea, for the idea requires the complete determination of all conditions. The critique of judg-

9. Salomen Maimon, *Gesammelte Werke* (Hildesheim, 1965–71): "In my view, the knowledge of things in-itself is nothing but *complete* knowledge of phenomena."

ment—that Leibnizianism of immanence—elaborates a philosophy of the as-if, a logic of hypotheses, precisely so as to remedy this shortcoming in subsumption and specification. We must finally agree that there remains a side to the phenomenon-for-itself that is not taken up into the interior, "where the phenomenon is not yet genuinely posed as phenomenon, that is, as suppressed [*aufgehoben*] being-for-itself" (*PE*, I, 124; *PG*, 115; *PM*, 196). The laws of nature are characterized by a contingency that appears in two complementary aspects: either law does not express the entirety of phenomenal presence, in which case the phenomenon still keeps as a possible in-itself an uncoordinated variety, or there is a multiplicity of empirical laws which cannot be gathered into the unity of a simple law of which they would be the specifications. The problem posed by moving from the phenomenon to its law reappears in the problem of the plurality of laws.

We could try to subsume all laws under the unity of a single law. Newton, for example, presents phenomena as diverse as the free fall of a body on earth and the general planetary movement around the sun (as expressed in the more specific laws of Kepler) as universal gravitation. But ever since his Jena dissertation on planetary movement, Hegel had tried to show the error of such a reduction: it can only reach an abstract formula which, though it has, no doubt, the merit of setting forth lawfulness as lawfulness, completely obscures the qualitative diversity of the content. Are we then to give up difference as genuine qualitative difference in order to attain unity, or are we to give up unity in order not to lose this difference? With this, we are at the heart of the problem of phenomenal identity and reality. Hegel's solution is not to continue to contrapose the two terms but rather to seek their union in a dialectical relation which for him is "absolute concept," or infinity.

The concept of law—the unity of differences—clashes not only with the empirical plurality of laws but also with law itself. For it expresses the *necessity* of the connection among terms which appear as distinct in the statement of the law—space and time, for example, what attracts and what is attracted, etc.— in such a manner that in the thought of this connection, in the thought of this unity, "understanding [difference] returns once more into the interior, understood as simple (indivisible) unity. This unity is the internal *necessity* of law" (*PE*, I, 125; *PG*, 116; *PM*, 197).

IV. EXPLANATION: THE ANALYTIC NECESSITY OF LAW

LET US CONSIDER a particular law, for example, that of falling bodies, or of gravitation, or of positive and negative electricity. Each law contains a concrete difference—space and time or positive and negative electricity—and it expresses the relation between these two factors. This relation, or concept of the law, which we can also call force, indicates the necessity of law in analytic form. But this necessity is not a necessity, for we cannot see how either factor joins with, or becomes, the other. By the very fact that one term of the law is posed, the other is not posed. And if, finally, we pose the necessity of their relation by starting with a force—weight, for example, or electricity in general—then this necessity is merely a verbal one, for we must then explain why this force expresses itself in this or that specific difference, why, for example, the nature of weight is such that weighty bodies fall according to an unchanging and precise law which contains a difference, such as that of space and time, and even states it in a mathematical formula, $d = \frac{1}{2} gt^2$.

The problem Hegel poses here is that of the necessity of relation, a question which Hume had posed as that of "the necessary connection" and which Kant claimed to answer in the *Critique of Pure Reason*. We know that for Hume everything that is different (in representation) is separable and nothing that cannot be separated is discernible. For what can discernment grasp where there is no difference?[10] Hume's conception forbids us abstraction while it renders the necessary connection impossible. As Hegel notes in the Jena *Logic*, what is posed by Hume and Kant is a diversity of substantive terms which are indifferent to each other, terms such as sensuous representation offers, or seems to offer.[11] In this case, Hume is entirely justified in denying necessity and in seeing it as merely an illusion. "In fact, necessity is only substance envisaged as relation or as the being-one of opposite determinations which are not, like material terms that are absolutely for-themselves, absolute substantive terms or qualities, but are in-themselves such as to bear on

10. Hume, *A Treatise of Human Nature*, book I, part I, section 7.
11. Jena *Logic*, p. 48.

another, are essentially the opposite of themselves." [12] As for the identity that understanding claims to reach in the process of its explanation, it is a formal identity, a tautology which in no way alters the diversity of the terms. For Hume there exist only substantive elements (Hegel says "substances") which are not interrelated, which remain for-themselves and are connected together *from outside*. Thus, for understanding, identity remains analytic and is a tautology, while sensuous diversity remains diversity. This identity does lead to a synthesis, but only to an empirical synthesis that lacks necessity. "This identity remains simply a tautology and this diversity is only a specific being-for-itself of substances; identity and diversity remain external to each other; the relation of diverse substances is in no way necessary, because this relation is not internal to them." [13] What is needed for this relation to become internal? As Hegel will show, it would be necessary that each determination be conceived as infinite, that is, as other than itself. In this case, space by itself becomes time, and time becomes space. Relation is no longer imposed on substantialized determinations from the outside; it is the very life of these determinations. We can then understand what relation implies: dialectical life. For relation is neither an abstract unity nor an equally abstract diversity; it is their concrete synthesis, or, as Hegel said of life in his early works, "the bond of the bond and the nonbond," "the identity of identity and nonidentity." [14]

Instead of thinking through this dialectic which alone confers necessity on relation, Kant failed really to answer Hume: "Kant did the same thing as Hume." Hume's substantive elements, which follow each other or come into juxtaposition and are reciprocally indifferent, remain indifferent for Kant as well. That these elements are called "phenomena" and not "things" changes nothing. Kant began with Hume's diversity and added to it the infinity of relation, but this addition remains external. Necessity, the infinity of relation, is something separate from diversity. Diversity is phenomenal and pertains to sensuousness; necessity is a concept of the understanding. Each of the two moments remains for-itself. "For Kant, experience is indeed the bond between concept and phenomenon, that is, it renders the

12. *Ibid.*
13. *Ibid.*
14. The first phrase is from Hegel's *Early Theological Writings*, p. 312; the second, from Hegel's study "Differenz," p. 77.

indifferent terms mobile (*mobilmachen*). Outside their relation, each of these terms remains for-itself, and the relation itself, qua unity, is external to that which is related." [15] Thus Kant did not truly grasp *relation as infinite*.

We have referred to this illuminating passage from the Jena *Logic* because it seems to us to shed light on the dialectic concerning the laws of nature—the first immediate elevation of the sensuous world to the intelligible. Since this elevation is immediate, it does not yet express the totality of the phenomenal world. In it, the phenomenon is not yet posed as phenomenon, as suppressed being-for-itself, and this shortcoming appears in the law itself as the indifferent difference between its terms. The law does not express the whole phenomenon, which keeps for itself its instability and its development, or (and this comes to the same thing) it expresses it immediately in the form of a difference that is stable and lacks necessity. We can grasp here one of the most profound characteristics of Hegel's thought: to introduce life and becoming into thought itself instead of giving up thought and returning to the phenomenon—a phenomenon no longer cut up into substantive elements, as for Hume, but grasped in its ineffable becoming, in an immediate intuition. For Hegel, the immediate givens of consciousness furnish not a discontinuous sequence of terms but, as Bergson later showed, an inexpressible transition. It is by reintroducing life into the law (immediate relation) that thought will completely rejoin the phenomenal world, or (in Hegel's terminology) that the phenomenon will be posed in its integrity as a phenomenon, that is, as complete manifestation of its essence. That this is indeed Hegel's goal is expressed in an important passage of the preface: "Hence, the task now is . . . to make the universal actually present and to infuse spirit into it as a result of the suppression of determinate and solidified thoughts. But it is far more difficult to render solidified thoughts fluid than it is to render sensuous Dasein fluid" (*PE*, I, 30; *PG*, 30; *PM*, 94). Similarly, in an article written in Jena, Hegel justified a profound empiricism— that of the man of action, who intuitively grasps the becoming of reality without cutting it up in an arbitrary way—and contrasted it to the empiricism of understanding, which freezes and solidifies experiential determinations. But the philosophic method cannot be simply to return to this profound empiricism— to the ineffable of sensuous certainty—at the cost of giving up

15. Jena *Logic*, pp. 48–49.

thought. For this reason, philosophy must raise understanding to reason and render the determinations of thought mobile—that is, it must think dialectically.[16]

It is rather difficult to follow the transition from the world of laws—that immediate and inadequate replica of the phenomenal world—to absolute concept, that is, to infinity. Hegel begins by criticizing the explanations offered by understanding which, in search of necessity, discovers that necessity only within itself, in its own tautologies, while leaving its object unchanged. He then proceeds from this movement, which takes place only in understanding, to the movement in the "thing-in-itself"—to the dialectic that infuses life into the "quiescent rule of laws" and thus allows it completely to rejoin phenomena. This last transition seems to us the most difficult to follow, especially since Hegel makes it rather abruptly.

Seeking the necessity of law, understanding creates a difference that is not a difference and, recognizing the identity of what it has just separated, ends up with simple tautologies which it calls necessity. This, one might say, is the soporific virtue of opium. Why do bodies fall according to the law? Because they undergo the action of a force, weight, that is so constituted as to manifest itself in precisely this way. In other words, a body falls in this way because it falls in this way.

> The unique event of lightning, for example, is apprehended as a universal, and this universal is expressed as the law of electricity. Then, explanation sets down and summarizes the law that is in force as the essence of the law. This force is then constituted in a manner such that when it externalizes itself two opposite electric charges are generated and then cancel each other. In other words, *force is constituted exactly like law;* the two are said not to differ at all (*PE*, I, 129; *PG*, 119; *PM*, 201).

But force is posed here as the necessity of law. It is in-itself, and it remains what it is external to understanding while the differences—specifically, the very difference between force in-itself and the law by means of which force externalizes itself—devolve on understanding. "The differences are pure universal externalization (law) and pure force. But law and force have the same content, the same constitution. Difference, as difference in content, i.e., as difference in the thing, is therefore abandoned once more" (*PE*, I, 129; *PG*, 119; *PM*, 201).

16. The article in question is "Naturrecht," p. 343.

But the difference between understanding and its object in-itself, force, is also a difference of understanding. This difference, therefore, disappears in turn, and the thing itself, force in-itself, reveals itself as the movement which had at first been considered only a movement of consciousness. "But since the interior of things is the concept qua concept of understanding, this change came about for understanding as the law of the interior." This is the difficult transition we noted above; we move "from one shore to the other" (*PE*, I, 130; *PG*, 120; *PM*, 202), from the movement of an explanation that is different from its object to the very movement of the object, for this difference, too, is a difference in understanding. Change of form becomes change in content because the difference between form and content is itself part of the process. But in that case, analytic necessity, i.e., tautology, becomes a necessity of the content, i.e., synthetic necessity; tautology reappears in heterology [*hétérologie*] as identity in contradiction. At that point, we reach dialectical thought, that "unity of unity and diversity" which, according to Hegel, both Hume and Kant had missed. But let us dwell here on the procedure of understanding which Hegel calls "explanation" (*Erklären*). We might think that explanation is merely a matter of a verbal formula—opium makes one sleep because it has a soporific quality—and be surprised at the length of the description Hegel devotes to it. In fact, the procedure of explanation is a very general one: it goes *from the same to the same*. It establishes differences which are not genuine in order then rigorously to demonstrate their identity. This is the formal movement of understanding, a movement that is expressed in the abstract equation $A = A$, in which A is distinguished from A in order then to be identified with it. Every explanation, then, is tautological, or formal. But this procedure extends far beyond the soporific quality of opium. Many explanations which appear fruitful are in fact reducible to this formalism, to this lifeless equal sign. In his Jena *Logic*, Hegel gives examples: "Explanation is merely the production of a tautology. Cold comes from the loss of heat, etc. . . . For understanding, there can be no genuine qualitative change; there is only a *change in the location of the parts*. . . . The fruit of the tree comes from humidity, from oxygen, hydrogen, etc., in short, from everything that the fruit itself is." [17] Hegel thus reproaches the formalism of understanding for using an abstract formula of conservation

17. Jena *Logic*, p. 47.

to negate qualitative difference. Specifically, we may note that he does not believe in the fruitfulness of mathematical equations. Just as he criticized Newton's general law, without taking its mathematical implications into account, so, in this critique of explanation he attacks—at least implicitly—a mathematical science of the universe which, if not verbal in the usual sense of the word, is nonetheless merely a formal language, unable to preserve qualitative difference in the network of its equations. We need but look in the preface to the *Phenomenology* to find an explicit statement of this critique:

> The actually real is not something spatial as mathematics considers it to be. Neither concrete sensuous intuition, nor philosophy, burdens itself with such actual nonrealities as mathematical things. . . . Besides, by virtue of this principle and this element —and this is what the formalism of mathematical evidence consists of—knowledge traverses the equal sign. For what is dead, unable to move itself, can attain neither the differentiation of essence nor opposition, or essential inequality; it thus also fails to attain the change of opposed terms into each other, a change that is qualitative and is immanent movement, self-movement (*PE*, I, 38; *PG*, 37–38; *PM*, 103).[18]

Hegel is seeking a science that will remain a science without, however, giving up qualitative difference. The answer he found —the dialectic—is the result of a manipulation of qualitative difference such that difference is forced to its resolution by means of opposition and contradiction. "In general," Hegel wrote at Jena, "opposition is the qualitative, and since nothing exists outside the absolute, opposition itself is absolute; only because it is absolute does it suppress itself within itself." [19] By introducing contraction into thought, we avoid both the formalism of explanation and the empiricism of random differences. We introduce infinity into determinateness and in this

18. The preface contains a general critique of mathematical knowledge, a critique which reappears in the Major *Logic* with reference to the category of quantity. To the *formal* knowledge of mathematics, in which reflection (or mediation) is external to the thing itself (*PE*, I, 37; *PG*, 36; *PM*, 101), Hegel contraposes a *dialectical* knowledge which does not contain an alien mediation but is simultaneously the movement of the thing itself and the movement of our thought of the thing. Mathematics, in particular, is unable to think time—"the pure disquiet of life, the process of absolute distinction" (*PE*, I, 40; *PG*, 39; *PM*, 104).

19. Jena *Logic*, p. 13.

way rise above Schelling's philosophy of identity, a philosophy that fails to reconcile the identity of the absolute with the qualitative differences of manifestation. For such a reconciliation to be possible, "polarity" had to be pushed to the point of contradiction.

In contrast to content, which remains unchanged, the movement of explanation, then, is a pure movement, a formalism. But this formalism already contains what its object (the world of laws) lacks: it is movement within itself. "In it, however, we recognize precisely absolute change itself, the lack of which was felt in law. Indeed, considered more closely, this movement is immediately its own contrary" (*PE*, I, 129–30; *PG*, 120; *PM*, 201).[20] It poses a difference where there is none; it quickly identifies what it has just distinguished. It is the contentless instability of pure form which is straightway its own contrary. When we say "*A* is *A*," we both distinguish and identify. The equal to itself repels itself but also unites itself.

What is the result for content, for the interior, when this movement is noticed in it—the difference between content and form having been suppressed? The experience of understanding reveals that the law of the phenomenon itself is that differences which are not differences come into being. "In a parallel way, [understanding] experiences that the differences are of such a nature that they are not genuine differences and that they suppress themselves." Content, which is noticed through the at first formal movement of understanding, becomes the opposite of itself, and form, in turn, becomes rich with content. We have here "absolute concept," or infinity. But let us dwell on what Hegel curiously terms the experience of the "upside-down world." It is because the first, suprasensuous world (the immediate elevation of the sensuous to the intelligible) reverses, or upends, itself in itself that movement is introduced into it and that it is no longer merely a replica of the phenomenon but completely joins the phenomenon which in this way mediates itself in-itself

20. In other words, insofar as it is envisaged *only* in our understanding, the movement of our thought which establishes laws and *explains* them is formal. It is tautological: we distinguish in order then to show that what we have distinguished is identical. But insofar as it is viewed as a movement of the thing itself it becomes synthetic, for it is the thing itself that opposes itself and unites with itself. Explanation, then, is no longer *our* explanation; it is the very *explanation* of being that is identical to the self. Thus, thought and being are one.

and becomes manifestation of essence. We understand what Hegel meant when he claimed that there were not two worlds but that the intelligible world was "the phenomenon as phenomenon," i.e., "manifestation," which in its authentic development is only the self-manifestation of self.

V. THE TWO WORLDS AND THEIR DIALECTICAL UNITY

THIS EXPERIENCE of the inversion of the world is more common than we might think at first. Perhaps if we are to understand it, we should refer less to science or to Schelling's polarity than to the dialectic of the Gospels, which constantly opposes the apparent world to the true one. Whereas in the first transformation of the sensuous world we raise this world to essence only in an immediate way—by raising the difference it includes to universality without modifying it profoundly—we now reach a world that is the *inverse* of the first one. The difference between essence and appearance has become an absolute difference, with the result that we say that anything in-itself is the opposite of what it appears to be for-an-other. We could indeed agree with common sense that appearances are not to be trusted; that they must, on the contrary, be negated if their true essence is to be discovered. The profound and the superficial oppose each other as inner and outer. "Seen superficially, this inverted world is the contrary of the first one; the first world lies outside the inverted world which repels it as an inverted actual reality. Thus, one world is the phenomenon, and the other is the in-itself; one is the world as it is for-an-other, but the other, on the contrary, is the world as it is for-itself" (*PE*, I, 133; *PG*, 122; *PM*, 205). Thus, in the Gospels, what is honored in this world is scorned in the other; apparent strength is in fact weakness; hidden simplicity of the heart is in-itself superior to apparent virtue. In the Sermon on the Mount, Christ repeatedly opposes appearance—"it has been said"—to profound reality—"I say unto you." Hegel takes up this opposition of inner and outer and considers it in all its scope. What appears sweet is bitter in-itself; the north pole of a magnet is in its suprasensuous in-itself the south pole, and vice versa; the pole of oxygen becomes the pole of hydrogen. But Hegel passes from these examples borrowed from the science of his time to spiritual examples, which in our opinion manifest the genuine meaning of this dialectic.

He speaks in particular of the dialectic of crime and punishment, which recalls his early writings on religion. Punishment appears to be a vengeance externally imposed on the criminal; in fact, punishment is self-punishment. That which, viewed superficially, appears as a constraint is in its profound meaning a liberation. The hidden meaning is the reverse of the apparent meaning. Further, punishment, which appears to dishonor a man, "becomes in the inverted world the grace and pardon which safeguard the man's essence and render him honor" (*PE*, I, 133; *PG*, 122; *PM*, 204). We are reminded of Dostoevski's famous novel—and this is not the only time that we find intuitions in Hegel's dialectic which Dostoevski later developed.

The difference between phenomenon and essence, between apparent meaning and hidden meaning, has become so profound that it destroys itself; it is, in effect, absolute opposition, opposition in-itself, that is, *contradiction*.

> At this point, the interior is fulfilled as phenomenon. Indeed the first suprasensuous world was merely the immediate elevation of the perceived world to the universal element; as a copy, it had its necessary original in the world of perception, which still retained for itself the principle of change and alteration. The first reign of law lacked this principle, but now it obtains it as the world "upside down" (*PE*, I, 132; *PG*, 121; *PM*, 203).

Now, each determination destroys itself and becomes its other; it is thought through as infinity, that is, it destroys itself in a kind of movement to its own limit, a movement that Hegel had made the technique of his first, Jena, *Logic*.[21] But this logic of infinity makes sense only on condition that it not again make the two opposed worlds real as two substantive elements;

> Such oppositions between inner and outer, between the phenomenon and the suprasensuous, are no longer present here as oppositions between actual realities of two kinds. Nor do the rejected differences redistribute themselves into two substances that would support them and furnish them a separate substance —in that case, understanding, having emerged from the interior, would fall back to its earlier position (*PE*, I, 133–34; *PG*, 123; *PM*, 205).

21. Cf. our article, "Vie et prise de conscience de la vie dans la philosophie hégélienne d'Iéna," in *Revue de métaphysique et de morale*, XLIII (1936), 50; reprinted in *Studies on Marx and Hegel* (New York, 1969), pp. 3–21.

The phenomenon itself is negative, a difference between itself and itself.

> The actually real crime carries its inversion and its in-itself as a possibility in intention as such and not in good intentions. For the fact itself is the only truth of intention. But, as regards its content, the crime has its reflection back on itself, or its inversion, in actually real punishment. This punishment constitutes the reconciliation of the law with the actual reality that opposes it in the crime. Finally, the actually real punishment has its actual inverted reality within itself; it is, in fact, an actualization of the law, in which the activity that the punishment is suppresses itself. [From an act, it again becomes a quiescent and valid law], and both the movement of individuality against the law and the movement of law against individuality are extinguished (*PE*, I, 135; *PG*, 123–24; *PM*, 206).

The inverted world, therefore, is not to be sought in *another* world. It is present in this world, which is simultaneously itself and its other and which is grasped in its phenomenal entirety as "absolute concept," or infinity. It is possible to think this infinity—which Schelling did not grasp—if, instead of fleeing contradiction, we agree to think it through in the midst of determinate content, which thus becomes absolute determinateness, or self-negation.

> What must be thought through now is pure change, or opposition within itself, that is, contradiction. . . . Thus, the suprasensuous world, which is the inverted world, has both encroached upon the other world and included it within itself; for-itself, it is the reversed, inverted world, which is to say that it is the inverse of itself: it is both itself and its opposite in one unity. Only in this way is it difference as inner difference, as difference within itself; only in this way does it exist qua infinity (*PE*, I, 135; *PG*, 124; *PM*, 206–7).

Instead of being posed now in their sensuous externality, the terms of the preceding law are animated toward each other like positive and negative poles. Their being consists essentially in posing themselves as nonbeing and suppressing themselves in unity. But this unity, in turn, is not—like Schelling's absolute—isolated from multiplicity. It is a moment of the splitting, a specific term in opposition to diversity. According to an image in the Jena *Logic*, the absolute itself is anxious if the finite lies outside it, for then it is only relatively absolute or infinite. For that reason, it becomes concretely infinite only by splitting itself.

The unity of which we usually think when we say that difference cannot issue from it is itself, in fact, simply a moment of the splitting; it is the abstraction of simplicity vis-à-vis difference. But to say that it is the abstraction, and therefore only one of the opposites, is also to say that by itself it is the act of splitting. Since it is a negative, an opposite, this unity is rightly posed as that which includes opposition within itself. Therefore, the differences between the *splitting* and the *becoming equal to itself* are merely the movement of self-suppression (*aufheben*) (*PE*, I, 137; *PG*, 126; *PM*, 209).

What we reach in this way is "absolute concept," the genesis of which we have followed since the being of sensuous certainty. More concretely, it is "universal life, the world soul, the universal blood stream which is omnipresent and whose course is not disturbed or interrupted by any difference. Rather, it itself is all differences as well as their suppressed being; it pulsates without moving and trembles in its innermost being without disquiet" (*PE*, I, 136; *PG*, 125; *PM*, 208). We have here the synthesis of the ἀκίνητον and the κίνησις of which Plato spoke in the *Sophist*. It is manifestation that is manifestation of self by self, mediation of the immediate with itself. It is already self.

But if this is so for us, and if the concept, as universal life, presents itself to us, then consciousness has reached a new stage in its ascent; it has grasped manifestation as its own negativity instead of distinguishing it from both itself and its intelligible object. This dialectic of self-identity within absolute difference at first appears to consciousness in an immediate form as self-consciousness. In self-consciousness, indeed, the I is absolutely other, and yet this other is the I. Consciousness has become self-consciousness. Beyond certainty, truth is posed in that very certainty. Can it preserve itself as truth in this certainty that is pure subjectivity?

PART III

The Transition
from Natural Self-Consciousness
to Universal Self-Consciousness

Introduction / The Movement of Consciousness to Self-Consciousness

I. SELF-CONSCIOUSNESS AS THE TRUTH OF CONSCIOUSNESS

KANTIAN IDEALISM—as it was interpreted by the German philosophers who developed it further—might well be summarized in a formula which is not to be found in Kant's own writings: "Self-consciousness is the truth of consciousness." In the "Transcendental Analytic," Kant specifies the meaning of his deduction by asserting "that the conditions of the *possibility of experience* in general are likewise conditions of the *possibility of the objects of experience* and that for this reason [these objects] have objective validity in a synthetic a priori judgment." [1] When empirical understanding knows its object, that is, nature, and through experience discovers the multiplicity of the particular laws of nature, it fancies that it knows an other than itself. But the reflection which the critique of pure reason constitutes shows that this knowledge of an other is possible only through an originary synthetic unity such that the conditions of the *object*, specifically, of nature, are the very conditions of knowing this nature. In knowing nature, then, understanding knows itself; its knowledge of an other is a self-knowledge, a knowledge of knowledge. The world is "the great mirror" in which consciousness discovers itself. [2]

1. Kant, *Critique of Pure Reason*, trans. Norman Kemp Smith (London, 1961; New York, 1950), p. 194.
2. At the end of the chapter on understanding, Hegel writes, "There is much self-satisfaction in explanation because in explanation consciousness is, so to speak, in an immediate dialogue with

To be sure, Kant does not develop his thought to such an idealism. What understanding determines in nature is, so to speak, only the skeleton, the universal conditions, or the laws thanks to which a nature is a nature. There then remains an a posteriori, an indefinite diversity that is not actually determined by the a priori conditions of knowledge. "By nature, in the empirical sense, we understand the connection of appearances as regards their existence according to necessary rules, that is, according to laws." [3] It is certain laws, then, a priori laws, which first make possible a nature; empirical laws can occur and be found only by means of experience, and only in conformity to those originary laws without which experience itself would not be possible. The existence of an absolute a posteriori in Kant's philosophy culminates in a conception (already present in the "Transcendental Aesthetic") of the "thing-in-itself," a conception from which, although it was transformed at every stage of his philosophy, Kant was unable to free himself. Kant borrowed the notion of the thing-in-itself from perception, the most common of experiences, and it is at the level of perception that Hegel criticizes it. [4] The noumenon of the "Transcendental Analytic" is no longer the thing-in-itself of the "Transcendental Aesthetic," and the notion of a dialectic which limits knowledge and of an idea which commits knowledge to push back its limit, is of yet another order. Kant's realism of the thing-in-itself served as a target for all the philosophers of German idealism. For in condemning all metaphysics of the object, of being—and until then all metaphysics had more or less been a metaphysics of being—the *Critique of Pure Reason* and, especially, the "Transcendental Dialectic" sowed the seed of a quite different metaphysics, a metaphysics of the subject.

It is indeed important to Kant that nature, in the empirical sense of the term, as constituted by the transcendental understanding of the analytic, not be mistaken for what it is not and arbitrarily set up as thing-in-itself. We must become aware of

itself and enjoys only itself; it seems to be dealing with something else, but, in fact, it is engaged and occupied only with itself" (*PE, I*, 139; *PG*, 127; *PM*, 210). Its knowledge of nature is in fact a self-knowledge.

3. Kant, *Critique of Pure Reason*, p. 237.

4. On this "absolute a posteriori," see Hegel's study of Kant in "Glauben und Wissen," p. 244. On the most mediocre interpretation of the "thing-in-itself" as "a rock under the snow," see Hegel, "Skeptizismus," pp. 167, 209.

the phenomenality of nature. This phenomenality is not, as is often thought, the result of the subjectivity of the categories (insofar as it is transcendental, this subjectivity is identical to objectivity). On the contrary, this phenomenality—this finitude of our knowledge, we might say—is constituted by the nontranscendental subjectivity of matter, by the passivity, the receptivity, which understanding cannot do without. Nonetheless, the finitude of our knowledge exists only because understanding conceives the idea of an unlimited understanding but finds itself limited. The object of a finite subject must itself be finite.

II. Self-Consciousness as Practical Consciousness

Now the finite subject is not limited in the way that an object can be limited: an object does not know its own limit, which is external to it; the subject continually seeks to transgress its limit. It tends toward the infinite, the unconditioned. By virtue of this, this understanding (*Verstand*) is reason (*Vernunft*), but by the same token, it transgresses the very sphere of objects. This infinite is not an object; it is a task the accomplishment of which is forever deferred. It is no longer the concept of reason that regulates experience, as it does in the "Analytic of Principles," but that of the idea, an infinite practical task in relation to which all knowledge and all knowing are organized. For Kant, self-consciousness is not only the sole truth of consciousness; it is also practical consciousness, the negation of all finitude and, therefore, of any consciousness of an object. Already in the "Transcendental Dialectic," the idea as infinite task is not the thing-in-itself manifesting itself in experience; it does not extend the boundaries of understanding. Rather, it is a maxim of the theoretical will, an imperative for scientific thought. The idea extends understanding not as understanding but as will. It enlarges understanding not theoretically but practically, permeating all of understanding's experimental knowledge of finitude and summoning understanding to the infinite effort of transcending itself. The idea qua infinite task, self-consciousness qua practical I, is the moment with which Fichte starts in his attempt to reconstruct the unity of Kant's entire philosophy, the unity of the critique of pure reason and the critique of practical reason. Fichte's idealism is therefore a moral idealism (at least if we consider only the first *Science of*

Knowledge, the only one that Hegel knew and the one he analyzed in his first work, "Differenz"). This brief discussion of the development of Kant's thought from a Hegelian point of view has been necessary in order that we understand how on the one hand self-consciousness appears in Hegel's phenomenology as the truth of consciousness, the knowledge of the other as a self-knowledge, and how, on the other hand, this self-knowledge, self-consciousness, is more than the knowledge of the other, or of nature. Self-consciousness is essentially practical; it is the consciousness of transcending the knowledge of the other. Just as in the *Critique of Practical Reason* self-consciousness, autonomy, is conceived to be the negation of nature, and just as in the *Science of Knowledge* the practical I is conceived to be the infinite effort to rejoin the primal identity, the I = I, the thetic principle of the whole *Science of Knowledge,* so in the *Phenomenology* self-consciousness appears, in opposition to consciousness, as active consciousness. The positivity of consciousness becomes negativity in self-consciousness. It is quite true that this activity will at first be envisaged in its most humble form, as desire. But its development will show what desire entails and how, by opposing itself to the world, and to itself as a being of the world, it leads us to higher forms of practical consciousness.

This analysis will show us the insufficiency of theoretical consciousness and of practical consciousness, of consciousness and of self-consciousness. It will require a higher synthesis, reason, which, containing the identity of consciousness and self-consciousness, of being and acting, will allow us to pose the human problem in a new and different way.

III. LIFE AND SELF-CONSCIOUSNESS

a. *The absolute concept*

WHAT UNDERSTANDING SEES arising before it in objective form in this world, which inverts itself into itself and whose every determination is its own contrary, is the absolute concept, "universal life, the world soul." [5] Moreover, for itself consciousness becomes self-consciousness. Before moving on with our

5. Cf. above, part II, chapter 3.

study, we must try to specify the significance for the philosopher of this ontology of life and self-consciousness. In modern terms, it is the being of life and the being of self-consciousness that Hegel strives to think through. When he speaks of absolute concept or universal life, he proceeds not from a given, specific entity or from a determinate biological consideration but from the being of life in general. Similarly, he describes the very being of (human) self-consciousness, which emerges from this life. This development of self-consciousness at the heart of universal life will later show us how the self-certainty which human consciousness gains and which becomes for it a truth is the very condition of truth, or universal reason. We can speak of reason, of universal self-consciousness, only when (subjective) certainty takes the form of an (objective) truth and (objective) truth becomes self-certainty. Absolute concept, or the concept of concept, is what later appears in the *Logic* in the form of the three dialectical moments, the universal, the particular, and the specific. In the "Fragment of a System," Hegel had written that the movement from finite to infinite life is religion, not philosophy.[6] If later, in the *Logic,* he managed to express in rational form an intuition of the very being of life or of the self, which he had earlier declared could not be thought through, we should not conclude from this that nothing remains of the first intuition, the kernel from which his whole system developed. When, in the *Logic,* he wishes to explain the meaning of this concept, he uses images to give it meaning. The concept is omnipotence; it is omnipotence only through manifesting itself and affirming itself in its other. It is the universal which appears as the soul of the particular and determines itself completely in it as the negation of the negation, or as genuine specificity. Or, in yet other words, it is love, which presupposes a duality so as continually to surpass it.[7] The universal of the concept is not external to the particular and juxtaposed to it; in this separation, it is itself the particular, it is always both itself and its other. Similarly, the particular is particular only through contraposing itself to the universal. Now this contraposition is the negation of the particular, and, therefore, its return to the universal as negation of negation. As we see, the concept is nothing else than the self which remains itself in its alteration, the self which exists only in this self-becoming.

6. "Fragment of a System," in *Early Theological Writings,* p. 311.
7. *Logic, SW,* IV, pt. 2, 242 ff.

This intuition, with which Hegel started, cannot easily be conveyed in a perfectly clear manner. It can, perhaps, be compared to the intuition of the one of the first German philosophers, Jakob Böhme, whose speculative ambition was "to grasp the no in the yes and the yes in the no." It seems that in his research in human life—and Hegel was more interested in human life than in life in general—Hegel came to an idea similar to Böhme's. But whereas Böhme had especially tried to discover in man an image of the divine life, of the *mysterium magnum revelans se ipsum,* Hegel was more interested in human being. Hegel tried to give a remarkable logical form to his intuition, an intuition the irrational character of which (in the usual sense of the word) is undeniable. In order for this to be possible, understanding must shatter the framework of common thought, the thingism of perception, and even the dynamism with which understanding seeks to conceive cause and force. "For understanding, the omnipresence of the simple (the indivisible) in external multiplicity is a mystery." [8] Yet it is this nonseparation of the whole and the parts and their simultaneous separation that constitutes infinity, universal life, as "the bond of the bond and the nonbond" or as "identity of identity and nonidentity." It is this infinity that understanding meets when it comes up against separate determinations and the demand for their unity. In thinking these determinations through as infinities, that is, in discovering in them the movement by which they become their own contrary, understanding rises above itself; it becomes able to think the self—which by posing itself in a determination negates and contradicts *itself.* Taken in itself, this movement constitutes "universal life, the world soul." For itself, however, it exists in human self-consciousness as consciousness of universal life.

We see now why the passage of the *Phenomenology* that deals with self-consciousness begins by presenting us a general philosophy of life which is in-itself what self-consciousness will be for-itself.[9] Here, the movement from in-itself to for-itself will not be a mere change of form without a change of nature. Man's becoming aware of universal life is a *creative reflection.* If for Schelling life is a knowing that does not yet know itself and knowing is a life that knows itself—so that the identity of the

8. *Ibid.,* pp. 416 ff.
9. The chapter on self-consciousness begins with a general philosophy of life and living beings.

two is philosophical intuition—for Hegel, spirit is constituted only by the reflection of life in knowledge. And spirit is superior to nature precisely because it is nature's reflection. Life refers back to the consciousness of a totality which never is given in it for-itself. But self-consciousness knows itself as the genus (γένος) and, in this coming to consciousness, it is the origin of a truth which is for-itself at the same time that it is in-itself, a truth which, through the mediation of diverse self-consciousnesses, develops historically, a truth the interaction and unity of which alone constitute spirit.[10]

It would be wrong to say that the fundamental intuition of Hegelianism was "the being of life in general" qua *mobility*, for example. This ontology of universal life only serves as the basis for a conception of the being of man—of human existence, we would say today—a conception which had been Hegel's essential preoccupation much earlier, in the works of his youth. "To think pure life through, that is the task," he wrote in an often quoted early text. And he added: "The consciousness of this pure life would be the consciousness of what man is." [11] At that time, Hegel identified pure life with the being of man. Nevertheless, this pure life is not pure, that is, it is not abstracted from the determinate modalities of human existence; it is not abstract unity as opposed to a multiplicity of manifestations, such as, for example, the abstract intelligible characteristic as a universal of the concrete determinations of the empirical characteristic. "The characteristic, indeed, is merely abstracted from the activity"; it expresses merely "the universal of determinate actions." [12] But pure life transcends this separation, or this appearance of separation; it is concrete unity, which, in his early works, Hegel was not yet able to express in dialectical form.

This being of life is not substance but rather the disquiet of the self. According to a recent commentator, the fundamental intuition from which Hegel's philosophy issued is that of the motion of life.[13] This seems inadequate. The attributed adjective which recurs most frequently in Hegel's dialectic is disquiet [*unruhig*]. This life is disquiet, the disquiet of the self which has

10. Hyppolite, "Vie et prise de conscience de la vie dans la philosophie hégélienne d' Iéna," *Revue de métaphysique et de morale*, XLIII (1936), 45.

11. *Early Theological Writings*, p. 253.

12. *Ibid.*, p. 254.

13. Herbert Marcuse, *Hegels Ontologie und die Grundlegung einer Theorie der Geschichtlichkeit* (Frankfurt, 1932).

lost itself and finds itself again in its alterity. Yet the self never coincides with itself, for it is always other in order to be itself. It always poses itself in a determination and, because this determination is, as such, already its first negation, it always negates itself so as to be itself. It is human being "that never is what it is and always is what it is not." To those who are familiar with Hegel's early works on love, on destiny, or on positivity (that is, the historical determination of a people, a religion, or a man, which as his finitude opposes within him the demand for infinity), this intuition of human being appears indeed to be the starting point of Hegel's speculation. In the Jena period this intuition is expressed through the dialectic of the finite and the infinite.

While at Jena, Hegel became aware of the function of philosophy, and, more specifically, of his philosophy: to think through, even if in a nonthinking way,[14] the living relation between the finite and the infinite, which the "Fragment of a System" had presented as experienced only by religion. For this reason, Hegel criticized the reflective philosophy of Kant, Jacobi, and Fichte—a philosophy which never moves beyond opposition—and seemed to adopt Schelling's philosophy of intuition, which grasps the identity of the absolute directly in its various manifestations. But implicitly Hegel already opposed this philosophy which erases qualitative differences, reducing them to random differences of degree. Not only identity must be thought through, but also "the identity of identity and nonidentity," a formula that takes up again in technical language the earlier formula, "the bond of the bond and the nonbond." The oppositions are not to disappear: on the contrary, in order to think them through we must develop them until contradiction appears in them. "In general, opposition is the qualitative, and since nothing exists outside of the absolute, opposition itself is absolute; only because it is absolute does it suppress itself within itself."[15] The absolute, thus, is not alien to reflection or to mediation. It is not the abyss into which qualitative differences disappear, but is itself opposition. Opposition is a moment of the absolute, which thus is subject and not substance. This comes down to conceiving the no as being contained in the yes. This is a mystical image, an image of an absolute which divides and rends itself in order to be absolute and which can be yes

14. Cf. "Differenz," pp. 104–5.
15. Jena *Logic*, p. 13.

only by saying no to the no. But with Hegel, this mystical image is translated through the invention of a dialectical mode of thought whose value is due to the intensity of the intellectual effort which it actually realizes.[16] The *pantragedism* of the early writings finds adequate expression in this panlogism which, thanks to the development of difference to opposition and of opposition to contradiction, becomes the logos of being and of the self. As Spinoza saw, determinateness is indeed the result of a negation, but this negation which seems to delimit it from outside is its own, and for this reason, insofar as it is concrete or complete determinateness, insofar as it is an absolutely determinate mode, it is the movement of self-contradiction within itself, the movement of negating itself. "The true nature of the finite is to be infinite, to suppress itself as being. The determinate has, qua determinate, no other essence than this absolute disquiet not to be what it is."[17] The true task of philosophy is thus to develop the determinations which common understanding grasps only as abstractions, in their fixity and their isolation, and to discover in them what gives them life: absolute opposition, that is, contradiction.[18] "Absolute opposition, infinity, is thus absolute reflection of the determinate within itself, of the determinate which is an other than itself." Similarly, infinity itself, the negation of the finite, should not be thought of as a separate absolute, "a beyond opposition." According to its concept, infinity is the suppression of opposition and not the being-suppressed [*Aufgehobensein*] of opposition.[19] The latter is

16. Implicit in Hegel's philosophy there is a certain interpretation of Christianity according to which it was only through becoming a man and knowing death and human destiny so as to surmount them that God became God: "God without man is no more than man without God" (see part VI, chapter 3, below).

17. Jena *Logic*, p. 31. All these passages are from the chapter on infinity (pp. 26–34).

18. If we are to understand Hegel's thought, we must recall that *abstraction* is not only a psychological action, our abstraction, but that it inheres in *being* just as much as opposition does. As Hegel notes in the section on Kant in "Glauben und Wissen," p. 247, the understanding that thinks abstract determinations is both *our* understanding and *objective* understanding. This is put even more precisely in the preface to the *Phenomenology*: "This is the understanding of Dasein" (*PE*, I, 48; *PG*, 46; *PM*, 114); "thus, understanding is a development and as such it is rationality" (*PE*, I, 49; *PG*, 47; *PM*, 115).

19. This could also be translated "is the *act of transcending* [opposition] and not *transcendence* [of opposition]."

merely the void which opposition itself opposes. For this reason, the infinite is no less uneasy than the finite. "The annihilating disquiet of the infinite exists only through the being of that which it annihilates. The suppressed is just as much absolute as it is suppressed; it engenders itself in its annihilation, for annihilation exists only so long as there is something that annihilates itself." [20]

This philosophy is a philosophy that conceives substance as subject, being as self. The word *Selbst*, which Hegel uses so frequently, corresponds to the Greek αὐτός and means both I and same, *ipse* and *idem*, sameness and identity. Life is identity with itself, or, as Hegel says, borrowing Fichte's phrase, equality with itself. But as it is itself the self, this equality is at the same time the difference between self and self. Its being is the movement through which it poses itself as other than itself in order to become self. In a form that is still immediate, this being of the self is universal life, self only in-itself; but in its reflection, it is self for-itself, that is, self-consciousness. Life and self-consciousness, therefore, are related. If life is the self (in his early works Hegel sometimes calls life "pure self-consciousness") it reaches itself only in self-knowledge. "Life refers back to something other than itself." It is, therefore, knowledge, and consequently it is self-knowledge, for otherwise it would not be itself. Truth is not outside of life; "it is the light that life carries within itself." This light is the truth of life and reveals itself through and in life. Truth is born precisely in self-consciousness, and there it simultaneously becomes self-certainty.

b. *General philosophy of life*

The general philosophy of life results from a double movement, that from the unity of life (*natura naturans*) to the multiplicity of living forms or of differences (*natura naturata*) and that which, on the contrary, starts from distinct forms and discovers that same unity in and through them. These two movements merge in the vital process, in the "die and become," so that the splitting of the entity is as much a process of unification as that unification is a process of splitting. Thus life is a circular becoming which reflects back on itself. But its genuine reflection is its becoming for-itself, that is, "the emergence of self-con-

20. Jena *Logic*, p. 34.

sciousness," whose development reproduces in a new form the development of life. This general philosophy of life reconciles monism and pluralism, and synthesizes rest and motion: The essence of life "is infinity as the being-suppressed [*Aufgehobensein*] of all differences; it is pure rotational motion around its axis; it is itself at rest as absolutely uneasy infinity" (*PE*, I, 148; *PG*, 136; *PM*, 221). For it is self, and self is that which cannot genuinely oppose itself to an alien term. In the medium of life, all alterity is provisional, and the appearance of an other is immediately resolved into the unity of the self. Life, precisely, is this movement which reduces the other to itself and discovers itself in that other. This is why Hegel says that life is an independence (*Selbständigkeit*)[21] in which the differences of its movement have been resolved. And, he adds, the essence "is the simple essence of time, which in this self-equality has the solid and compact shape of space" (*PE*, I, 148; *PG*, 136; *PM*, 221). In a first moment we have the subsistence of distinct beings. The finite mode, as a particular living entity, poses itself outside universal substance, that is, it poses itself as though it were itself infinite and it excludes from itself the whole of life. Precisely this activity of posing itself for-itself is lacking in Spinoza's monism. For Spinoza, the finite mode appears as a negation and infinite substance alone is absolute affirmation. But if infinite substance is what *appears* in the finite mode, then this absolute affirmation must be apparent through that mode. This affirmation will manifest itself, then, by the fact that the distinct individuality will negate itself, will be the negation of its separation, that is, of its negation, and thus will bring about the rebirth of the unity of life. The particular living entity "thus emerges in opposition to universal substance; it disavows such fluidity, disavows continuity with the universal substance, and affirms itself as not being dissolved into it. Rather it maintains and preserves itself by separating itself from its inorganic nature and by consuming it" (*PE*, I, 150; *PG*, 137; *PM*, 222–23). Life, then, becomes the movement of these figures [of consciousness]; it becomes life as process. But in this movement, the separated living entity is by itself an inorganic nature, which is why "it consumes itself, suppresses its own inorganic reality,

21. Let us note that to translate *Selbständigkeit* as "independence" does not give us the *Selbst*. The self is independent because it identifies itself in the other and reduces that other to it. The medium of universal life is not the inert medium which we discovered at the start as the first form of universality.

feeds on itself, organizes itself from within." [22] Although death appears to arrive from outside and to be the result of an alien negation, as though the universe were suppressing a living individuality, it originates in fact in the living entity itself. Insofar as this entity is the process of life, it must die in order to become; its emergence vis-à-vis the whole is its own negation and its return to unity. "The growth of children is the death of parents," for this return is, reciprocally, the emergence of new individualities. Nevertheless, life does not fulfill itself in this becoming.

> Life is constituted by the totality of this circuit. It is not, as we earlier said, the immediate continuity and the compact solidity of its essence, nor the subsisting figure, the discrete, existing for-itself; nor is it their pure processes, nor yet the simple gathering up of these moments. It is the whole, developing, dissolving, and resolving its development, and remaining simple throughout this whole movement (*PE*, I, 151; *PG*, 138; *PM*, 224).

Yet with this result, life refers us back "to something other than what it is; it refers us to consciousness, for which it is as this unity or as genus" (*PE*, I, 152; *PG*, 138; *PM*, 224). The genus which for itself is genus, which is not merely what is expressed in vital development but which becomes for-itself, is *the I* as it appears immediately in the identity of self-consciousness. Thus self-consciousness is the truth of life. But with it another life begins, an experience which will grow in richness until it comes to include the whole development we have seen in life (*PE*, I, 152; *PG*, 138; *PM*, 225). In its immediate emergence it will be posed for-itself in opposition to universal life, and it will have to surmount that opposition. We shall follow its experience in the new element of self-knowledge. The spirit which self-consciousness will actualize after having risen to reason, to universal self-consciousness, is *for-itself* the unity and multiplicity which were involved in the medium of life. "Spirit as the entity of this process, as I, is what does not exist in nature. Nature is the development of the existence of spirit as I. In nature this development turns itself inside out; its interior appears only as the power that dominates specific living beings." [23] Death, that is, the negation of individualities and of living species, is for these beings the power that is alien to them; in fact, it is the unity of

22. *Realphilosophie*, SW, XX, 116.
23. Jena *Logic*, pp. 193–94.

life, the life of the genus, a life which does not yet know itself. That is why in pure life, in the life that is not spirit, "nothingness as such does not exist" [24]—a significant phrase which more profoundly than any other expresses the fact that the I of self-consciousness is not, properly speaking, a being. As a being it would fall back into the milieu of subsistence. But it is what for-itself negates itself and for-itself preserves itself in that self-negation. Self-consciousness as the truth of life, spirit as the truth of self-consciousness, leave nature far behind—nature which is spirit only for the spirit that knows it.

24. *Ibid.*, p. 194. But "we are the nothingness" (*Realphilosophie*, SW, XX, 80).

1 / Self-Consciousness and Life: The Independence of Self-Consciousness

SELF-CONSCIOUSNESS, which is desire, can reach its truth only by finding another living self-consciousness. Three moments—the two self-consciousnesses posed in the element of externality and also externality itself, the Dasein of life—give rise to a dialectic which leads from the battle for recognition to the opposition between master and slave, and from that opposition to liberty. Indeed, in accordance with an ever-recurring pattern in the *Phenomenology,* this dialectic which arises in the midst of externality transposes itself to the interior of self-consciousness itself. Just as the forces discovered by understanding, which appeared to be alien to each other, proved to be a unique force divided within itself—each force being itself and its other—so the duality of living self-consciousness becomes the splitting and reproduction of self-consciousness within itself. The independence of the master and the harsh education of the slave become the self-mastery of the stoic who is always free, regardless of circumstance or the hazards of fortune, or the skeptic's experience of absolute liberty, which dissolves every position except that of the I itself. Finally, the truth of this stoic or skeptic liberty comes to be expressed in unhappy consciousness, which is always divided within itself, a consciousness both of absolute self-certainty and of the nothingness of that certainty. Unhappy consciousness is the truth of this entire dialectic. It is the pain felt by pure subjectivity which no longer contains its substance within itself. Unhappy consciousness, the

[156]

expression of the pure subjectivity of the I, leads back, through the movement of self-alienation, to consciousness of substance. But this consciousness is not the consciousness described at the beginning of the *Phenomenology*, for being is now self, itself alienated. Self-consciousness has become reason.[1]

We shall follow this movement: the positing of self-consciousness as desire, the relation among self-consciousnesses in the element of life and the movement that recognizes self in the other, and, finally, the internalization of this movement in the three stages of stoicism, skepticism, and unhappy consciousness.

POSITING SELF-CONSCIOUSNESS AS DESIRE: DEDUCTION OF DESIRE

"SELF-CONSCIOUSNESS is desire in general" (*PE*, I, 147; *PG*, 135; *PM*, 220). In the practical part of the *Science of Knowledge*, Fichte discovered impulse (*Trieb*) to be at the base of theoretical consciousness as well as of practical consciousness, and he showed that the first condition of this sensuous instinct was "an instinct for instinct," a pure action in which the I strives to rediscover the "thetic" identity of self-consciousness. We have already compared Fichte's and Hegel's conceptions, and we shall not dwell on that comparison here. Why is self-consciousness desire in general? And, as we might ask in contemporary terms, what is the intentionality of this desire? What is the new structure of the subject-object relation that is being described here? Hegel deduces desire, and the necessity of the presentation of self-consciousness as desire, in a few dense lines. The starting point of this deduction is the opposition between self-knowledge and knowledge of an other. Consciousness was knowledge of an other, knowledge of the sensuous

1. In the chapter on phrenology, Hegel himself clearly summarizes this development from unhappy consciousness to reason: "Unhappy self-consciousness has alienated its independence and has struggled until it has transformed its *being-for-itself* into a *thing*. Thus, it has returned from self-consciousness to consciousness, that is, to the consciousness for which the object is a *being*, a *thing*. But that which is a thing is self-consciousness which, therefore, is the category, the unity of the I and being [the category]" (*PE*, I, 284; *PG*, 252; *PM*, 369).

world in general; self-consciousness, on the contrary, is self-knowledge, and is expressed in the identity $I = I$ (*Ich bin Ich*). The I that is an object is an object for itself. It is simultaneously subject and object; it poses itself for itself. "The I is the content of the relation and the very movement of relating. At the same time, it is the I that opposes itself to an other and exceeds that other, an other which for it is only itself" (*PE*, I, 146; *PG*, 134; *PM*, 219). This seems far removed from what is commonly called "desire." But let us note that this self-knowledge is not primary; self-consciousness is "reflection issuing from the being of the sensuous world and of the perceived world; it is essentially this return into itself starting from being-other" (*PE*, I, 146; *PG*, 134; *PM*, 219). Unlike Fichte, we do not pose the *Ich bin Ich* in the absoluteness of a thetic act in relation to which antithesis and synthesis would be secondary. The reflection of the I, which takes the sensuous world, the being-other, as its starting point, is the essence of self-consciousness, which, therefore, exists only through this return, only through this movement. "Qua self-consciousness, it is movement" (*PE*, I, 146; *PG*, 134; *PM*, 219). However, when we consider only the abstraction $I = I$, we have merely an inert tautology. The movement of self-consciousness, without which it would not exist, requires otherness, that is, the world of consciousness which in this way is preserved for self-consciousness. But it is preserved not as a being-in-itself, as an object which consciousness passively reflects, but as a negative object, as the object which must be negated in order that through this negation of the being-other self-consciousness establish its own unity with itself. We must distinguish two moments. "In the first moment self-consciousness exists as consciousness, and the complete extension of the sensuous world is maintained for it, but maintained only insofar as it is related to the second moment, i.e., the unity of self-consciousness with itself" (*PE*, I, 147; *PG*, 134; *PM*, 220). That is what we mean when we say that the sensuous world, the universe, stands before me now as no more than phenomenon, or manifestation (*Erscheinung*). The truth of that world now lies in me and not in it; that truth is the self of self-consciousness. I need only establish that unity by the movement that negates being-other and then reconstitutes the unity of the I with itself. The world no longer subsists in-itself; it subsists only in relation to self-consciousness, which is its truth. The I is the truth of being, for being exists only for the I which appropriates it and thus poses itself for itself. "This unity must become essential to self-consciousness, which is to say that self-consciousness is desire in general" (*PE*, I, 147; *PG*, 135; *PM*, 220). Desire is this movement of consciousness which does not respect being but negates it, appropriating it concretely and making it its own. Desire presupposes the phenomenal character of the world which exists for the self only as a means. The difference between perceiving consciousness and desiring consciousness can be put in metaphysical language even though neither consciousness is aware of this metaphysics. We have already glimpsed this difference in the first chapter of the *Phenomenology,* the chapter on "Sensuous Certainty":

> Not even the animals are excluded from this wisdom but, rather, they show themselves to be profoundly initiated in it. For they do not stand before sensuous things as though these were in-itself; they despair of this reality and, absolutely convinced of the nothingness of sensuous things, they grab them without further ado and consume them. Like the animals, the rest of nature celebrates the revealed mysteries that teach what the truth of sensuous things is (*PE*, I, 90–91; *PG*, 87–88; *PM*, 159).

THE MEANING OF DESIRE

SELF-CONSCIOUSNESS, then, is not "the inert tautology, I = I"; it presents itself as engaged in a debate with the world. For self-consciousness, this world is what disappears and does not subsist, but this very disappearance is necessary for self-consciousness to pose itself. Self-consciousness, therefore, is *desire*, in the most general meaning of the word. And the intentional object of desire is of a different order than the object intended by sensuous consciousness. Hegel describes this new structure of consciousness in a precise, although very condensed, manner. We should recall that in his first essays on the philosophy of spirit, especially in the "System der Sittlichkeit" written in Jena, Hegel had constructed a kind of philosophical anthropology in which objects were grasped not so much in their independent being as in their being-for-consciousness: as objects of desire, as material for work, as expressions of consciousness. In the same vein, the philosophies of spirit of 1803–4 and 1805–6 studied instruments, language, and so on, in an attempt to describe, and to present in an original dialectic, the human world as a whole and the surrounding world as a human world. All these dialectics must be presupposed if we are to understand the transition from desire to the encounter between self-consciousnesses, an encounter that is the precondition of social and spiritual life. The individual object of desire—this fruit I wish to pluck—is not an object posed in its independence. Insofar as it is an object of desire we can just as well say of it that it exists as that it does not exist. It exists, but soon it will no longer exist; its truth is to be consumed and negated, in order that self-consciousness might gather itself up through this negation of the other. From this arises the ambiguity that characterizes the object of desire, or, rather, the duality of the end intended by desire.

> Henceforth, consciousness, qua self-consciousness, has a double object: one is the immediate, the object of sensuous certainty and of perception, which for self-consciousness is characterized by negativity (that is, this object is merely phenomenon, its essence being to disappear); the other is precisely itself, an object which is true essence and which is present at first only in opposition to the first object (*PE*, I, 147; *PG*, 135; *PM*, 220).

The end point of desire is not, as one might think superficially, the sensuous object—that is only a means—but the unity of the I with itself. Self-consciousness is desire, but what it desires, although it does not yet know this explicitly, is itself: it desires its own desire. And that is why it will be able to attain itself only through finding another desire, another self-consciousness. The teleological dialectic of the *Phenomenology* gradually unfolds all the horizons of this desire, which is the essence of self-consciousness. Desire bears first on the objects of the world, then on life, an object already closer to itself, and, finally, on another self-consciousness. Desire seeks itself in the other: man desires recognition from man.

DESIRE AND LIFE

WE HAVE TRANSLATED *Begierde*, the word Hegel uses, as "desire" [*désir*] rather than as "appetite," [*appétit*] for this desire contains more than appears at first; although insofar as it bears on the various concrete objects of the world, it merges initially with sensuous appetite, it carries a much wider meaning. Fundamentally, self-consciousness seeks itself in this desire, and it seeks itself in the other. This is why desire is in essence other than it immediately appears to be. We have already shown that at each stage of the *Phenomenology* a certain notion of objectivity is constituted, a truth appropriate to that stage. It is less a matter of thinking individual objects than of determining the characteristics of a certain kind of objectivity. At the stage of sensuous certainty we dealt not with this or that particular sensuous "this" but with the sensuous "this" in general. At the level of perception we dealt not with this or that perceived object but with the perceived object in general. Similarly, at the level of self-consciousness, objectivity is defined in a new way. What self-consciousness discovers as its other can no longer be the merely sensuous object of perception, but must be an object that has already reflected back on itself. "Through such a reflection back on itself the object has become life." And, Hegel adds, "That which self-consciousness distinguishes from itself by considering it as an existent not only has, insofar as it is posed as an existent, the mode of sensuous certainty and of perception, but also is being reflected back on itself; the object of immediate desire is some living thing" (*PE*, I, 147–48; *PG*, 135; *PM*, 220). In other words, life is the medium in which self-consciousness experiences and seeks itself. Life constitutes the first truth of self-consciousness and appears as its other. As we ourselves have grasped it as the result of the previous dialectic, it is the term that corresponds to self-consciousness. At the level of self-consciousness, truth is possible only as a truth that experiences and manifests itself in the midst of life. All the more must we emphasize the duality of self-consciousness and life, a duality whose philosophical meaning we have already considered. Life in general is genuinely the other of self-consciousness. What does this opposition mean, concretely? What I, as self-consciousness, find facing me (*Gegenstand*) is life, and life is simultaneously irremediably other and the same. When in his early works Hegel describes the consciousness of Abraham, he shows how reflection shatters a prior and immediate unity. Abraham separates himself from himself. His life, and life in general, appears to him as an other than himself; yet it is also what is closest to him, what is most intimate and most distant.[2] To desire life, to wish to live—and all particular desires appear to aim at this goal—is only, it seems, to desire to be oneself. Yet this life that is myself—and biological life especially—escapes

2. *Early Theological Writings*, pp. 182 ff., and *Theologische Jugendschriften*, pp. 371 ff.

me absolutely. Considered as other, it is the element of substantiveness with which I cannot completely merge insofar as I
am a subject; it is "the universal, indestructible substance, the
fluid essence that is equal to itself" (*PE*, I, 154; *PG*, 140; *PM*,
227). But self-consciousness as reflection signifies the break
with life, a break the full tragedy of which will be experienced by
unhappy consciousness. This is why Hegel's abstract text has
such concrete implications. "But, as we have seen, this unity is
also the act of rebounding away from itself, and this concept
splits, giving birth to the opposition between self-consciousness
and life" (*PE*, I, 148; *PG*, 135; *PM*, 221). Self-consciousness,
"specificity" in Hegel's terminology, opposes universal life; it
claims to be independent of it and wishes to pose itself absolutely for-itself. Nevertheless, it will encounter the resistance
of its object. Thus the object of consciousness is as independent
in-itself as consciousness is: "Self-consciousness which exists
uniquely for-itself and which immediately characterizes its object as negative—self-consciousness which is at first desire—
will experience instead the independence of that object" (*PE*, I,
148; *PG*, 135; *PM*, 221).

OTHERNESS IN DESIRE

How DOES THIS EXPERIENCE, in the course of which I
discover that the object is independent of me, present itself?
We can say that it is born at first from the continuous reproduction of desire and of the object. The object is negated and
desire is quenched, but then desire arises again and another
object presents itself to be negated. The specificity of the objects
and the desires matters little; the monotony of their reproduction
has a necessity: it reveals to consciousness that the object is
needed so that self-consciousness can negate it. "In order for
this suppression [*Aufheben*] to be, this other, too, must be"
(*PE*, I, 152; *PG*, 139; *PM*, 225). Desire in general, then, is
characterized by a necessary otherness. This otherness appears
to be merely provisional in the case of this or that particular
desire; its essentiality results from the succession of desires.
"Indeed, the essence of desire is an other than self-consciousness, and this truth becomes present to self-consciousness
through the experience of the succession of desires" (*PE*, I, 153;
PG, 139; *PM*, 225).

During the course of this experience, I discover that desire is never exhausted and that its reflected intention leads me to an essential otherness. Yet self-consciousness is also absolutely for-itself. It must therefore satisfy itself, but it can do so only if the object itself presents itself to it as a self-consciousness. In this case indeed, and only in this case, "the object is I as well as object." Otherness, the necessity of which we have discovered, is maintained. At the same time, the I finds itself—which is the most profound aim of desire—and it finds itself as a being. Life is only the element of substantiveness, the other of the I. But when life becomes for me another self-consciousness, a self-consciousness which appears to me at once alien and the same, a self-consciousness in which desire recognizes another desire and bears on it, then in this splitting and reproduction of itself self-consciousness reaches itself. Here already we have the concept of spirit, which is why Hegel says here that spirit is present for us. "In this way the concept of spirit is already present for us. Consciousness will later experience what spirit is—that absolute substance which, in the complete freedom and independence of its oppositions, that is, of the various self-consciousnesses existing for it, constitutes their unity: the I that is a we, and the we that is an I" (*PE*, I, 154; *PG*, 140; *PM*, 227).

This movement from desiring self-consciousness to the multiplicity of self-consciousnesses suggests several comments: first of all, about the meaning of a deduction of this kind. "Deduction" is obviously an inappropriate word here, because the dialectic is teleological, that is, through exploring the horizons of desire it discovers the meaning of that desire and poses its conditions. The condition of self-consciousness is the existence of other self-consciousnesses. Desire is able to pose itself in being, to reach a truth and not merely remain at the subjective stage of certainty, only if life appears as another desire. Desire must bear on desire and discover itself as such in being; it must discover itself and be discovered; it must appear to itself as an other and appear to an other. In this way, we can understand the three moments that Hegel distinguishes in the concept of self-consciousness: "(a) its first immediate object is the pure, un-differentiated I, but (b) this immediateness itself is absolute mediation; that is, it exists only as the act of suppressing the independent object, only as desire." The satisfaction of desire is indeed the return to the first immediate object, the I, but it is a return one degree removed. It is no longer certainty but a truth; it is the I posed in the being of life and no longer presupposing itself. For this reason, "(c) the truth of this certainty is rather divided reflection, the splitting and reproduction of self-consciousness" (*PE*, I, 153; *PG*, 140; *PM*, 226). In this way, Hegel returns to the definition of spirit as opposed to nature and to life which he gave in his Jena philosophy. "In nature, spirit is spirit to itself, as spirit unaware of itself as absolute spirit, as absolute self-reflection which is not that absolute reflection for itself, which is not for itself the unity of a double knowledge discovering itself." [3] This unity of a double knowledge discovering itself is realized in the movement of the recognition of self-consciousnesses. One more thing needs to be said here, at least in order to characterize Hegel's venture: it would have been possible to present the duality of self-consciousnesses and their unity in the element of life as the dialectic of love. The importance attributed to love by the German Romantics, by Schiller, for example, and by Hegel in his early works, is well known. Love is the miracle through which two become one without, however, completely suppressing the duality. Love goes beyond the categories of objectivity and makes the essence of life actually real by preserving difference within union. But in the *Phenomenology*, Hegel takes a different tack. Love does not dwell sufficiently on the tragic nature of separation; it lacks "the seriousness, the torment, the patience, and the labor of the negative" (*PE*, I, 18; *PG*, 20; *PM*, 81). For this reason the encounter between self-consciousnesses appears in the *Phenomenology* as a struggle between them for recognition. Desire is less the desire that characterizes love than that of one desiring consciousness for the virile recognition of another desiring consciousness. The movement of recognition, thus, will manifest itself through the opposition between self-consciousnesses. Each consciousness, indeed, will have to show itself as it is to be, that is, as raised above life, which conditions it and by which it is still imprisoned.

THE CONCEPT OF RECOGNITION

WHAT CONSCIOUSNESS, as understanding, contemplated outside itself as the interplay of forces, which is only the experience of the mutual action of causes, has now moved to the

3. Jena *Logic*, p. 193.

heart of consciousness. Each force, each cause, seemed to act outside consciousness and, reciprocally, to be solicited by the outside. But understanding discovered that each force contained within itself what appeared to be alien to it. Such, for example, was Leibniz' monad. This process has now moved from the in-itself to the for-itself. Each force, each self-consciousness, knows now that what is external to it is internal to it and vice versa. This truth is now no longer thought by an alien understanding, but by consciousness itself, which, for itself, splits, reproduces, and opposes itself. "What in the interplay of forces was for-us, now is for the extremes themselves. . . . As consciousness, each extreme indeed moves outside itself, but its being-outside-itself is at the same time kept within itself; it is for-itself, and its being-outside-itself is for-it" (*PE*, I, 157; *PG*, 142–43; *PM*, 231).[4]

This dialectic expresses what Hegel calls "the concept of the mutual recognition of self-consciousnesses." This concept is at first for-us, or in-itself. It expresses infinity realizing itself at the level of self-consciousness, but then it is for self-consciousness itself, for self-consciousness which undergoes the experience of recognition. This experience expresses the emergence of self-consciousness into the medium of life. Each self-consciousness is for-itself and, as such, it negates all otherness. It is desire but a desire that poses itself in its absoluteness. Yet it is also for-an-other, specifically, for an other self-consciousness. It presents itself as "immersed in the being of life," and it is not for the other self-consciousness what it is for itself. For itself, it is absolute self-certainty; for the other, it is a living object, an independent thing in the medium of being; a given being, it is, therefore, seen as "an outside." Now this disparity must disappear—on each side—for each self-consciousness is both a living thing for the other and absolute self-certainty for itself. And each can find its truth only through having itself recognized by the other as what it is for-itself and by manifesting itself on the outside as it is within. But in manifesting itself, each will discover an equivalent manifestation on the part of the other.

4. The ontological relation of consciousness is also indicated in the following passage: "Each extreme is a middle term for the other extreme, a middle term by means of which it enters into a relation with itself and gathers itself up. Both for itself and for the other extreme, each extreme is an immediate essence which exists for-itself but which is for-itself only through this mediation." In other words, I am for-myself only in being for-the-other and only because the other is for-me.

"The movement, thus, is wholly and simply the movement of two self-consciousnesses. Each sees the other do what it does itself; each does what it requires of the other and therefore does what it does insofar as the other does it too" (*PE*, I, 156–57; *PG*, 142; *PM*, 230).

Self-consciousness, then, comes to exist ("exist," here, does not mean merely the Dasein which is characteristic of things) only by means of an "operation" which poses it in being as it is for itself. And this operation is essentially an operation on and by another self-consciousness. I am a self-consciousness only if I gain for myself recognition from another self-consciousness and if I grant recognition to the other. This mutual recognition, in which individuals recognize each other as reciprocally recognizing each other, creates the element of spiritual life—the medium in which the subject is an object to itself, finding itself completely in the other yet doing so without abrogating the otherness that is essential to self-consciousness. The concept of self-consciousness is indeed "the concept of infinity realizing itself in and by consciousness"; that is, it expresses the movement by means of which each term itself becomes infinite, becomes other while remaining self. This dialectic was already present in the development of life, but it was only in-itself; each term indeed became other, but its identity was so internal to it that it never manifested itself. Now self-consciousness itself opposes itself within being and yet recognizes itself in this opposition as the same. We must consider again the difference between a being that is merely alive and a self-consciousness. Self-consciousness exists as a negative power. It is not merely a positive reality, a Dasein which disappears and dies absolutely, crushed by what exceeds it and remains external to it; it also is that which at the heart of this positive reality negates itself and maintains itself in that negation. Concretely, this is the very existence of man, "who never is what he is," who always exceeds himself and is always beyond himself, who has a future, and who rejects all permanence except the permanence of his desire aware of itself as desire.

> To be sure, the discrete figure which is merely alive also suppresses its own independence in the very process of life, but when its difference ends, it ceases to be what it is. The object of self-consciousness, on the contrary, is equally independent in this negativity of itself, and is thus for itself genus, universal fluidity in the particularity of its own differentiation: this object is a living self-consciousness (*PE*, I, 154; *PG*, 140; *PM*, 226).

Let us repeat, for this is the simple meaning of this entire dialectic: human desire occurs only when it contemplates another desire, or, to put it in a better way, only when it bears on another desire and becomes the desire to be recognized and hence itself to recognize. The vocation of man—to find himself in being, to make himself be—is realized only in the relation between self-consciousnesses. We should recall that this being is not the being of nature but the being of desire, the disquiet of the self, and that, consequently, what we are to rediscover in being—or make actual in it—is the mode of being proper to self-consciousness. Hegel even doubts that the word "being" is appropriate to this form of existence: "To present oneself as pure abstraction of self-consciousness consists in showing oneself as pure negation of its objective mode of being or in showing that one is attached neither to any determinate Dasein nor to the universal singularity of Dasein in general—in showing that one is not attached to life" (*PE*, I, 159; *PG*, 144; *PM*, 232). To say that spirit is, is to say that it is a thing: "If we ordinarily say of spirit that it is, that it has a being, that it is a thing, a specific entity, we do not thereby mean that we can see it or hold it or stumble against it. But we do make such statements" (*PE*, I, 284; *PG*, 252; *PM*, 369). Self-consciousness thus is what exists through refusing to be. Yet this essential refusal must appear in being; it must manifest itself in some way. This is the meaning of the struggle for mutual recognition.

The whole dialectic about opposed self-consciousnesses, about domination and servitude, presupposes the conception of two terms: "other" and "self." The other is universal life as self-consciousness discovers it, different from itself; it is the element of difference and of the substantiveness of differences. The self which faces this positivity is reflected unity which has become pure negativity. The self now discovers itself in the other; it emerges as a particular living figure, another man for man. This split and reproduction of self-consciousness is essential to the concept of spirit, but we must not neglect the duality on the pretext of grasping the unity. The element of duality, of otherness, is precisely the Dasein of life, the absolutely other, and, as we have seen, this other is essential to desire. To be sure, the other is a self, and as a result I see myself in the other. From this two things follow: that I have gotten lost, since I find myself as an other—I am for-an-other, and an other is for-me; and that I have lost the other, for I do not see the other as essence but see myself in the other. This has, in Hegel's phrase, a double consequence. The other appears as the same, as the self, but the self also appears as the other. Similarly, the negation of the other, which corresponds to the movement of desire, becomes self-negation as well. Finally—as we shall see in the case of stoicism—the complete return into the self, while claiming to suppress all otherness, in fact merely leaves the other free of the self and thus leads back to absolute otherness. Being is then other but no longer self. One point is essential in this dialectic, a dialectic easy enough to grasp in the subtle interplay which it presents: otherness does not disappear. We can say that three terms are present, two self-consciousnesses and the element of otherness, that is, life as the being of life, being-for-an-other which is not yet being-for-itself. It is useful to distinguish these three terms, for as we shall see in the case of the master-slave relation, there can be a master and a slave only because there is animal life, an existence according to the specific mode of life. What sense would desire or work or enjoyment have if this third term did not exist? But in fact, if we look more closely, we see that there are only two terms, for the duality of the I, the fact of speaking of two self-consciousnesses, of a master and of a slave, is the result of this moment of nature, the result of the otherness of life. It is because this moment of life is given that self-consciousness opposes itself. Thus, we were right to begin with the self and the other, noting that the other now appears as a self, or—and this comes to the same thing—that mediation is essential to the *positing* of the I, though that need is generally not noticed by the consciousness engaged in experience.

> In this experience (Hegel writes somewhat further on), self-consciousness learns that life is as essential to it as pure self-consciousness is. In immediate self-consciousness (with which the *Phenomenology* starts) the simple I is the absolute object which, for us or in-itself, however (for the philosopher who apprehends this immediate self-consciousness according to its phenomenological genesis), is absolute mediation and has as its essential moment subsisting independence (the positivity of vital being) (*PE*, I, 160; *PG*, 145; *PM*, 234).

The Struggle for Recognition: The Fight for Life and Death

"Life," Hegel writes, "is the natural position of consciousness, independence (*Selbständigkeit*) without absolute negativity" (*PE*, I, 160; *PG*, 145; *PM*, 233). At the beginning, self-consciousness—which emerges as a particular form in the midst of universal life—is only a living *thing*. But we know that the essence of self-consciousness is *being-for-itself* in its purity, the negation of all otherness. In its positivity, self-consciousness is a living thing, but it is directed precisely against that positivity and it must manifest itself thus. As we have seen, this manifestation requires a plurality of self-consciousnesses. To begin with, the plurality lies in the vital element of difference. Each self-consciousness sees in the other only a particular figure of life and consequently does not truly know itself in the other, and, similarly, is an alien living thing for the other. Thus, "each is quite certain of itself but not of the other" (*PE*, I, 158; *PG*, 143; *PM*, 232). Its certainty remains subjective; it fails to attain its truth. For certainty to become truth, the other, too, must present itself as pure self-certainty. These two concrete I's, which confront each other, must recognize each other as being not merely living things. And that recognition must not initially be a merely formal recognition: "The individual who has not risked his life can of course be recognized as a person, but he does not attain the truth of this recognition of an independent self-consciousness" (*PE*, I, 159; *PG*, 144; *PM*, 233). All spiritual life rests on these experiences, experiences which human history has superseded but which remain its underpinning. Unlike animals, men desire not only to persevere in their being, to exist the way things exist; they also imperiously desire to be recognized as self-consciousnesses, as something raised above purely animal life. And this passion to be recognized requires, in turn, the recognition of the other self-consciousness. *Consciousness of life rises above life.* Idealism is not only a certainty; it also proves itself, or rather establishes itself, in the risk of animal life. That men are wolves, in Hobbes's phrase, does not mean that, like animal species, they fight to survive or to extend their power. Insofar as they are animals, they differ: some are stronger, others weaker; some more clever, others less so. But these differences are merely within the sphere of life, and they are, therefore, inessential. The fight of each against all is a fight not only for life but also for recognition. It is a fight—in which the spiritual vocation of man is manifested—to prove to others as well as to oneself that one is an autonomous self-consciousness. But one can prove that to oneself only by proving it to others and by obtaining that proof from them. To be sure, historians can cite many causes for the struggle against others, but those causes are not the genuine motives of what is essentially a conflict for recognition. The human world begins here:

> One can preserve one's liberty only through the risk of one's life— and through that risk one proves that the essence of self-consciousness is not existence, is not the immediate mode in which self-consciousness initially arises, immersion in the expanse of life; that there is nothing present in self-consciousness which, for it, is not a disappearing moment; that self-consciousness is only a pure being-for-itself (*PE*, I, 159; *PG*, 144; *PM*, 233).

Human existence, the existence of the being who is continually desire and desire for desire, breaks loose from the Dasein of life. Human life appears as of a different order, and the necessary conditions of a history are thereby posed. Man rises above life, which is nevertheless the positive condition of his emergence; he is capable of risking his life and thereby freeing himself from the only slavery possible, enslavement to life.

The struggle for recognition is a category of historical life, not a specific, datable moment in human history, or rather prehistory. It is a condition of human experience, which Hegel discovered through his study of the conditions of the development of self-consciousness. Self-consciousness, then, experiences the struggle for recognition, but the truth of that experience gives rise to another experience: that of relations of inequality in recognition—the experience of mastery and servitude. Indeed, if life is the natural position of consciousness, then death is merely its natural negation. For that reason, "the supreme test by means of death suppresses precisely that truth which ought to have emerged through it and simultaneously suppresses the certainty of oneself in general" (*PE*, I, 160; *PG*, 145; *PM*, 233). Though self-consciousness appears as pure negativity and hence manifests itself as negation of life, the positivity of life is essential to it. By offering its life, the I indeed poses itself as raised above life, but at the same time it vanishes from the scene. For death appears only as a natural fact, not as a spiritual negation. Therefore, another experience is necessary, an experience in which negation would be spiritual negation, that is, an *Aufhebung*, which preserves while it negates. That experience will present itself in the labor of the slave and in the lengthy elaboration of his liberation.

Through risking life, consciousness experiences it to be as essential to it as pure self-consciousness is. For that reason, the two moments which at first are immediately united separate. One of the self-consciousnesses rises above animal life; able to confront death and not fearing the loss of its vital substance, it poses abstract being-for-itself as its essence and seems thereby to escape the enslavement to life. This is the noble consciousness, that of the master, and it is recognized in fact. The other self-consciousness prefers life to self-consciousness: it chooses slavery. Spared by the master, it is preserved as a thing is preserved. It recognizes the master, but it is not recognized by him. The two moments, self and other, are here dissociated. The self is the master who negates life in its positivity; the other is the slave, a consciousness too, but only the consciousness of life as positivity, a consciousness in the element of being, in the form of thingness. We see a new category of historical life here (that of the master and the slave) which plays a no less important role than the former category. It constitutes the essence of many historical forms, but it constitutes only a particular experience in the development of self-consciousness. Just as opposition among men leads to domination and servitude, so, by a dialectical reversal, domination and servitude lead to the liberation of the slave. Historically, genuine mastery belongs to the laboring slave and not to the noble who has merely risked his life and thrust aside the mediation of the Dasein of life. The master expresses the tautology I = I, immediate abstract self-consciousness. The slave expresses the mediation essential to self-consciousness (but which the master fails to notice) and frees himself by consciously carrying out that mediation.

In this new experience, the life element, the medium of life, becomes a new self-consciousness (the specific figure of the slave) and immediate self-consciousness (that of the master) poses itself facing it. Whereas in the prior experience the life element was only the form of the emergence of differentiated self-consciousnesses, it is now integrated to a type of self-consciousness. The two moments of self-consciousness, self and life, confront each other now as two unique figures of consciousness. This is the case throughout the *Phenomenology.* Just as master and slave oppose each other as two figures of consciousness, so noble consciousness and base consciousness, and sinning consciousness and judging consciousness, oppose each other until finally the two essential moments of every dialectic are simultaneously distinguished and united as universal consciousness and individual consciousness.

DOMINATION AND SERVITUDE

THE DIALECTIC OF DOMINATION and servitude has often been expounded. It is, perhaps, the best-known section of the *Phenomenology,* as much for the graphic beauty of its development as for the influence it has had on the political and social philosophy of Hegel's successors, especially Marx. It consists essentially in showing that the truth of the master reveals that he is the slave of the slave, and that the slave is revealed to be the master of the master. The inequality present in the unilateral form of recognition is thereby overcome, and equality reestablished. Self-consciousness is recognized, legitimized, initself—in the element of life—as well as for-itself: it becomes the stoic consciousness of liberty. It is noteworthy that Hegel is interested here only in the individual development of self-consciousness; he will show the social consequences of the recognition he discusses here only in the part of the *Phenomenology* that deals with spirit. There, the juridical world of persons, the world of Roman law, corresponds to stoicism. For the moment, however, we are not concerned with that extension of the dialectic. We need only consider the education of self-consciousness under slavery, and the truth of that education in stoicism. Hegel's argument draws on all the ancient moralists (and we can find a similar treatment of the categories of domination and servitude in Rousseau). Let us also note that this historical category not only plays an essential role in social relations, in relations between peoples, but also serves to translate a certain conception of the relations between God and man. In his early works, Hegel used this dialectic in his discussion of the Jewish people and of man living enslaved to the law, and even in his discussion of Kant's philosophy. He dealt with it in a special way in his "System der Sittlichkeit," but it was in the *Realphilosophie* of Jena that he elaborated it in the precise way in which it is later developed in the *Phenomenology.*[5]

5. In the *Early Theological Writings* Hegel envisions the relations between God and men among certain peoples as a relation between master and slave. He speaks of man's enslavement to law in Jewish legalism as well as in Kantian moralism. In these conceptions there is no possible reconciliation between the *universal* and the *particular.* It is important to note this if we are to understand the

The relation between master and slave results from the struggle for recognition. Let us first consider the master: he is no longer merely the concept of consciousness for-itself, but its actual realization, that is, he is recognized as what he is. "It is a consciousness existing for-itself which now relates to itself through the mediation of *another* consciousness, of a consciousness whose essence is to be synthesized with independent being, or with thingness in general" (*PE*, I, 161; *PG*, 146; *PM*, 234–35). This passage already contains the contradiction inherent in the state of domination. The master is master only because he is recognized by the slave; his autonomy depends on the mediation of another self-consciousness, that of the slave. Thus his independence is completely relative. Moreover, in relating to the slave who recognizes him, the master also relates through that intermediary to the being of life, to thingness. He relates in a mediated way both to the slave and to the thing. Let us consider this mediation which constitutes domination. The master relates to the slave through the intermediary of life (of independent being). In fact, the slave is, properly speaking, the slave not of the master, but of life; he is a slave because he has retreated in the face of death, preferring servitude to liberty in death. He is, therefore, less the slave of the master than of life: "That is the yoke from which he has been unable to free himself through struggle, and that is why he has shown himself to be dependent, having his independence in thingness" (*PE*, I, 162; *PG*, 146; *PM*, 235). The being of the slave is life. Hence, he is not autonomous; his independence is external to him—in life and not in self-consciousness. The master, however, has shown himself raised above that being; he has considered life as a phenomenon, as a negative datum, which is why he is the master of the slave by means of thingness. The master also relates to the thing through the intermediary of the slave; he can enjoy things, negate them completely, and thus affirm himself completely. For him, the independence of the being of life and the resistance of the world to desire do not exist. The slave, on the contrary, knows only the resistance of that being to desire and cannot, therefore, attain the complete negation of this world. His desire encounters the resistance of the real, and he is able only to elaborate things, to work on them. Servile labor is

___

transition from the concrete master-slave relation to unhappy consciousness, which contraposes the universal and the particular within consciousness.

the lot of the slave, who in that way arranges the world so that the master can negate it purely and simply, that is, enjoy it. The master consumes the essence of the world; the slave elaborates it. The master values negation, which grants him immediate self-certainty; the slave values production, that is, the transformation of the world—which is "a delayed enjoyment" (*PE*, I, 165; *PG*, 149; *PM*, 238). But the master's self-certainty in his dominance and his enjoyment is in fact mediated by the being of life, or by the slave. Mediation has been made real in another consciousness, but, as we have seen, it does not thereby become less essential to self-consciousness. Besides, recognition is unilateral and partial. The slave acts on himself as the master acts on him: he recognizes himself as a slave. His actions are those of the master; they do not carry their own meaning, but depend on the essential action of the master. But the slave does not act on the master as he acts on himself, and the master does not act on himself as he acts on the slave. The truth of the master's consciousness thus lies in the inessential consciousness of the slave. But how can slave-consciousness be the truth of self-consciousness when it is alien to itself and when its being lies outside it? Yet in its development, in its conscious mediation, it genuinely makes independence real. It does so in three moments: *fear, service,* and *labor*.[6]

SERVILE CONSCIOUSNESS

WHEN THE SLAVE FIRST APPEARS, his being lies outside his consciousness; he is a prisoner of life, submerged in animal existence. His substance is not being-for-itself but the being-of-life, which for a self-consciousness is always being-other. Nonetheless, the development of the notion of servitude will show us that in fact slave-consciousness brings about the synthesis of being-in-itself and being-for-itself; it carries out the mediation implicit in the concept of self-consciousness.[7]

6. Hegel characterizes the condition of domination very sketchily, for if the master genuinely existed he would be God. In fact, the master believes that he is *immediately* for-itself, although mediation, which is essential to the movement of self-consciousness, dwells not in him but in the slave.

7. The path of mastery is a dead end in human experience; the path of servitude is the true path of human liberation.

In the first place, the slave regards the master outside him as his own essence, his own ideal. For insofar as the slave recognizes himself as a slave, he humiliates himself. The master is the self-consciousness that the slave himself is not; and liberation is presented to the slave as a form that is outside him. This humiliation (the slave's recognition of his own dependence) and the slave's positing outside himself of an ideal of liberty which he does not find within himself constitute a dialectic that will reappear at the heart of unhappy consciousness when man, as consciousness of nothingness and of the vanity of his life, will stand opposed to divine consciousness. In Hegelian language, the master appears to the slave as *truth,* but as a truth that is external to him. Yet this truth is also in him, for the slave has known fear, has feared death—the absolute master—and all that was stable within him has been shaken. In that fundamental anguish, all the moments of nature to which he adhered as a consciousness immersed in animal existence dissolved. "This consciousness experienced anguish not concerning this or that thing, not at this or that instant, but concerning the entirety of its essence, for it has felt the fear of death, the absolute master" (*PE,* I, 164; *PG,* 148; *PM,* 237). The master did not fear death, and he raised himself immediately above all the vicissitudes of existence; the slave trembled before it, and in that primordial anguish he perceived his essence as a whole. *The whole of life* appeared before him, and all the specificities of Dasein were dissolved in that essence. For that reason, the slave's consciousness developed as pure being-for-itself, "but such a pure and universal movement, such an absolute dissolution of all subsistence, is the simple essence of self-consciousness, pure negativity, pure being-for-itself, which is in that consciousness itself" (*PE,* I, 164; *PG,* 148; *PM,* 237). Human consciousness can take shape only through this anguish throughout the *whole* of its being. At that point, specific attachments, the dispersion of life in more or less stable forms, disappear, and in that fear man becomes cognizant of the totality of his being, a totality never given as such in organic life. "In pure life, in life which is not spirit, nothingness does not exist as such." Moreover, the slave's consciousness is not only the dissolution in him of all subsistence; it is also the gradual elimination of all adherence to a determinate Dasein. For in service—in the particular service of the master—that consciousness disciplines itself and detaches itself from natural Dasein.

Fear and service cannot by themselves raise the slave's self-

consciousness to genuine independence; it is labor that transforms servitude into mastery. The master is able to satisfy his
desire completely; through enjoyment, he completely negates
the thing. The slave, on the other hand, comes up against the
independence of being. He can only transform the world and in
that way render it adequate to human desire. But it is precisely
in that apparently inessential action that the slave becomes able
to give to his own being-for-itself the subsistence and the permanence of being-in-itself. Not only does the slave shape himself
by shaping things; he also imprints the form of self-consciousness on being. Thus, in the product of his work, he finds himself.
The master attains only a transitory enjoyment, but the slave
attains, through his labor, contemplation of independent being
as well as of himself. "This being-for-itself externalizes itself in
labor and passes into the element of permanence; laboring
consciousness thus comes to the intuition of independent being
as an intuition of itself" (PE, I, 165; PG, 149; PM, 238). The
labor of the slave thus attains the authentic realization of being-
for-itself in being-in-itself. The thingness before which the slave
trembled is eliminated, and what appears in that element of
thingness is the pure being-for-itself of consciousness. Being-in-
itself, the being of life, is no longer separate from the being-for-
itself of consciousness; through labor, self-consciousness rises to
its self-intuition in being. Stoicism will manifest to us the truth
of this intuition of self in being-in-itself. In every case, for such
a liberation to come about, all the elements we have distinguished must be present: primordial fear, service, labor. In the
absence of that primordial fear, labor does not imprint the true
form of consciousness on things. The I remains immersed in
determinate being, and its proper meaning remains only an
empty meaning: it is stubbornness, not liberty.

> When the entire content of natural consciousness has not been
> shaken, that consciousness remains in-itself part of determinate
> being; then, meaning itself is simply stubbornness [der eigne Sinn
> ist Eigensinn], a liberty still in the midst of servitude. As little, in
> this case, as pure form can become its own essence, can that form,
> considered as extending beyond the specific, be universal forma-
> tion, absolute concept. It is merely a specific skill which domi-
> nates something specific but does not dominate universal power
> or objective essence in its totality (PE, I, 166; PG, 150; PM, 240).

This universal power, this objective essence—the being of
life—is now dominated by a consciousness which is not content
to negate it but discovers itself within it, and puts itself on stage

within it as a spectacle for itself. Self-consciousness has thus become self-consciousness in universal being: it has become *thought*. But this thought, of which labor was the first sketch, is still an abstract thought. The freedom of the stoic will be a freedom only in thought, not an actual and living freedom. Many more developments are needed before self-consciousness can realize itself completely.

2 / The Liberty of Self-Consciousness: Stoicism and Skepticism

IN THE PRECEDING STAGE, self-consciousness emerged immediately from life, of which it was the first reflection. In its abstract form, it reached only a purely vanishing state. For the abstraction "I = I" excludes all otherness and is expressed concretely in pure enjoyment. But as enjoyment was merely the negation of the being of life, self-consciousness could not thereby actualize itself in a subsisting form or acquire a stable being. In confronting each other in the interplay of recognition, living self-consciousnesses began to emerge from the medium of life. But while, by dint of courage, the master's consciousness posed itself above life, only the slave's consciousness proved able to dominate that objective being—the substance of being—and to transpose the I of self-consciousness into the element of being-in-itself. Tested through anguish and disciplined by service, self-consciousness became the *form* which found its *matter* in being-in-itself and inscribed itself therein. Being-in-itself and being-for-itself are then no longer separate. Self-consciousness now gains not only living independence but also liberty, which pertains to thought. The concept of liberty presents itself in stoicism and is further developed in skepticism.

STOICISM AND THOUGHT

WHAT HEGEL HERE CALLS "THOUGHT," and what allows him to speak of the liberty of self-consciousness, manifests itself as the truth of the whole preceding movement. That is, the effort of thought and the labor of the concept appear as the higher form of the labor that molded the world and impressed the pure form of the I onto being. Thus the I, which discovers itself in being and discovers itself there as consciousness, allows us to define liberty. This liberty first arose in world history in the form that it took in Stoicism—which is the name not merely of one particular philosophy but of a universal philosophy that is a part of the education of every self-consciousness. If one is to be a free self-consciousness, one must at some point in one's life be a stoic—and in the country of Montaigne and Descartes, the scope of this Hegelian description is evident. Moreover, the passages we shall comment on can be compared, *mutatis mutandis,* to Pascal's famous conversation with M. de Sacy.[1]

Self-consciousness is no longer a *living* self-consciousness; it is now a *thinking* self-consciousness. The stage that the development of self-consciousness reaches here is that of thought. What does this mean, and how has the transition been effected? Let us consider the slave's consciousness, which appeared to us as the truth of the master's consciousness. For the slave's consciousness, essence is being-for-itself; the slave's consciousness regards the master's consciousness as its ideal but finds itself driven back within itself. On the other hand, through his own labor the slave's consciousness becomes for him an object in the element of being. The form of self-consciousness "as the form of the thing that is formed appears in the being of things" (*PE,* I, 167; *PG,* 151; *PM,* 242). The slave does not yet know that this form is consciousness itself, because for him the two moments (that of the master's consciousness, which he regards as being outside him, and that of the form that he imprints on things) are separate. But for us, this is not the case. For us, who philosophize about the development of consciousness, what is manifested is the emergence of the universal form of self-consciousness which has gradually appeared in human labor. From this

1. The comparison has been made by Jean Wahl, *Le Malheur de la conscience dans la philosophie de Hegel* (Paris, 1929), p. 165. Hegel himself quoted Pascal ("Glauben und Wissen," p. 345).

point on, self-consciousness and being-in-itself are not separate: "Being-in-itself, or thingness, which received form through labor, is a substance in no wise different from consciousness" (PE, I, 167; PG, 151; PM, 242). We may recall the elaboration of the notion of form throughout the whole of classical philosophy. For Aristotle, form was opposed to matter as a statue is opposed to bronze. But the notion of form that we reach is universal. It is no longer a specific form which imprints itself on a given matter but the form of thought in general, the pure I. Hegel seems to lead us here from Aristotle's concept of form to the modern Kantian or Fichtean concept.

Thus, to the extent that it is able to become an object to itself without thereby losing itself and vanishing, self-consciousness is now thinking self-consciousness. To think is to make real the unity of being-in-itself and being-for-itself, of being and consciousness; "for to think means to be an object to oneself, not as an abstract I but as an I which at the same time has the signification of being-in-itself; or so to relate to objective essence that it have the signification of the being-for-itself of consciousness, for which it is" (PE, I, 168; PG, 151–52; PM, 242–43). Both parts of this definition are essential. On the one hand, the I must acquire subsistence and genuinely become its own object; on the other hand, it must show that the being of life is not valid for it as absolute other, but is itself. To think, precisely, is not to portray to oneself or to imagine, which supposes that the I is in an alien element and requires only that the I "may accompany all my portrayals." To think is to conceive, and the concept is simultaneously a distinct being-in-itself and my pure being-for-me (PE, I, 168; PG, 152; PM, 243).[2] In conception, I only appear to go beyond myself. The distinction is resolved as soon as it is made. The I discovers itself in being and consequently remains close to itself in that otherness. But thought also signals the liberty of self-consciousness. Thinking self-consciousness is free self-consciousness; freedom is defined by the notion of thought. Thought and will become identified, so long as we do not confuse will with stubbornness (a liberty that remains within the bounds of servitude). To be free is not to be

2. This is a definition of conceptualization as an act of thought. "But for me the concept is immediately my concept. In thought I *am free* since I am not in an other but remain absolutely near to myself and since the object, which is essence for me, is, in an indivisible unity, my being-for-myself. My movement in concepts is a movement within myself" (PE, I, 168; PG, 152; PM, 243).

either master or slave, not to discover oneself in this or that situation in the midst of life; it is to behave as a thinking being in all circumstances. In its highest form, thought is will because it is the self-positing of self. And will is thought because it is knowledge of itself in its object. Stoic liberty represents precisely this identity of thought and will.

Does this definition of thought lead us to the end point of the *Phenomenology*, or only to a particular, still imperfect, stage on the road of experience? The ideal proposed here—to rediscover oneself in being, the possibility for the I to settle in the element of externality without thereby leaving itself—is indeed characteristic of Hegel's idealism. Yet the stage reached here is only a stage, for the unity realized in it is still an *immediate* unity. "This figure is thinking consciousness in general; its object is the immediate unity of being-in-itself and being-for-itself" (*PE*, I, 168; *PG*, 152; *PM*, 243). The concept at this stage is not yet the penetration of thought into the variety and the plenitude of being. As yet, that penetration is only *postulated,* and for this reason Hegel raises against stoicism the objection he had raised in his youth against Kant.

Now that we have seen how this phase of the development of self-consciousness presents itself to us, we must follow the experience of it that consciousness enters into and demonstrate its inadequacy. This experience is indeed that of stoicism which could arise "as the universal form of the world spirit" only "in an era of universal fear and slavery but also only in an era of a universal culture which had raised education and culture to the level of thought" (*PE*, I, 169–70; *PG*, 153; *PM*, 245). This form of world spirit will present itself with a more concrete signification in the course of the very development of spirit. After the disappearance of the happy city, in which nature and spirit were harmoniously merged in such a manner that natural differences had spiritual significance and all spiritual significance was expressed in a moment of nature—e.g., divine law in the woman Antigone and human law in the man Creon—imperialism arose and was most completely realized in the Roman Empire. The I then was no longer bound to a particular nature; it posed itself in its sovereignty, as *person*. And, in some respects, Roman law corresponds to Stoic philosophy. In fact, however, this liberty of the I is a liberty only in thought, a liberty that leaves existence on one side and poses itself on the other in such a way that the truth of this world of abstract persons will be similar to what skeptic confusion is for self-consciousness, and will lead only to an unhappy consciousness in the social and ethical domain.[3]

The Liberty of Stoicism

THE LIBERTY OF STOICISM is in effect defined by the negation of prior relations. Differences within life which had presented themselves with a certain subsistence now lose all meaning. No concrete situation can stand up to a thought which seeks only to maintain itself. The position of master or of slave no longer counts. The object of desire or of labor posed in a consciousness, or by means of an alien consciousness, is no longer the goal. The only goal now is the equality of thought with itself: "The liberty of self-consciousness is indifferent to natural Dasein" (*PE*, I, 170; *PG*, 153; *PM*, 245). But for this reason, stoic liberty remains abstract, not vital, a liberty in thought but not in actuality. The stoic who wishes to live in accord with nature discovers that all his tendencies have in common only this disposition to live in accord with nature. What he does and the concrete situation in which he is matter little; what counts is the manner in which he behaves, or rather, the relation he establishes between the situation and himself: the essential is to preserve one's liberty "as well on a throne as in chains, in the midst of any dependency of one's specific Dasein." The genuinely free man rises above all the contingencies and the determinations of life. The art of morality is compared not to the art of a pilot—"it is not a technique that has a particular end in view"—but to that of a dancer: it is a means of being on top of any situation and of preserving oneself in one's liberty. But in that case reflection is split, according to Hegel's terminology. Pure form again separates itself from things, for the essence of such a liberty is only thought in general, "form as such, which, detached from the independence of things, returns into itself" (*PE*, I, 170; *PG*, 154; *PM*, 245). Things, in turn, manifest themselves as opposed to thought, and this opposition can be seen in subsisting determinations, which are alien to pure thought. The opposition that then feeds the

3. Hegel recapitulates this whole dialectical movement in discussing the development of spirit (*PE*, II, 44 ff.; *PG*, 342 ff; *PM*, 501 ff.). Cf. part V, chapter 2, below.

whole skeptic argument is that between the *particular* content of the concept and its *universal* form; content and form are juxtaposed, not merged: they separate. The content appears to be grasped by thought, but this grasp remains superficial. In fact, form in its universality stands contraposed to content in its particular determination. This reflection, which is the result of stoicism, is the basis of all skeptic liberation. Stoicism limits itself to affirming the coherence of thought through all the various contents of experience. Free self-consciousness thus rises above the jumble of life and preserves for itself that lifeless impassiveness that has been so much admired in the Stoic sage. But the determinations remain what they are. Thought extends itself and affirms itself, but the determinations exist, and their particular being, arbitrarily raised to the level of the universality of thought, maintains itself in its particularity. Dogmatism appears in this thought, which arbitrarily erects one or another determination to the status of dogma. At this stage, pure thought does not contain its own content.

> Stoicism was embarrassed when it was questioned, according to then current terms, about the criterion of truth in general, that is, on the content of thought itself. To the question "What is good and true?" it again offered in answer thought itself without content: the true and the good consist in rationality. But this equality of thought with itself is again only pure form in which nothing is determinate. Thus the universal expressions "true" and "good," "wisdom" and "virtue," at which stoicism necessarily stops, are no doubt generally edifying, but since they cannot in fact lead to any expansion of content, they soon engender boredom (*PE*, I, 171; *PG*, 154; *PM*, 246).

Thus free thought remains formal here, formal in the sense that having disengaged the essence of pure thought from all the differences within life, it is able to surmount all those differences and rediscover in them the essentiality of thought. But in that case, form only superficially affects a content which, in spite of everything, preserves its specificity and tends to affirm itself as a content that remains given. Similarly, in the world of law, juridical recognition transforms *de facto* possession into property, but this transformation merely clothes with universality a world that preserves its contingency. When thought, reflecting back on itself, determines itself as pure form, the differences within life, differences of social position, remain. The given content which, in spite of everything, remains impermeable to thought is the being-other which emerges at the end point of this experience of dogmatism "as determinability become permanent" (*PE*, I, 171; *PG*, 155; *PM*, 246).

Nonetheless, stoicism represents the first notion of will as thought. Stubbornness was the permanence of the I in a concrete determination, a particular form of servitude. The stubborn person has not risen above a life and a situation of which he remains the prisoner; he finds not the pure I, but the I that is still bound to a nature that he has not made. His goal is an alien goal presented by nature; his desire and his labor remain limited to a particular sphere. "The multifarious expanse of life distinguishing itself within itself, the differentiation and the complication of life, is the object on which desire and labor act" (*PE*, I, 169; *PG*, 152; *PM*, 244). The stoic is able to have a universal will. He does not will this or that determinate thing; he wills himself in every content. Yet the duality of a content that thought does not engender and thought which is equal to itself finally cannot but manifest itself. It is not the stoic but the skeptic who realizes the genuine negation of these determinations which claim an absolute value qua determinations.

SKEPTICISM

THE SAME RELATION pertains between stoic self-consciousness and skeptic consciousness as between master and slave. The master was only the concept of independent self-consciousness; the slave was its actual realization. Similarly, the stoic raises self-consciousness to thought, to the universal form which is the form of all determinate content. But this positing of the I as a thinking will is abstract, and it finally results in a separation: on one side the form of thought, on the other the determinations of life and of experience. These meet only superficially. Form remains what it is, that which is posited by thought; so, too, do the determinations, which preserve their absoluteness and are not penetrated by the self-conscious I. In this way, the master affirmed his independence but confessed himself unable to actualize that independence in the midst of life; only the service and the labor of the slave could penetrate the substance of life and imprint it with the I. So too, skepticism, penetrates all the determinations of experience and of life; it shows their nothingness, dissolving them in self-consciousness.

In skepticism, form is no longer merely the *absolute positivity* of thought; it is omnipotent *negativity*, which, indeed, is the genuine signification of form. It is the infinity of negation, and it is as such that it must finally manifest itself. "Skepticism is the realization of that of which stoicism is merely the concept; it is the actual experience of freedom of thought, a freedom which in-itself is the negative, and which must necessarily present itself as such" (*PE*, I, 171; *PG*, 154; *PM*, 246). Indeed, form is infinity, the absolute concept, and, as such, it is the negation of every particular determination, the soul of the finite (which is never to be what it is). Whereas stoicism isolates form and allows determination which has become permanent to fall outside it, skepticism discovers that *omnis determinatio est negatio*. In stoicism, self-consciousness reflected itself in the simple thought of itself, "but vis-à-vis this reflection, independent Dasein, or determination that has become permanent, in fact fell outside the infinity of thought. In skepticism, on the contrary, the complete inessentiality and dependence of that other becomes manifest to consciousness" (*PE*, I, 171; *PG*, 155; *PM*, 246).

THE MEANING OF SKEPTICISM IN HISTORY

SKEPTICISM AS HEGEL CONCEIVES IT—a necessary moment of the development of self-consciousness—has nothing to do with modern skepticism, e.g., the phenomenalism attached to Hume's empiricism. In his Jena article, Hegel had dwelt precisely on the difference between ancient Skepticism, the Skepticism of Pyrrho's tradition, and modern skepticism. The latter is a negation of all metaphysics. It claims to show the impossibility of moving beyond experience, and it limits itself to authenticating the "unshakable certainties" of common sense. Since we cannot know things-in-themselves, we should cultivate our garden and simply oppose all ventures which claim to go beyond the experience of common sense, either in order to reach truths in-themselves or even, under the guise of a critical philosophy, to found experience. Ancient Skepticism, on the contrary, was directed against the unshakable certainties of common sense. The greatest Greek metaphysicians, Plato, for example, could be considered Skeptics because they showed the nothingness of sensuous determinations as these are ordinarily taken. This Skepticism, which Pyrrho had inaugurated, connecting it to several strands of Oriental thought, is the dissolution of everything that claims to posit itself with a certain independence or stability with regard to self-consciousness. All the differences within life, the determinations of experience in knowledge, the concrete and particular situations in the ethical world, are in fact only differences within self-consciousness. They have no being by themselves; they exist relative to others. The human illusion is to take them as stable and to accord them some positive value. To dissolve this stability, to show the nothingness of the determinations which man vainly grasps, is the function of a Skepticism which is nothing other than the experience that human consciousness has of the dialectic. Later Hegel will show that ancient comedy—we might also mention romantic irony—is an art form which corresponds to this Skepticism. In this comedy, the solid determinations admitted by thought are prey to a dialectic which manifests their inanity. Everything which claims to pose itself with some value vis-à-vis self-certainty is shown in its vanity. The finite is finite, that is, it is nothingness, but the consciousness which thus affirms itself as superior to any destiny, to any particularity, enjoys itself. The consciousness of ancient comedy, which succeeded tragic consciousness, is the raising of the I above all the vicissitudes of existence. That is why Hegel, who had already spoken of ancient comedy in his article on natural law, says of it in the *Phenomenology*:

> What this self-consciousness intuitively contemplates is that, within it, that which assumes the form of essentiality vis-à-vis it is resolved in its thought, in its Dasein and its action, and is given up to its mercy; it is the return of everything that is universal into the certainty of itself and the complete absence of essence [and of fear] from all that is alien, a well-being and a relaxation of consciousness such as can no longer be found outside of this comedy (*PE*, II, 257; *PG*, 520; *PM*, 748–49).[4]

This comparison between Skepticism and ancient comedy, curious though it may at first appear, was quite necessary in order to clarify what Hegel meant here by skepticism, and what connects the Greek Skeptics to Ecclesiastes: "Vanity of vanities, all is vanity." Skepticism, as Hegel envisages it, is similar to the skepticism of which Pascal speaks, a skepticism that leads

4. For the opposition between ancient comedy and tragedy in the article "Naturrecht," see pp. 385 ff.

human consciousness to the double feeling of its nothingness and its grandeur. How else can we understand the passage in which Hegel defines this skepticism: "Thought becomes perfect thought annihilating the being of the multiply determined world, and the negativity of free self-consciousness becomes, at the heart of this multifarious configuration of life, real negativity" (*PE*, I, 171–72; *PG*, 155; *PM*, 246)?

It is here that self-consciousness reaches absolute certainty of itself. It is not only the abstract positing of itself, as in stoicism; it is the positing of itself through the actual negation of all otherness. It is the self-certainty obtained through the annihilation of all the determinations of existence; it is the exploration in depth of subjectivity. For this reason, this happy consciousness, rising above all the vicissitudes of Dasein, will discover its own misfortune and unhappiness, entangled as it is in what it constantly negates. Skeptic consciousness will become lacerated consciousness, divided within itself, unhappy consciousness. This development moves from stoicism, the still abstract concept of free self-consciousness, to unhappy consciousness through the intermediary of skeptic consciousness. How does skeptic consciousness become a consciousness divided within itself, two consciousnesses in one?

Skeptic consciousness is the very experience of the dialectic. But whereas, in the preceding stages of the phenomenological development, the dialectic occurred, so to speak, without the knowledge of consciousness, now it is its deed. Sensuous consciousness believed that it held truth in the immediate "here," but it saw its truth disappear without understanding how this was possible. Perceiving consciousness posited the thing outside of its properties and imagined that it had thus found a stable position, but in fact, although it did not understand how this was possible, that stability still escaped it. Henceforth it is consciousness itself that will eliminate this other that claims objectivity. "As skepticism, on the contrary, this dialectical movement has become a moment of self-consciousness. No longer does it happen that what is for it the true and the real disappears without its knowing how; it is this self-consciousness which in the certainty of its freedom eliminates the other that tries to pass itself off as real" (*PE*, I, 173; *PG*, 156; *PM*, 248). Thus consciousness procures for itself the unshakable certainty of its liberty; it brings its experience of liberty to light and raises it to truth. Thus nothing subsists except absolute self-certainty. All values, all positions, are values and positions of the I, but that I is not this or that particular contingent I, the vanity of which is also manifest; it is the very depth of subjectivity which is manifested only in this negative action with respect to all particular content. As in romantic irony the poet discovered himself by considering the many characters whom he played to be hollow and ephemeral, so self-consciousness becomes sure of itself through the annihilation of all the forms of being. "What disappears is the determinate or the difference which, in one way or another, from wherever it may come, imposes itself as solid and immutable difference" (*PE*, I, 173; *PG*, 156; *PM*, 248). The infinity of self-consciousness is now revealed in its annihilating action.

However, skepticism has not yet risen to consciousness of itself; it is merely the joy of destruction, dialectical action as purely negative. We must see how skeptic consciousness can pose its own self-certainty. It is clear that it can only do this through the negation of what is other; hence it is itself bound to this otherness, and that is why its duality must manifest itself. It does not yet itself have a genuine consciousness, for if it did it would be unhappy consciousness. The skeptic contraposes the equality of the I to the disparity of the differences. But that equality is in turn a difference, and contraposed to it there is a disparity. This is why skeptical irony turns on itself. This absolute self-certainty is contraposed to what is not itself and hence discovers itself as opposition, that is, as a particular consciousness. For this reason Hegel can say: "But in fact, this consciousness, instead of being a consciousness equal to itself, is here finally nothing but a contingent imbroglio, the dizziness of a disorder which continually engenders itself. This is what this consciousness is for itself, for it is consciousness itself that nourishes and brings forth the movement of this confusion" (*PE*, I, 174; *PG*, 157; *PM*, 249). The contradiction of skeptical consciousness manifests itself clearly here, but not yet completely for itself. On the one hand, it rises above all the vicissitudes of Dasein; it negates the concrete situations within which it immerses itself and takes them for what they are, pure contingencies, inessential differences whose inessentiality, precisely, it manifests; but on the other hand, as it admits itself, it remains caught in these situations, continuing to see and to hear, to obey the orders of the master whose inanity it nevertheless knows. The same is true of the man who proclaims that all is vanity and that life is but the shadow of a day. In this very thought he rises above all vanity and poses authentic self-certainty in its sublime grandeur, but at the same time he himself appears as a contingency. By lowering himself he rises, but as soon as he rises and claims to reach that immutable certainty he descends anew. His immutable certainty is in contact with ephemeral life, and the eternity of his thought is a temporal thought of the eternal. Thus the subjectivity of self-consciousness is a double consciousness. At times it places the world in parentheses and rises above all the forms of the being that it constitutes; at other times it is itself caught in this world of which it is only a contingent fragment. More precisely, these two poles cannot be separated, and self-consciousness knows it duality and the impossibility of remaining at one of these moments. Self-consciousness, then, is the pain of the consciousness of life which is simultaneously beyond life and in it. But skepticism is not yet this consciousness, for it does not gather up the two poles of this contradiction into itself.

> If equality is pointed out to this consciousness, then it in turn points out disparity. And when precisely that disparity which it has just pronounced is firmly held up before it, it then moves to the other side and points out equality. Its chatter is in fact the quarrel of stubborn young people, one of whom says *A* when the other says *B* and says *B* when the other says *A*, and who through the contradiction of each with himself give to both the satisfaction of remaining in contradiction with each other (*PE*, I, 175; *PG*, 158; *PM*, 250).

Yet the truth of this skeptical consciousness is unhappy consciousness insofar as it is the explicit consciousness of the internal contradiction of consciousness. Henceforth it will no longer be the case that an I will confront another I in the midst of universal life, or a master oppose a slave from the outside; with stoicism and skepticism the two consciousnesses have become the split of self-consciousness within itself. Every self-consciousness is double for itself: it is *God and man* at the heart of a single consciousness.

3 / Unhappy Consciousness

UNHAPPY CONSCIOUSNESS is the fundamental theme of the *Phenomenology*. Consciousness, as such, is in principle always unhappy consciousness, for it has not yet reached the concrete identity of certainty and truth, and therefore it aims at something beyond itself. The happy consciousness is either a naïve consciousness which is not yet aware of its misfortune or a consciousness that has overcome its duality and discovered a unity beyond separation. For this reason we find the theme of unhappy consciousness present in various forms throughout the *Phenomenology*.[1]

Nonetheless, unhappy consciousness, in the strict sense of the term, is the result of the development of self-consciousness. Self-consciousness is subjectivity constituted as truth, and this subjectivity must discover its own inadequacy and experience the pain of the self that fails to reach unity with itself. As we have seen, self-consciousness is the reflection of consciousness on itself; this reflection implies a split from life, a separation so radical that consciousness of it is consciousness of the unhappiness of all reflection. As Hegel says, "consciousness of life, of Dasein, and of its acts is only pain concerning that Dasein and those acts. For it is conscious only that its contrary is essence and that it is nothing" (*PE*, I, 178; *PG*, 160; *PM*, 252). This passage concretely defines the misfortune of self-consciousness. Consciousness of life is a separation from life, an opposing re-

---

1. See, for example, "The State of Law" (*PE*, II, 44; *PG*, 342; *PM*, 501), and "The Truth of the Enlightenment" (*PE*, II, 121; *PG*, 407; *PM*, 590).

flection: to become aware of life is to know that true life is absent and to find oneself thrown back on nothingness. This feeling of disparity within the self, of the impossibility of the self coinciding with itself in reflection, is indeed the basis of subjectivity. We should not be surprised that Fichte's early philosophy, for example (the only one that Hegel knew), which is a philosophy of subjectivity, of self-consciousness, should end with an unhappy consciousness. Nor should we be surprised that the chapter on unhappy consciousness in the *Phenomenology* occasionally reminds us of Fichte's first philosophy, as interpreted by Hegel.

HISTORICAL INTRODUCTION

HEGEL HAD REFLECTED ON the unhappiness of consciousness from the time of his first theological works. We can even say that the essential preoccupation of those early works was to describe the unhappiness of consciousness in its most diverse form in order to define the essence of that torment. At the time, Hegel was preoccupied with extraindividual entities—with the spirit of a people, or with a religion—and he envisaged the Greeks as the happy people of history and the Jews as the unhappy people. He also viewed Christianity as one of the great forms of unhappy consciousness. The Jewish people is the unhappy people of history because it represents the first total reflection of consciousness away from life. Whereas the Greek people remain in the bosom of life and attain a harmonious unity of self and nature, transposing nature into thought and thought into nature, the Jewish people can only oppose itself constantly to nature and to life. Through this opposition, it discovers a subjectivity more profound than that of the Greeks and prepares the way both for Christian subjectivity and for the reconciliation between self and life, on which Hegel's philosophy is a commentary. Hegel's early studies of Abraham are well known. Abraham left the land of his fathers and shattered his links with life; he is now merely a "stranger on the face of the earth." [2] The same is true of his descendants; Abraham so to speak, is their symbol. This people will carry the essential lacera-

2. "Volksreligion und Christentum," in *Theologische Jugend-schriften*, p. 37.

tion within itself; it will be unable to love. For what is love? Love is the original identity which precedes any reflection. In man's love for the nature that surrounds him, for his family, for his people, the infinite is immanent in the finite. The whole, or unity, is immediately present in the parts. Separation is still only potential. But with reflection, man splits off from the living milieu and opposes himself to it. From then on, the opposition can become so deep that the infinite becomes the beyond and the finite becomes the here-below. The God of Abraham, of Isaac, and of Jacob is conceived in his sublimity to be beyond all given, finite reality. But for the same reason all of given reality is reduced to its finitude and becomes incapable of representing the infinite. The Jewish people is condemned unceasingly to fall back into an idolatry that knows itself to be idolatry. Reflection, which Hegel particularly studied in the case of Abraham, culminates in the separation of the finite and the infinite. Consciousness of the infinite is joined then by consciousness of finitude, and all existence is reduced to a finite Dasein:[3] there is no longer a living bond between the finite and the infinite. That is what Hegel meant when he wrote that "Abraham could not love." Judaism is the religion of the sublime and of the separation of man from God. It expels freedom from the ever-changing I, and poses it beyond mankind. In Jean Wahl's phrase, it is "stoicism in reverse."[4] In stoicism, man rises directly to the divine; self-consciousness immediately poses itself as free. In Judaism, man feels himself to be nothingness. He is the thought of all finitude and God necessarily remains a beyond that is never reached, the only negation of the finite. There is, however, a progression in the history of the Jewish people, and that progression leads us to Christianity. With Abraham and later with Moses, man sets against himself an immutable God as his essence and places himself on the side of nonessence; with David and the prophets, he rises toward that

3. For this reason, according to Hegel, the Jew knows the finite as finite through attaching himself to it, and that knowledge makes the attachment an inevitable *sin*. In Christianity there is a more profound detachment from all the goods of the world. But that detachment culminates in a destiny that Hegel defines in a more and more profound manner. Besides, it is against the background of Judaism that Christianity appeared (*Early Theological Writings*, pp. 224 ff.).

4. Wahl, *Le Malheur de la conscience dans la philosophie de Hegel* (Paris, 1929), p. 167.

immutable; with Christianity, contact is established between the immutable and the specificity of existence, and a new reconciliation becomes possible—a reconciliation that is all the more profound for the depth of the preceding separation. Only an infinite cleavage can give rise to an infinite reconciliation.

But Christianity is not yet the genuine reconciliation; it leads to a new form of opposition. In his early works Hegel's attitude toward Christianity is rather ambiguous. At times he seems to consider it the source of the unhappiness of consciousness, and he contraposes to it the happy life of Greece: Socrates is contrasted to Christ.[5] But at other times Hegel emphasizes the profoundness of Christian subjectivity and views ancient paganism as merely an inferior form, a stage of immediateness which must vanish and engender higher forms of spiritual life. In this view, ancient tragedy serves as a prelude to the tragedy of Christ. This is the gist of the studies Hegel wrote in Bern and, especially, in Frankfurt ("The Spirit of Christianity and Its Fate"). It was in Bern that Hegel wrote a preliminary sketch of unhappy consciousness,[6] studying the transition from the ancient world to the modern world and showing how the ancient citizen discovered his essence in his city and in the gods of his city: the Greek was free through his participation in the polis. But a rupture occurred: the individual was reduced to himself and was unable to discover his essence within himself. Christianity offered a religion that corresponded to this state of the spirit. The dogma of original sin explained man's misfortune to him. Certainly Christ is not—like the transcendent God, God the Father, or the Judge—the infinite that is always separate from the finite; instead, he is the union of the universal and the specific. Yet in this form, man's specific consciousness remains separated from Christ. It is a different separation, but it is still there: reconciliation will genuinely be brought about only in the unity of spirit.

This reminder of the modalities of unhappy consciousness (the unhappiness of the Jewish people and then of Christian consciousness) was necessary, for in the development of self-consciousness we shall see Hegel's early studies transposed to a truly philosophic level.

5. *Theologische Jugendschriften*, p. 32.
6. This passage may be found in *Early Theological Writings*, p. 151; our analysis of it is in part V, chapter 2, below.

THE TRANSITION TO UNHAPPY CONSCIOUSNESS

WE CAN EASILY UNDERSTAND the transition from skepticism to unhappy consciousness. As Jean Wahl has written, "The skepticism Hegel is thinking of is Pascal's rather than Montaigne's; it is the skepticism of Ecclesiastes, posing the infinite essence of God on the nothingness of the creature and failing to reconcile the idea of the finite with the idea of the infinite."[7] Indeed, the skeptic relates all the differences in life to the infinity of the I, and thus discovers their nothingness. But he simultaneously knows himself as a contingent consciousness, involved in the meanderings of existence and unable to free himself from them. For this reason, skeptical consciousness is in-itself, though not yet for-itself, the consciousness of a contradiction. By contrast, unhappy consciousness discovers this contradiction and sees itself as a split consciousness. At times it rises above the contingency of life and reaches authentic and immutable self-certainty; at other times it lowers itself to determinate being and sees itself as a consciousness caught up in Dasein. Changeable, having no essence, "it is the consciousness of its own contradiction" (*PE*, I, 176; *PG*, 158; *PM*, 250).

The consciousness of life which discovers that life as presented to it is not genuine life but only contingency is here identified with the consciousness of contradiction, that is, the consciousness of the I that is internally rent. The misfortune of consciousness is contradiction, the heart of the dialectic; contradiction is the particular misfortune of consciousness. We see how the pantragedism that characterizes Hegel's early work is identified with the philosopher's panlogism. We must now further consider the intimate split within the I in order to characterize self-consciousness. To be a merely living self-consciousness is to be able to rise to independence and reject slavery, but this independence within life is transformed into freedom with respect to life. Concrete situations, the situation of the master and that of the slave, are, strictly speaking, inessential to the free self-consciousness of the stoic: Epictetus is no less free than Marcus Aurelius. Once this point is reached, the problem of master and slave is internalized and located within self-consciousness itself. To be a self-consciousness is to be able

7. Wahl, *Le Malheur*, p. 163.

to free oneself of all the determinate situations that may arise, to reach the I as an essence in relation to which the flow of life is merely an appearance. But this pure I, this free I which the Stoic sage claimed to bring into actual reality, in fact discovers its truth in the dialectic of the skeptic, in the anxiety and instability of a consciousness that is never at rest and that continually transcends its situation and the experiences it encounters. Thenceforth, the I is shattered. "Even for-itself, this new figure of consciousness is thus the split consciousness that it has of itself: as a consciousness liberating itself, immutable, and equal to itself, and as a consciousness absolutely entangled in its confusion and self-reversals" (*PE*, I, 176; *PG*, 158; *PM*, 250). This rending is such that neither consciousness can pose itself without the other, as we already learned from the restless oscillation of skeptic consciousness. Reflection splits us off from life, but it thereby contraposes essence to nonessence. It considers life as lacking essence, and contraposes to it infinity, or essence. Conversely, this separated infinity, which transcends Dasein, exists only in the specificity of self-consciousness. Thus, it is itself bound to the contingency of life and, as a result, the very consciousness of the immutable is affected by the consciousness of life. How can this separation (between master and slave) within consciousness be overcome?

> In this way, the splitting that attributed the respective roles to two specific beings—the master and the slave—comes to be situated in only one. The split of self-consciousness within itself, a split essential to the concept of spirit, is by that very fact present, but the unity of that duality is not yet present; and unhappy consciousness is self-consciousness as split essence, as yet only entangled in contradiction (*PE*, I, 176; *PG*, 158; *PM*, 251).

This unhappy consciousness is *subjectivity*, which aspires to the repose of unity; it is self-consciousness as consciousness of life and of what exceeds life. But it can only oscillate between these two moments as the subjective anxiety which does not discover its truth within itself. Thus self-consciousness, the reflection of life, appears to us as the elevation to freedom. But this elevation is subjective anxiety, the impossibility of escaping a duality that is essential to the concept of spirit. Yet the import of the dialectic of unhappy consciousness is its transcendence of its own misfortune. Through this transcendence, self-consciousness will surmount its subjectivity and agree to alienate it and pose it as a being. But then being itself will have become self-consciousness, and self-consciousness will be being. Such will be the new union of self-consciousness and consciousness. We must follow this movement, the end point of which will be the actualized alienation of self-consciousness. We shall consider in succession unhappy consciousness as a changeable consciousness in the face of immutable consciousness, then the figure of the immutable for that consciousness—the concrete universal for subjectivity—and then the problem of the union of reality and self-consciousness. If we are to give historical examples, the first stage corresponds to Judaism and the second to early forms of Christianity. The third stage leads from the European Middle Ages to the Renaissance and to modern reason. But these are only historical examples—as Stoicism and Skepticism were. What Hegel really wants to describe is the education of self-consciousness, the elaboration of subjectivity, which leads back to the consciousness of being.

CHANGEABLE CONSCIOUSNESS

HEGEL BEGINS by indicating the direction of this whole development. Unhappy consciousness is not yet the living spirit that has entered existence. In abstract terms, what characterizes spirit, the absolute of Hegel's system, is the union of unity and duality. Self-consciousness is not yet able to pose itself absolutely in unity. Yet the metaphysical solipsism which seems to force itself on any consciousness which rises to genuine self-certainty is an untenable position. In the domain of life, one self-consciousness meets another; this meeting is the most disturbing fact of existence. There is a point of view on the universe other than mine, and this other point of view is just as valid as mine. Moreover, I exist only insofar as I am recognized by the other and only insofar as I myself recognize that other. Self-consciousness, thus, is split to its very depths. It stands contraposed to itself, and it experiences itself as another self-consciousness. Master and slave are now God and man. But if, as is admitted, man does not exist without God, then conversely God does not exist without man. Yet unity cannot absorb one of the consciousnesses into the other. They stand contraposed to each other in such a way that unhappy consciousness is the continual transition of one self-consciousness to the other. "Since within each consciousness unhappy consciousness must include an other it is immediately expelled anew from each of them precisely when it thinks that it has attained the victory and the repose of unity" (*PE*, I, 176–77; *PG*, 158–59; *PM*, 251). "Inasmuch as [self-consciousness is] this transition, the act of one self-consciousness looking into another," it is a unity within its duality. This mediation is spirit itself existing; it will realize itself as the history of spirit. But with spirit, opposition entails unity and unity entails opposition, while with unhappy consciousness opposition still dominates. "The unity of the two [self-consciousnesses] is also its essence, but for-itself [unhappy consciousness] is not yet this very essence, not yet the unity of the two self-consciousnesses" (*PE*, I, 177; *PG*, 159; *PM*, 251).

The first form of opposition is that between the immutable and the changeable, between essence and nonessence, or, to take a concrete example, between God and man according to Judaism. But God is not yet the concrete universal, which is why Hegel first uses the adjectives "immutable" and "simple" in contrast to "changeable" and manifold." When consciousness later represents its essence to itself in a more highly developed form, the adjectives "universal" and "specific" will be contraposed. God will be the universal, and man the specific. But the unity of the universal and the specific will be realized in the Christian Incarnation.

Let us consider the first moment of the opposition. Skeptical consciousness becomes unhappy consciousness. It discovers the nothingness of its particular life. The consciousness of its Dasein, of its presence in the world, is simultaneously a consciousness of the nothingness of that particular and changeable situation. For the other consciousness is for it the consciousness of an immutable and simple self-certainty. Reflection, therefore, is truly adversary. Genuine self-certainty is posed as essence beyond life, while changeable and manifold life is posed as a here-below, a nonessential. The words "essence" and "nonessence" are chosen deliberately: they show that the two poles are related. Because it is the consciousness of this contradiction, consciousness stands on the side of changeable consciousness and it appears to itself to be the nonessential. Judaism, Hegel says, poses essence beyond existence and God outside of man. By recognizing the duality of the extremes, I stand with the nonessential. I am merely nothingness; my essence is transcendent. But that my essence is not in me but posed outside of me necessarily entails an effort on my part to rejoin myself so as to free myself from nonessence. Human life, thus, is an unceasing effort to attain itself. But this effort is futile, because immutable consciousness is posed as transcendent *a principio*. "This is why we witness a struggle against an enemy, a struggle in which victory is really defeat: to reach one pole is to lose it in its contrary" (*PE*, I, 178; *PG*, 159–60; *PM*, 252).[8] The *ascesis* of the unhappy consciousness to liberate itself is itself a changeable and manifold consciousness. Liberation is *ipso facto* a falling back into the nonessential. As Hegel wrote in his early notes, either the ideal is within me, in which case it is not an ideal, or it is outside of me, in which case I can never attain it. In the passage we are discussing, consciousness of the separation is dominant—the consciousness of the Jewish people, which alienates its own essence and poses it as a transcendent term. The Jewish people

> is not conscious of being the active essence that it should be in-and-for-itself. It poses its essence outside of itself and by virtue of this renunciation [alienation] it opens for itself the possibility of a higher Dasein—a Dasein in which it would bring its own object back into itself, a higher Dasein than it would have had had it remained immobile in the midst of the immediateness of being (*PE*, I, 282; *PG*, 250; *PM*, 366).

For the greater the opposition from which spirit returns into itself, the greater is the spirit. But God is conceived as the inaccessible master and man as the slave. The historical category of master and slave is transposed into a religious category. Man humbles himself and poses himself as nonessence, and then seeks to rise indefinitely toward a transcendent essence.

Hegel's description of this first form of the opposition is reminiscent of Fichte's system and of his interpretation in the *Science of Knowledge* of Kant's *Critique* as the primacy of practical reason. "From beginning to end," Fichte wrote to Reinhold, "my system is nothing but an analysis of the concept of freedom." And, he added, "The content of the *Science of Knowledge* is simply this: reason is absolutely autonomous; it is only for-itself, but for it there is only itself."[9] But a philosophy

8. Hegel insists that in-itself the split consciousness is single. For this reason, "the position that it attributes to the two cannot be a mutual indifference. . . . It is itself immediately these two consciousnesses, and for it the *relation between the two* is like a relation between essence and nonessence, with the result that nonessence must be suppressed" (*PE*, I, 177; *PG*, 159; *PM*, 252).

9. Fichte, *SW*, II, 279.

of freedom such as this results, as Hegel noted from the start, in the self's inability truly to grasp itself in its freedom, in its thetic identity. The ideal is correctly posed from the start, in the first principle: the absolute I. But this absolute I, this thesis, is beyond all dialectic. The absolute I posed at the start must not be confused with the finite, practical I which tends toward the absolute (the I posed at the end of the first *Science of Knowledge*). According to Hegel, the highest synthesis that Fichte attained was only an expression of unhappy consciousness. The I grasps itself as finite, and only as finite. But at the same time it is infinite (as it must be if it is genuinely an I), and it aspires to transcend its limit, struggling to rejoin a thesis which is always beyond it. Thus, this whole philosophy of freedom culminates in the irremediable duality of the finite I and the absolute I, in a synthesis which is the ever-renewed effort of the I to attain itself, an effort which, because it is condemned in advance to fail, is merely a false infinite.[10] Referring to Kantian autonomy, Hegel had written that "instead of being outside me my master is now posed within me," but the master-slave relation subsists even more strongly. In reconstructing the whole of critical philosophy from the point of view of practical reason, Fichte achieved only this internalization of the master-slave opposition. The I that was to be free has only the consciousness of its nothingness. Its freedom is beyond it. "That is why this consciousness undertakes its ascent to the immutable. But such an ascent is itself this consciousness and is, therefore, immediately a consciousness of the contrary, that is, consciousness of itself as specific being." The synthesis, which in its unceasing effort to reach an absolute I grasps only a finite I, remains a finite synthesis, a reflection that does not reflect on itself. If it were to reflect on itself, it would see that the absolute I is simultaneously the finite I, and that opposition is only a moment—just as the first position was.

THE FIGURE OF THE IMMUTABLE

JUDAISM, which is the consciousness of the separation of man and God, leads to the Incarnation, which is the con-

10. On this point, see Hegel's analysis of Fichte's thought in "Differenz," p. 53: "The result of the system does not lead back to its starting point."

sciousness of their union. But the meaning of unhappy consciousness, so to speak, changes here. Hitherto, it was the consciousness of the vanity of a life which did not contain its essence but had to seek it in a transcendent term, in "an entity beyond being." Now, the consciousness of life and of specific existence will become more profound. The misfortune of consciousness will be identified with specific existence itself, with subjectivity, which now will no longer lack essence, but whose essence will continuously elude the consciousness that seeks to grasp it. "At the same time, that essence is the inaccessible beyond which eludes the gesture that seeks to grasp it, or, more precisely, which has always already eluded it" (*PE*, I, 183; *PG*, 164; *PM*, 258). Christianity, of which German Romanticism claims to be an interpretation, is the feeling—if not yet the thought—of the infinite value of specific existence. "Love that which will never reappear." In a paradoxical manner, the particular life situation is joined to the transcendent pole which unhappy consciousness had at first posed outside itself. The transition from "an entity beyond being" to "an entity joined to being" (*PE*, I, 180; *PG*, 161; *PM*, 254) is effected. Unhappy consciousness is not tied to one of the poles of the contradiction; it discovers itself as the movement that surmounts the duality.

> From that point on, it undertakes its ascent to the immutable. But such an ascent is itself that consciousness and is, therefore, immediately a consciousness of the contrary, to wit, a consciousness of itself as specific being. By the very fact that the immutable enters consciousness, it is at the same time touched by specific existence and is present only with it. Instead of specific existence having been destroyed in the consciousness of the immutable, the immutable continually reappears in it (*PE*, I, 178; *PG*, 160; *PM*, 252–53).[11]

The specific destiny of consciousness is concentrated in this ascent, an ascent admirably evoked by the Psalms and the Hebrew prophets. The destiny of consciousness is to surmount itself, but the wish "deliver me from myself; deliver me from my nothingness" is specific consciousness itself. Thus, the destiny of

11. The progression that Hegel indicates here (which corresponds to the Jewish prophets) seems to be the following: at first, changeable consciousness contraposes itself to its essence (it is the relation between the two only *for us*); then it becomes *for its own self* the movement of subjectivity, the ascent. From that point on, the two terms must be connected for it in the *figure* of the immutable, but that figure is still alien to it.

this consciousness is to know that in surmounting itself it still remains within itself. The ascent itself is the consciousness. This is why the immutable can be attained only at the heart of specific existence and why specific existence occurs only in the ascent to the immutable. Thus, the wisdom of Solomon must be embodied in a concrete being: the son of David. Henceforth, we see the rise of specific existence at the heart of the immutable, and the rise of the immutable at the heart of specific existence: "Who sees me, has seen the Father." The immutable, then, is no longer the transcendent pole which reflection opposes to life; it is conjoined to being and it presents itself as a figure (*Gestalt*). Hegel's analysis now will bear on the relation of self-consciousness to this figured, *embodied* immutable.

The embodiment of God, the figure of the historical Christ—which is the unity of the universal and the specific, of immutable consciousness and changeable consciousness—is therewith produced for consciousness. There is an immediate unity of universality and specificity, of eternal truth and historical existence: "I am . . . the Truth and the Life." Thenceforth, the unity sought by unhappy consciousness is realized for it, but it remains an immediate unity, and thus one not free from contradiction. In its relation to Christ, Christian consciousness will discover itself to be an unhappy consciousness. Hegel distinguishes three possible relations between consciousness and its essence. First, qua specific consciousness, consciousness contraposes itself to the immutable. Man is nothingness; God is Master and Judge.[12] This Hegel calls the reign of the Father. Second, God takes the form of specific existence, so that this specific existence is the figure of the immutable, which is thus clothed with the full modality of existence; this is the reign of the Son. Third, that existence becomes spirit; it has the strength to discover itself in spirit, and it becomes consciousness for-itself of the reconciliation of its specific existence with the universal. This is the reign of the Spirit. The first reign corresponds to the first figure of unhappy consciousness that we studied, the absolute separation of consciousness within itself; the second corresponds to the figure of the immutable; the third, to the reconciliation by means of which unhappy consciousness will be surmounted (*PE*, I, 179; *PG*, 160; *PM*, 253).

12. "For consciousness, the first immutable is merely the alien essence *condemning* specific existence" (*PE*, I, 179; *PG*, 160; *PM*, 253; my emphasis).

We are writing from a phenomenological, not a noumeno-logical, point of view. What comes from God and what comes from man, grace and free will, cannot be separated. But here we are considering only the unilateral experience of conscious-ness, not the movement in-and-for-itself of absolute spirit (*PE*, I, 179; *PG*, 161; *PM*, 253).[13] In any case, the immediate has taken sensuous shape for consciousness; it is thus no longer the entity beyond being, but the entity conjoined to being, and it is caught up in the dialectic of the sensuous this. By virtue of having taken on form and having presented itself to self-consciousness through the senses, the immutable necessarily vanishes and, in the form that it has taken on, becomes as inaccessible to consciousness as the transcendent beyond was. First, the immediate unity of universal and specific is realized, and this immediateness puts the unity at a distance from self-consciousness. The disciples saw Christ and they heard his teaching: on one occasion the divine manifested itself in the world. But then it vanished into time, and self-consciousness knew that "God himself was dead." "It follows necessarily from the nature of the entity joined to being, from the actual reality that it has taken on, that this entity vanished in the course of time, and has come to be far away in space: he dwells at an absolute distance" (*PE*, I, 180; *PG*, 162; *PM*, 255). God became man. There is an irreducible historicity in this, which spirit must, nevertheless, overcome in order that this presence be raised beyond the historical now, in order that it be *aufgehoben*. The romanticism, the historicity, must be preserved, but it must be tied to rationality. The two must blend. In his early works on the positivity of religion, on the destiny of Christianity, Hegel had meditated on that historical element and on the effort of self-consciousness to assimilate it. The God who is dead is no more accessible than the God who never knew life. Yet the Incarnation has a *universal meaning*. Through it, the whole problem of the unity of actual reality and self-consciousness is posed anew.

13. In-itself, that is, for us, the movement is double and recipro-cal: specific consciousness rises to God, but God realizes himself in specific consciousness. "Thus, the immutable consciousness is simul-taneously specific consciousness, and the movement is also the move-ment of immutable consciousness. . . . But insofar as these con-siderations pertain only to us, they are inappropriate here" (*PE*, I, 179; *PG*, 161; *PM*, 254).

UNITY OF ACTUAL REALITY
AND SELF-CONSCIOUSNESS

THE LAST PART of the development of unhappy consciousness leads us to the unity of consciousness and self-consciousness, to what Hegel calls "reason." Before following the rich and concrete details of Hegel's argument, let us call to mind the meaning of the whole development. Unhappy consciousness expresses subjectivity essentially; it expresses the for-itself as opposed to the in-itself, or, as Hegel also says, specificity as opposed to universality. Thus, unhappy consciousness is the culmination of self-certainty's endeavor to be its own truth for itself.

We see that unhappy consciousness constitutes the counterpart and the complement of the consciousness of comedy, which is perfectly happy by itself. In comic consciousness, the whole divine essence returns; in other words, it is the complete alienation of substance. Unhappy consciousness, by contrast, is the tragic destiny of self-certainty which must be in-and-for-itself. It is the consciousness of the loss of all essentiality in this self-certainty, and specifically of the loss of self-knowledge—of substance as well as of the self; it is the pain that is expressed in the harsh phrase "God is dead" (*PE*, II, 260; *PG*, 523; *PM*, 752).[14]

Self-certainty, the for-itself, is precisely what can never attain itself; it is the subjectivity which is only "the movement, lacking substance, of consciousness itself" (*PE*, II, 86; *PG*, 377; *PM*, 550–51). All these phrases express the continuous escape from oneself, the impossibility for the for-itself, for self-certainty, which must be in-and-for-itself, to coincide with and be adequate to itself. Self-certainty cannot be in-itself without losing itself and becoming a thing. It is a perpetual transcendence toward a never given adequation with itself. Consciousness is never what it is; it rejects every determination—every concrete, given situa-

14. It seems to me that in this passage Hegel expresses the essence of the misfortune of consciousness. Consciousness is subjectivity (a certainty of itself) which *must be in-and-for-itself*. But it discovers, on the contrary, that its self-certainty is a loss of itself. As absolutely for-itself, it cannot be in-itself. It will thus have to alienate itself, make itself *be*, so as to rediscover itself in being as an *existing spirit*.

tion—in which one might try to enclose it. This incessant flight of self-consciousness from itself is expressed in skepticism. But skepticism does not know itself. It does not know that this negativity is the misfortune of self-consciousness, which, in its subjectivity, always aims to transcend itself, to reach an in-itself that would simultaneously be for-itself—an intention that at first glance appears self-contradictory. Self-consciousness wishes to be self, to pose itself in its identity with itself. But this identity is not given as a thing; everything that is given is negated by self-consciousness. Thus, self-certainty experiences itself as a changeable consciousness, as a consciousness which can never wholly be itself. It projects its own transcendence outside itself and onto an *immutable,* a universal, which, by definition, lacks nothing and is both in-itself and for-itself. For if what consciousness seizes as that toward which it transcends itself were merely in-itself, that transcendence would culminate in the annihilation of consciousness. This is the meaning of Hegel's phrase quoted above, "the tragic destiny of self-certainty which must be in-and-for-itself"—and which, we might add, being for-itself—negativity—discovers that it cannot as self-certainty be simultaneously in-itself and for-itself.

Consciousness claimed to grasp a truth in-itself but fell back to a certainty that was only for-itself. Certainty claims to attain itself, but it does so only by alienating itself. Thus, when unhappy consciousness has divested itself of its subjectivity and has itself become a thing, objectivity—substance—will be reestablished. As a result of this double movement, a movement that constitutes the meaning of Hegel's idealism, spirit appears. "One [aspect of the movement] is that by which substance alienates itself from its substantiveness and becomes self-consciousness; the other is that by which self-consciousness alienates itself and becomes thingness, or universal self" (*PE,* II, 263; *PG,* 525; *PM,* 755). Thus, the whole development of unhappy consciousness expresses the development of subjectivity which renounces itself and which through this self-negation reestablishes an objectivity. But that objectivity is no longer the pure and simple in-itself; it has become the in-itself for-itself, or the for-itself in-itself, a substance that is at the same time subject, a substance that poses itself as what it is. Most contemporary thinkers deny the possibility of such a synthesis of the in-itself and the for-itself, and it is precisely on this ground that they criticize Hegel's system as a system. They generally prefer what Hegel calls "unhappy consciousness" to what he calls "spirit." They take up Hegel's description of self-certainty which fails to be in-itself but which, nonetheless, exists only through its transcendence toward that in-itself; but they abandon Hegel when, according to him, specific self-consciousness—subjectivity—becomes universal self-consciousness—thingness—a movement through which being is posed as subject and subject is posed as being. They accept Hegel's phenomenology but reject his ontology. We shall not enter this debate here. We wish only to elucidate as clearly as possible the endeavor of the *Phenomenology*. There can be no doubt about the meaning of the dialectic of unhappy consciousness. As Hegel put it explicitly: "Self-consciousness which reaches its fulfillment in the figure of unhappy consciousness is only the torment of the spirit struggling to rise again to an objective state but failing to reach it" (*PE*, II, 203; *PG*, 473; *PM*, 685).

The unity of in-itself and for-itself first presents itself to self-consciousness as its essence beyond life, as the immutable. Then that essence presents itself to self-consciousness as incarnate: the immutable has become a concrete figure, a specific self-consciousness just like unhappy consciousness. "Thus, the unity of specific self-consciousness and immutable essence" (*PE*, II, 203; *PG*, 473; *PM*, 685) is realized for self-consciousness, but insofar as it is for self-consciousness it is not yet itself, not yet living spirit. Specific self-consciousness is not yet posed as universal self-consciousness. We shall now consider this development in detail. At its end point, specific self-consciousness will renounce its one-sided subjectivity and pose itself as a transcended specificity. This transcendence, manifesting itself as a new figure, will be reason: a consciousness of itself as of being and of being as of itself, a unity of the concept existing for-itself, that is, consciousness, and the object that is external to it. "Reason, the truth that is in-and-for-itself, is the indivisible identity of the subjectivity of the concept and its objectivity and universality." [15]

The development from Jewish consciousness to Christian consciousness makes this unity possible. In Jewish consciousness, the in-itself is always beyond for lacerated consciousness; in Christian consciousness, that beyond is grasped as united with subjectivity, with a self-consciousness. The concrete universal, unity, is indeed posed, but—and this is the meaning of the Incarnation—it is posed only immediately. It is not yet raised

15. *Encyclopaedia*, p. 379.

to the level of spirit; subjective consciousness has not yet itself become the concrete universal. Thus, the itinerary unhappy consciousness follows is that of Christian consciousness, which Hegel conceptualizes in the form of the subjectivity of the Middle Ages or in the form of Schleiermacher's romantic subjectivity. Jewish consciousness was a consciousness of the nothingness of human existence, and of the fruitless effort to transcend that nothingness. God was external and beyond the specificity of consciousness; he was the transcendent, the abstract universal. But that split consciousness appeared to us as itself the unity of the two extremes. As a result, the object of unhappy consciousness—what, for it, is essence—is no longer the formless immutable but, on the contrary, the unity of the immutable and the unique. "Who sees me, has seen the Father." Christ, as he appeared against the background of the Jewish world and manifested himself to his disciples, is the realized unity of God and man, of transcendent truth and specific subjectivity. For this reason, the attitude of Christian consciousness is quite different from that of Jewish consciousness. "What is henceforth the essence and object of lacerated consciousness is the at-oneness of the specific and the immutable, whereas in the concept, its essential object was only the abstract immutable, without figure" (PE, I, 181; PG, 162; PM, 255). Consciousness must now turn away from the separation that characterized the concept of unhappy consciousness and realize within itself the unity that came to be for it in the form of the historical Christ. This is why "this consciousness must raise its relation, initially external, with the figure of the immutable (which is like a relation with an alien actual entity) to absolute at-oneness." [16] The disciples saw in Christ the unity which the Jewish world and its prophets had sought. But that unity remained for them a truth alien to their own consciousness. Christ is there, in space and in time; in him the immutable has become "thinking specificity," self-consciousness. But he remains posed before unhappy consciousness as a "sensuous and opaque entity, with all the rigidity of an actual thing" (PE, I, 180; PG, 161; PM, 255). The unity that is the essence and the object of self-consciousness is posed outside it; it is a presence "which is by no means a perfect and authentic presence yet, but one carrying the imperfection of an

16. Jean Wahl has aptly written, "This external relation will be transformed in such a way that after the Jewish God and after the Christian God we have Spirit" (Le Malheur, p. 192).

opposition." Hegel again discusses the presence of Christ to his disciples, a presence that is not yet the immanence of spirit, in the section of the *Phenomenology* that deals with "revealed religion," as well as in the *Lectures on the Philosophy of Religion*. And we can find numerous preliminary studies in Hegel's early works.[17]

Unhappy consciousness is then considered in the same way that self-consciousness was: as in-itself, as for-itself, as in-and-for-itself. Considering it as pure consciousness, we must ask what its essence is and how it attains it. As being-for-itself, we see it manifest itself to itself as desire and labor, through the negation of the here-below. And we see the truth of the entire process of unhappy consciousness in its awareness of its being-for-itself in asceticism and in Christian resignation.

The object of unhappy consciousness, as pure consciousness, is the unity of the immutable and the specific. But unhappy consciousness does not relate to its essence through thought: it is the feeling of this unity and not yet its concept. For this reason, its essence remains alien to it; it has not yet completely overcome the duality that is characteristic of unhappy consciousness. To be sure, as feeling it is duality transcended. It is neither the abstract thought of the stoic nor the pure anxiety of the skeptic. But insofar as it is not the concept, not the authentic thought of its self-feeling, unhappy consciousness falls back to its divided state, separate from itself. The soul of the disciple is quite certain that it is known and recognized by a God who is himself a specific soul. But this certainty is only a feeling: a nostalgia like Jacobi's *Sehnsucht*, a pious fervor (*Andacht*) which is pointed in the direction of thought but is not itself the thought of existence. The feeling of the divine which this consciousness has is a shattered feeling, precisely because it is only a feeling. It does not discover itself, does not possess itself as an authentic truth, a truth immanent in self-consciousness, a truth that would be its own knowledge. In Christ, the Christian soul knows the divine as thinking specificity, but not yet as universal specificity. "Sought after as a specificity, consciousness is not a universal and thought-through specificity. It is not the concept but something specific, like an object, something actually real, an object of immediate sensuous certainty—and, therefore, an object such that it has already disappeared" (*PE*, I, 183–84; *PG*, 164; *PM*, 258).

17. See, for example, *Early Theological Writings*, pp. 182 ff.

What Christian consciousness lacks is the thought of its feeling. It fails to transcend the stage of immediate contact between pure thought and specificity: Christ is indeed God for it, but it itself is not Christ, it has not internalized the truth that is revealed to it from outside. "One thing is not the case for unhappy consciousness: that its object, the immutable—which essentially for it has the figure of specific existence—is unhappy consciousness itself, the specific existence of consciousness" (*PE*, I, 182; *PG*, 163; *PM*, 257). Thus, self-consciousness remains unhappy because its essence—the unity of the immutable and the specific—remains a beyond for it, a truth which it does not find within itself and with which it cannot coincide. Self-consciousness oscillates, therefore, between the "empty darkness of a suprasensuous beyond and the colorful appearance of the sensuous here-below" without being able definitively to enter the "spiritual light of presence" (*PE*, I, 154; *PG*, 140; *PM*, 227).

Disciple, crusader, and romantic fail to reach the concept of spirit. They kneel before the cross, or they undertake Crusades, but in both cases they reach only the feeling of their own misfortune, only a consciousness of the disappearance of what for them is essence. That essence, whether as beyond or as here-below, forever eludes them. Hegel views the Crusades as a historical symbol of a metaphysical truth. Seeking to possess his object as a sensuous presence, the Christian must necessarily lose it. He always finds himself in the presence of the "tomb of his own life," and he must experience the pain that is expressed in the Lutheran hymn: "God himself is dead." But that tomb remains a sensuous reality; "it therefore becomes the prize of a struggle and an effort that must necessarily end in defeat" (*PE*, I, 184; *PG*, 164; *PM*, 258). When, in the *Philosophy of History*, Hegel again deals with the metaphysical significance of the Crusades, he quotes Christ's words: "Why do you seek among the dead him who lives? He is not here; he is risen." [18] In the sorrow of the disciple before the cross, and in the failure of the Crusaders to hold the tomb of Christ, consciousness learns that insofar as specific existence has disappeared, it is not genuine specificity (*PE*, I, 184; *PG*, 164; *PM*, 258). The disappearance of the tomb is "a disappearance of disappearance." [19] And consciousness thus becomes able to find specific existence

18. *The Philosophy of History*, p. 393.
19. Hegel uses the phrase "the disappearance of disappearance" to define objectivity at the level of spirit.

as genuine, or universal. Christ is no longer merely the historical Christ who existed only to vanish. He is the spiritual community, the man-God, who is *truth that has become for-itself.*

But unhappy consciousness cannot conceive this truth, for if it did, it would transcend itself as self-consciousness. It is the pain of human consciousness, which knows that truth must be transcendent to it, that it must incessantly transcend itself in order to reach truth, and yet that this truth cannot be lacking to the for-itself of consciousness, to subjective certainty. The concrete universal was realized for unhappy consciousness one day in Christ. But having failed to internalize that revelation and to understand its spiritual meaning, having failed to think it through conceptually, consciousness fell back into a separation from its essence.

We must now consider this consciousness as it acts on the world. As pure consciousness, it fell back within itself. Its pain, at least, and its feeling of divine absence belong to it, and for this reason it returns within itself and manifests itself externally only as negativity, in desire and in labor. Thus, self-consciousness in general appeared to us to be negating the world so as to find itself. But now this negation will take on a different meaning. In its action on the world, self-consciousness will seek a new realization of its unity with the immutable. The meaning of its labor is to reach that communion. Negation must go so far as to negate itself in asceticism and alienation—to be the negation of the negation—and, by so doing, reestablish the universal.

The pious soul (*Gemüt*) has given up seeking its essence outside itself. "In-itself, or for us," Hegel says, "it has discovered itself, since although, for-itself, it feels its essence to be separate from it, that feeling is, in-itself, a feeling of itself; it has felt the object of its pure feeling, and it is itself that object" (*PE,* I, 184; *PG,* 164–65; *PM,* 259). For this reason, this consciousness will seek itself and, as we know, it will be able to objectify its certainty of itself only by acting on the world: in desire, in labor, and in enjoyment. The world exists only to provide it with the occasion to discover itself and to pose itself for-itself as it is in-itself. Disciple and crusader now return within themselves and find sanctification in labor. What, then, is the meaning for this consciousness of desire, of labor, and of enjoyment?

We have already noted that the very being of self-consciousness, its becoming for-itself, was its action (*Tun*). The world, which was in-itself for consciousness, in the strict sense of the term, is preserved for self-consciousness, but only as a vanishing moment. Self-consciousness is desire and labor; it negates the world that presents itself to it and thus affirms itself in its independence. Is this also true for unhappy consciousness, which has withdrawn into itself and has sensed its essence within itself? Is the world on which its labor acts, on which its desire bears, and from which it draws its enjoyment, still that vanishing here-below over which it triumphed? The meaning of the here-below has in fact been changed by the Incarnation; as a whole, the here-below has become a figure (*Gestalt*) of the immutable. "This actual reality is a figure of the immutable. For the immutable has received specificity within itself, and since qua immutable, it is a universal, its specificity means in general actual reality as a whole" (*PE*, I, 185; *PG*, 165; *PM*, 260).[20] Jewish consciousness contraposed the world to God and contraposed man, as a being-in-the-world, to the eternal; now, the world has itself become a figure of God, since God has embodied himself and presented himself as a specific self-consciousness. Bread and wine are no longer things null in themselves, which consciousness appropriates; if by his own action man makes them emerge from the ground and consumes them it is because "the immutable itself abandons its own figuration and yields it to him as enjoyment" (*PE*, I, 186; *PG*, 166; *PM*, 260). The vanishing here-below is no longer merely that: like unhappy consciousness, it is an actual reality broken into two fragments, "which in only one aspect is in-itself a nothingness, but in another is a consecrated world" (*PE*, I, 185; *PG*, 165; *PM*, 260). In his later lectures on aesthetics, Hegel says that the Incarnation transvalues all of sensuous reality, which becomes more profound and reflects itself on itself for consciousness. Sensuous existence becomes a symbol. It is not what it is, and if it yields itself to consciousness it does so because the immutable itself makes a gift of it to man. Consciousness, therefore, does not attain through its action a feeling of absolute domination over the here-below. Its desire, its labor, its enjoyment—in a word, its action—only seem to originate in it. Man thinks that he acts, but in fact he is directed by God. This is all the more so if we

20. We see that self-consciousness progressively rediscovers consciousness. The world that it negated becomes a figure of the immutable. Posing itself as alienated in this world it completely re-establishes the position of being.

consider the action of consciousness rather than the passive reality on which that action bears. Consciousness acts, but in so doing it sets in motion powers that do not originate in it. Its aptitudes and its talents are a being-in-itself, a being which consciousness uses but which it has received through the grace of God. In this action specific consciousness, too, is in-itself. "This aspect belongs to the immutable beyond, and it is constituted by the aptitudes and the efficacious power of consciousness, a gift from outside, granted to consciousness by the immutable" (*PE*, I, 186; *PG*, 166; *PM*, 260). On all sides, action is reflected toward a transcendental goal. Active consciousness merely appears to act. Inside and outside it, God acts, just as the master was the true subject of the slave's action. "For what the slave does is, properly speaking, the action of the master; being-for-itself, essence, are the master's alone." Both in its withdrawal into itself and in its action in the world, unhappy consciousness merely experiences the transcendence of its own essence. Its action is reflected beyond it. It is not genuinely autonomous, as self-consciousness claims to be. The truth of its self-certainty is a transcendent goal, which condemns it no longer to contain its own certainty. The relation of master to slave reappears here within consciousness itself. Human consciousness poses itself as slave consciousness; its essence, mastery, is beyond it in God, whom Hegel here still calls the immutable, or the universal.

Does unhappy consciousness, then, not realize concretely its communion with its beyond? On the one hand, indeed, the immutable offers itself to it and allows it to act; on the other hand, unhappy consciousness recognizes its dependence with respect to the immutable, as the slave recognized the master; "it forbids itself the satisfaction of consciousness of its independence and attributes the essence of its action to the beyond rather than to itself" (*PE*, I, 187; *PG*, 167; *PM*, 261). Acting consciousness humbles itself in its thanksgiving, in the recognition of God. Does it not, then, achieve communion with the transcendent? Hegel especially emphasizes this humiliation of unhappy consciousness which reaches communion with God through its recognition of him. Man, who poses himself as autonomous insofar as he is active being, man who works on the world and draws his enjoyment from it, nonetheless recognizes himself as passive.

This recognition of God, who alone acts, is man's essential

action. As the slave recognized the master and posed himself as slave, so human consciousness poses itself as passive and dependent. It renounces its domination. But through a dialectical reversal which we have already seen several times, the humiliation of man, who attributes everything to grace and grants himself nothing, is in fact an elevation. For it is man himself who poses God. Man recognizes the master, but that recognition emanates from him. In posing himself as the lowest he is the highest. Thus, self-consciousness fails to divest itself of its freedom, fails truly to alienate it. Self-consciousness glorifies God and denies man's freedom, but that, precisely, is its grandest act—which is why it does not allow itself to be duped by its thanksgiving. "Consciousness feels itself here as specific existence, and it does not allow itself to be duped by the appearance of its renunciation. For the truth of this consciousness remains the fact that it has not abandoned itself" (*PE*, I, 188; *PG*, 167; *PM*, 262). Specific existence—the subjectivity of self-consciousness, man—cannot for its own self pose itself in its absolute freedom without renouncing that freedom. But that renunciation, too, is its deed. In its action (and its action is its being, for action is the being of self-consciousness) it poses itself as being-for-itself. But while doing so, it discovers the hollowness of that being-for-itself. Its essence always eludes it—as does that of the slave who sees himself outside of himself in the guise of the master—and yet the act of posing itself outside itself, the act that transcends it, is still itself. Thus, the truth of this consciousness that is for-itself is the humiliated consciousness that is elevated through its humiliation, a consciousness which, like the slave's in the earlier dialectic, attains a new form of liberation. The truth of slave consciousness was *stoic* consciousness; the truth of unhappy consciousness will be the *ascetic* consciousness of the saint which intends to annihilate its own specificity in order thereby to become a more profound self-consciousness.

From this arises the third stage in the development of unhappy consciousness, the stage of renunciation and alienation, by means of which specific consciousness alienates its being-for-itself and genuinely transforms itself into a thing, but gains, thereby, a much higher truth. In posing itself as a thing, through asceticism, obedience, and the alienation of its own particular will, consciousness discovers—or we discover for it—that the thing is a manifestation of the self and that the self is universal self and universal being-for-itself. The Middle Ages prepared the way for the Renaissance and reason's certainty that, in-and-for-itself, it is the whole of truth. The medieval church prefigured modern reason, for it is a form of concrete universality. Let us consider this third stage. It depicts the Christian of the Middle Ages who completely alienates his self-certainty, his self, and who thereby poses the universal self, reason. The middle term, which connects the specific self of consciousness with the universal, is the church, "the agent of God, representing one of the extremes to the other" (*PE*, I, 190; *PG*, 169; *PM*, 264). Hegel briefly summarizes the three moments. Christian unhappy consciousness is first an aspiration, an emotion that has not arrived at genuine self-expression. This first state, which Hegel calls the concept of unhappy consciousness, is a "musical state of soul"; it is the state of soul of the disciple at the foot of the cross, or of the crusader, the immediate encounter of the beyond and the here-below. The aspiration of the religious soul is no longer directed toward an unformed beyond. As God has made himself man, it seeks him in an immediate contact, a contact that is, so to speak, as much external as internal. Self-consciousness knows itself to be recognized by another soul, which it recognizes. This "struggle of feeling" (*PE*, I, 188; *PG*, 168; *PM*, 263) has not yet come to realization: it is in-itself, not for-itself.

The second moment expresses the becoming for-itself of religious consciousness. The world is sanctified by the presence of the divine within it. Desire, labor, enjoyment, thanksgiving: these are all occasions for the soul to commune with its essence. But that communion is still marked by a contradiction. Having been in the world, consciousness has indeed experienced itself as real and acting, as "consciousness whose truth is to be in-and-for-itself." The second moment is the realization of the first. But since in that first moment consciousness is only feeling and does not conceive itself as concrete universal, this realization is the realization of a consciousness that lacks essence. Its humiliation is in fact a return within itself, a separation from the universal. The third moment, therefore, will be the consciousness that the soul comes to have of its nothingness in the face of the universal. The Christian ascetic corresponds to the Stoic sage, but his holiness is of a different order from that wisdom. He has become aware of the vanity of his self. His actual action becomes the action of nothing; his enjoyment becomes the feeling of his misfortune. "Action and enjoyment thereby lose all universal content . . . ; they withdraw into specificity, toward which consciousness is directed so as to suppress it." Hegel describes the world view of the ascetic who directs all his attention to his particular nature in order to combat it, and he shows the internal contradiction of such a struggle against oneself: "The foe is always reborn in defeat, and consciousness, instead of being freed of its foe, always remains in contact with it and forever views itself as tarnished" (PE, I, 189; PG, 168; PM, 264). This perpetual consciousness of guilt, of evil within oneself, is characteristic: it culminates not in the proud character of the Stoic sage, but in a character that is "as unhappy" as it is wretched (PE, I, 189; PG, 169; PM, 265).

But the self-negation of the ascetic is effected through the mediation of the idea of the immutable, and negative relation finally acquires positive signification. Through this, a new unity, which is the end point of unhappy consciousness, comes to be realized in-itself. Unhappy consciousness must develop to the point of complete self-negation in order that through that negation it may discover its universality. "For unhappy consciousness, being-in-itself is its beyond, but in the course of its development unhappy consciousness has accomplished the following: it has posed specificity in its complete development—the specificity that is actual consciousness—as its own negative, that is, as the objective extreme" (PE, I, 195; PG, 175; PM, 272). This self-negation on the part of specificity culminates in the universal self which does not yet know itself as such; only we, philosophers, see in the medieval church the universal self which, as such, later appears in the form of reason. The self, being-for-itself, must alienate itself and thus become the unity of selves, universal self rediscovering itself in being. This being-for-itself of the in-itself is spirit.

The mediation between specific consciousness and the immutable, then, is brought about through a clergy and a church. The content of the mediating action is the destruction of specific consciousness as such and, simultaneously, its advance to universality. At first, it rejects itself qua specific will, it abandons its freedom of choice and of decision. Then, through the sacrament of penance, it frees itself from the guilt of action: "When action consists in following an alien decision, it ceases—with respect to acting and to the will—to be the particular action of the person" (PE, I, 190; PG, 169; PM, 265). The fruit of its labor, and enjoyment, are still retained by consciousness, but it renounces these in part through almsgiving and fasts. Consciousness ends by surrendering its very independence, agreeing to what it does not understand.[21]

But in-itself this self-alienation realizes a universal will—in-itself, not for it. For it cannot yet rediscover itself in its alienated will. Only we are able to see the emergence of universal will in the negation of specific will. This new stage is the unity of consciousness (the in-itself) and self-consciousness (the for-itself), that is, reason.

21. Church rites and ceremonies in Latin. Self-consciousness has completely alienated its inner and outer freedom in favor of a church. But specific will, negated in this way, is linked to the universal; *in-itself*, it is universal will. We shall return to the transition from *church* to *reason* in the next chapter.

PART IV

Reason in Its
Phenomenological Aspect

1 / Reason and Idealism

HEGEL CONSIDERS the same dialectical movement in the *Propaedeutic* and in the *Encyclopaedia* as in the *Phenomenology:* the movement expressed in the three moments, consciousness, self-consciousness, and reason. For consciousness, in the strict sence of the term, the object is an other than the I; its object is being-in-itself. But the development of consciousness leads to self-consciousness, for which the object is only the I itself. At first, this self-consciousness is specific, for it is for-itself only immediately. It excludes the object of consciousness so as to pose itself as independent and free. The education of self-consciousness is the movement through which it rises from this exclusive specificity to universality. Specific self-consciousness becomes universal self-consciousness. The desiring I becomes a thinking I. At that point, the content of consciousness is in-itself as well as for consciousness. Knowledge of an object is self-knowledge, then, and self-knowledge is knowledge of being-in-itself. This identity of thought and being is called "reason" (*Vernunft*). It is the dialectical synthesis of consciousness and self-consciousness, but this synthesis is possible only if self-consciousness has within itself genuinely become universal self-consciousness. In-itself, the I is universal; it must become so for-itself. As a result, its determinations will appear as the determinations of things and its thought about itself will simultaneously be thought about the object. As we see, the notion of reason corresponds to idealism, in the most general sense of the word. In the *Phenomenology* Hegel stresses the relation between reason and idealist philosophy in general. In the *Propaedeutic*, as well as in the phenomenological section of the *Encyclopaedia*, the dialectical movement is presented in a far more schematic and summary manner. Before studying the section on reason in the *Phenomenology* we shall briefly consider the transition from self-consciousness to reason as it appears in the two later books.[1]

In the *Propaedeutic*, after discussing the dialectic of master and slave, Hegel shows how the education of the slave leads him to universality: "The alienation of arbitrary will constitutes the moment of genuine obedience (by teaching the Greeks to obey, Pisistratus made Solon's laws actually effective. When the Athenians had learned to obey, the master became superfluous)."[2] Obedience and service train the will and transform the specific I into a universal I. Similarly, in labor man learns to defer his enjoyment and to express in objective being the determinations of thought. Man alienates his I, but that alienation is the conquest of universality. The I is no longer isolated. It transcends itself by discovering other I's within itself: it recognizes and is recognized. "Universal self-consciousness is the intuition of self as a nonparticular self that in-itself is universal. Thus it recognizes itself as well as other self-consciousnesses within it and, in turn, it is recognized by the others."[3]

The idea of a truth in-itself, as it will appear at the level of reason, cannot be separated from the idea of a multiplicity of specific I's and of communication among them. It is in this way that we are to understand the necessity of the education which raises self-enclosed man to consciousness of his universality. The reciprocal recognition of I's is a moment of the truth, as it is a moment of every virtue. "This (universal) self-consciousness is the basis of every virtue, of love, honor, friendship, courage, self-sacrifice, and fame."[4] Thus, reason appears as the first result of the reciprocal mediation of self-consciousnesses, a media-

---

1. In both these works *reason* is *truth in-and-for-itself*, and consequently phenomenology ends with it and a new element, the concept, is born. But such is not the case in the *Phenomenology of Spirit*, in which reason is considered as it is manifested in the *history of knowledge*. The reconciliation of universal and specific comes about only later. This is why I have called this part of my book "Reason in Its Phenomenological Aspect."

2. *Propaedeutic*, pp. 208 ff.

3. *Ibid.*, p. 209.

4. *Ibid.*, p. 210.

tion which accomplishes the universality of self-consciousness. In the absence of that universality, which at this level is still abstract, no truth would be possible. We can see here one of the characteristics of Hegel's idealism, which distinguishes it from Kant's, for example. For Kant, the "I think which must be able to accompany all my representations" is in a sense suspended in a void. For Hegel, to be sure, it is the concrete I, but it is a concrete I which through its relation to other I's has risen to universality. Truth transcends man, but it is nonetheless a human truth and it cannot be separated from the formation of self-consciousness.

This truth is no longer the being-in-itself of consciousness; it is at once (objective) truth and (subjective) certainty. It is a truth that is a subject, a self-development. It is in this way that we must understand the synthesis that reason represents, as well as the self-conscious reason that spirit (*Geist*) finally becomes. In the *Propaedeutic,* Hegel defines reason as follows:

> Reason is the supreme unification of consciousness and self-consciousness, of knowledge of an object and knowledge of self. It is the certainty that its determinations are objective, that is, that they are determinations of the essence of things, as well as being our own thoughts. In one and the same thought, it is both self-certainty (subjectivity) and being, or objectivity.[5]

"Reason," Hegel continues, "signifies a content which not only is in our representations but also contains the essence of things, a content which is not alien to the I, given from without, but is produced by the I (*von ihm erzeugt*)." We can see Schelling's philosophy of identity (an identity of subjectivity and objectivity) in this conception. But in the *Phenomenology,* that identity is the result of a journey of culture, the result of a development of consciousness and of self-consciousness such that truth is impossible without the reciprocal recognition of self-consciousnesses and their elevation to the universality of thought, and such that this truth, too, is not a being-in-itself—something beyond the act of becoming aware—but is self-knowledge, subjective certainty as at the same time objective reality.

In the *Encyclopaedia,* as in the *Propaedeutic,* Hegel discusses the same dialectical movement, from universal self-consciousness (the dialectic of master and slave) to reason. But he indicates why universal self-consciousness is reason before it is spirit. The transition from universal self-consciousness to spirit

5. *Ibid.;* cf. *ibid.,* p. 27.

—the I that is a we and the we that is an I—might seem more natural than the transition from universal self-consciousness to reason. For reason appears not to consider the multiplicity of I's but only the identity of truth and certainty, of being-in-itself and being-for-consciousness. We move from a concrete development—for example, the relation between master and slave—to a metaphysical thesis, the thesis of idealism, or of identity. Indeed, when Hegel discusses universal self-consciousness in the *Encyclopaedia,* he writes:

> The concept—that manifestation which universally reflects self-consciousness—which knows itself in its objectivity as a subjectivity identical to itself, and therefore knows itself to be universal, is the form of consciousness of the substance of every essential spirituality (family, fatherland, state) as well as of virtues. But all this can still remain formal; content is still lacking.[6]

For this reason, what at first presents itself in the new element of universality is only the unity of the concept existing for-itself (consciousness) and the externally present object. Reason is not yet spirit, for spirit is the result of reason's development; spirit is reason that knows itself and exists for its own sake.

In the *Phenomenology* these distinctions are even more important. Reason is envisaged as a particular moment of the development of consciousness (in the broad sense). It corresponds to the *form* of substance, while spirit is the substance that becomes subject. This form of substance is attained when, for-itself, self-consciousness becomes universal, when it carries within itself the element of knowledge which is the identity of being-in-itself and being-for-consciousness. This element has been engendered by the whole prior dialectic of master and slave, of stoicism, of skepticism, and of unhappy consciousness.

More than either the *Propaedeutic* or the phenomenological section of the *Encyclopaedia,* the 1807 *Phenomenology* is really a concrete history of human consciousness.[7] This history of con-

6. *Encyclopaedia,* p. 379.
7. What is the difference between reason in the 1807 *Phenomenology* and reason in the System? In the System, reason is genuinely the identity of in-itself and for-itself. Consequently, from then on phenomenal consciousness is *transcended.* But in the 1807 work reason is the phenomenal manifestation of reason, and consequently the unity of in-itself and for-itself is envisaged as it appears, still *for-itself,* to human consciousness. Only at the end of the work, in the dialectic of the remission of sins, is the "internal opposition of the concept" genuinely surmounted. See part VII, below.

sciousness, for which its own objective Dasein is world history, is much more highly developed than the outline Hegel preserves in his later system, which loses more and more of its connection to the history of the world spirit. Thus in 1807 Hegel envisages the transition from unhappy consciousness to reason as the transition from the medieval church to the Renaissance and modern times. In unhappy consciousness we saw the complete alienation of specific self-consciousness. For unhappy consciousness, which was only the painful feeling of skeptic negativity, being-in-itself was beyond it. It felt the inadequacy of the subjectivity from which it was unable to emerge, and its beyond was present to it as a God who would reconcile subjectivity and objectivity, the specificity of self-consciousness and the universality of the in-itself. Thus specific self-consciousness would be able to rediscover itself in God and simultaneously gain universality, to become universal self-consciousness while remaining self-consciousness. "Later," Hegel writes with respect to religion,

> self-consciousness which reaches its fulfillment in the figure of unhappy consciousness is only the torment of spirit struggling to rise again to an objective state but failing to reach it. The unity toward which self-consciousness tends, a unity of specific self-consciousness and its immutable essence, thus remains beyond it. The immediate Dasein of reason, which springs up for us from that torment, and its particular figures contain no religion because self-consciousness knows itself or seeks itself in immediate presence (*PE*, II, 203; *PG*, 473; *PM*, 685).[8]

The self-consciousness which is at once universal and specific and which serves as the transition to the reason of modern times is the medieval church. The specific I genuinely rises to universality through the intermediary of the church—an intermediary which constitutes a universal community, speaks a language which individuals do not always understand, collects donations from individuals, and forms a general will born from the alienation of specific wills.

> Consciousness has torn away its being-for-itself and made a thing of it . . . . In this development, consciousness' unity with the

8. We have already quoted this passage, which summarizes the signification of unhappy consciousness, in the last chapter—but without the last sentence, which indicates the transition from unhappy consciousness to reason.

universal has also come to exist for it, a unity which, because the suppressed specific is the universal, does not for us lie outside consciousness and which, because consciousness maintains itself in its own negativity, constitutes in consciousness as such the very essence of consciousness (*PE*, I, 195; *PG*, 175; *PM*, 272).

The middle term between the universal and the specific, between the in-itself and the for-itself, is the unity (represented here by the church) that has an immediate knowledge of the two extremes and relates them to each other. "This middle term is the consciousness of their unity, a unity it announces to consciousness, thereby announcing itself to itself; it is the certainty of being the whole of truth" (*PE*, I, 195; *PG*, 175; *PM*, 272).[9] Such indeed is reason: consciousness' certainty that it is the whole of reality, the whole of truth, certainty that this truth is not beyond but is immediately present to consciousness. Yet such a certainty is possible only through the alienation of specific consciousness, an alienation that raises self-consciousness to universality without, however, entailing the disappearance of consciousness itself. The alienation of self-consciousness is a spiritual movement, not an abrupt shift from one term to another (in this case, from the specific to the universal). Self-consciousness preserves itself in the transition—which is what Hegel means by the obscure parenthetical remark, "since consciousness preserves itself in its own negativity." In death—envisaged as purely phenomenal at the level of universal life—the specific becomes universal but without preserving itself in that loss of self. But in the spiritual death that is the alienation of specific self-consciousness, consciousness preserves itself in its very negativity. The self becomes the universal, but, as though by a rebound, the universal is posed as the self. Specific and universal, self and being-in-itself, exchange determination: truth becomes subjective and subjectivity acquires truth. Reason, a particular moment in the general development of consciousness and of the *Phenomenology*, is this immediate unity which results from the whole prior dialectic and presents itself to consciousness as a new figure, having allowed its whole genesis to be forgotten entirely.

This moment corresponds to the Renaissance and to modern times; it follows the Crusades and medieval Christianity. The

9. Hegel speaks of a syllogism whose extreme terms are the immutable and the specific; the middle term, living mediation, is at first the church and then modern reason. This middle term is the concrete universal.

world then is offered to consciousness as a present world, and no longer as a here-below or as a beyond. Consciousness knows that it can discover itself in this world, and it undertakes the conquest and the science of this world.

> Only after the sepulchre of its truth has been lost, only after the abolition of its own actual reality has itself been abolished, when for self-consciousness in-itself the specificity of consciousness has become absolute essence, does self-consciousness discover this world as *its* new actual world, which now interests it qua permanent as it had earlier interested it qua vanishing. For the subsistence of this world becomes for consciousness a truth and a presence that are its own, in which consciousness is certain to enter only into the experience of itself (*PE*, I, 196; *PG*, 176; *PM*, 273).

Earlier, consciousness sought to escape the world; it worked on the world, or it tried to withdraw from the world into itself. Its essential concern was to save itself and its salvation was for it always beyond presence. Now it wishes to rediscover itself in this world and there to seek its own infinity. For this consciousness, knowledge of the world is self-knowledge: "The world is its mirror." From this arises man's interest in exploring the earth and in the natural sciences. In his history of philosophy, Hegel speaks of "a reconciliation between self-consciousness and presence"; and in the *Philosophy of History*, he writes, with reference to modern times, "A third important phenomenon we must mention is that outward surge of spirit, man's fervent desire to know his earth." [10]

IDEALISM AS A PHENOMENON OF SPIRIT

IN A GENERAL WAY, idealism is characterized by the two reciprocal propositions: "The I is all of reality" and "All reality is the I," propositions which come to define consciousness of the world as a self-consciousness and self-consciousness as a consciousness of the world. The term "world" (*die Welt*) corresponds perhaps to this new stage of experience. Hitherto, being-for-consciousness was not a world; it was, for self-consciousness, merely an alien reality to be set aside. Idealism is the characteristic philosophy of the modern world; in the chapter of the

10. *The Philosophy of History*, p. 410.

Phenomenology entitled "Certainty and Truth of Reason," Hegel describes it as expressing the new behavior of consciousness with regard to the world.

> Since self-consciousness is reason, its hitherto negative behavior with regard to being-other is transformed into positive behavior. Until then, consciousness had been concerned only with its independence and its freedom—with a view to saving itself and maintaining itself for itself at the expense of the world and of its own actual reality, both of which appeared to it as the negative of its essence. But as reason that has become assured of itself, it has made peace with them and can endure them. For it is certain of itself as reality; it is certain that all actual reality is nothing else than it. Its thought is immediately actual reality; thus, it behaves toward that actual reality as idealism (*PE*, I, 196; *PG*, 175–76; *PM*, 272–73).

What is novel in this passage is not the very general definition of idealism, as the doctrine according to which there is nothing opaque or impenetrable to the I, but rather the presentation of idealism as a "phenomenon of the history of spirit." This originality was noted by Nicolai Hartmann in his fine work, *Die Philosophie des deutschen Idealismus*. Whereas earlier German philosophers, Fichte and Schelling, for example, had presented idealism as a philosophical thesis (Fichte appealing to a fundamental intuition of self-consciousness and Schelling to an originating principle of identity) Hegel encounters idealism on the historical path of the self-development of self-consciousness. "The point is this: idealism is not a theory or a system, but a *phenomenon* of spirit. . . . Consciousness enters into the experience of reason; that experience, raised to knowledge, is idealism." [11] Hegel was aware of the originality of his presentation, which is why he showed the defects of an idealism that offers itself straight off as a philosophical thesis and neglects the historical preconditions of that thesis.

Reason and idealism (which is the philosophy of reason) are faulty in that for consciousness caught up in experience they are immediate truths. Reason is the certainty consciousness has of being all of reality. And this certainty is presented to phenomenal consciousness immediately. For phenomenal consciousness has forgotten the whole formative path that has led to reason. That path is known only to the philosopher, who follows

11. Hartmann, *Die Philosophie des deutschen Idealismus* (Berlin and Leipzig, 1929), II, 113.

the development of the experiences of consciousness; it is not known by consciousness itself, which, at each stage, is reborn to an absolutely new life, forgetful of its past, of its having-become: the series of phenomenal consciousnesses in the *Phenomenology* is like a series of metamorphoses. "So, too, idealism sets forth that certainty immediately, in the form of the equation I = I, in the sense that the I that is my object is the only object, . . . that it is all of reality and all of presence" (*PE,* I, 197; *PG,* 176; *PM,* 273).

The immediateness that characterizes both reason's certainty and idealism constitutes the latter's defect and leads it to self-contradiction. Instead of being an absolute idealism, it is a one-sided idealism which as a whole proves unable to justify knowledge and experience—for example, the semi-idealism of Kant or the subjective idealism of Fichte. In order to give its certainty the character of truth, reason sets itself to work as theoretical reason and as practical reason, actually knowing the world (knowledge of nature, of human individuality, and of the relation between them); it realizes itself in the world as a self-consciousness sure of being able to pose itself and rediscover itself in being. Before following this concrete development of reason, Hegel considers idealist philosophy and shows how its claim remains empty. He has in mind particularly Kant's and Fichte's idealism, and his arguments are similar to those in his earlier Jena study, "Differenz," and to the more technical elaboration in "Glauben und Wissen," in which he discusses Kant's philosophy as a whole.

For the philosopher who rethinks the phenomenological development, idealism is the result of a lengthy formation which constitutes the necessary historical presuppositions of this philosophical thesis. "Self-consciousness is not only all of reality for-itself; it is also all of reality in-itself because it becomes that reality, or rather demonstrates itself to be such" (*PE,* I, 197; *PG,* 176; *PM,* 274). It demonstrates itself to be such in the course of the prior dialectic of intending the this, of perception, and of understanding. In that dialectic, being-other disappears as being-in-itself. Consciousness supposed a being-in-itself that was absolutely independent of it, but it came to experience the hollowness of that supposition. For being-in-itself was always shown to be in-itself for it and therefore always disappeared before it. Consciousness also demonstrates itself to be all of reality in the course of the complementary experience of self-consciousness, for which being-other vanished for itself insofar as it was only for-it. In the struggle between skeptic liberation and unhappy consciousness, the I renounces a representation which can exist only for specific consciousness and rises to a universal thought.

> Thus, these two aspects alternated: in one, essence, or the true, had for consciousness the determination of being; in the other, essence had the determination of being only for consciousness. But these two aspects are reduced to one single truth according to which what exists, the in-itself, exists only insofar as it exists for consciousness, and what exists for consciousness is also in-itself (*PE*, I, 197; *PG*, 177; *PM*, 274).

The impenetrable thing-in-itself and the subjective solitude of the I are both superseded. But these two routes—that of consciousness seeing the phantom of being-in-itself vanish before it, and that of self-consciousness which in the course of its harsh and lengthy formation sees the disappearance of an essence that exists only for it, for it qua specific consciousness—are both prerequisites for the positing of a truth which is both in-itself and for consciousness, a truth such as only idealism can conceive. "But for the consciousness that is this truth that road is behind it, and it forgets that road when it immediately rises up as reason; or again, reason, rising up immediately, rises up only as the certainty of that truth" (*PE*, I, 197; *PG*, 177; *PM*, 274). It only asserts that it is all of reality; it does not think that assertion through conceptually. The conceptual thinking through of that assertion would be its own historical development, which lies behind it. But the development of a truth is the in-itself of that truth, and in the absence of the movement by means of which it arises, it is merely an assertion. This is what is most original in Hegel's philosophy, the reconciliation of the history of thought with thought itself. "The immediate manifestation of truth is the abstraction of its present being, the essence and the being-in-itself of which are the absolute concept, that is, the movement of its having-become." Several lines later, Hegel expresses this relation between truth and its history more concretely:

> Consciousness determines its relation to being-other (to its object) in various ways according to the extent that the world spirit has become aware of itself. How the world spirit recognizes itself and immediately determines itself and how it determines its object at

each stage, or how it is for-itself, depends on what it has become, on what it already is in-itself (*PE*, I, 198–99; *PG*, 178; *PM*, 275–76).

CRITIQUE OF EMPTY (SUBJECTIVE) IDEALISM

IT IS ON THE BASIS of this consideration that Hegel criticizes the idealist thesis in the abstract form in which it appears in the works of Kant and Fichte. To be sure, Fichte appeals to the self-consciousness of each specific consciousness to discover within itself the pure intellectual intuition which is the precondition of each consciousness. But in basing his truth on that appeal (on the I = I that no consciousness can challenge since it is only a matter of thinking oneself, and since "unless they don't know what they are saying all men think themselves, for they all speak about themselves" [12]), Fichte is forced also to accept the other truth, equally present in empirical consciousness, namely, that "there is for me an other; an other is object and essence for me" (*PE*, I, 198; *PG*, 177; *PM*, 275). The self-consciousness of the idealist is juxtaposed to the consciousness of an object, a thing alien to the I. "Thus, only when reason emerges as reflection from this contraposed certainty does its affirmation present itself no longer merely as certainty and assertion but also as truth—and not as one truth among many but as the only truth" (*PE*, I, 198; *PG*, 177; *PM*, 275). Without the dialectic we have left behind us, idealism runs the risk of posing itself as a thesis against an equally valid antithesis, in which case it would be prey to a contradiction similar to that of skepticism. In spite of its claim to absorb all of reality into the I, Fichte's idealism is no more than a modern form of skepticism or, better, of unhappy consciousness which oscillates endlessly between two irreconcilable terms. But it is an unhappy consciousness that is unaware of its misfortune. Whereas skepticism expresses itself negatively, idealism expresses itself as a positive truth, despite the fact that it is marked by the same contradiction as skepticism. For idealism, truth is the unity of apperception, the I = I; yet it is condemned to an untrue knowledge of the

12. Fichte, *Sonnenklarer Bericht an das grössere Publikum über das eigentliche Wesen der neuesten Philosophie: ein Versuch die Leser zum Verstehen zu zwingen* (Berlin, 1801).

other: "It is involved in an immediate contradiction, for it affirms as essence something that is split and absolutely self-opposed: the unity of apperception is also the thing which—whether it is called an alien shock, or empirical essence, or sensuousness, or thing-in-itself [*Ding an sich*]—always remains the same in its concept and is forever alien to that unity" (*PE*, I, 203; *PG*, 181; *PM*, 280). These objections to Fichte's subjective idealism are the same as those in Hegel's earlier article "Differenz." The starting point of the system, that the I is all of reality and is equal to itself, does not coincide with the end point, at which the I must (*soll*) be equal to the I. In the face of this empty requirement, reality is born as a not-I which will never be completely absorbed. Thus, despite its positive claim, this idealism has "a double meaning, an ambiguity as contradictory as skepticism." From the start of his philosophical career, Hegel denounced this contradiction between what Fichte's realism claims and what it in fact realizes: "I = I is transformed into I ought to equal I." [13] "The result of this formal idealism is an opposition between an empirical realm that lacks unity—a contingent multiplicity—and an empty thought." [14]

Idealism falls into this contradiction because it affirmed as true the abstract concept of reason, the unity of reality and of the I in the still abstract form of the category. Genuine reason, which we are studying at this stage of the *Phenomenology*, is not so inconsistent. It knows that it is only the (subjective) certainty of being all of reality, and does not yet take that certainty to be truth. It seeks to test it out, to raise it to truth. In this attempt it sets about learning about the world and acquiring genuine content. Concrete reason moves from the certainty of being all of reality to its truth, which is knowledge of reality. It builds up a science of nature and observes nature so as to discover itself within it and thereby advance to truth what at first was only a subjective certainty.

The difference between idealism (a philosophical system that gives out as truth a certainty that is still subjective) and the concrete reason of the *Phenomenology* is clear. In the *Phenomenology*, reason seeks its truth, whereas idealism proclaims that truth without having tested it out and without having justified it historically. Thus idealism is abstract; it remains at the stage of the category—the unity of being and the I—and does not know

13. Hegel, "Differenz," p. 53.
14. "Glauben und Wissen," p. 323.

development. It does not transcend the opposition between the a priori and the a posteriori, and it does not know genuine synthesis, which is the synthesis of the a posteriori and the a priori itself. But reason that is actually engaged in knowing nature and action will be able to discover itself and to substitute for formal idealism a concrete idealism in which the I and the universe are adequate to each other in a monism of spirit.

2 / The Observation of Nature

REASON—the certainty of consciousness that it is all of reality—is not, like idealism, a philosophical assertion which, inasmuch as it fails to deliver what it has promised, remains gratuitous and formal. Knowing that it is merely a certainty, it undertakes to acquire truth by putting itself to work and by realizing a knowledge of the world. It does not stop at the "pure I," Fichte's abstraction. "Reason suspects that it is a more profound essence than the pure I, and it must demand that multifarious being, difference, become for the I its own" (*PE*, I, 205; *PG*, 184; *PM*, 281–82). For this reason, the section that Hegel devotes to reason corresponds to the development of science from the Renaissance to his own time. That science is a knowledge which claims to originate in experience but which contradicts that claim by the manner in which it establishes and seeks out its truth. It is interested not in the sensuous as such but in the concept that resides in the sensuous. Reason is not passive vis-à-vis reality: it questions experience, and by questioning nature it manages to discover in experience a concept, which is nothing other than the presence of reason itself in the midst of the content. In the world that is offered to it, reason discovers itself; the knowledge of experience is a self-knowledge. Thus, we return to the thesis that idealism expressed gratuitously in the form of the equation $I = I$ or, with Schelling, in the form of identity. The empirical sciences—which Hegel does not scorn "since there is nothing that is not in experience" (*PE*, II, 305; *PG*, 558; *PM*, 800) and since the a priori is necessarily revealed in the a posteriori—culminate in a philosophy of nature that is a first mirror of the I. According to Hegel, there is no discontinuity between a science of the world and a philosophy of nature like Schelling's. The only question is whether such a philosophy of nature can fully satisfy the I, that is, whether the I rediscovers itself absolutely in nature, or whether there remains in nature an irreducible contingency such that the concept is only sketched in it but not actually presented. In the latter case, reason would have to return from nature back to itself; instead of observing the world, it would observe the I, or human individuality, in its relation to the world and, more specifically, in relation to that which indicates its presence in the world—the body. Hegel's phenomenology is a *phenomenology of spirit*. Nature is not the concept but only the concept's past, and reason cannot truly satisfy itself by observing it. Even less can it grasp the I by observing it, for observation freezes the concept in being, although the concept is not being but becoming, the self-positing of self. For this reason, though the philosophy of nature and more generally all the natural sciences must play a part in the phenomenological development in which consciousness learns to discover itself and to rediscover itself as spirit, it cannot have (as Schelling and, for a time in Jena, Hegel thought it could) a preponderant role. Theoretical reason will give way to practical reason: instead of discovering itself the I will pose itself; instead of ascertaining itself it will create itself. Practical reason, which emphasizes the aspect of the for-itself in the unity of the category (instead of the in-itself, which theoretical reason emphasized), is in turn revealed as too exclusive, and we are then led to a new synthesis, to a reason that is both theoretical and practical, objective as well as subjective; a reason which, having become conscious of itself and having become its own world, is spirit.

THEORETICAL REASON; NATURAL PHILOSOPHY

BACON, GALILEO, AND DESCARTES are closely linked in our minds to the origin of a genuine science of nature. This science only appears to reproduce the movement of perception and of understanding. In the chapter on perception and understanding, Hegel attempted to eliminate definitively the thing-in-itself, the suprasensuous world, as an existent beyond phenomena. By contrast, in the section on observing reason—a reason which envisages the description of things, the classification of species, the laws of nature, in short, a system of nature that is much closer to Schelling than to Newton—he tries to ascertain the degree to which nature can offer reason a reflected image of itself.

The passages we are about to study are important to an understanding of Hegel's system, for they express an essential movement of the development of consciousness and of knowledge. It is reason, indeed, that seeks itself in nature. But it seeks itself as an immediate reality. Thus, at the end of its attempt, it discovers itself in the system of nature, but as a thing, a being, and not as an act; it discovers itself as one discovers one's own past, and not as the movement whereby one makes oneself what one is. Nature, then, is indeed a certain expression of the I—as Schelling affirmed against Fichte (who reduced nature merely to the opposition needed for the I to pose itself). But it is not the genuine expression of the I. The absolute as nature must be transcended; the absolute must be posed as spirit. (Hegel's thought on this last point developed from the time of his arrival in Jena, when he had adopted Schelling's philosophy.) "Spirit is higher than nature" because it reflects back on itself and is therefore subject, whereas nature is merely spirit straying outside itself, the I absorbed in its intuition and lost in being. This is a second reason why we are interested in these passages: they allow us to specify (and perhaps to notice the development of) Hegel's philosophy of nature.

Observation, the attitude of consciousness, bears on characteristics. To observe is to congeal the concept in being and consequently to seek the concept only as a being and to seek the I as an immediate reality.

> Reason, as it immediately rises up, as the certainty of consciousness that it is all of reality, takes on its proper reality in the sense of the immediateness of being; similarly, it assumes the unity of the I and objective essence, in the sense of an immediate unity, a unity in which reason has not yet separated and reunited the moments of being and the I, or in the sense of a unity that reason does not yet know (*PE*, I, 205–6; *PG*, 184; *PM*, 282).

Genuine unity, on the contrary, will be a dialectical unity. The I is not immediately in nature; it is alienated in it, lost in it, so that it can there rediscover itself. It is this movement of separation and unification that constitutes the very life of the absolute. And in order to be able to think through this separation and unification, reason must first know itself as dialectical reason. The result of the observation of nature and of the I in nature is paradoxical, but it merely expresses the attitude taken by reason qua observing reason.

> Consciousness observes, that is, reason wishes to discover itself and to possess itself as an object in the element of being, as an actually real mode having a sensuous presence. Consciousness of this observation believes and states that it wishes to enter not into the experience of itself but into the experience of the essence of things qua things. If this consciousness so believes and says, it is because although it is reason it does not yet have reason as such as its object (*PE*, I, 205; *PG*, 184; *PM*, 282).

If consciousness knew the absolute knowledge of reason as the essence common to nature and the I, it would no longer be a phenomenological consciousness, and we should have transcended the *Phenomenology of Spirit*. We should then be able, in the element of absolute knowledge, to think reason through for itself. Instead of a phenomenology, the *ascesis* of a consciousness tainted by knowledge of the other, we should have an ontologic [*une ontologique*], precisely the logic that Hegel wrote after the *Phenomenology*. Hartmann noted the importance of this passage in which Hegel indicates the two possible directions of his research, the *Phenomenology* and the *Logic* (which later leads to the *Encyclopaedia*), that is, to a philosophy of nature and to a philosophy of spirit, each having its origin in the logos of this ontological logic.[1] "If consciousness recognized reason as the essence both of things and of itself, and if it knew that in its authentic figure reason can only have a presence in consciousness, it would seek reason in the depths of its own being rather than in things" (*PE*, I, 205; *PG*, 184; *PM*, 282).[2] It could then go back to nature and contemplate therein its own sensuous expression, directly grasping that expression as concept. (This example corresponds to the philosophy of nature in the *Encyclopaedia*.) In the *Phenomenology*, reason, unaware of itself, is as yet in Hegel's phrase merely the "instinct of reason." It can attain itself only through the detour of observing things. As an instinct, it is a presentiment of itself but not a self-knowledge.

1. Hartmann, *Die Philosophie des deutschen Idealismus* (Berlin and Leipzig, 1929), II, 114–15.
2. This self-knowledge by reason alone is the deduction of the categories, logos. We see the difference between "reason in its phenomenological aspect" and reason in-and-for-itself.

Thus, in observing things, reason seeks itself. "For observing consciousness, only the nature of things is unfolded through this process, but for us, what it itself is, is unfolded. As the result of its movement, it will become for itself what it is in-itself" (*PE*, I, 206; *PG*, 185; *PM*, 283). As we said above, a paradoxical result! Observing reason indeed immediately discovers itself as a thing. In phrenology, which is the end point of observation, the I appears to itself as "a bone." The I discovers itself as "pure and simple being." The concept of this representation is that "to itself, reason is entirely thingness, and thingness that is solely and purely objective" (*PE*, I, 205; *PG*, 184; *PM*, 282). The identity of thought and being is posed here as the end point of observation, but also as the transitional hinge between observation and action. By means of action, consciousness, which has failed to discover itself in being, will claim to pose itself in it.

From the Observation of Things to the Observation of the Organic

HEGEL FOLLOWS the development of observing reason from the description of things to the search for and verification of laws. According to the outline indicated in the introductory chapter to the section on reason, when consciousness assumes the movement of knowledge the object is posed as the immutable true, while when consciousness rises to self-certain and fixed truth, the object is posed as the movement itself: "Object and consciousness alternate in these reciprocal and contraposed determinations" (*PE*, I, 201; *PG*, 180; *PM*, 278).[3] For the movement the calm unity is the other, while for the unity the movement is the other. In the most elementary case, the description of natural objects, the first form of empirical knowledge, the object at first is what remains equal to itself. As Aristotle said, "There is a science only of the general." In this sense, consciousness seeks to discover in experience ever-new genuses to describe. The movement of description is within knowledge; it

3. This alternation between the *immutable true* and the *movement of thought* is typical of Hegel's thought. Truth is present in its absoluteness as "Bacchic delirium . . . but this delirium is also a translucent and simple repose" (*PE*, I, 40; *PG*, 39; *PM*, 105). Thus, consciousness distinguishes the *true* as a fixed object from the *movement of knowledge*, but this distinction vanishes in the absolute which includes mediation within it.

is a superficial extraction of the universal out of the sensuous. But this universal by itself lacks life. Consciousness is not the understanding of the universal but only its recollection, its memory (*Gedächtnis*), a memory which is not merely the internalization of the portrayal of external being but also a description of that being. What most closely corresponds to this stage of knowledge is language. As the poet, especially the epic poet, grants things the seal of universality and the form of thought by saying them, so by naming things we raise them from sensuousness to thought. In his first philosophy of spirit (the *Realphilosophie* of 1803–4), Hegel stressed the *mnēmosynē* of the ancients, the memory of things which is simultaneously a memory of words. Purely sensuous intuiton is superseded. "In the name the empirical being is suppressed . . . it becomes something ideal. The first action by which Adam established his domination over the animals was to name them, negating them as existing and making them ideal for him." [4] We have dwelt on the role of language—the importance of which we saw in the first chapter of the *Phenomenology,* at the moment of sensuous certainty—because Hegel returns to it throughout the book. Language is genuinely the Dasein of spirit. That things can be said, that their external existence can be expressed in a description, is already a sign that in-itself they are concepts, that the human logos is at once the logos of nature and the logos of spirit.

Nevertheless, description is a very superficial mode of knowledge, and it quickly reaches its limits. Even at this level nature manifests its contingency. "Description cannot know whether what appears to it to be in-itself is not a contingency. That which bears the mark of a confused, immature product so weak that it could barely develop beyond elementary indeterminateness cannot even claim to be described" (*PE,* I, 208; *PG,* 186; *PM,* 285). Reason, then, seeks and analyzes the characteristic signs of things; it wishes no longer merely to describe, but also to classify. The object of knowledge now is the hierarchy of genuses and species, which corresponds most closely to a science like ancient biology. The point is to reach a system of things such that simultaneously knowledge is possible through it and nature itself is expressed in it. There is an opposition between natural classifications and artificial classifications: "On the one hand, characteristic signs must merely serve to enable knowledge to distinguish things from one another. But on the other hand,

4. *Realphilosophie,* SW, XIX, 211.

what is to be known is not the nonessential of things, but that through which they detach themselves from the universal continuity of being in general, split off from the other, and come to be for-itself" (*PE*, I, 208; *PG*, 187; *PM*, 286). It is not enough to "count" characteristics, as Linnaeus did; they must be "weighed," as Jussieu did. We must note the primal continuity of being from which genuses, species, and individualities detach themselves. The separation effected by knowledge may be artificial if it fails to reach being-for-itself, but what corresponds to it in nature is precisely the movement through which living beings pose themselves for themselves and in their specificity are contraposed to the universe: "The distinctive signs of animals, for example, are drawn from claws and teeth, for in fact not only does knowledge distinguish one animal from another in this way but the animal itself thereby distinguishes and separates itself: it maintains itself for-itself with these weapons, separate from the universal" (*PE*, I, 209; *PG*, 187; *PM*, 286). The opposition between the universal and the specific—and more profoundly, at a different level, between the universe and the I—is the theme of Hegel's philosophy. It is the separation that must be overcome without either of the terms being swallowed up by the other. In its lowliest form, it already appears in the classification of living things. Animals rise to being-for-itself; plants only reach the threshold of individuality. And below the level of plants, distinction cannot be thought, for things—matter, substantialized quality—are lost in relation. What can be thought is no longer the separate term but the relation, and in this way we move from a science that seeks only to classify and to discover *types* and specific differences to a science of *laws*. The order of nature as an order of genuses and species is an ideal order which nature does not realize. "Observation, which kept these differences and these essentialities in good order and thought that in them it held something fixed and solid, sees its principles overlapping each other, sees transitions and confusions form, and sees what it had taken to be absolutely divided bound together and what it had taken to be bound together split apart" (*PE*, I, 210; *PG*, 188; *PM*, 287–88). At a certain level, the animal kingdom and the vegetable kingdom merge, and reason's distinctions are no longer justified. Although for Hegel the science of living beings, of the organic, is not a science of the evolution of beings (for such an evolution within nature can only be for him an ideal sequence) his conception is not absolutely opposed to what later became the theory of evolution.

We note the search for laws, which replaces classification, only in passing, for we have already discussed it with reference to understanding. Hegel returns here, at another level, to something he has already indicated. Understanding observes relations, not fixed determinations; it grasps the genuine nature of determinateness, which is to reveal itself as a moment in a process. The instinct of reason claims to discover law in experience, but in fact it destroys in law "the random subsistence of actual sensuous reality." Sensuous determinations then appear as abstractions; they are meaningful only in relation to other sensuous determinations, and this relatedness constitutes the concept of the internal necessity of law. To be sure, observation thinks that it sets forth the law of coexistence or a random sequence. But it errs—as does the pure theoretician who does not move beyond what ought to be and contraposes the necessity of law to every experience. "What is valid universally is in fact universally valid; what must be is in fact, and what merely ought to be but is not is completely void of truth" (*PE*, I, 211; *PG*, 189–90; *PM*, 289). The manner in which laws are established by induction (according to analogies) is clearly empirical and it leads to no more than a probability. But the notion of probability merely signifies the imperfect way that truth is present for consciousness. Reason also knows the necessity of law, and the immediate universality found in experience leads to the universality of the concept. Stones fall not only because we have seen them fall but also because they are in a relation to the earth, which is expressed as weight. Sensuous universality is the sign of a necessity that reason elucidates in experience. Rather than purely and simply observing, reason experiments, that is, it "purifies law and its moments so as to raise them to conceptual form" (*PE*, I, 213; *PG*, 191; *PM*, 291). At first, positive electricity is manifested as the property of certain bodies, and negative electricity as the property of others. Thanks to experiments, which seem to immerse the concept ever more deeply in the sensuous, the moments of law are freed from adherence to particular Daseins and become what in the physics of Hegel's day were called matters: heat, electricity, etc. They lose their corporeality but they remain present. Thus pure law is freed from the sensuous, a sensuous that has been transformed by experiments. It is as if an experiment were a *sensuous conception*, an elaboration of the sensuous which reveals within it the necessity of the concept. It raises the concept, which had been submerged in being, and makes it appear as what it is: the dynamism of nature, rather than the static universal of description or classification. But this concept is concept. It is relation, but it is also unity, the return to itself from being-other. In accordance with the outline consistently repeated in the *Phenomenology*, this unity within relation appears to consciousness as a new object: the organic. The organic is no longer law as the relation of terms which lose themselves in each other. It is law as the unity of a process which preserves itself in its becoming-other. Whereas law provided diversity within the concept, the organic, as finality or interiority, provides the unity of the concept—without being able to express it in an exteriority or a genuine separation of the terms.[5]

OBSERVATION OF THE ORGANIC

THE PROGRESSIVE DEVELOPMENT in the object corresponds to a progressive development in the consciousness that is conscious of the object. In the sensuous experience of the inorganic world, the necessity of law was not for-itself but only in-itself. But its being-for-itself was only the reflection of consciousness. Now, this reflection becomes the object of consciousness which, consequently, can rediscover itself therein. The "organic" is such an object. In the organic, Hegel says, the concept becomes for-itself; "it exists as concept. Thus, in the organic what had hitherto been merely our reflection exists." Inorganic nature does not truly reach selfsameness [*ipséité*], the self, unless we consider a concrete totality such as the earth, which Hegel calls "the universal individual." The essence of the inorganic thing is in fact a particular determination, which is why it becomes concept only in its connection to other things. But the thing does not preserve itself in that connection; it is only *for-some-other;* it does not reflect on itself in the process of relating to other things. Indeed, the inorganic is characterized by this absence of reflection. The living being is a relatively closed system, not because it hasn't endless interchanges with an

5. We can clearly see the parallelism here between the concrete objects of reason and reason itself (a parallelism already sketched in Schelling's transcendental idealism). "That which truly is the result and the essence now rises up for consciousness, but as an *object;* since this object is precisely not a *result* for consciousness . . . it rises up as a particular kind of object" (*PE,* I, 219; *PG,* 196; *PM,* 296).

external environment, but because "it maintains itself within its very relation." "In organic essence, all the determinations by means of which that essence is open to an other are bound to each other under the control of simple and organic unity" (*PE*, I, 215; *PG*, 193; *PM*, 293). Thus the organic is *necessity realized*, and no longer merely the necessity of a relation for consciousness. It is absolute fluidity which dissolves within itself every determination.

In the presence of this new object, which contains the prior development of consciousness, the instinct of reason continues its quest for laws, but the search proves vain. The first type of law that is possible is that which delineates the relations between organic being and its environment, between organic being and the inert elements of inorganic nature, air, water, climate, zones. These elements are particular determinations, and they lack reflection on themselves, that is, they present themselves as being for-others. Organic being, by contrast, is perfectly reflected on itself, and thus it negates the determinations by means of which it comes to relate to these external elements. Yet the relation exists: there are in nature birds, fish, furry animals, and so on. "The organic has the elemental being around it and also represents it in its own organic reflection" (*PE*, I, 216; *PG*, 194; *PM*, 294). The contemporary term for what Hegel means is "adaptation." The living individuality is adapted to its environment. It reflects that exteriority in its own interiority. But adaptation is ambiguous on several counts. There is no truly necessary juncture between air and the wings of a bird, or between water and the shape of a fish. On the one hand, the variety of organic forms gives rise to numerous exceptions to the rules, or laws; "on the other hand, the concept of the sea does not entail the concept of the structure of the fish, nor the concept of air the concept of the structure of birds" (*PE*, I, 217; *PG*, 194; *PM*, 295). We come upon a contingency here, with regard to the concept of nature as Kant formulated it in the "Transcendental Analytic." Adaptation is the living being's response to its environment, not a passive intake of the environment like the modification of fluid by the shape of the vase in which it is contained. In the *Critique of Judgement*, Kant had been struck by the contingency we see in living forms when we try to explain them by a sequence of efficient causes. He had advanced a teleological explanation in order to remedy that contingency, but such an explanation is outside nature and derives not from determining judgment but from reflecting judgment.

If, for example, we note the structure of a bird, we say that, according to the *nexus effectivus* in nature alone (without reference to a particular kind of causality, that of ends [*nexus finalis*]) it is all contingent in the highest degree—which is to say that considered as a simple mechanism, nature could have used different forms . . . and that we can hope to find the a priori reason only outside the concept of nature.[6]

"Since necessity can no longer be conceived as the internal necessity of essence," Hegel writes,

> it also ceases to have a sensuous Dasein and it can no longer be observed within actual reality. It has vacated actual reality. No longer in real essence, it is a teleological relation, a relation external to the related terms, and thus is rather the contrary of a law. It is thought that is completely freed from necessary nature, thought which abandons necessary nature and moves about for-itself above it (*PE*, I, 217; *PG*, 195; *PM*, 295).

In order to banish the contingency, the indeterminateness, that understanding discovers in nature, we must rise above the related terms (air, bird). The concept, then, is presented as transcendent to nature as defined by Kant—the ensemble of phenomena governed by laws. The concept is no longer law but finality, the concept of goal, and this now is the new object of observing reason—an object which, apparently, it can encounter neither in nature, since it locates it *beyond,* nor within itself, since this object is *its* object. But Hegel—who follows Schelling here, and develops ideas that were in the *Critique of Judgement* —tries to show that the concept is immanent in organic nature, and that the goal, the end, is neither outside nature nor outside human understanding. "But observing reason does not recognize the concept of goal in organic nature; it does not know that that concept is not somewhere else, in an understanding, but exists right here, as a thing" (*PE*, I, 220; *PG*, 197; *PM*, 299). Nature is not just the world, a variety of sensations informed by an alien understanding; it is raised above finitude. It is, as Aristotle saw, an activity that is a goal for-itself. According to Hegel, Kant was on the verge of considering it as such.

> Kant recognized that in-and-for-itself it is possible that the mechanism of nature (the relation of causality) and the teleological technicism [*technicisme*] of nature are one. This does not

6. *Critique of Judgement* trans. James Creed Meredith (Oxford, 1911), pt. 2, p. 18.

mean that nature is determined by an idea that stands contraposed to it, but rather that what according to the mechanism appears to be absolutely separate in an empirical linkage of necessity (one term is the cause, the other the effect) is, on the contrary, linked at the heart of an originary identity taken as the initial term and in an absolute manner. Although for Kant there is nothing impossible in this, it is merely a way of envisaging things, he holds to the view that nature is absolutely divided and that the activity of knowing nature is a purely contingent faculty of knowing, absolutely finite and subjective—which he calls the human faculty of knowing. He calls transcendent that rational knowing for which the organism, qua real reason, is the superior principle of nature and the identity of the universal and the particular.[7]

Kant admits the impossibility of explaining living nature without having recourse to teleology, but on the one hand finality is outside nature for him and is part of our subjective reflection, and on the other hand it is conceivable in-itself only for an intuitive understanding that is not ours. If for Schelling, on the contrary, nature is a subject-object, it is not lacking in activity; it is a goal by itself. And it is the organic that realizes for consciousness the unconscious wisdom of the concept, the self-feeling that animal life reaches. But this self-feeling, this unconscious finality of nature, is like a first reflection of self-conscious reason which in part will rediscover itself in it. What Hegel wants to show in his discussion of the concept of goal is that reason exists in organic nature, and that it exists imperfectly. When he summarizes this whole process somewhat further on, he writes:

> The organic process is free only in-itself, not for-itself. The being-for-itself of its freedom enters the scene with the goal. In the goal, being-for-itself exists as another essence, as a self-conscious wisdom that is outside the process. Observing reason then turns toward that wisdom, toward spirit—the concept existing as universality, or the goal existing as goal—and its own essence becomes its object (*PE*, I, 283; *PG*, 251; *PM*, 367).[8]

Contradictions can be found in these expressions. Organic nature manifests an immanent finality; it is the goal in-itself, un-

7. "Glauben und Wissen," p. 256. According to Hegel, this passage is an interpretation of Kant's philosophy.
8. In the preface, referring explicitly to Aristotle, Hegel dwells on the importance of an immanent finality (a self-becoming, a circular process), which is characteristic of his entire thought (*PE*, I, 20; *PG*, 21; *PM*, 81–82).

conscious wisdom; but simultaneously, in the concept of goal organic nature refers to another essence, spirit, which is self-conscious wisdom. Yet Hegel's thought is clear. He rejects a purely mathematical conception of nature like Newton's, and he criticizes Fichte's conception of a nature reduced simply to what stands contraposed to spirit. But he also rejects Schelling's and Goethe's view of nature as a manifestation of genuine reason. Reason, which observes and which seeks itself, in part discovers itself in nature, but only in part. The philosophy of nature does not satisfy reason's need to think itself. What reason observes in nature is only a moment of itself; nature always refers to spirit, as in the chapter on understanding life referred to self-consciousness. The theme that was merely broached at the level of life and the becoming aware of life is now dealt with at the level of the knowledge of nature. Hegel, who in his early works had dealt exclusively with human phenomena and had left the phenomena of organic life to one side, discovered his own dialectic in Schelling's philosophy of nature. He seems to have adopted that philosophy for a time, and the major part of the Jena *Realphilosophie* was devoted to a search for the concept in Schelling's philosophy of nature. But Hegel gradually detached himself from that philosophy, and already in the *Phenomenology* he saw in nature the fall of the idea, a past of reason, rather than an absolute manifestation of reason. From then on, the philosophy of nature plays an essential role in Hegel's system (for spirit cannot do without nature), but a subordinate one. Nature will never be more than the other of spirit, and spirit will genuinely realize itself only in objective spirit, in human history, in art, religion, and philosophy. Hoffmeister noted Hegel's evolution here, and he outlined Hegel's relation to Schelling on this point.[9] Schelling thinks nature directly; Hegel thinks nature through the knowledge of nature—which for him was the philosophy of nature of his time. Thus, Hegel's system would have been much the same even if that philosophy had been quite different, so long as it was not purely mechanistic. "Nature," Novalis said, "is a magical petrification of God, which in knowledge finds itself liberated." The conceptual character of Hegel's dialectic is due to Hegel's having reflected on the knowledge of nature rather than on nature itself. Goethe, whose thought was quite close to Hegel's at times, was indignant over Hegel's reduction of the

9. Cf. J. Hoffmeister, *Goethe und der deutsche Idealismus* (Leipzig, 1932), pp. 61 ff.

development of nature to a logical dialectic. In a letter to Seebeck, written in 1812, he quoted the passage in the preface that deals with the succession of plant forms and commented that "it is impossible to say anything more monstrous." But what Goethe did for nature, Hegel did for human history, which was his true field. In contrast to Schelling, then, Hegel sought to rediscover the concept, selfsameness, in nature. And, more than Schelling, he was led to note the qualitative differences in the realization of the concept, differences between organic and inorganic nature, and between vegetable and animal life. Whereas Schelling tried everywhere to find degrees of realizing one and the same intuition, Hegel was more sensitive to qualitative oppositions, especially to oppositions that have significance in the fields of the for-itself and of human experience. Having at the beginning appeared to adopt Schelling's philosophy of nature, Hegel drew further and further away from it. Seeking to give nature a conceptual transparency, he abandoned it more and more to itself and saw in it the fall of the idea. He ended by limiting nature to its mere manifestation and its spirit to its apparent being. He gradually limited the broad ideas of ether, light, and fire to empirical phenomena, and excluded speculative analogies.[10] Nature then is posed as being-for-some-other, and its own spirituality disappears. The result is that in nature reason is contingent. This contingency (a contingency with respect to meaning and the idea, not with respect to this or that empirical explanation or to a possible empirical determinism) finally overwhelms the expression of the concept in Hegel's view of nature. "Nature is a contingent reason." And it appears as such in the overview Hegel reaches at the end of the chapter.

But when we consider organic being, we discern in it the first realization of the concept, in the form of finality ($\tau\epsilon\lambda os$). Organic being is in fact the real goal; and it is its own end, preserving itself in its relation to others.

It is precisely in natural essence that nature reflects itself in the concept, and that the moments that in necessity are posed externally to each other (cause and effect, the active moment and the passive moment) are gathered together into a unity. What we have here emerges not only as the *result* of necessity but because what emerges has returned into itself; the last thing to come, the result, is also the initial term that began the movement and it presents itself to itself as the goal that it actually realizes.

10. *Ibid.,* p. 77.

The organic does not produce anything, it merely preserves itself; what comes to be produced is already as much present as it is produced (*PE*, I, 217–18; *PG*, 195; *PM*, 296).

This passage contains the crux of Hegel's thought on the teleological activity that the concept is, the self-production of self, the circular process in which the result emerges not only as a result but implies a first term which in the result becomes what it is. Necessity is no longer an external bond; it is the immanence of the self in its development, its selfsameness. Kant had already characterized natural objects as objective ends: "But in order to call what we recognize as a product of nature a 'goal' more is needed, if that is not a contradiction. I should say at the outset that a thing exists as a natural goal if (albeit in two senses) it is its own cause and its own effect." [11] The tree reproduces itself according to species and as an individual, with regard to the details of its organized parts, as though the whole were immanent in the parts and were their directing idea. But although Kant judged that such an archetypal understanding, which could go from the whole to the parts as well as from the parts to the whole, was possible, he denied that it was a possibility for humanity. But in that case, finality is for us merely an inevitable explanation, valid only κατ' ἄνθρωπον and not κατ' ἀλήθειαν. The existence of natural goals culminates in a maxim of reflective understanding which can have no objective value: "We men are allowed only this limited formula: we can conceive and understand the finality that must serve as the basis of our knowledge of the internal possibility of many natural things only if we portray nature and the world in general as the product of an intelligent cause." But in that case, the living being, organized and organizing itself, is not grasped as the presence of the concept in nature, nor is finality genuinely understood as the circular process which is a "becoming of the having-become," and which, according to Hegel, we find in the very essence of reason, in the development of the self. In the preface, Hegel expressed his intention, the very movement of the *Phenomenology,* as follows:

What we have said can also be expressed this way: reason is action in accordance with a goal. . . . The result is what the beginning is, because the beginning is the goal. In other words, the actually real is what its concept is only because the immediate as goal contains within itself the self, pure actual reality. The

11. Kant, *Critique of Judgement*, pt. 2, p. 18.

actualized goal, actually real existence, is movement, a development advancing toward its unfolding. This disquiet is the self
(*PE*, I, 20; *PG*, 22; *PM*, 83).

This development of the self, this mediation of the immediate,
is no doubt the fundamental intuition of Hegelianism. A number
of familiar philosophical formulas, some to be found in Aristotle
(the transition from potentiality to action, determined by the
immanence of that action in that potentiality,[12] the explanation
of meaning through an intentional analysis, the development of
a truth which is already possessed in-itself but which becomes
for-itself by negating its immediate form), help us to get a
sense of the conception of the self, the concept, which Hegel
made the cornerstone of his philosophy. In all cases, life and the
living things that are its expression realize in nature the still
immediate form of the concept. Thus we see how the instinct of
reason discovers itself in life. "That instinct rediscovers itself
here, but it fails to recognize itself in what it discovers" (*PE*, I,
218; *PG*, 196; *PM*, 296). The concept of the goal, to which observing reason rises, is present as an actual reality, as the organic in nature. Simultaneously, actual reality is the concept of
which we are cognizant. But observing reason does not attain
itself, because what it sees immediately is only an external relation. The related terms—the living individual and his environment, or organs in their reciprocal relation—are immediately
independent. But their activity has a meaning other than its
meaning for sensuous perception. Here already we see the guile
of reason, of which Hegel will write more profoundly with regard to history. Necessity lies hidden in what is happening;
it reveals itself only at the end. What the organic reaches in
the movement of its activity is itself. There is only an apparent
difference between what it is and what it seeks. "Thus, it is the
concept itself." Self-consciousness is constituted in the same
manner. "Thus, it finds nothing in the observation of organic
nature but this essence; it discovers itself as a thing, as a life"
(*PE*, I, 219; *PG*, 196; *PM*, 297). But, split into consciousness of
the other and self-consciousness, it finds both goal and thing but
fails to see the one in the other. For it, the goal immediately
falls outside the thing and implies an understanding. And since
at the same time the goal is objective, present to self-conscious-

12. Hegel writes, "The immobile which itself is the driving force;
thus, this immobile is subject" (*PE*, I, 20; *PG*, 21; *PM*, 81).

ness as a thing, it eludes self-consciousness' consciousness and appears to it to have its meaning in *another* understanding. Thus, the instinct of reason cannot see reason itself in organic life. This entire development is a critique of Kantianism, which recognizes the reality of goals in nature but separates the end from the real and refers the teleological explanation to an understanding that is not ours. Nature, then, is not apprehended as a first reflection of reason.

> Spirit that is cognizant of itself can recognize itself in nature and return to it. Only this reconciliation of spirit with concept is its true deliverance and redemption. The idea of the philosophy of nature is this liberation of spirit from the yoke of matter and of necessity. The goal of these lectures has been to offer an idea of nature and to oblige that Proteus [spirit] to reveal itself in its genuine form, to rediscover in the whole world the image of ourselves, to show in nature the free reflection of spirit—in a word, to recognize God in his immediate and sensuous existence rather than in the spirit's intimate contemplation.[13]

EXTERIOR AND INTERIOR

OBSERVATION HAS TURNED from inorganic things, which have shown themselves to be moments of a process, terms of a law, to organic being, in which "nature is reflected on itself." This reflection on itself of nature is the existence of the concept, which hitherto was the link among the moments of the law. This is why it grasps genuine necessity in the living being and that necessity offers itself to it as a new object, the concept of goal, or finality. We saw how Kant recognized this finality in living nature but was nonetheless unable to think it through within nature and had to transcend both nature and human understanding in order to realize the concept of a goal. Understanding carries out a projection out of nature through thinking the "as if," but this transcendence is rejected by the new observation, which however maintains Kant's opposition between actual reality and the concept, seeking only to give it a form compatible with its own manner of proceeding. Indeed, observation "seeks the moments in the form of being and of perma-

13. This passage is quoted by Archambaut, *Hegel* (Paris, 1911), p. 27. Cf. Hegel, *Encyclopaedia*, p. 211.

nence, and since organic totality essentially consists in not containing these moments in static form nor allowing them to be found within it, consciousness transforms the opposition into an opposition that conforms to its point of view" (*PE*, I, 222; *PG*, 198; *PM*, 300). Kant separated the concept of goal from actual reality, finality (teleology) from the organism given in nature. Now, in a new attitude of observing reason, one of the terms will appear to observation as the interior and the other as the exterior. Observing reason now seeks a new kind of law, which can be formulated as follows: *the exterior is the expression of the interior.*

It may appear overly scrupulous to follow the development of Hegel's thought here, for his critique is directed at a philosophy of nature that is no longer ours. He lengthily and even ponderously dwells on what he considers the errors of the science of his time, and it is difficult for a contemporary reader to follow him. Yet our task would not be completely fulfilled if we failed to try to explain at least in a general way the significance this critique has for him and to justify, if possible, the space he devoted to it in the *Phenomenology*. Let us once again note the sequence of the objects of observing reason, each of which results from, and condenses, the experience that precedes it. Laws established by understanding as the relation among inorganic matters present their immanent unity in the organic. Grasped as the universal concept, as finality, they are cut off from the concrete activity of the organism. The two terms are then envisaged as two concrete, observable realities, the interior and the exterior. The interior is no longer "a suprasensuous substratum of nature"; it has become observable in its own right. "The interior, as such, must have an exterior being and a figure, just as the exterior as such does. Indeed, the interior itself is an object; it is posed as existing, and as present for observation" (*PE*, I, 223; *PG*, 199; *PM*, 301). The interior is the concept of organic life, given to observing reason. The exterior is that same life in the element of being, as an ensemble of living forms, or as anatomical systems. This external presence of the interior may indeed appear paradoxical, but it results from the attitude of observation, which wishes to find its object as a given object. Let us, then, accept this new opposition and see where it leads.

The interior is the organic concept, but observation, unable to examine it as a concept, fails to grasp it in an adequate form. The interior presents itself in the universal form of the three moments that Kielmeyer and, later, Schelling distinguished in organic being: sensitivity, reactivity, and reproduction. In the *Realphilosophie* of 1803–4 and in that of 1805–6, Hegel especially emphasized these moments. They are the three moments of the concept of organic being, a being which is its own end, and they result from this autofinality. The living being is reflected on itself; it dissolves inorganic being in its universal fluidity. This is the moment of sensitivity, which already heralds the theoretical function. But if the living being were only reflected on itself, it would be dead being and pure passivity. It is also turned toward the other, and that capacity for action, or reaction, is what is called its "reactivity" and what will later be the practical function. These two properties are moments of the concept, and each exists through the other. Their conceptual contraposition is qualitative. The complete organic being (Hegel distinguishes between animal and vegetable here) reflects itself in its action on others and acts in its own reflection. Thus, the dialectical unity of sensitivity and reactivity is reproduction: "Reproduction is the action of the total organism reflected on itself; it is its activity as goal in-itself, or as genus (*Gattung*), an activity in which the individual repels himself away from himself, and either duplicates his organic parts by engendering them, or reproduces the whole individual" (*PE*, I, 224; *PG*, 200; *PM*, 302).

Assimilation (the organic's procedure against the inorganic) and the production of self by self (the procedure of preserving oneself) take on their full meaning only in the movement of generation—a movement essential to life and basic to Hegel's whole philosophy of life. The living individual, as he is presented in the Jena *Realphilosophie*, is the universal in relation to the inorganic elements of which he is the unconscious conception. (He idealizes the elements; he is their negative unity.) He thus poses himself for himself and preserves himself. But that self-preservation is simultaneously universal, and the living individual transcends himself in the process of generation. He is himself through being universal, through being life rather than this or that particular living being. That is why after having assimilated inorganic being the living individual, as infinite idea, behaves toward himself as though he were the other; he splits himself and opposes himself in a diversity that is concretely realized in the diversity of the sexes. "The idea of organic individuality is genus, universality. It is infinitely an other for itself, and in that being-other it is itself. . . . The individual is the idea, and he exists only as the idea. Thus the individual is marked by the contradiction between being the idea and at the same time being something other than the idea." [14] Hence the living individual is an impulse never satisfied. He always goes beyond himself to the suppression of his own determinateness, which culminates in the cycle of generations. In his philosophy of nature, and especially in his philosophy of the organic, Hegel, despite his conceptual ponderousness, sometimes rises to a profound view of life—for example, in this idea of the inseparability of the individual and the genus, or in the idea of illness, according to which the universal is manifested to the living being inside himself in such a way that man is posed as the "sick animal." [15]

But in the *Phenomenology* Hegel is less concerned with a conceptual philosophy of nature than with a critique of the manner in which observing reason takes up the moments of the concept. Instead of being viewed as moments of a dialectic, sensitivity, reactivity, and reproduction are taken as observable general properties whose laws are to be sought. One of these laws results from a comparison between sensitivity and reactivity: according to it, these vary in inverse proportion to each other. Hegel strives at great length to demonstrate the meaninglessness of such a law. Since reactivity and sensitivity are two moments of the concept of the organic, they correspond to each other as do positive and negative numbers, or the two poles of a magnet. Their relation is a qualitative one, and when it is expressed in a quantitative form we reach a tautology and organic being itself is lost sight of.

> The qualitative opposition that is characteristic of them thus enters the realm of magnitude. And then laws come into being such as that according to which sensitivity and reactivity vary inversely in magnitude (as one increases, the other diminishes), or, to formulate it more appropriately, taking magnitude itself as the content, the magnitude of something increases when its smallness diminishes (*PE*, I, 227; *PG*, 203; *PM*, 305).

Hegel's critique here is a critique of the category of quantity and, more specifically, of Schelling's philosophy which, according to Hegel, was unable to think qualitative oppositions and tried to find, in the form of powers and degrees, one and the same absolute intuition in all of reality. Quantity is random

14. *Realphilosophie*, SW, XIX, 130.
15. *Ibid.*, p. 186. "The illness of the animal is the development of spirit."

determination. To express the real quantitatively is to efface qualitative oppositions, to banish the concept in favor of random difference, and hence to stop at homogeneous identity which cannot internally distinguish and oppose itself.

Hegel's conceptual and dialectical philosophy is opposed to a mathematical philosophy of the real—not only in the sense of Newton, but even in that of Schelling, who sacrificed qualitative diversity to the *powers* of absolute intuition. In the preface to the *Phenomenology*, Hegel emphasized the nonconceptual nature of mathematics: "For what is dead and cannot move on its own cannot reach the differentiation of essence, or opposition, the essential disparity. Neither, therefore, can it reach the transition from one position to another, qualitative and immanent movement, automovement. Indeed mathematics considers only magnitude, the inessential difference." Far from wishing to understand nature with the help of differences in magnitude, Hegel sometimes tries to introduce conceptual difference into mathematics itself.

> What splits up space into its dimensions and determines the bond among them and in them is the concept. But mathematics leaves this out of account. For example, it does not consider the relation of line to surface, and when it compares the diameter of a circle to its circumference it comes up against their incommensurability—a genuinely conceptual relation, an infinite which is beyond the grasp of mathematical determination (*PE*, I, 39; *PG*, 38; *PM*, 103–4).

We may be surprised that Hegel's critique is directed not only against Newton (as it is in his thesis on the planetary orbits) but also against Schelling, whose philosophy of nature we generally think of as qualitative. But in fact, Schelling was unable to deal with quality because he had not managed to express it dialectically—or conceptually, which means the same thing for Hegel. He stopped at a fundamental intuition of reason and of nature and failed to conceptualize genuine differences as conceptual differences in nature. Thus, as a philosophy of powers and not of the concept, his philosophy of nature remained a philosophy of random difference, of magnitude. The passages of the *Phenomenology* under discussion here are especially difficult to understand because of the diversity of Hegel's intentions in them. On the one hand, he follows the path that progressively leads observing reason from the observation of inorganic things to the observation of the whole of nature and then to the observation of self-consciousness itself. On the other hand, he shows the imperfect character of observation, which fixes in being that which it observes and reduces becoming to a permanent reality. Hegel also uses this criticism to denounce the errors of a certain philosophy of nature, perhaps even of any philosophy of nature that claims that it can express the absolute adequately in nature.

In fact, laws relating sensitivity and reactivity as distinct terms prove hollow, because those moments are not distinct but are only moments of a concept. Similarly, laws claiming to draw a correspondence between these organic moments of the interior and exterior anatomical systems would also be hollow. We might think of linking sensitivity in general with the nervous system, reactivity with the muscular system, and reproduction with the organs of reproduction, that is, linking organic functions with anatomical organs. But the major organic functions go beyond particular systems and are not delimited in the way that portions of exteriority are: "Given that the organic is in-itself the universal, its essence consists rather in having these moments in an equally universal form in actual reality, that is, in having them as a process imbuing everything, not in giving an image of the universal in an isolated thing" (*PE*, I, 232; *PG*, 207; *PM*, 310). Moreover, anatomy considers only cadavers, not living beings. And it is physiology that allows anatomy to delimit its systems, not the reverse. If we cease to consider organs as parts of a whole we strip them of their specific being, their organic being. Thus, the law that observing reason claimed to have reached— that *the exterior is the expression of the interior*—is shown to be inaccessible by virtue of the very nature of the organic. Organic being does not present distinct aspects which can correspond to each other; each of its parts is caught up in the movement of its resolution. The whole of organic being is movement and transition from one determination to another: it is already concept, not thing. For this reason, the establishment of laws— even of the kind "the exterior expresses the interior"—is no longer possible.

Hegel explains this impossibility at greater length when he again discovers the meaning of law. In establishing these laws, understanding was itself the transition from one determination to another. When it moved from the universal to the specific, from essence to exteriority, it contained movement. But that movement, which is the movement of knowledge, has now become an object for it. What understanding sees in life is the movement of knowledge in its universality. The moments of law are no longer congealed determinations; they change immediately into each other. Organic unity cannot be split up into isolated determinations. For this reason, understanding speaks only of an *expression* of the interior by the exterior, an expression which leaves content unchanged and culminates in a formal distinction, that is, in a distinction without a difference. "Understanding has grasped the very thought of law here, whereas previously it had only sought laws whose moments rose up before it with specific content" (*PE*, I, 233; *PG*, 208; *PM*, 311). In the *Realphilosophie* Hegel wrote, somewhat more obscurely, "Life cannot be conceived on the basis of an other [than it]; it is knowledge itself existing. Knowledge knows itself through itself and not through something else, and we come to know the organic precisely when we know that it is that unity, knowledge existing." [16] The movement of knowledge is itself a life, and life is the existence of knowledge. What observing reason contemplates in the transcendence of law is itself as an object in the form of life.

Yet when observation wishes to discover laws at any cost, it obliterates conceptual differences and returns to random differences, to numerical series. These numerical series—the hierarchy of living beings which, according to Schelling, corresponded to the degree of the development of organic forces— lead us to examine in its own right the exterior of the organic.[17] That exterior is the system of life organizing itself in the element of being. This system gives rise to a multitude of living beings, ranging from the least differentiated to the most fully developed. If previously the interior was the movement of the concept, it is now "the particular interior of the exterior." On the one hand, the living being is for-others, it faces outward; on the other hand, it is reflected on itself. "Actual organic essence is the middle term which connects the being-for-itself of life with the exterior in general, being-in-itself" (*PE*, I, 236; *PG*, 211; *PM*, 315). But this being-for-itself is infinite unity which lacks content and so assumes content in the exterior figure—which appears as the process of that exterior figure. That negative unity is also the substance of all living beings. "This concept, or this pure freedom, is a unique and identical life even though the figure, being-for-another, can sometimes play many different kinds of

16. *Ibid.*, p. 134.
17. Schelling, *SW*, I, 387.

games" (*PE*, I, 237; *PG*, 211; *PM*, 316). There is no necessary connection between this pure life, the substance of the multiplicity of living forms, and the living forms themselves. "The river of life is indifferent to the nature of the wheels that it turns" (*PE*, I, 237; *PG*, 211; *PM*, 316). Hence, the multiplicity of living forms can be related to the unity of life only in a random way. Living beings can be subsumed under life in general by means of numbers.

> Number is the middle term of the figure that joins indeterminate life to the actually real life; it is simple like the first and determinate like the second. What exists in the interior as number must be expressed by the exterior as a multifarious actual reality, as a kind of life, as color, etc., in general, as the total multitude of the differences that develop in manifestation (*PE*, I, 237–38; *PG*, 212; *PM*, 316–17).

Universal life expresses itself in the series of figures only in contingent form. Life, Hegel writes further on, does not have a genuine history. To be sure, Schelling had tried to view the series of living beings as the progressive development of one and the same life. But the quantitative gradation through which a number, a power of life, is held to correspond to differences present in exteriority neglects qualitative phenomena, conceptual differences, which, moreover, cannot adequately be expressed in terms of such an externalized life. The essential point, to which Hegel returns in his final view of nature, is that a philosophy of life cannot be a philosophy of the concept (which negates itself and preserves itself in its development). Only consciousness has a history; only consciousness presents the genus, the concept for-itself. Only the *Phenomenology of Spirit* could be written, not a phenomenology of life, which would only have culminated in random differences. Hegel is condemning a philosophy of life such as Bergson later developed in his *Creative Evolution*, and in opposition to such a philosophy he elaborated, in 1807, a philosophy of consciousness and of spirit. We should note in passing that Hegel cannot be faulted for ignoring empirical sciences; he is interested only in the *meaning* of those sciences, in what they signify for philosophy. In rising to the concept of goal, observing reason had glimpsed the finality in life as the meaning of life. But although this meaning is present in organic vitality, it refers to consciousness, which alone manifests it. Similarly, nature as a whole can present to reason only an inconsistent reflection of itself.

Before gathering all this knowledge about nature into a global view, Hegel returns to inorganic nature. Indeed, observation of the organic as exteriority is itself a return to inorganic nature. In considering inorganic nature, we can try to form a series of bodies according to a continuous gradation. Schelling, for example, had attempted to formulate an ideal genesis of inorganic bodies according to the relation of their specific weight to other properties. But this attempt too was fruitless: "The attempt to find series of bodies which, through a law that related two simply paralleled aspects, would express the essential nature of those bodies must be considered a thought that knows neither its proper task nor the means of carrying it out" (*PE*, I, 242; *PG*, 216; *PM*, 321).

Schelling distinguished specific weight from other properties. Specific weight, weight divided by volume, expresses a certain degree of filling up space. In Kant's philosophy of nature this filling up is envisaged dynamically. Instead of a homogeneous matter with emptinesses that would explain the apparent diversity of things, Kant thought of fullness as a dynamic degree. The specific weight of a body, then, in relation to general gravitation valid for all bodies, would express the being-for-itself of that body, its interiority. But this interiority offers itself up to observation and is one property among others. It is measured and expressed as a number. Thus, one could try to classify bodies according to their specific weight, attempting to draw a correspondence between the essential property that expresses their being-for-itself and the multitude of their other properties. One of these other properties appears to be especially important: cohesiveness, that is, the resistance bodies put up to external modification. If the density of a body constitutes its being-for-itself, its cohesiveness constitutes its being-for-itself in being-other. Density, thus, is analogous to sensitivity and cohesiveness is analogous to reactivity. But unlike living beings, inorganic bodies do not preserve themselves in alteration. Hence, cohesiveness is merely a common property, the degree of a body's resistance to modification. In inorganic being, all these properties are juxtaposed and indifferent to each other. This disconnected multiplicity contradicts the possibility of a genuinely conceptual comparison of bodies. Thus any ideal genesis of bodies according to which their specific weight would correspond to other, multiple and changeable, properties appears impossible (*PE*, I, 241; *PG*, 215; *PM*, 319–20).

Reason in Nature

THUS, INTERIOR AND EXTERIOR present themselves differently in organic and in inorganic being. In the case of inorganic being, the interior is one property among others; in the case of organic being, the interior, being-for-itself, is in-itself universal; it is genus—the unity of being-for-itself and negativity (*PE*, I, 243; *PG*, 216; *PM*, 322). Thus, the organic does not present its being-for-itself, its specificity, in the element of being; yet in that element that specificity is in-itself universal. The living being does not show its essence as an external determination; it transcends all determinations: it is life, that is, universal specificity. Nevertheless, this universal specificity is not developed in life in its own right. It is present in life only in the negative movement that transcends all determinations. Universal life, the genus, is expressed in specific living beings who are genus not for themselves but only *in-itself*. Conversely, although the whole of inorganic nature, envisaged as a whole (earth, zones, climates, and so on), constitutes a universal individual, it lacks living specificity. Caught between these extremes—the genus, which specifies itself in species, and earth, the universal individual which acts on him—the specific individual is only an imperfect expression of life. He is not yet the consciousness which contains all these moments and develops them within himself, not yet the consciousness which alone is universal specificity *for-itself*.

In this manner, life as universal manifests itself either as the interior of the living being, without a means of expression proper to it—as the process of the living being's life which finally negates that being in the uninterrupted production of other living beings—or as a multiplicity of formal species. If the universal preserved its moments within itself and presented them in a dialectical development as the self-transcendence of self, it would be the concrete universal, human consciousness.

But such is not the case with the phenomenon of life. Life is realized outside the genus in distinct species, and this specification culminates in numerical gradations. But these species themselves depend on the terrestrial environment. Earth modifies the organization of living beings, an organization which thus results from a double process: "This activity of the genus becomes a completely limited enterprise to which the genus can give an impulsion only within these powerful [earthly] elements and which, interrrupted everywhere by their unchecked violence, is shot through with gaps and failures" (*PE*, I, 246; *PG*, 219; *PM*, 325). On the one hand, there is the series which the genus tries to establish outside itself in the element of indifferent being, in the form of particular species; on the other, the continuous action of the external environment—and in between, the specific living being, which in-itself is a universal (a unity of being-for-itself and negativity) but which presents that unity only in the movement of its life, in an ever-renewed development, and does not come to be universal, the unity, for its own self. Life has no history: "It dashes immediately from its universal to the specificity of Dasein, and the moments that are united in that actual reality produce development as a contingent movement."

Thus, reason, which seeks to discover itself in nature, manages only to view itself as life in general (*PE*, I, 247; *PG*, 220; *PM*, 326). It finds traces of the concept and beginnings of laws everywhere, "but we always remain at the stage of the intentions of nature" (*PE*, I, 248; *PG*, 220; *PM*, 327). A philosophy of nature (understood as organic life) stops either with the ineffable intuition of life as a whole or with a multiplicity of living beings and of reciprocally external species. Unlike the life of spirit, organic life is not a history that unites specificity and universality in a universal specificity. And for this reason, the instinct of reason which seeks itself in being must move from the observation of organic nature to the observation of human self-consciousness.

3 / The Observation
of Human Individuality

REASON OBSERVES THE WORLD in order to justify the still instinctive conviction that the world expresses it, and thus it is led from object to object. The instinct of reason is the basis of the empirical sciences which are gradually constituted by moving from nature to man. But this empiricism, which gives the "empty mine" [*Mien vide*] a positive content, is vitiated by the attitude it adopts. Reason observes, that is, it immobilizes and congeals the content that it claims to grasp. "Observation is not knowledge itself, and it does not know knowledge. On the contrary, it reverses the nature of knowledge by attributing to it the figure of being" (*PE*, I, 251; *PG*, 223; *PM*, 331). It vainly seeks "an image of the universal in an isolated thing," and it therefore fails to understand both life and thought.

The higher observing reason rises, the more it misses its object. Description and the classification of things correspond to a certain logic of being which is adequate to elementary existents. But the logic of essence and that of the concept transcend observation. We should conceive rather than describe; we should grasp the movement of intelligence in content itself, grasp the production and not the product. But by its very nature, the movement of intelligence eludes observation; observing reason is itself this movement—necessity—when it sets forth laws of nature "the moments of which are simultaneously things and abstractions" (*PE*, I, 249; *PG*, 221; *PM*, 329). But although it is the movement, that movement is not for-it. It itself is the concept of the determinate things that form the terms of the law, but only when it considers organic life does that necessity become for it a specific object.

But in becoming an object, organic life congeals for observation. Its principle becomes that "the exterior expresses the interior," a principle whose hollowness is most clearly evident in the observation of human individuality. In this domain especially, we see that interior and exterior cannot be regarded as two congealed determinations at once identical and distinct. We shall gauge the ambiguity of the verb "to express," which replaces the relation among the various moments of the law, and we shall see that to pose here an interior for-itself and there an exterior equally for-itself is illusory. Hegel denounces the unacceptable consequences of this principle in his discussion of physiognomy and phrenology, two sciences that were much in vogue in his time.

Before dwelling at length on the studies of the expression of human individuality and of the correspondence between the movement of self-consciousness and the shape of the skull, Hegel briefly discusses logic (formal and transcendental) and psychology. He criticizes them severely albeit briefly. We may well be surprised by the purely negative character of this analysis, as well as by its brevity. For there seems to be a disproportion between the lengthy analyses of organic science and of Kielmeyer's law and the no less lengthy analyses of physiognomy and phrenology on the one hand and the very short discussion devoted to the laws of thought and to the observation of active consciousness (psychology) on the other. It has been said that when Hegel was writing this chapter he did not yet know the precise scope of his introduction to speculative philosophy. If the *Phenomenology* had been meant to end with individual reason, with the observation of inorganic and organic nature, it would have led to a speculative logic that would have appeared at the same time as the preface, in which case it would have sufficed, for the purpose of announcing a new logic, to point out the inability of observation to understand reason. "It suffices," Hegel wrote,

> to have indicated in a general way the invalidity of what are called the laws of thought. A more precise argument would pertain to speculative philosophy, in which such laws are seen for what they truly are, that is, as specific vanishing moments, whose truth

is merely the whole of the thinking movement, and is knowledge itself (*PE*, I, 251; *PG*, 223; *PM*, 331).[1]

We can only make plausible conjectures about the process of composing the *Phenomenology*, but it would seem that Hegel progressively became aware of the scope of his introduction to science and that it was perhaps in spite of his original plan that that introduction became a totality of spiritual phenomena and not merely a negative critique that would lead straightway to a logic and to speculative philosophy in general. Be that as it may, Hegel presents his critique of a logic that considers the laws of pure thought or general concepts in isolation and fails to discern in them moments of the unity of thought, as though his own logic were to follow directly and replace the false conception of "pure thought" with a new conception of the logos.[2] Similarly, Hegel's critique of psychology—the study of acting self-consciousness—appears to herald a new philosophy of spirit in which the dialectical development of the faculties of spirit would be considered, rather than these faculties being taken in isolation. "Psychology ought at least to be surprised that so many contingent and heterogeneous things can jointly exist in spirit, as though in a sack, all the more as these things reveal themselves not as inert and dead things but as restless and unstable processes" (*PE*, I, 253; *PG*, 224; *PM*, 332–33).[3]

This chapter seems indeed to suggest that Hegel wished to replace a formal, inorganic logic with his ontological logic and to replace a psychology that remained empirical with a philosophy of spirit (subjective, objective, and absolute). But, caught up in his own argument, he was led to show in the *Phenomenology* itself how individual observing reason becomes practical reason and how individual practical reason becomes meaning-

1. For a discussion of the composition of the *Phenomenology*, see part I, chapter 3, above.

2. Hegel, like Fichte, bases formal logic (the principle of identity) on transcendental logic: "The I poses itself as I; I = I." Hegel's logic is a thought which thinks *itself*. Thus, it has a content: the logos. In the *Phenomenology* Hegel briefly indicates his conception of *form*: "This content is essentially form itself . . . the universal splitting into its pure moments" (*PE*, I, 250; *PG*, 222; *PM*, 330).

3. In the Jena *Realphilosophie*, Hegel tried to present a philosophy of spirit as a development of intuition, memory, imagination, language, etc. This is a matter not of juxtaposed faculties but of a concrete dialectic which expresses the movement of the self.

ful only through a common task which transcends individuality in a community of self-consciousnesses. Thus Hegel moved, almost inevitably, from reason to spirit, developing the introduction to absolute knowledge at considerable length and including in it an entire philosophy of spirit.

The transition from life to self-consciousness effected by observing reason is a crucial transition in Hegel's philosophy. We have already studied this transition with reference to self-consciousness and the genesis of the concept; we returned to it in discussing the impossibility of reason grasping itself in life.[4] Life exists only through the living beings who are examples (*Beispiele*) of universal life. In them, the concept—the genus, or the movement of generation—does not yet exist for itself. Living beings are born, they develop, they reproduce, and they die. And this movement of generation is repeated indefinitely, as monotonous as it is profound. The processes of self-preservation and generation merge, for the specific living being affirms itself at the expense of the universal only by negating every determination, including that thanks to which it itself is a particular form. The specific individual poses himself as a living being by transcending himself and annihilating himself. But this transcendence, which is evident in the case of illness, when one organic element fixes on itself and isolates itself from the total process of life, does not here exist for-itself. Death, instead of being the absolute form of negativity—the negation of the negation rejoining the universal in its authentic specificity—is a natural, and not a spiritual, negation. Only self-consciousness is the "concept existing as concept," the genus as such—the unity of being-for-itself and pure negativity (*PE*, I, 249; *PG*, 221; *PM*, 329).

The genus is presented as "pure thought," but observation is unable to apprehend this unity of universality and specificity, the living truth of form that transcends all its moments by showing their inadequacy and their abstractness. Thus, this negativity of form appears to observing consciousness when it considers acting human individuality, "which is for-itself in such a way that it suppresses [*aufhebt*] being-other and its actual reality is its intuition of itself as the negative" (*PE*, I, 251; *PG*, 223; *PM*, 331).[5]

4. See part III, chapter 1, and part IV, chapter 2, above.
5. The negativity that appears as the "thinking movement" is "the principle of individuality," *being-for-itself*. What reason observes is

But observation stands facing individuality and watches it act. If it limits itself to describing and classifying individual behavior it misses its object, which, in the specific self-consciousness, is always universal spirit.

> To apprehend distinct and concrete individualities in such a way as to describe one man as having an inclination to this and another as having an inclination to that is much less interesting than enumerating the species of insects or mosses. For since these species belong essentially to contingent specification, they allow observation to take them in this specific way and without concept. But to take conscious individuality spiritlessly and as a specific phenomenon in the element of being is to contradict the fact that the essence of human individuality is the universality of spirit (*PE*, I, 253; *PG*, 225; *PM*, 333).

Hence, observation must try to grasp conscious individuality as the expression of universal spirit, that is, as the expression of its world, which is a spiritual world. How does an individuality become what it is, if not by reflecting within itself the social milieu, the religion, the mores of its time and the particular historical situation in which it is placed? On the one hand there is the environment, being-in-itself, and on the other, individuality, being-for-itself. But such a separation is ambiguous: individuality does not mirror the world passively, it transforms it—as Napoleon did, for example. The two moments that observation distinguishes are so closely merged that to explain great men by their environment, as Taine did, is in fact to explain nothing. The world that acts on a determinate individuality is not the world in-itself but the world as it is for that particular individuality. The world that acts on us is already "our world"; we see it through ourselves. And we can come to know an individual's world only if we begin with that individual. We can specify an influence only if we know the person who undergoes it, and thereby determines it. In order to act on an individual, the world must already have particularized itself and it must present itself as the world-of-this-individual. The individual's world can be conceived only by starting with the individual himself. "There is no being-in-itself that can be distinguished from the action of

---

this negativity insofar as it appears in the *action* of an individuality, in its behavior vis-à-vis being-other. This behavior consists in *adapting oneself* to that being-other or *adapting* the being-other *to oneself*. The psychological problem here is that of the relations of an *individuality* to the *world*.

the individual. The individual is what his world is. But the world is what moves the individual." It follows from this that "psychological necessity is a phrase so empty that it is entirely possible that what must have exercised that influence could just as well not have done so" (*PE*, I, 256; *PG*, 226–27; *PM*, 335). Instead of considering being-in-itself and being-for-itself in their separateness, the unity of the two terms, the spiritual world and individuality, must be grasped. Reason is then led to observe individuality no longer as a reflection of the putatively given environment, but as a *concrete whole* in its own right. How can human individuality be observed both in its originality and in its universality? Hegel envisages this problem at length in his discussion of physiognomy and phrenology.

PHYSIOGNOMY AND PHRENOLOGY

WE MAY WELL BE SURPRISED by the length of the discussion Hegel devotes to the pseudo sciences of physiognomy and phrenology. But we must not ignore the importance that their contemporaries attributed to the work of Lavater and of Gall. Lavater had published, in Leipzig in 1775–78, his *Physiognomische Fragmente zur beförderung der menschenkentniss und menschenliebe,* which Lichtenberg soon critcized. Gall had not yet written when Hegel was writing the *Phenomenology,* but he was already known, for he had traveled from city to city in an attempt to spread his doctrine and in the process had given rise to certain scandals. Some time after Hegel, Comte rather uncritically adopted Gall's principal theses. Hegel, by contrast, put forward in 1807 a stringent and judicious critique of these principles, if one a bit ponderous and tedious for our taste. We should note that the problem is more general than we might think at first. What is in question, in fact, is the relation between spiritual individuality and its most immediate expression, the body. In many passages in this chapter Hegel poses the problem of the relation between "body and soul" in an original manner, and it is in this that we are interested. Observation, then, no longer bears on nature in general or on life but on the human individual, the self. It tries to ascertain the laws of the objective knowledge of that individuality. It has been shown that determination of individuality by the environment in general—the physical environment or especially the spiritual environment

—is impossible. Yet this relation between the individual and his human environment had been taken as the basis of "the law of individuality"—though what was important was not so much the environment as the individual's basic disposition to accept or reject this or that influence. The problem Hegel now poses is logically that of the "basic nature" of individuality. Does something of this sort exist, and can the self be reduced to a nature that it has not itself created?[6] We must recall that the attribute of observation presupposes the fixation, the internalization, of what is observed. Thus, observation cannot know action qua action. It only discovers action's manifestation in the element of being. When it considers action, it interprets it as an interiority which must find its expression in a fixed and given product. Ever since the discussion on the observation of life the fundamental theme has remained "the exterior expressing the interior."

Observation here seeks the "visible presence" of "invisible spirit." Now the body is the exterior of individuality on two counts. It expresses the basic nature of the individual, "that which he himself has not made"[7] and that by virtue of which he is a "being-in-itself" with innate aptitudes and functions. It also expresses the being-for-itself of the individual, what he is and does qua acting consciousness. The body is the expression of both the innate and the acquired.

This being, the body of determinate individuality, is the basic characteristic of that individuality, that which it itself has not made. But since at the same time the individual is only what he has made; his body is also the expression of himself as engendered

6. The problem of individuality (*Individualität*), which in the human world represents the concrete form of what in the concept is the moment of specificity (*Einzelheit*), is posed by the following definition: "Individuality is what its world is qua *its* world . . . ; it is only the unity of being as already given and being as constructed, a unity whose aspects are not external to each other" (*PE*, I, 256; *PG*, 227; *PM*, 336). As the negation of negation, specificity must manifest itself at the heart of individuality as the transcendence of all determinations.

7. The phrase is Hegel's (*PE*, I, 257; *PG*, 227; *PM*, 338): "What individuality itself has not made," its primordial nature (dispositions and functions not yet put into play), constitutes the initself of individuality—in the double meaning of "thing" and "power." How can individuality be before it exists? How can there be in it a preexistent given? This, for Hegel, is the fundamental problem of individuality.

by him, as well as a sign that he has not remained an immediate thing. But it is a sign in which the individual offers to knowledge only what he is insofar as he brings his primordial nature into play (*PE*, I, 257; *PG*, 227–28; *PM*, 338).

The opposition between the in-itself and the for-itself is thus transposed at the very heart of individuality to an opposition between its particular nature and the active putting into play of that nature. The body is the total expression of given and acting individuality, *what it is for-others*.

Hegel first shows that strictly speaking the organ qua organ is purely a transition, an action that realizes itself (the hand that works, for example, or the mouth that speaks), and that as transition alone it is not susceptible to being observed. Exteriority then lies in realized action, in speech or in deed, but these acts in turn lie in the element of being. Either the individual recognizes himself absolutely in them, in which case they are only interior (since they are what they are only for the consciousness that posed them in being), or he refuses to recognize himself in them (for they are what they are only as pure exteriority, as givens to other individuals). Thus, observation neglects the accomplished act, which either says too much or too little, and tries to know the individual subject who has accomplished it. At this point, the bodily organs take on new signification: they are not merely the moments of a transition but are also present for the observer; they are being-for-others, and they offer themselves as the middle term between pure interiority and pure exteriority. The hand is the organ of labor, but it can also be considered as presenting within itself the structure of labor, the individual traits that correspond to innate dispositions or acquired habits. Thus we would be able to read the individual's destiny in his hand, knowing a man without needing to consider the entirety of his life as a whole. "The hand is the animated craftsman of his destiny; one can say that it is what man does (*PE*, I, 261; *PG*, 231; *PM*, 343). But one need not stop with the hand. The voice, too, can be studied, as can handwriting, and so on. Such observation of individual interiority in the form of the body leads us directly to Lavater's physiognomy. The organs are considered no longer as channeling action but as facial traits which by themselves accomplish nothing exterior but rather express the individual's opinion about his own action. These traits directly express individuality's reflection on itself. They allow man to be known not insofar as he acts, but insofar as he has an intimate opinion about his action: they are the external trace of the most profound interiority. "Thus the individual is not silent in his external activity and in his relation to it. For he is simultaneously reflected in himself, and he externalizes that reflection. The individual's theoretical activity, or his discourse with himself about his own activity, is also intelligible to others, for that discourse is itself an externalization" (*PE*, I, 263; *PG*, 232–33; *PM*, 344). We can see on a person's face whether he means what he says and does.

Hegel criticizes this physiognomy on two counts. In the first place, he criticizes the contingency of the correspondence between the individuality's intentions and its multiple facial traits. The language of expression can dissimulate as well as convey thought. The interior becomes indeed the "invisible made visible," but it is not necessarily bound to a specific appearance. For convention plays a part in expression, and one can even learn a method of deceiving others.[8]

Hegel's second criticism is more profound, for in addition to physiognomy it condemns a whole conception of individual psychology. In his indiscriminate love for mankind, Lavater claimed to reach the most hidden intentions, those which are not actually realized in action. Thus, observation takes the completed act as an inessential exterior and the subject's own conjecture about his action as the essential interior. "Of the two aspects that practical consciousness includes, intention and action, observation chooses the first as the true interior. That interior putatively has its more or less inessential externalization in the accomplished act and its genuine externalization in its own bodily shape" (*PE*, I, 265; *PG*, 234; *PM*, 346–47). What the readers of *Werther* wanted, and what Lavater provided them with, was a study of sentiment, a study of the individual soul fully reflected on itself and far from any act that might betray it. But does such a psychology have any meaning? The individual makes conjectures about his own actions: he may have an opinion about himself that differs from what he is, if by what he

---

8. "What must be an expression of the interior is simultaneously an expression in the element of being, and it thereby falls back into the determinateness of being, which is absolutely contingent for self-conscious essence" (*PE*, I, 263; *PG*, 233; *PM*, 345). In acting, individuality is its very body. But taken as exteriority, the body remains an ambiguous sign. That is why individuality can "pose its own essence only in its deed," and not in the nonessential features of its face (*PE*, I, 264; *PG*, 234; *PM*, 346).

is we mean what he actually does. And in a natural physiognomy we already spontaneously make conjectures about intentions on the basis of facial movements. Can such a relation of two conjectures give rise to laws, or does it show itself to be as arbitrary as the starting point of such a study? "It is not the criminal, the thief, that is to be known but the capacity to be one" (*PE*, I, 265; *PG*, 235; *PM*, 347). An accomplished act has a universal character: it is a crime, a theft, a good deed. But intentions, the individual's conjectures about himself, are infinitely more subtle —as are all the conjectured details of facial traits. We are no longer in being but in the act of aiming at the "this." A psychology of this kind is forever lost in an infinity of nuances, nuances which are never adequate for stating the interior as such. This conjectured interior is ineffable and inexpressible by its very nature. The pure interior is malleable, infinitely determinable: *it transcends its false indeterminateness only through action.* "This false infinity is annihilated in the accomplished act: [. . .] we can say what an act is. It is a this, and its being is not merely a sign but the thing itself. It is a this and the individual man is what the act is" (*PE*, I, 267; *PG*, 236; *PM*, 349–50). Any other psychology would merely be a psychology of the imagination, engendering subtle and inexhaustible inventions. Similarly, it is in action that man transcends his body, considered as an immobile structure, as the indefinitely interpretable indication of what may or might be. An observation of man that limits itself to this false interior and this immediate exterior negates human reality: that man must recognize and rediscover himself. "To be sure, individuality, entrusting itself to the objective element, accepts being altered or reversed when it becomes a product. But what constitutes the nature of action is that it can be either an actually real being which maintains itself, or merely an intended action which vanishes without leaving a trace" (*PE*, I, 268; *PG*, 237; *PM*, 350).

In criticizing physiognomy as a science, Hegel does not so much deny the resemblance that may exist between expression and the individual soul as attack the claim that one can know man by analyzing his intentions, without respect to deeds and actions. What is wrong is observing reason's practice of isolating exterior and interior, and then claiming that they correspond. But such a correspondence cannot rectify the initial error, which was to pose a pure exterior and a pure interior each distinct in its own right. Qua object, the body is an abstract exteriority; the individual soul, qua inactive subject, reflected far from its action in the world, cannot be grasped. It is indeed the case here that "the interior is immediately the exterior and vice-versa." But observing reason does not suspect that this dialectic exists.

With phrenology, observing reason discovers its error. This false science reveals, better than physiognomy did, the impasse in which observing reason is caught. The skull with its bumps and its depressions is not a sign that expresses conscious individuality; it is a pure thing (*Ding*). Yet in this thing observing reason claims to discover the particular exteriority of spirit. Although the absurdity of physiognomy was not evident to everyone, that of phrenology is manifest. The instinct of reason presents the result of all its research in the form of an infinite judgment: "The reality of spirit is a bone" (*PE*, I, 272 ff.; *PG*, 241 ff.; *PM*, 355 ff.).

Of course, this judgment tries to mask its own absurdity from itself by advancing various pseudoscientific considerations. Cerebral fibers are spoken of; spiritual activity is made to correspond to areas of the brain and these areas are said more or less to act on the cranium. Little thought is needed to see that these explanations are unintelligible. Why should a highly developed spiritual activity express itself in a more extended area of the brain, which in turn determines the shape of the skull?[9] Such quantitative considerations are meaningless. Of course, although forced to abandon the attempt to understand, we do not give up all representations of a relation. Observation needs but consider experience: it notes a connection between a spiritual faculty and a cranial bump in the way that the housewife notes that "it always rains when she does the laundry" (*PE*, I, 277; *PG*, 246; *PM*, 361). In doing so, observation is guided by its instinct, according to which "the exterior must express the interior," and also by analogy to animal skulls—although it is hardly possible for us to put ourselves in the animal's place and judge what psychological being corresponds to the cranial structure we observe (*PE*, I, 279; *PG*, 247; *PM*, 363).

In order to establish this factual correspondence through experience, it is necessary to break down the spirit into ossified faculties, just as the spatially extended skull is broken down into distinct parts. This breaking down, which transforms living spirit into a "sack of faculties," is first of all the result of a psychological analysis specific to a given epoch, an analysis which

9. See Hegel's lengthy analysis of this matter (*PE*, I, 273 ff.; *PG*, 241 ff.; *PM*, 355 ff.).

then claims to justify itself by cerebral localizations which in fact only it has made possible. Observation progressively materializes self-conscious spirit so as to render it adequate to the *caput mortuum* that is to express it. If experience undercuts the relations that have been established on its basis, a new expedient may be used: the individual has dispositions which could have been actualized but which in point of fact had no occasion to manifest themselves. This way of isolating dispositions in order to make them correspond to cranial regions is characteristic of phrenology, and it shows us the end point of observing reason which isolates interior and exterior and ends by making them immediately identical.[10]

"Spirit is a thing." This infinite judgment is paradoxical in that it immediately connects two terms that have nothing in common. Yet it says something that we know, something that observing reason searched for unawares. That reason, or rather that instinct of reason, sought itself in being. It has now found itself. It sees itself as a thing, and moreover, as the most abstract thing, as the thing most lacking in signification. Thus, this judgment has a profound meaning, in contrast to its apparent absurdity. It sets forth the truth of idealism: the identity of thought and being. But this identity must be taken as a concept and not as a portrayal. The instinct of reason, which limits itself to representation, must move on from this infinite judgment to the judgment of reflection, and rise from immediateness to mediation.

We started with self-consciousness which reached the culminating point of its subjectivity in unhappy consciousness but simultaneously strove to alienate that subjectivity and to pose it as being. When accomplished, that alienation manifested itself to us as the certainty of the reason that was sure it would find its own realization in the world. With the moment of phrenology, Hegel leads us to the second stage of that realization. In the first stage, reason existed as consciousness; in the second it exists as self-consciousness. In the first, the category was the immediate unity of being and thought, and this immediate unity is what comes to light in the infinite judgment we have just considered; in the second stage the category has the form of

10. These *dispositions*, which may or may not manifest themselves, are the false conception of *primordial nature* as the being-in-itself of individuality. They correspond precisely to the pure and simple being-in-itself that the *skull* is.

being-for-itself and no longer that of being-in-itself. What this means concretely is that reason refuses to discover itself in being and wishes to pose itself. The object, being, is then determined as a negative term and the aspect of mediation, or negation, predominates. A negative attitude with respect to the world succeeds the positive attitude that characterized the first stage; an active self-consciousness succeeds a contemplative self-consciousness. It is this new moment in the development of the category that Hegel studies next. To be sure, this new moment will be no less partial in its way than was the first, and it is only the concrete unity of these two moments, self-consciousness existing in-and-for-itself, that will genuinely bring reason to fulfillment and will raise it to spirit.[11]

11. Observing reason dealt not with itself but with things; only *for us* did it seek itself in things. Now, what was for-us has become *for-it:* "To itself, it is *itself* the goal of its action, whereas in observation it dealt only with things" (*PE*, I, 285; *PG*, 253; *PM*, 370). The thing now is no more for it than a negation to be negated, for observing reason has become negativity, mediation. Its goal—its project—is itself as pure and simple negation. But the truth of this negativity will be the discovery of a new synthesis.

4 / Active Reason
and Modern Individualism

The Transition from Observing Reason
to Active Reason

THE OPPOSITION between knowledge and action plays a crucial part in Kant's philosophy and in the philosophical systems derived from it. In Kant's work, there is a practical philosophy, which is essentially a philosophy of freedom, and a theoretical philosophy, which is the product of understanding and which leads us to a phenomenal understanding of nature. The *Critique of Judgement* shows both the necessary distinction between the two realms and the need for their synthesis. But the synthesis of the knowing I and the practical I, of nature and liberty, cannot easily be realized. This was the major problem confronting Fichte and Schelling. In Fichte's work, the practical I predominates: it is the infinite effort to pose itself absolutely. The theoretical I merely explains the resistance that liberty must encounter if it is to be self-conscious liberty. The obstacle is nature, and liberty is what is of value.[1] The I, which is essentially a practical I, cannot be assimilated to a thing, to some substratum. Its being, if it is still appropriate to use that term, is not a natural being, a given being; it is production rather than a product; it is infinite negativity. Nature, the not-I, exists merely in order to allow the I to affirm itself by negating that which negates it. For Schelling, by contrast, nature and liberty are reconciled in an intuition of the absolute, an intuition con-

1. By *liberty* we mean the goal of *liberation:* "To be free is nothing; becoming free is all."

ceived on the model of esthetic intuition. We know that from the time of his arrival in Jena Hegel recognized the differences between Fichte's and Schelling's systems and that he, too, tried to conceive a novel synthesis of thought and practice, and of nature and liberty. For Hegel, the model of this synthesis is human history. The life of a free people, collective organization, is the great work of art.[2] Hence, his attempt to present absolute spirit as a social organization, in the manner of Plato's *Republic*. The people is ethical substance, and the people is said to be free when harmony reigns between the whole and the parts, between the general will and individual wills. The "System der Sittlichkeit" (*Sittlichkeit*, which we translate as "ethical order," is contraposed to *Moralität*) and the article on natural law are representations of the human city in which all the moments of spirit are grasped and developed as abstractions in relation to the collective organization. This first philosophy of Hegel's might be called a philosophical anthropology. We can understand the individual only if we link him to the life of the polis of which he is a member. But in the dialectical method specific to Hegel each of the moments of that life is envisaged by itself. In developing each of these moments and seeking out its meaning, we discover its inadequacy and are led to the higher moment that includes it. We rise from "the most humble exigencies of human consciousness" to a representation and a thought of the whole. This whole is an individual people which thinks itself through as a universal spirit and thereby manages to rise above its still specific being. But this elevation of self-knowledge above being and of the act of becoming aware above immediate life creates a cleavage in the beautiful ethical harmony. Thus Hegel, who tried at first to represent the organized human polis as an ideal work of art soaring above history, was gradually led to the history of the world spirit, to the succession of particular peoples each of which represents a moment of universal spirit. As Hegel rose above Schelling's notion of intuition (in which "spirit never turns in on itself") to reflection, to mediation, to the concept, he came more and more to introduce the history and development of the world into his philosophy of spirit. One may say that this

2. The idea of ancient democracy, in which man was a citizen in a city that appeared to him as his conscious deed, was widespread in Hegel's time and, as is well known, it had played an important role in the French Revolution. At the start of his Jena period Hegel did not yet mean by "absolute spirit" spirit's self-knowledge as art, religion, and philosophy (cf. "System der Sittlichkeit").

had already occurred in the 1805–6 *Realphilosophie*. The knowledge that spirit has of itself is more than the existence of that spirit; it is a reflexive reconquest. The modern world, in which "morality" rises above the ethical order and seeks to rediscover it, is more than the ethical world in which the unity of specific and universal was immediately realized. To be sure, reflection, which stands opposed to life and to the beauty of the immediate, is a rending. But this rending is necessary if spirit is to accede to a higher figure. "The greatness of spirit is directly proportional to the magnitude of the opposition from which it returns to itself" (*PE*, I, 282; *PG*, 250; *PM*, 366).

The introduction into the philosophy of spirit of world history, of the concept, and of the act of becoming aware overturns the perspectives of that philosophy. Hegel's thought with regard to the historicity of human life is far from clear, not only in the 1805–6 *Realphilosophie* but even in the *Phenomenology*. "The concept," he wrote in 1805, "is simultaneously an immobile work of art and a world history." [3] The idea of collective organization still floats above history, yet now it is grasped in the movement of the concept, which is defined as the form of mediation. In the *Phenomenology*, spirit is ethical substance, the life of a free people, a life in which each specific consciousness exists insofar as it is recognized by the others, exists, we might say, through its ontological link with the other specific consciousnesses. The life of spirit is only "in the independent actual reality of individuals, the absolute spiritual unity of their essence" (*PE*, I, 290; *PG*, 256; *PM*, 377), and spirit is fully realized only in the organic life of a people. For us, philosophers who witness the development of phenomenal consciousness, the object henceforth is spirit as ethical substance.

But before we pursue the development of the ethical substance from its immediate form to its self-knowledge (which will be expressed in religion), we must consider specific self-consciousness, which, as active reason, as practical I, exists at the heart of this substance, and follow its experiences, which raise it from its isolation to spiritual substance. The gallery of figures presented by the *Phenomenology*—pleasure and necessity, the law of the heart and the delirium of presumption, virtue and the course of the world, and, finally, individuality which in-and-for-itself knows itself to be real—is a representation of specific consciousness, sure of itself, launched into the world in search

3. *Realphilosophie*, SW, XX, 273.

of its own happiness, and learning that its happiness is conceivable only in social organization, in the ethical life. At that moment, specific consciousness discovers what we, philosophers, have already reached: spirit as the reality of the we. All the figures in Hegel's gallery correspond to forms of individualism in his time. We must try to justify their appearance at this moment of the phenomenological development, or at least closely examine the various justifications that Hegel advances.[4]

THE TRANSITION from observing reason to active reason first occurs at the end of the chapter on phrenology. The result that observing reason has reached is paradoxical: it is expressed in the infinite judgment "that the being of spirit is a bone." But this judgment should not surprise us, for at first glance it is not different from the judgment of common consciousness, which attributes being to spirit. "If we ordinarily say of spirit that it is, that it has a being, that it is a thing, a specific entity, we do not thereby mean that we can see it or hold it or stumble against it. But we do make such a statement, and what is said is genuinely expressed in the proposition that the being of spirit is a bone" (*PE*, I, 284; *PG*, 252; *PM*, 369). Further, the judgment of observing reason results from the very attitude of consciousness, which instinctively seeks itself as self in being. When it becomes reason, consciousness is immediately the synthesis of the I and being, and this immediateness is expressed as being. In observing things, organic life, nature, even human individuality, reason seeks immediately to discover the self, not to produce it by means of its own activity. It congeals interior and exterior and makes the exterior the immediate expression of the interior. It should come as no surprise that at the end point of its endeavor observing reason reaches a kind of materialism which formulates "the self as a thing." Besides, this judgment has a profound conceptual significance, all the more profound because representation of it is foolish: if it understood itself, it would be the fulfillment of life. To say that the self is being is to say that it is infinite expanse, that is is wholly posed in objectivity, and that in becoming nature it becomes quasi-external to itself.

But thus far the category has been envisaged only in a one-

4. The difficulty of such a justification is not that the dialectical development from one form to the next can not be conceptualized, but that the series of *concrete figures* borrowed from the age (Faust, Karl Moor, Don Quixote) seems rather strange as a sequence.

sided manner. The synthesis of being and I is not expressed in a single judgment or proposition; it requires mediation or negativity. We must say both that "the I is being" and that "the I is not being." This positive and this negative judgment are both necessary developments of the infinite judgment, the terms of which are mutually incompatible. In this way, the transition from observing reason (which seeks only to find itself as a thing) to active reason (which seeks to produce itself) is effected.

> Thus, the present object is determined as a negative object, but over and against it consciousness is determined as self-consciousness; in other words, the category which in observation traversed the form of being is now posed in the form of being-for-itself. Consciousness no longer seeks to discover itself immediately; it seeks to produce itself by means of its own activity. Whereas in observation it dealt only with things, now it is for its own self the goal of its action (*PE, I, 285; PG, 253; PM, 370*).

If in the preceding stage (observing reason) consciousness thought that it sought things but in fact sought itself, it is now cognizant of its search and is for-itself what it had been only for us. It wishes to make rather than discover itself. Its action, which had been our object, has become its object. Thus, we have moved from theoretical to practical reason, from reason in the element of consciousness to reason in the element of self-consciousness. The details of this transition may appear somewhat artificial. Why, for example, did Hegel use phrenology rather than, say, contemporary French materialism (which he had discussed in "Differenz" [5]) to show that "being is not in fact the truth of spirit"? We must admit that here as elsewhere it is difficult to justify Hegel's particular choices among the various experiences of consciousness. What is important is to note that the transitions have meaning for us, for the philosopher, and that therefore the particular experience—chosen no doubt for its topical value—is less important than the general signification it presents. Hegel himself was fully aware of the difficulties one might have following the twists and turns of his argument, and he felt it necessary repeatedly to offer retrospective justifications and to recapitulate the course of his thought. But so long as we keep to the whole, the thought is clear. Observing reason discovers the self as a being, or a thing presupposed by its endeav-

5. Pp. 96–97.

ors, and it therefore turns away from this positing of self, which is a negation of self, and becomes active reason. Active reason, in turn, is shown to be partial, and we must then envisage a new synthesis: *individuality*, which within itself reconciles the in-itself and the for-itself, and reconciles being and the negation of being in actual action. The truth of this acting individuality is objective spirit; once again we enter a new realm of experience.

Now that we have tried to justify the transition from observation to action, from reason that knows the self as a being to reason that produces itself by means of the negation of that alien being,[6] we must consider the particular experiences Hegel chose to express the steps undertaken by active reason. Let us begin by noting that active reason is still individual. In-itself, it is, to be sure, universal, for it is reason, but it still belongs to an individuality; it is not yet "reason that is itself a world," or reason that is spirit. It is the reason of specific individuality, and it is studied as such in the section of the *Phenomenology* that is called "Reason." "Reason is consciousness' certainty that it is all of reality," but it is not yet truth that has become self-certainty. The world—which henceforth is the appropriate word for reason's object—is its world; it discovers itself in the world or produces itself in it. But reason itself is not yet for its own self the world. Reason, we may say, is subjectively universal but not yet objectively universal; it is not spiritual substance itself. Thus, the reason which belongs to this or that specific self-consciousness rises to its truth only when it is actually realized, and it is actually realized only in the development of *objective spirit.*[7] "Reason becomes spirit when its certainty of being all of reality rises to truth, and when it knows itself to be conscious of itself qua its world and of its world qua

6. This "alien being" is no longer alien in the way that it was at the stage of simple self-consciousness, a stage that has long since been transcended. It is alien only inasmuch as it is immediate, and rational self-consciousness knows that this immediateness is a pure appearance that will be transcended: "It is a certainty for which the immediate in general has the form of something suppressed, so that its objectivity is valid now *only as a superficial layer the interior and the essence of which are self-consciousness itself*" (my emphasis).

7. In the *Phenomenology* Hegel does not use the term "objective spirit"; he uses terms which, in the terminology of the *Phenomenology*, are equivalent to it: "true spirit" and "spiritual substance."

itself" (*PE*, II, 9; *PG*, 313; *PM*, 457). Spirit is reason that is no longer merely subjective certainty but also truth and substance. As we have already pointed out, this ultimate synthesis is present in the human world and in the history of peoples. Thus, the end point of our studies is spirit, and spirit, qua the life of a people, qua ethical organization, is already present for the philosopher who witnesses the experiences of consciousness. For this reason, Hegel asserts the significance of these experiences before describing them and presents us already with the concept of spirit: "In the concept we glimpse the ethical world" (*PE*, I, 289; *PG*, 256; *PM*, 374). We shall follow individual consciousness from its initial impulse to realize itself to its discovery of the concept of spirit. At first, active reason is cognizant of itself only as an individual, and it must produce its reality in the other. But then it rises to universality and thinks spiritual essence. That essence —human deeds, morality, coming to light for consciousness—

is the real substance to the heart of which the preceding formations return as though to their foundation. Thus, the formations are merely specific moments of the development of the basis; they detach themselves and indeed manifest themselves as independent figures. But in fact they have a Dasein and an actual reality only insofar as they are supported by the foundation; and they have their truth only insofar as they are and remain in it (*PE*, I, 289; *PG*, 256; *PM*, 375).

In other words, spirit does not follow the development of active reason in the way that one event follows another. Spirit is already there; it is already given as the basis of all experience. Specific consciousness has only to discover that spirit is the truth of its subjective reason. The individual, who claims to realize himself in the world as being-for-itself, must gain (or regain) his substance, spirit. According to Hegel, specific individuals exist in the midst of the spirit of a people as vanishing magnitudes: they emerge as for-itself, but they are right away submerged in the spirit that constitutes them and that at the same time is their deed. Universal spirit is the milieu in which specific individuals subsist, and it is the product of their activity. There is a reciprocal action here, between the whole and the parts, between universal and specific, which makes for the very life of spirit. But this life must be a self-knowledge; it must reflect back on itself, for in its immediate form it is still a universal spirit in the element of being. What especially interests us in the *Phe-*

nomenology is precisely the movement of knowledge, the reflection outward from immediateness. The ethical life of a
people, the substance of spirit, exists only through self-knowledge. For this reason, the happy condition of immediateness,
ethical harmony, can be considered as both the starting point
and the end point of the development. We can just as well say
that the individual detaches himself from the whole of which
he is a part and shatters that immediateness so as to pose himself for-itself, as that he gains immediateness by engendering
spiritual substance through his own movement: the two representations are equivalent (*PE*, I, 292; *PG*, 258; *PM*, 378). In the
second case we begin with individual practical reason intending
to pose itself in being, to rediscover itself as another self in
"thingness." The individual seeks his happiness and through his
experiences he moves beyond his first, natural impulses: he rises
from specific consciousness to consciousness of himself in other
selves, to spiritual substance. In this vein, Fichte followed the
development of the practical I from its insipid search for a com-
fortable happiness, through the will to power, to the moral will.
"These specific moments have the form of an immediate will or
a natural drive reaching its own satisfaction, which becomes, in
turn, the content of a new drive" (*PE*, I, 295; *PG*, 260; *PM*, 380).
Step by step, individual self-consciousness is led to ethical substance, which then emerges as the truth of the development of
the practical I. But in the first case, on the contrary, ethical
substance is abandoned; the individual cuts the tie that binds
him to the whole and claims to be self-sufficient in setting his
own end. Each moment of substance is then posed as absolute
essence. "Ethical substance is reduced to a predicate which lacks
(the determination of the) self and whose living subjects are
individuals who must fulfill their universality on their own and
provide their own destination [determination]" (*PE*, I, 295; *PG*,
260; *PM*, 380). Such, for example, is the modern individualism
manifested in all the heroes of Romanticism, literary heroes who
expressed a general aspiration of the times. In this case, the experience that specific consciousness enters into culminates in a
reflective reconquest of ethical substance. Consciousness loses
its illusions. It sees that what it had taken as its destination is
worthless; it gains not the immediate substance it has left behind
but the thought of that substance. "Following one way, the goal
that the impulses reach is immediate ethical substance; following the other, the goal is consciousness of that substance and,

properly speaking, consciousness such that it is a knowledge of that substance as its own essence" (*PE*, I, 296; *PG*, 260; *PM*, 381).

We can see that in essential respects the two representations coincide. In one, the practical I is posed in its isolation, and it reaches substance by transcending its impulses; in the other, the I voluntarily splits off from substantive and immediate life and rises to the thought of substance, to morality. In fact, although the first way appears to be more in accord with the law of phenomenological development, Hegel follows the second way, explaining that it is more appropriate to the spirit of the times (*PE*, I, 255; *PG*, 226; *PM*, 335). Individualism must be considered in its various forms: the desire for immediate enjoyment, the heart's protest against the established order, virtue in revolt against the course of the world. In viewing these experiences of specific consciousness, which qua for-itself stands opposed to reality, we rise to the thought of the individualism that overcomes this opposition between its goal and the reality opposed to it, and that in the movement of its activity is in-and-for-itself. In observation, individual reason was in-itself; in its negative activity it is for-itself; it will be in-and-for-itself in the individuality that wishes only to express itself in being. Indeed, in its last figure (virtue), the goal of being-for-itself becomes the in-itself, that is, it is identical to actual reality. From then on, individuality is posed in its activity as in-and-for-itself.

THREE FORMS OF INDIVIDUALISM

a. *Pleasure and necessity*

WE SHALL PURSUE three forms of the development of active self-consciousness. The question is essentially one of the relations of specific individuality to the world order, the latter understood not as nature but as social reality, as the human order. The world is no longer nature, as it was for observing reason; it is now other men. First, specific individuality seeks to pose itself in being and to enjoy its specificity, its uniqueness. Then it transcends that first conception of self and rises to universality.

The two terms that are contraposed are the specific and the universal, individuality for-itself and the universe. Self-consciousness, which is for-itself and which has left knowledge and thought behind it like dim shadows, claims to realize itself immediately. Like Goethe's first Faust (the only one then known), it disdains understanding and science, the supreme gifts granted to men, and gives itself over to "the earth spirit" (*PE*, I, 298; *PG*, 262; *PM*, 384). It wishes to discover itself, and that will is no longer, as it was in the case of observation, unaware of itself and reduced to an instinct; it projects itself as a goal, and thus opposes itself to an objective reality which appears to stand over and against it but which has only a negative value for it. This individuality resembles the abstract self-consciousness that was pure desire and that intended the destruction of the other, which dialectic, as we recall, culminated in domination and servitude. The case now is somewhat different. At this level, self-consciousness is reason. The other now is nothing more for it than an appearance "the interior and the essence of which are self-consciousness itself" (*PE*, I, 288; *PG*, 255; *PM*, 374).

Thus, we take up at a higher level the experiences we have already described with reference to self-consciousness (as we took up again the experiences of consciousness when we discussed observation). These experiences have a different meaning now. Self-consciousness is the category for-itself, which means that it consciously seeks itself in objective being. It knows that in-itself the other is its own selfsameness. It is certain that the discovery of self in the other—a general definition of happiness that is not platitudinous as is the Enlightenment's definition—is possible and even necessary. That self-consciousness is the category for-itself means that it is the developed category. It is no longer the immediate identity of independent being (thingness) and the I, but their mediate identity. At first, I and being stand contraposed to each other as goal and discovered reality. But then they unite beyond that separation, and this mediation is expressed in action.

Before we abandon Hegel's abstract language and show the truly concrete meaning of this experience, let us note the transformation of the other which for a moment appears to oppose self-consciousness. It was at the level of reason that the other became the world (*die Welt*). Self-consciousness, *stricto sensu*, confronts an other, and reason has as its other a world, a world that exists for man, who knows it. But this notion of the world, valid at the level of observing reason, is further transformed at the level of active reason. The world, then, is a spiritual world, what today we would call a "social world." In Hegel's terminology, ethical substance will be revealed to consciousness, or, following the other way of presenting this dialectic, will rise within consciousness to the thought of itself. Human individuality, which seeks its happiness in the world, seeks it in other selves which it wishes to assimilate. The self is for the self, and if thingness appears between them it is because the self is not immediately for the self but is simultaneously thing and being-for-itself, or being-for-others and being-for-itself.[8]

We can now easily follow Hegel's description of the experience of the "individualism of enjoyment." What Hegel has in mind is primarily sensuous love, although this is never made explicit. The pleasure—which simultaneously is a desire for pleasure—that the individuality seeks to actualize is above all the pleasure of rediscovering oneself in another individuality. This Faustian eroticism later opposes its titanism, just as the taste for beautiful moments to be plucked will oppose the demand for unceasing self-transcendence. At this stage, transcendence, the universal, does not yet exist for the specific consciousness, which only desires its unique specificity and claims to pluck it "as one plucks a ripe fruit which offers itself to one's hand" (*PE*, I, 298; *PG*, 263; *PM*, 385). This is a description of the hedonism of every epoch, albeit, to be sure, a refined hedonism. To transcend this hedonism will be the deed of individuality itself, the result of its own experience. And the critique of this hedonism need not come from elsewhere, from a philosopher, for example, who in some way intervenes in the dialectic and judges its value. For specific consciousness itself —which is for-itself only insofar as it has withdrawn into itself and has abandoned the universality of knowledge and of mores —enters into this dialectic and discovers the contradiction between the specific and the universal. That contradiction is for-it, for it is self-consciousness and no longer merely living Dasein. In the realm of life in general the essential moment is the genus, or generation. Living individuality, which, inasmuch as it is individuality, is for-itself, can find itself only in a complementary individuality (a condition that is expressed by sexual

8. The first goal of individuality "is to become self-conscious as a specific essence in the other self-consciousness, to reduce that other to itself." Since self-consciousness is reason, the identity is presupposed in-itself; it is merely the immediate presentation of the other for me, his being-for-others, that must be transcended (*PE*, I, 297; *PG*, 260; *PM*, 381).

difference). Individuality knows itself, in the Biblical sense, in an other. And that other individuality is itself. But the genus, life qua universal, that is expressed in this movement is a continuous "die and become." Living individuality does not genuinely attain itself in the other; it is swallowed up by the other, and another individuality rises up in place of the unity that is never realized *for its own self*. The generations succeed each other: "The growth of children is the death of parents."

We rediscover this movement of the genus, which is life itself, as the universal. But it is for consciousness, although it was not for the living being, which is why self-consciousness in general can survive its own experience and another figure can emerge from this experience as its truth.

Let us consider the experience of the individuality which seeks only its specific enjoyment.

> It reaches its goal, but precisely in reaching it it experiences what the truth of that goal is. It conceives itself as this specific essence existing for-itself. But the actualization of such a goal is the transcendence [*Aufhebung*] of that goal, for self-consciousness becomes an object to itself not as this specific self-consciousness but rather as the unity of itself and the other self-consciousness. It becomes object to itself as suppressed [*aufgehobenes*] specific, or as universal (*PE*, I, 299; *PG*, 263; *PM*, 385–86).

At this stage the universal, to which life ever refers but which it never actualizes, is for man, but in its poorest, barest form—as death, perhaps, but a death at every instant. In all enjoyment, our specificity is abolished as specificity and we die; we consume ourselves at every instant. In voluptuousness we remain desire, and desire aspires to voluptuousness. The annihilative power of the universal is for self-consciousness itself, which experiences it as necessity, or as destiny. We experience the fragility of our specificity, which has posed itself for-itself, and we see it shatter against the universal. "The absolute rigidity of specificity is pulverized when it encounters actual reality, which is not only equally solid, but continuous as well" (*PE*, I, 301; *PG*, 265; *PM*, 387).

The tragedy here is that this necessity, or destiny, appears incomprehensible to man, and that therefore the consequences of his actions remain impenetrable mysteries for him. Man discovers the truth of his experience only in the absurd power that incessantly annihilates him. But he fails to understand that power; he is unable to give it content, to ascribe to it a meaning that would be the meaning of his destiny and in which he would genuinely recognize himself. "This transition of his living being into dead necessity manifests itself to him as an inversion void of mediation" (*PE*, I, 301; *PG*, 265; *PM*, 388). It is the transition from life to death, from voluptuousness to annihilation. It is only enjoyment, the movement of disappearing; it is not thought, in which destiny would be cognizant of itself in the action of consciousness and in which the action of consciousness would recognize itself in its destiny.

This necessity, of which men always complain and against which they always collide, nonetheless is for-them; we can even say that it is the category, emerging from the confined milieu of self-consciousness and exposing itself in the element of exteriority. For-itself, this category was indeed the I as difference (relation and unity). And this is precisely what necessity without content is: the solid connection among these abstractions —which qua abstractions do not exist independent of one another—in such a way that all are posed as soon as one is posed. Thus, man sees himself as the plaything of a necessity that is as barren as his specific desire to enjoy was abstract and limited. Man is annihilated by an inexorable mechanism which continuously recurs through various contents which he has not yet thought through. This contradiction—which is similar to that of the ineffable sensuous "this," which immediately becomes the least determinate universal—is for the consciousness that must assume responsibility for it (since the contradiction *is* for consciousness). But in taking responsibility for it, consciousness transcends that poorest of all figures, active reason; it reflects it within itself and a new figure of consciousness appears in which the universal is immediately bound to desire. Hegel calls this figure "the law of the heart."

b. *The law of the heart and the ravings of presumption*

We have observed the first form of active reason, the pursuit of an unreflecting enjoyment of the world, an experience of pure hedonism which culminated in the feeling of an absurd necessity that annihilates individuality. The figure that succeeds this is richer and more concrete; in it, necessity no longer appears as an inexorable destiny outside self-consciousness. Thanks to reflection, the necessity which was for individuality has moved within individuality, which now knows its desire for happiness as a necessary desire, a desire that has a universal value. Individual self-consciousness is universal for its own self while it is simultaneously a desire to enjoy the world and to discover itself therein. If we assimilate the notion of universality to that of law, an order that in principle is valid for all, we can say that in this new embodiment, self-consciousness has risen above its initial specificity and has included within its desire the very idea of a law. But this relation is immediate, which is why the law which does not yet exist and is only a goal of action is called "the law of the heart." [9]

We might be surprised at this phrase at first. But we should recall that Hegel was thinking of the sentimentalism of his time, of Rousseau, whom he had read throughout his youth, of Goethe's *Werther,* and (as is evident from a number of allusions at the end of the chapter) of Karl Moor in Schiller's *The Robbers,* the *Kraftgénie* of *Sturm und Drang.* To say that law is the law of the heart is to say that individuality's desire, its immediateness, and its naturalness have not yet been overcome, that we must unhesitatingly follow our natural inclinations, that what drives us to pleasure is never bad so long as we have not been perverted by society. The first impulse is always good, which is to say that nature is no longer considered exclusively specific; it is immediately in accord with a universal law which governs all individualities. If each person follows the promptings of his heart, everyone will partake of the immediate joy of living. "What individuality actualizes is itself law; its pleasure is also, therefore, the universal pleasure of every heart" (*PE,* I, 304; *PG,* 267; *PM,* 392). How can we not think of Rousseau here?

Nonetheless, the law of the heart is not actualized. It is for-itself in consciousness, as the immediate union of law and desire. We might say that it is an intention which must test itself through contact with a reality other than itself. That reality is the contrary of what is to be realized, that is, it is the separation between law and heart, their living contradiction. The world that self-consciousness now contemplates is, as we have seen, one in which a meaningless necessity crushes individualities that avidly desire to enjoy their specificity. This world confronts self-consciousness, and self-consciousness does not

9. It is a "natural order," but it is universal, and opposed to the "ruling order," which then is viewed as an unfounded appearance. It is important to note here that in this second figure the universal has passed over into self-consciousness rather than remaining external to it.

know that it is a product of this world. It therefore discovers that in this world law is arbitrarily separated from the individual heart. Hence, the order that rules this world is only an apparent order, "an order of constraint and violence which contradicts the law of the heart" (*PE*, I, 303; *PG*, 267; *PM*, 391), and which is borne by a suffering humanity groaning beneath its yoke. The individualism of Rousseau and, later, Romantic individualism are the heart's protest against this violence directed at human individuality. Man must be freed—which does not entail setting men in opposition to each other but, on the contrary, reconciling them. For my good is the good of humanity and, considered in its immediate relation to my intention, it presents only "the excellence of my own essence," the purity of my heart (*PE*, I, 304; *PG*, 267; *PM*, 392). Man must also be reconciled with himself. In this visible world where the heart's desire is separated from order, I am incessantly in conflict with myself. *Either* I resign myself to obeying an alien order and live deprived of self-enjoyment, absent from my acts, *or* I violate that order and find myself deprived of the consciousness of my own excellence. Thus, this "human and divine order" (*PE*, I, 305; *PG*, 268; *PM*, 393) is an illusory order, and the individual must replace it with the order of his heart: the law of the heart must be realized in the world.

But the experience that individuality has entered into at this stage of its development is, once again, deceptive. How can the law of the heart, valid only insofar as it is bound up with a specific heart, be realized? No sooner is it actualized than it escapes the particular heart that gave it life. "Precisely through being actualized, the law of the heart ceases to be a law of the heart; it takes on the form of being and it becomes a universal power to which the particular heart is indifferent. Once the individual establishes his own order, he can no longer recognize it as his own" (*PE*, I, 305; *PG*, 268; *PM*, 393). This divergence between the original aim of the heart and actual action in the universal element of being expresses the tragedy of human action. "Thus, the individual has taken leave of himself; he grows for himself as universality and he purifies himself of specificity" (*PE*, I, 305; *PG*, 269; *PM*, 394). His action is both his own and external to him. He fails to recognize the purity of his intention in it, and yet he cannot completely disown it. For in wishing to act he agrees to make reality his goal and he demands that the realization be tested out. "The individual has in fact recognized actual universal reality, for to act means to pose one's essence as a free actual reality, that is, to recognize actual reality as one's essence" (*PE*, I, 306; *PG*, 269; *PM*, 394). Hegel makes this point many times in the *Phenomenology,* with reference to the "moral world view" and the "beautiful soul": we do not have the right to refuse to recognize ourselves in reality, for we have wished to act; we have made the actuality of the goal the very goal of our action.

Thus, when it realizes itself, the law of the heart experiences the same failure as that experienced by specific desire when it sought only its own enjoyment of the world. But the later experience is fuller and more concrete. In realizing the law of my heart I become aware of my opposition to the laws of other hearts, or rather, since I cannot deny the universality of law, I find the hearts of other men abominable and detestable. Schiller's Karl Moor, for example, becomes indignant and calls men "a hypocritical race of crocodiles." In realizing myself as an individuality that wishes to be universal, I take note of myself as a stranger to myself, engaged in a sequence of actions that are both mine and not mine. I am *alienated* from myself. But I then discover that the human and divine order, about which I complained that it was a meaningless necessity, is the expression of universal individuality, or of the interplay of individualities exposing—each in turn and each to the others—the content of their own hearts, each claiming universality. What I am faced with is myself. The social order is my deed, though it is no longer consonant with my heart. "What this actualization means is that qua universal, individuality becomes an object to itself, but an object in which it fails to recognize itself" (*PE*, I, 307; *PG*, 270; *PM*, 395).[10]

The truth of this dialectic is the contradiction that harrows self-consciousness and tears it apart. Self-consciousness affirmed the law of its heart as alone genuinely real and essential, and it believed the ruling order to be merely an appearance. It now discovers that since it itself acts, that order is also its own essence and its own deed. In this consciousness essence is immediately nonessence and nonessence is immediately essence. This contradiction is, properly speaking, the madness in which

---

10. We should note that universal individuality "is the result of an interplay of individualities, each laying bare the content of its own heart"; it is "necessity enlivened by individuality." "Human and divine order" is an allusion to the order of the family and the order of the city. Cf. *PE*, II, 15; *PG*, 317; *PM*, 462.

consciousness is submerged insofar as it experiences itself as a contradiction. Madness is not due to the fact that what is essential or real for consciousness in general is inessential or unreal for a particular consciousness. Consciousness in general always subsists in human madness, and hence the madman is simultaneously cognizant of both the reality and the unreality of his object. The consciousness of reality and the consciousness of unreality are not split apart from each other; it is in its innermost self that consciousness is upset.

But consciousness still escapes this contradiction, or at least tries to, by casting out of itself the perversion that lies within it: here we have *the ravings of presumption*. In order to save itself from destruction, it denounces its perversion as an other than itself. It views that perversion as the deed of individualities, but of contingent individualities which, according to it, have introduced this ill into a humanity that was naturally good. "Fanatical priests and corrupt despots aided by their ministers, who seek to avenge their own humiliation by humiliating and oppressing others, are considered to have invented the perversion of the law of the heart that is exercised to the unspeakable misfortune of a deceived humanity" (*PE*, I, 309; *PG*, 272; *PM*, 397). Hegel is specifically thinking of Schiller's Karl Moor here, the apostle who becomes a bandit chief and discovers at the moment of his fall that "it is mad to wish to make the world more beautiful through crime, or to maintain law through anarchy," and, before the astonished bandits, surrenders to the forces of law. At the same time, these priests and despots are considered the authors of the human misfortune that all revolutionaries of the time denounced. But how can a contingent individuality invent an order and be able externally to impose it on humanity? What a puerile fancy, what a barren explanation! To be sure, the social order is the work of individuality, but not of a particular individuality: it is the immediate result of the *interplay* of individualities.

Let us consider this order, which is the truth of the whole dialectic we have just followed. As mad consciousness declared, it is the law of all hearts, and it is also a perverse order. But, in a different light, it is a stable and universal order, since it is the law of all hearts. It demonstrates that it is a valid law—that it has been exposed to the light of day and has undergone the test of reality—in the resistance that a particular heart encounters when it attempts to actualize itself.

Subsisting laws are protected against the law of a single individual because they are not an unconscious, empty, dead necessity, they are a spiritual universality, a substance in which those in whom that substance has its actual reality live as individuals and are cognizant of themselves. Thus, even if they lament and complain that the universal order conflicts with their inner law, even if they assert their heart's desire over and against that order, in their heart they are in fact attached to that order as their essence. If that order were taken from them or if they excluded themselves from it, they would lose everything (*PE*, I, 310; *PG*, 273; *PM*, 398).

Nevertheless, despite the reality in-itself of the order, it is a perverse order. For it is actualized only through individuality, which is its form. It results from a conflict of each against all, an "interplay of individualities" each of which seeks to assert its wishes and collides with the wishes of others. What appears as public order and valid law is in fact "the way of the world." It is the appearance of a regular and consistent functioning, but only an appearance. For its content is rather the "nonessential interplay of the consolidation of singularities and of their mutual dissolution" (*PE*, I, 311; *PG*, 273; *PM*, 399).

Thus, *in-itself* the order is universal, but in its development or its *manifestation* it is the interplay of uneasy, ever-changing individualities. Just as for understanding the unstable phenomenon stood over and against the in-itself before it became the expression of the in-itself, so now for the new figure of consciousness which emerged from that experience the universal order, insofar as it is in-itself, is contraposed to the inconsistent interplay of individualities. To realize the truth of this in-itself is simply to set aside the individuality that perverts it. The new figure, then, is virtue, the consciousness that wishes to annihilate individual egoisms in order to allow the order to appear as it is in its truth: virtue takes up arms against the way of the world. We have seen how self-consciousness encounters, standing over and against it as its truth and its universal, ever higher and ever more concrete forms. At first, self-consciousness confronted necessity; now it confronts the way of the world, the interplay of egos which through the reciprocity of their interchanges and the elaboration of their actions produce this manifestation of the universal. "That in which consciousness failed to recognize itself was no longer dead necessity but a necessity embued with life by universal individuality" (*PE*, I, 307; *PG*, 270; *PM*, 395).

c. *Virtue and the way of the world*

The "knight of virtue" whom Hegel presents in satirical form reminds us of Don Quixote and of all romantic reformers who in their heads overturn the world but prove incapable of anything except speeches—ideologues, denounced by Napoleon, and so prevalent in Hegel's time. Perhaps Hegel recalled the time he himself enthusiastically wrote to Schelling about Kant's *Sollen*, describing it as alone capable of awakening slumbering spirits and leading them out of bourgeois conformism. The virtue in question is not Greek or Roman virtue, the "solid content [of which] was in the substance of the people" and which did not pursue a nonexistent good or revolt against the way of the world on principle. It is a virtue void of essence, externalizing itself only in pompous and hollow speeches.

> Such ideal essences, such ideal goals crumble like empty phrases which excite the heart and leave reason empty . . . ; these declamations express, in their determinateness, only this content: the individual who claims to act for such noble goals and who speaks such fine phrases is valid in his own eyes as an excellent being. He puffs himself up, swelling his own head and other people's but attaining only an empty bloatedness (*PE*, I, 319; *PG*, 280; *PM*, 409).

We can see from these quotations the burden of Hegel's critique of such virtue which has departed from ethical substance and asserts itself against the way of the world. Hegel's realism, which later reappears in his critique of a "moral world view," stands opposed to the unrestrained idealism of these utopians (*Weltbesserer*). This kind of virtue vainly struggles against the way of the world and finally discovers that it is not as bad as it had claimed. It errs in always contraposing the ideal and the real in such a way that the ideal can never be actualized and, consequently, it never goes beyond speeches.

Virtuous consciousness distinguishes between the in-itself of the world's course (the universal, in which "it believes") and the actual reality of that course (in which the universal is realized in an imperfect figure). This realization is the result of individuality, whose perversity we have seen in the last two chapters.

What was then for-us is now for virtuous consciousness, which fails to recognize in individuality its own origin. Virtuous consciousness sees specific individuality pursue its own enjoyment in the world and shatter against brutal necessity. It also sees individuality expose the law of its heart to the world and encounter a general resistance from other individualities such that although the universal is, to be sure, realized in the process, it is realized in a distorted way. It appears in the "phenomenon" of the way of the world as the law of nature, but in a perverted way. Only the negativity of this universal, not its positivity, shows through in the way of the world. In its actual reality, the way of the world pertains to individualities—their specific enjoyment and their mutual conflicts. Virtue proposes to "pervert once again the already perverted way of the world" (*PE*, I, 314; *PG*, 276; *PM*, 404). For it has discovered the source of the ill. The way of the world is corrupted by its being-for-itself, individuality. Thus, virtue denounces human egoism and brings forward the language of the preceding form of consciousness on this point. But it adds the idea of a complete sacrifice of individuality. Virtuous consciousness contraposes law (which is the universal, in the positive sense) and individuality. Rather than immediately uniting them, as the law of the heart did, it distinguishes them by essence. For this reason, virtuous consciousness thinks that by destroying individuality within itself it transforms the real order. Inversely, in the way of the world, law is inessential and individuality becomes dominant. It subjugates the good and the true, which are in-itself, and transforms them from interiority to exteriority. Thus, law and individuality are moments common to both virtue and the way of the world. Although their respective positions are reversed their common presence in both prevents virtue and the way of the world from being completely separable. Virtue itself inheres in the way of the world, from which it is unable to disengage itself completely, and the way of the world inheres in virtue, as the vicissitudes of their struggle will demonstrate.

For virtue, the good, the universal, is in-itself. It is virtue's goal, and it has not yet been actualized. Virtue can only believe in its ideal; this faith is a consciousness of a nonpresence. Yet virtue knows—and this is the meaning of its faith—that to say that the universal is in-itself is to assert that it constitutes the *interior* of the way of the world, and that it cannot fail to triumph. Virtue postulates a primal unity of its goal and the essence of the world's course, while admitting that in phenomenal presence they are separate. Thus, its struggle against the way of the world is in fact a sham. And virtue itself is unable to take the struggle seriously. For its major argument, the snare in which it tries to catch its opponent, is precisely the belief that although for-itself the way of the world is not good, it is good in-itself, and that it must necessarily become for-itself what it is in-itself. Virtue distinguishes the in-itself from being, the basis of things from their manifestation. But in the last analysis this distinction is merely verbal, for if the in-itself is not for-an-other it is a pure and simple abstraction. What does not manifest itself does not exist. The essence of essence is to manifest itself—and the essence of manifestation is to manifest essence.[11]

This distinction between the in-itself and being-for-an-other vanishes in the course of the struggle between virtue and the way of the world. Virtue appears to the way of the world as a potentiality that has not yet come into play. It consists of "talents, abilities, strengths" which are put to good use by virtue but misused by the way of the world. These nonactualized dispositions make up "a passive instrument which, governed by the hand of free individuality, is completely indifferent to the use to which it is put; it is lifeless matter with no independence of its own, and it can be misused in the production of an actual reality that entails its destruction; it can be formed and bent in any way, even to its own degeneration" (PE, I, 315; PG, 277; PM, 405). In the course of the struggle these dispositions, which otherwise remain "somewhere in the rear, as a slumbering consciousness," become actual in fact. Owing to acting individuality, they are transformed from in-itself to actual realities for consciousness. In its struggle, virtue discovers them everywhere, already *actualized* in various figures:

> Virtuous consciousness takes up arms against the way of the world as against something that stands opposed to the good. But what the way of the world presents to consciousness in the struggle is the universal, not merely as abstract universal but as the universal brought to life by individuality and existing for-an-other, i.e., the good actually real. Thus, wherever virtue encounters the

11. Here we can clearly see the meaning of this whole dialectical development. The two terms that were opposed in acting reason (inner and outer, the in-itself and being-for-others) are identified in *action*, which is actual reality. There is not a goal (the negation of the other) and an other (an appearance to be negated); the movement of individuality is the union of the two.

way of the world it is in contact with positions that are the essence of the good itself—the good which as the in-itself of the way of the world is inextricably enmeshed in all the manifestations of the way of the world, and whose Dasein is the actual reality of that way (*PE*, I, 316; *PG*, 278; *PM*, 406–7).

Thus, either virtue is in, and inextricably linked with, the way of the world, in which case the good that it proposes is an already existing good, a good that inheres in ethical substance, or it separates itself from the way of the world and asserts a distinction which can only be verbal. Virtue is a faith which can lead to no genuine presence. Thus, the struggle between virtue and the way of the world manifests the concrete identity of the adversaries. This is so because Hegel poses virtue in the form of "talents, abilities, strengths" which can be actual only by dint of individuality. Similarly, in the chapter on the "moral world view," we shall see that the great man, the man who, like Caesar or Napoleon, makes history, is an actualization of the universal. To be sure, the consciousness of the "valet of morality" can explain the great man's actions by petty and low motives; these motives play a part in the action inasmuch as the action is the action of a particular man. But this is only a partial explanation. "The great man is what he has done, and we must say that he has willed what he has done and has done what he has willed." The so-called virtuous consciousness errs in showing such action in an unfavorable light, and in so doing it reveals its own pettiness. Moreover, although it fails, in judging, to act, it wishes to pass off its inactive judgment as an act.

At the end point of its experience, virtue discovers that the opposition it had set up between individuality for-itself (which would be the phenomenon) and the in-itself of the good and the true is invalid. The in-itself is realized for consciousness through the action of individuality and, therefore, is inseparable from its manifestation. Hegel made things easy for himself by posing the in-itself as a disposition, a potentiality distinct from its actualization. There are no dispositions apart from the acts that give them concrete signification—unless we are merely speaking of an abstraction and the consciousness of virtue based on an abstraction which is void of reality. The way of the world is not as bad as it seemed, since it is the realization of a virtue which without it would slumber forever in some nether region. The way of the world and virtue are no longer contraposed as they were at the beginning of this dialectic due to the arbitrary disjunction of the in-itself and the for-an-other by a consciousness of virtue which talks instead of acting and believes rather than actualizes.

But if virtue vanishes into the way of the world, the way of the world, conversely, can no longer be thought as a being-for-itself that is distinct from being-in-itself. Virtue and the individuality of the way of the world share a false view of human action. Individuality may fancy that it acts egoistically, and may explain all individual actions with reference to conscious egoisms. But it only proves thereby that it is ignorant of the true nature of action. When I act, even if I subtly explain my action by egoistic considerations, I transcend myself, and I actualize potentialities of which I was unaware. Thanks to my act, what was in-itself becomes actual. I imagine myself to be limited to my own individuality, but in fact I more or less embody a universal that transcends me. I am not only for-itself; I am also in-itself. Virtue was mistaken in distinguishing the in-itself from the for-itself. And the individuality of the way of the world was equally wrong in distinguishing them and claiming to subdue the good and the true. The meaning of this whole dialectic is expressed in a proposition which already sets forth the concrete universal: "The movement of individuality is the reality of the universal" (PE, I, 320; PG, 281; PM, 411). Human action in the world transcends individual man, who thinks that he acts for himself. But transcendence is possible only through individual men. We must think through the unity of individuality, which in its action is simultaneously in-itself and for-itself. This action is the development of the universal, which is inseparable from its manifestation.

> Because its principle was individuality, the way of the world necessarily perverted the good, but individuality is the principle of actual reality. Indeed, it is thanks to this consciousness that what is in-itself is also for-an-other. The way of the world perverts and upends the immutable. But in actual fact it reverses and upends it from the nothingness of abstraction to the being of reality (PE, I, 318; PG, 280; PM, 409).

At this point we reach a new concrete synthesis, the actual action of individuality (an action that is no longer merely for-itself vis-à-vis a being-in-itself and that no longer contraposes its goal to actual reality): an action that is simultaneously in-itself and for-itself. Observing reason was a (solely contemplative) universal consciousness that instinctively sought itself in reality; its truth is that reality has *meaning* only for man, who is for-itself. Henceforth, meaning is separated from that of which it is the meaning, and human individuality is posed as active reason. It projects its meaning as a goal outside the reality that it negates. This individual consciousness is specific, and it stands opposed to the universe. But this opposition in turn does not hold up. Human individuality is not cut off from reality; it is itself the reality that creates itself, the synthesis fulfilled in action. We shall now consider this action of individuality in-and-for-itself, action in which goal and reality stand contraposed only at one moment and then come together in a development. We approach the substance of spirit, or the thought of that substance, which in turn is revealed as subject. The dialectical development we have just studied is interesting in that it allows us the better to understand "Hegelian realism." Any idealism of the *Sollen*, any separation of idea from actual reality, must be set aside—from which it does not follow that a reality without meaning replaces an ideal without reality. Rather, what must be thought through is that "the idea seeks reality, and reality seeks the idea," and only the development of man in his actual action is concrete.[12]

12. The three experiences that we have considered can be summarized as follows: Individuality began by contraposing the *for-itself*, as a *goal*, to the *in-itself*, the given reality. This *for-itself* grew progressively richer, and in the last experience (that of virtue) the *in-itself* became the *goal*. But at that point the *goal* rejoins *given reality* and the distinction between them becomes a mere abstraction. We return to actual reality, but to actual reality as *action*.

5 / Human Works and the Dialectic of Action

AFTER CONSIDERING the individuality that is in revolt against the way of the world because the world opposes its ideal—whether that ideal is the immediate enjoyment of the world, or the law of the heart, or virtue—Hegel considers individuality that is "real in-and-for-itself." For this individuality, reality is not a resistance to be overcome, for it is directly in the midst of the world and it wishes only to express itself. Its goal is not the negation of the real world: it is itself a part of the world, and, conversely, the world is the world of individuality. Thus, what is essential is to act for the sake of acting; to manifest on the outside, in the pure element of exteriority, what the individuality already is within itself, its *basic and determinate nature.* Insofar as individuality is this basic nature, it is in-itself; insofar as it expresses it, or carries it "from within to without, from the not-seen to the seen" (*PE*, I, 324; *PG*, 284; *PM*, 416), it is for-itself. Its existence as an act is only the actualization of its essence. The objective world and conscious individuality are now conjoined in one reality. This reality is the deed (*Tat*). "Action is in its own right its own truth and actual reality. For it, the presentation and expression of individuality is in-and-for-itself the goal" (*PE*, I, 323; *PG*, 284; *PM*, 415).

The concept of action has become essential, and it is now our object. With the concrete action of individuality we shall see the unity of subjectivity and objectivity, of observing reason and active reason, come into being. Hence, Hegel's title for this chapter, "Individuality That Is Real In-and-for-itself." By studying this transitional chapter between reason and spirit and noting the new signification that the world takes on for self-consciousness, we can discover one meaning of Hegel's work. But before we elucidate the dialectic that the *Phenomenology* presents at this point, let us indicate several of the concrete significations of this chapter.

Emile Brehier correctly notes that "after considering the heroes of Romanticism, Hegel turns his attention to specialists, teachers, and artists, who ascribe absolute value to their work,"[1] "a spiritual animal kingdom," in Hegel's graphic phrase. Each individuality begins by limiting itself to a self-enclosed task, wishing only to express its nature. Then, when it rises above its transitory and limited work, it justifies itself in its own eyes and to others by claiming that in a modest way it has contributed to a more general cause, to a universal task. But that task is still conceived in abstract form, and the more limited and partial the actual work is, the more abstract that form is. This general justification—the artist labors for the beauty of art, intellectuals advance science by their patient and scholarly research—is properly speaking the honesty of consciousness, an honesty which, as we shall see, is in fact quite deceptive. The thing itself (*die Sache selbst*), which is actuality for the self-consciousness of individuality, is only a very general predicate applicable in turn to each particular moment of action. But this "thing itself," conceived as the action of everyone and of each one, becomes the new subject of experience, first as spiritual essence and then as concrete spirit.

In order to justify Hegel's name for one of this chapter's major developments—the spiritual animal kingdom (*das geistige Tierreich*) (*PE*, I, 324; *PG*, 285; *PM*, 419)—we began by noting the first concrete interpretation it presents. But we must not neglect the very general dialectical interpretation of this moment of phenomenological experience. For more than any other, it casts light on the orientation of Hegel's thought. In reason in general we saw a mode of self-consciousness which tried to adopt a positive stance toward being (the in-itself in general) instead of standing opposed to it. Being is then no longer a thing-in-itself, a pure being-other, but has become the world, where individuality (the form in which self-consciousness presents itself) seeks itself unknowingly. It discovers itself, to be sure, but in the form of a determinate, static being which is the opposite of its ontological disquiet. Hence, self-conscious individ-

1. Emile Brehier, *Histoire générale de la philosophie* (Paris, 1926), II, 742 ff.

uality again stands contraposed to the being-in-itself of the world. The for-itself of reason succeeds its in-itself; projects succeed being. But we saw in the last development of acting reason —the knight errant who sought to enthrone virtue in the way of the world—that this opposition no longer holds. The goal that self-consciousness pursues is verbally opposed to the given reality. The in-itself of the way of the world, which is the same thing as virtue's ideal, does not differ from being-for-an-other, or the discovered actual reality. This in-itself changes from potentiality to action in its manifestation; the way of the world is merely the in-itself realized. Thus, goal and being-in-itself are shown to be the same as being-for-an-other and discovered actual reality (*PE*, I, 322; *PG*, 283; *PM*, 414–15).

In concrete terms we may say that the opposition between active reason's ideal and the objective world no longer holds. The objective world, which appears as being-for-an-other, is the very world of acting individuality. Being-in-itself, that is, the universal, and being-for-itself, that is, individuality, interpenetrate each other closely. The talents, abilities, and strengths that were potential in the way of the world are realized through the efficacy of acting individuality. The concept of conscious individuality that we had at the beginning of the section on reason —the complete fusion of being and self (the in-itself in the for-itself)—then appears. The acting self is simultaneously being and self; it is *the category that has become conscious of itself*. We have seen the category develop in the element of being (in which it was observing reason) and then in the element of the self (in which it was acting reason). Now, these two moments of the category unite dialectically: human individuality is the self-conscious category. There is no objective being here that can be contraposed to the self, no self that stands opposed to being and is for-itself without being in-itself: "the self is being and being is the self." "The object of self-consciousness is the pure category; self-consciousness is the category become conscious of itself" (*PE*, I, 323; *PG*, 284; *PM*, 415). What the observation of human individuality was not able to bring to light completely (because it was only observation) is realized at this stage of the dialectic.

Individuality is what its world, inasmuch as it is *its* world, is. It is itself the bounds of its own action, the bounds in which it has presented itself as an actual reality. It is only the unity of being as already given and being that is constructed, a unity whose aspects are not external to each other, as was the case in the representation of psychological law—one aspect being the world in-itself as present, and the other individuality for-itself (*PE*, I, 256; *PG*, 227; *PM*, 336).

There is not a world in-itself and an individuality for-itself; the world is the world of individuality, and individuality is the meaning and the expression of the world. Being-other and self cannot be separated so as to be compared. In its truth, self-consciousness is what remains self in its being-other, what discovers and produces itself through the mediation of that otherness.

At the level of consciousness—in the strict sense—there really was a being-in-itself. At the level of self-consciousness, that in-itself was elaborated in the master-slave dialectic by a human consciousness that was able to rediscover itself in it. At the stage of reason, the in-itself finally becomes the world (*die Welt*)—a far more concrete term which is meaningful only in reference to self-consciousness rediscovering itself therein. But this world does not yet genuinely appear as the *work* of self-consciousness. This is why we had to consider first the presence of the self in the world as an inauthentic presence, as a presence in-itself, so to speak, and then the opposition between the self and the world that, insofar as it is a superficial stratum of reality, has become being-for-an-other. Finally, as active individuality, individuality became the unity of for-itself and in-itself. In this moment, action is the essence both of individuality and of reality. Action is the concrete whole; we must act for the sake of acting. "Since individuality itself is actual reality, the matter of action and the goal of action lie within action itself. Thus action appears as a circle which moves on its own, freely and in a vacuum; without encountering any obstacle, it grows at times and shrinks at times, and, perfectly satisfied, frolics by, and with, itself" (*PE*, I, 323; *PG*, 284; *PM*, 415).

At the end of this chapter reality will appear as the work of self-consciousness, but of a universal self-consciousness which transcends individuality. This work of all and of each, this world engendered by self-consciousness, in which the notion of an opaque and impenetrable thing (*Ding*) will vanish and be replaced by a new notion of objectivity (*Sache*) corresponding to the Greek πρᾶγμα, will open for us the "world of realized reason," spirit. What remains to be transcended if spirit is to be reached is the individuality that is *right* but is not *reason*. But as we observed in the dialectic of desire and in that of the master and slave, this individuality is meaningful only because it reflects itself and rediscovers itself in other individualities. When the world of individuality becomes a we (an I that is a we and a we that is an I), when mediation among consciousnesses becomes actual, then the work will be the work of all and of each. Objective reality as a thing would be dissolved in a new reality, in spiritual essence. In this manner, an idealism (which, although its intentions are quite different, resembles Kant's idealism in some of its formulations, e.g., the category, the unity of self and being) is justified by phenomenological (one can as well, at times, say "anthropological") procedures. What Hegel presents through such formulas is a concrete idealism. Truth is engendered by action and is guaranteed by the mediation of consciousnesses. Life itself is self-consciousness, and the essence of self-consciousness is always to rediscover itself in being-other, to be self through the mediation of an always reborn otherness. At the end point of the dialectic we are studying, the opaque thing of consciousness (*Ding*) which at the level of reason became the world (*die Welt*)—but the world of acting individuality (*Sache*)—becomes first spiritual essence (*das geistige Wesen*) and then reason which itself is its own world: spirit (*Geist*).

Let us observe this dialectic in greater detail. The first moment is the *work;* the second the *thing* itself (*die Sache selbst*), i.e., spiritual objectivity at the level of action. The third moment is the thing itself as the *work of all and of each.* Yet the self of individuality becomes universal self, and its object—which henceforth is all of truth (*PE*, I, 343; *PG*, 301; *PM*, 438)—is spiritual essence, the thought of the ethical world.

I. THE WORK AS TRUTH OF INDIVIDUALITY

WE MUST NOW CONSIDER self-consciousness as the consciousness of a human individuality. But this individuality is simultaneously an acting self-consciousness, and the various moments of being-for-itself that we have transcended in the prior dialectic appear in it anew. But they appear simply as moments that follow each other, and they are meaningful only in the context of the whole of action.

Since that individuality is real in-itself it is an originarily determinate individuality. It is an originary nature because it exists in-itself; it is originarily determinate because the negative dwells at the heart of the in-itself and the latter, insofar as it is determinate, is a quality. Thus, considered merely as a being-in-itself, prior to the process of action, individuality is a particular nature; it is defined by a content specific to it. We have encountered this nature at the stage at which reason observed human individuality and ascribed to each individuality a delimited sphere of being—a body, an environment, an irreducible given: "What it itself has not created." This originarily determinate nature is the starting point of the dialectic of individuality. In considering individualities in this way, in the particularity of their nature, within the limits of their specific determinateness, we can speak of a *spiritual animal kingdom*. Each individuality is what it is, and it cannot think of stepping outside its own sphere. At first glance, this spiritual kingdom appears to be a natural kingdom. But the individual is viewed as a determinate content, a nature, only when his being, and not his action, is envisaged. For action is negativity: "Thus, in acting individuality, determination is resolved in negation in general, in the *summum* (*Inbegriff*) of every determination" (*PE*, I, 326; *PG*, 286; *PM*, 420).

This distinction is essential to the dialectic that follows. Negativity is manifested in two complementary aspects. In being, encrusted in the in-itself, it is a determination (*omnis determinatio est negatio*); in action, it is the very movement of negativity. It is impossible to act without determining oneself, but action is what determines. Thus, what in the in-itself is quality, delimitation of being, is in action a movement. And the movement of negativity will appear as the truth of this whole process. There is a primacy of existence over essence here, which will soon appear. Nonetheless, we must follow active individuality in its own concept of itself and ascertain whether the reality of its experience corresponds to its concept.

We begin with this originary and determinate nature which individuality neither wishes nor is able to transcend—and which, besides, does not seem to limit action. Consciousness is the act of relating to oneself; it is for-itself, and it must maintain that equality with itself in the element of originary nature: it must remain itself in its own determinateness.

The originary determinateness of nature is then only a simple principle, a transparent universal element within which individuality remains so free and equal to itself that it unfolds its differences without hindrance and in its actualization is a pure reciprocal relation with itself. Similarly, indeterminate animal life takes its life breath from the elements of water, air, and earth (and, within earth, from more highly determinate principles) and immerses all its moments in these principles. Yet despite this limitation by the elements, it maintains control of its moments and maintains itself as an entity—remaining, inasmuch as it is a particular organization, the same universal animal life (*PE*, I, 325; *PG*, 285–86; *PM*, 419–20).

Thus, while expressing a particular nature which is the specific sphere of its being, self-consciousness remains equal to itself, unrelated to any other. In this description we see the concept of individuality "real in-and-for-itself," an individuality that is simultaneously a nature and a self-consciousness within that nature, an individuality that does nothing but be for-itself what it already is in-itself. There is only a transition from potentiality to action, a transition that is the whole mystery of action. By right, this individuality can only experience joy. "The individual can only be cognizant of the pure expression of himself—from the darkness of possibility to the light of presence, from an abstract in-itself to the signification of an actually real being. He can be certain that what rises up before him in this light is the same as what slept in the darkness" (*PE*, I, 330; *PG*, 290; *PM*, 425). Action, existence in the modern sense, merely actualizes originary nature. The individual becomes what he is in-itself, and nothing more. What he is in-itself is his nature; what he is for-itself is the development of what he is for his consciousness. Thus, in this view, each individuality as it develops for-itself becomes the actualization of an originary essence, of a primordial nature which constitutes it. As a given nature, it could never transcend itself and would only express itself. If we are to know whether the experience entered into by this individuality coincides with its concept we must study it in the movement of action.

In action, the originarily determinate nature presents itself in line with the differences that characterize action. At first, the whole of its action is present to acting consciousness as a *goal*, a goal which is its own and which is contraposed to present reality. Then, the movement from goal to reality, the *means*, must be considered—internal as well as external means. The third moment is the object, "when it is no longer the goal which the person acting is immediately cognizant of as his own, when it is an object outside of the person who acts, and is an other for him" (*PE*, I, 326; *PG*, 286; *PM*, 421). This third moment is the work, the expression in the element of being of what the individuality was by itself, before acting. But according to the concept of this individuality, no difference can arise among these various moments. The goal is the originary nature of individuality. How could one wish to do anything but actualize one's nature? What project would go beyond us? We can only will what we already are; "if we were to represent consciousness as passing beyond this content and wishing to advance another content to actual reality, we should be representing it as a nothingness laboring in the void" (*PE*, I, 327; *PG*, 287; *PM*, 421).

Actual reality, then, the reality present to consciousness before it acts, cannot be different in-itself from the originary nature of the individual. We have moved beyond the moment at which the reality of a world existed in opposition to individuality. Only the appearance of an opposition remains. When we are about to act, the world that offers itself to us as the matter of our action is not in-itself distinct from us. It is already the external revelation of what we are within. It is an objective world only for the individuality that recognizes itself therein. "The being-in-itself of this actual reality contraposed to consciousness is diminished to the point of being no more than an empty appearance" (*PE*, I, 327; *PG*, 287; *PM*, 421). It is our world, and only our world, that we see in it. By our *interest* in this or that aspect of it we discover ourselves in it.

One could, of course, object against this notion of the complete actualization of individuality that the problem of action seems to lead to a vicious circle. How can an individuality recognize its originary nature before it acts? I know what I am only after I have acted. Yet in order to act I must portray as my goal precisely what I am. But this is circular only in theory, not in actual action. If "action is the development of spirit as consciousness" (*PE*, I, 327; *PG*, 287; *PM*, 422), all the moments interpenetrate and, properly speaking, action has no beginning. I always confront a certain situation, my situation of being-in-the-world, which reveals by my interest in it my originary nature and shows me what is to be done. As for the means, they immediately connect my interest and the situation, and they express my nature—as talent, inclination, and so on. The external means, the real means, are the transition from the interior to the exterior which leads to the deed, in which individuality discovers itself as it is, in the element of exteriority. But with the deed the possibility of discrepancy is introduced. For the deed is something determinate; it is an actual reality in the element of being. And negativity has become inherent in the deed itself as quality. When I act, I become an other to myself. Consciousness, on the other hand, is negativity in general—the universal process of action. Hence, consciousness which withdraws from the deed and contemplates it has again become, in relation to that deed, universal consciousness. Although Hegel does not introduce the reciprocal relation of other individualities yet, it is clear that "the other" that I become is my being-for-others.

Thus, the originary nature of an individual is related to his consciousness only in the deed—the deed that is abandoned by the action that brought it into being. This nature is expressed as a determinate quality, the deed which condenses within it the whole dialectic of action. The question we must now ask is how individuality, real in-and-for-itself, can preserve its concept in the deed. In fact, it is precisely through wishing to preserve its concept that it transforms it and makes it meaningful. To begin with, consciousness can compare its works to those of other individualities and thus discover quantitative differences among individualities. A qualitative difference—between good and bad —cannot occur here. In fact, it is not at all clear what a bad work might be according to the concept with which we began. As the *expression* of an individuality, every work is a positive thing. The only possible comparison among works is the comparison that has meaning within individuality itself. The originary nature of an individuality is the in-itself and the criterion by which to judge the work. But the work is no more and no less than the expression of an individuality. There is no reason to boast, or to lament, or to regret. The individual always obtains his goal; his work is himself (*PE*, I, 330; *PG*, 290; *PM*, 425).[2]

II. THE THING ITSELF

WHAT IS THE EXPERIENCE of consciousness when it compares its works, deposited in the universal milieu of objec-

2. "Nothing is *for* individuality that has not come to be *through* it; there is no actual reality that is not its nature and its action; there is no action or in-itself of individuality that is not actually real" (*PE*, I, 330; *PG*, 290; *PM*, 425). Let us note that in this first moment of the dialectic individualities are posed as monads: "Indifferent to each other, each relates only to itself." The development of the dialectic will suppress this "mutual indifference."

tive being, to its earlier concept of itself? The work is the genuine expression of real in-and-for-itself individuality; in it individuality exposes to the light of day the originality of its nature. What we are, inasmuch as we exist in a determinate manner, can be seen in our works. The artist expresses his original world view in his work, a world view that is specifically and exclusively his; the intellectual puts his labor and the result of his research into the work—he is entirely in the work.[3] According to its concept of itself, individuality, as we saw, admits no difference between its goal and the reality it takes on, no difference between the means used and the goal pursued. By being expressed, originary nature is immediately bound up with the self in such a way that there is no reason now to distinguish that nature (as being-in-itself) from its actualization (as a work). For the I, there can be an in-itself only through the mediation of action. It is only through what we do (what in the work becomes a being-for-others) that we learn what we are;[4] only through action (negativity as movement and development) that originary nature (talents and abilities) is transformed from potentiality to reality. But consciousness, as the movement of action, as the negativity in the act, is distinct from the works in which this negativity is exclusively inscribed as a particular determination. Acting consciousness *transcends* its work and becomes the *universal* milieu in which that work is something particular. Thus, a difference between the work and acting consciousness is introduced, a difference which contradicts the concept consciousness had of itself.

The passage in which Hegel describes the difference between consciousness and its work contains, in a condensed form, the major articulations of the dialectic we are discussing:

> The work is the reality that consciousness accords itself; it is in the work that the individual is for consciousness what he is in-itself in such a manner that in the work he comes to be for universal consciousness, not a particular consciousness. In the work, consciousness has presented itself in general in the element of universality, in a determinateless region of being. The consciousness that withdraws from its work is in fact universal consciousness, because in that opposition it becomes

3. "This distinctive coloration of the spirit," Hegel writes, "must be considered the only content of the goal and, exclusively, as reality" (*PE*, I, 326–32; *PG*, 287–92; *PM*, 420–27).

4. "Thus before he is led to actual reality through action the individual cannot know what he is."

absolute negativity or action vis-à-vis its work, which is determinate consciousness. In this way, consciousness goes beyond itself as a work, and is itself the space that lacks determination and that is not filled by its work (*PE*, I, 331; *PG*, 290–91; *PM*, 426).[5]

In order to understand this argument, we must emphasize again the double role played by the negative. In the in-itself, negativity is congealed in being and therefore appears as a static determination; but in action, the becoming for-itself of consciousness, negativity is an act: it is the process of pure mediation. The I, Hegel writes in the preface, is "pure mediation," simple becoming. "Mediation is the moment of the I which is for-itself; it is pure negativity or, reduced to its pure abstraction, simple becoming" (*PE*, I, 19; *PG*, 21; *PM*, 82). Insofar as it acts, consciousness is the absolute negation of all otherness. It is equal to itself within this negating movement and that equality constitutes its universality, its form, to which no determinate content can be adequate. But this opposition was only latent in the concept of individuality, for in that concept the work was not yet posed as external to individuality but was only at the stage of active possibility. But action is the necessary transition from the possible to being, and in being, the possible becomes a determination. Thus, the act, which is this transition, always leads to a determination but is not itself a determination. The consciousness of individuality now becomes the universal form—a determinateless region of being—in which any determination is possible but only as limitation and negation. What I see in my work is a particular and contingent content, not the universality of the form, the self-equality of self-consciousness. I go beyond my work, which is to say that I transcend my originarily determinate nature and find it inadequate to my action qua action. Self-consciousness—equality with itself within being-other—now, as self-equality, stands contraposed to being-other. Thus, we appear to revert to the previous stage, that of romantic idealism, in which the individual always opposed the world instead of identifying with it.

The opposition that individual consciousness here reaches at

---

5. Since the discovery of the here as universal here at the beginning of the *Phenomenology*, we have known that consciousness itself is a "determinateless region of being." Already for Fichte, in his interpretation of Kant, space was the I as possible universal intuition. Hegel's image is drawn from this.

the end of its experience was its starting point in preceding dialectics, in which it rebelled against a reality which it experienced as alien and dead. It began by carrying its project within itself, but it ended by discovering that only reality could be its actualization and its truth. Here, on the contrary, individuality began with the conviction of an equality between reality and the self but comes to discover that they are opposed. Indeed, the determinateness of the work is not only the *content* of actual reality but also the *form* of that reality vis-à-vis consciousness—which means that the actual reality present in the work is what manifests itself as the opposite of self-consciousness: it is *the determinateness of all reality, contraposed to the movement that determines.* "In this aspect, it appears as an alien actual reality which as soon as it is found vanishes from the concept. The work *exists,* that is, it is for other individualities, and it is for them an alien actual reality in whose stead they must pose their own actual reality in order, by means of their action, to gain a consciousness of their unity with actual reality" (*PE,* I, 332; *PG,* 291; *PM,* 427). We can see from this passage that there is a reality (in the narrow sense of the word) only because there is a being-for-others.

Vis-à-vis consciousness, the being of the work is an objective being, a being-for-others. Hence, in that work the individuality opposes not only itself but also other individualities;[6] it becomes for-them. We are about to return to the dialectic of intersubjectivity that we seemed to have abandoned after discussing the master and the slave. But now the dialectic of intersubjectivity will lead to a work that genuinely expresses universal self-consciousness by being the "common work," "the work of everyone and of each one."

Opposition, which served as the starting point of the preceding dialectic (the opposition between self-consciousness and reality), now reappears in a new form and as a result. But in fact, that opposition was presupposed. When consciousness undertakes an action, it presupposes the originary nature as in-itself, and "that nature is the content of pure accomplishing for the sake of accomplishing." But "pure action is form equal to itself, to which, consequently, the determinateness of originary nature is unequal" (*PE,* I, 332; *PG,* 292; *PM,* 427–28). The in-itself

---

6. We might add that it opposes itself only because it opposes other individualities. In action, I become an other for others and hence for myself. But it is only in this relation that I exist.

(originary nature) can be taken as concept here, and action as reality. As in the case throughout the *Phenomenology,* concept and reality are contraposed. There is a discrepancy between originary nature (the being either of the individuality or of the work) and action. "Action is the originary concept, as absolute transition or as becoming." "In its work, consciousness now experiences the discrepancy between the concept and the reality lodged in its own essence. Thus, in its work, consciousness becomes to itself what it is in truth, and its empty concept of itself vanishes" (*PE*, I, 333; *PG*, 292; *PM*, 428).[7]

Deposited in the alien milieu of reality, the work is shown to be contingent, and it unfolds the possible contradictions among the moments that previously (in the concept) appeared to us to be harmoniously united. In the element of subsistence all the moments become indifferent to each other. That my goal corresponds exactly to my nature is a contingency. (I might have been mistaken about myself and have sought to realize something inappropriate to what I am.) That the means chosen were those appropriate to the goal is equally contingent. (A given artist may have a noble goal but be unable to discover the technique that would suit his purpose.) And reality itself opposes the individual's action: "Chance can smile as well as frown on a poorly chosen goal and on poorly chosen means" (*PE*, I, 333; *PG*, 293; *PM*, 428–29).

This latest opposition—once again between reality (objectivity) and the concept (subjectivity)—summarizes all the earlier ones. Self-consciousness is not only for-itself; it also is for-others. It is not only subjective; it also is a thing, an objective manifestation. But what the *Phenomenology* as a whole traces is the transcendence of this fundamental opposition which we have seen in all its aspects. Are we about irretrievably to fall back into it, or are we to reach a genuinely new form?

At this point, Hegel rises to a new notion of actual reality, a new notion of objectivity, which we may call "spiritual objectivity" and which Hegel calls *die Sache selbst.* Hegel uses this phrase, which usually denotes the purest objectivity and which in English would be "the thing itself," to go beyond the *contingency* of the work while maintaining the *necessity of the*

---

7. Indeed, the work will appear not as a determinate thing—which is what it appears to be at first—but as a movement; it will be variously interpreted by others. As a determinate thing it will *disappear*, and this movement of disappearing will allow consciousness to transform its concept of "objective reality."

action.[8] In the limited and ephemeral character of its work consciousness has discovered the contingency of its own action. But the unity and the necessity that characterized the action are present nonetheless. "Goals are related to actual reality; this unity is the concept of action" (*PE*, I, 334; *PG*, 293; *PM*, 429). The content of the experience which consciousness has just gone through is the work that disappears and maintains itself, the work that subsists through the vicissitudes of particular deeds: the necessity of action, the necessity of the unity of being and action. Works appear in reality as actions. They are negated by other works; they vanish. But what subsists and becomes actual reality is precisely this *negation of negation*, this infinite movement which transcends each particular deed by integrating it into a *universal essence*.

Thus the negation of the work disappears together with the work, in "a disappearance of disappearance" (*PE*, I, 334; *PG*, 293; *PM*, 429). For reality, in the naturalistic sense of the word, is transcended here. What is posed is the unity of that reality and self-consciousness. Thus the true work is not this or that ephemeral work, this or that objective reality (in the materialist sense of the word), but the higher unity that we have been seeking since our discussion of the concept of thing (*Ding*), a unity of being and self-consciousness. This unity is the thing itself (*die Sache selbst*). Hegel puts great emphasis on the difference between the thing of perception (*Ding*) and the spiritual thing, the human thing (*Sache*) that we reach here. Later, Hegel writes in the *Logic*, that the logos is the thing itself (*die Sache selbst*) inasmuch as it is the identity of thought and being. Here, the meaning of this identity is more readily apparent. It is the identity of acting self-consciousness and being. "The genuine work is the thing itself (or the cause) which asserts itself and is experienced as permanent independently from the particular thing which is the contingency of individual action, the contingency of circumstances, means, and actual reality" (*PE*, I, 335; *PG*, 294; *PM*, 430).

The "thing itself" is actual reality envisaged as the work of

8. In the ontological logic, what Hegel means by the thing itself (*die Sache selbst*) is the unity of thought and being. To say that thought is the thing itself is to say that it is identical to being and that being is thought. But here, the thing itself is discovered as "the action of universal self-consciousness." Hence it is the *subject*, "being that is I, or the I that is being." But let us recall that this subject entails intersubjectivity—the reciprocal relation of all individualities.

self-consciousness, the real at the level of creating consciousness, which we have been seeking as the category. But in the form in which it first appears the thing itself is not yet the concrete subject, spirit as the joint work of individualities which transcend their particularity and through their community realize a world that is the existence of reason: "the *I* that is a *we* and the *we* that is an *I*." This genuine work, the spiritual subject as history, has not yet been posed. In order for that to happen, the thing itself must be transformed from a universal predicate to a subject. And this requires a consideration of the interplay of individualities, which, as we have noted, repeats in another form the mediating movement of self-consciousness.

For the moment, the thing itself—the abstract cause, we might say—is the predicate that consciousness attributes to each of the moments of its action in order to grant them validity. It advances consciousness, which is still submerged in an originary nature, to the dignity of an honest consciousness. For consciousness is honest to the degree that it reaches "the idealism" (*PE*, I, 337; *PG*, 296; *PM*, 432) that spiritual objectivity expresses when it proclaims the true as the thing itself. What matters is to reach the form of universality which, though it is not yet that of Kant's moral subject, does seem to correspond to the honesty of the French moralists, from Montaigne to La Bruyère—an honesty thanks to which man, qua individual, rises above animal nature and reaches an already ideal notion of what is valid in-and-for-itself as reality.

The "thing itself," Hegel writes, is the "copenetration (which has become objective) of individuality and objectivity" (*PE*, I, 336; *PG*, 295; *PM*, 431). Self-consciousness then sees its true self-concept, in which it becomes cognizant of its own substance, come into being. The substance of self-consciousness is this self-equality that subsists through all otherness—the humanization of the in-itself, which reveals its meaning and through which, in Montaigne's phrase, the world becomes the mirror of consciousness. But in the consciousness we are considering, which is still an individual consciousness, the thing itself is merely the abstract work that is equally appropriate to each of the moments of action, taken as particular subjects.

> For this consciousness, the various moments (the originary determination or the thing of a particular individual, his goals, his means, the action itself, and actual reality) are on the one hand specific moments which it can set aside and abandon in favor

of the "thing itself." But on the other hand, the thing itself is the essence of these moments and, consequently, it is in each of them as its abstract universal and it can be the predicate of each (*PE*, I, 336; *PG*, 295; *PM*, 431–32).

III. THE INTERPLAY OF INDIVIDUALITIES; TRANSITION TO THE UNIVERSAL SELF

IF WE CAST a retrospective glance at the forms of the behavior of consciousness since the beginning of the *Phenomenology*, we notice a progressive "deobjectification" [*désobjectivation*] of being-in-itself and a universalization of self-consciousness. At first, consciousness related to things; subsequently, as we have seen, it related to works. It now becomes a behavior with regard to the "thing itself," and here Hegel speaks of idealism. But the deobjectification has a complementary aspect which we must not overlook. The more spiritual the object of consciousness becomes, the more it reveals itself to self-consciousness which discovers itself therein, the more real it becomes (in a new sense). The dissolution of its being-in-itself entails no loss on its part of anything essential; to the contrary, it unveils its genuine essence. Punning on the term, "in-itself," as Hegel does himself, we may say that being-in-itself becomes what it really is in-itself. The "thing itself" is present only in the revelatory knowledge and the action of subjectivity. It is as much a real thing as an action of self-consciousness, as much objectivity as suppressed objectivity. A better way to put it is that the "thing itself" is the thing seen through the action of self-consciousness. A work has no value by itself. It acquires value when it is authenticated by the development of self-consciousness, when, through the test of time, it has found its meaning for spirit. But this experience is beyond the stage at which we find ourselves here. It is the world of spirit, the world that is spirit and that will soon be the thing itself. And this world requires that not only individuality but the interplay of individualities, their interaction, be considered. We have already encountered the categories being-for-itself and being-for-an-other in the emergence of self-consciousness. We meet them again now. Self-consciousness is necessarily *for-itself* and also *for-others;* it is selfsameness, but it also appears as objectivity. We observed this duality in the immediate encounter of living self-consciousnesses. The advent of self-consciousness, which is the self-consciousness of life, is both an objectification and a suppression of objectification.[9] The work, too, is for-others. But it is also for-me. The "thing itself" by means of which the disappearance of the work is negated, and through which self-consciousness qua necessary action overcomes natural objectivity, is simultaneously the *thing of an individual* and the *thing of other individuals*, a difference in form which calls to mind the difference that was already present at the stage of force. Force was for-itself but also for-an-other. Hegel himself points out the similarity: "At this point, a movement which corresponds to that of sensuous certainty and to that of perception [and, we should add, to that of understanding] develops" (*PE*, I, 337; *PG*, 295; *PM*, 431). In our opinion, a higher stage of the dialectic always sheds light on a lower stage, and when Hegel spoke of the being-for-itself and the being-for-an-other of force he was already thinking of relations among self-consciousnesses.

Thus, honest consciousness will seek to justify its action by relating it to the universal criterion that the "thing itself" is for it. But since this criterion is abstract at first, it will be able to apply it to each particular moment and its honesty will be revealed as illusory.

> When consciousness fails to reach the "thing itself" in one of its moments or in one signification, then by that very fact it appropriates it in another moment; consequently, it always obtains the satisfaction which according to its concept it must enjoy. However things turn out, it will always have reached the "thing itself," for the latter is the universal genus of these moments and the predicate of each of them (*PE*, I, 337; *PG*, 296; *PM*, 432).

Let us suppose that consciousness does not realize its goal; it has at least willed it, and that is what is essential, that is the thing itself. Or let us suppose that because circumstances were unfavorable it did nothing. It can still quote the fox: "The grapes are sour; I think I'll leave them for some knave." The thing itself, in this case, was precisely the unity of reality and the desire of consciousness. Or let us suppose that great events are occurring around it—one of Napoleon's campaigns, for example

---

9. Cf. our discussion of the struggle for recognition, part III, chapter 1, above. Each self-consciousness is *for-itself,* but it is simultaneously an *object* for another self-consciousness. It is through the negation of this objective character that it forces the other to recognize it.

—without its taking part in them. Honest consciousness then takes as the thing itself its ineffective interest in these events. It becomes interested in that, and that plays the role of the side it could have chosen.

In gathering up these various moments—to which the predicate "thing itself" is always applicable—honest consciousness must finally discover its dishonesty, the contradiction lodged within it. Pure action is essentially the action of a particular individual and, simultaneously, an actual reality, a thing. Similarly, what we call "actual reality" is the action of an individual as well as action in general. This is why at times the individual fancies that he is dealing with the thing itself as an abstract thought and at other times that he is dealing with it as his thing. But in either case, he is prey to a dialectic. When he believes that he wills only the thing in general it is his thing that he is thinking of. When he believes that he wills only his thing it is to the thing in general that he gives himself up. When we consider the *interplay of individualities* this difference in content becomes a difference in form; between *being-for-itself* and *being-for-others*. In other words, when an individual consciousness exposes one of the moments on the outside, it keeps the other for itself. A reciprocal deception arises. But individuals deceive not only each other but also themselves: consciousness is never where one thinks it is.[10]

When I labor and I display my work, I claim, for example, to be laboring for the love of science. My only interest in the work is the general advancement of knowledge. At least, that is how I present myself to others. And at first the others see it this way—which is why they show me that they have already accomplished my work and that what I have done is useless or, alternatively, why they offer to help me. But they are soon disappointed, for they discover that I am interested not in the work in-itself but in the work insofar as it is mine. Being-for-others was not the same as being-for-itself. Of course, what is true of me is equally true of everyone else, and they are wrong to complain. "They discover that they have been deceived, but they themselves wished to deceive in the same way" (*PE*, I, 341; *PG*, 299; *PM*, 436–37). Conversely, when we claim to be interested in the work only insofar as it is our work we are soon

10. When the individual believes that he is working for a universal cause, he is following his own interest; when he believes that he is following his interest, he is working for a cause that transcends it.

led to discover that we are interested in the thing itself. To create, to work in general, is it not to wish to emerge into the light of day?

> But when they [act and thus] present themselves in the light of day they immediately contradict thereby their allegation that they wish to exclude the light of day, universal consciousness, and the participation of everyone else. The actualization is rather an exposition of what is one's own in the universal element by which this thing that is one's own becomes, and must become, everyone's (*PE*, I, 341; *PG*, 299–300; *PM*, 437).

As soon as a work is begun, others flock to it, in Hegel's phrase, "like flies to fresh milk" (*PE*, I, 341; *PG*, 300; *PM*, 431), and wish to know how they are involved in it.

The double contradiction of content (thing in general and my thing in particular) and form (being-for-itself and being-for-others) must be resolved in a higher synthesis, in which the thing itself rises from being an abstract predicate to being a concrete subject. It then becomes the thing which, by being my thing, is everyone's as well: the thing which is for-me by being for-others and which in its being-for-others is being-for-me. This thing belongs to everyone and to each one—a common work, qua common, in which individualities and the interplay of their mutual deceits are transcended but in which each rediscovers itself as universal self. This thing is spiritual essence; "it is an essence whose being is the action of the specific individual and of all individuals, and whose action is immediately for-others (is a thing) and is a thing only qua the action of all and of each: it is the essence that is the essence of all essences [, spiritual essence]" (*PE*, I, 342; *PG*, 300; *PM*, 437–38). This is indeed the category, "the I which is being and being which is I." But whereas earlier the category was determined as the unity of thought and being and in this way was for thought, now it is for real self-consciousness which thereby becomes all of content. For now all content enters into this spiritual essence and is part of the world that is the work of self-consciousness. That world is spirit: *the work of all and of each*. We have transcended individual consciousness, which, for its part, having moved from nature to honesty and from honesty to morality and the thought of the ethical world, has risen to universal self. To be sure, inasmuch as it belongs to an individual consciousness, the thought of the ethical world is not yet real spirit, but only thought—a thought that is discussed in the subchapters on legislative reason and the reason that examines laws. But these two chapters merely serve as a transition to the new world that has been foreshadowed since the dialectic of self-consciousnesses: the world of spirit, in which the self is posed in *substance* and substance is posed in the *self*.

IV. Legislative Reason and the Reason That Assays Laws

WE HAVE REACHED the stage of spiritual essence as "the work of all and of each." The abstract "thing itself" that could be the general predicate of all the moments of an individual's action and thus confer a certain universality on them is now the "absolute thing" (*PE*, I, 343; *PG*, 301; *PM*, 440), a "thing" beyond which it is impossible to advance since it is simultaneously universal being and the self of that being. Individuality has transcended the particular nature in which it seemed to be enclosed; it has risen to self as universal self. Conversely, the formal "thing itself" acquires its content and its differences in acting individuality. The universal is no longer contraposed to specific consciousnesses; rather, it finds in them its own concrete content. This is the universal of "pure consciousness," a universal which is also "this-self." Hegel adds to these determinations of spiritual essence (to be in-itself and to be for-itself) that of being true. At this stage, truth is equivalent to certainty for consciousness; it is the ethical world in which being is simultaneously self. And this world is "the will of this-self." Thus, Hegel comes to define truth as the unity of being and action, the human work—a work that is both in-itself and for-itself, a work that is the category.[11]

The consciousness we are discussing is the consciousness of ethical substance, ethical consciousness (*PE*, I, 344; *PG*, 302; *PM*, 440). Yet it remains an individual consciousness, and when it poses ethical substance within itself it upends it and ascribes

11. The object of consciousness now is "the absolute thing" "(which no longer suffers from the opposition between certainty and truth, between the universal and the specific, between the goal and its reality), the absolute thing whose Dasein is actual reality and the action of self-consciousness" (*PE*, I, 343–44; *PG*, 301–2; *PM*, 440). Let us note that this truth, which is also a deed, is a life and is in-itself only in the for-itself of consciousness.

to it either the form of contingency or that of a formal knowledge. The experiences we shall now comment on (legislative reason and the reason that examines laws) have a double implication. On the one hand, they lead to the self (which is still separate from substance) being posed in the very midst of substance. On the other hand, from the point of view of substance and of spiritual essence in general, they lead to granting actuality to substance; they raise it to spiritual actuality. Hegel summarizes this double process at the beginning of the next chapter:

> In fact, qua specific entity, this consciousness is still separate from substance. Either it prescribes arbitrary laws to substance, or it presumes that it possesses in its knowledge, as such, the laws as they are in-and-for-itself and it regards itself as the power that appraises them. Or, from the point of view of substance, we may say that this substance is spiritual essence that exists in-and-for-itself but is not yet consciousness of itself. The essence that exists in-and-for-itself and simultaneously knows itself to be actual as consciousness and represents itself to itself is spirit (*PE*, II, 9; *PG*, 313–14; *PM*, 457–58).

We reach this new level of experience when ethical substance becomes conscious of itself and when consciousness actually becomes consciousness of substance. For the moment, we are still on the *path* of that realization. The individual self is still distinct from the substance of which it is the self, and substance is still separate from this self. "I am within ethical substance when law is in-and-for-itself for me; thus, ethical substance is the essence of self-consciousness, but self-consciousness, in turn, is the actual reality, the Dasein, of that substance: it is its self and its will" (*PE*, I, 355; *PG*, 312; *PM*, 453). We recall that at the beginning of the dialectic of acting reason Hegel proposed to lead individuality to the thought of substance, and that he defined that thought of substance as *morality*. But since it is only an individual's thought it remains distinct from ethical substance and is equally the *possibility of immorality*. It is in this form that we shall now consider it.

In the first place, individual self-consciousness believes that it immediately knows what is just and good. It proclaims edicts that must be immediately valid: "Everyone must tell the truth," or "Love your neighbor as yourself." But these edicts prove inadequate to the necessity that they claim to express. They manifest a contingency which derives from the individuality of the consciousness that formulates them. We must tell the truth, but to do so depends on our knowing the truth and that knowledge depends on circumstances and on individual conviction. This is all the more true for the second command, which we must understand to mean "Love your neighbor intelligently, for a stupid love might harm him even more than hatred would" (*PE*, I, 346; *PG*, 304; *PM*, 443). Thus, when examined, these laws lose their immediateness and are shown to be arbitrary, just as arbitrary as the specific consciousness that formulates them. The contingency of these particular contents is transcended by substance qua universality and necessity. But when the individual claims to legislate, his edicts appear to emanate from a particular self-consciousness and to be arbitrary orders, the commands of a master. In substance, these orders are not only orders; they exist and are valid in-itself. They are in-itself, but their proclamation by a particular consciousness gives them an arbitrary character which does not correspond to their absolute nature.

The self which has thought through universality and necessity still has a last resort. Instead of legislating immediately, it can examine the laws. Their content is already given; consciousness is merely the unit of measure which tests content in order to ascertain its validity (*PE*, I, 348; *PG*, 306; *PM*, 445). Thus we come to Kant's rule, which proclaims nothing but the general condition in which a maxim can be established as a universal law. But this manner of testing an already given content can proclaim nothing but tautologies. Let us take the case of property, for example. Property is a concrete determination, a particular content. If we wish to ascertain whether property exists in-and-for-itself, that is, without reference to anything else, we can equally say "property is property" and "nonproperty is nonproperty." If, on the other hand, we consider its relation to need and to the human person, then property is as self-contradictory as nonproperty (the community of goods). It would be quite remarkable, Hegel notes, "if tautology, the principle of contradiction, which is recognized only as a formal criterion of the knowledge of theoretical truth (that is, as something that is equally indifferent to truth and to nontruth) should be something more for the knowledge of practical truth" (*PE*, I, 351; *PG*, 308; *PM*, 449).

Indeed, the examination of laws may already be the beginning of the immorality of an individual consciousness. "Similarly, the second moment, insofar as it is isolated, signifies the process of examining laws, of moving the immovable, and it signifies the audacity of knowledge which by dint of reasoning frees itself from absolute laws and takes them as something arbitrary and alien" (*PE*, I, 352; *PG*, 309–10; *PM*, 450).

In each case, individual consciousness has appeared in its negative behavior toward ethical substance. Substance has appeared only in the form of the particular individual's will (to legislate immediately) and knowledge (to examine law by oneself). It exists only as the must-be of an edict that lacks actual reality, or as the knowledge of a formal universality.

> But since these modes have been suppressed, consciousness has returned into the universal and these oppositions have vanished. When these modes are no longer valid in their separateness but only qua suppressed [*aufgehoben*], spiritual essence is actual substance. And the unity in which they are only moments is the self of consciousness, which henceforth is posed within spiritual essence and raises that essence to actual reality, to plenitude, and to self-consciousness (*PE*, I, 353, *PG*, 310; *PM*, 451).

Laws are not the arbitrary edict of an individual consciousness. They are not based on the will of an individual, but rather are valid in-itself: "Law is the pure absolute will of everybody, and it has the form of immediate being," "This pure will," Hegel adds, "is not thereby a command which simply ought to be; it exists and it is valid. It is the universal I of the category that immediately is actual reality. And the world is nothing else but this actual reality" (*PE*, I, 353; *PG*, 310; *PM*, 451).

Thus, consciousness has suppressed itself qua specific consciousness; it has effected the *mediation* by which laws lose their arbitrary character. It is only because that mediation has been accomplished that consciousness again becomes the self-consciousness of ethical substance. Essence is self-consciousness, and self-consciousness is the consciousness of essence. We have reached spirit, insofar as spirit is the concrete substance, reason posed as being—"the individual who is a world" (*PE*, II, 12; *PG*, 315; *PM*, 460).[12]

---

12. This world, which seems to realize the equilibrium of substance and self, of truth and certainty—spiritual substance—will nonetheless be itself only in a history in which the two moments oppose each other anew but as moments of spirit. Thus, spirit, in turn, will be itself only through its mediation, only by alienating itself so as to reconquer itself: "This becoming of spirit as such will be history."

PART V

Spirit:
From Spiritual Substance
to the Self-Knowledge of Spirit

Introduction

THE *Phenomenology* sets itself a double task: to lead naïve consciousness to philosophical knowledge and to lead individual consciousness to emerge from its would-be isolation—its exclusive being-for-itself—so as to raise it to spirit. Individual consciousness must be shown its ontological relation to other beings-for-itself in the very heart of its being-for-itself. Thus, individual self-consciousness raised itself to universal self-consciousness through the struggle for recognition, the opposition between master and slave, and, finally, unhappy consciousness, which, by alienating its subjectivity, led us to reason. Hegel had already noted the end point of the dialectical development of self-consciousness at the beginning of his section on self-consciousness:

> When a self-consciousness is an object, the object is I as well as object. In this way, the concept of spirit is already present for us. Later, consciousness will experience spirit: that absolute substance which, in the perfect freedom and independence of its oppositions, that is, of various self-consciousnesses each of which is for-itself, constitutes their unity—an *I* that is a *we* and a *we* that is an *I* (*PE*, I, 154; *PG*, 140; *PM*, 227).

Spirit here appears as the experience of a *cogitamus* and no longer merely that of a *cogito*. It presupposes both the transcendence of individual consciousnesses and the maintenance of their diversity within substance. It is at the heart of individual consciousness itself that we discover its necessary relation to other individual consciousnesses: each is for-itself and at the same time for-others; each requires recognition from the other in order to be, and, reciprocally, each must recognize the other.

[321]

This conflict, which allows them to exist, is both preserved and transcended at the level of spirit. Thus spirit is the truth of reason: universal self-consciousness has itself become a being in-and-for-itself. This being, in turn, develops for us in the dimension of history and unfolds its vital content. Spirit, thus, is at first immediate, like a nature; it then opposes itself and makes itself other so as to regain itself. But in this reflective regaining it internalizes itself and becomes the self-knowledge of spirit. What Hegel, in the *Phenomenology*, calls "spirit" (*Geist*) is the experience of *objective spirit* becoming *absolute spirit*. We can now understand what Hegel wrote in the preface to the *Phenomenology*: spirit is at first immediate; it is in-and-for-itself "inasmuch as it engenders its own spiritual content," that is, insofar as it makes its own history and is its own development, but it is not yet in-and-for-itself *for itself*; it is not yet "the knowledge of spirit by spirit" (*PE*, I, 23; *PG*, 24; *PM*, 86). This self-knowledge of spirit is philosophy itself; it is truth which has also become certainty, a vital truth that knows itself. The titles of the chapters of the *Phenomenology* dealing with spirit proper reveal the movement and meaning of this dialectic: "True Spirit," "Spirit Which Has Become Alien to Itself" (the general movement of alienation and opposition), "Self-certain Spirit." The direction of this movement is always from substance to subject, from spirit that merely exists to the self-knowledge of spirit. The fundamental thesis of the *Phenomenology*, that "the absolute is subject," is reasserted here. But in order that this thesis acquire its full meaning, Hegel had to move beyond individual self-consciousness, which is able to found history only on the historicity of its own being, and reach the *reality* of universal self-consciousness. Reason, of course, was universal self-consciousness, but only potentially, not in any action. In action, that reason becomes a world, the world of spirit, or of human history. In this history, spirit must know its own self; it must progress from truth to certainty.

Spirit is a "we": we must begin not with the *cogito* but with the *cogitamus*. Spirit is history: it becomes what it is only through a historical development because each of its moments, in making itself essence, must realize itself as an original world, and because its being is not distinct from the action through which it poses itself.[1] Spirit is knowledge of itself in its history:

1. "Each moment, since it is a moment of essence, must come to present itself as essence" (*PE*, I, 293; *PG*, 259; *PM*, 379). This is

it is a return to itself through, and by means of, that history, a return such that nothing alien subsists in or for spirit and such that spirit knows itself as what it is and is what it knows itself to be (this being of spirit is nothing but its very action). These are the three fundamental theses of Hegelian idealism. We shall discuss the third later: it is the one that raises the greatest difficulties, for it leads the *Phenomenology* to an ontology and results in the transcendence of all transcendence and in the most perfect equanimity within the perpetual disquiet and instability of history. Let us consider at present only the first two theses.

The problem of the multiplicity of self-consciousnesses has always been the stumbling block of philosophies. According to the realist, I know the other at first only through his body or his being-for-an-other, which alone is given in my sensuous experience. In Kant's *Critique of Pure Reason,* on the other hand, the problem of the other's consciousness does not seem to arise. An idealist like Kant is concerned with the universal conditions of all experience and tries to establish the general laws of subjectivity which are simultaneously the laws of everything that can present itself to me as an object. But how can an object of my experience be, in other respects, a subject? To be sure, the "I think" is the apex of the Kantian edifice. But that *cogito* is a *cogito* in general, the common sense of individual consciousness; the question of *transcendental intersubjectivity* is not really posed. Yet the other, too, appears in my experience, and it does so as a particular object; it is an object-subject, the conditions of whose possibility Kant did not study. We know, by contrast, the importance which in our own time Husserl, for example, attached to the problem of the multiplicity of self-consciousnesses. He wished to show that the world—qua objective world for-me—referred back to alien subjectivities. According to Husserl, only the complementarism of points of view on the world makes possible the notion of the objectivity of the world.[2] This *intersubjectivity* has also been considered as an original "phenomenon" of our experience, which Heidegger has called *Mitsein.* According to Heidegger, this being-with is consti-

---

an indication of a method specific to Hegel: each particular moment of spirit—wealth, state power, family, etc.—must present itself as the essence. And it is in the course of these presentations (which sometimes are embodied in a historical epoch) that each is transcended.

2. Husserl, *Cartesian Meditations,* trans. D. Cairns (The Hague, 1960), Meditation V.

tutive of human reality and is as much a part of it as is being-in-the-world.[3]

We call these contemporary works to mind only the better to indicate the importance of the relation among beings-for-itself in the *Phenomenology*. Hegel wishes to rediscover Kant's I in general by starting with individual self-consciousness. The "I exist" of one self-consciousness is possible only through another "I exist," and it is a condition of my very being that an other be for-me and that I be for-an-other.[4] The encounter of self-consciousnesses which are objects for each other and must reveal themselves to each other in experience as subjects is integral to transcendental philosophy. The *cogito*, reason, is possible only on the basis of that relation. The possibility of a universal thought arises in the element of mutual recognition. The truth that appears at the level of reason presupposes the existence of self-consciousnesses, and would not exist were it not for the phenomenology of self-consciousness as our study has revealed it.

This presupposition, which seems forgotten in the phenomenology of reason, regains its full meaning in the transition from reason to spirit. Truth must appear as spiritual substance, the work of all and of each. For this reason, the phenomenology of reason must, on its own, result in a phenomenology of spirit proper.

The universal self-consciousness which Hegel claims to reach, then, is not Kant's "I think in general" but human reality as an *intersubjectivity*, a we which alone is concrete. Spirit is this we precisely insofar as it simultaneously brings about the unity and the separation of I's.[5] The universal I is *right* but not

3. Heidegger, *Being and Time*, trans. John Macquarrie and Edward Robinson (New York and London, 1962), § 26.

4. Let us note the originality of Hegel's solution (which we have already emphasized while discussing the *struggle among self-consciousnesses* and the *common human work*): I am for-myself only through becoming an object for the other: "The doubling of self-consciousnesses is essential to the concept of spirit." Self-knowledge presupposes the other whom it simultaneously poses and excludes.

5. Sartre has criticized Hegel for an "ontological optimism" which consists in his placing himself above the various self-consciousnesses which he contraposes and unites: "For individual consciousnesses are moments of the whole, moments which by themselves are *unselbständig* [not independent], and the whole is a mediator between consciousnesses." J.-P. Sartre, *Being and Nothingness*, trans. Hazel Barnes (New York, 1956), p. 243.

yet itself *reason*. In other words, it must become what, in-itself, it already is; in order to pose itself as being, it must pass beyond the immediate unity of the for-itself and the in-itself, of the I and being. Spirit is precisely this reason which exists, this category which develops as history. "Reason becomes spirit when its certainty of being all of reality rises to truth, and when it knows itself to be conscious of itself qua its world and of the world qua itself" (*PE*, II, 9; *PG*, 313; *PM*, 457). This world is the self of spirit, which means that it gives rise to itself and develops itself but at the same time discovers itself. For the self exists only insofar as it knows itself as self. We can now understand the second thesis of Hegel's idealism, "spirit is history." We might say, in contemporary philosophical terms, that if self-consciousness was *historicity,* spirit is now *a history.* In his introduction to his presentation of spirit, Hegel rapidly summarizes the argument up to that point. Reason was merely the first reconciliation of the individual and the universal. Self-consciousness which, having passed through the test posed by unhappy consciousness, has become free self-consciousness, becomes capable of universality. For it, then, the object is no longer a pure and simple in-itself but a "world," a universe in which it instinctively seeks itself. The category becomes the concept of reason—not merely by right, through an unrealized requirement, but in actual fact, for that world is revealed to science as reason itself. To be sure, this result is inadequate. Qua nature, the world does not genuinely express reason itself. Reason merely discovers itself in this being-other, which implies that it was lost, alienated in being. As Hegel wrote, "Spirit is what discovers itself and presupposes itself as lost." Nature is this spirit outside itself, external to itself. Reason thus discovers itself as in-itself in nature, in-itself in both senses of the term. It discovers that it is the in-itself, that it is being as compactness, which, so to speak, does not have any perspective on itself. So we come to say that spirit exists in the way that a skull exists. But reason also discovers that this nature is potentially spirit, spirit in-itself, spirit for the spirit that knows it, and in that knowledge grasps the essence of its object and reveals it as it is capable of being known. However, this immediate discovery of the self is only one moment of the category, which is mediation as well as immediateness. Therefore, in developing only the aspect of mediation, reason poses itself by opposing what is and negates the immediate truth of itself as constituted by nature. "The category given to intuition, the thing discovered, henceforth enters consciousness as the being-for-itself of the I, an I which now knows itself in objective essence as the self" (*PE*, II, 9; *PG*, 312; *PM*, 457), that is, as what reflects itself, what always refers back to itself in the other. But this continual negation of objective essence, in turn, ends in defeat, and the category is finally grasped in the action and the works of the individual entity, grasped as the unity of the in-itself and the for-itself. The category has then become the thing itself (*die Sache selbst*), human work. It is indeed in-and-for-itself in the earlier sense, but it is for-others, too, as well as for-me. It is spiritual essence, the human fact, and no longer the thing of nature. Spirit is thus the genuine development of that universality which self-consciousness reached as reason. As spirit, reason has become the we. It is no longer the subjective certainty of discovering itself immediately in being or of posing itself through negating that being; it knows itself as this world, as the world of human history, and, conversely, it knows this world to be the self.

The dialectical development of this world in three ages (immediate spirit, spirit alien to itself, and self-certain spirit) which correspond to three periods of universal history (the ancient world of Greece and Rome, the modern world, from the feudal age to the French Revolution, and the contemporary world, that of Napoleon and Germany in Hegel's time) presents serious difficulties of interpretation. Why does Hegel begin this development of spirit with the polis? Are we to see it as a truly historical development or as an exposition of the different moments of spirit? Or are we to agree with Rosenzweig that at the time Hegel was writing the *Phenomenology* he had abandoned his earlier conception of the state, a conception to which he was to return in the Berlin *Philosophy of Right*?[6]

It is difficult to answer these questions precisely because Hegel's thought remains ambiguous and the relevant passages of the *Phenomenology* are open to various interpretations. But although we cannot reach a perfectly clear solution to these fundamental problems, we can nevertheless, on the basis of an examination of the development of Hegel's earlier works, reject certain interpretations and define what remains obscure. First of all, Rosenzweig's thesis seems to us to be unacceptable. "In the

---

6. Rosenzweig, *Hegel und der Staat* (Oldenburg, 1920). Rosenzweig's thesis, which we shall discuss further on, leads to an interpretation of the *Phenomenology* according to which "Hegel was never further from his state absolutism" than in that book.

Phenomenology," he writes, "the state is no longer what is most exalted; it yields that position to morality and morality, in turn, will soon yield it to religion." [7] In that case, we would have to agree that there was a break between Hegel's earlier work and the *Phenomenology*, as well as between the *Phenomenology* and the later work. According to this view, the ideal of the *human city*, expounded in the "System der Sittlichkeit" and in the "Naturrecht," is abandoned in favor of a *City of God*. Later, the argument continues, Hegel returned to his divinization of the state, although we cannot clearly indicate the relation between, on the one hand, objective spirit and the universal history of nations and, on the other, absolute spirit as art, religion, and philosophy. Rosenzweig's argument is supported only by the order of the chapters of the *Phenomenology*. Hegel begins with the ethical idea (*Sittlichkeit*), which, indeed, is the substance of spirit in which the self, qua being-for-itself, tends to be absorbed. He then shows how the self emerges from this harmonious totality and becomes its destiny. But this immediately universal self can no longer find itself: it is the unhappy consciousness of history. This world is the world of alienation and culture, the modern world, which culminates, after the great movement of liberation of the eighteenth century, in the French Revolution. But the French Revolution foundered on the Terror. The sublime effort of a people to reconcile heaven and earth, to realize the state concretely as general will, was, in fact, a historical fiasco. Spirit then flees to "another earth" (*PE*, II, 141; *PG*, 422; *PM*, 610) and becomes moral spirit.[8] Rousseau's general will is apparently succeeded by Kant's moralism and by the internal revolution accomplished by German idealism. This revolution culminates in the self-knowledge of the spirit, and this self-knowledge expresses itself in the new element of religion, an element destined, in turn, to find its truth in absolute knowledge, in philosophy. If we were to interpret this sequence literally, we should have to conclude that Hegel gave up the ethical ideal: that he noted the failure of the French Revolution to overcome all alienation in the objective spirit, and that he raised above the state, which is unable to manifest the absolute idea, first the moral vision of the world and then religion. According to

7. *Ibid.*, II, 19.
8. In a letter to Niethammer (April 28, 1814), Hegel boasts of having predicted this "reversal" in the book he "finished on the eve of the battle of Jena."

this view, the failure of the general will's aspiration to realize itself in a people is followed by the appearance of the religious community, which alone is able to embody the self-knowledge of spirit. The citizen is succeeded by the moral subject and then by religious spirit.

But this interpretation seems to us to run counter to the very text of the *Phenomenology*. Religion does not succeed objective spirit in the way that one historical event follows another. When objective spirit grasps itself as subject and becomes aware of being *creative spirit,* which throughout history, and at the heart of its own history, reconciles the infinite and the finite, the universal I and the specific I, then the philosopher who in the *Phenomenology* says "we" discovers in this reconciliation a new element of knowledge, the self-knowledge of spirit. At that moment, a new history, the history of religion, appears in history. It is the development of this self-knowledge that Hegel studies in the phenomenology of religion, but he does not claim thereby to negate the spirit that creates its own history. This can be clearly seen in the discussion of absolute knowledge, a discussion that is obscure because of its concentration. There Hegel asserts the need to reconcile the spirit that *represents* itself to itself in religion with the spirit that *develops* [*se fait*] in history. The intuition of the divine (as an other) must be reconciled with the self-intuition of the divine (the subject spirit which makes history) (*PE,* II, 299; *PG,* 554; *PM,* 795).[9] In Christianity, God is represented as subject, but that is still only a representation. It is necessary to advance from that representation to the concept, that is, to the subject spirit which simultaneously alienates itself in history and, in that alienation, knows itself as itself: "the concept in its truth, that is, in its unity with its alienation" (*PE,* II, 299; *PG,* 554; *PM,* 795).[10] It is up to philosophy, up to absolute knowledge, to be this very concept. What does this thesis mean concretely? Does it imply that religion disappears into a humanism? What does it mean with regard to the problem of God? We shall investigate these questions later in interpreting various passages. For the moment,

9. "Nicht nur die Anschauung des Göttlichen, sondern die Selbstanschauung desselben" (*PE,* II, 299; *PG,* 554; *PM,* 795).

10. If it is the destiny of Christianity that "church and state, divine service and life, spiritual action and action in the world cannot coincide" (*Early Theological Writings,* p. 301), then the reconciliation that Hegel effects in "absolute knowledge" is the most difficult of all.

it seems to us proven that the *Phenomenology* is not the transition from the idea of the state to the religious idea that Rosenzweig apparently thought it to be.

The development of the various moments of spirit clearly has a direction, which corresponds to a historical development. At first, spirit is considered as substance; at the end point of its development, it is viewed as subject, indeed as the subject that creates its own history. Now the polis, of which Plato's *Republic* was, as it were, the idea, was ignorant of this subjectivity. The self-reflection of spirit is discovered by the modern world, both in its bourgeois culture ("bourgeois" here as opposed to "citizen" in the ancient sense) and in its religion (a faith in a beyond that is radically cut off from the terrestrial world but constitutes its foundation). Spirit had to reflect on itself in order truly to become what it had been only in-itself, in order to assume its being and discover itself as its own author. This reflection was fulfilled in a history; it is the transition from the ancient world to the modern and contemporary worlds. Today the state can no longer be merely substantive like the Greek city; it has become a self-certain spirit, expressed through the historical action of a Napoleon, even though a bourgeois world, in which each thinks that he works for himself but in fact works for all, still subsists. This transition from substance to subject, from true spirit to self-certain spirit, is what the *Phenomenology* presents.[11] If in the last chapter of the section on spirit Hegel does not actually speak of the state, it is not because the state has disappeared as the supreme form of world spirit and yielded its position to a moral subject or a contemplative soul, but because in that chapter Hegel considers only the novel aspect that spirit takes on when it grasps itself as subject. Thus, we prefer Martin

---

11. We must distinguish being-for-itself as the *absolute form of the idea* (as opposed to being-in-itself as an objectivity that has not yet been absorbed into that form) and being-for-itself as the *second moment* of every dialectic (as opposed to being-in-itself as the first moment). Thus, in the first sense, objective spirit is in-itself vis-à-vis subjective spirit, but in the second sense subjective spirit is the in-itself (the first moment of the dialectic). The first meaning allows us to understand the *Phenomenology* as the transition from in-itself to for-itself, from substance to subject; the second allows us to understand the development of each of the various moments of the system. The *Phenomenology* grasps this absolute form of the idea and reduces all substance to it: "Being-for-itself is the pure certainty of itself, the pure concept existing for-itself as infinite universality" (*Encyclopaedia*, p. 354).

Büsse's recent interpretation to Rosenzweig's. Rather than opposing the theses of the *Phenomenology* to those of the *Philosophy of Right*, Büsse has tried to demonstrate that the differences between the two books are due to a difference in point of view. What the *Encyclopaedia* presents as the development, in-and-for-itself, of the concept, the *Phenomenology* presents as a *prise de conscience* of that concept: "Both the *Phenomenology* and the system are presentations of absolute spirit, but they are different presentations." [12] In the *Philosophy of Right*, which is a moment of the system, each articulation appears in the absolute element. The opposition between essence and knowledge plays no part here, and the *prise de conscience* characteristic of the *Phenomenology* is no longer the moving force of the dialectic. Abstract right, morality, the state are both content and form, objective essence and self-knowledge. In the *Phenomenology*, of course, all the moments of the concept are presented according to the internal opposition between in-itself and for-itself, between essence and knowledge. The moments of spirit are all presented in the *Phenomenology*, but they are presented in the order of their emergence with respect to the knowledge spirit gains of itself, with respect to the *prise de conscience*. For this reason, the end of the development, self-certain spirit, is not the negation of the substantive state and its submersion in a new form of the world spirit, but the emergence of the self-consciousness of spirit from its substantiveness, the emergence of the for-itself aspect of the in-itself, which, as general will, is always the state. Hegel himself points out that the development is in accordance with the development of the *prise de conscience*: "Spirit is the ethical life of a people inasmuch as spirit is immediate truth—the individual who is a world. Spirit must progress to the consciousness of what it immediately is; it must suppress that beautiful ethical life and, through a sequence of figures, reach self-knowledge" (*PE*, II, 12; *PG*, 315; *PM*, 460). This passage is consonant with the circular movement of Hegel's argument. Spirit becomes what it immediately is. The beautiful ethical life, the ancient city, with which Hegel begins because it is for him the first genuine form of a harmonious organization of the human city, is also the goal that history pursues. But in order to become what it already is in-itself, spirit must renounce immediateness; it must regain itself and deepen itself as the

12. M. Büsse, *Hegels Phänomenologie des Geistes und der Staat* (Berlin, 1931), p. 84.

subject of its history. The phenomenology of spirit proper develops this transition from immediate spirit to subject spirit. But, as we have seen, the figures of this development have historical signification, as Hegel explicitly tells us: "These figures differ from the preceding ones in that they themselves are real spirits, genuine actually existing entities; rather than being merely figures of consciousness, they are figures of a world" (*PE*, II, 12; *PG*, 315; *PM*, 460). The correspondence between the ancient, modern, and contemporary worlds and the moments of the dialectic of the spirit's *prise de conscience*—ethical world, world split into a here-below and a beyond, moral world view—is not arbitrary. The meaning of the dialectic here is the very meaning of history. *The prise de conscience is a history.* And Hegel's early works make this clear to us.

At the start of his stay in Jena, Hegel had tried to present the absolute idea as the most beautiful organization of the human city; the greatest work of art is the organic city. In the "System der Sittlichkeit" and in his article "Naturrecht," as in Schelling's intuition, creative spirit must forget itself in order to pose itself absolutely. These works of Hegel's present the ideal of a city which floats above history, independent of its vicissitudes. All the moments of human life—need, enjoyment, labor, tools, language, etc.—become truly significant only in the context of that totality, which philosophy must present. Despite the beauty and validity of certain passages, these works of Hegel's seem oddly archaic. The polis and the Platonic ideal mingle with eighteenth-century states in a completely unhistorical exposition. What we have here is the idea of the *Volksgeist,* and not yet the idea that becomes itself in the course of a history. "Philosophy," Hegel wrote at the time, "demands the most beautiful form for the absolute moral idea, and, since the absolute idea is intuition, spirit recognizes itself therein with no reflection on itself independent of intuition. For this reason it is absolute spirit and perfect morality." [13]

It can be said that Hegel had not yet found himself in this first exposition; he does not even seem here to have been up to the level of his first theological works. But gradually, as he discovered his originality with respect to Schelling, he became

13. "Naturrecht," p. 416. At this point, "absolute spirit" is realized for Hegel in the perfect figure of the spirit of a people and not in the absence of figure (*Gestaltlosigkeit*) of cosmopolitanism or of abstract human rights, a universal republic which would be the opposite of ethical vitality (*ibid.,* p. 415).

aware of the necessity of the *prise de conscience,* and he contraposed the concept to intuition. From that moment on, the ideal of the ancient city was relegated to the past. The substantive spirit of antiquity became the modern spirit, and history no longer appeared alien to the absolute idea. This conception of spirit as history and as *prise de conscience* dawned in the *Realphilosophie* of 1803–4 and 1805–6: "Spirit is higher than nature"; it is the concept, that is, the subject which rises above intuition, in which it was completely absorbed in its works. The world spirit transcends the spirit of a people.[14] The difference between the ancient world and the modern world is not only recognized but also judged: "Freedom of the self was not truly known by the Greeks, by Plato or Aristotle," and the infinite subjectivity of Christianity makes a return to a city like the ancient polis impossible.[15] This evolution is irreversible. Henceforth spirit is inseparable from a history. For it itself is history: it exists only in producing its own being.

If we compare our study of the evolution that is manifest in the Jena works with our analysis of the passages of the *Phenomenology,* we will understand why Hegel began his dialectic of spirit by presenting the ancient city, and also why for him the direction of that dialectic—from substance to subject, from true spirit to self-certain spirit—corresponds to a real historical evolution. It was indeed in the course of this historical evolution that spirit asserted itself as the subject of its own history and secured itself through the most profound opposition—that between its essence and its Dasein, between its beyond and its here-below.[16] At the end point of the reflection back on itself, merely true—merely objective—spirit becomes subject spirit. The *Phenomenology* means to establish precisely this reality of the concept, this possibility for all the content of experience to appear as the work of the self. For that reason, at the end of the section on spirit, spirit will appear to itself as remaining itself in its alienation, as the subject of history. It is this history that will be *constituted* as the equality of spirit (of itself to itself) in the inequality of becoming—the vital reconciliation of universal self and specific self.

14. SW, XX, 272–73.
15. *Ibid.,* p. 251.
16. In Hegel's 1805–6 lectures it seems that philosophy is to transcend the dualism of religion and spirit that has a Dasein. In the *Phenomenology* absolute knowledge seems to bring about this reconciliation. "Philosophy is man in general" (*SW,* VII, 273).

But the interest of the *Phenomenology*, as well as its difficulty, lies less in its general theses than in the detailed interpretations it presents. Though the general movement is easily discernible—Hegel in fact continually restates it, showing it in an
ever-new light—the detailed analyses keep getting tangled. It
sometimes seems as though, forgetting the whole, Hegel lingers
overlong at specific moments: he interprets various historical
events, tries to elaborate their signification, and presents a
moment as though it were absolute essence. We must, therefore,
analyze each of the moments of the development of spirit (ethical spirit, spirit alien to itself, and self-certain spirit) for its
own sake, yet without forgetting that the true is the whole and
that each of these moments has meaning only through its position in the general dialectic.

1 / Immediate Spirit

IMMEDIATE SPIRIT: THE EMERGENCE OF THE SELF

AT FIRST, spirit exists immediately; it is there as a historical given, i.e., the existence of a people—a community of individuals aware of themselves as living in the concrete totality of a people.[1] We have moved beyond the abstract moment at which the individual, as self-consciousness, stood contraposed to his world, trying to realize concretely an ideal found only in himself. The world now is reason made real, and self-consciousness is not contraposed to it; on the contrary, self-consciousness now recognizes itself in the world immediately. As at the beginning of the *Phenomenology*, certainty and truth seem identical. Spirit exists; it is substance. And specific certainty, the consciousness of that substance, merely presents a contrast to this universal, which is its goal and its in-itself. There is, to be sure, a distinction, that implied by consciousness itself. But the distinction between specific and universal, between individual and genus, is not an opposition. "As universal essence and as goal, substance presents a contrast to itself as individualized entity." But spirit is not merely the substance of

1. This "historical given" is analogous to the "primordial nature" which human individuality finds within itself at first—that which it has not made. Further, the problem of *individuality* is posed anew with respect to a *people*. But now *the individual himself is a world*, a *totality*, without, however, being the cosmopolitan absence of figure which Hegel consistently denounces as incompatible with the vitality of the concept. This individuality will appear as universal in the negation of negation, which for a people is the moment of war.

[334]

individuals; it is also their work, which is why individual consciousness actualizes substance in making it its own deed, and, conversely, why substance, which at first is only an in-itself (abstract universal spirit) becomes actual and alive in ethical action. The "unity of self and substance" is thus realized (*PE*, II, 14; *PG*, 316; *PM*, 462).

Hegel tries to explain and justify the distinctions in *content* which appear here; we shall limit ourselves to conveying an outline of his argument. The first moment, immediateness, is characterized by the fact that the self does not yet appear as the power of the negative, contraposed to its being. Ethical self-consciousness, Antigone's, for example, or Creon's, adheres immediately to its action, to the content that it intends to actualize. The self, here, is an ethical nature, a *character*. Action, and only action, will cause the self to emerge in its abstract independence and will pose it as *person*, free of any concrete content. The end point of this dialectic is the resolution of the "beautiful ethical life" in a world of abstract persons valid in and of themselves. From then on, substance is dissolved in the realm of persons, and spirit is posed in its externality to itself. In the modern world of alienation, spirit can no longer be what it is; it must always oppose itself.

The first moment, the beautiful ethical life, does not lack differences, but these differences are not yet oppositions. As we have already noted, substance splits into goal and consciousness, genus and individual. But the law according to which consciousness splits extends to substance too, and the content of substance then manifests itself as human law and divine law, element of specificity and element of universality.[2] Hegel is describing the Greek city here, and he represents the decline of that city through a study of ancient tragedy. Human law corresponds to the explicit laws of the city, the social and political life of a people; divine law corresponds to the penates, to the family, which is the kernel and, as it were, the potentiality of this world. Hegel tries to explain this division of substance according to the law of consciousness by showing that the very activity of self-consciousness is already present in the city and its government. "Spirit of this kind can be called human law because it has the

---

2. The split (*Entzweiung*) according to the law of consciousness continues to appear. The specific opposes the universal, but substance too divides according to the same law, and family and city reflect and oppose each other.

form of actuality conscious of itself" (PE, II, 16; PG, 319; PM, 467). The law of the city is public; everyone knows it, and it manifests itself externally as the expression of the common will of the citizens. As we read in the Antigone, "man has given laws to cities." The spirit of the people, then, appears in full light; it already appears as self-positing and, consequently, it stands contraposed to its other, to that from which it detaches itself, just as a plant rises and manifests itself on the outside while its roots remain sunk in the earth. The division of substance into human law and divine law, manifest law and hidden law, is brought about by the movement of consciousness which grasps being only in contrast to an other and sets off the figure of consciousness against a background of unconsciousness. Human law and divine law, the city of men and the family, complement each other, though each is other for the other. Human law expresses the actual action of self-consciousness; divine law, therefore, has the form of immediate substance, or of substance posed only in the element of being. The former is already an action, the latter the background against which that action stands out and from which it emerges. "Another power, divine law, opposes this public manifestation" (PE, II, 17; PG, 319; PM, 467). Thus, the family is the substance of ethical life as pure and simple immediateness, that is, as nature. "Spirit emerges from the depths of nature," and ethical spirit, the spirit of the city, emerges from the depths of the penates and family life. Thus, two oppositions appear, oppositions which for the moment are only distinctions: that between specific and universal and that between family and people. Hegel first shows us the complementary relation between these moments of immediate spirit, moments whose unity will constitute the beautiful totality, true spirit as totality, or infinity. Later, we see how action, "which alone disturbs the quietude of substance" (PE, II, 244; PG, 508; PM, 733), causes the self to emerge in its negative power. Greek tragedy, that of Aeschylus and Sophocles, represents the opposition between ethical self-consciousness and a destiny that entails the disappearance of the beautiful ethical totality: "In fact, through this movement, ethical substance becomes actual self-consciousness; this-self becomes what is in-and-for-itself, but the ethical order is destroyed" (PE, II, 15; PG, 318; PM, 463).

Because the ethical order is immediate, it must be undone, but because that immediateness is a beautiful moment in the development of spirit, spirit seeks always to rediscover it and reflectively to reconstitute it. To say that spirit exists immediately is to say that it is still nature, that morality is custom (έθος), that the self immediately knows the laws of its action. The substantive content of the act is given; subjectivity does not oppose it from the infinity of its being-for-itself. In his early works and in the philosophy of his Jena period, Hegel insisted, against Kant, that immediateness was a necessary condition of moral action. For no decision is possible without a certain presence of what must be done—an existential "this." The legislative activity of a formal consciousness does not culminate in action, and an examination of laws is already a slide toward immorality. But in the ethical world which we have just distinguished from modern morality, spirit knows itself as a nature and that nature is known as spirit: content does not oppose form but has spiritual meaning. We know the various ways in which Rousseau's contraposition of nature and culture influenced Hegel's generation. For Hegel and for Hölderlin, of course, there was no question of a "state of nature," a barbaric period prior to civilization; rather, they postulated a realized harmony between spirit and its world, the harmony of a spiritual life that was also natural without the painful opposition between self and the content of its life, between the infinite demand of the self and the finite given of its action. Hegel's contemporaries, and Hegel himself, saw Greece as a paradise lost, a moment of spirit's youth. They sought the land of the Greeks, as Goethe wrote in his *Iphigenia,* with the eyes of the soul: "Das Land der Griechen mit der Seele suchend."

The organic ideal of the life of a people, an ideal which Hegel conceived at Jena, was modeled on the Greek city. And much later, in the *Philosophy of History,* as in the *Phenomenology,* Hegel presented the essence of Greek character as "the beautiful individuality" produced by spirit which transforms nature into its own expression:

> The genius characteristic of the Greeks is the plastic artist who makes a work of art out of stone. In this molding, the stone does not simply remain a stone, but neither is its form a merely external garment. Contrary to its nature, it becomes an expression of the spiritual, and it is thereby transformed. Conversely, in order to express his idea, the artist needs stone, colors, sensuous forms. Without that element, the idea cannot become an object of his thought; he can neither be aware of it nor objectify it for others.[3]

3. *Philosophy of History,* p. 239.

This full realization of spirit existing as meaning in the objectivity of a nature makes that spirit true spirit, spirit which has not yet descended to the depths of subjectivity or posed itself as absolute negativity. "As ethical spirit, therefore, Greek spirit is the political work of art." The ἔθος exists there as the very being and will of the soul and of particular subjectivity. The individual does not yet exist as absolute specificity; he exists only as the *citizen* of a free people, a people that poses itself within the limited confines of a concrete city as a beautiful individuality, "a political work of art." That people is indeed an individuality. The formless Oriental despotism no longer holds sway, and the Roman opposition between the dominance of the state and the freedom of the individual qua abstract person is not yet arisen. For this reason, the Greek state is essentially *democratic*. The state is the work of its citizens; it has not yet, in its abstract necessity, become their destiny.

> Since the Greeks will, and perform, justice in the form of custom and habit, that form is the solid element and does not yet include reflection or the subjectivity of the will, the enemies of immediateness. The public interest can, therefore, be entrusted to the will and the decisions of the citizens. The Greek constitution must be democratic, for no principle yet exists which might oppose the ethical will or prevent its realization. The citizens are not yet aware of the particular or, therefore, of evil; among them, objective will has not yet been shattered. The goddess Athena is Athens itself, that is, the real and concrete spirit of the citizens. But divinity ceases to reside among the citizens when the will withdraws into itself, into its inaccessible refuge of knowledge and consciousness, and establishes the infinite separation between the subjective and the objective.[4]

In the pages following this passage, Hegel explains why the modern world cannot reconstitute that democracy, that immediate link between general will and individual will. "Subjective freedom, which in our society constitutes the particular form and the principle of freedom and is the absolute basis of our state and our religious life, could appear in Greece only as destruction." Interiority was not far from the Greek spirit, and it was soon attained, but it dashed Greek society to its ruin. For the constitution was unaware of that determination, had foreseen nothing with regard to it, and had not made provision for it. "We can assert that in the first, and true, form of their freedom

4. *Ibid.*, p. 252.

the Greeks had no moral consciousness (*Gewissen*); the habit of living for the native land ruled among them without any reflection." [5] There is a passage in the *Philosophy of History* which reproduces the discovery Hegel had made immediately preceding the writing of the *Phenomenology*, a passage which casts light on the opposition between the immediateness of true spirit and the split between faith and knowledge, between state and individual, that characterizes modern culture: "[The Greeks] did not know the abstraction of a state, which our understanding considers essential; their goal was the vital native land, this Athens, this Sparta, these temples, these altars, this manner of living together, this milieu of citizens, these mores, these habits. For the Greek, his native land was a necessity outside of which he could not live."

The presentation of this ethical spirit in the *Phenomenology* entails the presentation of two spiritual totalities, family and city, which, as we have seen, are contraposed to each other as shadow is to light. Hegel's reconstruction here is based on the great opposition between human law and divine law which appears in the plays of Aeschylus and especially in Sophocles' *Antigone*. That opposition is in fact an opposition between the masculine and the feminine. "Primal nature," which the I has not made and which at first appears as the brute given of sexual distinction, acquires a spiritual signification precisely by virtue of that givenness. In accordance with the immediateness of ethical spirit, the great natural distinctions have *meaning*, and, for the consciousness that discovers it, that meaning is immanent in the distinction. Yet in this way nature is transcended, for value is attached not to it but to the meaning in it. The natural element merely stimulates man; he can consider only the spiritual element which he has formed from it. The Greek solves riddles posed to him by nature. "The attitude which senses, which hearkens, which avidly grasps significations, is represented for us by the image of Pan." [6] Nature is grasped by spirit, and in that nature spirit discovers itself, though without knowing explicitly that it does so.

Thus the two sexes overcome their natural essences and, in their ethical signification, appear as diverse natures which share between them the differences that ethical substance accords itself. Thus, the two universal essences of the ethical world, divine law and human law, take on their specific individuality in self-

5. *Ibid.*, p. 253.
6. *Ibid.*, pp. 234–35.

consciousnesses which are differentiated in nature because ethical spirit is the immediate unity of substance and self-consciousness, an immediateness that is manifested simultaneously in reality and in difference qua the Dasein of a difference in nature (*PE,* II, 26; *PG,* 327; *PM,* 478).

Natural difference becomes spiritual difference: Antigone is womankind as Creon is mankind. Man rises from the substantive milieu of the family to human law, which is a positive law; he builds the city and finds in it his self-conscious essence. "But the sister becomes, or the wife remains, the manager of the house and the keeper of divine law"; her law, in accordance with her own nature, is not a positive, written law: it does not refer to human works but expresses the immediateness of the substantive element which simply exists. Hence, this law is unwritten and its origin unknown: "Not now or yesterday but always this law has lived; no one knows when it appeared." [7] These two laws complement each other and in their relation constitute the movement and life of ethical substance as infinite totality. "Human law proceeds, in its living movement, from divine law, the law that obtains on earth from subterranean law, the conscious from the unconscious, mediation from immediateness; and, similarly, human law returns to its starting point" (*PE,* II, 27; *PG,* 328; *PM,* 478–79). Their union is like the union of man and woman and, like that union, ethical substance in its totality is simultaneously a nature and a spirit.

Hegel studied the family, the city, and the transition from the one to the other so as to cast light on their spiritual meaning. Let us first consider the human city that is an individuality. It expresses itself in government as the self of all.[8] Whereas custom and publicly known law constitute the element of universality, simple and indivisible individuality is spirit qua government. The life of this whole asserts itself in a double movement of *expansion* and *contraction.* Specific individuals can become aware of their being-for-itself because the force of the whole flows in them and separates, so to speak, into distinct families. But this expansion, which might culminate in negating the

7. From the *Antigone,* quoted by Hegel, *PE,* I, 359; *PG,* 311; *PM,* 452.

8. This government will later become *self-certain spirit,* the acting spirit of history; here, it is still presented only as substance. In his 1805–6 lectures on "Philosophy of Spirit," Hegel says that in the modern state, government is spirit *certain* of itself (no. 2, pp. 262–63).

simple individuality of social spirit, the government, is negated in turn by war, which, in its negative action, contracts the particular systems which are in the process of splitting off from the whole. In the absence of war, individuals would return, through enjoyment and the acquisition of wealth, to a state of pure and simple nature. As the negation of a negation, war makes them aware once again of their dependency.

> Lest they take root and solidify in their isolation, that is, lest the whole be allowed to disintegrate and spirit to evaporate, government must unsettle their intimacy from time to time by war; through war, it must disturb their order, which is becoming habitual, and violate their right to independence, just as government must make those individuals who, submerged in that order, detach themselves from the whole and aspire to inviolate being-for-itself and to the security of the person feel, through forced labor, their master, death (*PE*, II, 23; *PG*, 324; *PM*, 474).[9]

In this way spirit exists as the individuality of a people and not in an abstract form. Negation is present here in a double form: as the individuality of a people, spirit is a determinate national spirit, and every determination is a negation; but the determination of individuality which, grasped in its Dasein, is a *negation* manifests itself in its action as *negativity*. War is the negativity that overcomes nature and "prevents submergence in natural Dasein far from ethical Dasein; it preserves the self of consciousness, brings it up in freedom, and cultivates its strength." In spiritual individuality, the self of spirit rises above its determination, but that is already a destiny, and, as we shall soon see, the determinate individuality of a people perishes through the negativity that preserves it. This idea of the tragedy of spiritual existence, which is merely foreshadowed by the description of the ethical order in repose, will soon manifest itself in action in the world. In fact, tragedy is characteristic of spirit itself: "Tragedy is the representation of the absolute position." [10]

The citizen thus brings his work to fruition in the service of the community that he builds. The labor of his life is his death, his universal becoming, yet that death appears as a contingency, as a fact of nature the spiritual signification of which is not evident. The role of the family, of *divine law*, is to rescue death

9. We see how Hegel grasps universal individuality as the negation of negation and thereby moves from pantragedism to panlogism.

10. This sentence is from Hegel's Jena article "Naturrecht," pp. 384–85.

from nature and make of it essentially "an action of spirit." As Hegel envisages it here, the ethical function of the family is to assume responsibility for death. The fundamental problem of the *Phenomenology* is to know what spirit has to "take upon itself": "Nothing, it appeared at first; but, as we shall see at the end, everything." [11] The family is a natural community. "Man finds the flesh of his flesh in woman, but the spirit of his spirit in the city." [12] In the union of man and woman, in the immediate recognition of love, nature prefigures the spirit of the city. But the family is not only a fact of nature; as ethical substance, it has a spiritual meaning which transcends the natural moment. It is not, therefore, grounded in the immediate determination of sentiment: "The ethical relation among family members is not that of sentiment or of love" (*PE*, II, 18; *PG*, 320; *PM*, 468). The ethical essence of the family is not constituted by the many determinations which may appear in it. Some of these remain too close to nature; others foreshadow the transition from the family to the order of the city and have, therefore, only negative signification with respect to the family. For example, the production, preservation, and enjoyment of goods concern needs, and pertain only to vital desire. Of course, the family would be inconceivable in the absence of the familial property which determines it as a substantive totality. But that property serves to satisfy the vital needs of contingent individuals. On the other hand, through its higher destination, economic life is also connected with the universal, although in a mediated way, without the individual being directly aware of it. The individual believes that he labors for himself or for his family; in fact, he takes part in an action which makes sense only in the context of the whole. If the essence of the family is not defined by economic life, neither is it defined by the education of children. Indeed, education, which "takes the individual being as a totality and through a series of efforts produces him as a work" (*PE*, II, 19; *PG*, 321; *PM*, 469), culminates in the dissolution of the family: it transforms the family member into a citizen. We must look elsewhere to see the family's ethical action on the specific. The specific, the individual, must indeed be the goal of the family, if the family is viewed outside the whole of ethical substance, as an autonomous spirit and not as a moment. In order that the individual be viewed accord-

11. Bréhier, *Histoire générale de la philosophie* (Paris, 1926), II, 739.
12. "System der Sittlichkeit," p. 465.

ing to ethical spirit and not according to nature, in order that he not be viewed according to his existence (insofar as he no longer belongs to the family), he must be a *universal individual*. "The goal of the family is the individual as such," but since the ethical is in-itself universal, it cannot bear on contingent individuality but only on the idea of individuality, on what individuality becomes as a shadow, when it is freed from all the accidents of life. Ethical action "concerns not the living but the dead, the one who gathers himself up out of the long sequence of his fragmented Dasein into a single, final configuration, and who has risen out of the disquiet of contingent life to the quietude of simple universality" (*PE*, II, 19; *PG*, 321; *PM*, 470). It concerns the individual, indeed, but the individual "Tel qu'en lui-même enfin l'éternité le change" [Mallarmé]; not the active self of the citizen, but the familial self. The family, thus, is a religious rather than a natural association. None of its other functions can truly characterize it as an ethical totality. The family is the worship of the dead; it reveals the spiritual meaning of death.

Death is the movement of the individual into the universal; in merely living nature, the species transcends the individual in a way such that this negation appears external. The individual does not carry his own death within himself. Death, thus, is natural negation: "It is natural negativity and the movement of the specific as existent, a movement in the course of which consciousness does not return into itself and become self-consciousness" (*PE*, II, 20; *PG*, 322; *PM*, 471). Death, then, would be a fact of pure nature in the spiritual world. The dead person becomes a pure thing, prey to elemental individuality, to the earth, or to other living beings (*PE*, II, 21; *PG*, 323; *PM*, 471–72). "Leave him unburied," Creon says, "a dinner for the birds and for the dogs." But death inaugurates the life of spirit. This movement into the universal occurs within a community: "Death is the achievement and the highest labor that the individual as such undertakes for the community" (*PE*, II, 20; *PG*, 322; *PM*, 471), which is why the preeminent function of the family is to restore to death its true meaning, to remove it from nature and to make of it a spiritual action. "Death seems only the immediate natural outcome, not the action of a consciousness. Consequently, the duty of the family member is to embrace this aspect, too, so that his ultimate being, universal being, not belong to nature alone and not remain something irrational, but be the result of an action in which the rights of consciousness are asserted" (*PE*, II, 20; *PG*, 321; *PM*, 470). The family replaces the action of nature with its own; it unites its member with the bosom of the earth, transforming him into a δαίμων. The family community, as it appears in the ethical world, gives meaning to death. The specific self is raised to universality; it is the late this-one but a late this-one who, qua spirit, continues to be. We see how Hegel rediscovers the essence of the ancient γένος and interprets it in his own system. As he wrote in the preface, "The life that carries death with it and maintains itself in death is the life of spirit" (PE, I, 29; PG, 29; PM, 93). And, writing about the struggle for recognition which opposes men to each other, he notes that death is merely natural negation which does not preserve as it negates, which is not spiritual Aufhebung. The family here substitutes itself for nature and raises the dead to the universality of spirit. Indeed nothing is more terrible for ancient man than not to receive the highest honors to which he is entitled (as specific) (PE, II, 20 ff.; PG, 322 ff.; PM, 472 ff.). Hector begs his enemy not to leave him without burial: "Return my body so that the Trojans may give me my due in funeral pyre."

Such is the ethical nature of the family. But as a concrete totality, it includes, as does the city, particular moments which result from the split in consciousness. Here we find those determinations which we set aside while seeking the spiritual meaning of the family. Love between man and woman is the highest moment of natural life. It expresses the natural and immediate recognition of one self-consciousness by another. The family is not only this immediate self-knowledge in the other, which Hegel considered love to be in his early fragment and which stands contraposed to the difficult recognition of man by man described in the Phenomenology; it is also the cognizance of that mutual being-recognized, which is thus the substantive element of family life. But this recognition is only a foreshadowing and, as it were, an image of actual spirit. The actuality of an image "lies in an other than itself" (PE, II, 24; PG, 325; PM, 475). Love between parents is realized externally, in the child. "The growth of children," Hegel wrote in the Jena Realphilosophie of 1805–6, "is the death of parents."[13] Their love has become another "whose development is that very love and into which that love vanishes. The flow of passing generations achieves its perma-

13. No. 2, p. 202. "Love becomes an object to itself." It contemplates itself in an other who is its negation. "The natives of North America kill their parents; we do the same."

nence in a people" (*PE*, II, 24; *PG*, 325; *PM*, 475).[14] Later, in the *Philosophy of Right,* Hegel expressed the same idea:

> The unity of marriage—which, as substantive, is interiority and feeling but, as existence, is separated into two objects—becomes in children an existence for-itself and, qua unity, an object. Parents love children as their love, as their substantive being. From the natural point of view, the immediate existence of the person of the parents becomes a result here, a continuing sequence in the infinite chain of generations which reproduce and presuppose each other. In this manner, the spiritual simplicity of the penates manifests its existence in finite nature as a species.[15]

Nevertheless, these various relations—between husband and wife, between parents and children—are not purely spiritual. Since a discrepancy is still present in them, recognition is affected by an element of naturalness. The love of man and woman does not return into itself; it escapes out of itself and onto that other that is the child. The devotion of parents for their children remains affected by the touching contingency of "being aware of one's own actuality in the other and of seeing being-for-itself develop in that other without being able to recover it—for the other remains an alien actuality all its own" (*PE*, II, 24; *PG*, 325; *PM*, 475). Genuine spiritual relation contains its return into itself; its becoming-for-itself is simultaneously its own preservation. But in parental love, nature appears as an irreducible otherness, and that otherness is a passion, a particularity within spiritual universality. If for parents the child is the being-for-itself of their love, which stands outside them, then, conversely, children see their nonorganic nature, their in-itself, in the figure of their parents; they attain being-for-itself and their own self-consciousness only "through a separation from the source, a separation in the course of which the source dries up."

Drawing on Sophocles' *Antigone,* Hegel sees the relation of brother and sister, by contrast, as pure and unmixed. Brother and sister are free individualities for each other: "They are of the same blood, which however attains peace and equilibrium in

---

14. In this ethical world the self does not exist yet except as a *shadow:* "It is the suppressed here and thus a universal self, but its negative signification has not yet been converted to this positive signification." We shall see the beginning of its realization in the first type of self, the person (*PE*, II, 204; *PG*, 474; *PM*, 686).

15. *Philosophy of Right,* p. 117.

them." For this reason, a sister has the most profound presentiment of ethical essence, of the free relation of one self-consciousness to another. But she can have no more than a presentiment, for family law, of which femininity is the guardian, does not appear in the light of day; it is not an explicit knowledge but remains a divine element withheld from actuality. From the ethical point of view, a woman finds in her husband and children only her universality; the relation of specificity remains bound up for her with pleasure and contingency and is thus not itself ethical. At the hearth of ethical rule, the question is not of this husband or these children but of a husband and children in general. "Woman's relations are founded not on sensuousness but on the universal" (PE, II, 25; PG, 326; PM, 476). Man, on the other hand, earns the right to desire through his sacrifice for the totality, by finding his universality in the city. In the family, he finds his self as specific and no longer as universal. But if specificity enters into woman's relations, it is not purely ethical. Insofar as woman's specificity is purely ethical, it is irrelevant; and woman is barred from self-recognition as this-self in an other. Her pure recognition, unadulterated by naturalness, arises in her relation with her brother. "For a sister, a lost brother is irreplaceable, and her highest duty is to him." Hegel quotes Antigone here: "If a husband dies, another can replace him; if a son dies, I can have another; but I cannot hope for the rebirth of a brother."

It is in her brother that the sister becomes aware of individual self; but then the spirit of family shifts into the consciousness of universality. The brother abandons the elemental and negative realm of the family so as to conquer and bring about concrete ethical rule, the self-conscious spirit of the city. With this, we have spent enough time on Hegel's close and often ingenious (rather than convincing) interpretations of Sophocles' tragedy. Family and city, which are presented here in an immediate form, cannot disappear from the life of spirit. That these moments do not reappear in the subsequent developments means only that spirit's becoming aware of itself—true spirit becoming self-certain spirit—no longer needs to pay particular attention to them. We shall dwell only on those moments in the history of spirit which translate the aspect of for-itself by developing the oppositions noted in this starting point. These moments are abstract person, culture, and self-certain spirit. Thus Hegel's dialectic of the family and much of his dialectic of the city—

expansion and contraction, economic life and war—retain for him a validity independent of the historical moment at which they appeared in their most adequate form. The Greek city, in which the citizen rises immediately to universality, and the Greek family, in which the specific self is saved from death itself and preserved in his universal specificity, form a beautiful totality in which universal and specific do not yet stand opposed. In this totality, substance, as a people, is an individual substance and is not yet present as destiny—abstract universality contraposed to individuals. And the self is present only as a shadow, as the blood of a family, and not yet as negative specificity, the exclusion of everything that is other. These two moments develop until they oppose each other: destiny comes to swallow up the individualities of the ethical realm, and the individualities lose their immediate character and become the abstract self of persons. At that point, ethical substance has perished. This double signification of destiny and of the specific self of the ethical world is set forth in a later passage of the *Phenomenology:*

> In the ethical world, we saw a religion of the lower world: a belief in the frightful and unknown night of destiny—pure negativity in the form of universality—and in the fury of the departed spirit—the same negativity in the form of specificity. In the latter form, absolute spirit is indeed self, and it has a presence—the presence of the self which can exist only as present. But the specific self is that specific shadow which has cut off from itself the universality of destiny. It is indeed a shadow, a *suppressed this-one*, and thus universal self, but its negative signification has not yet been converted into this positive signification (*PE*, II, 204; *PG*, 474; *PM*, 685–86).[16]

Hegel will further examine the essence of tragedy as such; his study of the ethical world—no longer as immediate beautiful totality but insofar as tragic opposition arises within it as the result of action—will show how concrete substance becomes a destiny which is all powerful and just, albeit negative with respect to the self, and how the self emerges from the subterranean world in which it exists merely as suppressed this-one.

Before we leave this static representation of the ethical world to consider what it becomes in the tragedy of genuine action, let

16. Cf. Hegel's interpretation of the state as *destiny* rather than as the expression of the *common will*, and, later, as *power* (Rosenzweig, *Hegel und der Staat* [Oldenburg, 1920], pp. 80 ff., 102 ff.).

us note that it includes all the prior moments of "the realization of individual self-consciousness." [17] Insofar as it was abstract, this self-consciousness could not discover itself in nature. Now, ethical life (mores) is the truth of that individual reason, for here these mores are what reason discovers. But simultaneously, they are a being that is the action and product of the consciousness that discovers them. The anxious quest for self-enjoyment, the law of every heart, virtue: these take on their true meaning. In the family the specific individual finds himself as another self-consciousness; the destiny that expels him from the family is the law of the city. This law of every heart is the universal order in which each participates as citizen. Virtue, then, is no longer an empty abstraction; it realizes that toward which it tends. Through the sacrifice it requires from the individual, it makes essence into a present reality. It can, therefore, enjoy its sacrifice in the universal life that it contemplates. Formal reason finds in the ἔθος the living content which eluded it when it claimed to legislate or to test laws. As for the totality of substance, it splits, indeed, into human law and divine law, but each of these laws seems to confirm the other. Human law leads the individual toward the universal through the trial of death, the absolute master; it moves from light to shadow. Divine law bears death and raises it from nonactuality to actuality; it leads from shadow to light. Human law devolves upon man, divine law upon woman. This totality remains self-contained; it is measure and tranquillity, that is, justice—a justice which is neither a transcendental law beyond the self-present totality nor a pure arbitrariness whose equilibrium is assured by the mechanism of mindless chance. The vengeance which recoups the injury an individual has suffered emanates from himself, from his Erinys. His individuality and his blood survive in the family. For the rest, the only injury an individual can truly suffer in this world is one that comes only from a natural fact that lacks spiritual signification. But nature is transformed in this world and is penetrated by spirit. Death itself becomes an action of consciousness. In his section on religion, Hegel will name this beautiful moment in the life of spirit: its self-representation is the religion of art. Indeed, beauty is this immediate unity of nature and spirit.

17. For a discussion of all these moments (immediate enjoyment, the law of the heart, virtue) see part IV, chapter 4, above. Each of these moments which made themselves essences is taken up again in ethical totality as a moment.

Tragic Action: The Self as Action

In his early works and in his Jena writings, Hegel thinks of spirit—the absolute—as tragic. In the Jena article on natural right, after characterizing the ethical world, the life of a people, as the highest manifestation of the absolute, Hegel writes that tragedy is "the representation of the absolute position." In comedy, on the contrary—the divine comedy of Aristophanes or modern bourgeois comedy—spirit appears raised above all oppositions: either oppositions appear in it for a moment as shadows which are then dispelled in its pure self-certainty, or it is itself caught in oppositions, trapped in the finite in such a way that the absolute is revealed to it as nothingness and illusion.[18] For this reason, comedy, which is the absence of destiny, always expresses the victory of specificity, of subjectivity withdrawn into itself. It is, therefore, merely the laughter of impotence, and it finds its tragic destiny within itself, in its own inadequacy. Thus we see again that tragedy expresses the very life of spirit. The ethical world, the calm subsistence of which we saw above, is spirit only because tragedy is revealed in it. Tragedy will make substance appear as destiny, and the truth of this destiny is the emergence of the self, the subjectivity of being-for-itself (in other words, ancient comedy, in which "the oppositions and the finite are like shadows without essence"). The truth of this emergence of subjectivity will, in turn, appear in the alienation of spirit, in modern comedy, in which the finite is asserted as such and claims an illusory independence. Modern bourgeois society, the world of culture, is the truth of the disappearance of ancient destiny into the self, as Hegel explained in his tract on natural right. Comedy, then, separates two ethical zones so as to leave each with its own validity: in one zone, the oppositions and the finite are shadows, without essence; in the other, the absolute is an illusion. The genuine and absolute relation is that

---

18. The first case corresponds to ancient, Aristophanic comedy; the second to modern, bourgeois comedy in which the self, as a character, takes what is merely finite to be absolute—money, for instance—and is caught up in a dizzying dialectic. Although he vainly tries to stabilize the finite and to pose it as in-itself, it eludes him—in accordance with its inner law. In ancient comedy the self laughs at itself on stage; in modern comedy only the audience laughs. Cf. Hegel, "Naturrecht," pp. 384 ff.

each appears seriously in the other, each enters into a living relation with the other and is the other's serious destiny. Thus, absolute relation is indeed represented in tragedy. In the section on religion, Hegel again considers the significance of tragedy and comedy for the representation of spirit. We have referred to this passage on the transition from ancient tragedy to ancient comedy and from ancient comedy to the modern comedy which is its destiny, because it sheds light on the entire development of objective spirit which Hegel is to follow. In the beautiful ethical nature we have just discussed, in which the two moments, family and city, "complete each other" in such a way that, in Plato's phrase, which Hegel repeats, that totality is "an eternal living," [19] the self has not yet emerged in its rights as specific individuality. Indeed, no action has been accomplished, but action is the actual self. With action, tragic contradiction enters the world and leads it toward its necessary decline. Substance will then appear to self-consciousness as destiny. This opposition between self-consciousness, caught up in a particular form (divine or human law), and substance, raised from its immediateness and become the abstract universal (necessity as destiny), is the tragic opposition whose development we shall study. For us, of course, the truth of this necessity, of this destiny, is the self of self-consciousness, but in that case the ethical world has perished and another world—which, in the Jena article, is defined by modern comedy—has come to light: spirit is alienated from itself. This entire development is summarized in the following passage:

> What appears in this world as the order and the accord of these two essences, each of which confirms and completes the other, becomes, through action, a movement of opposites into each other, a movement in the course of which each appears as the nothingness, rather than the confirmation, of itself and of the other; each becomes the negative movement, the eternal necessity of a terrible *destiny*, a necessity that swallows up in the abyss of its simplicity both human and divine law, and, with these, the two self-consciousnesses in which the Dasein of each lies. It is a necessity which for us passes over into the absolute being-for-itself of a self-consciousness that is purely specific (*PE*, II, 30; *PG*, 331; *PM*, 484).[20]

19. *Ibid.*, p. 389.
20. The transition from ancient world to modern world, from citizen to bourgeois or to Christian (a necessary split, for the bourgeois lives in finitude and therefore poses his essence beyond his actuality, thus giving rise to the double world of spirit alien to

The *Phenomenology*, like a symphony, continually presents the same themes but in different forms. The fundamental theme is that of the opposition between the universal and the specific, substance and subjectivity, being and self. We have seen the consciousness of the universal vanish in the specificity of self-consciousness. But, qua subjectivity, self-consciousness is unhappy consciousness which has lost substance. We shall rediscover that unhappy consciousness at the end point of the tragedy of the ethical world. It will appear in its objective form, in the history of spirit, in the Roman world, in the harsh politics of empire and the turning inward of persons, and it will develop in the modern world of culture. At that point, spirit will be self-alienated. This is the equivalent, in the objective, social, and political order, of unhappy consciousness.[21] The meaning of this pain of subjectivity becomes clear later in the vision of the absolute granted to us by religion. The religion of art will culminate in absolute self-certainty, and man will be the truth of tragic destiny. But, as in the case of unhappy consciousness, that infinite self-certainty will be unable to pose itself without negating itself. The Christian God-man himself will have to die; subjectivity will have to deepen itself to the point of restoring substance, just as substance had submerged itself into subjectivity. The self will then be the absolute subject which rediscovers itself in the tragedy of its alienation, the concept which preserves itself in objectivity, remains close to itself, and, in its subjectivity, becomes objective to itself. Substance indeed becomes subject; the universal and the specific are reconciled while remaining opposed. But this opposition (unhappy consciousness, the world of alienation, and Christianity all take up the same theme at different levels) cannot disappear from the life of the absolute. Hegel had already said this in the Jena article quoted above. Explaining why "tragedy is the representation of the absolute position," he wrote: "The absolute eternally performs this tragedy to itself. It eternally engenders itself in objectivity.

---

itself) is well represented by the transition from ancient to modern comedy. This transition is the tragic destiny of absolute self-certainty, which now is necessarily alienated from itself.

21. We summarize here what in the *Phenomenology* is developed in stages: (1) in the dialectic of self-consciousness (cf. part III, above); (2) in the development of objective spirit, the unhappy consciousness of history or self-alienated spirit (cf. part V); (3) in the development of religion, the moment of Christianity or of the dead God (cf. part VI, below).

In that concrete figure of itself it yields to passion and to death, and rises majestically from its ashes." [22] This is the "die and become" of the divine, which is thus identical to the human; God becomes man, and man becomes God. The God-man becomes a man-God, but the torment of subjectivity is the torment of the self which, having posed itself in its absolute self-certainty, discovers only its own finitude and is lost in the finite. Yet this alienation is necessary in order that the self become what it already is immediately.

We shall now consider the notion of destiny and the related notions of tragic opposition, action and guilt, and knowledge and ignorance—notions which play a large part in the elaboration of Hegel's philosophy. In his early theological writings, Hegel studied the relation of a particular people to its destiny. It was in Frankfurt in 1787–1800 that, according to his sister, Hegel personally experienced the anguish of his epoch, as he studied the destiny of the Jewish people and the destiny of Christianity.[23] In his earlier stay in Bern, Hegel had tried to make sense of the *positivity* of a historical religion which opposed the Enlightenment's pure religion of reason and refused to sacrifice the richness of concrete life and the breadth of historical changes to a dry and narrow concept of human nature. In Jena, he came to see the irrationality of human life and the impossibility of thinking the transition from finite life to infinite life according to the rules of discursive understanding. Yet since infinite life, the ἓν καὶ πᾶν, is immanent in finite life, neither can exist without the other. But understanding freezes them in objectivity, and, therefore, can never reunite them. Now the concept of destiny is pregnant with meaning and seems to go beyond the analyses of reason, but by that very fact, it is a means for thinking the opposition that action introduces into human life. The separation of man from his destiny and his reconciliation with it through love constituted a new way of grasping the relation

22. "Naturrecht," p. 384.
23. Cf. K. Rosenkrantz, *Hegels Leben* (Berlin, 1884), p. 80. We may say that while in his Bern period Hegel thought of historical experience, the *given*, as positivity (today we would say "facticity") and contraposed it to abstract reason, in his Frankfurt period that given became an individual *destiny*. The elaboration of the concept of destiny and its substitution for that of positivity was one of the essential stages in Hegel's movement toward pantragedism. His transition from this pantragedism to a *panlogism* was a new step forward—or perhaps a step backward.

between finite and infinite life. Thus Hegel—without naming it or clearly being aware of it—elaborated a dialectical philosophy which moved from the pantragedism of his youthful period to the panlogism of his maturity. This notion of destiny, which reappears in the *Phenomenology*, seems to be at the heart of Hegel's view of spirit. Kant had noted that the idea of destiny can have no legitimacy for those who wish to judge things from the point of view of experience and of reason. But Jaspers, who quotes Kant's remark, adds, "The idea of destiny regains its significance for the person who stands in a borderline situation; the validity of destiny as a concept cannot be demonstrated, but destiny can be experienced." Hegel rises from that life experience of his Frankfurt years to an identification of destiny with the concept. In the *Phenomenology*, he writes, "It is the spirit of tragic destiny that gathers up all the individual gods and the attributes of substance into one pantheon, into spirit conscious of itself as spirit." (*PE*, II, 262; *PG*, 524; *PM*, 754).

What is this destiny that Hegel borrows from the tragic view of human existence, a view which, with Hölderlin and before Nietzsche, he perceives to be the somber background of Hellenic serenity? We must distinguish destiny in general—actual reality (*Wirklichkeit*), that world history which becomes for Hegel the tribunal of the world—from particular destinies which transpose the original pathos of individuals and peoples into the real. Nothing great occurs without passion, which is to say that every human action bears a characteristic finitude and is inadequate to infinite life. It is the deed (*Tat*) that introduces separation into pure life and raises man's destiny before him as alien. But this destiny of an individual or a people—Hegel had studied the destiny of the Jewish people and that of Christianity through characteristic individuals, Abraham and Christ—is nothing but the manifestation in actual reality of what these individuals or peoples are qua pathos. Thus a particular destiny is the revelation of a determinate pathos in a history. "Destiny is what man is"; it is his own life, his own pathos, but it appears to him as "having become alien." "Destiny," wrote Hegel in Frankfurt, "is consciousness of oneself, but consciousness of oneself as an enemy." [24] And in a passage of the *Phenomenology* which we have yet to study, he repeats Sophocles' words: "Because we suffer, we recognize that we have failed." But, in the same work, Hegel had already noted that "destiny is merely the explicit

24. *Early Theological Writings*, p. 232.

manifestation of what determinate individuality is in-itself as original internal determinateness" (*PE*, I, 261; *PG*, 231; *PM*, 342).[25] Only actual action, then, reveals the pathos of individuality in objectivity. It is our own life that appears to us as an externality. And, in order to feel guilty (that is, to experience our own finitude), we do not need a law which condemns us and to which we can never be reconciled because it is by nature always alien to us: through our actions, we ourselves call forth our own verdict. To be sure, by separating itself from us our destiny shows us that we are not pure infinite life, purely at one with being; it is our nonorganic nature, that in us which is not infinite life. But by contraposing it to us, we can confront it and reconcile ourselves with it through love, through an *amor fati* which is both a "die and become," and in which man finds his highest reconciliation with destiny in general, with world history—which for Hegel is the highest consciousness of freedom.[26] That reconciliation, in which my destiny is integrated into destiny in general, simultaneously negated and preserved in it, is the final harmony of tragic representation; it makes actual reality appear, substance in its necessity, just destiny in its omnipotence. Of course, the pathos of individuals and peoples subsists: Antigone and Creon are eternal figures. But they are stripped of their exclusiveness; they are *aufgehoben*. In the ancient world, the calm of this reconciliation appears only as forgetfulness, as "the vanished-being of actual reality, . . . the quiet of the whole within itself, the still unity of destiny, . . . simple Zeus" (*PE*, II, 252; *PG*, 516; *PM*, 743). But in the Christian world, that destiny becomes the subject, *spirit conscious of itself as spirit*. As has been noted, Hegel's notion of destiny is quite different from his contemporaries' conceptions of it.

> The transition from individualist thought to historical thought was similar to a parallel change in the concept of destiny. Just as for the Kantians and the pre-Romantics history and law were but a series of wrenches inflicted on pure reason, a series of compromises with sensuousness, so in Schleiermacher's monologues destiny appeared merely as the eternally hostile course of nature,

25. In its largest terms the problem Hegel poses here is the problem of individuality.

26. On the evolution of the notion of destiny, on the separation of life, and on reconciliation through love, see *Early Theological Writings*, pp. 232 ff.

as the entirely external brutality of fate which flouts and defies the I that is sure of its freedom.[27]

But in Hegel's earlier writings, and in the *Phenomenology*, destiny is no longer this brutal force; it is interiority in exteriority, the manifestation of the I on the outside. And when the individual succumbs to his destiny, spirit regains its freedom by transcending him. The moment of the fall is also the moment of salvation. We have already seen in the *Phenomenology* how the individual who sought his own specificity in being, who sought immediate self-enjoyment, recognized himself in brutal necessity. The law of the heart understands only itself in what is opposed to it and in what in actual fact expresses the law of all hearts. Similarly, virtue cannot overcome the way of the world because that way is not blind, brutal force, but, on the contrary, is that which alone can give virtue meaning.

After these remarks on Hegel's novel conception of destiny, we are better able to understand the meaning of the tragic action which opposes divine law to human law, Antigone to Creon. Out of the clash of their pathos, with which self-consciousness identified itself, the all-powerful rights of the ethically real, of substance become necessity, are born. They are no longer the illusory knowledge of a right that overwhelms the individual as character. That knowledge discovers through its action that it is also ignorance, and the self thereby opposes necessity, the negativity of destiny. But *for us,* the truth of that destiny will be the universal self, simple self-certainty. Ethical substance as immediate individuality, the presence of spirit in the midst of a particular nature, will have perished, and infinite subjectivity will have come to light. "The self appears only insofar as it is attributed to characters, not as the medium of movement. Nevertheless, self-consciousness—simple self-certainty—is in fact negative power, the unity of Zeus, the unity of substantive essence and abstract necessity; it is the abstract unity to the bosom of which all returns" (PE, II, 253; PG, 517; PM, 744). The ethical world becomes the world of subjectivity and of abstract persons, of Christianity and of the Roman Empire.

Hegel conceives of this transition from the life of the city to the Roman Empire, from the ethical world to the world of ab-

27. P. Bertrand, "Le Sens du tragique et du destin dans la dialectique hégélienne," *Revue de métaphysique et de morale*, XX, no. 2 (April, 1940), 170.

stract persons, through a general interpretation of Greek tragedy, or more specifically—since in Euripides' plays the conception of tragedy and destiny is no longer present in its pure form— through an interpretation of Aeschylus and Sophocles. In his article on natural law, which we have already cited, Hegel interprets the *Eumenides* as posing and solving the problem of the unity of divine law and human law in the city. At the end of the play, peace is concluded between the Erinyes and the Athenian people, between the avenging goddesses, who represent the ancient law of blood, and Apollo. The old and the new orders are reconciled through the instrument of justice created by the Athenian state. The conflict between the Furies and the Olympian gods is a conflict between the lower world and the upper world, between the ancient pact and the new order of the city, an order in which there exists a bond stronger than blood.[28] These two worlds are united and inseparable: "Manifest spirit draws its force from the lower world. The self-certainty experienced by a people, a self-confident and self-affirming certainty, possesses the truth of its oath joining all into one only in the unconscious and silent substance of all, in the waters of forgetfulness" (*PE*, II, 40; *PG*, 339; *PM*, 495). *Knowledge* is lost in its origin, *ignorance*. In this chapter of the *Phenomenology*, the main texts in question are *Antigone* and *Oedipus*, but the great tragedy *Eumenides* is present in the background. In *Antigone*, the two laws which, according to Hegel, constitute the two essences of the ancient spirit are opposed in content. This opposition in content between powers in the ethical world, symbolized by Antigone and Creon, must be surmounted by an opposition in form, that between knowledge and ignorance, an opposition inherent in every self-consciousness. It is this latter opposition that appears in *Oedipus*, for example, and that allows the universal notion of destiny to be conceived. Through these oppositions, Hegel is able to envisage the decline and dissolution of ethical essence in general, the end of municipal life and of the beautiful totality, which spirit seeks ever to restore in its history but which —since it was merely true, immediate spirit—had to vanish.

> This determination of immediateness implies that nature generally intervenes in the action of the ethical world. The actuality of the action merely manifests the contradiction and the seed of corruption which the beautiful harmony and the tranquil

28. "Naturrecht," pp. 385 ff.

equilibrium of ethical spirit contain in the very midst of that tranquillity and that beauty. For the unconscious repose of nature is ambiguous: it masks the self-conscious disquiet of spirit (*PE*, II, 43; *PG*, 342; *PM*, 498).

We first discover this determination of immediateness in the individuality of the ethical world, an individuality which is not abstract self but a *nature* and, in the most profound sense of the word, a *character*. "This decay of ethical substance and its move-ment into another figure are thus determined by the fact that ethical consciousness is directed toward law in an essentially immediate way" (*PE*, II, 43; *PG*, 342; *PM*, 498). In ancient tragedy, unlike modern drama, there is no unique individuality who is raised above the determinations of action and to whom a problem of contingent choices is posed. There is no free will, that is, no problem that has the form "either/or." What we have is a pathos which genuinely expresses one of the moments of ethical substance. In later tragedy (Hegel is thinking of Eurip-ides) "that pathos is lowered to the level of passion, to con-tingent, nonessential moments which the chorus (which has no self) praises, to be sure, but which cannot constitute the char-acter of the heroes and which these heroes cannot set forth and respect as their essence" (*PE*, II, 253; *PG*, 517; *PM*, 744). The ethical character, on the other hand, Antigone, for example, is an individuality which bears the meaning of its action within itself and knows immediately what it must do. It belongs by its very nature (as woman or man) either to divine or to human law and, for it, *that* particular law is ethical law *as such:* it is cognizant of that law as *its* essence and as essence *as such*. It is resolute, but its resolve is fused with its very being and does not follow from conscious deliberation. "This immediateness of its resolve is a being-in-itself and, therefore, simultaneously has, as we saw, the signification of a natural being. It is nature, not the contingency of circumstances or choice, that assigns each sex to one of the laws" (*PE*, II, 31; *PG*, 332; *PM*, 485). In this determination of character, in this indissoluble unity of a spirit and a nature, there is an ethical beauty that indeed will have to be found in a different form in the further development of spirit. For without such determination genuine action is im-possible. We shall see later how self-certain spirit discovers within itself—no longer in an alien nature but as its own de-termination—the immediateness necessary for action. At that point, the problem of knowledge and ignorance is again posed, this time definitively.[29] But for the moment, prior to action, that problem is not yet posed. Creon condemns Polyneices without hesitation; he suffers no inner conflict. And Antigone hesitates no more than he: she is fully identified with what she will do, she belongs to divine law. When hesitation appears in ancient tragedy, it is evidence not of a moral conflict but, only of weakness in the face of action. Like Antigone, Orestes does not discuss the deed he must do; he knows it from the very god of light. It is important to see the essence of tragic conflict clearly: "As, on the one hand, the ethical order consists essentially in that immediate decision—for consciousness, therefore, only one of the laws is the essence—and as, on the other hand, ethical powers are actual in the self of consciousness, they come to exclude each other and to be opposed" (*PE*, II, 32; *PG*, 332; *PM*, 485). The opposition is necessary, because, qua character, self-consciousness adheres to one of the laws as *the* law. The opposition in ethical consciousness is not between a duty and a passion, or between two duties (collisions which, showing the absolute in opposition to itself, would be comic), but between "duty and a lawless reality." "Opposition appears as an unfortunate clash between duty and an actuality devoid of right." Ethical consciousness then sees right on one side and wrong on the other and seeks, by force or by cleverness, to impose its own law on the actuality it faces. Antigone sees only a contingent human violence in Creon's orders, and Creon sees only criminal disobedience and woman's stubbornness in Antigone's deed. The tragedy is not that of a good will opposed to a bad will but of the coexistence of two wills, of two self-consciousnesses, which, each fully adhering to law, reject and fail to recognize each other: that recognition follows the action and shows up the earlier ignorance. Then, self-consciousness abandons its partiality, comes to know itself in *its destiny*, and discovers *destiny* as the actual reality of the unity of substance.

In order that the recognition of the other be possible after the action and that this be the work of consciousness and not a merely externally imposed result, self-consciousness itself must, as it acts, provoke the contradiction; the contradiction must be the deed of self-consciousness. With this we come to the nature of *acting*. First of all, self-consciousness must act. By acting it implicitly recognizes the rights of the real: "The goal of action

29. Cf. *PE*, II, 168 ff.; *PG*, 445 ff.; *PM*, 642 ff. and, for our interpretation, part VI, chapter 2, below.

is the actuality of the goal." But for self-consciousness that real is no longer an alien world: "It has drunk from the cup of absolute substance the forgetfulness of any partiality of being-for-itself" (*PE*, II, 33; *PG*, 333; *PM*, 487). Self-consciousness, therefore, does not see actuality as something that can pervert its action, reverse its meaning, and bring about through the world's malice a nonethical realization of an ethical goal. At this stage, self-consciousness sees action only as the necessary transition from what is thought to what is. Its absolute right is to find its own self in reality. "The absolute right of ethical consciousness is that once an action is finished the figure of its actuality should duplicate what that consciousness knows" (*PE*, II, 33; *PG*, 333; *PM*, 487). Action is necessary, for it "leads the goal, the substance merely thought, to fulfillment." But it is merely a transition; through it, the in-itself becomes a deed. And yet it is through action that the opposition between knowledge and ignorance is introduced: in action, "the opposition between the known and the unknown is born in consciousness, and the opposition between what is conscious and what is unconscious is born in substance. The absolute right of ethical self-consciousness comes to clash with the divine right of essence" (*PE*, II, 33; *PG*, 332; *PM*, 486).[30] The absolute right of self-consciousness is to find only what it knows in the result of its action. But having attached itself to one law to the exclusion of the other, and having taken that law for law as such, it necessarily calls up the other law, which is closely bound up with the first law. Consciousness believes that the ethical world reveals itself to it as it is, but that world is reality, and it is therefore double: it is *in-itself* as well as *for consciousness*. The right of essence to split into two laws, then, must also appear when self-consciousness acts. Here again we find a dialectic that is inherent in action and which appeared in its elementary form with regard to "real individuality in-and-for-itself." We saw then that although every acting consciousness believed that it was only translating its project into the element of being, in fact, it experienced in its work a transformation of the project itself and through that work discovered itself to be other than it had thought. Although the moral and ethical character of self-consciousness changes

30. It will be noticed that the opposition that is essential to action, and which was presented and transcended in earlier stages (cf. all the chapters on individuality), reappears here in a new form—as the opposition between the divine right of essence (non-knowledge) and the right of self-consciousness (knowledge).

the content of this dialectic, it does not change its structure. "To act is precisely to move the immovable, to produce externally what at first is merely enclosed in possibility, and thus to join the unconscious to the conscious, what is not to what is" (*PE*, II, 36; *PG*, 336; *PM*, 490). But this right of essence, which appears at the time of ethical action, is not to be looked for anywhere but in self-consciousness itself. It is self-consciousness which, by acting, rises from its immediateness and poses the split. In becoming the acting element, the self simultaneously negates and recognizes the right of the actuality contraposed to it, for it wishes to inscribe its project in that actuality: "The goal of action is the actuality of the goal." The existence of an unconscious element in substance, corresponding to ignorance in consciousness, is illustrated by the story of Oedipus. Actuality does not appear to consciousness as it is in-and-for-itself; the son does not see the stranger who attacks him as his father nor the queen whom he marries as his mother. In a beautiful passage in his early work, Hegel thinks the tragedy of human existence through in the following way: one must assert one's right and in so doing oppose reality. But then one must either recognize the value of reality—including the possibility of other rights, against which I collide, a tragic contradiction—or refrain from asserting one's right in reality, which is to recognize the inactuality of, no longer to believe in the reality of, that right, a no less tragic contradiction.[31] In acting, ethical self-consciousness leaves immediateness and produces the split; becoming aware after the fact of the finite and partial character of its decision, it necessarily experiences itself as *guilty*.

"Because we suffer, we recognize that we have failed." This guilt must be distinguished from what the moderns call "moral responsibility," just as ancient character must be distinguished from free will. What has passed from an intention to an alien milieu, which has changed its purity, cannot be distinguished here from what that milieu has added to the intention. "The action itself is this split, the act of posing itself for itself and in the face of this posing an alien actual exteriority" (*PE*, II, 35; *PG*, 334; *PM*, 488). That such an actuality exists, precisely as an alien term, depends on the very fact of acting and is a result of it. For that reason, every human action is guilty; "only the absence of action is innocent, the state not even of a child but

31. This is the dialectic of the "beautiful soul": *Early Theological Writings*, pp. 233 ff.

of a stone" (*PE*, II, 35; *PG*, 334; *PM*, 488).[32] This guilt, which is bound up with action, is also a crime (*Verbrechen*), since the action counters another equally essential law. It violates it by adhering exclusively to one of the laws of substance, which is to negate the other. But since the two laws are united in essence, "the fulfillment of one calls forth the other as an injured essence which, because of the action, is henceforth hostile and demands vengeance" (*PE*, II, 36; *PG*, 335; *PM*, 489–90). Whether it adheres to divine law or to human law, self-consciousness recognizes itself in its action. But that recognition has an unexpected result. For what it sees asserted are the rights of substance as actual reality, rights which negate the partiality and exclusiveness of the moment that had been made into an absolute.[33] But then ethical goal and actuality are no longer separate and the recognition is only a return to inactive ethical sentiment which knows that only uprightness has any worth. Insofar as it was character, ethical individuality disappears, unable to survive the decline that ethical power, of which it was the self, undergoes at the hands of the opposing power. These two laws, each of which is expressed by a different self (which contradicts the unity of the self), must each suffer the same destiny. "It is only in the equal submission of both sides that absolute right is fulfilled and ethical substance appears as the negative power which swallows up both sides, as omnipotent and just *destiny*" (*PE*, II, 38; *PG*, 337; *PM*, 492–93).

We have dwelt on this dialectic because it includes some of Hegel's most remarkable analyses of tragedy, character, and the conditions of human action. The *self* as pure negative unity (as specific individuality) and *destiny* (substance no longer qua beautiful individual totality but qua necessity and negative unity), both only potentially present in the ethical world, appear at the end point of this movement, a movement in which the partiality of character is dissolved. This opposition between self and destiny expresses the decline of ethical essence and a transition into another world. Let us briefly indicate the meaning of

32. This guilt, which is *inevitable* since it is linked to our finitude, reappears in the higher dialectic of spirit. Cf. part VI, chapter 2, below, and *Early Theological Writings*, pp. 224 ff.

33. This "exclusiveness" was contained in decision itself, as the necessary separation between knowledge and nonknowledge, between light and darkness. "Decision is *in-itself* the negative which contraposes an other, a something alien, to the decision that knowledge is" (*PE*, II, 36; *PG*, 335; *PM*, 490).

this transformation, a transformation closely related to the preceding dialectic.

The story of Eteocles and Polyneices is a good illustration of the seeds of contradiction in the ethical world. Wishing to give metaphysical meaning to every concrete given, Hegel interprets the struggle for power between the two brothers as an example of the opposition between nature and self-consciousness and as a starting point for the opposition between divine law and human law. The adolescent emerges from the unconscious being of the family and becomes the individuality to be found in a community. But that this individuality appears in the guise of two brothers is a contingency of nature. (For priority of birth can have no intelligible signification in the purely human order of the city.) This contingency has rights over self-consciousness, for spirit, here, is present only in an immediate unity with nature; it is not yet *true spirit*. Nevertheless, from the human point of view, the brother who is, in fact, in power and who defends the city is in the right; the one who attacks it in the wrong. Creon, who represents human law and the dictates of human government, is right, then, in according burial honors to one brother and denying them to the other. But although the spirit of community thus triumphs over the rebellious principle of specificity, that principle is not defenseless: its being is in the family and in divine law. "Self-conscious spirit engages in battle with unconscious spirit" (*PE*, II, 40; *PG*, 339; *PM*, 494). To be sure, Antigone must succumb to the actual law of the city, for she represents only a subterranean law, a law which at first is defended only by "a bloodless shadow"—weak and unreal specificity. But for all that, this underground law is the root of actual spirit, and therefore the supreme right of the community becomes the community's greatest wrong. The dead person whose rights have been injured by the community can find equally effective instruments to avenge him: other cities. These, becoming hostile, devastate in *war* the community that has dishonored and shattered the familial piety that is its own strength. These wars among cities—we have already seen how they suppress the centrifugal forces that arise in the midst of the human city—appear contingent. In fact, they express a *necessary dialectic* which leads individual ethical substance to its foundation.[34]

34. This is the transition from national spirit, which is an *individuality*, to empire, which contraposes *persons* and abstract *state*.

This general development can be summarized as follows: the unconscious spirit of the penates is defeated by the self-conscious spirit of the city; that individual spirit of cities, in turn, disappears in a spiritless empire. "As at first only the penates were swallowed up in the spirit of a people, so, as a result of their individuality, the vital spirits of peoples are swallowed up as they pass into a universal community, a community whose simple universality lacks spirit and is dead and whose vitality is the specific individual qua specific." For Hegel, who had seen eighteenth-century universalism and Napoleon's empire, spirit could only live embodied in diverse peoples, in concrete historical realities. Else, the substance of spirit loses its individuality and becomes a lifeless universality. Yet this multiplicity of peoples in history cannot be posed as a goal; they come to play their various roles in the course of history. In this case, we see how through the dissolution of the ethical city war realizes the abstract universality of spirit and the actuality of the specific self. War has a double function: on the one hand, it is needed by governments to combat the centrifugal action of the penates—individualization into families under the direction of the feminine, the principle of specificity; on the other hand, it makes manifest the contingent particularity of each city. Although the city appeared to have defeated the feminine principle of specificity, the latter avenges itself: "Through intrigue, femininity—the eternal irony of community—transforms the universal goal of government into a private goal." [35] The specific individual is then no longer merely a bloodless shadow or a representative of the common will; he appears as actual self. War requires the strength of youth and the ambition of conquerors. Although the community can maintain itself only by repressing the spirit of specificity, it simultaneously calls on it as the mainstay of the whole. "Indeed, the community is a people; it is itself individuality and is essentially so for-itself only because other individualities are for-it, because it excludes these and knows itself to be independent of them." The fate of the city depends on the very principle that it represses, which is why the ethical order dissolves. Human and divine law lose their

35. In "Naturrecht" (p. 372) Hegel had placed considerable emphasis on war, which transforms the original individuality of a people into an infinite individuality (negating its negation): too lengthy a peace leads to a submersion of spirit in naturalness. This thesis reappears, albeit in less romantic form, in the Berlin *Philosophy of Right*, pp. 208 ff.

individuality in the unity of substance. Substance itself, detached from naturalness, becomes negative and simple destiny, but, simultaneously, the self becomes actually real. Imperialism succeeds municipal life; exclusive self becomes actual reality. What will this new world of spirit—comparable to the moment of self-consciousness in the first part of the *Phenomenology* —be?

2 / The First Form of Spiritual Self

IN THE ETHICAL WORLD, spirit existed immediately. But immediate existence is unsuitable to spirit, and, therefore, we have witnessed the decline of beautiful spiritual individuality. The ethical world is succeeded by a world of torment and alienation. Spirit stands contraposed to itself: on the one hand, it perceives its essence to be beyond its reality; on the other, it appears to itself in this world as external to itself.

Nonetheless, the truth of the ethical world is the emergence of the self, which, as such, did not yet exist in it. This self is immediately universal: it knows itself as the abstract person who is valid in-and-for-itself. This actuality of the self, its recognition and its validity, are the elements of the new world of spirit into which we are entering. How is this world precisely the reverse of what it appears to be? How does *realized* self-certainty give birth to a world in which the self can no longer find itself? We shall find the answers to these questions in the dialectic of the *state of law* (PE, II, 44 ff.; PG, 342 ff.; PM, 501 ff.). There we find reproduced in the universe of spirit the dialectic we have already encountered in the history of the formation of self-consciousness (the movement from stoic consciousness through skepticism to unhappy consciousness). But this movement is a general movement of the history of spirit, and not the particular movement of a self-consciousness. And if the ethical world corresponded to municipal life and the Greek city, this universal *realization* of the self corresponds in the world spirit to the disappearance of municipal life and the development of the Roman Empire.

Before analyzing this dialectic as it appears in the *Phenome-*

nology, we shall study its sources in Hegel's early works. Hegel first discussed the unhappy consciousness of history, which corresponds to the transition from the Greek city to Roman despotism and from paganism to Christianity, in "The Difference between Greek Imagination and Positive Christian Religion," a text he wrote while in Bern.[1] The principal traits of unhappy consciousness appear in this text, although the term itself does not. Let us also note that before abstractly presenting the split of the I within itself, Hegel discovered that unhappy consciousness in a *historical phenomenon.* In the *Phenomenology,* the analyses of unhappy consciousness proper (in the section on self-consciousness) and of the alienation of spirit (in the chapter on the state of law) are separate. But they were elaborated together, and the one that in the *Phenomenology* appears later was indubitably earlier. Hegel first discovered what later was to be unhappy consciousness in general in a certain transformation of the world spirit, a transformation from which issued the modern world.

The text in question deals with the transition from paganism to Christianity. Hegel drew on the historical works of Gibbon and Montesquieu, but he dealt with the historical problem as a philosopher. "The suppression of pagan religion by Christianity was one of the most astonishing historical revolutions; the study of its causes must occupy, most particularly, the philosopher of history."[2] This revolution was preceded by a hidden and continuous transformation of the world spirit, a transformation more important than the events, which alone impressed contemporaries. The transition from the Greek city and municipal life to the modern world and its religion cannot be accounted for in so simple a manner as certain supporters of the Enlightenment believed. The demise of paganism was due not to the sudden activity of critical spirit but to a social and spiritual transformation of the human world. "How could a religion which had for centuries been rooted in states and had a close connection with the constitution of the state, disappear?"[3] Today, we do not consider the pagan deities worthy of belief, yet the wisest men of antiquity fully believed things that today strike us as absurd.

1. *Early Theological Writings,* pp. 151 ff. In his translation, Knox drops Hegel's title, "Difference between Greek Imagination and Positive Christian Religion."
2. *Ibid.,* p. 152.
3. *Ibid.*

We must understand first of all that the religions of the Greeks and the Romans were bound up with the whole of ancient life. Each was the religion of a people and, as Hegel notes, of a free people. When freedom was lost religion lost its power: "The change from freedom to despotism entailed the decline of ancient religion; the latter lost its hold over souls when freedom became an empty word. . . . What use are the fisherman's nets when the stream is dry?" [4] The ancient citizen was unaware of the liberty of conscience; in the ancient city the modern notion of free will would have made no sense. For the young Hegel, freedom in the Greek city expressed simply the harmonious relation between individual and city. The ancient citizen was free to the extent that he merged with his city, that the will of the state was indistinguishable from his own will. He was as unaware of a limitation on his individuality as of an external constraint imposed by a dominating state. "The idea of his native land, of his state, was the invisible reality, the highest thing for which he labored; it was the final goal of his world." [5] Hegel quotes Montesquieu, for whom the principle of a republic was *virtue*, virtue in the sense of a civic, not an individualistic, morality. "The ancient citizen was free precisely because he did not contrapose his private life to his public life." The state, therefore, was not for him an alien despot. "As a free man, he obeyed the laws he had imposed on himself—he sacrificed his property, his passions, and his life for a reality which was his own." This was a living totality, and pagan religion was but the expression of that beautiful individuality. The ancient citizen placed the eternal part of himself in his city. The problem of the immortality of the soul could not, therefore, be raised for him in the way that it is for us. "Cato turned to Plato's *Phaedo* only when the highest order of things—his world, his republic —was shattered. Then he fled to a still higher order of things." [6]

But this city—immediate spirit—was dissolved in wars and was succeeded by an imperialism that leveled all. The *citizen* as such disappeared, and in his place the *private person* appeared. The individual turned in on himself: "The picture of the

4. *Ibid.*, p. 153.
5. And, Hegel adds, this final goal was present for him; it was a reality. He himself contributed to the presentation and the maintenance of that reality (*ibid.*, p. 222). We should note that Hegel uses the term "idea" here for the first time, to denote this *final goal*, this reality which contains its own *meaning*.
6. *Ibid.*

state as a product of his activity disappeared from the citizen's soul; the burden of the state was carried by only a few persons, and sometimes by only one—the others were but cogs in a wheel." This mechanical image allows us to understand what Hegel calls in the *Phenomenology* a "spiritless relation." The abstract domination of the state and the individual's interest, limited to his own preservation, replaced the beautiful living relation between the individual and the whole. "All activity and all goals relate merely to the individual; there is no further activity for a whole, for an idea." [7] *Private property* is the goal of the individual, and each individual can consider the state only as an alien power which he tries to bend to his own interest. "Everyone works for himself or, by constraint, for another individual." The citizen's rights become merely the right to the security of property, "which now fills the entire world of the individual." [8] What Hegel later describes in the *Phenomenology* is this social atomism and its correlates: domination by a "world master" and the universal, but only formal, relation of law.

From then on, ancient religion could no longer make sense. In this misfortune of the world new faiths appeared and Christianity—which in Tübingen Hegel called a "private religion" as opposed to "the religion of a people"—became dominant. "In that situation, man had to flee the world in order to find something absolute. He had to become aware of the corruption of the world and wander from the here-below (the prose of the world) to the beyond (the reconciliation with the infinite, which is unrealized here below)." This separation between self and its essence characterizes the world of spirit become alien to itself. The living unity and the self-presence which held sway in the ancient world are succeeded by the dualism of here-below and beyond.

This social and spiritual transformation from ancient to modern world, from citizen to private person, was so important for Hegel that he returned to it in his Jena article on natural law. What he wrote there was not much different from the earlier text, but it foreshadowed more closely the dialectic presented in the *Phenomenology*. "Private life succeeded life lived for the state, and with private life the formalism of abstract law appeared, a law which freezes the specific being and poses him

7. *Ibid.*, p. 156.
8. *Ibid.*

absolutely." [9] This formalism of law, the reign of the person valid in-and-for-itself, characterizes the chapter of the *Phenomenology* which we shall now discuss.

The general movement of the dialectic Hegel presents here is easy to grasp. The compact substance of spirit has dissolved into the world of persons, and the abstract I which is no longer bound up with determinate content becomes our object. The beautiful ethical individuality is replaced by the *juridical person;* the living relations of ethical individualities are replaced by spiritless, legal equality, juridical recognition. But that formalism is never adequately matched by the content that this I gives itself. Possession, when recognized, becomes property. Thus in the first part of the Berlin *Philosophy of Right,* Hegel immediately connects the abstract law of persons with private property.

Yet the content that the I gives itself in the form of private property is a finite content which in its development escapes juridical formalism. The I can no longer find itself in this content, for the latter belongs to an alien power: "Content belongs to an independent alien power other than the formally universal: chance and whim" (*PE,* II, 47; *PG,* 345; *PM,* 504). When the I discovers the externality of this content, the latter reflects back on itself and is gathered up into the person of a world sovereign, an alien domination. Thus the world of persons, in which universal self-certainty is actually realized, is a world in which the I eludes itself. When it poses itself immediately, it tests its own finitude; it sees itself outside itself either in the form of a real content from which it is distinct but which is its work, or in the form of an absolute essence which, like unhappy consciousness, it must pose beyond this finite world. "The universal validity of self-consciousness is the reality that has become alien to it. That validity is the universal actuality of self, but such a validity is immediately its surrender: it is the loss of the self's essence" (*PE,* II, 49; *PG,* 346; *PM,* 506).

This stage of the dialectic, then, is a bridge between the ethical world and the world of culture. It presents a critique of individual relation and communication insofar as these are merely

9. "Naturrecht," pp. 381–82. Let us note that the *Phenomenology* presents this emergence of the *person* in history whereas in the *Philosophy of Right* Hegel considers the notion of law as the first moment of the dialectic that expresses the concept of law in-and-for-itself. Hegel pointed out this difference in approach in a note in the *Philosophy of Right,* p. 105.

juridical. The abstract recognition and the formal equality of persons, which has replaced the living unity of spirit, is a poor substitute for the development of a concrete content which, having left the unity of spirit, now develops on its own. This content is the world of private men, the transformation of properties. Thus when the ancient citizen becomes the private man, abstract self is realized. But in becoming realized, it discovers its own externality to itself. This self does indeed make the world, but the world appears other to it, just as its own essence appears to it to be alien to the finite world. Hegel's description has a historical reference (it corresponds to the moment of the Roman Empire), but it also has a more general bearing. This passage of the *Phenomenology* allows us to understand the first part of the Berlin *Philosophy of Right* and the influence which that analysis of abstract law and the juridical relation among persons had on Marx. "The actual content, or the determination of what is mine —be it a matter of external possessions or of internal wealth or poverty of spirit or character—is not contained within that empty form and in no way concerns it. Content thus belongs to an independent power" (*PE*, II, 46; *PG*, 344–45; *PM,* 504).

Certain passages of the *Philosophy of History* cast light on the historical context of this dialectic and specify concretely each of its moments: validity of the person, contingency of the person, world ruler. The development in question is that from the Greek to the Roman world.

> The Greek principle showed us spirituality in joy, serenity, and enjoyment. Spirit had not yet withdrawn into abstraction. . . . Abstract universal personality did not yet exist, for spirit had first to adapt itself to the abstract form of universality, which subjected humanity to a harsh discipline. In Rome, thenceforth, we find the free universality, the abstract freedom, which on the one hand set the abstract state, politics, and force above concrete individuality, completely subordinating the latter, and on the other hand created in the face of this universality the freedom of the I within itself—a freedom which we must be careful not to confuse with individuality.[10]

The Roman world, especially the period of empire, serves here as a transition from spirit that is still immediate to the modern world.

In the first moment of spirit, the self did not yet exist by itself; it was present only in its living bond with its substance—

10. *Philosophy of History*, p. 278.

as *citizen* of a particular city or as *blood* of the family. "But now it emerges from its inactuality" (*PE*, II, 44; *PG*, 343; *PM*, 501). This reflection of substance into the self is necessary, and at the end point of the development of spirit substance will indeed become subject. But here we find only the *first type of self*, the self *immediately* universal and therefore *contradictory*.

> Its Dasein is recognized-being. Just as the person is self void of substance, so the Dasein of the person is also abstract actuality. The person is valid and, precisely, is valid immediately. The self is the point that is immediately at rest in the element of its being. This point exists without separation from its universality, and hence self and universality have neither movement nor mutual connection. The universal exists with no distinctions within it, and it is not the content of self. Nor is the self filled by itself (*PE*, II, 170; *PG*, 446; *PM*, 645).[11]

In the world of culture, by contrast, the self, by willfully alienating itself, poses the universal outside it and is thus able to give itself content of its own. Reciprocally, the universal receives the self within it and becomes actual. In this way a second form of the reflection of spirit is prepared, a *second type of spiritual self*.

But in the moment we are studying, the self is merely an abstract form juxtaposed to a contingent content. The living spirits of peoples have vanished into a spiritless universal community: the pantheon of Rome. Only the specific individual, qua specific, has vitality, and he serves as the content of the abstract person. The universal "has split into atoms which constitute the absolute multiplicity of individuals"; this dead spirit is "an equality in which, insofar as they are persons, all are of equal value" (*PE*, II, 44; *PG*, 342–43; *PM*, 501). In the *Philosophy of History*, Hegel summarizes this evolution as follows:

> The living body of the state and the Roman mentality which inhabited it as its soul are now reduced to the specification of inanimate private right. The political organization has dissolved into the atoms of private persons—just as when a physical body rots each of its parts acquires a life of its own, which, however, is nothing but the wretched life of worms.[12]

11. Thus, in reflecting itself as self, spirit becomes (1) the immediate self (the abstract person), (2) the self opposed to itself (specific will and general will), (3) the self as acting subject, as the creator of history.

12. *Philosophy of History*, p. 317.

Abstract order, which corresponds to the validity of the person, is an order of law which the great Roman jurists gradually elaborated. Their work—which led Leibniz to say that demonstrations in law were hardly less rigorous than those in geometry—culminated in a mechanical form of understanding. The person is recognized-being in-and-for-itself, but the recognition has no content and can establish only external links among individuals. The period between the reign of Augustus and that of Alexander Severus (250 A.D.) is considered to be the great era of legal science. But it is also the period of the most ruthless domination, a period in the course of which all the ancient civic and religious institutions died out as despotism grew. There is indeed no mediation between the person I am in law and the contingent content that constitutes me in other respects. The old substance of the people was reflected back into destiny, and empty destiny is "nothing but the ego of self-consciousness" (*PE*, II, 44; *PG*, 343; *PM*, 501); we can now see what comes of that abstract self-certainty. The mediation of stoicism leads to skepticism, and the skeptic unveils the contingency of actually existing content. The individual who (in vain) knows himself to be a person appears alone face to face with an alien domination which crushes him. "The emperor's will ruled over all; beneath him was an absolute equality. . . . Private law developed, and it perfected that equality. . . . Indeed, individual rights consist in a person's having validity as a person in the reality he accords himself—in property." [13] Law is no longer a sacred and mysterious chant handed down obscurely within the family; it emerges from rituals and becomes public. In fact, according to Hegel, it is the world of law that Stoicism expressed in thought. Primitive law was grounded only on authority and tradition; it was an imposed rule (*jussum*). Under the influence of Stoic philosophy, it becomes the manifestation of natural equity. According to a contemporary definition, human law is *quod naturalis ratio inter omnes homines constituit.*

But the independence of Stoic consciousness was the independence of a thought withdrawn into itself, a thought which neglected content and determinate situations.

> In its flight from actuality such a consciousness reaches only the thought of independence. It is absolutely for-itself insofar as it does not attach its essence to any given Dasein, claiming instead to abandon Dasein, and poses its essence only in the unity of pure

13. *Ibid.*, p. 317.

thought. In the same way, the law of persons is attached neither to a richer or more powerful Dasein of the individual as such nor to a universal living spirit, but rather to the pure entity of its abstract actuality, or to that entity qua general self-consciousness (*PE*, II, 45; *PG*, 343–44; *PM*, 502).

This is why stoicism found its truth in skepticism and skepticism was the actual consciousness of the contingency of content. But in thinking the contingency which it always seeks to overcome, skepticism itself, as consciousness of contingency and finitude, is a contingent and finite consciousness, a consciousness which ever becomes alien to itself and, consequently, is unhappy. The case is the same with the abstract juridical person. In the reality that it accords itself (property), the juridical person can find only the contingency and finitude of its content. "Consequently, consciousness of law experiences in its own actual validity the loss of its reality and its complete inessentiality: to call an individual 'person' is to express contempt" (*PE*, II, 47; *PG*, 345; *PM*, 504). Thus, paradoxical as the contrast may appear, the Roman world which Hegel calls the world of "abstract interiority" is the world of finitude, the *prose of the world*. Possession, a factual state, becomes property, a legal state. But that recognition, which raises the I for-itself to an I in-and-for-itself, in no wise changes the contrast. As Hegel later wrote in the *Philosophy of Right*, "Equality could only be the equality of abstract persons as such, and therefore the whole field of possession, this terrain of inequality, falls outside it." [14]

Content thus reflects back on itself, as form, too, had done, and the abstract person *withdrawn into itself* is opposed by a no less abstract domination, an arbitrary external power. The validity of the person has led us to the contingency of the person; that contingency culminates in the thought of the "world ruler" in whom the entire movement and development of content is gathered up.

For the small property owner in the provinces, the world ruler, or, to use the term from the *Philosophy of History*, the *monas monadum*, symbolizes the content that is alien to his personality. "The individual's destiny lies in the emperor's favor, or in violence, in ruse, or the inveigling of an inheritance." Instead of a small republic in which each citizen directly feels himself a living member of the community, *pax romana* appears, extended over the world. Thus the *state* has become the in-

14. *Philosophy of Right*, p. 317.

dividual's *destiny*. On the one hand, there are abstract persons who exclude each other and assume reality only through their property; on the other hand, there is the continuity and unity of these exclusive persons, but a continuity and unity external to them: this is the despotism of the emperors, of the world ruler, of the *real God*.[15] Hegel takes pleasure in showing how this "solitary person" is constituted, facing everyone and representing the master of this world. In its isolation, the person of the emperor is powerless; it asserts itself and has value only through the masses of subjects who stand facing it. This world ruler, worshipped like a god, is the weakest of creatures. His formal self is unable to contain the leashed powers that arise within him. "Knowing himself to be the sum of all actual powers, this world ruler is the gigantic self-consciousness which knows itself as actual God. But since he is only a formal self unable to restrain his powers, his movement and his self-enjoyment are a gigantic orgy" (*PE*, II, 48; *PG*, 345; *PM*, 505).[16] Indeed the "prince of this world," denounced by the Christians and worshipped by the pagans, is aware of himself only through the destructive violence he exercises on his subjects. So he too is external to himself— like the master, whose truth lay in the slave who labored for him.

Such then is the new world that is born from the dissolution of the ethical world: it is a world in which the self has become actually real, but it is also a world in which the self is always external to itself. In this "world misery" man could only withdraw into philosophy and reflect on his inessentiality. "The consciousness of this actuality driven back into itself thinks its own inessentiality" (*PE*, II, 48; *PG*, 346; *PM*, 506). In the *Philosophy of History*, Hegel wrote, more concretely, that in this period

> Man sought repose in philosophy, which alone remained able to provide a solid prop existing in-and-for-itself. For the systems of the time—Stoicism, Epicureanism, and Skepticism—though contraposed, all culminated in the same result, viz., to make spirit in-itself indifferent to everything that reality represented. . . . But that internal reconciliation through philosophy was itself abstract in the pure principle of personality. For the thought which,

15. *Philosophy of History*, p. 320.
16. "By virtue of the principle of his personality, the subject has only the right to possess, and the *person of persons* (my emphasis) has the right to possess everybody. Hence individual right is simultaneously resolved and without right. The misery of this contradiction, however, is the *education of the world*" (*Philosophy of History*, p. 320).

as pure, took itself as object and reconciled itself to itself was completely without object, and the unshakable firmness of Skepticism made the absence of a goal precisely the goal of the will. This philosophy knew only the negativity of all content. It was only the advice that despair offered to a world in which nothing solid remained.[17]

Through the voluntary alienation of its subjectivity, unhappy consciousness prepared for reason. So too, the immediately universal self which gives rise to a world and which is no less immediately its own contrary must voluntarily alienate itself. That alienation allows the constitution of a new reign of spirit, a reign at the end of which the self will have *made* itself universal. This reign is that of *spirit alien to itself* which opposes *immediate spirit*. In the reign of the latter, the self existed *immediately*, either as the expression of one of the masses of substance (divine law or human law), or in its pure abstract validity; in the former, it exists in the movement of *mediation*: it acquires content through the renunciation of its immediate self-certainty, and that content, in turn, is imbued with the self. This double movement is the movement of *culture*.

17. *Ibid.*, pp. 317–18.

3 / The World of Culture and Alienation

WE HAVE SEEN immediate, natural spirit dissolve into a world of private persons. The spiritual substance with which we began has become the formal relation of specific individuals in whom the self has taken refuge as pure (abstract) self-certainty. We have gone from substance to self, from the objective and natural social order to private persons who exclude each other. Now we must reverse our direction and approach a second type of self, a self whose will is genuinely universal and which includes within itself the entire substantive content of spirit. "The first self was valid immediately; it was the specific person. The second, which returns to itself from its alienation, will be *universal self*—consciousness grasping the concept" (*PE*, II, 52–53; *PG*, 349; *PM*, 511).[1] This self, which will be historically embodied in the "absolute freedom" of the French Revolution, is the result of culture and of the preceding civilization, of which it is simultaneously the culmination and the negation. The world (in the spiritual sense of the word which we have indicated) will be no more than the expression of the will of that self; better, it will be that will itself.[2] The end point of the dialectical development, however, will not yet be reached,

1. Whereas the first type of self lacked content, the result of alienation is that the second type presents the content of substance as self.
2. "For it, the world is exclusively its will, and that will is universal will" (*PE*, II, 131: *PG*, 415; *PM*, 600).

[376]

for this second type of self, having overcome all alienation, will not make an existing world, a reality detached from itself, out of its universal will. "The universal . . . is the object and the content of the self, and its universal actuality. But it does not have the form of Dasein free from self. Therefore, it attains no plenitude in the self, no content, no world" (*PE*, II, 170; *PG*, 446; *PM*, 645). In that *absolute freedom* spirit will not manage absolutely to discover itself in the other while simultaneously preserving the form of otherness. Yet Hegel takes the historical events he is discussing, which he witnessed—the revolutionary thought of the eighteenth century, the Enlightenment's struggle against faith, the French Revolution, and the domination of Napoleon—as a metaphysical *code*, and he seeks to draw from these events a philosophy of spirit.

The period preceding these events, from the Middle Ages to the eighteenth century, is first studied as the period of culture, or civilization (*Bildung*). The word has a very general meaning for Hegel. It covers *intellectual culture* as well as *political* and *economic culture*. But we will be able to see its fullest meaning only after we have specified the meaning of the related term "alienation" (*Entäusserung*). For culture is the alienation of immediate self, which we have seen emerge from ethical substance and starting with which we must see the reconstitution of that substance "in which spiritual powers arrange themselves into a world and thereby maintain themselves" (*PE*, II, 51; *PG*, 348; *PM*, 510). Unlike the first world of spirit, the second is not a harmonious totality quietly resting in itself; it is a torn, divided world, a world of spirit *become alien to itself* (*entfremdete*). At first reading, the passage in which Hegel expounds the meaning of the term *Entäusserung* and prepares us for subsequent developments is quite obscure. We shall try to explain it before following the stages of culture, which will lead us to the philosophy of the eighteenth century and to the French Revolution.

In the first dialectical moment in the development of spirit (the moment of primal and immediate unity), opposition, Hegel writes, is as yet implicit in consciousness. That consciousness is at one with its essence, immediately at one. We may also say that this spirit exists immediately: consciousness lives it as one lives mores or customs whose origins are unknown and which are not thought of as being distinct from the self that lives them. The second dialectical moment, opposition, is entirely different. Opposition derives from the actuality of the self, which was not present as such in the ethical moment. In that first moment, "consciousness does not take itself to be this particular exclusive self, and substance does not have the meaning of a Dasein excluded from the self, a Dasein with which the self could become at one only through its estrangement while at the same time having to produce substance" (*PE*, II, 50; *PG*, 347; *PM*, 509). This sentence contains the burden of what Hegel wants to show: on the one hand, the fundamental opposition between self and substance, an opposition which was not present at the preceding stage but which we are now to encounter; on the other hand, how that opposition is to be overcome in the *double* movement of culture. Indeed, we shall see that by alienating its immediate self-certainty, its natural being, the self binds itself to the universal and makes itself substantive, or universal, while in that same action producing and giving life to that very substance. The self becomes substantive when substance becomes actual. There is no need to belabor the first point —the opposition between self and substance—for we have already shown how that opposition is necessarily produced under the conditions of private law. Substance is the content of ethical life which eludes the self and appears to it as a progressively more alien, progressively more objective, reality. What spiritual consciousness lived at first as its immediate world— mores, familial and social life, the power of the city—has now become for the insular and exclusive self an other, an other which is not however absolutely other. For this reason, the need to discover oneself in the other is at least present. And since that content is the substance of spirit, spirit can think of itself only as separated from itself, as having become alien to itself. This opposition between self and substance contains in summary all future oppositions, which merely develop it. Just as when self-consciousness emerges from universal life that life is for it simultaneously same and other and it can exist only by opposing that life and discovering it within itself, so the previous ethical substance becomes for the self that other which is the same and which it must take into itself again.[3] The distinctive characteristic of this stage of spirit is that that substance has become for the self an alien world in which it no longer recognizes itself. "The world then is determined as being an externality, the

3. For a discussion of this opposition between self-consciousness and universal life, which is repeated here as an opposition between spiritual substance and the self, see part III, chapter 1, above.

negative of self-consciousness" (*PE*, II, 50; *PG*, 347; *PM*, 509).
But we must not forget that we exist in spirit and that the content which stands contraposed to us as a world cannot be a
thing-in-itself or even a nature (as in the dialectic of reason).
It is merely spirit that *exists*, as opposed to spirit that *knows
itself;* it is the world of immediate self, which, when it is thus
posed in its exclusiveness, no longer discovers itself. "But such
an actuality is also immediately its reversal; it is the loss of the
self's essence" (*PE*, II, 49; *PG*, 346; *PM*, 506). That is why the
Dasein of this world is also a work of self-consciousness, albeit
"a work in which self-consciousness fails to recognize itself."

In the world of (private) law, content—gathered up in the
domination of the world master—appears to the self as a contingent and wholly external content. It is the product of dis-
located elements, of specific individualities, and it continually
negates itself and transforms itself. But that development is precisely the movement of the self which, thanks to its alienation,
finally gives that content consistency and order. It produces
spiritual substance as its work, "but the external actuality which
the ruler of the world of law includes in himself is not only that
elementary essence, which appears to the self in a contingent
manner; it is also its labor, negative rather than positive. It
acquires its Dasein through the alienation peculiar to self-
consciousness, its renunciation of its essence (*Entwesung*)"
(*PE*, II, 50; *PG*, 347; *PM*, 509). Here we reach the second point:
the development of culture by means of alienation. The immediate, isolated self, the private person of law, which thinks
that it is in-and-for-itself, discovers its own poverty: it becomes
aware of a "world misery." Although this *prise de conscience*
appears to result from the violence of a domination exercised
over it, in fact, it is itself that discovered world, and it destroys
itself. Immediate self sheds its immediateness; it cultivates itself,
alienating its *natural rights* in order to gain substantiveness. In
this manner, it constitutes substance whose Dasein is the very
alienation of the self. That substance indeed acquires a consistency and a permanence thanks to the movement of the self,
which renounces its immediate state and poses substance as the
self.

> Nevertheless, the action and the development by means of which
> substance becomes actual are the very estrangement of personal-
> ity, for the self which is valid in-and-for-itself immediately, that is,
> without estrangement, lacks substance and is the plaything of
> tumultuous elements. *Its* substance is therefore its very aliena-

tion, and alienation is the substance in which spiritual powers arrange themselves into a world and there maintain themselves (*PE*, II, 51; *PG*, 348; *PM*, 510).

In that double movement of the self toward essence and of essence toward self, substance becomes spirit, that is, a unity conscious of itself, of the self, and of essence. By virtue of the process of alienation, however, self and essence remain alien to each other—or, at least, their genuine unity is posed *beyond actual presence*, in *faith*. "Spirit is consciousness of an actuality that is objective and free for-itself. The unity of self and essence stands in contrast to that consciousness; pure consciousness stands over against actual consciousness" (*PE*, II, 51; *PG*, 348; *PM*, 510). Thus spirit now has a *double* consciousness of itself. On the one hand, spirit discovers itself in an objective world; on the other hand, the need for unity of self and essence is still posed. That unity is not realized in this world in which spirit remains alien to itself in the movement of culture: it is *beyond* this world. Consciousness of that unity is *pure*, not *real* consciousness: "Presence stands immediately contraposed to its *beyond*, which is its thought and its being-thought [*Gedachtsein*]; conversely, this thought stands contraposed to the *here-below*, which is its actuality that has become alien to it" (*PE*, II, 51; *PG*, 348; *PM*, 510).

This dualism is characteristic of spirit that has become alien to itself: it is the sign of the *unhappy consciousness* of spirit. We have referred to a passage from Hegel's early work, in which he studied the birth and development of Christianity during a transformation of the ancient world. The individual no longer adhered to himself in the world. "In that condition, man had to flee the world so as to find something absolute outside it." Man is outside himself, but that separation entails a corresponding unity, a unity, however, which can have no presence since for the self all presence is now external. "Despotism expelled man's spirit from the earth. The loss of freedom led him to safeguard his eternity, his absolute, by locating it in a divinity; the misery of the times led him to seek and find his happiness in heaven. The divine became progressively more objectified as slavery and corruption extended their sway." [4] Thus *faith* appears as the requirement for a unity beyond the separation experienced by consciousness. That unity stands opposed to actual reality and transcends it. For consciousness, however, this

4. *Early Theological Writings*, p. 162.

unity has an *objective* character, a character of exteriority, precisely because it is the reverse of the world of culture and is a new form of alienation. Hegel's use in his early works of the term "objectivity" in the sense of "positivity" foreshadows a difference between unhappy consciousness and faith. *Unhappy consciousness*, which was a subjective aspiration, a nostalgia for an unrealized unity, differs from the *consciousness of faith*, which is consciousness of an objectivity, which, however, is beyond presence. Hegel distinguishes *subjective* unhappy consciousness from the *objective* faith of the world of culture more precisely: in unhappy consciousness, content is merely desired by consciousness; "in believing consciousness, on the other hand, [. . .] it is the essentially objective content of representation, a content which generally flees actuality and therefore lacks the certainty of self-consciousness" (*PE*, II, 273; *PG*, 533; *PM*, 766). That content is still the substance of spirit, but it is now projected beyond presence. Faith is a flight from the present world, but it becomes *another world*, which, for all that it is the world of the beyond, appears no less external and objective. Faith and culture stand contraposed, but both are forms of the alienation of the self. The self—the centainty of self-consciousness—has become alien to itself in the one world as well as in the other. Starting with his early theological works, Hegel repeatedly reflected on the split between God and Caesar which Christianity introduced into the modern world. Christ teaches that his "kingdom is not of this world" and requires that men "render unto Caesar the things which are Caesar's and unto God the things that are God's." From then on, man lives in a double world: the world of action, which is the world of the earthly city, of the state, and the world of faith, which is the world of the City of God. But these two cities oppose each other radically. The earthly city has an actual presence for consciousness, but its essence lies beyond itself. Whereas that city is an actuality that lacks thought, the City of God contains the thought-out essence of man. But that essence is cut off from real presence and lacks actuality. In the courses on "Philosophy of Spirit," which preceded the *Phenomenology*, Hegel showed the importance that this dualism and the need to overcome it have had in human history. The distinction that man makes between his "actual self" and his "absolute self" is perhaps a "last resort" [*pis aller*].[5] "Religion lends confidence to the individual, allows

5. Hegel uses the French phrase (no. 2, p. 268).

him to believe that the events of the world are reconciled with spirit," that the course of things is not a blind necessity. "Religion is the representation of spirit, the self that has unified its pure consciousness and its actual consciousness." [6]

In the *Phenomenology*, Hegel repeatedly discusses the dualism he wishes to surmount, a dualism which expresses the torment of spirit obliged to live in one world and to think in the other. He presents it in various aspects and distinguishes, more or less felicitously, *unhappy consciousness, faith*, and *religion*. The faith under consideration here is no longer the depth of subjectivity whose pain we saw in unhappy consciousness. Unhappy consciousness is the subjective self-consciousness we find in certain Christians of the Middle Ages for whom the beyond has not yet become objective essence, i.e., a content which, though it is merely thought, is as solid and rigid with respect to the self as is the present world. The faith of the modern world (culture), on the contrary, presents the content of representation in objective form. In the modern world, in which objective faith struggles with pure intellection—in the Reformation and in the Enlightenment—the content of faith is objective; it is *in-itself*, and it lacks the certainty of self-consciousness. Although it is a *flight* from the actually real, faith shares the characteristics of that actuality. "What we are discussing here is not the self-consciousness of absolute essence insofar as it is in-and-for-itself, not religion, but faith, insofar as it is a flight from the actual world and, therefore, not in-and-for-itself. Thus the flight from the realm of presence immediately implies a double direction" (*PE*, II, 54; *PG*, 350; *PM*, 514).[7] In rising from actual consciousness, consciousness of the present world, to pure consciousness, consciousness of thought and of essence, spirit finds a new duality, a new form of alienation. It finds *pure intellection*, which reduces everything to the self, as well as *pure essence*, which is thought that lacks the movement of intellection. Faith is merely one element; the other is concept. And the faith of the world of culture stands contraposed to concept. This opposition will appear in the Enlightenment's struggle against faith. Hegel's subtle distinctions between unhappy consciousness and faith and between faith and religion have historical signification. Religion—as a dialectical moment, as Hegel studies

6. *Ibid.*, pp. 268 ff.
7. The direction of the *in-itself* and the *for-itself*.

it in the course of the *Phenomenology*—will be the spirit's awareness of itself. But before that stage, religion appears only in certain, necessarily partial, aspects. Faith, as man's awareness of an essence beyond presence, is the term contraposed to self-consciousness as pure intellection. The conflict between this faith and the Enlightenment, a conflict which began perhaps at the time of the Reformation and the Renaissance, expresses a moment in the development of spirit. But in its originality and its wholeness, religion in-and-for-itself has a different meaning, a meaning which must be set forth as such.[8]

Despite these complexities, which make the *Phenomenology's* interpretations somewhat puzzling, the general meaning of the opposition between pure consciousness and actual consciousness is clear. In the ethical world—the first world of spirit— spirit was its own presence to itself. There was nothing that implied a negation of self-consciousness. The spirit who died retained a presence in the blood of kinship. The power of government was the self of all. "But what has presence here is valid as an actuality that is only objective and whose own consciousness is beyond itself. . . . Nothing has an immanent spirit grounded in itself; everything is outside itself in an alien spirit" (*PE*, II, 52; *PG*, 348, 349; *PM*, 511). Thus the totality of this world is not a unique spirit which remains within itself: it is alienated from itself, alien to itself qua totality. From this results the double world: two realms—the actual world and the world of faith—reflect and oppose each other as though in a mirror. Each exists only by virtue of the other; each is alienated in the other. Their common truth is precisely the self-discovery of self in each of them: in the one, in the form of the final spirit of culture, the vanity of all content; in the other, in the form of the Enlightenment. "The Enlightenment disturbed spirit's place in the kingdom of faith by introducing into that world utensils of the world here below, which spirit cannot deny as its property because its consciousness belongs to this world as well" (*PE*, II, 53; *PG*, 349; *PM*, 512). At the height of its culture, the self has gained universality and reduces everything to itself. It has denounced the alienation whereby man transposes the world here-below to the beyond; that is, it reduces these two worlds into

8. On the difference between the aspects of religion which appear prior to religion as a totality (a form of absolute spirit) does, see *PE*, II, 203 ff.; *PG*, 473 ff.; *PM*, 683 ff.

one, in which, overcoming all self-alienation, spirit becomes *absolute freedom.*

I. THE ACTUAL WORLD: CULTURE

THE SPIRITUAL WORLD is the world of culture (*Bildung*) and of alienation (*Entäusserung*), two terms that we have already encountered. The slave becomes the master of the master and rises to genuine self-consciousness, which he is in himself, only through the process of culture—the formation of being-in-itself. It is in labor that slave-consciousness manages to externalize itself; in forming things, it forms itself. It renounces its natural self—a slave to desire and the Dasein of life—and by so doing gains its genuine self. Human self emerges from the being of life when it comes to dominate "universal powers and objective essence in their totality" (*PE,* I, 166; *PG,* 150; *PM,* 240).[9] At the stage of the *Phenomenology* we have reached, objective essence is no longer the being-in-itself of life; it is the being of *spiritual substance.* It is that substance, as still abstract in-itself, that self-consciousness gains and dominates through its culture. In the development of self-consciousness, the human self rose above the universal being of life, and appeared as the proof of that being, by giving it the form of self-consciousness and *taking on* from it being-in-itself. In the present development, the self must master social substance. The dialectical movement is the same. "The individual here has objective validity and actuality by virtue of culture" (*PE,* II, 55; *PG,* 351; *PM,* 514–15). Just as the being-in-itself of things acquired meaning through human labor, abstract in-itself, substance that is merely thought, becomes an actual reality through culture. Reciprocally, determinate individuality rises to essentiality, just as the empirical consciousness of the slave became through labor and service a universal consciousness. The term "alienation," too, is familiar to us. Unhappy consciousness rose to the universality of reason through the alienation of its pure subjectivity. "Culture" and "alienation" are akin in meaning: the determinate individual cultivates himself, and forms himself to essentiality, through the alienation of his natural being. More precisely, for Hegel, the cultivation of the self is conceivable only by the mediation of

9. Cf. part III, chapter 1, above.

alienation, or estrangement.[10] To cultivate oneself is not to develop harmoniously, as in organic growth, but to oppose oneself and rediscover oneself through a rending and a separation. The moment of rending and of mediation is characteristic of Hegel's concept of culture, and it allows us to make clear the originality of Hegel's pedagogy (in the widest sense of the word) with respect to rationalist and humanist pedagogy (that of the adherents to the Enlightenment and of certain classical humanists).[11] Hegel had already conceived this notion of culture at the time of his earliest writings. Life develops only through self-opposition: it starts with naïve unity (in Schiller's sense) and rediscovers itself only after a moment of separation and opposition. This circular movement—this self-pursuit which is the life of the self—is the foundation of Hegel's dialectical schema. The first moment of any development is that of immediateness, of nature; it is a moment which must be negated. In that immediateness the self is in fact outside itself. It exists but it must become what it is, and in order to do that it must oppose itself: the self can gain its universality only through that opposition—the alienation that is culture. "Starting from the undeveloped unity of the beginning," Hegel wrote in his early writings on religion, "life has traversed, through culture, the circle which leads it to an achieved unity." [12]

Culture, then, has a very general sense here: it is the result of an alienation of natural being. The individual renounces his natural right, his immediate self which was recognized only as such in the state of law.

> This equality with everyone is not the equality of law, not the immediate being-recognized and the immediate validity which are due merely to the existence of self-consciousness; self-consciousness is valid because, through the mediation of estrangement, it has made itself consonant with the universal. The spiritless universality of law takes in any modality of character

---

10. The term "estrangement" (*extranéation, Entfremdung*) is stronger than the term "alienation" (*aliénation, Entäusserung*). It implies not only that the natural self gives itself up, alienates itself, but also that it becomes *alien* to itself. Hegel always uses "estrangement" in speaking of the fundamental opposition between good and bad.

11. For a study of Hegel's concept of culture see W. Moog, "Der Bildungsbegriff Hegels" in *Verhandlungen des dritten Hegelkongresses vom 19 bis 23 April 1933 in Rom* (Tübingen, 1934).

12. *Theologische Jugendschriften*, pp. 378 ff.

or of Dasein and justifies all equally. But here, the valid universality is the universality which has become, and it is because of that becoming that it is actual (*PE*, II, 55; *PG*, 351; *PM*, 514).

In the pedagogy of the Enlightenment, the individual rises to reason by a continuous progress, following a linear path upward; in humanist pedagogy, there is a kind of spontaneous and harmonious development of all the forces of nature. According to Hegel, by contrast, there is a moment in education in which the self becomes unequal to itself and negates itself, thereby gaining its universality: that moment is the moment of *alienation,* or estrangement.[13]

The first moment of the development of the self through culture is the formation of the gentleman [*honnête homme*], the education of the individuality which estranges its immediate nature. The substance of individuality, its true originary nature —that which, consequently, it is in-itself and must become for-itself—is precisely this alienation of the natural self. "The alienation of its natural self is thus the individual's goal as well as its Dasein; it is both the transition of thought-out substance to actuality and, conversely, of determinate individuality to essentiality" (*PE*, II, 55; *PG*, 351; *PM*, 515). Hegel returns here to the concepts we have already seen in the discussion of determinate individuality (the spiritual animal kingdom) and gives them the signification appropriate to this world of spirit. Indeed, the self knows itself here as specific self, but in this spiritual world its reality lies only in its universality. It can see itself no longer as this particular self but as having absorbed universal substance into itself. "This claim to individuality is only intended Dasein, and it reaches no stability in this world, in which only that which renounces itself and, consequently, is universal, gains actuality." The differences among individuals are reduced to an inequality in the *energy of the will,* but the goal and the content of will are borrowed from substance. This is not to say, as we shall soon see more clearly, that the self has not a certain *will to power* to appropriate substance by actualizing more and more effectively the alienation of natural

13. Life in general is characterized in Hegel's early works as being a *development* only through being an *opposition*. Each "stage of its development is a separation necessary if it is to gain all the richness of life for itself." To cultivate oneself is to become a stranger to oneself, to lose oneself so as to regain oneself. Thus, education presupposes *opposition*.

being. But the world thus reached is a world in which the self has formed itself to the point of universality. That culture—which is a negation of the natural self such that at its most refined point, in seventeenth-century French society, for example, the "I becomes hateful" or takes on truly universal signification while, simultaneously, the universal is realized in concrete individualities—is culture in knowledge as well as social culture. Hegel almost quotes Bacon's phrase, "Knowledge is power": "The greater the culture of an individuality, the greater its actuality and its power" (*PE*, II, 56; *PG*, 351; *PM*, 515).[14] On the other hand, using Goethe's translation of *Rameau's Nephew*, Hegel emphasized the disdain that people in such a world have for what has preserved in-itself the *specificity of a nature* and has not cultivated itself. As Littré's dictionary correctly says, " 'type' [*espèce*] is said of people in whom one sees no worth." "These types," Diderot said, "play you dirty tricks and make you their accomplice to the point of turning decent people against you." [15]

Thus the formation of the self is the alienation of its natural self, its education toward the universal. But that alienation is also an estrangement. The self no longer discovers itself within itself. By becoming universal, it becomes *alien to itself*. The self-coincidence of self, which was the essence of the first world of spirit, begins progressively to be more and more lacking, and in the eighteenth century that lack is held to warrant the desire, commended by Rousseau, for a return to nature, or at least to the natural.[16]

But this first moment which we have just considered is only one aspect of alienation. While the self becomes substantive, or universal, substance becomes concretely real. The alienation of the self is its alienation in substance. Political and social organization is, therefore, the product of that alienation. To be sure, that organization of substance appears to the individual self as an alien actuality—that appearance is the very character

14. It is remarkable that Hegel should use the term "power." It is a will to power that animates the self in the real world.

15. Diderot, *Rameau's Nephew*, trans. Jacques Barzun and Ralph H. Bowen (New York, 1956) p. 58. Although known in Germany in Goethe's translation, Diderot's book was not yet known in France.

16. The precise allusions to French culture of the seventeenth and eighteenth centuries, and to Diderot's and Rousseau's critiques of that culture, are quite clear in this part of the *Phenomenology*.

of this world. In fact, however, it is its deed; it is the other aspect of culture, understood in the broadest sense of the word. "What appears here as the power of the individual, under whose domination substance falls and is thereby suppressed, is precisely the same as the actualization of that substance. For the strength of the individual consists in his making himself equivalent to substance, that is, alienating his self, thus posing himself as objective substance in the element of being" (PE, II, 57; PG, 352–53; PM, 516–17). Let us also emphasize the will to power, which seems to be manifest in the self's effort to conquer substance. Ambition, the desire for political power or wealth, forms the motive force of the alienation of the self which makes itself substantive and simultaneously animates substance with its own life.

The word "alienation" had already been used by such political thinkers as Hobbes, Locke, and Rousseau who, in various and differing ways, had considered the problem of the alienation of the natural self. If indeed we begin with the *state of law*, considered by Hegel in its most general form to be the immediate affirmation of natural law, we must ask how the person renounces all or some of his rights, a renunciation that is the condition of social life. We recall the phrase with which Rousseau defined the social contract: "These clauses, of course, are reducible to one, viz., the total alienation of each associate with all his rights to the whole community." [17] For Hobbes, individual rights were alienated not to the community but to the sovereign. Hobbes, indeed, knew only individuals. We know from passages in the "Philosophy of Spirit" that Hegel explicitly thought that alienation constitutes community. In those passages, Hegel studied the realization of social substance by the "formation of the individual," and he quoted the theory of the *Social Contract*. "We imagine the constitution of the general will," he wrote, "as if all the citizens gathered and deliberated and as if a majority vote created the general will." [18] In this picture, we conceive a necessary movement, that by which "through self-negation" the individual rises to the universal. But in history alienation is not effected quite that simply, and at first the general will appears to the individual as alien, as other. That general will is the in-itself of the individual, what he is to become. Thus there can be

17. *The Social Contract.*
18. No. 2, p. 245. Hegel uses the same terms in the 1805–6 courses on the "Philosophy of Spirit" (*Entäusserung, Bildung*) as in the *Phenomenology*.

no question of a *contract,* even a tacit one, which as such would constitute the general will. "The whole precedes the parts," as Aristotle had said,[19] and social substance appears to the self as an alien reality which that self must appropriate by alienating itself. "The general will must first constitute itself on the basis of the will of individuals, and it must constitute itself as general so that individuals will appear to be its principle and its element. But in fact, the general will is the original term and the essence." The general will is "the in-itself of individuals," their substance, but that in-itself appears alien to them, as what they must become through culture. Thus, the child sees in his parents his in-itself which appears alien to him. This separation between the universal and the self is characteristic of the development of spirit. We must follow the movement by which substance, the in-itself, which at first is only an immediate concept, is realized through the movement of self-consciousness, through its culture and its alienation—a movement through which the self, conversely, takes on substantive reality. Substance becomes subject when subject becomes substance.

We saw the same problem posed in the first world of the spirit, the ethical world, but then it did not yet entail the necessity of alienation. Substance—as universal essence and as goal —was realized through ethical action, which, moreover, promoted the self to substantiveness. But it is precisely action that in its development untuned the immediate world, posed immediately the unity of self and substance, and brought out the self as the only genuine reality. Here the *judgment,* and later the *reasoning* of self-consciousness take it on themselves to actualize alienation, to infuse life into the substance of spirit, and to cultivate the self till it attains essentiality. Of course, the words "concept," "judgment," and "reasoning" must be understood in a specifically Hegelian manner. What is in question is a logical expression of a concrete process as well as a concrete illustration of a logical movement. Concept corresponds to the posing of immediate terms; judgment expresses the relation of self-consciousness to those terms; reason is the mediating movement which alone animates the moments and raises them out of their immediateness. The spiritual world we are now considering is the world of estrangement, a world in which each moment is alien to itself. Indeed, the self never discovers itself

19. In a marginal note in the 1805–6 course, Hegel notes, "Aristotle: by nature the whole precedes the parts" (p. 245).

in this world; it is only their internal negativity that animates the moments and constitutes their incessant becoming-other. "The self is conscious of being actual only as suppressed [*aufgehobenes*] self" (*PE*, II, 57; *PG*, 353; *PM*, 517). It never coincides with itself, nor with any of its objects. Each term, insofar as it is self, is external to itself; it refers to another term which it does not include but which it presupposes at the same time that it poses it. This spiritual world is constituted precisely by that exteriority and *relativity* of the moments. "Nothing (in that world) has an immanent spirit grounded in itself; everything is outside itself in an alien spirit" (*PE*, II, 52; *PG*, 349; *PM*, 511). Just as in the *Logic* the immediate categories of being are succeeded by the reflective categories of essence—the universal relativity in the midst of which nothing remains immediate and everything refers to something other and takes on meaning through that other—so here the world of nature-spirit which coincides with itself is succeeded by the world of culture-spirit, in which the self is always outside itself. However, these moments, which reciprocally presuppose each other, maintain a rigidity which prevents them from changing immediately into their opposites. Thought freezes that opposition in the most general way possible through the opposition of *good* and *bad*, terms which cannot coincide with each other at all. This is not to be understood as a distinction between moral *good* and *evil*, but rather, as Hegel says, "in the most general way possible": they express in pure consciousness only the complete impossibility of one term becoming the other, the necessity of a radical separation, of an unbridgeable dualism. Yet we, who understand the process as philosophers, know that "the interchange of opposites is the soul of that fixed and solid Dasein, and that estrangement is its life and foundation" (*PE*, II, 58; *PG*, 353; *PM*, 517). This spiritual world is as a whole the world of estrangement; thus, its life and its development consist exclusively in the movement by means of which one moment becomes the other, gives it consistency and receives its own consistency from it. Thus what is solidified as good for consciousness engaged in experience will be bad, and vice versa. *Noble consciousness* will be revealed as *base* (or vile) *consciousness*, and *base consciousness* as *noble consciousness*. At the end point of this dizzying dialectic whose hidden soul is the self seeking to rediscover itself beyond estrangement, "the estrangement will be estranged, and everything will thereby recover itself in its own concept" (*PE*, II, 58; *PG*, 353; *PM*, 517): the self will return to itself in absolute laceration. We must now follow this dialectic, from immediate concepts, through the judgment of self-consciousness, to reasoning—a dialectic which in the midst of mediation will lead to the rediscovery of the self. Just as in the *Logic* concept, that is, the self in its autonomous development, succeeds the reflective world of essence and freedom succeeds necessity, so at the end point of the world of culture a free, because universal, self will emerge. The dialectic of noble and base consciousness will be succeeded by the dialectic of the French Revolution.

Hegel considered the moments of substance as they are immediately, or in themselves (concept), then as they are for self-consciousness (judgment), and finally as they become through the mediation of the alienation of the self (reasoning or syllogism).

a. *The moments of substance in themselves*

Hegel's argument about the moments of substance can easily be grasped in the abstract, for it is always the same: substance first is *in-itself*—it is being that is *equal to itself;* but as such it is the abstraction of its otherness and the contrary of itself. Thus it is being-for-some-other, or disparity with itself. Finally, in that otherness it is its return to itself, its becoming for-itself.[20] Being-in-itself, being-for-some-other, and being-for-itself: these constitute the dialectical moments of substance which qua totality is being-in-and-for-itself. According to Hegel, this dialectic can be seen in the natural elements, air, water, fire, earth:

> Air is permanent essence, purely universal and transparent; water, by contrast, is essence that is always offered and sacrificed; fire is their life-giving unity, which ever resolves their opposition by breaking up their simple unity into oppositions; earth, finally, is the solid core of this organization and the subject of these es-

20. This dialectic recurs throughout Hegel's work. It corresponds to the three moments of the concept: the universal, the particular, the specific. Self-equality *excludes* otherness, which is to say that it supposes it and that it is not truly self-equal. Every positing is a positing only because it is the negation of a negation and thus a return to the *in-itself* in the *for-itself.*

sences and their processes, of their origin and their return (*PE,* II, 58; *PG,* 353; *PM,* 518).[21]

Whatever we may think of this particular argument, which indicates how Hegel wished to apply his dialectic to Schelling's philosophy of nature, the thought behind it is clear: it is impossible to pose *abstract identity* without posing *otherness*. The identity of the in-itself, precisely, is an abstraction, and because it is an abstraction it is the contrary of itself; it is for-some-other. As we know, this negativity within positivity is the hallmark of Hegel's dialectical schema, the intuition with which he began.[22]

At this stage of the argument, the moments of spiritual substance, which were foreshadowed by the elements of nature, are the primitive in-itself (the good) and the becoming for-itself of this essence through its negation, negated essence (bad). The subject of this opposition, which always either divides substance into these opposed terms or reunites them, is self-consciousness.

> In the first essence it is conscious of itself as being-in-itself; in the second, through the sacrifice of the universal, it acquires the development of being-for-itself. But spirit itself is the being-in-and-for-itself of the whole. That whole splits into permanent substance and substance sacrificing itself, and also takes up substance once again in its own unity—a devouring flame which consumes substance as well as the permanent figure of that same substance (*PE,* II, 58–59; *PG,* 354; *PM,* 518).

The life of substance is that life of spirit which splits internally, separating itself from itself, and through that separation rediscovers itself. The moments we are considering at this stage—the universal in-itself and the becoming of being-for-itself—correspond to the community (the simple will of all) and the family (individualization in the penates) in the ethical world. But the later moments lack the internal unity and immediateness of the earlier ones: their characteristic of being strangers to each other must appear.

For *pure consciousness,* these moments are the abstract essence of good and bad, the positive of in-itself and the negative of negated in-itself. In the first essence individuals find their

---

21. This comparison between "spiritual masses" and "natural elements" seems strange to us. But in his Jena period Hegel attempted to find his own dialectic in Schelling's philosophy of nature.

22. On this point see part III, introduction, above.

universal foundation; in the second, they find "their unceasing return to themselves" (*PE*, II, 60; *PG*, 354; *PM*, 519), the permanence of their becoming for-itself. But these moments are also *objective* for self-consciousness: they appear in real forms, the first as state power, the second as wealth. Whereas in the ethical world the community was immediately the will of all and the self was not separated from that will, which was identical to a nature, in this spiritual world, become alien to itself, community appears as a reality external to specific consciousness; for self-consciousness, it appears as a power of the objective state, a power from which self-consciousness distinguishes its pure thought of the good. Similarly, the specificity of the family, as wealth, has become the becoming-other of the in-itself. To be sure, this transition from the family (γένος) to wealth derives its justification from the shift we have already noted through the moment of law and property. From then on, the two opposed terms are no longer genuses, like community and family, but rather the universal and the specific. The same dialectic which we saw in substance in general arises in state power and wealth, which express substance as objective being-in-itself and objective being-for-some-other. State power is the universal work—the absolute thing itself—within which the universality of individuals is expressed; it is "the work of all and of each" which we defined as the "thing" at the level of spirit. But the fact that this work also draws its origin from the action of individuals is lost. Yet this is an abstraction, and for that reason the simple, ethereal substance of individuals is such only if it appears, becomes for-some-other, and is expressed in the individualization of economic life in general, of wealth or of national resources. "Through the determination of its unalterable equality with itself, this simple ethereal substance of their life is being; it is, therefore, merely being-for-an-other. Thus, in-itself, it is immediately its own opposite: it is wealth" (*PE*, II, 60; *PG*, 355; *PM*, 520).[23] Wealth, in turn, is a universal essence, although it is an incessant becoming-other, a perpetual mediation. But this universality results from a trick:

23. If we are to understand this argument properly we must distinguish the moments of substance for *pure consciousness* (good, bad, their separation, and their unity) from the moments of substance for *actual consciousness* (state power and wealth). This separation between pure consciousness and actual consciousness is what characterizes the world of *alienation*.

Within this moment, each specific entity believes that it acts so as to further its own selfish interests. In this moment, each entity has the consciousness of being for-itself and, therefore, it does not take the moment as something spiritual. But considered from the outside, this moment is such that the enjoyment of each leads to the enjoyment of all, that each labors for all as well as for himself, and that all labor for each. Consequently, the being-for-itself of each is in-itself universal; selfish interest is only intended, never made actual. Nothing can be done that is not to the advantage of all (*PE*, II, 60–61; *PG*, 355; *PM*, 520).

State power and wealth, thus, are the objective essences of this world, and in the face of them stands self-consciousness, which, qua pure consciousness, contains essence, as essence, in the ideal form of the opposition between good and bad. State power is the universal of individuals; it is stable law in contrast to the instability of the specific being. It is also government and authority, which coordinate the specific movements of the universal work. The common source of individual wills, as well as their common product, is expressed in state power. But, on the other hand, wealth—the economic life of the whole people— is also a universal essence, albeit not directly, in the manner of state power, but thanks to an interplay of mediations. If we consider a people's economic life as a whole, we discover a hidden harmony which results from the interaction of the individual labor and the individual enjoyment of all the members of the people. Hegel had especially emphasized this dialectic of wealth in the Jena courses on "Philosophy of Spirit." He had just read the German translation of Adam Smith's *Wealth of Nations* and had seen in that book an illustration of his own dialectic.[24] From the point of view of being-for-itself, wealth corresponds to its development for-itself. Each labors and enjoys himself on his own behalf. This is the moment of multiplicity in the unity of substance. But thanks to the division of labor, the labor of each serves the collectivity and is only a fragment of the total labor. The individual imagines that he is assuring his own specific life; his conscious intention does not reach "the thing itself." Yet his enjoyment conditions the labor of others and assures it a possible outlet. Thus, as producer and as consumer, the individual is the victim of an illusion when he erects what is

24. Course on the "Philosophy of Spirit," 1803–4 (no. 1, p. 239). Hegel quotes from Garve's German translation of *Inquiry into the Nature and Causes of the Wealth of Nations* (Breslau, 1794–96).

merely his own goal into a universal goal. Without knowing it, he realizes the life of the whole (the whole understood as diversifying itself in the multiplicity of individual lives). This is why Hegel emphasizes the permanent and universal nature of the moment of mediation in substance: "This absolute dissolution of essence, in turn, is permanent" (*PE*, II, 59; *PG*, 354; *PM*, 519). State power and wealth correspond to what in the last *Philosophy of Right* Hegel calls the "state" and "civil society" (or bourgeois society—*die bürgerliche Gesellschaft*). In the ancient world, community and family correspond as two reflections of one substance. In the modern world, the opposition is between the state—as general will in which the individual is directly universal—and bourgeois society—in which the individual realizes the universal only indirectly. It was in his Jena years that Hegel became aware of the importance of bourgeois society, the economic world, which had, so to speak, replaced nature and on which the individual now depended as on another nature.[25]

b. *These moments for self-consciousness: Judgment*

Self-consciousness does not merge with the objective essences, state power and wealth; as pure consciousness (of good and bad), it distinguishes itself from them. And that distinction between self and actuality is characteristic of the world of alienation which we are now discussing. But self-consciousness is also "the relation between the individual's pure consciousness and his actual consciousness, between the entity thought through and objective essence; it is essentially judgment" (*PE*, II, 61; *PG*, 356; *PM*, 521). The individual knows himself as free with regard to power and wealth. He thinks that he can choose between them, or even choose neither; he contains essence as the pure thought of good and bad. But he must judge, that is, connect his thought to the actual reality that is present to him. We can see that there are two possible judgments. According to one, state power is the good because it is the in-itself of individuals, and wealth is the bad, or nothingness, because it is merely the

25. Course on the "Philosophy of Spirit," no. 2, pp. 231 ff. Hegel's texts on the economic world (the accumulation of wealth, the opposition between wealth and poverty in the modern world, the new nature constituted by civil (or bourgeois) society—"blind movements on which the individual depends")—are remarkable in view of their early date (1805–6).

becoming-other, merely the movement of being-for-itself. According to the other, wealth is the good because it expresses self-consciousness in its being-for-itself, and state power is the bad because in it "self-consciousness finds action denied qua specific action and subjected to obedience" (*PE*, II, 63; *PG*, 357; *PM*, 523). In both cases, self-consciousness sets itself up as judge and raises the essences above what they immediately are. (Immediately, state power is self-equality, the in-itself—or the good —in the abstract, and wealth is perpetual disparity, or being-for-itself.) Self-consciousness makes these essences what they are in-itself; what is important now is not their immediate determination (their equality or disparity in themselves) but their mediate determination (their equality or disparity with self-consciousness). But self-consciousness contains both moments, being-in-itself and being-for-itself. Thus it relates in opposite ways to these essences, and since they appear by turns as the contrary of what they appeared to be at first, their characteristic alienation from themselves begins to appear. We have tried to follow as closely as possible the developments through which Hegel moves from the immediate determinations of state power and wealth to their mediate determination (a mediation due to the judgment of self-consciousness). Let us also note that since self-consciousness exists in-and-for-itself, *and as* essence, it realizes these moments absolutely.

> What is good and bad for self-consciousness is simultaneously good and bad in-itself, because self-consciousness is the medium in which the moments of being-in-itself and being-for-itself are identical. It is the actual spirit of objective essences, and judgment is a demonstration of its power over them, a power which makes them what they are in-itself (*PE*, II, 62; *PG*, 356; *PM*, 522).

Thus two possible conceptions of state power and wealth appear; these conceptions have concrete signification.

In one system the essence of the individual is realized through a common unity which rules and orders the life of a whole people. In universal law and in the government's command the individual discovers what makes up the heart of his action, what allows him to actualize himself concretely, what accords meaning to him. In wealth, on the contrary, the individual finds only an ephemeral consciousness and enjoys himself as specificity. In this system the good is the unity of all, participation in political life; wealth merely separates individuals and opposes them to each other, and it must be superseded if the individual is to exist essentially.

In the alternative system—which corresponds to an individualistic form of thought popular in the eighteenth century—power is bad; the oppression before which the individual is constrained to bow must be reduced to the minimum. The true good is wealth, which allows each individual to rise to self-consciousness. This individualization of essence, correctly understood, does not so much oppose individuals to each other as it reunites them in-itself. "In-itself, it signifies universal prosperity" (*PE*, II, 63; *PG*, 357; *PM*, 523). The enrichment of each is thought to realize the good of all. Interference by the state, on the contrary, is the oppressive power which stands in the way of the expression of all. "That in a given case wealth withholds its gifts and that it is not obliging to every need is a contingency which does not prejudice its necessarily universal essence—to spread to all specific beings, to be a many-handed donor" (*PE*, II, 63; *PG*, 357; *PM*, 523). In these two systems, a hierarchical organization of society confronts a liberalism whose essence is concern for the interests of the individual, interests which, all things considered, contribute to the interests of all.

"But in each of these judgments there is an equality and a disparity. . . . There is a double equality and a double disparity. What is given is an opposite relation to the two real essentialities" (*PE*, II, 64; *PG*, 358; *PM*, 524). Equality and disparity, which were at first immediately posed in the moments themselves, later appeared to us in the relation of self-consciousness to those moments, a relation which alone allows them genuinely to be. But we saw that that relation is self-contradictory: it gave rise to a double equality and a double disparity. We must rise still higher and consider equality and disparity neither in the moments taken immediately nor in the relation of self-consciousness to the moments, but in self-consciousness itself. In this manner we rise to spirit, the being-in-and-for-itself of the whole. Equality and disparity will then appear to us as two concrete figures of self-consciousness. If we envisage equality as the essence of self-consciousness itself, we will reach *noble consciousness*, the consciousness that is adequate both to state power and to wealth. If we view disparity as the essence of self-consciousness, we will reach *vile* or *base consciousness* (*niederträchtige*). Thenceforth, our problem will be the opposition between *noble consciousness* and *base consciousness*. The disparity between these two types of self-consciousness reproduces at a higher level that between *master* and *slave*. *Noble conscious-ness* is defined by its adequation to the real political and social world. It respects state power and endeavors to remain in obedi-ence to it; it sees in wealth the satisfaction of its being-for-itself, "recognizes the one who grants it enjoyment as a benefactor and considers itself bound in gratitude to him" (*PE*, II, 65; *PG*, 359; *PM*, 525).[26] This is the state of mind of an aristocracy in an organic society in which as yet no revolutionary ferment is stirring. Noble consciousness is conservative insofar as it recog-nizes the established order and accepts it: the power it obeys, the wealth it receives as a gift. Equality—adequation—is the precise characteristic of noble self-consciousness, its essence. *Base consciousness* is quite different. It is constrained to obey the constituted power, but in doing so it hides an internal revolt. It seeks wealth, which makes possible enjoyment, but above all it sees in wealth a disparity with its own essence, that which in wealth is ephemeral and unsatisfying. Thus it receives wealth but hates the benefactor. Base consciousness is consciousness in revolt, consciousness which, essentially, is always discrepant. Now—just as the slave was the truth of the master, and the master was, without knowing it, the slave—so base conscious-ness will be revealed as the truth of noble consciousness and ever-unsatisfied consciousness as the truth of satisfied conscious-ness. The revolutionary nature of Hegel's dialectic (which Marx noted) is unmistakable. Although the implications of Hegel's system are conservative, the advance of the dialectic is revolu-tionary, whatever Hegel's intention may have been. Nonetheless, the opposition between noble consciousness and base conscious-ness is not reducible to an opposition between two social or economic classes. The drama has a psychological and even a metaphysical character to the degree that the essence of self-consciousness is in question. The self of noble consciousness is posed in the mode of equality and that of base consciousness in disparity. But the genuine self can only discover itself through the most profound rending, through essential disparity. The world of alienation thus necessarily reveals base consciousness,

26. Thus, Hegel moves from the moments of substance (as they are for us) to the relation of self-consciousness to these moments (self-consciousness' judgment). He then envisages *equality* and *disparity* as two possible types of self-consciousness: noble con-sciousness and base consciousness. This movement conforms to the general schema of phenomenological experiences.

consciousness disparate with itself, to be the truth of the whole process.

c. *The forward motion of the moments in themselves: The mediating syllogism*

Thus far we have seen what the moments of substance were as the predicates of the judgment of self-consciousness. But these predicates have not yet been raised, through the alienation of self-consciousness, to spiritual being. The mediating movement of the syllogism has not yet occurred. That is the movement we shall consider in attending to the development of noble consciousness which, through its alienation, makes state power and wealth actually real. We know indeed that state power becomes real only through the alienation of the natural self and, conversely, that that self acquires essentiality only through that same alienation. Such will be the mediating process which actualizes the two terms, noble consciousness and state power, or noble consciousness and wealth. As a result of that mediation, state power and wealth will become subjects rather than remaining inert predicates.

> These determinations are immediately essences; they have not become what they are; they are not in themselves self-consciousnesses; that for which they are is not yet their animating principle; they are predicates that are not yet subjects. By virtue of this separation the whole of spiritual judgment is shattered into two consciousnesses, each of which is bound by a one-sided determination (noble consciousness and base consciousness) (*PE*, II, 65; *PG*, 359; *PM*, 526).

This development of the moments is simultaneously the self's conquest of its universality. The spur to this development will be the process of alienation. At first, noble consciousness constitutes state power by alienating its natural being. Thereby, it wins esteem, both from itself and from others: the development of a feudal regime culminates in a monarchy. But noble consciousness will appear ambiguous to us in its sense of honor, and it will approach, for us, base consciousness, which is always on the verge of revolt. Through an even more complete alienation (produced by language), state power will be constituted as personal self (in absolute monarchy). In this way noble consciousness will gain wealth. But wealth having then become in-itself, we shall see all consciousness become base consciousness, unequal to itself. At that supreme moment of alienation, culture truly appears as the world of lacerated consciousness. Diderot's *Rameau's Nephew* offers us a description of that lacerated consciousness, of a prerevolutionary state of mind. The spirit of culture will emerge completely for itself. The successive stages of this dialectic suggest an actual historical development. The modern nations were formed from feudal regimes. They became monarchies through a weakening of the nobility. And absolute monarchy, as we see it in the France of Louis XIV, is the supreme moment of this development; it is the sign of a decline. This decline can be seen in the substitution of wealth for state power as the essential, with the result that although the two dialectics (that of state power and that of wealth) are contemporaneous by right, they appear to succeed each other in a necessary order. It seems indeed that for Hegel the description of an extreme culture and of a lacerated consciousness corresponds to French society of the late eighteenth century, which heralds the birth of a new spirit.[27]

Transition from the feudal regime to monarchy: Alienation of noble consciousness

At first, noble consciousness recognizes state power as goal and as absolute content. It sees this power not as a personal monarch whom it must obey, but only as a substantive reality to which it must sacrifice itself. By taking a positive attitude with regard to that power, it takes a negative attitude with regard to its own natural existence. This consciousness is "the heroism of service," the virtue which sacrifices specific being to the universal and, in so doing, carries the universal to Dasein. There is a double alienation here: with regard to content, noble consciousness renounces its particular goals and its naturalness and becomes thereby an essential will, a will that desires the universal as such; through this alienation the substance of the state, which hitherto had been only in-itself, enters existence— not yet as government or as personal decision, but at least as power in action, as recognized and existing universal.

27. Cf. Jean Hyppolite, "La Signification de la Révolution française dans la *Phénoménologie* de Hegel," *Revue philosophique* (Sept.– Dec., 1939), p. 321; English translation in *Studies on Marx and Hegel* (New York, 1969), pp. 35–69.

In this way, noble consciousness gains essentiality. Able to renounce its life, it alienates its natural being. But "being that has become alien to itself is the in-itself." Losing the immediateness of natural existence, noble consciousness becomes suppressed immediateness, or in-itself, and it thereby gains esteem in its own eyes as well as the respect of others. Such is the "proud vassal," whose sense of his own value stems from his renunciation. Hegel calls this feeling "honor," thinking perhaps of Montesquieu, who considered honor the essential principle of an aristocratic monarchy. But in renouncing particular purposes, and even his life, the "proud vassal" does not renounce his self. He is willing to sacrifice himself for the state, but not when the state is incarnated in a specific will. He has alienated his natural Dasein but not his self itself. "This self-consciousness is the proud vassal who acts for state power, but only when state power is an essential, not a personal will" (*PE*, II, 67; *PG*, 365; *PM*, 528). For this reason, the honor gained through this alienation—this personal sense of the universal—is an equivocal mixture of arrogance and virtue. Unless the nobleman actually dies in combat, there is no proof that the truth of his nobility is anything more than the self-love which La Rochefoucauld described in the early seventeenth century. "Being-for-itself, will which has not yet been sacrificed qua will, is the inner spirit of the social hierarchy, spirit which in speaking of the universal good reserves its own particular good for itself and tends to use the mere rhetoric of universal good as a substitute for action" (*PE*, II, 68; *PG*, 361; PM, 528). In Germany, especially, the feudal regime extended itself to the point of preventing the complete realization of state power; the inner spirit overwhelmed genuine public spirit. But in France, as Hegel showed, it was possible for the feudal regime to lead to the absolute monarchy and to the full and actual realization of state power.[28] Thus, when the heroism of service stops short of actual death we cannot know whether noble consciousness does not at bottom identify with base consciousness, a consciousness "always on the verge of revolt."

If state power is to exist as a personal self, there must be an alienation greater than that of natural Dasein. This further alienation also manifests an essential moment of spirit: *language*. In the alienation of natural Dasein noble consciousness can prove its nobility only through death. But death is merely a

28. See Hegel's study "Die Verfassung Deutschlands."

natural negation. When living self-consciousnesses wish to prove to each other their truth as pure being-for-itself, they can only die in combat. But then death is also the end of the act of recognition. Thus, an alienation of the self must be found in which "being-for-itself surrenders itself as completely as in death while preserving itself in that very alienation" (*PE*, II, 68; *PG*, 362; *PM*, 529). The negation must be a spiritual negation which preserves at the same time as it negates; it must be an *Aufhebung*. Now the only way to go beyond the natural alternatives of posing and negating is to find an exteriority of the I such that that exteriority still remains I. According to Hegel, language is that exteriority—which henceforth will allow us to understand the world of culture, the world of spirit alien to itself. In the alienation peculiar to noble consciousness, the content of language is only *advice*, which is communicated for the universal good. But in the face of *advice*, state power has no will; it is unable to choose among various opinions concerning the universal good. State power is not yet government; it is not yet the actual power of the state.

Language as the actuality of estrangement, or culture: The absolute monarchy of Louis XIV

In language qua language, this-specific I can become external to itself and move up to universality; the universal, reciprocally, can become I. Up to this point, language has been considered only with regard to its content: in the ethical world it served to express essence as law and commands; in the world of the alienation of natural being it expressed essence as advice. Now, language is to play a role qua language. Its very form will realize that which is to be realized. "But here [language] receives its own form as its content; it is valid as language. It is the force of speech as such that realizes what is to be realized" (*PE*, II, 69; *PG*, 362; *PM*, 530).

Indeed, language is the only spiritual alienation of the I that offers a solution to the problem we have posed. In language "the for-itself specificity of self-consciousness as such enters existence in such a way as to be for-others." The I that is expressed is learned; in its very disappearance it becomes a universal contagion. "Thus, this disappearance is immediately its permanence.

It is its own self-knowledge, the knowledge of a self which has passed over into another self, one that has been learned and is universal" (*PE*, II, 70; *PG*, 363; *PM*, 531).

The two opposing terms, the self of consciousness and the universal, become identified with each other in language— spirit's logos which makes the I a universal and by that very fact makes the universal an I. The function of language is precisely to say the I, to make the I itself a universal. Thus, language is a moment of the spirit; it is the logos, the middle term of intelligences. It must make spirit appear as the self-conscious unity of individuals. From the very beginning of the *Phenomenology*, language has appeared in this aspect. When consciousness wishes to grasp the present moment or the privileged place given it as its own, the only words it finds are "here" and "now," which are universal terms. When it wishes to name itself, I, *this*-I, it names what is most universal, the I in general (*PE*, I, 84; *PG*, 82; *PM*, 154). In saying "I," I say what every other I can say. I simultaneously express myself and alienate myself; I become objective; I move from a specific self-consciousness to a universal self-consciousness. That universal self-consciousness which results from the alienation of the specific self is precisely what is to be realized. And language alone can realize it. Language gives the world of culture a spiritual being. The courtier's language will make the state an I which in its specificity is a decision-making and universal I. The language of the basest flattery will raise wealth to essentiality. The language of laceration will be spirit itself, self-alienated and having become transparent to itself in its disparity. Not only does the individual renounce his natural existence so as to form himself through service; he also alienates himself in expressing himself. He says what he is and in so doing he becomes universal. He can then discover himself only as a universal being. Thus, we will best be able to understand the self's becoming universal if we study the self's expression in the development of culture—its alienation in a language. At the end point of that development, language will have become the universal consciousness of human culture that we find in French thought of the eighteenth century.[29]

29. At the end of the *Phenomenology* (*PE*, II, 184; *PG*, 463; *PM*, 667; cf. part VI, chapter 2, below), Hegel returns to the role of language as the *universal self-consciousness* which remains self in universality. Thanks to language spiritual substance as such enters existence and finally exists as spirituality.

The language of flattery

In the first place, the language of flattery brings about what the alienation peculiar to the noble consciousness could not—the actualization of state power. Language is now the middle term between the extremes of universal and specific, substance and self, and it reflects each of these extremes back into itself, posing it as the contrary of itself. State power, an abstract universal, is reflected back on itself and becomes a specific I, a decision-making will. Correspondingly, noble consciousness alienates its pure being-for-itself and is reflected back on itself, receiving in exchange for that alienation the actuality of substance, that is, wealth. But in this reflection, noble consciousness shows itself to be as disparate as base consciousness.

> Its spirit is the completely disparate relation: on the one hand, in its honor it retains its will; on the other hand, it abandons its will and in that abandonment it partly alienates its interiority, thereby reaching the greatest disparity with itself, and partly subjugates universal substance and renders *it* unequal to itself. Clearly, the determination that noble consciousness had when, in judgment, it was compared to base consciousness has vanished, and by this very fact, base consciousness itself has vanished, having reached its goal: to encompass universal power under being-for-itself (*PE*, II, 73–74; *PG*, 366–67; *PM*, 535–36).

This passage clearly shows us the meaning of this whole development of the dialectic of spirit. Just as the I rose through the service and the labor of the slave to the in-itself and retrieved the substantiveness of being for the self, so in this world of spirit spiritual substance is gradually conquered by self-consciousness. It is transformed from *substance* to *subject*. Wealth is but one stage in this development. If the self alienates itself and becomes substantive, it is so that substance in turn will show itself as self-certainty, as the subject of its own history. But in wealth, the self-alienated self will come to discover itself in the most profound laceration.

Let us first consider the evolution of noble consciousness and the corresponding evolution of state power. Noble consciousness and state power both decompose into extremes. State power is the abstract universal, a common good; it is not yet a will and a decision; it does not yet exist for its own sake. Noble consciousness, by contrast, has renounced its natural being and has sacrificed itself in service and obedience, but it has not alienated its pure self. Being-in-itself exists only potentially in noble consciousness, in the form of honor and self-esteem, while the self remains actual. "But in the absence of alienation the acts of honor of noble consciousness and the advice of its insights remain equivocal, dissembling the internal reservation of particular intentions and of one's own will" (*PE*, II, 69; *PG*, 362; *PM*, 529). This seems almost one of La Rochefoucauld's maxims, showing up the self-love that subsists in those acts that appear most noble, acts inspired by feelings of honor and glory. There is only an apparent difference here between noble consciousness and base consciousness ever on the verge of revolt. When the "pure being-for-itself of will is kept in reserve," the obedience of service is always impure. On the other hand, in return for its alienation in service noble consciousness has been granted only honor, not actual power. The universal is actual only in the power of the state, whereas the self is actual only in noble consciousness. The *language of flattery* will permit the one alienation that is still necessary, and will grant the I to the state and real power to the I.

In the language of the court, noble consciousness alienates its very I. The nobleman becomes the courtier and shifts from "the heroism of service" to "the heroism of flattery": "The heroism of silent service becomes the heroism of flattery" (*PE*, II, 71; *P.G.*, 364; *PM*, 533). This eloquent reflection of service raises "this power, which at first is only in-itself, to being-for-itself and to the specificity of self-consciousness." Henceforth, this power can say "L'Etat c'est moi." Hegel's dialectical argument is in fact a commentary on Louis XIV's famous phrase. When the nobleman becomes a courtier, the structure of the state is upset. The state is no longer beyond self-consciousness, a universal that is merely thought; it becomes, in the terms of court language an "unlimited monarch." "Unlimited": the term corresponds to the universality of the concept in language; " 'monarch': language too elevates specificity to the summit" (*PE*, II, 72; *PG*, 365; *PM*, 533). Only the king has a proper name that is known by all. Individuality is immediately universal, and universality is immediately individual. Behind these dialectical formulations, we see the reign of Louis XIV. What Taine later called the "classic spirit" was already described by Hegel. Whereas the courtiers have completely alienated their selves, their pure inner certainty, only the sovereign, in this artificial world, preserves his nature,

In the 1806–7 course on "Philosophy of Spirit," Hegel had noted that "the majority of individuals, the people, face one individual, the monarch. He is all that remains of nature; nature has taken refuge in him. Every other individuality is valid only insofar as it is alienated, only by virtue of what it has made itself into." [30] The king still has a proper name that is known and recognized by all, and the succession of kings follows the order of nature. But this "exclusive individuality" can be the power only if the nobles *recognize* it, if, in Saint-Simon's phrase, "through assiduity and baseness [they become] valets." "As for the unique one, he knows himself as the universal power because nobles not only are ready to serve state power but stand grouped around the throne like an ornament, constantly telling the one who sits on it what he is" (*PE*, II, 72; *PG*, 365; *PM*, 534).

But state power, having thus been actualized, is, in fact, alienated; it too has become alien to itself. It depends on the noble consciousness which has posed it in its solitary specificity. It is no longer the in-itself, but rather the in-itself negated. "Noble consciousness, the extreme of being-for-itself, receives the extreme of actual universality in exchange for the universality of thought which it has alienated" (*PE*, II, 73; *PG*, 366; *PM*, 534). In a general way, we can say that substance, the in-itself of state power, has become a moment of the consciousness that has dominated it. Noble consciousness has exchanged its honor for pensions and material advantages. Power is no longer the in-itself that is beyond self-consciousness; it is what self-consciousness appropriates, the suppressed essence, wealth. Of course, it still subsists as an appearance, but it is now no more than this movement: "to pass through service and homage into its contrary, the alienation of power." Finally, nothing remains to it but its "empty name" (*PE*, II, 73; *PG*, 366; *PM*, 535).

At that moment, all spiritual substance has become dependent on self-consciousness, which has alienated itself to gain that dominance. The only object that subsists in the face of the self and still resists it is wealth. But wealth is not the in-itself, it is not the essence which state power, in the strict sense, was; it is rather suppressed in-itself, and the self-consciousness that makes it the essence must see itself alienated in it. Self-consciousness then must rediscover itself in wealth. We have had occasion to think of La Rochefoucauld; here La Bruyère comes to mind: "Such people are neither relatives nor friends, neither citizens

30. No. 2, p. 252.

nor Christians; perhaps they are not men: they have money." In the 1806–7 course on the "Philosophy of Spirit," Hegel had noted the profound transformation in the modern world, which made wealth the object of the I. Money becomes the "existing material concept," and man's self is alienated in the blind movements of the whole of economic life. "The opposition between great wealth and great poverty appears." But this inequality, which almost necessarily increases in society, is also a laceration of spirit. The individual sees his self outside himself, in a thing which is neither the universal, devoid of self, that characterized state power, nor the naïve nonorganic nature of spirit. The contradiction cannot be overcome. The self alienates itself not into another self or into a spiritual power, but into a *thing*. It depends on a thing in which it can no longer discover itself, though that thing is the exact incarnation of its works. For this reason, Hegel noted in the course from which we have just quoted, "the inequality between wealth and poverty becomes the sharpest laceration of will; it becomes internal revolt and hatred." [31]

In the *Phenomenology*, the alienation of the self in wealth expresses the moment of the most profound laceration, and it is therefore the dialectical development that returns the self to itself.

> Noble consciousness finds itself facing its self, as such, which has become alien; it encounters it as a solid actual object which it must receive from another solid being-for-itself. Its object is being-for-itself, i.e., what is its own, but because that is an object it is also immediately an alien actuality which is being-for-itself proper, or will proper. That is, consciousness sees its self at the mercy of an alien will (*PE*, II, 75; *PG*, 367–68; *PM*, 537).

When the power of the state is completely realized and becomes a specific I, it is already negated and only an appearance of it remains. For it is entirely subjected to being-for-itself. It is not yet, however, substance that has completely returned into the self; that return, which marks the end point of the dialectic of culture, does not occur at first. The negated in-itself is only being-for-an-other; it is essence which sacrifices itself and which spreads, without yet being for-itself. Such indeed is wealth, the object which is now presented to the self, just as state power was before. "Wealth is indeed the universal, subjected, to be sure, to consciousness, but not yet, by that first suppression, returned

31. *Ibid.*, pp. 232–33.

into the self" (*PE*, II, 74; *PG*, 367; *PM*, 536). In order that the last stage of this dialectic be reached, the self must finally have its self as its object, as self; alienation must in turn be alienated; the self must be able to discover itself as identical to itself in its being-other. In that moment, spirit rediscovers itself as self, no longer as the immediate self of the world of law, but as the self that has become universal within itself and knows itself in every otherness. This absolute self, raised above substance, having penetrated substance and reduced it to self, is the rationality of the Enlightenment, the idealism of intellection and of the Enlightenment. Rationality will present the metaphysics of the Enlightenment—the French Revolution—which attempts to make the Enlightenment real.

Hegel observes the relation between self-consciousness and wealth as he had observed the development of the relation between self-consciousness and state power. This relation too is the result of an alienation. Noble consciousness has had to renounce its self, to renounce what was innermost in it, in order to make the state actually real and to make itself its actual master. For this reason, the self appears alien to noble consciousness, as the will of the monarch who accords or fails to accord the promised enjoyment. The alienated self has become wealth, being-for-some-other, which makes being-for-itself possible. In this manner, consciousness contemplates its alienated self in the form of wealth. Its object is nothing other than itself, but itself having become alien to itself. Thus, in the final dialectic of observing reason, the I discovered itself as a *thing*, a judgment which although seemingly the most puerile, was in fact the most profound.[32] The relation thus established between self-consciousness and wealth is open to a whole dialectical development which is quite different from the development of the relation that obtains between self-consciousness and state power. The alienation in this case is much more strongly marked. For this reason, it leads to a becoming aware of alienation, such as does not appear in the preceding moment; it leads to the disintegration of spirit as a whole. Concretely, it leads to a situation which we can call "revolutionary" if we refer to certain terms Hegel uses and to precise allusions in the *Phenomenology* to eighteenth-century France.

32. When observing reason formulated the judgment that "the being of spirit is a bone" (*PE*, I, 284; *PG*, 252; *PM*, 369).

First of all, noble consciousness, which is adequate both to state power and to wealth, fails to notice the internal contradiction of its alienation. It accepts gifts and it is grateful to the donor. But just as in its relation to state power noble consciousness turns out to be identical to base consciousness, so with regard to wealth too its actual experience will reverse its immediate judgment. In fact there will be only one type of consciousness, and it will be discrepant to the whole social order, a consciousness internally rent and in revolt. Wealth, which is but the suppressed in-itself, becomes the conscious goal when it is raised to the dignity of essence. The desire for wealth for its own sake is cynically admitted, and that wealth comes to signify the precondition of being-for-itself. Consciousness see its self depending on an alien will, and the feeling of that dependence, together with hatred of the benefactor, replace respect and gratitude. What consciousness awaits from another is its absolute object, its enjoyment in-and-for-itself. But what allows it to receive that object is "the chance of a moment, a whim, or some other random circumstance." This contradiction necessarily appears to consciousness. Consciousness enters into the experience of it, and that is why "the spirit of gratitude is equally the feeling of the deepest abjectness and the deepest revolt" (*PE*, II, 75; *PG*, 368; *PM*, 537–38).

In this relation of self-consciousness to wealth, the impossibility for the I to discover itself as a thing appears. The I "sees that its self-certainty, as such, is that thing which is most empty of essence; it sees that its pure personality is absolute impersonality." Thus, it arrives at the infinite judgment that "wealth is the self," an opposition that is much more deeply felt than the opposition that was expressed in the phrase "L'Etat c'est moi." In being completely realized as an object, the self is negated: it is repudiated insofar as it seeks to rediscover itself. But the self is fundamentally inalienable. Negated, it negates what negated it: it is "elasticity" itself.

> Reflection, in which the self receives itself as an objective entity, is the immediate contradiction that is posed at the heart of the I. Nevertheless, qua self, this consciousness stands immediately above that contradiction; it is absolute elasticity which suppresses anew the suppressed-being of the self and repudiates the repudiation. That is, when its being-for-itself becomes alien to it, and it rebels against receiving itself as something alien, it is for-itself in this rebellion (*PE*, II, 76; *PG*, 368–69; *PM*, 538).

The world of culture becomes aware of itself as a world of alienation. The self discovers itself in that self-contradiction and considers itself the essence of the world. Such is the language of
laceration.

The language of laceration

The general corruption of the body politic by wealth, considered as essence, entails the disappearance of the differences
between noble consciousness and base consciousness. The *ancien
régime* depended on this distinction and on its firm preservation.
But the nobility, which had devoted itself to serving the state,
alienated its honor and demanded genuine power, money, in exchange. The state, then, is no more than a means; it has indeed
been transformed into wealth, which is "self-consciousness existing as universal gift." Hegel views this transformation as a profound revolution in the texture of spirit, and he describes it both
as it is on its own and as a dialectical moment in which spirit
realizes itself and prepares to reach a higher self-consciousness.
The self receives substance, and the most extreme form of the
alienation of self-consciousness (that which takes place when
substance is realized as wealth) leads—precisely because it is
the most extreme form—to its own reversal. This entire dialectical development is summarized in the following passage:

> In reaching its spirituality thanks to the principle of individuality,
> universal power (which is substance) receives its self only as a
> name; and when it is actual power it is instead self-sacrificing
> impotent essence. But that abandoned essence, deprived of itself,
> i.e., the self that has become a thing, is rather the return of es-
> sence into itself. It is being-for-itself which is for-itself; it is the
> existence of spirit (*PE*, II, 79; *PG*, 371; *PM*, 541–42).

This entire development—the formation of noble consciousness,
its service and its virtue, its opposition to base consciousness that
is in revolt against the universal order, the development (thanks
to the formation of noble consciousness) of state power, which
at first is impersonal, its subsequent realization as an absolute I
(which accompanies the transformation of the noble into a
courtier), and finally the actual transformation of power into
wealth as the object of self-consciousness—prepares a consciousness of the dialectic of the self, a consciousness that is fulfilled in
language. The world of alienation will appear to itself; its self
will finally emerge as the "existence for-itself of spirit."

Noble consciousness becomes in actuality what base consciousness was. These values and distinctions now have a merely formal meaning. Although they subsist, they contain no truth; they are merely a façade behind which a new world is fashioning itself. To be sure, there is a difference in this world between two types of consciousness—that of the wealthy man who dispenses gifts and that of the client who receives them—but this difference is not an essential one. Both types of consciousness are characterized by laceration; there remains briefly a certain unawareness in wealthy consciousness. The wealthy man is indeed familiar with the power of wealth. He knows that what he distributes is the I of others; and his right hand knows full well what his left hand is doing. Wealth is no longer an original and naïve condition of life. "Wealth shares the abjectness of its client, but arrogance replaces revolt" (*PE*, II, 77; *PG*, 369; *PM*, 539). Hegel's whole argument about the arrogance of the rich man and the baseness of the poor client is inspired by Diderot's satire, *Rameau's Nephew*, which Goethe had just translated. Hegel interpreted Diderot's text as the expression of a general depravity of society, as the self-consciousness of an extreme culture.

The wealthy man's consciousness is the arrogance which thinks that it supports an alien I by the gift of a meal and that it thereby brings his innermost being under submission. This is a clear allusion to Diderot's text. Rameau's nephew describes to the philosopher how he behaves toward the rich man who feeds him, and he gives a portrait of that man, who likes to see his client grovel at his feet:

> My hypochondriac with his head swallowed up in a nightcap down to his eyes looks like an immovable idol with a string tied to its chin and running down beneath his chair. You wait for the string to be pulled but it is never pulled; or if the jaw drops it is only to let out some chilling word, from which you learn that you have not been understood and that your apish tricks have been wasted.[33]

In the state of mind depicted by Diderot, Hegel sees a self-consciousness that is equal to itself in its greatest disparity with itself, "the complete liberation from every bond, the pure laceration in which—the self-equality of being-in-itself having become completely disparate—all that exists in the mode of equality, all

33. *Rameau's Nephew*, pp. 40–41.

that subsists, is lacerated, and which consequently lacerates in the first place opinion and feeling with regard to the benefactor" (*PE*, II, 77; *PG*, 369; *PM*, 539). This intuition of being-for-itself as destructive of everything that subsists, as the refusal of immediate equality, and as a perpetual mediation with itself, is characteristic of Hegel's conception of spiritual self-consciousness. Diderot's description provided Hegel with an illustration of his own conception. The rich man sees "that bottomless depth which has neither foundation nor substance" as merely a common thing—a plaything of his mood, an accident of his whim. His spirit, therefore, is absolutely superficial. But the client's case is different. He can rise through his depravity and his humiliation to a consciousness of the self. The rich man, on the other hand, does not gather the disparate moments together, and he cannot, therefore, become aware of this world of alienation.

Hence, we must consider the consciousness of the poor client, and, in his becoming aware of himself, perceive the very consciousness of culture, the spirit peculiar to this world. After reading Goethe's translation of the book, Schiller wrote to Körner that *Rameau's Nephew* "is an imaginary conversation between a nephew of the musician Rameau and Diderot. The nephew is the ideal of the vagabond parasite, but among vagabonds of this type he is a hero and while portraying himself he simultaneously satirizes the world in which he lives." This idea shows us what Hegel was at first able to see in the book: the portrayal not merely of the eccentric but also of the world that is reflected in him. Further, in that world's (a world that is alien to itself) becoming aware of itself, Hegel saw the consciousness of extreme culture and of the laceration that results from that culture. And Hegel appreciated the dialectical nature of the book. Rameau's nephew is a strange character who completely resists definition. He is always other than he is thought to be, "a compound of elevation and abjectness, of good sense and lunacy. The ideas of decency and depravity must be strangely scrambled in his head." [34] He frankly shows himself as he is, but he never recognizes himself in any particular aspect. He is never what he is, always outside himself, and, when outside himself, returning within himself. Hegel had already said that man "is what he is not and is not what he is." Diderot's description offered Hegel the satire of a world, a concrete example of human self-consciousness, and, with regard to the dialectical development under dis-

34. *Ibid.*, p. 8.

cussion, the result of the culture in which the I is always alien to itself. Rameau's nephew humiliates himself and plays the part of a base man, but he finds in this depravity an occasion to assert his dignity. Only as soon as this dignity becomes manifest it appears ridiculous to itself: "A certain dignity attaches to the nature of man that nothing must destroy. It stirs in protest [with regard to boots. Yes, with regard to boots]."

Hegel notes that the dialogue puts two very different characters face to face: the respectable philosopher and the bohemian. The philosopher wishes to preserve a number of fixed values; he is frightened by the bohemian's dialectical reversals and by his incessant transformations. Yet he is forced to recognize the frankness of his interlocutor: "I was confounded by such sagacity and such meanness, such correct ideas and such false ones, by so general a perversion of feeling, such complete turpitude, and such uncommon frankness." The decent soul of the philosopher cannot adapt itself to such a perpetual reversal of values. Indeed, Hegel too often tries to evade the consequences and the logic of his own dialectic. But in Diderot's dialogue, truth is with the bohemian. For he sees everything in the world for what it is, to wit, the opposite of what it appears to be. One of the chapters of *Rameau's Nephew*, "Gold is All," can help us analyze the passages in the *Phenomenology* that discuss the depravity brought on by wealth. "What a hell of an economy: some men are replete with everything while others, whose stomachs are no less importunate, whose hunger is just as recurrent, have nothing to bite on." [35] But in a world in which gold is all, spirit is always alien to itself, and each moment is its own contrary.

> Good and bad, the consciousness of good and the consciousness of bad, noble consciousness and base consciousness: none of these hold true. They pervert themselves into each other, and each is its own contrary. . . . Noble consciousness is base and abject, and abjectness changes into the nobility of the most refined freedom of self-consciousness (*PE*, II, 79; *PG*, 371; *PM*, 541).

The bohemian strips the veil off a world and a social system which have lost their substantiveness, a world whose moments lack all stability. The consciousness of this loss transforms action into a stage comedy and pure intentions into hypocrisy. Ambition and the desire for money, the wish to master power, these are the truth of this comedy. But having frankly laid out "what

35. *Ibid.*, p. 84.

everyone thinks but does not say," the nephew draws himself up: he is proud of his pure frankness. He raises his self above the baseness he has portrayed, and through the cynical admission of that very baseness he reaches equality with himself within the most complete laceration. Hegel's analysis of "lacerated consciousness" may remind us of the analyses of "skeptic consciousness" and of "unhappy consciousness." But it is original on two counts (in addition to the dialectic of insult and humiliation that one finds again in the world of Dostoevski): the lacerated consciousness is specifically the consciousness of the end of a certain world (it is perhaps a *prerevolutionary state of mind*, expressing a civilization which, becoming aware of itself, has lost all naïveté, all self-coincidence, and all substantiveness and which in that becoming aware negates itself); it is also, generally, the *final consciousness of every culture*. That the nephew expresses a prerevolutionary state is clear: "Vanity: There are no [fatherlands] left. All I see from pole to pole is tyrants and slaves." [36] Hegel explicitly says that this shows the end of a world: "The demand for this dissolution can be addressed only to the very spirit of the culture in order that it return from its confusion back into itself, thus gaining a still higher consciousness" (*PE*, II, 82; *PG*, 374; *PM*, 546). The study of lacerated consciousness allows Hegel to advance from the world of culture to another world. Having rediscovered itself, self-consciousness will be either faith or pure intellection. For the time being, it is merely "the scintillating language of wit," which pronounces the vanity of the vanishing world and which tears everything apart. [37]

The language of wit, which pronounces the vanity of the world of culture, is, Hegel quotes Diderot, "a musical language which accommodates and mixes some thirty different tunes: French and Italian, tragic and comic, tunes of all kinds." [38] The respectable consciousness of the philosopher, by contrast, wishes to keep to the melody of the good and the true in a harmony of tone.

> It considers each moment a stable essentiality; it is the inconsistency of an uncultivated thought that does not know that it

36. *Ibid.*, p. 35 (translation modified).
37. Hegel will use this dialectic of the vanity of the content of the actual world (power or wealth) to move to *faith* (the consciousness of an essence that is beyond this world) and to *intellection* (the Enlightenment's critique of this world and of faith).
38. Quoted by Hegel (*PE*, II, 80; *PG*, 372; *PM*, 543).

does the opposite as well. The lacerated consciousness, on the contrary, is the consciousness of perversion and specifically of absolute perversion. The concept is dominant in it, the concept which gathers together thoughts which respectable consciousness considers far apart. Its language, consequently, sparkles with wit (*PE*, II, 80; *PG*, 372; *PM*, 543).

The sparkling language of wit is not merely the language of the tragicomic bohemian; it is the truth of the world of culture—a truth which the naïve, nondialectical philosopher cannot understand. It is the language of an entire society which can hold itself in esteem only insofar as it can, in select circles, declare frankly and with verve the hollowness of its world. It continues to benefit from the existing order, but it knows itself to be superior to that order, an order which serves it only as an object on which it can exercise its judgment, "sparkling with wit." Nonetheless, as Diderot notes, nobody can think this way and condemn the established order without noticing that he thereby renounces his own existence. Language, the universal judgment made on the world of culture, is the truth of that culture and its spirituality. The Dasein of this spirit is universal speech and the judgment that tears everything apart, a judgment in the light of which all the moments that should be valid as essences and actual members of the whole dissolve. "A judgment of this sort plays the game of self-dissolution with itself too" (*PE*, II, 79; *PG*, 372; *PM*, 542–43).

This universal language pronounces the hollowness of culture and contains its truth. It contraposes its negative dialectic to the decent soul who even by giving imaginary or real examples cannot maintain the good and the true in their purity—"for to portray the good in the form of a specific anecdote is the worst way to speak of it" (*PE*, II, 82; *PG*, 374; *PM*, 545). And if simple consciousness demands the dissolution of this world and a return to nature, it cannot address itself to the isolated individual; even Diogenes in his barrel was conditioned by his society. The world as a whole must be transformed and must rise to a higher form. There is no question of spirit falling back to innocent nature and rediscovering the simplicity of the natural man. Rousseau's work, which was the most negative of its century but by that very token prepared the way for a new positivity, is not to be understood in this way. The return to nature can signify only the return of spirit within itself, "thus gaining a still higher consciousness" (*PE*, II, 82; *PG*, 374; *PM*, 546).

But this return has already occurred. The *language of laceration* is the reflection of spirit back on itself. On the one hand, this reflection may signify the rise of spirit above the reality it has constituted, in which case spirit is impelled beyond the world of culture: "It is deflected from this world to heaven; its object is the beyond of *this* world" (*PE*, II, 83; *PG*, 375; *PM*, 546). We know that the spirit of culture and alienation has its counterpart in the world of faith, a world parallel to the world of culture. On the other hand, that spirit is the reflection of the world of culture in the self, which knows and pronounces the hollowness of *this* world. Its interest is then merely the judgment on the hollowness of the whole culture. The self still focuses on the real world, but it retains a spiritual interest in it only constantly to criticize it.

> The hollowness of all things is its own hollowness; it itself is hollow. It is the self which is for-itself, which can not only judge and chatter about everything but can also express wittily in all their contradictions both the solid essences of actuality and the solid determinations posited by judgment; those contradictions are their truth (*PE*, II, 83; *PG*, 375; *PM*, 546).

The self gains power and wealth, and it is then dissatisfied. It continues to desire power and wealth and to do everything possible to acquire them, but when it has acquired them it knows that they are nothing in-itself; that *it* is their power, and that they are hollow. Thus, it transcends them in possessing them, and its highest interest is to become aware of their hollowness. "This hollowness depends on the hollowness of all things for its own self-consciousness; thus it engenders that hollowness itself and is the soul that sustains it" (*PE*, II, 83; *PG*, 375; *PM*, 547). Hegel is thinking here of the brilliant French society of the eighteenth century, of the conversations and of all the critical thought, which culminated in the negation of the cultural world and in the experience of the return of spirit into itself, in Rousseau. But the critique of the hollowness of all things remains negative and can grasp no positive content: "The positive object is now only the pure I itself, and lacerated consciousness is in-itself the pure self-harmony of self-consciousness returned to itself" (*PE*, II, 84; *PG*, 376; *PM*, 548).

Thus, the cultural world leads us to become aware of it as a world of the alienation of the self. This act of becoming aware is a return of spirit to itself, a transcendence of alienation. This transcendence will appear in two guises in Hegel's dialectic. Parallel to the real world of culture there is a world of *faith* into which spirit flees to regain its unity with its essence, and there is *pure intellection*, the self which has gained its own universality through culture and is able to reduce to itself all the content that appeared alien to it. The conflict between faith and the Enlightenment, a result of the alienation of spirit, remains caught up in that alienation, although it is in order to end and definitively surmount the alienation of spirit that the Enlightenment struggles against faith. At the end of this struggle, according to the Enlightenment, heaven will descend to earth and absolute freedom will appear.

II. Faith and Pure Intellection

THE CULTURAL WORLD, the world in which spirit has become alien to itself, has a counterpart in another world, the world of faith. In a development parallel to the development of spirit that we have just discussed, *actual* consciousness comes to stand contraposed to *pure* consciousness, consciousness of realized spirit to the consciousness of the essence of spirit, and the here-below to the beyond.

We know that this split is characteristic of the modern world. Man lives in one world and thinks in another. In the cultural world, he seeks power and wealth, which are the objects of his desire. But in acquiring them he transcends them. He knows that they are hollow and that pursuit of them cannot satisfy. In possessing them he does not reach himself.

> Power and wealth are the supreme goals of the self's effort; it knows that through renunciation and sacrifice it molds itself to the universal and manages to possess it, and that in that possession it attains universal validity. Power and wealth are the recognized actual forces, but the validity that the self reaches through them is hollow. Precisely when the self has acquired them it knows that they are not autonomous essences, that it is itself their power, and that they are hollow (*PE*, II, 83; *PG*, 375; *PM*, 547).

This knowledge of the hollowness of the cultural world, of the powers in which the self has realized, or rather alienated, itself, is a knowledge of the nothingness of the world and the immediate ascent of spirit to another sphere. This world, in which by forming itself the self actualizes its will to power, now appears only on the near side of essence; it is not the *true* world, although it is the actually *given* world. "Faith," Malebranche wrote, "teaches us that the things of the world are vain and that our happiness does not lie in honors and in wealth." [39]

Thus, unlike the first world of spirit, the world of culture is not self-sufficient. As a "totality" it is alien to itself, and it implies a truth that lies outside it. As it is a here-below it refers to a beyond. That beyond is the thought of this world itself, yet it constitutes its reflection. It appears now to the pure consciousness of spirit in faith. Hegel envisages faith as the counterpart of the world of alienation and shows how it is a *flight* which is also conditioned by the real world which it flees. Faith is the thought of spirit, to be sure, but it is a thought that does not yet know itself as a thought and that therefore appears contaminated by the element of which it is the other. That is why although in-itself faith is thought—"the principal moment in the nature of faith, a moment that is usually neglected"—it appears, once it has entered self-consciousness, only as a *representation* of self-consciousness itself, an objective being that is negative in the positivity of its content. "But inasmuch as thought enters consciousness, or pure consciousness enters self-consciousness, this immediateness carries the signification of an objective being, a being that dwells beyond the consciousness of the self" (*PE*, II, 88; *PG*, 379; *PM*, 553).[40]

If we try to express Hegel's idea of faith as simply as possible, dispensing with his terminology, we come to the following: Faith is a flight from the real world; it is a representation of spirit beyond the determinations of this world. Yet, as in a play of mirrors, the same substance appears at times in the guise of the powers of the world and at times in the guise of absolute being, in the guise of God. "The absolute object is nothing but the real world raised to the universality of pure consciousness" (*PE*, II, 89; *PG*, 380; *PM*, 554). The content of this faith is the content of the Christian revelation, spirit in-and-for-itself in the

---

39. It is not by chance that we quote Malebranche here (*Recherche de la vérité*, book IV, chapter 4). He expresses especially well the duality of reality and essence that Hegel wishes to note.

40. In penetrating *immediately* to self-consciousness, pure thought, the essence of spirit, is contaminated by the moment of reality; as a result, it is only *representation* and it takes on the form of an *other world*. In *intellection*, on the contrary, pure thought behaves negatively with respect to objectivity and reduces the whole of negative objectivity to the self (*PE*, II, 89; *PG*, 380; *PM*, 554).

form of the three persons of the Trinity. In the first place, spirit is eternal substance, God the Father. But since the substance is spirit, it is not only in-itself; it becomes for-itself, and it realizes itself in the form of a transitory self given over to the Passion and to death, i.e., in the form of Christ. It then gathers itself up into its original simplicity. "Only when represented in this manner is substance represented as spirit." Thus, the three moments of spirit which we saw in the real world in the mode of alienation appear to believing consciousness in the form of the three persons of the Trinity. It is indeed the content of spirit in-and-for-itself that is portrayed here. But it is only *portrayed;* that is, believing consciousness does not grasp the necessity of the *transition* from one moment to another—the movement through which substance forms itself as subject, actualizing itself and preserving itself within that actuality, in its substantiveness. The Christian Trinity appears to believing consciousness in the element of representation. Each of the persons is envisaged in its unalterable unity, and an unintelligible *event* presents the transition from one person to the other. Believing consciousness knows that "God became man and dwelt among us," but this development of divine substance is not a necessary development, it is not the very expression of substance as spirit. "These persons form a necessary series only for us; for faith, their difference is a static diversity and their movement is an event." Inasmuch as the object of believing consciousness, God, participates in the real world through his Son, believing consciousness is still part of the real world. Yet—and Hegel had made the same observation with regard to unhappy consciousness, whose subjectivity stands contraposed to the objectivity of faith—its participation in the real world does not suffice to reabsorb the moment of the beyond. If God was made flesh and dwelt among us, he nonetheless remained an alien reality in that incarnation. "And the beyond merely took on the determination of being spatially and temporally distant" (*PE*, II, 91; *PG*, 381; *PM*, 553).[41]

Believing consciousness rises immediately above the real world, but it carries that world within itself. Thus it thinks its essence, but does not know that it is a thought. The content of

41. Hegel has already presented the dialectic of the incarnation of God in his discussion of unhappy consciousness (*PE*, I, 180; *PG*, 162; *PM*, 255). He returns to it in his discussion of "revealed religion," viewing spatiotemporal *distancing* as a sensuous manifestation of *mediation:* "The past and distance are merely the imperfect form" of mediation (*PE*, II, 270; *PG*, 531; *PM*, 763).

spirit in-and-for-itself appears to it, but it appears as a world, as an *other* world, as an other *positive* reality that is different from it and whose provenance is unknown. This is the positivity, the exterior authority presented by faith, that was denounced by the eighteenth century's critique and that Hegel (who agreed on this point with the Enlightenment) viewed in his Bern *Life of Jesus* as an impurity: "When you revere church statutes and state laws as your highest law, you overlook the dignity and the power that allow man himself to create the concept of divinity." [42] Precisely inasmuch as the world of faith is an *other* world, it is not the thought of spirit; unlike religion, it is not spirit in-and-for-itself. Hegel here subtly distinguishes faith and religion. At the end point of the *Phenomenology*, religion, that is, spirit rising to the consciousness of its own content, finds the dialectic proper to it: it is viewed as absolute spirit's becoming aware of itself. But here, it is only a moment in the development of self-alienated spirit—the moment that stands contraposed to *actuality*—and therefore it is only a *faith*.

Faith is different from unhappy consciousness. The latter was the expression of the deepest subjectivity, which is why it failed to reach *objectivity*. Its content was not yet posed as the substance of spirit, but was merely ardently desired: unhappy consciousness was the soul's nostalgia, not the spirit's thought. It was a pious fervor and the soul's direction toward thought (*Andacht*). "As fervor, its thought remains a formless tumult of bells, a warm mist; it is a musical thought that fails to attain the concept, which would be the only immanent objective modality" (*PE*, I, 183; *PG*, 163; *PM*, 257). In the faith of the world of culture, the subjective Christian piety of the Middle Ages gives way to the objectivity of substance. What appears to believing consciousness is the essence in-and-for-itself of spirit, the content of truth. But precisely as a *content*, it carries in its objective presentation the mark of the alienation of spirit. Religion, Hegel wrote later, reunites within itself *the subjectivity of unhappy consciousness and the objectivity of believing consciousness.*[43] Hegel further specifies the characteristics of the content of faith

42. *Theologische Jugendschriften*, p. 89.
43. In characterizing revealed religion, Hegel writes: "The content has already presented itself as the representation of unhappy consciousness and of believing consciousness"—in unhappy consciousness as the subjective content "desired by consciousness," in believing consciousness "as the essence of a world deprived of self" (*PE*, II, 272–73; *PG*, 533; *PM*, 766).

by distinguishing it from the *in-itself of stoic consciousness* and from *virtuous consciousness*. For the stoic, thought was merely a *form* that received an alien *content* into it. For faith, thought itself is the content; its object is not a mere form. For virtuous consciousness the in-itself was indeed the essence of reality, but it was an unrealized essence, an *ideal* that was not yet present. For believing consciousness, the in-itself is not an ideal to be realized; it is thought of as actual, although it is posed beyond actuality. Thus, the object of faith is neither the form of thought nor an ideal: it partakes of both. It is the essence of spirit, which, in its self-alienation, perceives itself as beyond itself.

Nevertheless, since "this pure consciousness of absolute essence is a consciousness alien to itself," it must contain its otherness within itself. It is a flight from the actual world and at first glance its other appears to be that world. But it must contain its other within its own heart. Thus, it presents itself as engaged in a conflict. "Pure consciousness is thus alien to itself within itself, and faith constitutes only one aspect of it." The other aspect, as Hegel notes, has already been born for us: it is the aspect of pure self-consciousness—the movement that we discovered in the dialectic of the world of culture, a movement that attacks the subsistence of each of the moments of the world and transforms it into its contrary. If *faith* is the thought of the content of spirit, it stands contraposed to the movement of *intellection*—the movement of the self which rejects all otherness and transmutes all objects into the self. As the totality of life stood contraposed to the self-consciousness of life, and immobile truth stood contraposed to the anxious search for the true, so faith, as the content of the substance of spirit, stands contraposed to intellection, the universal self which reduces everything to itself and rejects all content which appears in an objective form alien to the self.[44] Faith can present itself only as engaged in an unending conflict with reason (Hegel says "intellection," *Einsicht*). This conflict at the heart of pure consciousness is now our subject.

44. The supreme synthesis of Hegel's thought is this unity of *movement* and *repose*, a unity of the disquiet of the self (temporality) and the eternity of essence. For this reason truth in-and-for-itself is "Bacchic delirium . . . but this delirium is also a translucent and simple repose" (*PE*, I, 40; *PG*, 39; *PM*, 105). The two moments separate here as essence and self, faith and intellection. Cf. the discussion of life as repose and disquiet (*PE*, I, 148; *PG*, 135; *PM*, 220) and the discussion of the true and its movement (*PE*, I, 201; *PG*, 178; *PM*, 276). (For this unity the movement of truth is the other.)

The two terms which so radically oppose each other are not as distinct *for us* as they appear to be for each other. We see one and the same truth of self-alienated spirit in them.

> When we consider it as it is in truth, driven back into itself from the world that lacks essence and is merely disintegrating the world of culture), spirit is an inseparable unity both of absolute move-ment and the negativity of its manifestation, and of the essence of these two moments, satisfied by itself, and their positive repose. But these two moments, bound in general by the determination of estrangement, move apart as a split consciousness (*PE*, II, 87; *PG*, 379; *PM*, 552).

Content as an immobile truth, as an essence posed beyond in-tellection, characterizes faith; the movement of the self, turned against all objectivity, characterizes intellection. On the one hand, spirit perceives itself as a truth that is equal to itself, and is pure positivity. On the other hand, spirit is the self that pene-trates every content and reduces it to its own self; it is absolute negativity, the universal self. These two aspects are identical, for the concept is absolute difference which, as such, is difference from itself, that is, is not a difference at all. But they present themselves in opposition here, an opposition that seems the most profound possible.

Thus, the object of Hegel's study is the struggle between faith and intellection. These two terms present themselves as a turning away from the world of culture: faith is a *flight* from it; universal intellection is its *result*. The self, which has traversed the world of culture, has risen to universality. The natural dif-ferences that separated individuals have been overcome. There are no longer fundamental differences but only differences in magnitude—more or less powerful wills. In every individual spirit is one and the same universal acquired by culture. It re-veals itself as the self. On the one hand, the self reduces every-thing objective to the being-for-itself of self-consciousness; on the other hand, that being-for-itself has the signification of a uni-versal: "Intellection becomes the property of all self-conscious-nesses." The I, as it later appears in Kant and Fichte, has already been discovered here *by us;* idealism expresses the triumph of the universal self in a philosophic system. No longer can any-thing be contraposed to that self as a thing-in-itself. It will pene-trate every content that claims to be valid outside self-conscious-ness. It will comprehend such content, and, in so doing, make of it a moment of its own self. Similarly, the I will not be the exclusive property of this or that given individual but will be universal in everyone. The requisite universal self, resulting from the process of culture, precedes the reduction of being to the I in philosophic systems. Its universality is as yet no more than a *pure intention*. "Thus, pure intellection is the spirit that addresses every consciousness and proclaims: what you all are in yourselves, be for yourselves, be rational" (*PE*, II, 93; *PG*, 383; *PM*, 558).[45]

But intellection is confronted by the world of faith, which presents itself as an irreducible objectivity, as a content contaminated by that from which it is in flight. Intellection, then, struggles against faith on the pretext of actualizing the freedom of spirit. This struggle is realized in the sixteenth century with the Renaissance and the Reformation and in the eighteenth century with the Enlightenment. Hegel dwells principally on the struggle between the Enlightenment and faith. Critics have been surprised that in the *Phenomenology* Hegel did not discuss the Reformation at greater length. There does not even seem to be a clear allusion in the *Phenomenology* to what Hegel called "the revolution of the Germans." In fact, Hegel understood the movement of the Reformation as a first stage in the liberation of spirit. In the *Philosophy of History*, he compared Luther to Socrates and wrote that with Luther, "spirit began to return to itself" and rose to an "inner reconciliation." The Reformation was the beginning of the Enlightenment: "Faith preserved in the spiritual world the sensuous 'this' which it claimed to be escaping, and the necessary corruption of the church was due to this." [46] Faith became impure as a result of the admixture of thought and the sensuous, the immediate transposition of the real world into the world of thought. For Protestantism as for the Enlightenment, "religion must build its temples and its altars only in the individual's heart." And it must see that the objective thing presented for the worship of the faithful is nothing but a thing. Thus, the divine is completely separated from all intuition. In "Glauben und Wissen" Hegel had tried to show how Protestantism had contributed to the separation of *inner* from *outer*. In this way, the subjectivity that characterizes "this form of universal

45. Hegel also characterizes the movement of believing consciousness vis-à-vis the real world. Instead of thinking that world vain and going no further, it tries to reach "the consciousness of its union with essence." But that union is never realized, at least not by specific consciousness (*PE*, II, 90; *PG*, 381; *PM*, 555).

46. *Philosophy of History*, p. 412.

spirit, the principle of the Nordic peoples," was reached.[47] For this reason, the Enlightenment did not have in Germany the antireligious nature that it had in France. If in France the Enlightenment attacked theology it was because French theology was not yet internalized; faith had remained a faith in a suprasensuous beyond, that is, in a second world that was beyond the first one but that, like the first, was objectively given. The struggle for the liberty of spirit which Luther inaugurated was carried on by the Enlightenment. In the modern world, Hegel wrote in the *Philosophy of History*, "Religion cannot subsist without thought; in part, it advances to the concept; in part, forced to by thought itself, it becomes intensive faith or, if pushed to despair by thought, from which it flees completely, superstition." [48]

If our interpretation is correct, Hegel had no need to discuss the Reformation specifically in the *Phenomenology*, because that movement is part of the struggle between what Hegel calls "faith" and what he calls "pure intellection." The two terms appear together. The Reformation is only a moment in that struggle; the Enlightenment, on the other hand, is its culmination. In considering the Enlightenment's struggle against superstition, Hegel transcends Protestantism, which merely initiated spirit's freedom, attaining only its inner reconciliation. The Enlightenment finally met partial failure in eighteenth-century philosophy and in the French Revolution. Nevertheless, in subjective spirit faith still presents itself, albeit as pure subjectivity freed from alienation. Subjective spirit, which can be connected more directly to the Protestant revolution—an "unsatisfied Enlightenment" rather than an Enlightenment that submerges itself in finitude and finds its repose there—reappears in what Hegel calls the "moral world view." This world view, which corresponds to Nordic subjectivity and to the philosophies of Kant and Fichte, constitutes the original development of the Reformation.[49]

Thus the Reformation does play a part in the *Phenomenology*. Insofar as it opposes the theology of the beyond and fights it with the weapons of pure intellection, but also, on the other hand, insofar as the beyond still subsists in Protestant theology and pertains only to subjectivity, the Reformation is expressed in the moral world view, in the awakening of free subjectivity,

47. "Glauben und Wissen," p. 225.
48. *Philosophy of History*, p. 346.
49. Cf. the chapter on the moral world view in the *Phenomenology* and the Jena article "Glauben und Wissen."

which the *Phenomenology* specifically studies and which the article "Glauben und Wissen" related directly to Protestantism.

Pure intellection turned against faith comes to be called "the Enlightenment": it is the light that dispels shadows. At first, this struggle, which runs throughout the eighteenth century and claims to realize rationality in-and-for-itself, is negative. The Enlightenment triumphs over faith; it denounces the moment of the beyond that faith includes and shows faith to be superstition. But in the course of this struggle, pure intellection acquires a positive content: the Enlightenment's doctrine, its truth, which reveals itself as the most platitudinous utilitarianism, and the thought of the finite world. Emerging from this finitude, spirit is reconciled with itself. And the two worlds, earth and heaven, come together in one. This is the experience of the French Revolution which appears to be the end of the world of culture and of separation. Yet this experience too proves disappointing. With the Terror and with Napoleon, then, spirit rises to a higher form; it becomes self-certain spirit, which constitutes the third moment in the development of spirit.

4 / The Struggle between Enlightenment and Superstition

THE GREAT STRUGGLE of the eighteenth century, which pitted the philosophes of the *Encyclopedia* against those whom they considered the backward defenders of an already crumbling faith, the struggle of reason against faith, of the Enlightenment against superstition, was a recent phenomenon for Hegel. It was a struggle which foreshadowed new times, a struggle which entailed a revolutionary change in the "texture" of spirit. Sensitive as he was to historical changes, to visible and invisible changes in the world spirit, Hegel could hardly fail to devote to that struggle a discussion appropriate to the importance he attributed to it. He had to describe the revolution in spiritual life and to understand its significance. His prime model was "philosophical preaching" in France, which took on a more pronounced antireligious cast than it had in Germany (where the Reformation had already accomplished part of the task), and which culminated in a political revolution of considerable importance. To be sure, in 1807 Hegel no longer thought of the French Revolution as he had during his years at Tübingen; the course of events, the Terror of 1793 and the Napoleonic Empire, led him to change his views somewhat, as they did many of Hegel's contemporaries. But Hegel continued to affirm that there was in that political revolution a prodigious effort on the part of the world spirit to realize "the rational, in-and-for-itself" on earth. The world changed with the eighteenth century and the French Revolution. Despite his cautious conservatism, Hegel still wrote in the *Philosophy of History* that with the French Revolution, the thought, the concept of law, was suddenly asserted, and the ancient edifice of injustice could not withstand it. In legal thinking, a constitution was constructed on the basis of which everything was thenceforth supposed to stand. Never before, since the sun has been in the sky and the planets have turned around it, had man stood on his head, that is, based himself on the idea and constructed reality according to it. Anaxagoras had first said that νοῦς rules the world, but only now has man come to see that thought must direct spiritual reality. It was a superb sunrise. All thinking beings celebrated that era. A sublime feeling reigned; enthusiasm of spirit shook the world as though the genuine reconciliation of the world and the divine had occurred at precisely that moment.[1]

Of course, in the same book, Hegel criticized the revolution for having realized only formal principles and for having been unable to express concrete reason: "It's principle remained formal because it issued from abstract thought, from understanding, which is abstract insofar as it is immediate and which is at first the consciousness that pure reason has of itself." We shall see this critique developed throughout this whole study, but we must not allow it to blind us to the spiritual necessity that Hegel ascribes to the struggle. The French Revolution was born of thought; it emerged from the philosophy of the world elaborated during the eighteenth century:

> The sovereignty of the subject standing by himself was posed against a faith based on authority, and the laws of nature were recognized as the only bond between [phenomena]. Thus all miracles were challenged, for now nature was a system of known and recognized laws. Man was at home in nature and where he was at home was all that counted. Knowledge of nature made him free.[2]

Then thought extended its sway to the world of spirit and refused to recognize law and morality in a commandment that was alien to human reason. Thus a fundamental change in the development of spirit came about: the effort to transcend all alienation of the I.

> These general conceptions, deduced from actual and present consciousness—the Laws of Nature and the substance of what is right and good—have received the name of *Reason*. The recogni-

1. *Philosophy of History*, p. 447.
2. *Ibid.*, p. 440.

tion of the validity of these laws was designated by the term *Eclaircissement* (*Aufklärung*). From France it passed over into Germany, and created a new world of ideas.[3]

In the passages from the *Phenomenology* which we shall now discuss, both the historical moment and the general significance of the rationalism of the Enlightenment are considered. There was, to be sure, a philosophical doctrine, but it was a doctrine that spread throughout the whole of society and won over a whole people. We have already noted the opposition in *Rameau's Nephew* between the philosopher, who behaves formally while collecting the secrets of the bohemian, and the bohemian himself, who expresses the rending of the perverse and self-alienated world:

> There was in all he said much that one thinks to oneself, and acts on, but that one never says. This was in fact the chief difference between my man and the rest of us. He admitted his vices, which are also ours: he was no hypocrite. Neither more nor less detestable than other men, he was franker than they, more logical, and thus often profound in his depravity.[4]

At that point, the world of culture reaches its sharpest self-awareness and becomes a scintillatingly witty discourse that judges all aspects of its own condition. "This mirror of the world" is not yet pure intellection. For it wishes (impurely) to shine and, in the midst of that world, to manifest itself by its wit and by the originality of its corrosive critique. Self-consciousness still participates in the world it reflects. This is the time of the *salons* and of Montesquieu's *Persian Letters,* not yet the time of pure intellection which, having become the intellection of all, escapes this artificial world through the universality of its critical thought.[5] At first, the I still enjoys the artificial order of society. But the I knows itself to be superior to that order, which serves merely as an object on which it can exercise its judgment. One rises above the world by showing its vanity and, in the process, demonstrating one's own wit. One still lives in that world, but through one's wit one shows that one no longer believes in it. "Only the interest in having content for argument and frivolous

3. *Ibid.,* p. 441.
4. *Rameau's Nephew*, trans. Jacques Barzun and Ralph H. Bowen (New York, 1956), p. 76.
5. Hegel seems to distinguish two moments here, that of *The Persian Letters* and that of the *Philosophical Dictionary:* intellection's critique is progressively extended to the whole of society and becomes universal (in scope as well as in dissemination).

conversation maintains the whole and its articulations" (*PE,* II, 94; *PG,* 384; *PM,* 560).[6] Thus, consciousness still participates in the world of culture and, seeking to shine at its expense, helps to maintain it. But the emptiness of the content also expresses the emptiness of the self which knows that content to be empty. Therefore, when consciousness discovers that its judgment is universal it rises to *pure* intellection: "The scattered traits are gathered up into one universal image and make up one intellection belonging to everyone." At that point, the fact of "judging better" than others, the only remaining interest, disappears and "specific insight [*Einsehen*] is resolved into universal intellection [*Einsicht*]" (*PE,* II, 95; *PG,* 385; *PM,* 561).[7]

In this way, Hegel shows us how pure intellection is formed by a reflection back on itself of the world of culture, a reflection which also gives rise to the world of faith. Both faith and intellection result from the alienated spirit's attempt to overcome its alienation: faith is the transcendence of the world through the thought of its absolute beyond, the thought of the being of spirit; intellection is the return of spirit to itself as an act of thought, as the negation of all alienation. Henceforth, those two reflections oppose and confront each other in a fratricidal combat all the more violent in that they fundamentally express the same truth, the truth of spirit. Thought struggles with thought. In the beyond to which it aspires, faith knows, without knowing it, the very essence of spirit. But only content appears to it, not the form of intellection. In intellection, spirit still knows itself only as pure negativity; it is form which separates itself from content so as to negate it qua other. "At first," Hegel wrote in the *Philosophy of History,* "the principle of thought appears in its universality in abstract form, and it stands on the principle of contradiction and identity. Thus content is posed as finite, and the Enlightenment banished anything speculative from human and divine things." And in the *Phenomenology* he writes, "Faith and intellection are one and the same pure consciousness, but they are contraposed with regard to form: for faith essence is thought, not concept, and it is therefore something absolutely opposed to self-consciousness; whereas for pure intellection es-

6. By "masses" Hegel means the divisions of the social substance—community and family, social classes and estates, etc. At the close of the eighteenth century these "masses" have *being* only insofar as they furnish the *occasion* for wit's critique. The hour of their disappearance in revolution is near.

7. On Voltaire, see "Glauben und Wissen," p. 335.

sence is the self. Thus faith and intellection are negatives of each other" (*PE*, II, 95; *PG*, 385; *PM*, 561).

The defect of faith is that it presents itself as a beyond, as a content that is alien to self-consciousness; the truth of rationalism is that it asserts the absolute freedom of the spirit. That freedom had already begun to appear in Lutheranism: "Luther had secured to mankind Spiritual Freedom and the Reconciliation in the concrete: he triumphantly established the position that man's eternal destiny must be wrought out *in himself*. But the *import* [content] of that which is to take place in him—what truth is to become vital in him, was taken for granted by Luther as something already given, something revealed by religion." [8] What the Enlightenment denounces is precisely this given, this *positivity*.[9] In 1788 Hegel's professor at the Tübingen Seminary was a theologian named Storr. Storr, in the age of the French *Encyclopedia*, based all his teaching on the authority of Revelation. Starting with the sacred authority of Christ and the apostles, Storr—as a concession to modernism—even justified his method by appealing to Kant's philosophy. Critical philosophy had shown that human reason could not go beyond the knowledge of the sensuous world. Human reason, therefore, is incompetent to judge the validity of Revelation. In his book *Doctrinae christianae pars theoretica et sacris litteris repetita*, Storr wrote, "In hac causa ne habet quidem philosophia justam auctoritatem." [10] On the other hand, we know that in the first of his early works Hegel criticized such "positive religion," which imposes a content on human consciousness. The students at the Tübingen Seminary had read the French philosophes of the eighteenth century. And in Germany Lessing had praised religious tolerance; in his first essays, Hegel often quoted from "Nathan the Wise." According to Lessing, Revelation was necessary during the childhood of humanity. It prepared for a moral religion which corresponds to human maturity and which is the result of human reason.

The conflict between the Enlightenment and positive faith

8. *Philosophy of History*, p. 447.

9. Thus extending the work of the Reformation: "Now the principle has been established that this content is an actual content of which I can convince myself internally, and that everything must be brought back to this intimate foundation" (*ibid.*, p. 447; translation modified).

10. "In this matter philosophy has no proper authority" (Storr, *Doctrinae*, p. iv).

was one of the fundamental problems Hegel posed in his youth. The details of this conflict and its speculative implications are presented in philosophical form in the *Phenomenology*. Although Hegel was influenced by the Enlightenment in his youth and, despite profound differences, remained faithful to its rationalist spirit, his adherence to it was not unreserved. As early as the first Tübingen essays, there is a critique of any philosophy of understanding that is too dry and abstract to inspire human action. Following Rousseau, Hegel contraposed "subjective religion," a religion of the heart capable of directing the whole of human life, to an abstract theology, which at that time he called "objective religion." The Enlightenment, the critique carried out by understanding, can make us more intelligent. But it cannot make us better. It has no effect on our souls; it acts only negatively, and it thereby stands contraposed, in turn, to subjective religion. During that same period, Hegel drew an opposition between the "religion of a people" and "private religion": he was clearly aware of realities not known by the Enlightenment. We can already see in these texts a desire to go beyond the oppositions, to think religion through so as to preserve its speculative content as a manifestation of spirit's truth, without, however, denying the rights of self-consciousness to rediscover itself in its object. But it was not until "Glauben und Wissen," and later the text we are discussing here, written in Jena, that Hegel conceived of religion as a moment of absolute spirit, the moment of self-consciousness of spirit. From then on, the Enlightenment's critique, although correct, appears as merely negative. Eighteenth-century thought, which denied faith, had to be replaced by a thought in which everything that Revelation first offered in history to believing consciousness was assimilated to, and integrated in, spirit. The mistake of the Enlightenment was to offer a merely negative critique, to fail to grasp the content of faith and discover its speculative meaning. Religion must be thought through: Hegel prepares the way for Feuerbach.[11]

11. For a discussion of Hegel's early attitudes toward religion and the Enlightenment, see J. Hyppolite, "Les Traveaux de jeunesse de Hegel d'après des ouvrages récents," *Revue de métaphysique et de morale*, vol. XLII (July, Oct., 1935). In his early works, Hegel contraposes subjective religion to objective religion, the religion of a people to a private religion. He evaluates *positivity*, the historical element of a religion, in different ways. At times, he combats it; at other times, he contraposes it to the sterility of abstract human reason. A decisive development took place during his years in Frankfurt, when *positivity* became a *destiny*.

THE ENLIGHTENMENT SPREADS

PURE INTELLECTION is an example of the power of the negative that animates self-consciousness, a power we have already encountered, for example, in the strength of skepticism, "annihilating the being of the world in the manifold variety of its determinations" (PE, I, 171–72; PG, 155; PM, 246), unveiling the hidden dialectic of each determination posed as such to thought. We have also seen the power of the negative in theoretical and practical idealism. But in pure intellection it is raised far above these subordinate stages. "For pure intellection is born of substance, knows the pure self of consciousness as the absolute, and compares itself to the pure consciousness of the absolute essence of all actuality" (PE, II, 95; PG, 385; PM, 561). It is born of substance: that is, we have here no longer an abstract aspect of self-consciousness or of reason but a manifestation, a *phenomenon of spirit* as such. This pure intellection is the result of a culture that is bound up with collective life; it is a human experience in the full sense of the word. Spirit, "which always negates," emerges *in history* here and confronts the consciousness spirit has of itself when it knows itself only as an essence that is beyond it.

For the abstract reason of the Enlightenment, then, faith is the realm of error, the kingdom of shadows. In its denunciation of fundamental error, the Enlightenment distinguishes various moments. There is first the naïve consciousness of the masses, still submerged in childhood. Among the masses, error is only a weakness of spirit, a lack of reflection and, consequently, of a turning in on itself. But this naïveté is contraposed by a second moment, the ill will of the priests who, vain, envious, and anxious to maintain their prestige, seek to deceive the masses. They reserve thought for themselves and deceive everyone else. On top of these, there are the despots who, unenlightened, share the stupidity of the masses but use the lying clergy for their own ends. Thus they gain an "undisturbed control and the possibility of realizing their pleasures and whims" (PE, II, 96; PG, 386; PM, 562). Such is the world of error—error in-itself, so to speak— which the Enlightenment notes and, by a dialectical movement frequent in history, almost manages to create in its adversary. Sometimes when two principles are in conflict the idea that one has of the other transforms that other and introduces into it the evil which at first existed only implicitly.[12] In this description of the realm of error, we can see without difficulty Voltaire's notion of *l'Infâme*. In his *Oedipe*, written in 1718, we find the following:

> Les prêtres ne sont pas ce qu'un vain peuple pense,
> Notre crédulité fait toute leur science.
>
> [Priests are hardly what we fancy;
> Their wisdom is but our credulity.]

The weakness of the people and the hypocrisy of the clergy create the abominable fanaticism and hatred which have bloodied human history. In the play *Mahomet*, the duality of ignorance and hypocrisy is expressed in the opposition between Saïde and Mahomet. The former, expressing naïve and ignorant consciousness, can say

> Vous avez sur mon âme une entière puissance,
> Eclairez seulement ma docile ignorance
>
> [You have full power over my heart;
> My docile ignorance awaits your word],

while Mahomet poses as the earthly representative of God: "Ecoutez par ma voix sa volonté suprême [Hear, through my voice, his supreme will]."[13] This world is also depicted in Schiller's *The Robbers*, Hegel's use of which we have already seen.

Nevertheless, though the *Enlightenment* begins by unveiling that "logic of error" which perverts humanity, and by negating it seeks to free mankind and render it capable of truth, it cannot act on all the moments of error equally. The perverse intention of the priests escapes its reach, for that intention pertains to the being-for-itself of consciousness; its action, therefore, bears on the masses, who are still unconscious but who have the potential to be influenced by it. Naïve consciousness and self-conscious-

12. Hegel gives several examples of the "bad consciousness" (*mauvaise conscience*) that develops in one party as a result of the negative critique of the other, e.g., when religion agrees to discuss the historical basis of Revelation on its opponent's ground.

13. Voltaire, *Mahomet*, act III, scene 6.

ness, indeed, differ only in that the one is in-itself what the other is for-itself—which is why there was no serious obstacle to the rapid spread of the Enlightenment. It penetrated the substance of the masses, insinuated itself into them, and became a universal doctrine. A revolution in spirit was brought about even before people were clearly aware of it. Hegel quotes *Rameau's Nephew* here: "The foreign god takes his place humbly next to the native idol, little by little asserts itself and one fine day elbows out his fellow—before you can say Jack Robinson, there's the idol flat on its back." [14] This contagion calls to mind Beaumarchais's words on slander: "The evil is conceived; it is born; it crawls. It grows and grows and suddenly there is slander rising, whistling, swelling, growing before your eyes." "Now," Hegel wrote,

> an invisible and imperceptible spirit, it insinuates itself into all noble parts, it becomes mistress of the limbs and the guts of the unconscious idol . . . and if the infection overcomes all of the organs of spiritual life, then one fine day, a day whose dawn is not reddened by blood, there will be merely the memory of an old inexplicable story, the dead form of the preceding incarnation of spirit. The new serpent of wisdom raised for the people's worship has merely sloughed, painlessly, a shriveled skin (*PE*, II, 98–99; *PG*, 388; *PM*, 564–65).

The established powers are helpless against the epidemic. In undertaking the struggle they ascertain what is wrong, but the ill has already been done. The spread of pure intellection is comparable to the "expansion of a gas through an atmosphere without resistance." From then on, there is no longer in the spiritual mass a solid faith which genuinely opposes reason, as with two struggling adversaries; the adversary itself succumbs to the contagion, and its arguments are inspired by the spirit of its opponent. The same spirit holds sway in both camps. Of the confident faith of the past there remains only a memory, deeply buried in the "texture" of spirit. But when the new spirit has spread and has infected the whole substance, it reveals its precise nature and the signification of its conflict with faith. Arguments can be judged and their implications seen only retrospectively. *Thinking that it was criticizing the other, pure intellection criticized itself.* It is trapped in a polemic without seeing that it has negated itself as pure intention and pure intellection.

14. P. 67. We should note that Diderot applies these words to the Jesuits' conversion of the infidels.

THE OPPOSITION BETWEEN INTELLECTION AND FAITH

THE ANALYSIS OF THIS POLEMIC and of its implications is one of the most appealing passages in the *Phenomenology*. Free thought, pure intellection, as Hegel says, intends to liberate the human spirit from a fundamental error the origin of which cannot easily be discovered. That error is nothing other than the *irrational*. The Enlightenment finds an inconceivable world in the object of faith, a world alien to reason, a being-other whose otherness is irreducible. But how could that irrational have become the object of consciousness, an object, moreover, in which consciousness saw the expression of its own most intimate being? How was such an error possible? That pure intellection behaves negatively with regard to the object of faith proves that for pure intellection there is an absolute other. But pure intellection, reason, is the category, which "means that knowledge and the object of knowledge are one and the same. Thus what pure intellection sets forth as its other, what it sets forth as an error or a lie, can be nothing other than itself; it can condemn only what it itself is." And, Hegel adds to give the argument its full weight, "What is not rational has no truth; what is not conceived conceptually does not exist. Hence when reason speaks of an other than itself it is in fact speaking only of itself and in so doing it does not emerge from itself" (*PE*, II, 100; *PG*, 389; *PM*, 566).

In Hegel's conception of the conflict between the Enlightenment and faith, we find an attitude of reason toward religious faith completely different from the negative polemic dear to the eighteenth century. In-itself, or for us, that conflict does not contrapose two terms which differ in essence. Faith, its absolute object, and its worship do not constitute the other of reason. Human reason itself is unconsciously represented in them. There are many passages in Hegel's analysis that already suggest Feuerbach's interpretation of religion in *The Essence of Christianity*, a work in which Hegel's "absolute spirit" is replaced by a "philosophical anthropology." [15] To be sure, Feuerbach wrote that "religion is the dream of the human spirit." But Hegel had described faith as a "sleeping consciousness," as opposed to the

15. Feuerbach, *The Essence of Christianity*, trans. George Eliot (New York, 1957).

awakened consciousness of the Enlightenment.[16] Feuerbach will indeed say that his work merely presents "religion that has become conscious of itself, that is, completely disillusioned." But he shows in Christianity a consciousness that humanity has of itself qua species. Religion can be nothing but man's consciousness, not of the limitation, but of the infinity of his being. "Our task," Feuerbach writes, "is to show that the distinction between human and divine is illusory, that it is no more than the distinction between the essence of humanity—human nature—and the individual." Man's consciousness of God is indirectly man's consciousness of himself. Consequently, in the development of human thought, religion is not an alien body but a thought of spirit. Instead of viewing religion, as the Enlightenment did, as an adversary that must be purely and simply negated, both Hegel and Feuerbach view it as the highest expression of self-consciousness. But whereas Hegel still speaks of an absolute spirit whose self-consciousness lies in the human community, Feuerbach wishes to reduce that absolute spirit to a spirit that is only human: "Man, not Hegel's absolute spirit, is the center of religion." [17] Hegel, on the contrary, feared that such a reduction of spirit to the human, all too human, would culminate in the banality of a humanity sunk in its own finitude and incapable of transcending itself. In denying religion (Hegel says "faith," since as we have seen he reserves the word "religion" for the self-consciousness of spirit in the human community) the Enlightenment merely reached a philosophy of the finite and of the supreme being, the dullest philosophy that ever was.

We have quoted Feuerbach here because it is impossible, especially in discussiong this chapter of the *Phenomenology*, not to be struck by the similarity between his thought and Hegel's. Nevertheless, Hegel's absolute spirit exceeds human spirit even though its consciousness lies only in that spirit. And Hegel's "metaphysics" is different from Feuerbach's "anthropology." If for Hegel the essential problem of religion is the relation of God to man, it is important to emphasize that the complete reduction of the divine to the human entails a world view which eliminates all that is speculative and which, like comedy (tragedy alone expresses absolute *position*), culminates in a con-

16. "Faith lives in two kinds of perception. One is the perception of *slumbering* consciousness living purely in a thought with no concept" (*PE*, II, 120; *PG*, 406; *PM*, 588).

17. "The mystery of God," Feuerbach writes, "is but the mystery of mankind's love for itself" (*Essence of Christianity*, p. 289).

sciousness of insurmountable finitude. Whatever the case may be, since pure intellection is absolute concept, outside of which there can be nothing, it must err in seeing an other than itself in faith and its object, God. For reason, there is no genuine other, there is no irrational. What it fails to recognize is itself, and when it engages in its fierce polemic against faith it merely negates itself. All the determinations of faith are unconscious determinations of thought. When thought shows them up as illusions, it is itself that it denounces. What we first notice in reason's argumentation is a split within the concept, a struggle of self with self which can only lead to self-destruction. Reason vanquishes faith, but its triumph is such that, as Hegel noted in his article "Glauben und Wissen," faith is introduced into the very midst of reason in a new form, recognizing a perpetual beyond and thereby limiting itself to an empty hope.[18] Simultaneously, faith sees polemical, merely polemical, reason as the opposite of what it claims to be. A pure intention, it appears impure; the light of truth, it seems to be a lie and a deception. And its victory is expressed in a world view whose banality is in marked contrast to its original intentions and goals.

Let us consider for a moment the significance of intellection's struggle against faith. The Enlightenment accuses faith of, on the one hand, engendering its own object, God, and, on the other hand, receiving that object from the outside, as an alien essence imposed by the malice of "trickster priests." The Enlightenment argues that the God of believing consciousness is a pure fiction, by which it means that "what is absolute essence for faith is a being of its own consciousness, is its own thought, a product of consciousness" (*PE*, II, 101; *PG*, 390; *PM*, 567). But it *also* claims that the object of faith is alien to self-consciousness, that it is not its essence but, "like a changeling, has been substituted for that essence. . . . The Enlightenment expresses itself as though by the sleight of hand of the trickster priests something absolutely alien and absolutely other had been placed in consciousness instead of and in the place of essence" (*PE*, II, 103; *PG*, 391; *PM*, 569). Without belaboring the inner contradiction of this argument, we may note that the two moments that intellection sees in faith in fact correspond to the moments of its own object. In intellection, consciousness ap-

18. Cf. "Glauben und Wissen," p. 224: the triumph of the Enlightenment leads to a philosophy that reestablishes a faith, as we can see in the philosophies of Kant, Jacobi, and Fichte.

prehends its object simultaneously as itself and as an other. That object is in-itself and, as such, is other; but it is also the self of the consciousness that grasps it, it is for-it. *Consciousness produces it by understanding it.* The absolute essence of reason is in-and-for-itself. That object is its own object. It exists, and it is produced by the self. Thus, intellection's critique of faith is a critique of itself. When reason denounces the illusory or alien character of the absolute essence of believing consciousness, it denounces what constitutes reason itself: it fails to recognize itself.

Feuerbach later wrote that "in man's relation to external objects his consciousness of the object can be distinguished from his consciousness of himself, but in the case of the religious object the two consciousnesses are one. The sensuous object exists outside man; the religious object, on the contrary, is within him, it is the closest and most intimate of objects." [19] How can a mistake be possible here? Believing consciousness grasps its object, God, in an act of trust (*Vertrauen*); that trust is an expression of its own self-certainty. "This consciousness does not pose itself as lost and negated in its object; rather, it entrusts itself to it, that is, it discovers itself in it as that consciousness, or as self-consciousness" (*PE*, II, 102; *PG*, 390; *PM*, 568). God, here, is not an object which in its transcendence would negate self-consciousness; he is rather the inner certainty that consciousness has of itself. Nevertheless, in faith, that inner certainty appears to me as beyond me. It is God, insofar as I rise above my sensuous particularity and specificity. I am in God "as an *other* self-consciousness, that is, as a self-consciousness that has become alien to its particular specificity or, in other words, to its naturalness and its accidentalness" (*PE*, II, 102; *PG*, 391; *PM*, 568).[20] But I remain a self-consciousness in this experience, just as I do in the act of pure intellection apprehending itself in its object. Believing consciousness, finally, qua spirit of the community, the union of abstract essence and self-consciousness, establishes its certainty that it is in absolute essence through its worship, just as intellection produces its object by mediating what was at first an immediate certainty (*PE*, II, 102; *PG*, 391;

19. Feuerbach also writes that he wishes to discover in religion "the treasures hidden in the heart of man" (*Essence of Christianity*, p. xlii).

20. Let us note the similarity between this formula and Feuerbach's phrase, "religion is the consciousness of humanity as a *species*."

PM, 568–69). Hegel's language here foreshadows Feuerbach's, though Hegel adds: "That spirit is what it is only by virtue of the production of consciousness or, more accurately, it could not be what it is without being produced by consciousness. Indeed, as essential as production is, it is not essentially a unique foundation of essence but only a moment: essence is simultaneously in-itself and for-itself" (*PE*, II, 103; *PG*, 391; *PM*, 569). That is why God appears to believing consciousness as beyond it, as the moment opposed to the preceding *fiducia*. But just as the Enlightenment interprets the first moment as though faith *invented* its object, so it interprets the second moment as though faith *received* its object from an absolutely alien source, the lies of priests.

Indeed, faith oscillates between absolute trust, in which God loses his transcendence for it, and the feeling of the beyond, in which God appears to it as "impenetrable in his ways and means." Positive theology and negative theology express two complementary aspects of the life of faith. But when the Enlightenment says of the object of faith—the object that expresses the innermost being of consciousness—that it is forcibly introduced into consciousness from outside, it shows itself to be absurd. A people can certainly be deceived about sensuous things; it can be fooled into seeing brass as gold, or even a defeat as a victory. But it cannot be fooled about its own intimate consciousness of itself. Now the absolute essence of faith, precisely, is the object of a people's self-consciousness. "How can we speak of deception and illusion here? . . . How could illusion and deception be produced where in its truth consciousness immediately has self-certainty, where in its object it possesses itself, discovering itself there as well as producing itself? There is no longer even a verbal difference" (*PE*, II, 103–4; *PG*, 392; *PM*, 570).

To be sure, a people's faith, its consciousness of absolute essence, can be expressed awkwardly. But it cannot err. For it is what it thinks: religion is nothing other than spirit's consciousness of itself.[21] Since the nature of the absolute concept present in pure intellection is no different, what it fails to discern in faith is what it is itself. If only we interpret them, we see that reason and faith are not truly opposed; what Hegel tries to think through is their speculative identity.

21. On religion as "a people's intuition of its own spirit," see "System der Sittlichkeit," p. 467.

But the Enlightenment introduces the *disparity* of the concept into the *equality* of believing consciousness; it dissociates what in faith was immediately joined, and its arguments will make believing consciousness an unhappy consciousness which futilely seeks to rediscover its primal innocence but is unable to forget the point of view of reflection and dissociation. In that sense, the Enlightenment is victorious, and it intrudes into believing consciousness itself. After the struggle, faith becomes an unsatisfied, unsettled consciousness. Perhaps Protestant subjectivity—as Hegel views it in "Glauben und Wissen," or as it is expressed in the *Phenomenology*, in the chapter on the moral world view—corresponds to that unsatisfied enlightenment which faith becomes after its adversary's attack.

> Since faith lacks content and cannot remain in that void, since, when it rises above the finite, which is the only content, it finds merely a void, it is simply pure yearning. Its truth is an empty beyond to which no content any longer conforms. For now all is shaped differently. In fact, faith becomes the same thing as the Enlightenment, that is, the consciousness of a relation between the finite existent in-itself and the unqualified absolute, unknown and unknowable, except that the Enlightenment is satisfied while faith is a dissatisfied enlightenment (*PE*, II, 121; *PG*, 406–7; *PM*, 588–89).

Hegel's article already shows that it is impossible for modern consciousness to return to the naïve confidence of earlier times. For someone like Jacobi, faith is merely a desperate attempt to supersede reflection and the split between the finite and the infinite, a split which, as we shall see, results from the labor of the Enlightenment; it is a *salto mortale,* which cannot be carried out. The beautiful souls in Jacobi's novels always seek virtue, but they are never able completely to forget themselves. They retain a reflection back on themselves which takes the place of naïve generosity. The characters of *Woldemar* and of *Aus Eduard Allwills Papieren* have a moral beauty, a desire for virtue and faith, which is merely nostalgic yearning. They suffer because of the finitude which they can never renounce, and which they know to be finitude. They experience what Dante and Goethe called the sufferings of hell, "the eternal torture of being attached to oneself, of being unable to separate oneself from one's actions and of always coming back to oneself." [22] That

22. "Glauben und Wissen," p. 308.

split between the finite and the infinite—between the impurity of the finite realities of experience and the purity of an interiority without exteriority—is the doing of the Enlightenment as well as of the Reformation. Both demonstrated to believing consciousness the disparity that obtained between its consciousness of essence and its sensuous consciousness, between the beyond and the here-below. That disparity becomes manifest with regard to the three moments of faith: (1) its object, God, (2) its justification, and (3) its practices and rites.

Pure thought, infinite being-in-and-for-itself, is the object of believing consciousness, but that object still appears in sensuous form. Of course, this form is merely an empty form borrowed from finite reality. Believing consciousness does not think that God is a piece of wood or a piece of bread, the element of which was furnished by nature, which was transformed by man, and which must return to earth. Sensuousness is *also* present in believing consciousness, but the worship is not addressed to the wood or stone idol. There is simply a contamination of the two elements, a contamination about which believing consciousness fails to think. Yet the Enlightenment, behaving negatively with respect to its own object, claims that the absolute essence of faith is a stone or a piece of wood, that faith "has eyes and sees not." Thus, by seeing in the essence of consciousness only the contingent form in which "faith customarily anthropomorphizes essence and renders it objective and representable" (*PE*, II, 105; *PG*, 393; *PM*, 571), the Enlightenment transforms faith into superstition. Faith recognizes the validity of the criticisms leveled at it by the Enlightenment; it is unable to challenge them, and its naïve confidence is lost. The Enlightenment has revealed to it the mixture of the here-below and the beyond. Understanding expresses the finite as finite—wood as wood, stone as stone—and it separates the pure from the impure in such a way that believing consciousness will always fear anthropomorphism and will take refuge (as in the case of Protestant subjectivity) in an undefined yearning, in a fervor which fears all objectification, in "an art with no work of art." [23]

The Enlightenment practices the same dissociation with regard to the second moment of faith, the process of mediation and faith's search for its own foundation. It separates eternal

23. The phrase is from "Glauben und Wissen," p. 312. Cf. the pages Hegel devotes to the subjectivism of Schleiermacher, who nonetheless reached a higher intuition of the universe than Jacobi.

spirit and historical spirit and reduces the foundations of faith to merely historical justifications, which are open to the same criticisms as any other human testimony. Like every consciousness, faith includes a mediation which binds its certainty to truth. It portrays this mediation as *sacred history*. Christ, who is God made man, revealed spiritual truth to mankind. He came to bear witness to spirit; he asked to be believed in; he performed miracles. There is indeed a history in this. But believing consciousness does not dissociate the historical fact from its eternal meaning, though it knows that only spirit can bear witness to spirit. "Spirit itself bears witness to itself, either within a specific consciousness or thanks to the universal presence in it of the faith of all" (*PE*, II, 107; *PG*, 395; *PM*, 573). Christ said to his church, his spiritual community, "I am with you always, even unto the end of the world," and that spiritual presence, that immanence of spirit in the community, is the great truth on which faith is founded. It connects faith's subjective certainty to an eternal truth; it establishes a bond between the contingent and the necessary, between transitory events and eternity. The passage we have just quoted refers both to the inner faith of an individual consciousness and to the spirit of a universal church.

The behavior of the Enlightenment here is similar to its earlier behavior. It shatters the equality between history and spiritual signification; it considers history only as a succession of facts and the testimony of spirit becomes human testimony, less sure than the testimony of "newspapers about daily events" (*PE*, II, 107; *PG*, 395; *PM*, 573).[24] Faith allows itself to be won over by its adversary and, by responding on its adversary's own ground, it admits its defeat.

> If faith wishes to ground itself on history, or at least to confirm its content in the way the Enlightenment describes, if it undertakes to do so seriously and as though everything depended on it, it has already been seduced by the Enlightenment, and its attempts to ground itself and consolidate itself in this way are merely testimony of its own contagion by the Enlightenment (*PE*, II, 107; *PG*, 395; *PM*, 573).

24. In his Jena period (cf. "Glauben und Wissen," pp. 311–12) and even in the *Phenomenology*, Hegel insisted on the idea of the church. To be sure, that church is merely the prefiguration of absolute knowledge. (Cf. in the *Phenomenology* the section on absolute knowledge, the transition from the religious community to modern philosophy [*PE*, II, 306; *PG*, 559; *PM*, 801–2]).

The third moment of faith is the moment of action. Believing consciousness is not only a contemplative consciousness. Christ was a model; the goal aimed at by individual consciousness is the "imitation of Christ." In this endeavor, individual consciousness emerges from its contingency and its naturalness and becomes universal self-consciousness. Through worship and sacrifice, it proves to itself that it is able to attain a life that is no longer natural. It renounces enjoyment and property, the element that separates individualities, isolating each in its exclusive specificity. But the Enlightenment does not understand this sacrifice; it fails to understand how anything can be given up except in exchange for money. And this indeed is the law of the modern world: a rigorous exchange, which makes gifts and sacrifice appear absurd. But its misunderstanding of sacrifice shows that the Enlightenment's pure intention is in fact an impure intention, even a hypocrisy. "The Enlightenment still asserts as pure intention the need to rise above natural existence, above greed for the means of existence. But it considers it unreasonable and unjust to demand that that rise be demonstrated by deeds" (*PE*, II, 108–9; *PG*, 396; *PM*, 575). It admits interiority, but separates it from *works*, which strike it as empty.

In its polemic, the Enlightenment, which is at first purely negative, becomes real, and the question of what it becomes in its positive form is then raised. "If all prejudice and all superstitions are banished, the question of what remains must be asked: what truth does the Enlightenment reveal in their stead?" (*PE*, II, 109; *PG*, 397; *PM*, 576). That truth is the complete separation between absolute essence and finite reality. "Pure intellection has realized itself as its own contrary," which indeed conforms to the dialectical nature of the absolute concept. Pure intellection now sees in absolute essence only an "empty supreme being, unknown and unknowable"; on the other hand, it casts light on a finite world which becomes its only positive content. Thus sensuous certainty again becomes the truth of consciousness, though no longer naïvely, as at the beginning of the phenomenological experience, but with reflection and in opposition to an absolute being that is stripped of all attributes. Hegel here envisages eighteenth-century philosophy as the specific world view of the Enlightenment. It is an impoverished world view: just as sensuous certainty believes itself to be concrete and rich although for us it is the most abstract knowledge, so, when its structure is set forth, the philosophy of the Enlightenment is seen to lack all speculative content. Indeed, the foundation of that philosophy is the negation of everything that transcends *human* essence and *human* representation. When that negation puts itself forward as a positive doctrine it can only culminate in what we have already indicated. On the one hand, since all content illuminated by that intellection is shown to be a finite determination (wood as wood, stone as stone), since these finite things, which are reduced to their immediately-present-to-consciousness-being, are stripped of all meaning, absolute essence—being-in-and-for-itself—must be posed as void of content. "For pure intellection, absolute essence becomes a vacuum to which neither determinations nor predicates can be attributed" (*PE*, II, 109; *PG*, 397; *PM*, 576). The attitude of the Enlightenment culminates in a purification of all of man's representations of absolute being. Finally, only the abstraction of that negation, an abstraction now set up as a being, remains. Sensuous content, on the other hand, is taken into consideration and accepted as such. Human consciousness returns to sensuous experience, but it does so with the conviction that all other ways are unworkable: they have been tried, but they lead to dead ends. This is a negative proof—the only kind possible in these matters. Empiricism and sensualism are justified by the wanderings of previous philosophical research. Consciousness therefore must keep to its first truths. It exists as sensuous things do, with the same characteristic of specificity and exteriority, and with other actual things existing outside it. Thus the certainty consciousness has of *its own existence* is, like its certainty of other existences, the certainty of a *being-other*. Intellection does not find itself in what is thus posed before it. The "I am" is empirical, like the "*this* is," and these finitudes have become the sole field of human experience. Beyond them there is surely an absolute being, but nothing can be said about this being except that it exists absolutely.[25]

Nevertheless, a relation between absolute essence and finite existences, or rather a possible double relation, can be conceived. All finite determinations can be positively connected to absolute essence, in which case they are posed in absolute being: they actually exist. They can also be negatively connected to essence, in which case their being is a vanishing being: they are

25. This certainty of the *being-other* of the I as well as of the object has no mediation (no possible positive proof), for it is the immediate posing of the concept in exteriority, the starting point and the end point of the phenomenological dialectic.

then only for-some-other (*Seinfüranderes*) and no longer in-itself. Thus the two modalities of the relation of finite things to absolute essence, an essence toward which pure intellection cannot but tend—intellection always goes beyond itself as the only being-other (*PE*, II, 111; *PG*, 398; *PM*, 578)—are *being-in-itself* and *being-for-some-other*.

These two modalities, in turn, can be applied to any finite reality, and they lead to the fundamental synthetic concept of *utility*, a concept which contains the essence of the theoretical and practical philosophy of the Enlightenment. Things appear in themselves but they serve other uses. Man, too, is a finite reality which participates in this concept. It might be said that Hegel's argument here is rather artificial and that it laboriously works its way back to eighteenth-century utilitarianism and to the vague deism and the empiricism of the Enlightenment. But the argument is consonant with an argument we have already encountered several times in the *Phenomenology*, and its meaning is clear. Hegel wished to translate the world view held by many of the French Encyclopedists into his own dialectical language. What is crucial is to note the reduction of all speculative richness to purely human experience. The divine is negated, or rather, nothing is left of the divine but the empty form of the absolute, a form that can be applied to anything and that is equivalent to nothing in particular. This is an empty formalism. What remains is an ensemble of finite beings considered first in their absolute, and then in their relative, position. Each is in-itself; each is for-some-other. And the "human flock" as a whole must be considered from this point of view.[26]

Let us consider now what man becomes in this world view. "As he comes from the hand of God, man walks about in the world as in a garden planted for his sake." He is naturally good, and everything has been made for his delectation. We must understand this to mean that everything other acquires signification for man from its usefulness to him. Similarly, social bonds are justified by the mutual usefulness of men to each other. "As everything is useful to man, so man too is useful to man and his destination is to become a member of the flock

26. It will be noticed that this dialectic is analogous to that of the perception of a *thing*. But here, in the world of spirit, the relation is more concretely expressed as *utility*. The "world view" of the Enlightenment reduces man to a being of nature, which is why Hegel speaks of the "human flock." This *naturalistic* view of the world is opposed to the prior *religious* view.

useful to the community and universally obliging" (*PE*, II, 113; *PG*, 399; *PM*, 579). Morality in general is reduced to social morality, and social morality is expressed in utilitarianism. Man uses others, and he is used: that is the dialectical relation that brings men together. The relation is dialectical because each man poses himself simultaneously as an end and as a means and because, as in economic life, it is in seeking to pose himself as an end that man serves others: on the one hand, *homo oeconomicus,* and on the other a certain "social goodwill" which results from man's self-consciousness and from his awareness that he can use his reason to limit, or even to correct, nature. Even religion can no longer be conceived of other than as a relation of usefulness. It is regarded as man's search for the advantages he can draw from his relation to divinity. In this way, we reach the shallowest possible philosophy. In reducing everything speculative to the human, it seems that the Enlightenment reaches a world of no depth, a world in which things are only what they are immediately, a world in which individuals are shut up in their natural egoism and are linked to each other only by considerations of interest. This philosophical structure—being-in-itself, being-for-some-other, usefulness—applies to everything. It seems too abstract and too impoverished to express the finite richness which seems to constitute experience. But it supports the world of that experience and constitutes its *category.*

Nevertheless, the Enlightenment's human rights over faith cannot be denied: they are the rights of self-consciousness against the divine right of essence.[27] To the extent that believing consciousness is itself a self-consciousness and participates in the human, it cannot challenge those rights. Because faith, without being aware of it, mingled the finite and the infinite, it was a slumbering consciousness which the Enlightenment awakened. At times it was even a hypocritical consciousness, which fancied that by a partial sacrifice it gained the right to enjoy its property at ease (*PE*, II, 118; *PG*, 404; *PM*, 585). This was a mixture that could no longer be tolerated once it became conscious, and the Enlightenment, precisely, made faith become aware of itself and of its disparateness. From then on, there is no genuine difference between believing consciousness and the consciousness of the

27. We see once again the opposition between the *divine right* of essence and the *human right* of self-consciousness, an opposition which was first manifested between *nonknowledge* and *knowledge.*

Enlightenment. Believing consciousness is merely a "dissatisfied enlightenment" which recalls the lost paradise and preserves a nostalgia for the beyond. The consciousness of the Enlightenment believes itself to be a happy consciousness, satisfied with its world, but it too will have to overcome its own satisfaction and rise to a higher consciousness (*PE*, II, 121; *PG*, 407; *PM*, 589).

That rise becomes actual in the metaphysics that expresses the truth of the Enlightenment—a *materialistic* or *deistic* metaphysics which poses pure essence as the material substance of things or as the supreme being, representing its concept to intellection as an object. It develops for intellection the movement from the in-itself to being-for-an-other and from being-for-an-other to being-for-itself. But the concept finally presents itself as the self only at the end point of its becoming real. At that point, the Enlightenment reaches the highest truth accessible to it, the moment of *absolute freedom*. The self of self-consciousness reabsorbs all objectivity: "The world is its will." This absolute freedom gathers up into one world, that of the universal will, what had hitherto been separate, the here-below and the beyond. "The two worlds are reconciled; heaven comes down to earth" (*PE*, II, 129; *PG*, 413; *PM*, 598). It is in this way that Hegel introduces his discussion of the French Revolution.

IDENTITY OF MATERIALISM AND IDEALISM

STRANGE AS HEGEL'S ARGUMENT may seem at first, we shall try to justify it, primarily by showing to what historical doctrines and what movement of spirit it corresponds. In more accessible form, the same argument appears in the *Lectures on the History of Philosophy* with reference to eighteenth-century French philosophy. That philosophy, Hegel writes, is

> absolute concept, which directed itself against the whole realm of solidified representations and congealed thoughts, a philosophy which shattered everything fixed and which attained the consciousness of pure freedom. At the basis of this idealism is the certainty that everything that exists, everything that is valid as in-itself, everything, in short, is essence of self-consciousness; that neither the concepts of good and bad, of power and wealth, nor the congealed representations of God and his relation to the world, of his rule and the duties of self-consciousness with regard

to him, that nothing of this can be a truth in-itself outside self-consciousness.[28]

This polemic in favor of the freedom of self-consciousness, which Luther began but did not bring to completion, was continued, according to Hegel, by French philosophy and culminated in the correct, if still abstract, principle that, qua world of the spirit, the world is the realization of *will identical to thought*: "What is rational is actual and what is actual is rational."

After its victory, the Enlightenment began to split, according to its conceptions of absolute essence, into *materialism* and *agnostic deism*. These two sides are basically identical, but they do not reflect on the identity of being and thought, which Descartes perceived (*PE*, II, 125; *PG*, 410; *PM*, 594). They fail to see that what the one calls "matter" and the other "supreme being" differ only in their memory of the preceding culture.

> Difference lies not in the thing but only in the different starting points of the two formations, and in the fact that each side attaches itself to a particular point in the movement of thought. If they went further, they would meet, and they would know that what the one considers an abomination and the other folly is the same essence (*PE*, II, 124; *PG*, 409; *PM*, 593).

As it is the indefinite movement of self-consciousness, pure intellection is the distinction of differences which in their development are no longer seen as differences. Thus, pure intellection stands contraposed to itself and becomes its own object. That object is absolute essence, pure thought, which—in contrast to the movement of self-consciousness which continually separates itself from itself—is self-identical. We have already encountered this "distinction of the nondistinct" with regard to the dialectic of *life* and the *self-consciousness* that is consciousness of life. Self-consciousness poses itself as consciousness of differentiated content; over and against itself, it poses truth as immobile and beyond it. In this way, self-consciousness rediscovers its earlier distinction from faith. Qua self-certainty, pure intellection was contraposed to faith qua substantive truth. But now that truth has lost all speculative content, which is why it is *pure* thought, the supreme abstraction of the in-itself. Considered with regard to its purity, this abstraction can evidently be pure like pure matter, which is neither seen nor smelled nor

28. Hegel, *Werke* (Berlin, 1840). *Vorlesungen über die Geschichte der Philosophie*, ed. Michelet, III, 457.

touched—that abstract thing, that substratum the self-contradictory nature of which had been demonstrated by Berkeley—or it can be pure like the negative beyond of human self-consciousness, the "supreme being" in the philosophical expression of the time. Robinet, for example, whom Hegel quotes in his *Lectures on the History of Philosophy*, speaks in this way at the beginning of his work on the nature of a God who is the unique cause of the phenomena we call nature but whom we are condemned never to know. We can only call him "the unknown God." "The order that governs the universe is no more the visible sign of his wisdom than our limited spirit is a reflection of his intelligence." [29] D'Holbach, on the other hand, whom Hegel also quotes, tries in his *Système de la nature* to conceive "the great whole of nature" as a combination of matter and motion, a continuous chain of causes and effects some of which are known to us and some not yet known.[30] Materialism and atheism both insist on the positive aspect of absolute essence. Matter is positive being; the beyond of self-consciousness, as supreme being, is purely negative. But, as Hegel will show in his ontological *Logic*, insofar as this positivity is pure, it is negation. Indeed, in order to reach his substratum, the materialist must abstract from the sensuous thing; he speaks of the existent, but to the extent that this existent is the substratum of what appears to my senses, it is the result of an abstraction performed by thought. The thing that is merely thingness, and not this or that determinate thing offering itself to our consciousness in various aspects, is pure abstraction: it is thought itself.

Conversely, agnosticism, which speaks of a *beyond* of thought, could reappropriate the moment of positivity and of presence which it lacks (a moment contained in the term "matter") if it were to think that the simple immediateness of thought is nothing but being and that immediateness, the negative of self-consciousness, also is related to self-consciousness in negative judgment—that, therefore, immediateness is external to self-consciousness and is not to be conceived of as other than matter.

In actual fact, the Enlightenment's victory is even more profoundly manifest in that internal split. Its former adversary has entered it, and in dividing itself, the Enlightenment salvages its foe. The idea of a beyond, but an empty beyond which is only

29. *Ibid.*, pp. 470–71.
30. *Ibid.*, pp. 469–70.

negation, confronts the idea of a matter which appears to self-consciousness to be positive presence but which, in its purity, is in fact merely the supreme abstraction of thought. This abstract materialism, or atheism, and this deism, or agnosticism, can not even be developed into a *system of nature* and a *system of spirit*. For in order to be thought through as *nature*, nature requires a concrete development which is not contained in the mere idea of matter. And spirit, or God, requires the moment of *self-consciousness* internally differentiating itself—a moment that is not contained in the mere idea of a negative beyond.[31]

The World of Utility

BUT THE ACTUAL CONSCIOUSNESS of the Enlightenment transcends this abstract thought when it perceives the moments of its concept as differences displayed before it. It then conceives the spiritual world in the form of *utility*. It no longer sees itself as abstract essence, but as the movement of its concept developing in moments which, since they are themselves concepts, return into the *whole of the movement*. The moments are being-in-itself, being-for-an-other, and being-for-itself. Here too the Enlightenment replaces the concrete richness of social and moral relations as well as speculative thought with an abstract schema valid for all but serving only as a starting point. The relation of utility, which expresses this relation of self-consciousness to its object, is characterized by the perpetual *transition* from one moment to another, but not their complete unification. Yet the dialectic of utility tends precisely to that unification. In-itself, each thing is, qua being, the moment of essence that we considered above. But it is only a moment: the in-itself binds itself to some other thing, which absorbs it. That is, it is no longer in-itself; it has become for-an-other; it is what vanishes, the negation of the in-itself. But in that very vanishing it rises to being-for-itself. These moments succeed, but are distinct from, each other: "The moment of being-for-itself is indeed in the useful, but not in such a way as to invade the other moments (in-

31. What this "unconscious weaving" lacks in order to be nature is "the wealth of a matured life and spirit or God, the consciousness that distinguishes itself from itself" (*PE*, II, 124; *PG*, 409; *PM*, 593).

itself and being-for-an-other) so as to be the self" (*PE*, II, 127; *PG*, 412; *PM*, 596).

Let us express this dialectic concretely. Self-consciousness, being-for-itself, still has before it a world, social institutions, a subsisting spiritual reality which does not yet appear to it as its *own* work, as the expression of universal will. Yet this world is denied as soon as it is posed as in-itself: it is considered with regard to its utility and its relation to actual self-consciousness. But what does utility, the link between in-itself and for-itself, mean if not that the self is the sole reality, that the world must be my will in-and-for-itself? This unity of being and the concept is already apparent *for us* while self-consciousness is still in the world of utility. The useful is still an object, then, but it already foreshadows the resolution of object into subject, the reign of absolute freedom.

That reign, which should put an end to the alienation of the spirit, in which spirit's only object would be itself, and in which the world would be spirit's will (because that will, at first specific, would have become universal will in-and-for-itself), is the reign of the French Revolution. The Revolution puts an end to the alienation of internally divided spirit; it gathers together self-certainty (which in the world of culture was specific self-certainty, cut off from truth) and truth (which in the world of faith was a truth beyond self-consciousness). In the last paragraph of this chapter, which heralds the chapter on absolute freedom, Hegel summarizes this whole dialectic and shows its significance.

The *real* world (the world of culture) and the *ideal* world (the world of faith) have found their truth in the actual world of *utility*.

> The first world of spirit is the widespread kingdom of its Dasein which is dispersed and of its self-certainty which is singularized, just as nature disperses its life in an infinite variety of figures without their genus being present. The second world of spirit contains genus; it is the kingdom of being-in-itself, of truth as opposed to certainty. The third kingdom, the useful, is truth which is also self-certainty. The kingdom of the truth of faith lacks the principle of actuality, or of self-certainty as this specific individual. But actuality, or self-certainty as this specific individual, lacks the in-itself. The two worlds are reunited in the object of pure intellection. The useful is the object inasmuch as self-consciousness penetrates it with its glance and in that the object possesses the

specific certainty of itself, its enjoyment, its being-for-itself (*PE,* II, 128; *PG,* 413; *PM,* 597).[32]

Conversely, we may say that in this object specific certainty rises to the universality of knowledge, with the result that in this knowledge of self in the object certainty and truth are reconciled and "heaven comes down to earth."

Thus, this dialectic resolves the great dualism of the modern world. As life is dispersed in a multitude of living beings and of particular species which actually exist but which refer for their essence to a genus that is beyond them, so the world of culture was the world in which actual self-consciousness was realized without being able to discover its truth within itself. It reached only the consciousness of the vanity of its object—wealth and power—which it did everything to possess. It discovered that its truth was beyond its actuality. Yet that truth, which the world of faith offered to it as a beyond, lacked the actual certainty of consciousness. The third spiritual world, which is born out of the Enlightenment's struggle against faith and which actualizes pure intellect, reunites *that truth* and *that certainty.* It causes the in-itself to lose all positive content and reduces it to a vanishing moment. It transforms the world which stands contraposed to consciousness into a world which dissolves in consciousness. And it raises specific self-consciousness to the universality of thought. From then on, the object thought is no longer beyond the self, and the self is no longer merely individual self: the object becomes the realized self, and the self becomes universal will. Absolute freedom is thought as universal will—the self identical to the being that it poses immediately. But is not that immediateness still an abstraction, and can all alienation and all mediation be set aside in this manner? That is the problem that the French Revolution poses insofar as, after culture and faith, it is a conscious return to the immediate world of spirit, a return to the Greek city with which we began.

32. Thus, in the world of alienation the law of consciousness led to posing truth (the in-itself) on the one hand and self-certainty (being-for-itself) on the other. The result of that culture now is the *immediate transition* of one moment to the other, first as *utility* and then as absolute freedom, the passing over of specific will to universal will.

5 / Absolute Freedom and the Terror: The Second Type of Spiritual Self

ABSOLUTE FREEDOM AND THE TERROR

THE PRINCIPLE OF HUMAN FREEDOM is the truth of the preceding worlds. This freedom, which knows only itself, absolute freedom, is realized immediately in the French Revolution. Yet that revolution—of which in the *Philosophy of History* Hegel says that it "issued from thought"—is not the final term but itself appears as a dialectic. The immediate realization of the general will culminates only in the Terror, and the terrestrial city which claims to have absorbed the City of God appears as a new avatar of spirit. The immediate interchange between specific will and universal will oscillates between anarchy and dictatorship and fails to come to a stop at a world, at a stable organization.[1] The self-consciousness of spirit cannot *exist* without alienating itself. Therefore, it must transcend that immediateness, which is fatal to it, and express itself in different form, as a "moral world view": it must sink profoundly into subjectiv-

1. This is Hegel's essential criticism. This second type of "spiritual self," the *revolutionary citizen*, differs from the first, the *abstract juridical person*, in that the universal in him (the general will) is *his object, his immediate project. Mediation*, which characterized culture, now becomes the abstract *exchange* of specific self and universal self. The one passes over into the other (anarchy) or negates the other (dictatorship) *immediately*. As a result, although the "universal is the object and the content of the self, it does not have the form of the free Dasein of the self. Consequently, in this self it reaches no plenitude, no content, no world" (*PE*, II, 170; *PG*, 446; *PM*, 645).

[453]

ity. The political experience of revolutionary France is succeeded by the moral experience of German idealism, an experience that had its roots in the Reformation—the German revolution—and which found philosophic expression in the systems of Kant and Fichte.

In the *Philosophy of History*, Hegel wrote that the French Revolution "had its origin and its basis in thought." Now the highest possible determination of thought is freedom of the will. To say that the will is free is to say that it is aware only of itself, that it meets no obstacle, encounters nothing that is alien to it. For the only term that could be alien to the will would be a thing-in-itself, an irreducible opacity. But the notion of a thing-in-itself has just disappeared in the preceding world, the world of utility corresponding to the philosophical elaboration of the eighteenth century.

For that philosophical thought, a subsisting world still exists over against self-consciousness, but the essential predicate of that world is *utility*, which means that it is not in-itself. It opposes self-consciousness for a moment but then straightway disappears into it. What exists exists only insofar as it is useful, only insofar as self-consciousness can rediscover itself in it and adapt it to itself. Conversely, self-consciousness is no longer a particular consciousness whose intentions and goals are limited; it has risen to universality, and its concept, therefore, contains the essence of all actuality. "As pure intellection, consciousness is not specific self vis-à-vis which the object also stands as independent self. It is the pure concept, the self's glance into the self: the absolute sees itself doubled. This self-certainty is the universal subject and its conscious concept is the essence of all actuality" (*PE*, II, 131; *PG*, 414–15; *PM*, 600). The tension between universe and I is resolved, for the universe has become transparent to the I and the I has become universal. Thus man is like a creative god who resides completely in his works; these works are the terrestrial city. The self-knowledge of consciousness is a knowledge of all reality; it is simultaneously knowledge of being. "All reality is but spirit." For self-consciousness, "the world is nothing but its will, and its will is universal will" (*PE*, II, 131; *PG*, 415; *PM*, 600). Why was this idealism—of which the French Revolution was the expression—a historical failure? Why did it fail, given that it seemed to manifest in the history of spirit that equivalence between self-certainty and truth which the *Phenomenology* seeks? It is difficult to find a satisfactory answer in the short chapter Hegel devotes to the revolution, the

Terror, and the transition from that world to the new spiritual world of "the moral world view." Hegel notes that the French Revolution failed not because its principle was false but because it claimed to realize that principle immediately, and therefore abstractly. That immediateness is an abstraction and hence an error. Self-consciousness cannot be realized immediately; it must alienate itself and develop through opposing itself. Otherwise, it can reach no positive works, no world. It is absolute truth to itself only insofar as it is *pure* knowledge and *pure* will. But pure knowledge and pure will are immediateness that has been negated, that is, superseded and preserved. In other words, "just as the realm of the actual world is transformed into the realm of faith and intellection, so absolute freedom leaves its self-destructive actuality and enters another domain of self-conscious spirit, a domain in the nonactuality of which absolute freedom has the value of truth" (*PE*, II, 141; *PG*, 422; *PM*, 610). What we have here is an internalization of absolute freedom, which cannot exist immediately, that is, as a nature. Hegel's thought is quite obscure here. Although it could well culminate in a justification of the revolution, in fact, it interprets the failure of that revolution. Nor, it seems, does Hegel's thought lead us to a City of God above, or parallel to, the terrestrial city. For the "moral world view" fails in turn. Hegel's solution is not easily ascertainable.[2]

The transition from the world of *utility* to *absolute freedom* is clear enough. In the world of utility, there still remains an appearance of the thing-in-itself. If, for example, we consider existing institutions—the monarchy, parliament, constituted political bodies—we can say that in the world of utility these are no longer posed absolutely as institutions existing in-and-for-itself: they are justified only by their utility. Absolute monarchy is no longer accepted as a monarchy by divine right; it makes sense only insofar as it is useful. Social substance, to use Hegel's terminology, still exists but its Dasein is not a being-in-itself; it must be justified by virtue of its utility. But the concept of utility is internally inconsistent. It leads from being-in-itself to being-for-some-other, and from being-for-some-other to being-for-itself. The last moment is supposed to absorb the others and include them in its unity. The concept of utility raises the following

2. The dialectical transition is from the French Revolution to the moral world view, but the moral world view, in turn, is a moment that leads to a third type of spiritual self.

question: useful for what, useful in what sense? And the answer can only be universal self, the general will or the thinking will as Rousseau had already conceived it in the *Social Contract*. The general will, indivisible and inalienable, is the common self, the goal and the basis of the body politic. Thus in the world of utility, there is only an appearance of objectivity and of opposition to self-consciousness. In the thought of universal self, of the general will, nothing exists which, qua existent, is not an expression of that will. Let us repeat a sentence we have already quoted, for it summarizes the whole of Hegelian idealism: For self-consciousness, "the world is nothing but its will, and its will is universal will." What becomes realized must be an emanation of the general will. Law exists as law, both as objective and as an expression of my will. My will is my own, a specific will, but it is simultaneously thought, universal will, or, to use Rousseau's term, "general will."

In the *Phenomenology*, Hegel returns to passages from the *Social Contract*.

> This will is not the empty thought of a will posed in silent assent or in assent through representation. It is genuinely universal will, the will of every specific person as such. Indeed, will is in-itself the consciousness of personality or of any person, and must be like that authentic actual will, like the self-conscious essence of each and every personality, so that each person always does everything without splitting himself and so that what emerges as the action of all is the immediate conscious action of each person (*PE*, II, 131–32; *PG*, 415; *PM*, 600–601).

"Each of us in common," Rousseau had written, "puts his person and all his power under the supreme direction of the general will, and as a body we receive each member as an indivisible part of the whole."[3]

In rising to the general will each specific will is transformed from the will of a *private person* into the will of a *citizen*. This will wishes to participate directly and in an indivisible way in the total work and to rediscover its integral self at the heart of that total work. Society—whose will is the self-conscious state—is the work of all, and all must *be aware of themselves* in that work. Such is absolute freedom: direct participation in the common work and not the limitation of consciousness to a restricted task, a determinate task in the midst of the whole, whose relation to the whole is not immediately thought through. What must

3. *The Social Contract.*

be surmounted here is the particular alienation of self-consciousness, which enslaves man to a reality that is alien to him. Until this is overcome, like a biological organism, society is subdivided into particular spiritual masses. Its life is regulated by a law of differentiation, and each individuality is thus excluded from the universal by its concrete bond with a limited part of social life. There are constituted bodies, corporations, states within the state, just as there are distinct limbs within an organism. In his Jena works on the life of peoples, Hegel had endeavored to characterize social classes: peasants leading an elementary life, sustained only by a naïve confidence in the universal order; the bourgeoisie and the artisans moved by an abstract morality which was the expression of their own mode of life, of labor and exchange; the nobles and the military who alone attained the thought of the whole because their very function was to preserve and sustain that whole as whole.[4]

But henceforth, these divisions no longer have a *raison d'être*. They merely express the alienation of the general will present in each and every person. These spiritual masses disappear, therefore, and in their stead the *simple opposition between specific will and universal will* arises.

> In the element of being what made concept the object was its subdivision into separate subsisting masses. But when the object becomes concept, nothing subsisting remains in it: all its moments are shot through with negativity. It comes to exist in such a way that each specific consciousness rises from the sphere that had been attributed to it, no longer finding its essence or its works in that particular mass, and understanding its self as the concept of will and all masses as the essence of that will. Specific consciousness, then, can actualize itself only through a labor that is the totality of labor (*PE*, II, 132; *PG*, 415–16; *PM*, 601).

Individual consciousness then genuinely becomes universal consciousness in everyone; "its goal is the universal goal; its language, universal law, its works, the universal works." There is no longer a beyond since everyone can think of himself as the creator of spiritual being. At most, one can still speak, in recol-

4. The study of social classes and eighteenth-century estates (peasants, bourgeoisie, nobles) is carried quite far in Hegel's early works on the organic city. Gradually, he defined social divisions more precisely and he became aware of the modifications that modern life and modern mentality had introduced in the social masses. Cf. "System der Sittlichkeit" and the article "Naturrecht," (pp. 379 ff., 475 ff.), as well as the Jena "Philosophy of Spirit" (no. 2, p. 254).

lection, of the empty "supreme being" (*PE*, II, 132; *PG*, 416; *PM*, 602).

Yet this experience leads only to a failure, a failure manifested in the Terror of 1793. Hegel interprets the Terror in the language of his dialectical philosophy. The great human problem which the French Revolution had claimed to solve was that of the interpenetration of *substance* (spiritual reality in objective form) and self-consciousness. In the previous world substance existed as a term alien to the self, a self which thus was self-alienated. In the revolutionary world, that substance disappears: will cannot alienate itself.[5] "Consciousness allows nothing to be detached from it and to pass before it in the form of a free object. Consequently, it can reach no positive work; neither the universal works of language nor those of actuality; neither the universal laws and institutions of conscious freedom, nor acts and works by the will of freedom" (*PE*, II, 133; *PG*, 417; *PM*, 602–3).[6] The problem Hegel poses here can be reformulated as follows: on the one hand, if society is organized—divided into distinct and complementary moments—then it is indeed a concrete work. But in that case, it is not an immediately self-conscious work; it has become objective, an objectivity in which the I has alienated itself. If, on the other hand, man, as universal will, claims to think himself immediately in the state, and thus installs "absolute freedom on the throne of the world," then the concrete and objective work vanishes together with alienation, and all that remains is an abstract, and therefore purely negative, universal. That is the experience of the French Revolution and the dialectic of the Terror.

The spiritual masses disappear and are replaced by "the nation, one and indivisible." But the general will cannot create anything that would have the form of an independent object since that object would then stand contraposed to self-consciousness. It can create no positive work. Indeed, a *positive* work would be a new organization of society and thus mark a return to a social differentiation, which the revolution had overcome. "The work that might be attained by freedom becoming aware

5. At least not by making itself *objective*. There remains an alienation and a mediation, but only in the *immediate passing over* of the specific to the universal: "Thus, opposition consists in the difference between specific consciousness and universal consciousness" (*PE*, II, 137; *PG*, 416; *PM*, 602).

6. Hegel is talking about "state laws" and governmental "decisions."

of itself is this: as universal substance, it would make itself an object, a permanent being; that being-other would be difference at the heart of freedom" (*PE*, II, 133–34; *PG*, 417; *PM*, 603). Thus "a world" would be formed again, but in that world, individual consciousness would be cheated of direct participation in the whole. Sovereignty would lose its indivisible character and become differentiated into legislative, executive, and judicial powers; the mass of citizens would be organized into estates each having its own task. "The action and being of personality would thus be limited to a branch of the whole, to one kind of action and of being. Posed in the element of being, that personality would receive the signification of a determinate personality and would cease genuinely to be universal self-consciousness" (*PE*, II, 134; *PG*, 417; *PM*, 603). Thus specific self-consciousness resides neither in the positive work that is the organized state nor in the action and decisions of a government. In order that the universal reach action, it must indeed be concentrated in the entity of individuality and have a specific self-consciousness at its head. But other self-consciousnesses cannot immediately discover themselves in that specific self-consciousness which decides and acts; they are excluded from it, or at least, they participate in the "whole of action" only in a limited way.

For this reason, absolute freedom can produce neither a *positive* work (a constitution or a social organization) nor a *positive* action (a decision or a governmental act). "Only negative action is available to it; it is only the rage of destruction." This, precisely, is the dialectical meaning of the Terror. The abstract universal and the no less abstract specificity, the unitary and indivisible general will and the atomized dust-cloud of individuals, stand opposed. The only work possible for the general will is the continuous annihilation of that specific will which continually reappears. "Thus *death* is the only work and action of universal freedom, a death, more precisely, which has no internal significance and which accomplishes nothing. For what is negated is the point that is void of content, the point of the absolutely free self" (*PE*, II, 136; *PG*, 418; *PM*, 605).

The antithetical terms "anarchy" and "revolutionary dictatorship" are identified here, for specific will and universal will are immediately transformed into each other. In this system, government is no more than the faction in power. At the top of the pyramid an individuality holds power, but in the particularity of its decisions it manifests itself as individuality and thereby excludes all others. "What we call 'government' is merely the winning faction, and in the very fact that it is a faction lies immediately the inevitability of its fall. That it is the government conversely makes it a faction, and therefore renders it guilty" (*PE*, II, 136; *PG*, 419; *PM*, 605–6). If the government is always *guilty* insofar as it actually *acts*, then the inactive mass is always *suspected* by it. The general will, which does not act in a particular way (which would be contradictory), is withdrawn in inactive intentions; it is that simple interior which is aimed at in "the law of suspects."

Transition to Self-Certain Spirit; Objective Spirit and Subjective Spirit

THIS INTERACTION between specific will and universal will, which manifests itself only through the rage of destruction —the terror of death—is not without signification. In the first place, it shows that absolute freedom cannot be realized in an immediate form, and that alienation and mediation are necessary to the life of spirit. Absolute freedom had been thought through positively; in actuality, it is realized as pure negativity, as the absolute negation of the point of individuality. It is experienced as the terror of death, the absolute master. In the second place, that interaction assures the transition to a new world in which abstract negation is internalized and, in the form of moral will, becomes pure will and pure knowledge. Hegel calls this the "awakening of free subjectivity." Rousseau's *general will* becomes Kant's *pure will;* the world of the French Revolution becomes the moral world of German idealism—a transition to a creative subjectivity.

But let us consider the effect of the Terror on the mass of individual consciousnesses who had emerged from their assigned limited spheres.

> The organization of spiritual masses, to which the multitude of specific consciousnesses is assigned, is refashioned. The latter, who have felt the fear of death, their absolute master, lend themselves once again to negation and to difference, arrange themselves under the masses and, although they return to a factional and limited work, also thereby return to their substantive actuality (*PE*, II, 137–38; *PG*, 420; *PM*, 607).

Thus, spirit returns to its starting point, to immediate spirit and to the spirit of culture, and history begins ever anew its cyclical experience. Starting from its submersion in nature, in ethical substance, it rises through and due to culture to consciousness of that substance. But in so doing it alienates itself and becomes an *object* while, by a kind of endosmosis, substance becomes *subject:* "Thus ethical substance is the essence of self-consciousness but self-consciousness, in turn, is the actuality of substance, its *Dasein,* its self, and its will" (*PE,* I, 355; *PG,* 312; *PM,* 453). This cyclical philosophy of history appears in the following passage:

> Spirit is cast back from this tumult to its starting point, to the ethical world and to the real world of culture, which have only been refreshed and rejuvenated by the fear of the master which grips people anew. Spirit would have to repeat this cycle of necessity unendingly if the final result were only the total interpenetration of self-consciousness and substance. For in this interpenetration, self-consciousness, having felt the negative strength of its universal essence against it, would want to know and discover itself, not as particular, but only as universal, and would thus be able to bear the objective actuality of universal spirit, an actuality which excludes it insofar as it is particular (*PE,* II, 138; *PG,* 420, *PM,* 607).

We are presenting a hypotheses—which Hegel did not hold to absolutely—of a cyclical philosophy of history with three moments to each cycle: immediate spirit, culture (the moment of separation and mediation), and absolute freedom (the revolution against the alienation of spirit). According to this philosophy, the third moment leads back to the first and only rejuvenates spiritual substance. Revolutions and wars, then, Robespierre's dictatorship and Napoleon's achievement, serve to recreate social substance, to discipline individual consciousnesses anew by assigning them new spheres. The new world of spirit which emerges from revolution would not be completely similar to the first moment. Social divisions would be different. We know from the various philosophies of spirit which Hegel elaborated from 1802 to 1807 that under the influence of Napoleon he was led to a new view of social rank. The aristocratic model of the state was replaced by a new model, in which Hegel distinguished a petty bourgeoisie from an haute bourgeoisie, the latter carrying the sense of the universal. And he connects public opinion to a body of responsible functionaries—a new aristocracy akin to that of scholars. Napoleon gave Hegel a sense of the modern state, which Prussia would soon try to become, and this rejuvenated state replaced in Hegel's mind the earlier aristocratic state. But even though the objective spirit born in revolution is not completely identical to the preceding objective spirit, the principle is the same: it is necessary to return to an *objective spirit,* to a general will which renounces itself in making itself an object, a substance in the element of being. From that moment on, the same movement of alienation and revolt against that alienation must be repeated. Each revolution tries to overcome the opposition between substance and self-consciousness, but since it cannot succeed, revolution, like war, is limited to renewing social life and recasting it for a new restoration. With each succeeding cycle, the copenetration of substance and self-consciousness becomes more intimate. Perhaps self-consciousness could even know and discover itself in the actuality of universal spirit which, however, excludes it insofar as it is a specific self-consciousness. But Hegel does not hold to this hypothesis, which is too favorable to objective spirit. Spirit is subjective spirit as well as objective spirit; it is self-certain spirit, the creator of its own history. We must now consider spirit as subjective spirit, for "the absolute is not only substance but subject as well." "Absolute freedom" serves as the transition from substantive, objective spirit to creating, self-certain spirit, spirit that is self-knowledge. Creating spirit must in turn be reconciled with the universal, but this reconciliation leads to a new experience: absolute spirit, or religion. As we said at the beginning of this chapter, Hegel's thought here is quite ambiguous. Yet the movement that animates it seems to us to be such as we have described it. It is not so much that (as Rosenzweig thought) Hegel abandoned the philosophy of the state as the manifestation of the divine in the world—a philosophy which he held before and after the *Phenomenology*—as that he showed that objective spirit, substantive spirit, must interiorize itself and rise to subjective self-certainty so as to become the creator of its own history, as well as how that self-certainty must be reconciled with the universal, a reconciliation which is the very thought of religion, or absolute spirit. We cannot agree with Rosenzweig that "never in his philosophical career was Hegel more distant from the absolutism of the state than when he was writing the *Phenomenology*."[7] For self-certain spirit is still the

7. Rosenzweig, *Hegel und der Staat* (Oldenburg, 1920), I, 215. We have already discussed this passage in the introduction to part V, above.

state, envisaged as decision and creation; it is acting, albeit subjective, spirit. The third part of the section on spirit examines this subjective aspect. The first deals with immediate spirit, the second with spirit alien to, or alienated from, itself, and the third with self-certain spirit. Now subjectivity is not thought through with sufficient clarity in the notion of absolute freedom, but absolute freedom will serve as the transition to pure will, to moral interiority, which, in turn, leads to self-creating spirit.

Hegel portrays this transition in the following way: in absolute freedom the two contraposed terms are not a universe and a particular concrete consciousness; they have been purified, the first to the point of being universal will and the second to the point of being the self, specific will as such. Alienation, the exchange which takes place here, is of a different order from the earlier self-alienation of consciousness for the sake of honor or wealth, or the heaven of faith, or the utility of the Enlightenment. What self-consciousness gains in this self-alienation is "death stripped of meaning, the pure terror of the negative in which lies nothing positive, in which there is no plenitude" (*PE*, II, 139; *PG*, 421; *PM*, 608). This culture, then, is the highest culture, the supreme moment, from which a reversal must come about. *For us*, indeed, this self-negation must have a meaning other than its immediate meaning, which is the annihilation of the specific will. *Here too death must have spiritual signification.*

> In its actuality, this negation is not an *alien entity;* it is neither universal necessity that remains in the beyond, the abstract destiny into which the ethical world disappears, nor the specific accident of private ownership or of the whim of the owner, on which the lacerated consciousness sees itself dependent. It is universal will, which in its ultimate abstraction no longer contains anything positive and can give nothing in return for the sacrifice (*PE*, II, 139; *PG*, 421; *PM*, 608–9).

But it is precisely for this reason that absolute negation is immediately at one with self-consciousness; "it is the purely positive because it is the purely negative, and death stripped of meaning—negativity that lacks the plenitude of the self—is transformed in its inner concept into absolute positivity" (*PE*, II, 139; *PG*, 421; *PM*, 609). In other words, the universal will becomes my pure knowledge and my pure will.

For us, this death—the abstract universal—becomes the pure will, or the pure knowledge, which is immediately suppressed within self-consciousness. Unlike animals, man surmounts his own immediateness; the universal is not outside him. "He thereby knows that pure will as himself; he knows himself as essence, not as an essence that exists immediately" (*PE*, II, 140; *PG*, 422; *PM*, 609), as do revolutionary governments and anarchy, but as pure will and absolute self-knowledge. Spirit then passes into another realm: it becomes self-knowledge. Just as the kingdom of the actual world rose to the kingdom of faith and intellection, so the realm of absolute freedom and of the terror of death becomes the realm of *pure* will beyond immediateness, a pure will that is posed, beyond that immediateness, as identical to the self of consciousness. Self-certain spirit begins with the moral world view, which corresponds to the transcending of that immediateness.

PART VI

From the Self-Knowledge of Spirit to Absolute Spirit

1 / The Moral World View

SELF-CERTAIN SPIRIT is spirit that has raised itself above substantive or objective spirit and has become self-knowledge. Spirit knows itself, and this knowledge is its essence, just as self-consciousness raised itself above life by being knowledge of life. Before showing how this (subjective) spirit is capable of a new immediateness by becoming *acting and creative* spirit, we must delve into a new dimension: that of subjectivity. This new dimension corresponds to the moral world view, to the German idealism of Kant and Fichte. The critique of the moral world view will lead to the certainty of spirit acting (*Gewissen*), but at the same time to the reconciliation of this acting spirit (which is thus always guilty) with universal spirit. This reconciliation will be the self-knowledge of spirit, no longer merely as subjective spirit but as absolute spirit. This will be the phenomenology of religion.

We must therefore leave the earth, on which spirit remained objective and on which absolute freedom tried to actualize itself *immediately,* in order to consider that region in which freedom becomes more profound and grows into moral subjectivity, self-knowledge. The moral subject momentarily substitutes itself for the revolutionary citizen; Kant and Fichte's moral view of the world takes the place of Rousseau's *Social Contract.* We will examine in succession: (1a) the moral world view, (1b) the antinomies of this moral view and their resolution into acting consciousness; and (2) spirit sure of itself and its creative development.

The spirit we are now studying is self-certain spirit. It seems that within this spirit we see actualized for it what the whole

[467]

Phenomenology was looking for: the identity of knowledge and the object of knowledge. Indeed, whereas in the world of culture or that of faith, spirit, as a specific self, had its substance outside itself, now it bears it within itself. This substance is no longer an alien reality—power, or wealth, or heaven—but rather *pure duty*. If we consider the conception that Kant and especially Fichte had of the autonomy of the moral subject, we do indeed find the equivalence of self-certainty with truth that is expressed in the conception of a universal self-consciousness. The I can desire nothing other than itself. Its absolute goal lies within itself; it would be incapable of taking on the form of an alien end point. To desire power or wealth, to aspire to heaven as if to a truth beyond the subject's certainty of itself, these are desires that have been transcended [*aufgehoben*]; the subject can only desire itself in its self-certainty. This self-certainty is at the same time its truth. It seeks itself as universal self. That is why its self-knowledge is its one and only object—and in the "moral world view" this object is expressed as pure duty. "It is thus at this point that knowledge seems finally to have become perfectly equivalent to its truth; indeed its truth is this very knowledge and all opposition on either side has disappeared. It has disappeared not only for us or in-itself, but even for self-consciousness itself" (*PE*, II, 142; *PG*, 423; *PM*, 613). The keystone of the Kantian system is freedom, and freedom is the central theme of the *Critique of Practical Reason*. Self-consciousness is the autonomy of the moral subject which can desire nothing other than itself. "To will oneself," as universal self: therein lies freedom and morality. Pure will which wills itself is being in general or every being. Kant's critique of classical ontology is designed to prepare for a new ontology, in which being is no longer anything more than the subject that poses itself, an act and not an inert substratum. *Being is freedom.* In the first pages of the *Groundwork of the Metaphysics of Morals* self-consciousness is revealed as common moral consciousness.[1]

Before delving into this moral world view, Hegel shows how it reconciles the immediateness of ethical spirit and the mediation of the spirit of culture [*Bildung*]. "The knowledge self-consciousness possesses is thus its very *substance*. For self-

1. For Kant, self-consciousness is essentially pure moral consciousness, such as it is found in common consciousness. For Hegel, the *universal*, which appears to specific consciousness as *death*, is now interiorized. This universal is the knowledge that self-consciousness has, its absolute essence.

consciousness this substance is, in an indivisible unity, both *immediate* and absolutely *mediate*" (*PE*, II, 142–43; *PG*, 423; *PM*, 613). It is immediate: self-consciousness itself *knows and performs* its duty and for it the duty that is its absolute goal is not an alien reality; duty pertains to self-consciousness as if by nature. Thus, in characters, immediate spirit—ethical spirit—presented to us a complete fusion of being with its ethical destination. Antigone's femininity was a given of her nature with a spiritual signification. It was, in the full sense of the term, an irresistible vocation. This immediateness is found again in consciousness of pure duty, since pure duty is not something alien to self-consciousness, but its very essence. However, moral self-consciousness is not, like Antigone and Creon, a character, that is, a determinate and therefore partial nature; the moment of natural existence that characterized ethical spirit must now be overcome. Moral self-consciousness as consciousness of pure duty is universal consciousness; in effect, it is essentially the movement of self that consists of suppressing the abstraction of immediate Dasein and becoming consciously universal. This freedom is essentially a *liberation;* it is therefore simultaneously immediate and mediated. It is knowledge of its freedom that makes it free, and this knowledge presupposes mediation. Immediateness is not here a fact of nature; it has been regained reflectively. "Self-consciousness is absolutely free because it knows its freedom and it is precisely this knowledge of its freedom that is its substance, its purpose [*Zweck*], and its only content" (*PE*, II, 143; *PG*, 424; *PM*, 614).[2] The synthesis of immediate spirit, spirit of nature, and spirit that is alien to itself and has its object outside itself is now realized. Pure duty as object of consciousness expresses simultaneously what I myself am and what I am to become, the unity of the immediate and mediation. "To be free is nothing, to become free is everything."

Starting from these general givens, Hegel goes on to study more precisely what he terms the "moral world view." The expression *Weltanschauung*, which has had a curious history, is

2. Thus we are heading toward the third form of spiritual self. The first, person, was the self which *posits* itself and which merely *exists*. The second, which results from the world of alienation, was the immediate *negation* of this position, specific will negated by universal will. The third, which unifies the first two, is maintained in its own negation; it is spirit which, by being opposed to itself, is conserved in this opposition, *spirit creating its history*. The term "creative" is used by Hegel himself (*PE*, II, 187; *PG*, 460; *PM*, 663).

first used in the *Phenomenology* at this point. However, it corresponds quite exactly to the descriptions that Hegel gives in the *Phenomenology* of different attitudes of human consciousness. It is less a question of philosophical systems—stoicism, skepticism, moralism—than of ways of living and of looking at the universe. Although all these views of the world are linked to each other in such a way that they form what Hegel claims to be a scientific system, it is nonetheless true that he stops at each one of them, forgetting for an instant the structure in which it is a link, and rethinks it in its own terms. We have just seen the place that the moral world view occupies in the development of spirit. Immediate spirit—ethical spirit—led us to spirit alienated from itself, which had its object outside itself. This lacerated spirit brought us in turn to spirit that knows itself, that possesses itself in its absolute object, pure duty. But for a moment we must forget this dialectic in order to study on its own this world view, of which Kant's critical philosophy is an expression. This moral philosophy will be considered less as a speculative philosophy than as a way of living, and the contradictions it contains—immediateness and mediation—will be envisaged in their concrete form as contradictions lived by spirit itself in the course of its moral experience.[3] It is especially in the second part of this study, which deals with equivocal displacement, or transferals (*Verstellung*), that we will see these contradictions emerge in the experience of consciousness. Finally, consciousness discovers them itself, in such a way that it cannot avoid pharisaicalness or hypocrisy except by renouncing a purely moral world view and taking up another attitude.

Kantian morality will thus be considered by Hegel as a "moral world view." Consequently, it is not a question of the purely speculative analysis of a certain philosophy, but of examining "moralism." Kantian morality is taken as the expression of a moment of world spirit. The close relation between pietism and Kantianism has often been insisted on. During his youth, Kant was influenced by Spener's doctrine and by pietism through his mother and his teacher Schultz. Pietism, without directly being opposed to Lutheran orthodoxy, finds the source of religion in the will rather than in the understanding. It criticizes any external instruction in theology and proposes a return

3. Contradiction is misfortune only because it is a subject which opposes its self to itself.

to the primitive Christian community. Although a degree of mysticism is not completely absent from this movement, it is primarily a movement of moral purification: "It did not separate the moral renewal of man from his religious renewal. . . . To the extent that pietism loosened the bonds tying religious belief to dogmatic theology, it tightened or retied those attaching it to moral activity." [4] Undergoing simultaneously the influences of pietism and rationalism, Kant increasingly was to accentuate the doctrine's moralism and to avoid the specifically religious or mystical elements. In his early writings, Hegel had tried to write a *Life of Jesus* by following Kant's *Religion within the Limits of Reason Alone*. Like Schleiermacher, he discovered the difference between a "purely moral world view" and a "specifically religious view." [5] We know how Romanticism reacted against this Kantian moralism, and we will follow the evolution from Kantian moralism to other world views in the development of the *Phenomenology*. Before examining in detail the Hegelian dialectic which expounds and criticizes this moralism, we must emphasize its principal characteristics. Hegel's exposition is the account not only of a particular philosophy, but of a spiritual experience of which this philosophy is the expression. At this point human consciousness sees pure duty as its absolute; it locates the absolute in its unceasing effort to make itself independent of sensuous nature, of natural existence which is judged as inessential and yet which is always present. Not only will the contradictions of this moral world view appear to us, they will be revealed to consciousness itself in the course of its experience, proved by its actions. Moral consciousness (*das moralische Bewusstsein*, not *Gewissen*) will either have to renounce its moralism or consent to be what it thought it was not: instead of a pure and disinterested consciousness, a hypocritical and even envious one. The moral world view is constituted by the set of postulates of practical reason, which Kant sets forth at the end of his critique, but very broadly interpreted and rethought by Hegel. Hegel does

4. Cf. V. Delbos, *La Philosophie pratique de Kant* (Paris, 1905), p. 7.
5. The *Life of Jesus* that Hegel wrote at Bern is an attempt to think Christ within the categories of Kantian thought (opposition of morality, of the autonomy of the subject, to Jewish legalism). Christ is "the schema of morality." We know that Hegel gradually departed from this nonhistorical conception of Christ and rediscovered in him *positivity* and *destiny*.

not consider these postulates—as has sometimes been done—as mere appendages to the Kantian system which could be accepted or rejected without affecting the essence of critical philosophy. On the contrary, they appear to him as indispensable and required by the system. Kant's critique analytically dissects consciousness: the system of postulates is simply the necessary attempt to reconcile the elements of this analysis. By Kant's own admission, it is impossible to ignore the relation between virtue and nature, between the moral order and the order of the world. *Acting* consciousness is constrained to pose the problem of these relations and to posit a unification beyond their division. It must be said that the development of critical philosophy justifies this way of looking at the problem. The *Critique of Judgement* is a new attempt to unite what in moral consciousness had been posited as separate. Thus Hegel interprets here the postulates of practical reason as the part of the Kantian system that holds it all together.

Hegel's exposition does not merely claim to describe an experience that is valid for a moment in the history of human spirit. He describes an original structure of the life of spirit, capable of reappearing in various forms, and he ends with a penetrating critique of "pure moralism," a critique that occasionally makes one think of Nietzsche's later critique.

Exposition of the Problem

THE MORAL WORLD VIEW is entirely contained in the following presuppositions, which are precisely those of the Kantian system. (1) On the one hand, moral self-consciousness knows pure duty to be its essence: "Self-consciousness knows duty to be absolute essence, it is bound only by it, and this substance [duty] is its own pure consciousness, for duty cannot take the form of something alien to consciousness" (*PE*, II, 144; *PG*, 424; *PM*, 615).[6] Man thus identifies his self with the law of duty; he no longer considers it as exterior to his reason, as if imposed on him by some alien constraint. The certainty of the identity of the universal (pure duty) and self is the essence of moral consciousness. "Law is the true I within the I." It is in

6. We can say that the general interest of this whole analysis is to contrapose, in God as well as in man, *purity* and *efficacy*.

this sense that in moral consciousness we again come upon the original immediateness of spirit. (2) But, on the other hand, moral self-consciousness is only consciousness insofar as being-other is present to it and insofar as a process of mediation is added to the immediateness of pure duty. Self-consciousness still has a nature, a Dasein, which is not pure duty and which must be overcome. If law is the true I within the I, it is because there is an I that is not true I, a world that is not the true world. Moral self-consciousness is thus linked to a nature and this nature is contraposed to freedom and must be overcome. (3) There are thus two independent terms: freedom, in which self identifies itself with moral life, and nature, in which self is not able to find itself, but knows only its being-other. *Freedom* and *nature:* the entire effort of critical philosophy has consisted in separating the two, so that in a certain sense we have here, as it were, two realities independent of each other. "Since moral self-consciousness is so perfectly self-contained, it behaves toward a being-other in a perfectly free and indifferent manner; consequently, Dasein is a Dasein which is completely free-floating, which does not relate except to itself" (*PE,* II, 144; *PG,* 425; *PM,* 615). Hegel condenses this whole argument into the following proposition: "The freer self-consciousness becomes, the freer the negative object of its consciousness becomes as well" (*PE,* II, 144; *PG,* 425; *PM,* 615). For me the essential is to do my duty, and this duty has no relation to nature, whose phenomena are linked to each other by laws that are completely indifferent to that which constitutes my essence. Nature cares as little about moral self-consciousness as moral self-consciousness cares about nature. Nature is the "impassive theater." (4) However, the mutual independence of nature and morality is not as complete as we have just indicated, for the self-consciousness that partakes of both of them considers morality as *essential* and nature as *inessential.* There is thus a *subordination* of nature to morality at the same time that there is *indifference* of the one with respect to the other. These two hypotheses are no doubt contradictory, but it is precisely this contradiction that propels the entire moral world view, a contradiction which moral consciousness attempts to evade through the system of postulates made by practical reason. The problem is well put by Hegel:

At the bottom of this relation there is on the one hand the complete mutual *indifference* and specific *independence* of *nature* and *morality* (as moral goals and moral activity), but on the other hand there is also the consciousness of the exclusive essentiality of duty and of the complete inessentiality and dependence of nature. The "moral world view" contains the development of the moments present in this relation of presuppositions which are so fundamentally antithetical (*PE*, II, 145; *PG*, 425; *PM*, 616).

Nature and morality are indifferent with respect to each other and yet nature must be dependent on morality: a *synthesis* must therefore be postulated which reconciles these contraposed terms. This synthesis is presented *in-itself* in the first postulate (the harmony of happiness and morality), *for-itself* in the second postulate (the indefinite progress of moral self-consciousness via the harmony achieved between its nature and morality), *in-and-for-itself* in the third postulate (a divine legislator of the world in whom the two terms are fully identified).[7] But the contradiction at the bottom of this moral world view will become visible as these postulates develop. Moreover, the contradiction is contained in the notion of a *postulate* that bears on *being*. There is a certain analogy between Hegel's presentations of stoicism and of the moral world view, but there is also a difference which allows for a development specific to this world view, namely, the necessity for concrete *action* contained in the idea of *duty*. Moral consciousness not only contemplates its essence, it wills it; but to will means to will its realization, and this realization contains the moment of nature, the moment of actuality which was at first posited as alien to the moment of morality.[8]

First Postulate

WE BEGIN WITH A HYPOTHESIS which will be seen to be unacceptable during the course of our dialectic, but which seems at first unavoidable because it is the very statement of

7. Here Hegel advances to a general critique of the Kantian system. This synthesis in-and-for-itself is the *intellectus archetypus* which human understanding projects *outside itself*, but which does not actually exist except in its *concrete unity* with discursive human understanding.

8. That is why pure knowledge is presented here as *duty*. If self-consciousness had only to contemplate its object, it would not be acting. However, it must act; that is what reintroduces mediation into self-consciousness. Its object, or its essence, is presented as *duty*.

the moral world view. "There is a moral self-consciousness." It is by supposing the actual existence of this moral self-consciousness—which Kant came to doubt, for does a purely moral will exist?—that we can call for the unity of happiness and virtue. According to Kant's expression, "virtue is what makes us worthy of being happy."

Moral consciousness wills only duty; the motto that guides its conduct is the desire to obey the law out of pure respect for the law. Its intention is pure; what counts for it is that in every concrete action it aims for duty. But it does not limit itself to *knowing* duty; it *desires* to realize duty, for by definition it is an active consciousness which can not be content with knowledge of the universal. Action is indispensable and is contained in the very notion of duty. No matter what, one must act: do not lie, help your neighbor, and so on. What is important is not some particular concrete action, but the duty that is linked to it. Pure duty exists only because there are realizations of it in a world, in a nature which has been defined as completely independent of the moral order. The succession of phenomena follows a law that has no relation to moral law. Moral consciousness will therefore lead a tormented existence. It will become aware of the independence of nature, within which it acts, with respect to its purely moral intention. For it, happiness will be contingent: it may perhaps find happiness by acting morally, but then again it may not. "On the other hand, the amoral consciousness may perhaps by chance find its realization in a situation in which moral consciousness only sees an *opportunity* to act, but through this action does not manage to partake of the happiness deriving from the execution and enjoyment of achievement" (*PE*, II, 145; *PG*, 425; *PM*, 616). Happiness is now defined by Hegel not in its empirical form as the mere realization of desires, as Kant had defined it, but as the enjoyment of achievement, the plenitude of realization. The contingency of happiness is what makes Kant say that the unity of virtue and happiness is synthetic and not analytic. It is immoral to deduce virtue from happiness as the epicureans do, but it is impossible to deduce happiness from virtue as the stoics do.[9] Moral consciousness will therefore complain of the injustice which limits it to having its object only in the form of pure duty, and keeps it from seeing its object and from seeing itself actualized. This complaint about the injustice

9. *Critique of Practical Reason*, trans. Lewis White Beck (New York, 1956), p. 115.

of fate which allows the wicked to prosper and subjects the just to trials recalls the Biblical story of Job. Of course the fate of man on the earth is hard:

> Has not man a hard service upon earth,
>> and are not his days like the days of a hireling?

Nature merely gives him opportunities to act, but he cannot avoid complaining "in the bitterness of his heart" and he aspires to a different justice.

> Behold, God will not reject a blameless man,
>> nor take the hand of evildoers.
> He will yet fill your mouth with laughter,
>> and your lips with shouting.

There is an essential comparison between the fate of the just and that of the wicked:

> Why do the wicked live,
>> reach old age and grow mighty in power?
>> (Job 7:1; 8:20–21)

Moral consciousness cannot renounce happiness and keep this moment separated from its absolute goal. But because of his dualism, Kant conceives of happiness in a completely empirical way: "Happiness is the state of a being to whom everything happens according to his desires and his will." The *Critique of Practical Reason* conceives only of vulgar eudaemonism or pure morality. Hence the reluctance of these two terms to join each other. Schelling had already noticed Kant's vulgar concept of happiness, as dull and mediocre as that of the Enlightenment. "We can explain empirical happiness as a contingent congruence of objects with our selves. We can thus think through the impossibility of any connection of empirical happiness with morality, for the latter does not deal with a contingent congruence of I with not-I, but with their necessary congruence." [10]

But in his exposition of Kantianism, Hegel cannot accept this empirical conception of happiness. All his early works dealt with the search for a *happy consciousness* in history as opposed to an *unhappy consciousness*. For Hegel, happiness cannot be some pathological state determined solely by external circum-

10. Schelling, SW, I, 197. The definition of happiness in Kant is found in the *Critique of Practical Reason*, p. 129.

stances: it is the plenitude of realization, the act of "finding one-self again in one's deed." A people is happy in history when it manages to express itself in its deeds. Thus the artist who sees in his work an expression adequate to himself knows the joy of self-fulfillment. By demanding happiness, moral consciousness thus demands the intuition of itself in the real world. Duty lacks *Erfüllung,* lacks the reality which would give the acting in-dividual a feeling of his actuality. "The moment of attaining the goal of duty fulfilled, a goal which has become objective, is specific consciousness which has an intuition of itself [which regards itself] as actualized, that is, it is enjoyment" (*PE,* II, 146; *PG,* 426; *PM,* 617). This moment is not to be found im-mediately in morality, understood solely as a disposition to act, but only in the concept of the realization of morality. The sover-eign good or the supreme goal is thus the concept of realized morality, of the reign of virtue on earth. We must therefore postulate an accord between the natural order and the moral order. This postulate is not the wish of a consciousness, but a demand of reason; it is included in the very concept of morality, the true content of which is "the unity of pure consciousness and specific consciousness" (*PE,* II, 147; *PG,* 426; *PM,* 618).

The first postulate concerned the in-itself. In-itself, natural order and moral order—despite the apparent independence from each other with which they are presented—should be congruent. But it is up to specific consciousness as such to *make* this unity *for it.* This brings us to the second postulate.

Second Postulate

Nature is not only the completely independent and exterior world in which consciousness as an object has to realize its goal; it "also exists at the very heart of consciousness as *its* nature." Man is a natural entity, he is directly linked to the exterior world by impulses and inclinations which influence his action. This nature, which is *my* nature, is contraposed to moral volition in its pure form. However, originarily these two terms are present within a single consciousness. Each of them, sensu-ousness and pure thought, is in-itself a unique consciousness (*PE,* II, 147; *PG,* 427; *PM,* 618). But mediation is essential to morality; that is, the two moments are presented as contraposed to each other. We have not a divine will, but a moral will. Kant considers the attempt to unite the two terms immediately and to link pure duty to a natural inclination dangerous mysticism. "We are not volunteers to duty, we are merely its soldiers." A finite creature in whom reason and sensuousness are necessarily opposed is no more capable of a spontaneous attachment to practical law than of an intellectual intuition of suprasensuous objects.

Moral life thus consists in the struggle against one's nature, in the effort to transform spontaneous nature and to make it conform to the law of pure duty. Unity must indeed be aimed at, but this unity cannot be the originary unity, for that unity is the immorality of nature. Rather, it will be a unity that must be conquered. "Only such a unity is actual morality, for in it is contained the opposition by means of which the self is consciousness, or first becomes actual self, self in deed and at the same time universal. In other words, that mediation which, as we see, is essential to morality is expressed here" (*PE*, II, 148; *PG*, 427; *PM*, 619). Morality realizes itself by adapting nature to itself instead of adapting to nature; it is the complete transformation of sensuous being in order to make it conform to pure moral will. The unity thus achieved is something which precisely cannot be present, for the only thing that can be present is the opposition between my inclination and the moral imperative.

This unity is therefore *postulated:* it does not exist, for what exists is consciousness, or the tormented opposition between sensuousness and duty. But this postulate does not deal with the in-itself, since the unity to be realized is conceived of as the work of the acting subject. However, this unity nevertheless remains a postulate, for it is ultimately rejected. We must therefore postulate an *indefinite* life in order for the subject continually to make moral progress (Kant's postulate of immortality).[11] But by now the contradiction of this moral world view is on the verge of appearing explicitly. It remains hidden only by the fog of indefinite progress, a progress which can never attain a final point, since that end would be the end of all *effort,* the return to *nature,* and the negation of *morality* as such.

11. Kant, *Critique of Practical Reason*, pp. 126–27: "Since [the conformity of will to moral law] is required as practically necessary, it can be found only in an endless progression to that complete fitness."

Perfection is thus not actually accessible; it must be considered solely as an *absolute task*, that is, in such a way that it will always remain a task to be fulfilled. . . . Strictly speaking, we must say that the determinate representation (of this goal) cannot be of interest and should not be searched for, because that would culminate in contradictions—contradictions of a task which should remain a task and yet be fulfilled, of a morality which should no longer be consciousness, which should no longer be actual (*PE*, II, 149; *PG*, 428–29; *PM*, 620).

Such is the constitution of the first two postulates of this "moral world view." The first concerns the final goal and the second the progress of consciousness as such. These must be related to each other, just as in real action the goal of a particular consciousness is related to the ultimate goal.

THIRD POSTULATE

THIS RELATION leads to the third series of postulates which are in-and-for-itself and which resolve the contradictions in which moral consciousness gets bogged down when it wants to act concretely. These last postulates resolve the first two by positing a *consciousness other* than actual consciousness, that of a *divine legislator of the world*. But in fact, to do this only displaces the fundamental contradiction of moral consciousness, that of pure duty and actual reality, into the *portrayal* of a divine legislator. Concrete action is always presented *hic et nunc*, as a particular case, which conceals within it different modalities. There is not one law, but determinate laws, each of which, in order to adapt itself to the diversity of opportunities for action, has a particular content. But the particularity of content borrowed from nature is contraposed to pure duty, and pure duty is the only object which consciousness should propose for itself. The inevitably incomplete concrete knowledge of the circumstances of action is contraposed to the pure knowledge of this moral consciousness, which wills and knows only duty in general. Then how can it act? This is where the divine legislator of the world intervenes. He sanctifies *determinate*, limited duty. The transition from morality to religion is *also* found in Kant. Religion consists of making us see each and every duty as one of God's commandments. "In this manner theology leads directly to religion, that is, to the recognition of our duties as divine commands." [12] This is not, as one might think, a principle of heteronomy. The existence of this other consciousness is an inevitable postulate; it guarantees us the possibility of realizing the sovereign good in the world. The motto for action is not the fear of God or the desire to please him; it is always the will to pure duty.[13] However, through this maxim, multiple duties are consecrated as being multiple. The divine legislator unites in himself what is separate in us, the universal and the particular. Within a consciousness (that is, for-itself), he represents the harmony of duty and reality which was posed in-itself in the first postulate.

Thus moral consciousness *projects* outward from itself into *an other* consciousness the unity of content and form, of the particular and the universal which it refuses itself, and sees in this other consciousness the sign of immorality. "The first consciousness (that is, ours) contains pure duty, which is indifferent to every determinate content; duty is merely this indifference toward content." But the other consciousness contains the equally essential relation with action (for with the notion of pure duty and pure knowledge alone, it is impossible to act *in concreto*) and the necessity for determinate content: "If various duties are valid for this other consciousness as determinate duties, it is because content as such is as essential for it as is the form by virtue of which content is duty." The necessity for content rests outside our consciousness in that of the divine legislator, "who is thus the mediation between determinate duty and pure duty and the reason that determinate duty also has validity" (*PE*, II, 151; *PG*, 430; *PM*, 622).

However, we act, and in acting, from the instant the act takes place and is not merely the thought of action, we behave like this other consciousness. We will the particular, for otherwise we do not seriously will; we take reality as our goal, for we wish to accomplish "something." Thus duty, as pure duty, is found in an other consciousness, in that of the legislator of pure duty, and it is divine for us only through the mediation of this other consciousness. In both hypotheses we have just made,

12. Kant, *Critique of Judgement*, trans. James Creed Meredith (Oxford, 1911), pt. 2, p. 159.
13. *Ibid.*, p. 2. In his *Critique of Practical Reason* (p. 129) the postulate of a "Divine Legislator" appears as morally necessary: "Therefore the highest good is possible in the world only on the supposition of a supreme cause of nature which has a *causality* corresponding to the moral intention."

we are led to divide our consciousness and *to posit in the other consciousness what we cannot posit in ourselves; in every instance, it is what we are not* and *on the other hand is what we were in the opposite instance.* This other consciousness is present, sometimes as sanctifying the particular as such, sometimes as sanctifying pure duty or the abstract universal. It is by going from one of these hypotheses to the other that we conceal the contradiction in the moral world view, which rests on the radical separation of nature and duty, and of content and form. The critique of Kant which Hegel presents here goes further than a critique of his "moral view" of the world; it also takes aim at his dualism of *finite understanding* and *infinite understanding.*

Insofar as the moral world view alone is concerned, we see clearly where its contradictory starting point leads it: it posits pure duty as within itself, then beyond itself; it posits reality as outside itself, then within itself; it comes to the point of "portraying morality only in the following form": in the first instance it reunites actuality and pure duty by positing itself as moral self-consciousness which exists and acts, but at the same time it portrays this unity to itself as an object which would be a negative of self-consciousness. Thus this unity falls *outside* self-consciousness as harmony in-itself. Its self is therefore no longer any actually existing moral self-consciousness. Insofar as it exists in actuality, it is no longer moral.

In the second place, starting from the proposition that there is no actual moral consciousness, the moral world view can only come to the conclusion that there is no moral actuality. Then it is pure duty that is beyond (from that point on, the postulate that demands felicity for the just is without moral foundation, since there are no just men).

Finally, in the third instance the moral world view gathers the two preceding hypotheses together into a "representation" or "portrayal": there is an actual moral self-consciousness; there is no actual moral self-consciousness. This portrayal avoids contradiction only by the continuous passage from one term to the other, from actuality to pure duty or from pure duty to actuality. *Each passes in turn for the other.* Actual reality is captured in the portrayal of an other consciousness as pure duty, and conversely.[14] The other consciousness only serves to hide this passage. "In this manner the first proposition—there *exists* a

14. Cf. in particular Kant, *Critique of Practical Reason*, p. 127.

moral self-consciousness—is reestablished, but closely linked to the second—there *exists* no moral self-consciousness—that is, a moral self-consciousness *exists*, but only in the portrayal of it, or again there is precisely none, but one is validated as moral by an other consciousness" (*PE*, II, 155; *PG*, 434; *PM*, 626–27). The difficulties of Kant's moral world view lie in the rigidity of his dualism and the necessity of going beyond it. Consciousness finally grasps its object as knowledge and will, that is, as self, but at the same time by contraposing knowledge and will to actuality it posits them as outside itself, as pure knowledge and pure will, in the form of a nonactual universal. For Kant, self is, one might say, posited beyond self and, since self is the unity of these two moments, since it is simultaneously actuality and pure duty, it can never arrive at self-certainty as truth. Its truth is indeed the self, but this truth is still alien to it; it always displaces it, without perceiving this dialectic which constitutes it.

In general, Kantian philosophy did not see that knowledge of nature is also a knowledge of self and that knowledge of self is a knowledge of nature. It did indeed posit unity as its truth, but by refusing any dialectical character to truth, it excluded truth from knowledge and fell into an unself-conscious dialectic. It is this dialectic that is expressed in Kant's moral world view, but since it is unconscious of itself, it falls into a series of transfers or displacements (*Verstellungen*) which become *equivocal* to the extent that it tries to avoid them. It is these displacements that remain to be considered. They lead to a kind of hypocrisy when moral consciousness persists in separating in its portrayal what it in fact unites in action. To avoid this hypocrisy, we will have to proceed to *acting spirit certain of itself which wills itself as reality and as universality*. The dialectic will of course be found again in this certainty of acting spirit, but it will be raised to consciousness of itself, and concrete self will become *for-itself* the unity of the universal and the particular, of the infinite and the finite, a dialectic and yet a positive unity, which Kant denied to human understanding and situated beyond in an infinite understanding.[15]

15. We may say that man would have become for himself "this other consciousness" that the moral world view displaces beyond man. The divine and the human resemble each other. Isn't that the entire meaning of Hegel's *Phenomenology*? (Cf. our chapter "Religion: Mysticism or Humanism?")

The Antinomies of the Moral World View: Displacement

HEGEL'S EXPOSITION of the moral world view is a critique of the whole of Kantian philosophy and not just of his practical philosophy. In the "Transcendental Analytic," Kant discovered a logic of truth *for us* which is not dialectical, and in the *dialectic* he saw a logic of appearances, which, though admittedly inevitable, is nonetheless the source of our metaphysical errors. He tried to avoid this dialectic by turning reason (as opposed to understanding) into mere practical reason and by demanding that moral faith or a system of postulates provide a truth which would no longer be entangled in this dialectic. But in fact this moral world view is "a web of contradictions," just as much as the cosmological proof was, according to Kant. Kant failed to see that the analytic was already a dialectic and that the dialectic on the other hand had positive implications. He was obliged to cast out beyond self-consciousness the unity that his system necessitated, to make unity an inaccessible term which under various names, depending on the moments of the development of his thought—thing-in-itself, noumenon, infinite understanding—is always contraposed to the self of consciousness. But the opposition of self and the in-itself, of immanence and transcendence, cannot be maintained as it is in his philosophy: for in effect the characteristic of this philosophy is "to know essence as oneself." Absolute truth cannot be beyond the self which *knows* itself or *wills* itself in its object. "Consequently consciousness seems to attain here its fulfillment and its satisfaction, for it can only find satisfaction when it no longer needs to go beyond its object because its object no longer goes beyond it." However, as we have pointed out, Kant does indeed posit the object outside the self. "But this being-in-and-for-itself [*Anundfürsichseiendes*] is also posited as something that is not free from self-consciousness, but that exists at the disposition of and by means of self-consciousness" (*PE*, II, 156; *PG*, 434; *PM*, 629). According to Hegel, this is the fundamental contradiction that pervades the entire Kantian system. Instead of culminating in a self-knowledge which would be knowledge of being, in speculative idealism, Kant's system culminated in positing the self beyond itself. In Kant, self-consciousness is consciousness of pure duty and of pure knowledge as opposed to consciousness of actuality, nature, existence, or whatever. Pure duty and knowledge are projected out to the beyond. We have no intuition of them, even though we tend toward them continuously. In modern terms, we might say that Kantian philosophy inaugurated a philosophy of "moral value" and that this goal, which is simultaneously beyond the self and exists only through and for the self, is precisely value and not speculative truth. However, it is just this value, taken as abstract universal, for which Hegel criticizes the moral world view. With obvious pleasure, he enumerates in detail the unreflected contradictions to which someone who starts down that path falls prey. These contradictions come to the fore as *equivocal displacements*. Someone is going to act; he posits or *locates* a thesis. But in order to act, or after having acted, he unconsciously *dislocates* it. Even if he is the dupe of these dislocations or displacements, he still maintains a certain intellectual honesty; but there comes a time when he can no longer be duped. At that point the already equivocal displacement becomes dissimulation or even hypocrisy. To avoid that, moral consciousness must come back to the moral portrait it paints of itself as concrete self; it must grant what Kant refuses to it, self-intuition, and become the certainty of spirit which has in this certainty its immanent truth. To be sure, the dialectic will reappear in this new situation, but it will take on an entirely different character. From the point of view of the whole *Phenomenology*, this exposition of Kantianism serves as a transition from spirit alienated from itself, that is, opposed to its substance, to self-certain spirit, which has its truth in self-knowledge. From this angle, Kantian philosophy indeed appears as *intermediary*. Spirit is expounded as not capable of having an object beyond itself, and yet as being forced repeatedly to posit an object outside itself.

We will now follow up the various postulates we have already described and sketch the interplay of the displacements in the moral world view performed by consciousness. We begin from the presupposition that there is an existing moral self-consciousness, that it has pure duty for its object and that it actually desires it, but that its essence contraposes moral self-consciousness to nature or to concrete Dasein, whose laws are asserted to be independent. The first postulate claims that in-itself the two terms are reconciled; but when moral consciousness acts—and it cannot not act—it does not take this in-itself seriously. "For to act is nothing other than the actualization of the inner moral goal, nothing other than the production of an actuality determined by that goal, or of the harmony of the moral goal and actuality itself" (*PE*, II, 157; *PG*, 435; *PM*, 630). Before acting, I may *believe* in this harmony, but when I act I actualize it; by giving myself body and soul to the act itself, I experience the presence of the accord which I posited as being beyond me. Thus I displace the thesis according to which this accord is always beyond me; in the presence of this harmony I experience what may properly be called enjoyment, which had been withheld from me and which was always supposed to be beyond me.

It is true that as soon as I have acted, I ascertain the insignificance of my particular realization with respect to the final goal; the deed is contingent and the goal of reason goes well beyond the content of this specific act. What must be posited as in-itself is the ultimate goal and limit of the universe. "Since it is universal good that should be realized, nothing good has been done" (*PE*, II, 158; *PG*, 436; *PM*, 631). Who, however, cannot see that to say this really displaces the question within the moral world view? What counts cannot be the ultimate goal, but moral action as such, which is indivisible. One single act of good will in the world and everything is done. "Moral action is not something contingent [*zufälliges*] and limited, for it has pure duty as its essence. Pure duty constitutes the only total goal [*Zweck*], and, therefore, despite any limitation of its content, an action, as an actualization of this unique total goal, is the fulfillment of the absolute total goal" (*PE*, II, 158–59; *PG*, 436; *PM*, 631). The goal has been fraudulently displaced; there had been a shift from pure duty to actuality, that is, to concrete realization in nature. Now this realization is abandoned, but consequently one no longer acts; one contemplates pure duty, which is the essence, while nature, which is independent according to its own laws, is allowed to go on as it pleases. But this is an untenable position, since the essence of pure duty implies the necessity of acting. One way or another, we must act, and pure duty must become the *law of nature*, which implies a realization that goes well beyond specific consciousness. But here the contradiction becomes manifest. What will happen when pure duty finally becomes the law of all nature? Duty—which is the only essence—will purely and simply be suppressed [*aufgehoben*], since it is defined by the resistance of nature; duty exists only when there is an *effort* and a corresponding resistance. "Moral action being the absolute goal, the absolute goal is that moral action never be present at all" (*PE*, II, 159; *PG*, 437; *PM*, 632).

Moral consciousness will displace the entire problem which we have just posed in the first postulate, that is, the totality of nature's in its relations with morality, and will take refuge on the ground of the second postulate, that of the relation of my nature (which is called "sensuousness") with pure duty. The two terms that contradict each other remain the same: empirical existence as against essence as pure duty and pure knowledge, but now we consider them at the center of consciousness itself. At this point the important thing with respect to morality, which is in-itself, is to perfect my nature or rather, since that term is ambiguous, to make my sensuous existence conform to that in-itself. Sensuousness cannot be eliminated, for without it action is impossible. "Consciousness does not take seriously the elimination [*Aufhebung*] of inclinations and impulses, since these are precisely *self-consciousness in the process of actualizing itself*" (*PE*, II, 161; *PG*, 438; *PM*, 633–34). *Nothing is done without passion.* Action implies a transition from pure consciousness to deeds, in which the middle term is constituted by inclinations and sensuousness in general. For moral action to exist it must needs give itself a sensuous form, must in its turn become an impulse. That is why the thesis of the elimination of sensuousness is displaced, and one speaks of a conformity of my sensuous nature to morality. But this conformity is not given, since my sensuousness possesses its own wellsprings; rather, what is given is immorality. One must therefore postulate a harmony in-itself, which should, in an indefinite progression, become for-itself. Kant clearly sets forth the question in the *Critique of Practical Reason* when he writes:

> However, the perfect conformity of will to moral law is sainthood, a perfection of which no rational being in the sensuous world is capable at any moment of his existence. Since, however, this perfection is nonetheless demanded as being practically necessary, it can only occur in a progression, leading to infinity, toward this perfect conformity. Following the principles of pure practical reason, we have to admit such a practical progression as the real object of our will.[16]

But here displacement is elevated to method: it has become progress ad infinitum, which is a perpetual displacement of the question. What would happen if will, as sensuous will, conformed to morality? In other words, what would happen if the

16. Kant, *Critique of Practical Reason*, p. 160.

problem were resolved? "Morality would renounce itself; in effect morality is consciousness of the absolute goal as *pure* goal and thus as existing in *opposition* to all other goals" (*PE*, II, 162; *PG*, 439; *PM*, 634–35). Without this opposition, or this mediation, there can be no morality, which is doubtless why the solution to the problem is put off indefinitely; one speaks of an *infinite task*, that is, one that must always remain a task. In that case, however, one should make progress in morality, approach a goal that will never be attained, like an asymptote to its curve. But if this is not a mirage, it is at least a new displacement of the question, since by definition increases and decreases have no meaning in the realm of pure duty. If we wanted to define them at all costs, we would surely have to speak of decreasing, since we would be approaching a state in which, struggle having ceased, there would no longer be any duty as such. In fact, "there is only one pure duty, only one morality" (*PE*, II, 162; *PG*, 439; *PM*, 635), and not different degrees which would open the way to the "indulgence of casuists or the insane presumption of enthusiasts." But we said "in fact." Now, in fact, there is a sensuous will which does not yet conform to pure duty and consequently, in fact, there is not an actual moral consciousness. However, we started from the presupposition that there was. Since morality should be perfect in order to exist, there is no moral self-consciousness, but rather imperfect moral self-consciousnesses which ought to be conscious of their imperfection. *It is here that morality is transformed into its opposite.* Now let us return to the first postulate, which demanded happiness for the just, with duty making us worthy of being happy. Since there are no just men, by itself the demand for happiness is in-and-for-itself. "Nonmorality thereby declares precisely what it is—it has to do not with morality, but with felicity in-and-for-itself without respect to morality" (*PE*, II, 163; *PG*, 440; *PM*, 636). Yet one complains of the injustice of fate, one sees that in the real world misfortune is visited on the just man and happiness comes to the wicked:

> But when I looked for good, evil came;
>   and when I waited for light, darkness came.
> . . . the wicked man is spared in the day of calamity
>   he is rescued in the day of wrath.
> Who declares his way to his face,
>   and who requites him for what he has done?
>   (Job 30:26; 31:30–31)

But this demand is without foundation, since there are no pure men; or rather the foundation is arbitrary, it resides in feelings that man hides in the depths of himself. He is envious, he suffers from the happiness of others, he is jealous of their success. "The meaning of this judgment is thus envy which covers itself with the cloak of morality" (*PE*, II, 163; *PG*, 440; *PM*, 636). The demand for happiness for others has the same arbitrary foundation; it expresses the good fellowship one has toward them, it hopes for contingent favor.

To salvage the moral world view, which has been bogged down in the contradiction between actuality, or existence, and pure duty, and has culminated in the antinomy "there exists a moral consciousness, there doesn't exist a moral consciousness," it only remains to carry out a displacement of consciousness itself and to situate *beyond,* in *an other consciousness,* what cannot be located *here-below* in our own consciousness. The entire previous dialectic up to now winds up with this displacement toward transcendence, opposing the in-itself to the self.

We recall that the third postulate (in the order in which Hegel sets them forth) is that of the divine legislator of the world. But this consciousness, which is not ours, is revealed to be sometimes the source of determinate duties, of the link between content and form, between the particular and the universal, and sometimes the source of pure duty as pure duty. *By positing duty as beyond our consciousness, we posit it as that which we do not take upon ourselves.*[17]

But to posit a beyond which exists only through our consciousness culminates in a final contradiction:

> Moral consciousness posits its imperfection in the fact that in it morality has a *positive* relation with nature and with sensuousness. In effect, moral consciousness considers the fact that morality has only a *negative* relation with nature and sensuousness to be an essential moment of morality. On the other hand

17. In the final chapter of the *Phenomenology* (see our part VII), Hegel shows that in the moral world view self alienates itself as *essence.* This moment corresponds to that of understanding (cf. part II, chapter 3), which sees the thing as interior or suprasensuous, beyond phenomena. The comparison between the moment of the thing (as essence) and this moment of the self (positing itself beyond self) is revelatory, according to Hegel, of the dialectical identity of self and being.

pure moral essence, being above the *struggle* with nature and sensuousness, does not have a *negative* relation with them. Thus all that remains in fact is a *positive* relation with them, that is, precisely what had been considered as imperfect, as immoral (*PE*, II, 115; *PG*, 442; *PM*, 638).

On the other hand, to speak of a pure morality with no relation to actuality is to speak of an inconsistent abstraction within which morality, will, and action lose all meaning. This moral divine legislator who would be above struggle but who would also be the essence of morality is a contradictory synthesis. In the Hegelian dialectic, as we shall see, the separation of infinite essence from finite existence is overcome. *Infinite essence fulfills itself in finite existence and finite existence rises to essentiality.* There is no abstract universal. Rather, the absolute self of spirit is this very reconciliation. The *abstract God* who would be above struggle is not *absolute spirit.*

But the "moral world view" only posits an in-itself distinct from the self in order promptly to make it into a moment of consciousness. Pure duty must be beyond actual consciousness, beyond existence, but it must also be within consciousness and, inasmuch as it is the beyond, it no longer means anything; it oscillates between immanence and transcendence. It cannot take seriously the distinction between self and in-itself, for what it propounds as in-itself it keeps within its own self-consciousness as a term that is merely thought, without actuality; it refuses any truth to that distinction. In some other consciousness, pure duty considers this unity of universal and existence the perfection of morality; within itself, it considers it the mark of imperfection. On occasion it posits actuality or existence as something that is nothing, at other times as the supreme reality. The formal contradiction "is the transposition beyond the self of that which the 'moral world view' must conceive as necessary." It covers up the contradiction in content, which is that between pure duty and actuality (which is inessential and yet indispensable). The moral world view must therefore renounce this *portrayal* of its truth in order to return within its certainty of itself. Within this certainty, as in a new immediateness, it discovers the unity of pure duty and actuality. This unity is its *concrete self* which no longer has a *portrayed* truth, but which knows immediately what is concretely just; and this certainty as *conviction* is its own truth to itself. The fraudulent dualism of the moral view is transcended; spirit knows itself without going beyond the self.[18]

18. An all-powerful God would be immoral; a pure God who, like Christ, would refuse the temptation of power would be ineffectual. And yet it is this reconciliation of purity and efficacy which must be actualized in the creative spirit, in *self-certain spirit*.

2 / Self-Certain Spirit: Self or Freedom (Third Type of Spiritual Self)

INTRODUCTION: GENERAL SIGNIFICANCE OF THE CHAPTER OF *Gewissen*

IN A WORK AS RICH, but also as complicated and involved as the *Phenomenology*, Hegel himself feels the need to look back and to summarize prior stages. That is the case in the final chapter of the section on spirit. He shows us the teleological meaning of the entire previous development, and insists on the various types of self which have been encountered in the course of this development (*PE*, II, 170; *PG*, 445–46; *PM*, 645):[1] the *abstract person*, which corresponds to the stoic's formal self-consciousness (immediate self, without alienation); the *revolutionary citizen*, whose object is the general will (the self of the alienated world), but a general will which is incapable of concretizing itself in an existing world; and finally *moral will*, whose truth is no longer alien to the spiritual subject (self which returns to itself enriched by the entire spiritual substance). Indeed, the Kantian system contains the apex of the idea of self, of the autonomous spiritual subject. It is this autonomy of the I which best expresses the most important

1. Thus the three types of self, which correspond to the three worlds of spirit, are: (1) immediate self, (2) the self which immediately negates itself in reality, and (3) the subject which *assumes* its history and poses itself in the very movement of mediation. In this chapter we see the development of this third self. Kantian moral volition was only the prelude to it. The first type corresponds to the unity of the *universal* and the *specific*, the second to their direct *opposition*, the third to their authentic mediation.

[491]

thought of German idealism, whose sources would have to be sought in the Lutheran Reformation and the principle of free examination. However, the idea of fully autonomous self is not really actualized in Kant's moral view of the world, or even in that of Fichte. The evolution of German idealism after Kant, such as Hegel already envisaged it in "Glauben und Wissen," leads us to a deeper and especially to a more concrete expression of the autonomy of the I. The works of Jacobi, Schleiermacher, Schelling, and Novalis allow us to go beyond the narrow limitations of Kant's moral world view, a world view which, moreover, gets bogged down in insoluble contradictions, continually contraposing a nature whose laws are independent to a will and a pure duty which are then condemned to remain ineffectual. In this view, acting self, spirit *creating* its destiny, posits itself, so to speak, beyond [*au delà*] itself, or beneath [*en deçà*] itself; it is never congruent with itself, that is, in fact, it *does not act.* But if we consider this self in its actuality, *at the very moment of action,* the contradiction of the moral world view is resolved: "the difference that lies at the very foundation of this world view is shown to be no difference at all and converges with pure negativity. Now this negativity is precisely the self, a *simple* self which is both *pure* knowledge and self-knowledge as *this* specific consciousness" (*PE*, II, 174; *PG*, 449; *PM*, 649). Nature and duty are no longer contraposed, so that human action—this pinpoint in the world—becomes impossible. Nature and duty are gathered into the organic unity of the self; and it is this free self, which no longer knows anything beyond itself, whose truth is the certainty it has of the truth, that constitutes the end point of this dialectic of spirit. We had started from a true spirit—an *objective spirit*—in which subjective certainty disappeared in an objective truth. After the mediation of culture and alienation, we arrive at a *subjective spirit* in which (objective) truth disappears in the subject's certainty of it. Spirit is no longer substance, but is entirely reflected in on itself; it has totally become *subject.* This is precisely what the self as *Gewissen* expressed, that is, *self-certain spirit.* Here, apropos of the evolution of spirit, one can verify the fundamental thought which presides over the entire Hegelian system and which the preface to the *Phenomenology* so clearly expressed: "According to my way of looking at things, which will be justified only by the presentation of the system, everything depends on this essential point: to apprehend and to express the true not as substance, but precisely also as subject" (*PE*, I, 17; *PG*, 19; *PM*, 80). At the end of this dialectical development concerning spirit, what emerges is the *subject creating its history*, a subject which has absorbed within itself the universal as its pathos (πάθος) instead of having the universal beyond it in the form of an abstract universal. Just as infinite life rises to self-consciousness of life, which is higher than life itself, so the substantive spirit of the family or of the Greek city, with which we began, is reflected in self-certain spirit which no longer knows anything beyond its internal conviction. Consciousness has been freed of any possible content, "it absolves itself of all determinate duty which ought to be valid as law. In the force of its self-certainty, it possesses the majesty of absolute αὐτάρκεια, omnipotence to bind and unbind" (*PE*, II, 182; *PG*, 456; *PM*, 658).

Hegel also takes up again the notion of the "thing itself" (*die Sache selbst*), with which he entered into the domain of spirit in the strict sense of the term. When human individuality was seeking to express itself truthfully, it encountered this notion of the "thing itself," the authentic human deed. But that was still a notion without content, an abstract predicate suitable for anything and strongly linked to nothing. This notion assumed its full meaning for us only when we saw it identified with the deed of each and every person, with reality as it is posed by man, a reality which then took the place of the *thing* (*Ding*) as a merely discovered thing of *nature*. The human deed acquired its substantiveness in ethical spirit, in the family and the people, in the social organism, of which individuality was at first the expression. It then acquired an *external existence* in the world of culture, in which spirit alien to itself grasped its object as given outside of it, in the form of power, wealth, heaven, usefulness, general will. But at that point, the "thing itself" lost the character of being a predicate; it became the subject "that acts." "In the end, in *Gewissen*, the 'thing itself' is *this* subject which knows within itself all its moments" (*PE*, II, 176; *PG*, 451; *PM*, 651–52).[2]

Thus Hegel again takes up his conception of the self and of the "thing itself" to indicate the signification of the entire dialec-

2. We can see how the prior notions are enriched and made more exact during the development of consciousness. The "thing itself," that is, objectivity at the human level, was only an *abstraction* prior to *spirit*. It acquired *substantiveness* with true spirit, *external existence* with spirit alien to itself, *subjectivity* in this last moment of the dialectic. We should add that the prior moments are conserved (*aufgehoben*).

tical discussion of spirit. Spirit has become the human subject creating its history, who no longer has the universal outside himself, who is no longer opposed to the universe, but who bears it and absorbs it in himself. Spirit is the free subject. True, someone may ask: what subject are we talking about? The question is indeed embarrassing, for the self in which substantive spirit reflects itself at the start of its development is just as much the self of natural individuality as it is universal self; at least that is what is suggested by taking up "the thing itself" again. The distinction between them, on which Kant's moral world view rested, has been shown to be untenable; *Gewissen* is precisely the good conscience which knows immediately the content of its individuality to be pure duty and pure knowledge, a consciousness which, at the point of its existential decision, gathers up

> the in-itself and the self, pure duty as pure goal, and actuality as a nature and a sensuousness opposed to the pure goal. When it has thus returned to itself, it is concrete moral spirit which no longer makes consciousness of pure duty into an empty norm which is opposed to actual consciousness; but rather, pure duty and nature, which is opposed to pure duty, are suppressed [*aufgehoben*] moments. In its immediate unity, this spirit is moral essence in the process of actualizing itself, and action is immediately concrete moral figure (*PE*, II, 171; *PG*, 446–47; *PM*, 646).

Acting spiritual individuality is concrete spirit as Hegel considers it here; and of course it is not impossible that he is thinking of the great men of action of which human history furnishes so many examples. If we want to understand the chapter on which we are attempting to comment, it seems that in addition to the romantic figures mentioned above, we must mention a particular figure who could hardly fail to haunt Hegel's imagination: Napoleon. Napoleon appears as the man of action who revealed to man his creative possibilities. Free spirit is creative spirit which does not stop to contrapose the abstract universal to actuality, but which acts and possesses essence through discovering the inner certainty of the validity of its act. It is the moment of creative decision that is described here, and the universal is absorbed into the development of this action instead of transcending it. In other words, the universal, instead of being an abstract in-itself, an inaccessible transcendence, as in Kantian moralism, has become a moment of human action, a *being-for-an-other*. As such, it has not disappeared, but rather has acquired concrete signification: the *recognition* of action by other individualities. It is this recognition which, as in the dialectic of self-consciousness,[3] expands the notion of human individuality to the concrete universal, which poses the self as a we via the mediation of other selves. The action of human individuality must be recognized in order to be authentic; it carries this demand with it and must be able to be translated into the element of universal self-consciousness. "The element which confers subsistence (we should say, which constitutes the *consistency* of an action) is universal self-consciousness" (*PE,* II, 184; *PG,* 458; *PM,* 660).

"What is the subject in which substantive spirit is reflected?" To this question, which we asked above, it seems that only one answer is possible: this subject is humanity considered in terms of its history, for it is only history that decides the truth of an action emanating from an individual self. But Hegel does not use the term "individual self." He restricts himself to elaborating a dialectic of acting self in which the specific and the universal are contraposed in a much more concrete form than in Kant's moral view. The specific is the man of action whose act is always finite, acting consciousness which, in its freedom, cannot avoid coming up against limitations and, consequently, discovering within itself, in its particular view taken as absolute, evil itself. The universal is judging consciousness, which is opposed to acting consciousness and which fails to perceive its own limits, limits which reside in the fact of not acting but merely judging. *Judging consciousness* and *sinful consciousness* are two figures of self-consciousness which, like those of the *master* and *slave,* or *noble consciousness* and *base consciousness,* exchange their respective roles. But in this dialectic, spirit reconciles evil within itself and becomes *absolute spirit.* The Christian dialectic of forgiveness of sins is the symbolic representation of a tragic philosophy of history in which the finitude of acting spirit is always converted within the ascending movement of spirit, in which the past awaits its *meaning* from the future. It is in this *Aufhebung* that spirit grasps itself as absolute, not in consciousness of sin but in consciousness of pardon for sins.

This is the transition to a new phenomenology, the phe-

3. Cf. the dialectic of "recognition" in the development of *self-consciousness* and that of the "interplay of individualities" apropos of the spiritual *animal spirit kingdom.* The universal, by becoming for-others, passes from Kantian transcendence to an immanence. It will exist in the development of human history.

nomenology of religion and of philosophy, of absolute knowledge which is the truth of philosophy. Before stressing this last part of the *Phenomenology* (which it is difficult still to call "phenomenology"), we will study more closely the last chapter on self-certain spirit. This chapter is important because of the detail of its analyses, which are sometimes close to what we would call today "existential analyses." First, Hegel considers *acting spirit, self, in its specificity* (the moment of the freedom of individual self in the process of acting, the moment in which law is made for man and not man for the law), then he considers *self-certain spirit in its universality* (the moment of the contemplative beautiful soul who ends up rejecting action so as to lose none of his purity), and finally *spirit becoming absolute* through the reconciliation of these two aspects. It is the dialectic of sinful consciousness and of judging consciousness which culminates in the Christian conception of forgiving sins, in the Hegelian *Aufhebung.*

I. *Gewissen:* ACTING INDIVIDUALITY

MAN IS ALWAYS CAUGHT UP in a particular situation; his individuality is inseparable from an empirical being, he exists here or there (Dasein), his acts are never general acts, but particular concrete acts, *a given case (ein Fall des Handelns).* Contemporary philosophy has insisted on just this necessity for man always to be in a situation and on the impossibility of transcending all situations to become pure I, essentially distinct from any empirical being, from any Dasein. I belong to a certain family, to a nation. When I want to act, I am already tied to a past. Thus I cannot absolutely will what I am without at the same time willing something concrete.[4] On the other hand, human will, unlike animal instinct, is not completely absorbed in this empirical being. A contemporary philosopher, Jaspers, has attempted to demonstrate the unity of the self and its empirical being as *historicity.*[5] Hegel's analysis of *Gewissen,* concrete moral consciousness, is not without analogy to Jaspers'. Doubtless, the differences are quite apparent. Jaspers fears nothing

4. Fichte had already noticed that one could only will by willing *something.*

5. Jaspers, *Philosophie,* Vol. II: *Existenzerhellung* (Berlin, 1932), p. 118 (*Geschichtlichkeit*).

quite so much as to see his philosophy confused with an absolute idealism, with a system which, like the Hegelian system, culminates in absorbing within a totality—even if it is infinite in Hegel's sense—all partial viewpoints, all world views, or all particular truths.[6] He objects less to the Hegelian affirmation that "the truth is the whole" than to the very possibility of such a totalization, which for him is a betrayal of *existence,* a word borrowed from Kierkegaard, who gave it its philosophical meaning by opposing it to the Hegelian philosophical tradition.[7] But, just as people have shown that the young Hegel was not so far away from Kierkegaard as the latter might have thought when he stood up against the Hegelian system as formulated in the *Encyclopaedia,* in the same way we can, we believe, compare what Hegel here calls *Gewissen* with what Jaspers calls the "historicity" of existence. This comparison will allow us to clarify certain difficult passages of the chapter we are studying. It will perhaps even allow us to understand better what Hegel means here by self—an indivisible unity of actuality and pure knowledge. The self, certain of its being, is already existence with its historicity. There can be no doubt that Hegel does not stop at a "clarification of existence," that he claims to go beyond the existent, which cannot step out of its unique and original view of the world to constitute an infinite totality, an absolute truth which, moreover, is *required* by every particular existent. In other words, as a philosopher, Hegel situates himself outside the existents whose experiences he has reconstituted; for Jaspers this is radical non-sense. For Jaspers, existence cannot *be* without consciousness of its finitude, and existence always comes up against a transcendence: it cannot leave its own truth to compare it to other truths, yet it demands an absolute truth which would be a single truth for all existents. This contradiction is the last word of Jaspers' philosophy, and that is why his dialectic remains an antinomy.[8] That is not the case with Hegel, who

6. The truth, said Hegel in the preface to the *Phenomenology,* is the whole. It is the possibility of this *whole* of existences that Jaspers rejects (see *Existenzerhellung,* p. 415: "Existenz unter Existenzen.").

7. On the relation between Kierkegaard and Hegel, see in particular J. Wahl, *Etudes kierkegaardiennes* (Paris, 1938).

8. Jaspers, *Existenzerhellung.* The paradox of understanding (*Verstand*) is the following: The truth is specific, and yet in relation to other truths there seem to be several truths, and yet again there is a single truth: absolute value and relativity should not exclude each other (p. 419).

claims to attain this transcendence with a *concrete universal*, with a universal self-consciousness that is *history* and no longer merely *historicity*. But if we read the volume that Jaspers entitles *Existenzerhellung* without prejudice, we realize that, in spite of his assertion that existence is "all the more profound the more it is narrow," he himself indeed describes, as does the author of the *Phenomenology*, "particular world views," and that he considers them as a philosopher and thus also elevates himself above them. This difficulty with Jaspers' position has often been noted, and it is beyond the scope of this work to take it up again. We merely wanted to excuse a comparison which might appear somewhat daring since the final results of the two philosophers can be contraposed so easily.

We will often translate *Gewissen* as "good conscience" [*bonne conscience*], because it is acting consciousness which "immediately knows and does" what is concretely just and which does not distinguish what appears just to it from what is just in-itself (indeed it has gone beyond the distinction between the in-itself and the for-it). *Gewissen* is quite different from the moral consciousness (*das moralische Bewusstsein*) of the preceding dialectic. The latter always contraposed pure duty and reality. Reality was a presence without depth and without signification; pure duty was without presence. Thus to will pure duty was indeed to will oneself, and the object of moral consciousness could not be other than the self, but at the same time it was beyond the self which is there, which is actual in concrete action. That is why moral consciousness did not act at all, despite its essence which demanded action; for duty as such is not merely the object of a pure knowledge, but is willed and must be realized. We have already shown all the antinomies of such a moral consciousness; let it suffice to repeat here with Hegel "that moral consciousness is not at all acting, does not actualize at all. For it, its in-itself is either abstract nonactual essence or else being as an actuality that is not spiritual" (*PE*, II, 175; *PG*, 450; *PM*, 650).

> According to this consciousness I act morally when I am entirely conscious of accomplishing only pure duty and not any other duty whatsoever, which in point of fact means that I don't act. But when I actually act, I am internally conscious of an other, of one actuality which is at hand and of another which I want to fulfill; I have a determinate goal and I fulfill a determinate duty. Therein lies something other than pure duty which is all one should propose to accomplish (*PE*, II, 173; *PG*, 448; *PM*, 648).

However, these contradictions in which moral consciousness gets entangled fade away at the very moment of action, since one way or another we must act, we must make a decision. If I am a head of state and placed in such-and-such a situation, I propose a determinate goal and I desire actually this concrete goal which is closely linked to the situation in which I am engaged. In the same way I administer the family inheritance, or propose that I help one or another of my friends. "The actualization of the goal is the goal of action." The opposition of pure duty and reality is resolved in the self, which is pure knowledge, self-knowledge, as well as actuality and being. Thus the Kantian analysis of moral purity culminated in complete impotence; while on the other hand authentic moral action always supposed *existential evidence*. I know what is to be done in this, my situation, and now, going beyond the separation of the in-itself and the real within the negativity of acting self, I adhere to what I will, because I freely will what I am. In a prior text written at Jena, Hegel had already stated that true action always supposed an existential this: "A determination that is raised to concept is by that very fact ideal, and the opposite determination can just as well be posed . . . on the other hand the expression of intuition contains a this, a living relation with which some possibility is strictly bound up, and any different possibility, or being-other, is absolutely negated. Immorality would reside in this being-other." [9]

Moral consciousness, which contraposed the in-itself to reality, also behaved like the *universal milieu,* within which multiple duties, each for-itself, were granted an unshakable substantiveness. From this new point of view, action was still impossible because it would always entail the *conscious* violation of some duty. But "*Gewissen* is rather the negative entity, the absolute self which annihilates these various moral substances. It is indivisible action: it conforms to the duty which does not accomplish some particular duty or other, but knows and does what is concretely just. Thus in general it is primarily moral action as action into which the prior nonacting consciousness of morality has passed" (*PE*, II, 172; *PG*, 447–48; *PM*, 647).

Here self is revealed to us as the negative unity of the moments that previously were distinguished. It reunites actuality and abstract duty; it grasps itself in its contingency as fully

9. "Naturrecht," p. 360.

valid, "that which knows its immediate specificity as pure knowledge and pure acting, as actuality and true harmony" (PE, II, 169; PG, 445; PM, 644). Concrete self, which Kantian moral consciousness had posited beyond man and continually displaced, is henceforth our topic.

At this point, human individuality, as Gewissen, appears to return to the immediateness of the ethical world. "Since self-certainty is also immediateness, it possesses Dasein itself" (PE, II, 170; PG, 446; PM, 645). It need not hesitate and equivocate continually about what should be done: it immediately sees what is just, it acts as if by instinct, guided by the voice of its conscience. The voice of conscience, of which Rousseau had spoken, "is to the soul what instinct is to the body." Hegel does not begin by criticizing this individual morality, although he soon shows the ambiguity of such formulas and reveals within good conscience (Gewissen) a bad conscience that is not yet aware of itself. We must act, and no action would be possible without the fusion of pure duty and concrete duty. Similarly, both Creon and Antigone knew what they had to do. The former fully adhered to human law, the latter to divine law. In the full meaning of the term they were characters. In them, nature coincided with decision. Thus indeed we seem to find the immediateness which made a kind of nature of the ethical world, and this return to original immediateness conforms with the Hegelian schema. All life is developed starting from an original immediateness, and returns to this immediateness after having gone through a period of splits and of mediation. With the coincidence that concrete self expresses, moral spirit again becomes natural spirit. What Kant called "sensuousness" and what he called "pure practical reason" now make up but a single self which is both acting and actual.

And yet there is a huge difference between immediate ethical spirit and Gewissen, which we are now considering. Ethical spirit was merely true spirit, substantive spirit, and we can literally say that in that world the self did not yet exist; it was merely an unreal shadow. The congruence between individuality and duty stemmed from the fact that this individuality simply expressed a law that was immanent in it. Creon did not hesitate to manifest the human law whose depository he by nature was; the same was true for Antigone in relation to divine law. But now, after the movement of culture, spirit has been entirely reabsorbed into the self, into free personality. In Hegelian language, ethical spirit was wholly truth but lacked absolute self-certainty.

Gewissen, by contrast, is purely self-certainty; it does not express a law, a true order; it is freedom of the self as originary fact, the source of all decisions. Antigone was ignorant of the origins of the law she followed. "Not now or yesterday but always this law has lived; no one knows when it appeared." She was merely its incarnation, and the immediateness of her decision expressed the perfection of this incarnation. Actual self, when it emerges from substantive spirit, the mores of the Greek city, or of the family, proceeds to win over to itself everything; it no longer recognizes that anything can have validity independent of its own internal certainty, its own conviction. Henceforth this conviction (*Überzeugung*) is its essence and not an immanent or external order.

> *Gewissen* recognizes no content as absolute for it since it is the absolute negativity of everything determinate. Thus it determines itself simply by itself. . . . Everything that was presented in preceding figures as good or bad, as law and right, is an other than immediate self-certainty, is a universal which is now a being-for-an-other, or, considered differently, is an object which, by mediating consciousness with itself, comes between consciousness and its own truth and separates consciousness from itself instead of constituting the immediateness of consciousness (*PE*, II, 178; *PG*, 453; *PM*, 654).

The essence of *Gewissen* is absolute conviction. To act according to its conviction, to determine itself by itself, finally to be concretely free in Dasein and not in some abstract and nonactual essentiality (as pure duty was): that is what characterizes the self of *Gewissen*. The self knows itself as absolute; it immediately experiences duty in its feeling of what for it is duty. It decides by itself and by itself alone. For it, freedom is the originary character of its decision, a character which Jaspers will seek in existence. Here Hegel emphasizes *conviction*. In the "Confessions of a Beautiful Soul," Goethe has his heroine express the same thought: "I would willingly leave my parents and earn my bread in a foreign land rather than act contrary to my thoughts," or again: "In the face of public opinion, my profound conviction and my innocence were my surest guarantees." [10]

But how can a conviction render authentic a content which is always determinate content, which pertains to the given situation of individuality and in a general way to what we call "sen-

10. In Goethe's *Wilhelm Meister*, "The Confessions of a Beautiful Soul."

suousness"? In that question, there is a link between conviction and the contingency of a situation, or of a sensuous content, which must become apparent at one time or another. The freedom of the self cannot help but be revealed as tainted with the arbitrary. Ultimately, this freedom will be *Willkür* [arbitrariness]. It is at that point that good conscience (*Gewissen*) discovers that it is bad conscience as yet unaware of itself; good conscience will know its finitude and will have the feeling of sin, of inevitable sin, "for only stone is innocent."

> Thus consciousness determines itself by itself, but the circle of self within which determination as such falls is what we call sensuousness. . . . Yet for *Gewissen* self-certainty is pure immediate truth, and this truth is thus its immediate self-certainty portrayed as content, that is, generally, arbitrariness of the specific being and the contingency of its natural unconscious being (*PE*, II, 178; *PG*, 453; *PM*, 654).

And yet we should not push the analysis ahead too quickly. It is too easy to denounce "the error of subtly confusing the subjective and the objective," as Goethe puts it;[11] less easy to avoid it, for it is perhaps unavoidable. Let us consider human actions. "Suppose a given case of action. This case is an objective actuality for the consciousness that knows. As *Gewissen*, that consciousness knows the case immediately and concretely, and at the same time the case exists only insofar as consciousness knows it" (*PE*, II, 171; *PG*, 447; *PM*, 646). Knowledge is contingent insofar as it is other than the object, but there this distinction is transcended. Dasein, the empirical situation that is mine at the moment that I am going to act, has become my original knowledge and, as such, this Dasein is grasped in the certainty that I have of myself. We proposed comparing this *unity of knowledge and being* with Jaspers' historicity.[12] Now let us attempt to interpret this passage from Hegel:

> But when the separation of the in-itself and the self is suppressed [*aufgehoben*], a case of action is immediately within knowledge's sensuous certainty as it is in-itself, and is in-itself only as it is in this knowledge. *Acting, as actualization, is thus the pure form of willing, the simple conversion of actuality, as an existing case in*

11. *Der Briefwechsel zwischen Schiller und Goethe*, ed. Emil Staiger (Frankfurt, 1966), Letter 56, p. 96.
12. Jaspers, *Existenzerhellung*, p. 119: "In the originary, here, being and knowing are indissolubly linked." Cf. also the critique of Hegel as representing a slippage of historicity, p. 147.

the element of being, into an executed actuality, the conversion of
the mere mode of objective knowledge into the mode of knowledge
of actuality as something produced by consciousness (PE, II, 171;
PG, 447; PM, 646; italics mine).

Now what can this conversion of knowledge to will, of a known
concrete case into a reality produced by acting consciousness,
mean? When I act, I am always in a certain situation and as
Dasein this situation—my race, my social milieu, the more or
less precise circumstances of my life at this moment—can be
the object of some knowledge. But here being, as it is in-itself, is
not distinct from knowledge of this being. The concrete situation exists only as it is for me. To say that "indeed its content is
determined by the interest of the consciousness that has an understanding of it" means that this concrete situation is not objective, in the sense of being determined by some impersonal
consciousness which could so to speak hover over the situation.
My free I thus appears linked to the facticity of a determinate
being, and this determinate being in turn is intimately joined to
my potentialities; it is known and at the same time willed, since
it is not a matter of contemplating it for the mere joy of contemplation, but of engaging it in the impetus of acting consciousness. I must convert the given situation into a situation
that I take upon myself or assume; I must transform an objective knowledge into a reality produced by consciousness.

Within what Jaspers terms "historicity," which evokes the
notion of *amor fati*, there is a conjunction between the facticity
of the situation and the freedom of existence which cannot be
thought through. I am free and my existence is merely potentiality, but never an indifferent potentiality; I am always caught
up in a history, which, however, is mine. And that is why it is
not only history but historicity. The history of a being that is
different from me is never historicity; it appears as an object
which has lost all potentiality, and by that very fact is distinct
from the knowledge I have of it. Here knowledge of the situation, determined by my concrete interest in this situation (*PE*,
II, 172; *PG*, 447; *PM*, 647), is no longer different from the situation itself; the situation is absorbed in my knowledge of myself
and this *knowledge* in turn becomes *will*. Reality is less contemplated than willed. The will is restricted by the limitations
of concrete knowledge, but in exchange knowledge carves out a
window onto potentialities. If a given case—a case in the *element of being*—is faithfully respected, that faithfulness is cre-

ative.[13] For this case is converted into "executed actuality"; this objective knowledge becomes knowledge of reality as if of something *produced* by consciousness. This *amor fati* is less a resignation to a reality that is given in its entirety than the creative acceptance of a reality that simultaneously imposes itself and becomes my work.

It seems to us impossible to comment seriously on this text without attempting the comparison which we have just begun. Otherwise what meaning could we give to this conversion of objective *knowledge* into *will*? Acting self cannot, if it wishes to act, take the position of an impersonal I in relation to which all situations exist at the same level. It is deeply set in its own view of the world; it posits this view not only as *a* truth, but as *the* truth. (We should recall that in Hegel this term is often equivalent to what we would call "value" today.) This truth is simultaneously its own and absolute. It is absolute by the *sincerity* of its conviction, and this sincerity of conviction has become the very essence of consciousness.

Here the "subtle confusion of the subjective and the objective" which we said was unavoidable again takes place. In Hegel's time, Rousseau and Jacobi, who was even closer to him in time, could have served him as examples. Jacobi clearly saw what Kant neglected: the aspect of individuality in moral consciousness. According to Hegel's definition, Jacobi's philosophy is "a dogmatism of finite existence and subjectivity," yet when it takes up arguments which oppose Kantian morality it describes the conditions of concrete moral action much better than Kant did. To abstract law, to the Kantian universal, Jacobi contraposes moral genius. Interpreting Jacobi, Madame de Stael says: "With respect to morality or poetry, the law can only teach us what we must not do. In all things, what is good and sublime is revealed to us only by the divinity of our hearts." *Gewissen* knows the vacuity of pure duty, and since we must act, it finds the positivity of action in its *moral genius*. In his Jena article Hegel praises the conception of the voice of conscience which we find expressed in this passage from Jacobi's letter to Fichte almost without reservation: "Yes, I am the atheist and the godless one who opposes that will which does not desire anything, I am the one who wants to deceive and lie as Pylades did when he presented himself in place of Orestes, the one who wants to kill as did Timoleon . . . because the law is made for man and

13. Gabriel Marcel's expression.

not man for the law." This moral individualism is capable of beauty and on occasion it rises to a point where it is a substitution for synthetic and living reason. In a passage of the *Phenomenology*, Hegel quotes Jacobi's formula almost literally: "Now it is the law that exists for the self, not the self for the law" (*PE*, II, 174; *PG*, 449; *PM*, 649). However, as Hegel remarks in the Jena article, moral beauty should not lack either of two aspects: "It should lack neither vitality as individuality, so that it does not obey a dead concept, nor the form of the concept and of law, universality and objectivity."[14]

That is why once again we find the universal aspect in acting self just as we find the individual aspect. Haven't we already said that, in the sincerity of my conviction, of my knowledge of truth, I posited *my* truth as *the* absolute truth? What does this demand for transcendence mean when, *seen from outside,* the conviction of the self can be attached to any random sensuous content and when it therefore has an undeniable arbitrariness and finitude? In fact, acting consciousness maintains itself "in the unity of being-in-itself and being-for-itself, in the unity of pure thought and individuality" (*PE*, II, 181; *PG*, 455; *PM*, 657), but *for us* this unity is already breaking down. Content and form are contraposed: "The immediate specificity is the content of the moral act, and the form of this act is precisely this self considered as pure movement, that is, as knowledge or specific conviction" (*PE*, II, 173; *PG*, 449; *PM*, 648–49).

Are we not coming back to Kantianism and consequently again falling into the contradictions of the moral world view? It does not seem so, for now the universal has acquired a concrete signification, it has become being-for-an-other, a *moment* of consciousness, instead of being an abstract beyond, an inaccessible transcendence. This moment is expressed as the *demand for the recognition of my conviction by other selves.* Similarly, self-consciousness existed only through the mediation of other self-consciousnesses.

Recognition of conviction

Gewissen has its own truth in the immediate certainty of itself. This certainty, as conviction, as pure self-knowledge, is

14. Hegel devotes a part of his article "Glauben und Wissen" to Jacobi (pp. 262–73).

duty. "Duty is no longer the universal passing by before the self; rather, in this state of separation, duty is known to have no validity. Now it is the law that exists for the self, not the self for the law" (*PE*, II, 174; *PG*, 449; *PM*, 649). This is rather obscure, but it is an extremely important dialectical transition in Hegel's argument. The universal is no longer transcendence, as it was in the moral world view. As the equality of conviction with itself, it is the foundation of good conscience, *Gewissen*. Conviction is the in-itself; the content of conviction is the for-itself, the difference of pure essence. It is on the basis of conviction that the figure of the content of action emerges, and for consciousness this basis becomes being-for-an-other, that is, precisely, a *moment*. Law is for the self. However, this moment remains essential or, more exactly, whereas the transcendence of the Kantian universal remained pure but nonactual, henceforth the universal becomes a real being; as a moment, it is an object of concrete consciousness: "And now duty by itself is something immediately actual and is no longer merely abstract pure consciousness" (*PE*, II, 175; *PG*, 450; *PM*, 650). Universality is conviction to the extent that this conviction presupposes the *relation among self-consciousnesses*. When I am convinced, I presuppose that my conviction is as valid for others as for myself; I seek or demand recognition for my conviction. We now have to look at this recognition. In an immediately concrete way it expresses the universality which has previously been nonactual. "*Gewissen* has not abandoned pure duty or the abstract in itself; rather pure duty is the essential moment which consists of behaving toward others as if it were universality. It is the element common to self-consciousnesses, and this element is the substance in which acts have subsistence and actuality, the moment of *becoming-recognized* by others" (*PE*, II, 175; *PG*, 450; *PM*, 650).

The distinction between *Gewissen* and *Bewusstsein*, so difficult to translate, allows Hegel to make the dialectical transition which we have tried to explain. For *Gewissen*, conviction and the content of conviction are not separable; they are *existentially* linked. But for *Bewusstsein*, the opposition necessarily reappears and duty turns into being, in the sense of spiritual being, the milieu of recognition. We may question the validity of the logical, or rather dialectical, argument by means of which Hegel proceeds from the abstract in-itself, from duty in the Kantian sense, to the concrete substance of mutual recognition by self-consciousnesses, but we can see immediately its signification and its importance. *Abstract universal becomes concrete universal,* duty beyond acting self becomes universal self-consciousness as human community. We should not be led into error by the fact that Hegel calls this element "being." The being in question is neither the abstract being at the level of sensuous certainty with which the *Phenomenology* started, nor being in the sense of a natural being. Being is now the spiritual milieu, the community of human self-consciousnesses linked to each other. It is only spiritual being which can give validity and consistency to my action. No doubt we must say, with the solipsist, "to each his own truth," but we also must add right away that everyone well knows that there is only one truth, and that his truth, in order to *exist,* must be *recognized.* The struggle for recognition on the part of self-consciousnesses, a struggle without which self-consciousness would not exist, since it needs the mediation of others in order to exist, prefigures this demand for the recognition of conviction which now is presented at a higher level and in a more concrete form.

When I act, my action expresses my own conviction in the milieu of self-consciousnesses. This action has meaning only in this milieu; its being is a spiritual being, its truth depends on recognition by others. To know what my action is worth, its signification, we must wait for it to be transferred from particular consciousness to the *milieu of universal consciousness.* This transfer at first appears to be a purely formal question. As soon as I act with conviction, my action must immediately be recognized: "This conviction is precisely the in-itself itself; it is self-consciousness in-itself universal, or being-recognized, and is consequently actuality. Thus what is carried out with the conviction of duty is immediately such that it possesses consistency and Dasein" (*PE,* II, 175; *PG,* 450; *PM,* 651). Such, at least, is the naïve belief of acting consciousness which has not yet surveyed the difficulties of this recognition, nor the inadequacy of every particular action to the knowledge of the conviction that accompanies it. And yet it is this conviction—in-itself universal —which must be expressed in the human milieu. This milieu must be universal self, everyone's self-sameness [*ipséité*]. The "thing itself" (*die Sache selbst*) is precisely the universal subject which contains the unity of selves.

Before showing how consciousness discovers this inadequation and at the same time the means of remedying it, language, which as logos expresses specific self as universal self, we should once again insist that we have just reached the concrete universal and that this is spirit as the mutual mediation of self-consciousnesses. Duty has lost the elevated position which it had in Kantianism and which made it into something inhuman and in fact unreal. In Kantianism duty had no Dasein, no presence. "Moral self-consciousness does not have this moment of being recognized, of pure consciousness which is there, and consequently it is not at all actualizing, not at all acting" (*PE*, II, 175; *PG*, 450; *PM*, 650). Now action is simply the expression of the specific content of moral self-consciousness in the objective element, at the heart of which this content is universal and recognized. And that it is recognized is precisely what makes action actual. What confers on action its consistency and its reality is human history, the community of self-consciousnesses in their mutual relations. The universal is there, it is universal self, and this universal self is already present within the interiority of the self in the form of conviction. It is this conviction that must find expression in the common milieu and consequently must remain linked to the very content of action.

But this is precisely what creates the whole difficulty. Consciousness will discover the arbitrary character of its action, the indeterminateness of its conviction, "the subtlest confusion of the subjective and the objective" which Goethe denounced in the feelings of the beautiful soul. Only in language, which states conviction, will consciousness find Dasein to be simultaneously specific and universal, the self-sameness of everyone. In this language of conviction specific acting consciousness will become a universal consciousness. Just as we have seen acting self from the angle of specificity, we will see the self stating its conviction from the angle of universality.

Indeterminateness of conviction

Duty is now only a moment linking self-consciousnesses to each other, but the content of duty is still borrowed from natural individuality, from *moral genius*. When I act, I know very well that I cannot conscientiously examine all the circumstances of my action. In fact, these circumstances go beyond the restricted circle of my knowledge and extend infinitely. I cannot know them all, and at this point *knowledge* comes up against *nonknowledge*. However, because it is my own knowledge, I accept my incomplete knowledge as sufficient and complete knowledge.

The same is true for the determination of duty. Only pure duty is absolute, but I know that pure duty is empty and I have to limit myself to the mere conviction that *this* is my duty. This conviction is essential, but in its turn it is as empty as pure duty. However, we must act; the individual must make a determination and he must make it by himself, that is, he must find it within his sensuous individuality.

Now any content can be posited as pure duty. Conviction remains formal. We can justify anything provided we are able to convince ourselves of the conformity of our action with duty by firmly holding onto the way in which the action can be considered as duty. Suppose I increase my property. It is my duty to think of preserving my life and that of my family, better yet, to foresee the possibility of being useful to others. If others discover something fraudulent in my action, it is because they take up another aspect of the issue. "By the same token the duty to affirm my own independence against others is fulfilled by what others call 'violence' and 'injustice'; what they call 'cowardice' fulfills the duty to preserve one's own life and to preserve the possibility of being useful to one's neighbor. On the other hand what they call 'courage' often violates these two duties" (*PE*, II, 179; *PG*, 454; *PM*, 654–55).[15] *Casuistry* is inevitable: what is inadmissible is to ignore the fact that conformity to duty resides in this knowledge. "Without this knowledge, cowardice would commit the stupidity of being immoral." Thus *Gewissen* is freed of any content, absolved of any determinate duty. *It chooses itself by itself*, but this freedom is also, as we have just seen, purely arbitrary.

This arbitrariness, which appears to us philosophers, is not yet manifest to acting consciousness which must itself experience it. The indeterminateness which we have just discovered must become conscious for the self itself. Once an act has been accomplished and is detached from the self as the fruit from a tree, it is a determinate act which is not necessarily recognized by other self-consciousnesses. Other individualities do not dis-

15. Hegel takes up again this whole critical analysis of *Gewissen* in the second moment of the *Philosophy of Right*. The first moment was the (objective) person; the second moment is the moral (subjective) subject; the third moment will be, in the state in general, a will which is simultaneously subjective and objective. In this passage in the *Philosophy of Right*, he makes reference to the *Phenomenology* ("Good and Conscience," pp. 86–104).

cover themselves in this act. The action that I have just performed is without doubt my action. In its determinate content I
have a knowledge of myself, I express my congruence with myself, with my conviction. Since conviction is in-itself universal,
all others should recognize themselves in this knowledge of the
I. However, things don't happen this way, and in fact the supposed congruence is disparate. Indeed, once it has been accomplished, the act is no longer self-knowledge, but "a determinate
act which is not congruent with the element of self-consciousness
in everyone and which is thus not necessarily recognized. Both
sides, acting *Gewissen* and universal consciousness which recognizes this action as duty, are equally free from the determinateness of this action" (*PE*, II, 183; *PG*, 457; *PM*, 659). That is
why recognition appears to be impossible here. On the contrary,
what is striking is the discrepancy between action and the universality of conviction.

II. THE UNIVERSALITY OF *Gewissen*

YET THIS UNIVERSALITY must establish its validity. The
act cannot be considered here, as it was in previous moments,
merely according to its material content. The act cannot be
stripped of its spiritual signification; it expresses a conviction
which is by rights universal, it is a knowledge which at the same
time ought to be universal knowledge. How can this universality
emerge and invest the act with spiritual being? Such is the problem that is posed at this point. We again quote the terms of the
problem: "Self must enter into Dasein as self; self-certain spirit
must exist as such for others" (*PE*, II, 184; *PG*, 458; *PM*, 660).
The being that mediates among self-consciousnesses cannot be
the effect (*Wirkung*) of action, since the self is no longer contained in this effect. It is *universal self-consciousness* which must
now *exist* and be actual. What then can the true mode of expression of the self be, a mode that both is objective, perceivable by
all, and yet despite this objectivity conserves within itself the
subjectivity of the self?

The answer is immediate: the Dasein of the self, as universal self, can only be language, logos. It is language that comments on action and expresses conviction; it alone states the
meaning of action. "Language is self-consciousness which is for-
others, which is immediately present as such and which, as *this*

self-consciousness, is universal self-consciousness" (*PE*, II, 184; *PG*, 458; *PM*, 660).

At the level of experience we have reached, the only adequate expression of self-certain self is not the act whose content always remains particular and contingent, but knowledge of the act by the acting subject. This knowledge is objectified in language. We have already seen the great importance that Hegel assigns to language. In the first moment of consciousness, sensuous certainty, language already revealed its nature to us: it states the universal and confers on it a sensuous presence, it is the authentic expression of spirit.[16] In the entire *Phenomenology*, language accompanies every important moment of the life of spirit, it incarnates the originality of every moment. Following his usual practice, Hegel at this point again takes up the different roles of language in order to stress the continuity of its function. In the ethical world, language expresses the objective truth that spiritual self-consciousness merely actualizes (which is why language there is only the expression of an impersonal social order); it propounds "the law or commandment" imposed on individual consciousness. This first form of language still lacks the self, as is required by this world; the legislator disappears in the face of the statement of what is valid in-and-for-itself. Thus language expresses the commandment which directs individual conduct and seems to emanate from a force superior to the I. There is another form of language in this first world of spirit, and that is the complaint, which is a lamentation in the face of terrible necessity. Here Hegel is doubtless thinking of Greek tragedy. At other points, apropos of religion in the form of art, he will come back to language as a spiritual work of art.

As we have seen, language also plays an essential role in the world of culture. For it is through its mediation that the I can completely alienate itself and the substantive state can acquire a personality. It is also language that states the laceration of the I that has become alien to itself. Only the literature of this epoch can express this spiritual division.[17]

Moral consciousness (in the Kantian sense) cannot but be

16. Cf. the commentary on this function of language in the study by Brice Parain, *Recherches sur la nature et les fonctions du langage* (Paris, 1942), pp. 143 ff. In the "System der Sittlichkeit" Hegel characterizes language as both the *instrument* and the *offspring* of intelligence.

17. We would recall Hegel's analysis of *Rameau's Nephew* (see above, pp. 411–16).

silent, since in it the self does not yet attain actual existence. But now, by contrast, it is language alone that universalizes the self that is certain of itself in its internal conviction.

> The content of the language of *Gewissen* is the *self that knows itself as essence*. It is that alone which language expresses, and this expression is the real actuality and validity of action. . . . In effect universal self-consciousness is freed from determinate action which merely is. This action, as Dasein, has no validity for consciousness; what counts is rather the conviction that this action is duty, and this conviction is actualized in language (*PE*, II, 185; *PG*, 459; *PM*, 661).

In response to this passage how can we avoid thinking of a literature which goes from Rousseau's *Confessions* to the "Confessions of a Beautiful Soul," by way of the *Sorrows of Young Werther*? What is important is not what the self has realized, for this determinate action is not necessarily recognized, but rather the assurance that the self gives of having acted according to its conviction. It is this inner assurance of the self, in the *Confessions* or in *Werther*, indeed in this whole literature of the I, which shines forth, which emerges and becomes actual. "This is the form that must be posited as actual, it is the self that is actualized as such in language, that proclaims itself as the true, and that precisely within language recognizes all selves and is recognized by them" (*PE*, II, 186; *PG*, 460; *PM*, 663).[18] Whereas the self becomes alien to itself and is alienated from itself in the language of the seventeenth century, in this new language the *self states itself* in its *inner certainty* as being *universal truth*.

The beautiful soul

However, little by little we have left the particular content of an action to consider what alone here is actual, the I, simultaneously as specific I and as universal I in the Dasein of language. Acting consciousness was considered in its universal aspect; now it becomes a contemplative beautiful soul. We

18. Thus language follows the progress of spirit which is coming to consciousness of itself; it proceeds from the objective order (*true* spirit) to self *certain* of itself (subjective spirit). Thus we have the language of the Greek world, the language of the alienation of the I, the language of being torn asunder, and the (Romantic) language which states the *I* as truth.

started our dialectic with *Gewissen* as acting consciousness; now we arrive at the dialectic of the beautiful soul. This dialectic will make us see rather a *self-contemplation* than a *determinate action* in the movement of the beautiful soul.

It is useful to follow the diverse significations that Hegel ascribes to the beautiful soul, which he borrows from the literature and philosophy of his own time. Thus we will see more clearly the transition from action to contemplation, a transition that terminates by making the beautiful soul into absolute self-consciousness (Hegel says "the pure concept") which sinks into the void of its subjectivity and becomes incapable of any positive action because it refuses to alienate itself, to give a determinate and external content to the concept. The beautiful soul (*die schöne Seele*) is first of all, as its name indicates, the happy soul which has found the means of reconciling through the beauty of its feelings a rigid conception of duty with the spontaneous inclination of nature. Such, for example, is Schiller's conception of it: "It is a soul in which the most difficult duties and the most heroic sacrifices which it obtains from instinct appear as the spontaneous effect of this very instinct. In it morality has become nature."[19] Through an aesthetic education, Schiller tried to reconcile the two terms which Kant so radically contraposed: freedom and nature. Although Kant had shattered the unity of human nature, he also tried to reconstitute it in a soul in which virtue would possess the grace of natural movements and nature would possess the spiritual meaning of moral life. Kantian moralism, the abstract idea of the universal and of law, would thus be transcended in a more *aesthetic* view of man. We know that the reconciliation of nature and duty was one of the themes of the early works of Hegel, who never accepted Kantian dualism. We ourselves have just seen in *Gewissen* spirit immediately certain of itself, spirit which does indeed reconcile within itself nature and morality.

However, the beautiful soul is not only concrete moral individuality; it tends to become more contemplative than active. This evolution may perhaps have been prefigured in its aesthetic formation; it is indeed "moral genius which has vitality in its concept" and here, as in the Jena work, Hegel refers to Jacobi. Yet Jacobi's characters, the Allwills and the Woldemars, are not just active; they perpetually turn back upon themselves. The invention through action that was implied by moral genius dis-

19. Schiller, *Von Anmut und Würde* (1793).

appears in favor of a quasi-aesthetic self-contemplation. Above all, these beautiful souls are concerned with perceiving their inner purity and with being able to state it. Concern for themselves never completely leaves them, as true action would require. Hegel again insists on this point in the work we have just quoted. In the *Phenomenology*, the transition from moral genius to self-contemplation is clearly indicated: "Its action is the contemplation of its own divinity" (*PE*, II, 187; *PG*, 460; *PM*, 663).[20]

In addition to an aesthetic character, this contemplation has a religious one. What the beautiful soul discovers within itself as an inner voice is a divine voice; its enjoyment of itself is at the same time an enjoyment of the divine within it. On this point Schleiermacher, according to Hegel, raised Jacobi's subjectivity to a higher degree. The idea, of which Hegel subsequently speaks, of a community of beautiful souls—the kingdom of God on earth—follows the line of this evolution from moralism to aestheticism to religion, a religiosity which retains an aesthetic element, as in *On Religion: Speeches to Its Cultured Despisers*.[21] In order to provide itself with an objective consciousness (*Bewusstsein*) of itself, the beautiful soul needs to participate in a community which states its universal self as the self of everyone. In these communities everyone acts according to the inspiration of his heart, yet each recognizes the others "by virtue of the discourse in which the self is expressed and recognized as essence" (*PE*, II, 187; *PG*, 461; *PM*, 664). What counts is less the action which, as such, has nothing universal about it, than the assurance that each gives to the others of the purity of his heart and of the sensitivity of his intentions. This knowledge of self as divine is *religion*, and this knowledge as object of intuition is "the speech of the community which states its own spirit" (*PE*, II, 188; *PG*, 461; *PM*, 665).

Here we should also think of the "Confessions of a Beautiful Soul" in Goethe's novel *Wilhelm Meister's Apprenticeship*. Before writing the novel, Goethe wrote to Schiller, "Last week I suddenly had a peculiar inspiration which happily is still with

20. In the early works, Hegel proceeds from the *active soul* to the *contemplative* soul mainly by the intermediary of *Christianity*, by Christ's "my kingdom is not of this world." On Christ as the "beautiful soul," cf. *Early Theological Works*, pp. 233 ff.

21. In "Glauben und Wissen," Hegel extends Jacobi with Schleiermacher.

me. I was struck with a desire to begin the religious section of my novel, and since the subject is based on the noblest deceptions and on the subtlest confusion of the subjective and objective, I needed a more intense concentration, to gather up my forces." [22] Goethe's beautiful soul is more contemplative than active; it is contraposed to the active Christian which Goethe described in the person of Nathalie: "The destiny of man is to be active, and every interval between actions should be occupied with learning about those exterior things which subsequently facilitate activity." Again, doesn't Goethe say in this work: "I revere the man who knows what he wants, progresses without stopping, knows the means with which to realize his goal and is able to understand and utilize those means?" So we should not be surprised at Novalis' judgment—whom Hegel perhaps intended to portray in the last features of his figure of the beautiful soul —on Goethe's novel. After praising it profoundly, as did the entire Romantic generation, he criticized the prosaic meaning behind its poetic façade. Goethe rejects the subjective idealism which neglects objective nature and concrete action in the world. The beautiful soul can only exhaust itself within itself and "in this transparent purity vanish like a formless vapor which dissolves in the air" (*PE*, II, 189; *PG*, 463; *PM*, 667).

In the *Phenomenology*, Hegel reproduces the entire evolution of the beautiful soul, and he insists above all on its contemplative character; it is subjectivity elevated to universality but incapable of going outside itself and, by truly acting, of "transforming its thought into being and of giving itself over to absolute difference." The portrait of the beautiful soul—that of Christ in the early works—did not have the pejorative nuance that it has in the *Phenomenology*. In order not to lose its purity, the beautiful soul of the early writings refused to confront destiny; it declined to defend its independence in the world, as an active soul engaged in struggle, but it did not have the cowardice of the passive soul incapable of defending its rights. To avoid this dilemma, it did not locate its rights in the things of the world, it refused power and wealth, and above all sought the kingdom of God in the intimacy of its heart.[23] However, "this

22. *Der Briefwechsel*, Letter 56, p. 96.
23. The dilemma was the following: either affirm the reality of its rights and thus the rightfulness of reality, or leave reality and thus affirm the irreality of its rights. In either case, one culminates with a tragic contradiction (*Early Theological Writings*, p. 234).

flight from destiny experienced the most terrible of destinies."
Its separation from the world was its destiny, and the greatest
innocence was not incompatible with the greatest sin.

In the *Phenomenology*, the portrait of the beautiful soul has
an entirely different signification, but it retains the features we
have just sketched. The beautiful soul is still "this flight from
destiny, this refusal of action in the world, a refusal which culminates in the loss of self."

Thus, by contrast with acting *Gewissen*, the beautiful soul
incarnates the subjectivity that satisfies itself within itself, and
through this haughty subjectivity preserves the universality of
spirit which the language of conviction has already manifested.
It becomes not the intuition of the divine, which still supposes
the distinction between essence—the divine—and the self, but
rather *"the self-intuition of the divine," absolute self-consciousness*. But this self-consciousness has lost its consciousness; the
object that appears to it is no longer distinct from itself. It loses
all truth in subjective certainty, in possessing the absolute intuition $I = I$, which Fichte denied to man but which Novalis
granted himself. "As consciousness, it is divided into the opposition between the self and the object which, for it, is essence, but
this object is precisely that which is perfectly transparent, it is
its self, and consciousness of it is only self-knowledge. All life
and all spiritual essentiality have returned within this self" (*PE*,
II, 188; *PG*, 462; *PM*, 665–66). Self-consciousness of absolute
life no longer has an object; it sinks into the darkness in the
midst of which substance has wholly been transformed into subject. Thus Novalis persisted "in stubborn impotence . . . in
ascribing to himself substantiveness, in transforming his thought
into being" (*PE*, II, 189; *PG*, 463; *PM*, 666). He preferred this
inner night to the distinct light of day, and said of himself: "An
ineffable solitude surrounds me since the death of Sophie; with
her, the entire world died for me; I am no longer from here below." But, in this self-consciousness which does not allow itself
any alienation, the self that is object cannot be in-and-for-itself;
it is only the dying echo of a self for which the world is but its
own speech coming back to it without having received the imprint of an authentic objectivity. "Nor does consciousness have
a Dasein, for the objective element does not manage to be a
negative of actual self any more than this self manages to arrive at actuality. It lacks the strength to alienate itself, the
strength to make itself into a thing and to support being" (*PE*,
II, 189; *PG*, 462; *PM*, 666).

In the conclusion of the *Phenomenology,* apropos of absolute knowledge, Hegel returns to this notion of the beautiful soul. Self-certain spirit attains absolute truth only through "unity with its alienation." It is not the subjectivity of the beautiful soul, which embraces within itself the entire substantiveness of spirit and reduces it to itself, that is the last word of philosophy, but rather both this universal subjectivity and the partiality of concrete action taken together. The beautiful soul and *Gewissen* as acting consciousness must be reconciled. What we have just considered, that is, the reconciliation of two moments of spirit, each of which is insufficient by itself, finally leads us to *absolute spirit.* The beautiful soul represents the universality of spirit which is certain of itself but which is determinate because it opposes the partiality of action. On the other hand, *Gewissen,* of which we spoke originally, represents acting but determinate spirit because its action is necessarily finite and limited. These two forms of the I certain of itself must each recognize its limit; acting consciousness must discover within itself the sin necessarily implied by its finitude, and universal self-consciousness must perceive this same finitude in its separation from the finite. This reconciliation of finite spirit with infinite spirit—but falsely infinite because separated from the finite—is the supreme dialectic of spirit: it expresses organic reconciliation at the heart of the most rending divisions. Such is the dialectic of the *forgiveness of sins* in which spirit by itself becomes absolute spirit, and is absolute spirit only in its becoming so.

III. Evil and Its Forgiveness

a. *The terms of the opposition*

THE OPPOSITION between nature and abstract universal as pure duty beyond the self could not be maintained. Spirit has become concrete moral spirit (*Gewissen*). But, starting from this concrete spirit which, in its immediate sense of itself, reconciles what the moral world view contraposed, a new opposition arises which appears to reproduce the one we thought we had left behind us. And that is just what the conclusion of the chapter on the moral world view hinted at (*PE,* II, 168; *PG,* 444; *PM,* 641). Spirit as universal ("for which universality and duty are the essence, whereas specificity, which, in contrast with the universal, is for-itself, is valid only as a suppressed [*aufgehoben*] moment") confronts "spirit as specific individuality, for which self-certainty is the essence relative to the in-itself or to the universal which is valid only as a moment" (*PE*, II, 191; *PG*, 464; *PM*, 668). Thus it appears that we have made no progress. However, now the opposition has taken on a concrete form; more exactly, it is two *figures* of consciousness that are presented to us, each containing the two moments—the universal and the specific—but with different values. What is more, it is starting from *Gewissen*, from inner self-certainty, that these two figures have developed; they have their common source in this certainty which is as much specific as it is universal, as much immediate knowledge as pure knowledge. One of them is *acting spirit*, positing in being its actuality as action and immediately convinced of the legitimacy of its action; the other is the *beautiful soul*, which little by little abandons the determinate content of action, declines to allow its life to be shattered and, in its pure subjectivity, states the universality of the I. Acting consciousness and the beautiful soul both incarnate in concrete figures what the moral world view restricted to a single consciousness in the form of an antinomy of abstract terms. At the level we have reached, it is impossible to speak of a pure nature of man, which has independent laws, but which is contraposed to a pure universality that is no less independent. It is spirit that, as a totality, divides itself, and this division, like the reconciliation that it requires, is present in Dasein thanks to language. Spirit in some way is *given* as *universal spirit* as well as *particular spirit*. The movement of each against the other, as well as the movement of each toward the other, should have a presence and give rise to a dialectic which is as representative and as concrete as that of master and slave, or that of noble consciousness and base consciousness. Thus despite certain appearances, the progress is considerable in comparison to Kant's moral consciousness. The portrait of acting consciousness and of the beautiful soul and the discovery in language of the Dasein of spirit allow us to contrapose infinite spirit and finite spirit within existence itself, and this opposition, through its own deepening, gives rise to their organic reconciliation.[24]

24. Apropos of unhappy consciousness or noble consciousness, we have already insisted on the character of the Hegelian phenomenology. It is a matter of arriving at a plastic figure (*Gestalt*) of the moments of consciousness. The universal and the specific, infinite spirit and finite spirit, are two concrete figures of consciousness here. In addition, each figure has the other enclosed within it and that is why opposition, becoming contradiction, and reconciliation, becoming identity, are possible.

b. *Finite spirit: consciousness of sin*

We are aware of the ambiguities of the dialectic which, following the text of the *Phenomenology*, we are now going to take up again, and we want to reserve the possibility of coming back to the plurality of its possible significations. This ambiguity, which opens the door to diverse interpretations, undoubtedly constitutes the richness of this philosophical text, but it is none-the-less troublesome for the historian. It is precisely the character of this dialectic, simultaneously *representative* (or symbolic, if one prefers) and *concrete,* that conceals its ambiguities.

Like Hegel, we will begin with sinful consciousness and then consider the other consciousness which in this opposition becomes judging consciousness. But sinful consciousness is nothing other than what we have called *Gewissen* or "good conscience" which, through a sort of internal reversal, must now become "bad conscience." One thinks of the witticism of a contemporary philosopher: "Good conscience is never anything but a refusal to listen to conscience (*Gewissen*)." [25] How can this consciousness, which knows immediately what it must do in this situation or in another, which is existentially linked to a concrete situation, become a sinful consciousness? There is a metaphysical postulate very often found in philosophers and theologians which might be stated thus: "Finitude is necessarily sinful." By virtue of the fact that spirit is finite, it is sinful. This finitude implies a limitation, an existential choice, which is confused with our own determinateness. "To exist is to commit the sin of limitation and to have the feeling of impotence." [26] Thus it is that Hegel can say that "only stone is innocent," since acting spirit must necessarily engage itself in the world, be something particular, and at the same time feels called on to surpass this inevitable particularity. This equation, of which one member is limitation and the other is sin, poses many problems. According

25. Heidegger, *Being and Time*, trans. John Macquarrie and Edward Robinson (New York and London, 1962), § 59. We quote this expression of Heidegger's, but the spirit of Heidegger's text is completely different from that of Hegel's. For Hegel, there exists negativity, guilt, the necessity for taking the negative seriously, *splitting*, but in spite of all that, there is *reconciliation.*

26. Jaspers, *Existenzerhellung*, p. 204. It is remarkable that Hegel uses the expression *Geworfenheit* for man's being (*PE*, II, 276; *PG*, 537; *PM*, 769).

to the sense in which one reads it, we interpret the very situation of man religiously or in a purely philosophical manner. We need not enter into this debate. Yet it is impossible not to discover in man this consciousness of a sin which is linked to his very existence, even setting aside questions of its origin. There is a certain narrowness to existence which constitutes its profundity but which is accompanied by consciousness of sin linked precisely to this narrowness and at the same time linked to an originary freedom, that is, a fundamental freedom which we can neither situate exactly nor refuse. In Hegelianism, acting spirit determines itself by itself, but at the same time it demands that its own truth be recognized as absolute truth. The demand for recognition of my conviction by others presupposes, as we have seen, the moment of universality which thus is present in *Gewissen*. Thus the contrast between the universality that it states in its words and the particular content of its action finally appears to it and it becomes *for its own self* consciousness of the evil which is in it, sinful consciousness.

> When it fills empty duty with a *determinate* content which it draws from itself, it acquires positive consciousness; it itself, as this particular self, procures content for itself . . . *Gewissen* becomes conscious of the opposition between what it *is for-itself and what it is for others*, the opposition between universality or duty and its own being-reflected outside duty (*PE*, II, 190–91; *PG*, 463–64; *PM*, 667–68).

Consciousness of evil is thus linked to the opposition between finitude in action and the element of mutual recognition between self-consciousnesses which is an immanent demand. I recognize the universal by stating my conviction to others, and I await *judgment*. In addition I know that the specific content of my goal is inadequate to this universality that I proclaim. If this opposition becomes fully conscious it is what is called "hypocrisy," and this hypocrisy must be unmasked; it is what universal consciousness denounces in sinful consciousness: "In the first place, the movement of this opposition is the formal establishment of equality between what evil is in-itself and what it expresses. It must become manifest that evil is evil, that is, that its Dasein is equal to its essence; hypocrisy must be unmasked" (*PE*, II, 191; *PG*, 464; *PM*, 669).[27] This equality is established

27. We should notice the contemporary resonance of Hegel's analyses: the opposition between *being-for-itself* and *being-for-others*, the internal demand for my *recognition* by others, and the need to be *judged*.

neither by verbal recognition of the universal—since hypocrisy is, as they say, the homage that vice renders to virtue—nor by consciousness insisting on its own inner law. That this law is merely consciousness' own means that it is not universally recognized. But duty has now taken the form of universal consciousness and specific consciousness claims to go beyond its existential solitude and, at least by its language, opens itself up to universal recognition.

c. *Universal consciousness*

Thus it is not by looking toward acting consciousness that we will find the means of establishing the equality we are seeking. Just as the consciousness of the master is revealed as the consciousness of the slave who ignores what he is, or just as noble consciousness ultimately appears as base consciousness, so too here universal consciousness in the form of judging consciousness reveals itself to us as identical with the sinful consciousness that it claims to judge. Let us therefore consider this consciousness in the concrete form of *moral judgment*. In the first place, this consciousness cannot manifest its universality merely by its judgment. When it stigmatizes hypocrisy as evil, it bases its judgment on its own law, just as evil consciousness based itself on its law; its zeal already performs the inverse of what it thinks it is doing: "It exhibits what it terms 'true duty' which should be recognized universally, as something that is not recognized" (*PE*, II, 193; *PG*, 466; *PM*, 670). But we must go further still. This consciousness exhibits itself to us as being itself evil and particular, and it is by perceiving the hypocrisy within itself that acting consciousness will come to confess, will open itself completely to the other by a confession which expects another confession. In effect, by opposing evil it judges instead of acting, and takes this nonreal judgment as a real action. "It has preserved its purity, for it does not act. It is hypocrisy which wants the fact of judging to be taken for an actual *action* and, instead of demonstrating uprightness through action, demonstrates it only by the proclamation of its own excellent dispositions" (*PE*, II, 193; *PG*, 466; *PM*, 671).[28] It thus places itself

28. As universal consciousness, Hegel is thinking here of the judgment of the masses on the great man (see the allusion to Napoleon which follows in the passage).

alongside the consciousness it judges; it is constituted like that consciousness.

However, this consciousness that judges or contemplates instead of acting only contemplates evil, and on this last point it again shows itself to be inadequate to the universality it claims to represent. If it does not act, it is in order to preserve its purity as a beautiful soul and not limit the infinite life within itself. But when it perceives evil in the first consciousness, it precisely breaks the concrete totality of action, separating what the life of spirit unites. Every real action must be viewed as a concrete whole—here Hegel thinks mainly of men of action and of the petty explanations that the consciousness of the mob has frequently given for their acts—that is, every real action is particular because it is linked to such-and-such a given individuality, but in its scope and general signification it is also universal in the sense of the concrete universal. Human action is always passion as well as action. "Nothing great is done without passion." Human action is the limited expression of individuality, and within this limit it is passion, but it is also the expression of spirit which acts *through* this individuality, and in that respect it is universal action.[29] Consciousness that judges shatters the concrete and living whole, "it illuminates action only in the light of particularity and pettiness" (*PE*, II, 194; *PG*, 467; *PM*, 672). In the act of a great man, it denounces the impure motivations which are merely a moment of action; it does not see that the great man "has willed what he has done and has done what he has willed," and tries to explain everything by the love of glory or the search for worldly or celestial felicity. "There are no heroes for the *valet de chambre*." Hegel quotes Napoleon's statement with the comment that inspired Goethe several years later: "Not because the former is not a hero, but because the latter is a *valet de chambre*" (*PE*, II, 195; *PG*, 468; *PM*, 673). In the same way, for judgment there is no action in which it cannot contrapose the specific aspect of individuality to the universal aspect of the action and thus play the role of morality's *valet de chambre* with respect to the person who acts. That is because infinite spirit exists only through finite spirit and, con-

---

29. We have already pointed out that for Hegel, beginning with the early works, and even more explicitly in the political works of Jena, universal spirit is not without "individual vitality." The *idea* always appears in the individual *figure*.

versely, finite spirit exists only through perpetually surpassing itself.[30]

When it sees itself in the consciousness that judges it, as in a mirror, consciousness engaged in action admits to the evil within it and opens itself to reconciliation. Its admission is a recognition of the continuity of its I with the other I; in return it expects the same admission, which would express their identity. But that is not what happens: judging consciousness persists in its judgment, it becomes the "hard heart" which confirms itself as evil by this *absolute will to isolation,* this rupture of continuity with others. Thus this universal consciousness, the beautiful soul which does not act, the consciousness which judges instead of acting, the hard heart which withdraws into its haughty silence, becomes the opposite of itself. Instead of being the continuity of the universal, in its inner self it becomes the discontinuity of the purely specific, because it has refused to open itself to the world, to consent to being. If it persists in its haughty attitude it degenerates, as did the beautiful soul, into a pure being, but a being without spirit. However, since equality has now been established, "to break the hard heart and raise it to universality is the same movement that has already been expressed through consciousness confessing." The "yes" of pardon which surges forth is the word of reconciliation, the recognition of the I in the other I—a remission of sins which causes *absolute spirit* to appear via this reciprocal exchange. Absolute spirit is neither abstract infinite spirit which is opposed to finite spirit, nor finite spirit which persists in its finitude and always remains on this side [*en deçà*] of its other; it is the unity and the opposition of these two I's. Thus the equation I = I assumes all its concrete signification if we *insist on its duality as much as on its unity.*

> The "yes" of reconciliation in which the two I's mutually give up their opposed Dasein is the Dasein of the I extended to duality, the I, which remains the same as itself and which, in its complete alienation and its complete opposite is certain of itself. This "yes" is God manifesting himself in the midst of those who know themselves as pure knowledge (*PE,* II, 200; *PG,* 472; *PM,* 679).

30. Cf. the passage in "Naturrecht," which puts forth the absolute as the *tragic:* "The universal realizes itself by giving itself up to passion and to death; the specific, on the contrary, raises itself through this *Aufhebung* to the heights of universality" (p. 384).

d. *Signification of this dialectic*

We have already indicated the wealth and ambiguity of the Hegelian dialectic of the forgiveness of sins. This is the place to come back to it. What meaning should we ascribe to this Christian dogma which, along with the Trinity and the Incarnation, Hegel makes one of the bases of his philosophical thought? Hegel is not a mystic; in Christian thought and in the sacred texts he is looking less for a religious experience than for a philosophical symbol. Already in his early works, which we would today call "existential," and in which the philosophical interpretation is less apparent, what he asks of these religious texts is a more direct knowledge of human nature. These texts do indeed present him with a living dialectic on which his own philosophical dialectic will be modeled.

When we speak of the ambiguity of the thesis of the remission of sins, we do not mean to say that its general philosophical signification is unclear, but rather that surrounding this philosophical signification there subsists a halo of concrete significations whose richness delights the commentator and alternatively whose multiplicity of possible interpretations brings him to despair. If it were merely a question of clarifying the philosophical scope of the opposition and reconciliation of infinite spirit and finite spirit, of the universal and the specific, the task would be easy; but Hegel's concrete presentation of them, which varies from one work to the next, cannot be considered as useless drapery: it is perhaps what we are most sensitive to today. The Hegelian dialectic, like poetry, is not independent of its form.

The dialectic of the remission of sins was presented for the first time in the Frankfurt fragment entitled *The Spirit of Christianity and Its Fate*, the same fragment which contains the portrait of the beautiful soul to which we alluded above.[31] From the point of view of justice, contraposing the universal of the law to criminal action, no reconciliation appears possible. What is done is done; the criminal will always be a criminal. "Before the law, the criminal is nothing but a criminal, but just as the latter is only a fragment of human nature, so too the former.

---

31. *Early Theological Writings*, pp. 182–301, especially pp. 224 ff., "The Moral Teaching of Jesus: (β) Love as the Transcendence of Penal Justice and the Reconciliation of Fate."

If the law were a whole and an absolute, then the criminal would be only a criminal." But "the sinner is a man, not an existing sin." By his act, he himself has called forth this hostile destiny in which he is foundering, and by confronting his destiny he raises himself above it.[32] Infinite life has been divided by action and aspires to a reconciliation, for *that life still exists in the criminal.* It is this discovery of life as love that is Christ's sublimity. "Wherever Christ found faith, he expressed himself forthrightly, saying, 'Your sins are forgiven you,' since for him faith signified the understanding of spirit by spirit, elevation above the law and above destiny." Christ had confidence in the spirit which did not yet exist for the believing sinner but toward which he was heading. To say that "Jesus recognized those who possessed harmony, love, within themselves, and thus went beyond their destiny, he didn't need a piecemeal understanding of human nature," means that he discovered the immanence of infinite life at the heart of finite life. "The Jews, on the contrary, could not understand the pardon of sins because for them there was an absolute separation . . . they had alienated all harmony, all love and had placed them in an alien being."[33] The idea that emerges from this passage is that of a living reconciliation substituted for a dead opposition. The fact still subsists, but as a past, a past that awaits its meaning from the future, a wound that can be healed, as Hegel says in a slightly different tone in the passage from the *Phenomenology* on which we are commenting: "The wounds of spirit heal without leaving scars. The facts are not imperishable, but the spirit absorbs them within itself, and the aspect of specificity that is present in facts, either as intention or as its [existing] negativity and its limit in the element of Dasein, disappears immediately" (*PE*, II, 197; *PG*, 470; *PM*, 676). Like all romantics, Hegel wants to think through the immanence of the infinite in the finite. But this leads him to a tragic philosophy of history; infinite spirit should not be thought through beyond finite spirit, beyond man acting and sinning, and yet infinite spirit itself is eager to participate in the human drama. Its true infinity, its concrete infinity, does not exist without this fall. God cannot ignore human finitude and

32. *Ibid.*, pp. 226 ff.
33. *Ibid.*, p. 239. It is in this passage that Hegel substitutes *destiny* for the *abstract universal* of law and thinks through the idea of a reconciliation through *love:* "This sensing of life, a sensing which finds itself again, is love, and in love fate is reconciled" (p. 232).

human suffering. Conversely, finite spirit is not a within-limits [*en-deçca*]; it surpasses itself, indefatigably drawn toward its own transcendence, and it is this transcending which is the possible healing of its finitude. Thus Hegelianism poses the problem of the unity of God and man, of their reconciliation which presupposes their opposition—what Hegel calls alienation.[34]

However, the dialectic of the remission of sins presents a few more particular characteristics in our passage from the *Phenomenology:* it contraposes the judge to the man who acts and once again deals with the question of communication among self-consciousnesses. The man who acts cannot isolate himself from others, from universal consciousness. He feels the need to be recognized which, as we have seen, is the fundamental human need. Self-consciousness exists only through the *mediation of recognition.* The recognition of self constitutes concrete spiritual being. Now, moral judgment appeared to be as evil as sinful consciousness could be. Commenting on the Biblical text "Judge not, that ye be not judged," Hegel discovers in judgment, which is sometimes that of the envious mob vis-à-vis the great man, that hypocrisy and baseness lie hidden under the veil of virtue. The judge of the action of others speaks instead of acting and always interprets action as evil, instead of discovering in it its possible universality. He becomes the "hard heart" who in turn isolates himself from the spiritual community. Evil appears as this very isolation, this break. To the confession of the other, "he contraposes the beauty of his own soul . . . the obstinate attitude of the character who is always equal to himself and the silence of the one who withdraws into himself and refuses to lower himself to an other" (*PE*, II, 196; *PG*, 469; *PM*, 674).

So many possible themes are intertwined in this dialectic that the critic can accentuate one or another at will and show how they have subsequently been developed. The critique of moral judgment, the motives which can inspire it, and the impurity of which becomes manifest upon analysis are to be found for example in Nietzsche; contemporary philosophy has insisted on the problem of the relations among self-consciousnesses, on the difficulties of communication and recognition, on which Hegel placed the greatest importance.

As we have already said, the general philosophical meaning

34. Cf. "Speculative Good Friday" in "Glauben und Wissen," p. 346. In the same way, Hegelian logic is the reconciliation of intuitive (divine) understanding and discursive (human) understanding.

of this entire dialectic does not present the same ambiguities; we have indicated it sketchily. The moral world view of a Kant or a Fichte situated the moral order, the good, beyond our world. Spirit is not realized here below, but then spirit resides perhaps less in what we accomplish in actuality than in the intention that inspires us. Such was the solution of Lessing, for whom the search for truth was the essential and was worth more than the static possession of this truth. Despite deficiencies and finitude, is it not the essential to aspire to the highest? Although this interpretation may appear quite similar to Hegel's, it is in fact far different.

The whole long history of errors that human development presents and that the *Phenomenology* retraces is indeed a fall, but we must learn that this fall is part of the absolute itself, that it is a moment of total truth. Absolute self cannot be expressed without this negativity; it is an absolute "yes" only through saying "no" to a "no," only by overcoming a necessary negation. Unity is only realizable by continual conflict and by perpetual surpassing. "The true life of spirit resides in this surpassing, not in the consciousness of sin which is always located within the limits [*en-deçà*], nor in the consciousness of a beyond which is always transcendent, but rather in the consciousness of the forgiveness of sins, of a reconciliation through opposition." [35] Such is the meaning that we should give to I = I.

In the *Lectures on the Philosophy of Religion*, Hegel will express this conception in a sharper form than in the *Phenomenology*:

> The determination that everyone remains what he is lies in the realm of finitude. He has done evil, therefore he is evil, evil is in him as his quality. But in morality and still more in religion, spirit is known as free, as itself affirmative, so that this limit within man, which goes as far as evil, is a nothingness for the infinity of spirit. Spirit can manage things so that what has happened has not happened. Action does indeed remain in the memory, but spirit rids itself of it—the finite, evil in general, is negated. [36]

However, this text does not sufficiently stress the pantragedism that we still find in the *Phenomenology*. Hegel's optimism is

35. Royce, *Lectures on Modern Idealism* (New Haven, Conn., 1919), p. 208.
36. *Philosophie der Religion*, part 3, "Die absolute Religion," pp. 172–73.

not that of Leibniz, for whom evil is only a partial point of view which disappears in the heart of the whole. Infinite spirit itself is not without finitude and negativity. At Jena, Hegel wrote that "the infinite is just as uneasy as the finite" and that without "the calvary of history, spirit would be lifeless solitude" (*PE*, II, 313; *PG*, 564; *PM*, 808).

God is not posited beyond human history as a transcendent judge; rather, human history itself is a revelation of God. Starting with the thesis of the remission of sins, a new field of experiences opens to us, a new dimension of human experience to explore: this will be the theme of religion. Absolute spirit *appears* to us, and it is the apparition of absolute spirit that the phenomenology of religion will study.

3 / Religion: Mysticism or Humanism?

HEGEL DEVOTES A LONG CHAPTER of the *Phenomenology* to religion. Apropos of religion, he speaks of art; he thinks that a religion in the form of art, as a moment of the development of religion, corresponds to Greek antiquity. It is only much later that he separates art from religion and conceives absolute spirit in three stages: art, religion, and philosophy.[1] Religion precedes absolute knowledge; it is already the portrayal of speculative truth, but within a particular element, that of representation or portrayal (*Vorstellung*). For Hegel religion is not what it was for the Enlightenment, an abstract deism, or what it was for Kant and even for Fichte, an extension of moral life, a postulate of practical reason. The moral idealism of Kant and Fichte had largely been surpassed by the writers of the time. Its insufficiency had been felt as much by Schiller in the aesthetic realm as by Schleiermacher in the religious realm. We have seen that in the *Phenomenology* Hegel criticizes a "moral world view," but to understand the difference between Hegel's conception of religion and that of Kant, we would have to go back to Hegel's early writings, to the time of Bern and especially Frankfurt. Whereas Kant tried to purify religion of every positive or his-

1. Even in *The Philosophy of Fine Art*, the distinction between art and religion is not very clear for Hegel. On the first expression of absolute spirit, as art, religion, philosophy, see "Differenz," p. 91. Concerning the intuition of the absolute, Hegel develops the thought of Schelling and speaks of art, religion, and speculation.

torical element and to conserve its essentials in a practical philosophy, by seeing a schema of pure morality in the person of Christ, for example, Hegel, who several times rewrote a *Life of Jesus*, attempts to integrate the *positive* elements of religion into philosophical speculation. For him, religion is specifically different from morality. As the *religion of a people*, it expresses a certain unique world view, and the contingent and historical aspects of this religion should not be neglected. "Man necessarily links his thought of the eternal with the contingency of his thought."[2] The consciousness that a people has of itself in history is what a religion can express, and as such it goes beyond the temporal circumstances that presided over its birth. Already for the early Hegel, religion is as much speculative thought as ethic. There is a "spirit of Hellenism," a "spirit of Judaism," and a "spirit of Christianity," and to these different spirits correspond different religions in history. The abstract religion of the Enlightenment, or Kant's "religion within the limits of simple reason," do not account for the originality manifested in religion, for the inspiration expressed in this self-consciousness of spirit.[3]

It was through this reflection on religion—which is not particularly mystical for Hegel, but which does not yet know itself as reflection—that his own thought was formed. Under the influence of his codisciple and friend Hölderlin, he sought to recover the spiritual meaning of Greek fantasy and myths, the religious sense of Greek tragedy. Like the Schiller of the *Letters on the Aesthetic Education of Man*, he saw in beauty the reconciliation to which Kant aspired, but which his analytic method never allowed him to encounter. "Beauty and only beauty can show that passivity does not exclude activity, that matter does not exclude form, nor limitation infinity."[4] Greek paganism had an intuition of humanity which was expressed in its gods, and its religion was essentially a work of art. We will come upon this conception again in the *Phenomenology* when Hegel in-

2. Hegel, *Early Theological Writings*, p. 171.
3. We could condense the whole problem which Hegel put to himself in his early works into the following formula: What *value* should be attributed to *positivity*, that is, to the historical, to *experience*? This *positivity*, which is a blot on the light of reason or of human nature, is sometimes considered by Hegel as an external determination, an obstacle to freedom, and sometimes as an essential moment of life. In Frankfurt, where *positivity* became a *destiny*, it took on its signification.
4. Schiller, *Werke*, XII, 102.

troduces, between the natural religion suitable to the peoples of the Orient and Christianity, an art-religion (*Kunstreligion*) which Schleiermacher had vainly attempted to make explicit.

Schleiermacher's *On Religion* is a work contemporary with Hegel's early works. These lectures on religion led in the same direction as Schiller's *Aesthetic Letters;* they contributed to orienting transcendental idealism toward an aesthetic and religious idealism. Schleiermacher's tone is completely different from Hegel's: it is the tone not of a philosopher reflecting on religion, but of a prophet seeking to communicate his spiritual enthusiasm to others. The preface to the *Phenomenology,* which alludes several times to Schleiermacher's work, contains a critique of this prophetic tone. But Hegel no more avoided his influence than had Schelling. He speaks of Schleiermacher in "Differenz," and in his Jena article rates him more highly than Jacobi. Schleiermacher claims a special position for religion within transcendental philosophy. Kant and Fichte reduced religion to a pure moral faith, neglecting its speculative content and failing to see that it perhaps contained an original synthesis of metaphysics (theoretical philosophy) and morality. "To want to reduce religion to what it is not, not to respect its originality, its specific meaning, is to show the greatest scorn for religion." Kant, who was so careful to distinguish between areas, ignored the area of religion which is "an intuition of the universe (*Universum*)." This intuition, which is the inspired expression of a community, depends on creative imagination which is, as Fichte saw, the highest faculty of man. "You must know that the imagination is the most originary element of man and that everything outside imagination is merely a reflection on it." The different points of view of man toward the universe, his way of experiencing the presence of the infinite in the finite, depend on the direction of the imagination. Schleiermacher makes a remark concerning theism which Hegel could have made: "It is surely an illusion to seek the infinite outside the finite, the thing opposed outside what it is opposed to." [5] When Hegel speaks of religious thought developing in the "element of representation," for example, he is perhaps influenced by Schleiermacher. But if Schleiermacher is careful to characterize the originality of religion in relation to morality and theoretical philosophy, his thought is much less clear when dealing with

5. Schleiermacher, *On Religion: Speeches to its Cultured Despisers,* trans. John Oman (New York, 1958), p. 125.

the limits of aesthetic intuition and religious intuition. For him, religion and art are like "friendly souls that sense their affinities." [6] He speaks of religion as if it were music: "Religious feelings, like sacred music, should accompany all man's actions." [7] Religion transforms the simple music of life into a harmony. He refers to priests as virtuosos, artists of religion, who communicate to the faithful the intuition of the universe in which moral faith and speculative knowledge mutually surpass each other. [8]

Hegel's thinking on religion, such as it appears in the *Phenomenology*, is far from these prophetic speeches, but it too sees in religion a higher form of spirit. Religion is *spirit's self-consciousness*. However, it is not yet absolute knowledge, for this comprehension of spirit by spirit is a comprehension in the element of representation, and that is doubtless why art is a moment of every religion and more particularly is characteristic of a certain form of religion. Hegel's hierarchy of natural religion, religion in the form of art, and revealed religion (Christian religion) was perhaps suggested by Schleiermacher. But whereas the latter is inclined to elevate religion above the philosophical thought of religion, or at least tends to confuse them, Hegel merely sees in religion, as in art, the prefigurative representation of philosophical thought. Absolute knowledge rises above religion, which indeed presents true content. But since it is in the form of a representation or portrait, this content *appears* to the religious community as an *alien* content. "The religious community does not yet possess the consciousness of what it is" (*PE*, II, 289; *PG*, 547; *PM*, 783). In Hegel's work, philosophy appears enriched by all that religion has to add and particularly by Christianity, of which philosophy claims to be the interpreter. But by raising knowledge above faith, concept above religious representation, doesn't Hegel singularly reduce the scope of religion, doesn't he himself open the path to an interpretation of religion which, like that of Feuerbach, preserves religion only to negate its essential elements?

6. *Ibid.*, p. 140.
7. *Ibid.*, pp. 51–52.
8. In his *Von Kant bis Hegel* (Tübingen, 1921, 1924), Kroner traces particularly well the evolution of German idealism, from Kant's moral idealism to an aesthetic and religious idealism, which was clearly conceived of by Hegel starting with this period, and then to the thought of this idealism as speculative idealism.

RELIGION IN THE *Phenomenology*

RELIGION, HEGEL TELLS US, was already present in the previous figures of consciousness. How could it be otherwise, given that the experience of consciousness, even if it does not know it, is always an experience of spiritual substance? *Understanding* has discovered a suprasensuous interiority beyond sensuous phenomena, but this interiority was lacking in the self of consciousness. *Self-consciousness,* as abstract self-consciousness, appeared to us as unhappy consciousness which projected its ideal of freedom beyond itself and which aspired to recover in objectivity the unity of itself with immutable consciousness (which for self-consciousness is only a *subjective aspiration*). Finally, apropos of *spirit,* we saw a religion of the lower world in which destiny was the annihilating night while the self, reduced to nothingness, had not yet been raised to true universality. In the *faith of the world of culture* or in the *religion of the Enlightenment,* as in the religion which extends the *moral world view,* consciousness knew a kind of religious experience as its own limits. And yet, Hegel tells us, until now we have regarded religion only from the point of view of consciousness, "but absolute essence in-and-for-itself, the *self-consciousness of spirit,* has not been manifested in these forms." If we believe this passage, then what characterizes the new field of experience into which we are entering is that it will be the (phenomenal?) manifestation of "the self-consciousness of spirit" (*PE,* II, 203; *PG,* 473; *PM,* 685).[9]

This is the formula, ambiguous on more than one count, that we must attempt to explain. It will allow us to understand how religion can by itself constitute a series of original experiences, a particular history within actual history, and will lead us to what we feel is the essential problem in this dialectic of religion: the relation between finite consciousness, which portrays to itself the divine or the infinite spirit, and this infinite spirit itself. In other words, we will have to ask whether we are

9. In this passage, Hegel summarizes all prior moments of consciousness from the point of view of religion. But in those moments, it was only a question of *consciousness* of absolute essence, not yet of the *self-consciousness* of this essence.

still dealing with a *phenomenology* or whether with the section on religion we are not already entering a *noumenology* (if we may be allowed to use this term formed on the model of "phenomenology").

"Religion is the self-consciousness of absolute spirit as portrayed by finite spirit." [10] That religion is the self-consciousness of spirit puts it in contrast to all prior experience, which was only experience for us, that is, for the philosopher, but which did not manifest itself in that way for phenomenal consciousness. In the first three sections of the *Phenomenology* (consciousness, self-consciousness, and reason) we have followed the development of an individual consciousness. With spirit, the object of experience became "a world," and in-itself this world was indeed spiritual substance; but it was not yet the consciousness of itself as spirit. It did not exist for its own self in the *element of self-knowledge*. This is why Hegel characterizes it as spirit in relation to religion—that is, spirit as immediate spirit which is not yet consciousness of spirit (*PE*, II, 207; *PG*, 476; *PM*, 689)—and also says: "Those figures of spirit which we have considered so far: true spirit, spirit alien to itself, and self-certain spirit, together constitute the consciousness of the spirit (and not yet its self-consciousness) which by opposing itself to its world does not recognize itself in that world" (*PE*, II, 205; *PG*, 475; *PM*, 687). Only at the end of its development, with *Gewissen* and the beautiful soul, does spirit attain consciousness of itself as its supreme truth. At that point it presents itself to us as "the Dasein of the I's which are expanded to duality, each I remaining equal to itself and in its complete alienation and in its complete opposite possessing self-certainty. It is God manifesting himself (*erscheinende*) in the midst of those who know themselves as pure knowledge" (*PE*, II, 200; *PG*, 472; *PM*, 679). Thus consciousness no longer comprehends a world or a beyond-itself which is always displaced, as in the moral world view, but rather spirit comprehends spirit, and this pure recognition of self in the other is the self-consciousness of spirit. Spirit which has developed itself from substance to subject has for itself become what it was only for us: it has become self-knowledge, and that is the starting point for a new reflection on itself. This

---

10. R. Kroner, *Von Kant bis Hegel*, II, 403. To resolve the difficulty we have just pointed out, Kroner adds, "But finite or phenomenal spirit itself is but the becoming of absolute spirit, absolute spirit becoming conscious of itself."

reflection is characterized at the end of the section on spirit by the term "God": "It is God manifesting himself in the midst of them." This *manifestation* of the divine has a unique history; it is the source of a particular phenomenology within phenomenology. The words of Saint Bonaventure could appropriately be applied to it: "itinerarium mentis in Deum."

However, we may ask why the self-consciousness of absolute spirit gives rise to a phenomenological dialectic which in turn is presented as *a series of imperfect figures.* If spirit has become *self-knowledge as spirit,* haven't we reached the end point of the phenomenological development? Spirit has finally managed to discover itself, it *exists* and at the same time it is *for-itself,* it no longer has a truth that is contraposed to its certainty. Rather, within this duality, which is always essential to the concept of spirit, the two terms are no longer alien to each other and each is spirit for the other. However, we must note that "the difference between actual spirit and spirit that knows itself as spirit or between spirit as consciousness and spirit as self-consciousness" (*PE*, II, 210; *PG*, 479; *PM*, 692) is not yet turned in on spirit. For those who have grasped the meaning of the dialectical reconciliation between finite spirit and infinite spirit, this difference is suppressed; but it is not immediately suppressed, when the concept of religion is merely posited.

Difference between consciousness and self-consciousness of spirit

Spirit that knows spirit is simultaneously self-consciousness and consciousness; it portrays itself to itself, and it is this *portrait of self* which is susceptible of being transformed into religion *until it is perfectly adequate and equivalent to what it claims to express.* The object which consciousness contemplates is always spirit and no longer an alien world (it is in this sense that religion is self-consciousness of spirit), but at the same time it is an object of consciousness, an object whose *form* is not immediately the complete revelation of *essence.* The different religions, which are also like aspects of a single religion, differ only by the form in which they present to consciousness the essence that is common to them, the self-consciousness of spirit.

The series of diverse religions which are produced also portray merely the diverse aspects of a single religion, or better, of every specific religion, and the portrayals that seem to distinguish one actual religion from another are to be found in each. But at the same time diversity should be seen as a diversity of religion. Indeed, as spirit is located in the difference between its consciousness and its self-consciousness, its movement has the purpose of suppressing [*aufheben*] this fundamental difference and of giving the form of self-consciousness to the figure that is the object of consciousness (*PE,* II, 212; *PG,* 481; *PM,* 696–97).

With religion, we have indeed reached a new realm of human experience. Spirit portrays itself to itself, it is for-itself self-knowledge instead of simply being the consciousness of its world as was the case in prior experiences. "The immediate unity of spirit with itself is the foundation, or pure consciousness, within which consciousness disintegrates" (*PE,* II, 210; *PG,* 479; *PM,* 693).[11] Henceforth the essence of spirit is that self-knowledge which constitutes absolute spirit, for spirit is absolute only insofar as it knows itself; its manifestation, however, is still imperfect in that it appears to itself under the veil of a form inadequate to this essence. But again, why does it appear to itself in this imperfect form, that is, by representing itself to itself as object? Is it not directly in its object what it is in its essence? Why is this necessity fulfilled only in manifest or revealed (*offenbar*) religion, in which the very form of the object of religious self-consciousness is identical (except for the element of representation which must still be transcended) with spiritual self-consciousness? Why this *progressive revelation,* which is at the same time a unique elaboration of religious consciousness, a consciousness which is always that of a spiritual community (a particular historical people or a religious community properly speaking)?

First, we can say that this progression is always necessary in Hegel's philosophy. "It is only the concept of religion that has been posited" (*PE,* II, 210; *PG,* 479; *PM,* 692). Spirit is now immediately self-knowledge, but this immediateness is always an origin; spirit must again become what it immediately is, it must *elaborate* itself in this new element of experience, the

11. We might say more simply: The new element that is reached is *spirit's self-knowledge.* But, *in this element,* spirit again poses itself as consciousness; it creates itself as the *figure* of itself and this *figuration,* which is more or less adequate to the element which is the foundation of this representation, transforms itself to the point of reaching what it *ought* to represent. At the end of this dialectic, spirit, knowing itself, will be, *for-itself,* what it at first was only *immediately.*

form of this self-knowledge. Thus it is not only *posited for us,* but it itself *posits itself.* This too general answer includes within it a particular answer which is more interesting and on which Hegel insists in his introduction to the dialectic of religion.

Spirit of religion is still *spirit in the world;* this difference, which we have surpassed ever since the thought of reconciliation (the dialectic of the forgiveness of sins), is not yet transcended for phenomenal consciousness. Actual spirit—for example, Eastern spirit, Greek spirit, the spirit of modern peoples—lives in a world, and as spirit within religion it is also spirit's self-knowledge. This spirit of religion presupposes all the moments of spirit (consciousness, self-consciousness, reason, immediate spirit); it is their simple totality or their absolute self. To the extent that they are related to religion, these moments are not represented in time; they become the attributes of spiritual substance which was their common profundity, the in-itself into which they return. But now this substance has made its appearance as a *whole,* and this totality is immanent in religion and in every particular religion. The dialectic of religion is thus *positive* (in relation to previous dialectics). The phenomenology of religion is no longer the phenomenology of consciousness rising to the certainty that spirit is the only truth. It is spirit itself which, having arrived at self-knowledge, seeks an expression adequate to its essence. Besides, only this history is truly a history, since "only the whole is in Time." It is this spirit which, as a totality, rises to absolute self-knowledge; and this movement, as the development of the whole, is a temporal movement. The succession of religions, of total spirit, takes on a historical form which is the expression of its internal development.

This historical development corresponds to the relation of actual spirit and spirit of religion.[12] A particular religion, although it presupposes every moment of spirit, possesses a certain determination which expresses through its consciousness *the spirit of the world which has in it its self-consciousness.* "For example, the incarnation of God presented in Eastern religion has no truth since its actual spirit lacks reconciliation" (*PE,* II, 214; *PG,* 482; *PM,* 698). Every religion does indeed contain representations which are to be found in all the others, but what counts is the one which authentically corresponds to its

12. "Actual spirit" is the same thing that we have called "spirit in the world." The spirit of religion is total spirit, as opposed to the spirit in the world which is characterized by a particular determination.

actual spirit, *the one it takes on* and in which this actual spirit truly knows itself. The history of religions, that is, of the self-knowledge of spirit, is simultaneously the history of the world spirit *which in religion knows itself as spirit.* Here we again come on the conception Hegel had of religion in his early works, where he saw in religion the mirror of a certain real spirit—Eastern spirit, Greek spirit, spirit of Judaism, spirit of Christianity—but in addition we find that the development of this self-knowledge is organized. Indeed, the foundation of religion is the self-knowledge of spirit; the end point of its development must therefore be this integral knowledge of spirit as spirit, a knowledge in which difference, which corresponds to a certain history of the world spirit, is overcome. At that moment, spirit knows itself in the figure of spirit, and there is a complete reconciliation between actual spirit which serves as its object and spirit of religion, or between consciousness and self-consciousness. The object by means of which spirit portrays itself to itself (its consciousness) is in the figure of spirit (it is identical to this self-consciousness or essence that is the basis of all religion); it is no longer simply a *symbolic object.*

Let us state this more simply. Our life in the world and our religious consciousness are distinct; hence our religious consciousness is still imperfect and our life in the world is still without true reconciliation. Our religious consciousness is imperfect because it uses the world in which we live as a sign or a symbol of absolute spirit. It is through the intermediary of this object—which in religion no longer has the character of pure objectivity, of a negation of self-consciousness—that spirit portrays itself to itself. But this object, the actual spirit of history, is simultaneously treated as a *symbol* (which does not respect its full rights), and grasped as being inadequate to what *it claims to represent.* We come back to the difference we started from, that between consciousness and self-consciousness. Spirit knows itself as spirit, but consciousness, by means of which spirit represents itself to itself as object, is inadequate to this absolute self-knowledge, and must move forward until this object has become the figure of spirit itself, knowing itself as spirit. This object, as world spirit, actual spirit, is not yet reconciled with its essence, infinite spirit.

To the extent that the spirit in religion represents itself to itself, it is indeed consciousness and the actuality included in religion is the figure and the clothing of its portrait. But the full right of actuality is not respected in this portrait: its right to be not merely a suit of clothes, but a free and independent Dasein. Conversely, since this actuality is not fulfilled within itself, it is a determinate figure which does not attain what it should represent, that is, spirit conscious of itself. In order for the figure of spirit to be able to express spirit conscious of itself, the figure should be nothing other than that spirit and it should make itself manifest to itself, or be actually what it is in its essence (*PE*, II, 206; *PG*, 475–76; *PM*, 688).

Thus the highest form of religion will be *revealed* religion, because then spirit will be given over to itself as it is in essence, because the actual incarnation of God, his death and resurrection in the community, will be the very Dasein of spirit knowing what it is; and at that particular moment, the world spirit or finite spirit will be reconciled with infinite spirit. It is this reconciliation, which at the starting point of this dialectic was merely ours, which will have become the object of consciousness. Actual spirit must ultimately become identical with absolute spirit and absolute spirit must know itself in actual spirit as absolute spirit.[13]

Difference and unity of the two dialectics

The dialectic of religion fulfills two different requirements, which must merge. On the one hand it is the *internal* development of a self-knowledge of spirit which portrays to itself what it is as spirit and, at first knowing itself immediately, must progress to the point of giving its very form to its self-expression. "Spirit is truly self-knowledge only by making itself into what it is." On the other hand it is the *reflection* of a certain world spirit which finds an ideal expression of itself in its religion. These two dialectics are but one because the progression of world spirit and that of the self-knowledge of spirit are correlative. The world spirit is the coming to be of the self-knowl-

13. Hegel's presentation is obscure, but the idea is simple: at the end of the dialectic of religion there will be no more surpassing; spirit in the world will be absolute spirit itself; there will no longer be either symbolism or transcendence. Spirit will contemplate itself, in its authentic figure, in its history. *Everything will be revealed.* However, even in revealed religion, there will still be a certain surpassing, due to the "element of representation," and that is why actual reconciliation occurs only in absolute knowledge.

edge of spirit as spirit. But in fact a religion does not go beyond the actual spirit that determines it. As Hegel says in the *Encyclopaedia,* "The correlative of an evil God, a natural God, is evil, natural men, men without freedom. The pure concept of God, spiritual God, has as its correlative free spirit. The portrait that man has of God corresponds to that which he has of himself and of his freedom." Thus the fact that religion is only a part of human existence and that the other part is the life of man in the world means that religion is imperfect. Religion is that part which serves man as a symbol for his consciousness and which determines his particular spirit.

General dialectic of religion

The general dialectic of religion constitutes a progressive *revelation* of spirit to itself. The first moment of this revelation is *natural religion,* in which spirit knows itself immediately. Thus the object which serves spirit as a portrayal of itself to itself has the form of being in general (consciousness) or of the master as opposed to the slave (immediate self-consciousness).

> Of course what constitutes the plenitude of this being is neither sensation, nor variegated matter, nor any other one-sided moment, goal, or determination; rather, this plenitude is spirit. This being is known by itself as all truth and all actuality. Yet this plenitude is not therefore equal to its figure; spirit, as essence, is not equal to its consciousness (*PE,* II, 210; *PG,* 479; *PM,* 693).

This form of immediateness is not appropriate for spirit; it corresponds to a God-substance and not to a God-subject. That is why the second moment of this revelation is that in which spirit knows itself in the figure of suppressed naturalness or of self; "this figure is thus *esthetic religion* because it is raised to the form of self through the production of consciousness, so that consciousness contemplates its operation or self in its object" (*PE,* II, 211; *PG,* 480; *PM,* 694). The world spirit reflected in this religion is the spirit of the Greek city, the Greek spirit. Spirit has surpassed the abstract immediateness of mere nature. In its own terms it has become finite self, the self which is a work of art but which lacks the depth of the first moment. These two moments are reconciled in a third moment: "self is just as much immediate self as immediateness is self." The Christian God, truly man and truly God, whose history is actual, replaces the Greek gods who portray the self as an objective work of art. Then spirit knows itself as in-and-for-itself, and because it is portrayed as it is in-and-for-itself, it is *manifest (revealed) religion*. This development of religion is the coming to be of the absolute self-consciousness of spirit which, though at first immediate, raises itself up to itself by the movement of its own mediation, or reveals its depth.

Phenomenology or noumenology

We come back to our initial definition: "Religion is the self-consciousness of absolute spirit as *portrayed* by finite spirit." The *portrayal* of absolute spirit by a people or a community in history is the phenomenal aspect of religion—which is what allows it to enter into a phenomenology or a study of appearances —but on the other hand the fact that it is a *self-consciousness of absolute spirit* would tend to make it a noumenology. Insofar as the dialectic of religion is a response to the development of world spirit which progresses to knowledge of spirit, it reverts to phenomenology, for each of its moments is an original phenomenon which is inadequate to the total truth; but insofar as it is an internal dialectic, a development of the knowledge of oneself and like a revelation of spirit to itself, it resembles a development of God and a real noumenology. Can these two aspects be reconciled? Do they not pose the fundamental problem of Hegelian theology? How can the viewpoint of finite spirit, that of man, be reconciled with the viewpoint (if we can use that term) of infinite spirit, that of God? Is religion the portrait that a finite spirit, man, draws of God, or is it the knowledge that God has of himself? For Hegel, the solution to this problem, however ambiguous it may be, is not in doubt. Religion is simultaneously the one and the other, and that is indeed what is indicated to us by what we took as our point of departure, "the thought of reconciliation," of the descent of infinite spirit and the elevation of finite spirit. Finite spirit, phenomenal spirit, is itself nothing other than absolute spirit becoming conscious of itself; that is why the dialectic of this relation dominates the entire history of religion. Even before absolute knowledge, religion is already the moment in which phenomenology is transformed into noumenology, in which absolute spirit reveals itself as such, *makes itself manifest to itself in manifesting itself to man.*[14] Absolute spirit, God, is not beyond the knowledge religion has of it, it is not a lifeless truth situated outside its manifestation; rather, its essence is to manifest itself in time and by so manifesting itself to manifest itself to itself in its eternity. It is self-knowledge in and through man, who thus participates in divine life. This revelation is complete only in Christianity, in which spirit is truly known and knows itself as it is. In all other religions the manifestation of spirit is incomplete and symbolic (which is the same thing) and that is why in those religions *man* is not truly reconciled with *God.*

The problem is thus that of *the unity of man and God,* of the finite and the infinite. In the *Encyclopaedia,* Hegel writes more clearly: "God is God only insofar as he knows himself; but in addition his self-knowledge is the self-knowledge that he has as man; and the knowledge that man has of God is continuous with the knowledge that he has of himself in God."[15] Thus the problem seems to be displaced; it becomes a problem of knowing whether we have to do with a *mysticism* whose sources are to be found in Meister Eckhart and especially in Böhme, or with a kind of religion of humanity, an *anthropology* such as will be found in Feuerbach. Mysticism or humanism?

Hegel liked to quote this text of Meister Eckhart: "The eye with which God sees me is also the eye with which I see him, my eye and his eye are but one; if God did not exist, I would not exist; if I did not exist, he would not exist." It is even more in the German mystic and theologian Böhme that we find the most extensive foreshadowing of Hegelian thought. In a passage from his *Lectures on the History of Philosophy,* Hegel opposes Böhme to Spinoza. For Spinoza, God is merely substance; he is not conceived as subjectivity, as subject, *Moïte.*[16] On the other hand, what Böhme is seeking is God as personal life, as subject and self-knowledge. During his entire life, the German mystic sought a reflection of God within himself, in the history of his subjectivity. For Paracelsus, man was a "microcosm," for Böhme a

14. One might say, with Jakob Böhme, "Mysterium magnum revelans seipsum."

15. *Encyclopaedia,* p. 481. We can see the opposition between Hegel and Schelling, who said, "The father of all things is in his unity as an inaccessible fortress" (*SW,* I, 4, 302).

16. Hegel, *Werke* (1844 ed.), XV, 273. In the *Phenomenology,* Hegel quotes Böhme concerning "the wrath of God" (*PE,* II, 279; *PG,* 539; *PM,* 773).

"microtheos." The *mysterium magnum* is the desire and will to manifest his mystery. "Böhme's entire theology," Boutroux has written, "is an analysis of the conditions of the possibility of absolute person." One must indeed say *person*. God is not the abyss (*Ungrund*), the unconscious source of everything that is; he is self-knowledge. He generates himself within himself and discovers himself. He is simultaneously time and eternity. His *Moïte* is already what Hegel calls *concept*, absolute self.

It is impossible to accuse Hegel of pantheism in the vulgar sense of the term in which "pantheism" makes one term of the opposition disappear into the other. Self-consciousness in God supposes finitude, and finitude in turn must be reconciled with the divine infinite, must surpass itself into infinity. For Hegel, God is the truth that knows itself; the self-knowledge that man has of God cannot exist outside divine life. But if Hegel rethinks mysticism, he is no mystic akin to those we have cited. We may therefore ask whether the life of God, his self-knowledge, will not be expressed completely in the knowledge that man has of himself as "universal self-consciousness." Is Feuerbach's interpretation—which absorbs God into man instead of absorbing man into God—the consequence of Hegel's philosophy of religion?

As Feuerbach says,

> Man, not Hegel's absolute spirit, is the center of religion. It is not I, but religion which adores man, even though it—or rather theology—doesn't want to admit it; it is religion itself which says: God is man, man is God. It is not I, but religion which refuses to admit an abstract God, a pure *ens rationis*; and the proof of it is that in religion God becomes man.[17]

But if Hegel does seem to lean toward this humanism, he rejects the complete reduction of God to man. He always maintained that to some extent man necessarily had to surpass himself. Man's greatest torment—a form of unhappy consciousness—is to be reduced to himself alone, to have absorbed the divine

17. Feuerbach, *The Essence of Christianity*, trans. George Eliot (New York, 1957): "God become man merely reveals man become God" (p. 335). "The consciousness that man has of God is the consciousness that he has of himself, but man does not know that his consciousness of God is his consciousness of himself. Religion is the first, although indirect, consciousness that man has of himself" (p. 281). Man, Hegel also says, is the spiritual hearth of the universe (*universum*).

into himself. If God himself is dead, what remains? A profound thought which foreshadows the themes, for example, of Nietzsche and Heidegger on the absence of God and on man's necessity for transcending himself.

Between this mysticism in which the life of humanity is a moment of divine life, of divine self-consciousness, and this philosophical anthropology which reduces God to man, what is Hegel's choice? He is certainly not a mystic and although he interprets and takes up for himself the formulas of certain mystics, he already sees in them the image of his own dialectic. Nor is his solution an anthropology in Feuerbach's sense. Hegel speaks of the *universal divine man* who succeeded the *God-man*, but his thought remains equivocal and opens the way to the diverse interpretations of his followers. Absolute spirit surpasses finite spirit and yet exists only through finite spirit, even if it is true that only in this reconciliation (which supposes both separation and unity) is spirit authentically absolute because it becomes absolute. As a whole, reading the pages of the *Phenomenology* that Hegel devotes to religion, along with the discussion of art, suggests a human interpretation of religion rather than an absorption of human life into divine life.[18]

I. NATURAL RELIGION

THE DEVELOPMENT OF RELIGION reproduces as a whole the general movement of the *Phenomenology*. Natural religion corresponds to consciousness; in it spirit appears to itself in the form of immediate being. Art-religion corresponds to self-consciousness, and in it spirit manifests itself to itself in the form of works of art. Revealed religion corresponds to reason, for in it spirit appears as it is in-and-for-itself. At the same time,

18. Hegel's effort to overcome the major Christian dualism, that of the *beyond* [*au-delà*] and the here-below [*en-deça*] appears to us as essentially characteristic of Hegelian thought. Isn't the aim of the dialectic of religion to arrive at a complete reconciliation of *spirit in the world* with *absolute spirit*? But then there is no longer any transcendence aside from historical development. In these conditions, Hegelian thought—despite certain formulations—appears to us quite distant from religion. The entire phenomenology appears as a heroic effort to reduce "vertical transcendence" to a "horizontal transcendence."

as we have seen above, each of these moments coincides with a real spirit in history. Hegel's erudition allows him to fill in this general framework, particularly in his last *Lectures on the Philosophy of Religion*. In the *Phenomenology* only the framework is given, and the most interesting and most concrete developments have to do with art-religion and the Christian religion.

In natural religion, spirit makes natural objects divine. It is the religion of light (that of the Parsis), then the plant and animal religions (the first Indian religions), and finally the spirit of natural religion, still operating instinctively, constructing pyramids and obelisks: it is an artisan before being an artist. But here the figure of the divine begins to lose the character of natural immediateness which it had at the beginning. Nature has already unconsciously been surpassed and spirit begins to recognize itself in a work of art. In its immediate form, spirit appears to itself as the light of the rising sun. The existence given to sensuous consciousness is not spirit, but this existence serves as a symbol for spirit, a symbol which is not the result of a reflection. The immediate certainty spirit has of its being merges here with the no-less immediate certainty of sensuous consciousness. If the depths of self-consciousness make up the night of essence, its revelation is the immediate manifestation of the sensuous world in the forms created by the dawning light. The absolute appears as "the Eastern light which contains and fulfills everything and is conserved in its formless substantiveness." As yet, this pure I is but a substance in which nothing attains consistency and reflects in on itself. "Its determinations are only attributes which do not succeed in attaining independence, but merely remain names of the One with many names" (*PE*, II, 215–16; *PG*, 484; *PM*, 700). In the movement of spirit, this Eastern *substance* must become *subject;* thus the sun rises in the East and sets in the West. But we are still quite far from this setting of the substance into itself and its transformation into subject conscious of itself as subject. In its first form this substance is the negation of the finite; only what has been sublimated shows through in creation. The actual spirit that finds its portrayal here is that of *Oriental despotism.* The infinite and the finite oppose each other without being able to be reconciled; the absolute takes the form of the all-powerful master whereas man has the form of the slave.

This "tumultuous life" which absorbs everything into it is, however, negativity *in-itself,* and it must appear as such in the

midst of the finite, which "borrows substance from its substance." The perception of natural forms, which are then divinized in their immediate "being-for-itself," is substituted for
immediate spiritual certainty. Infinity disintegrates into "an
innumerable plurality of spirits, some weaker and some stronger,
some poorer, some richer" (*PE*, II, 216; *PG*, 485; *PM*, 702). The
being-for-itself within natural figures is not yet spiritual self. In
order authentically to portray this movement of the divine in
the figure of man elaborated by Greek sculpture, spirit must
have raised itself above nature and have transcended nature
through working on it. The absolute, in this primitive figure of
being-for-itself, is at first imagined in plants, then in animals.
That is pantheism in the precise meaning of the term, that is,
the religion in which finite things are God. "The innocence of a
religion of flowers which is merely the representation of self
without the self, turns into the seriousness of a life engaged in
struggle, into the guilt of animal religion" (*PE*, II, 216; *PG*, 485;
PM, 702). The actual spirit which here finds its portrayal is
that of unsocial tribes, always struggling against each other.
The animal figures symbolize these spirits of elemental groups
which have no spiritual life other than that which the struggle
for the recognition of their independence gives them. These
tribes "fight each other to the death and come to the consciousness of particular species of animals as if of their essences."
In effect, they are nothing but "one animal life separating itself
from some other and conscious of itself without universality."
Just as, in the development of natural self-consciousness, the
truth of the struggle for life or death was the formation of the
slave who raised himself to a higher self-consciousness through
labor and service, so here "above these spirits of animals which
are only tearing each other apart among themselves, the artisan,
whose operation is not only negative but also peaceful and
positive, obtains the upper hand" (*PE*, II, 217; *PG*, 485; *PM*,
703). Self produces itself and elaborates itself in the thing it
produces, but at first this production of the self is unconscious.
Similarly, understanding conceived of itself within nature, but
did so unknowingly. This moment is that of the artisan spirit
and not yet that of the artist, "since the artisan has not grasped
the thought of himself." "It is a type of instinctive work like that
of bees constructing their hives" (*PE*, II, 218; *PG*, 486; *PM*,
704). Egypt, which at this date Hegel knew mainly through
Herodotus and the descriptions of the Greeks in general, corresponds particularly to the religion of the artisan. The result

of these abstract productions, inspired less by nature than by the forms of understanding, will be spirit's discovery, in its labors, of spirit. Unconscious work only progressively attains the portrayal of self. In the Pyramids, the self is deceased spirit, which remains internal and hidden, or else, as external self, it is the dawning light which gives the works their meanings.

However, the temple and the statue are elaborated gradually through the division and coordination of architecture and sculpture. The first portrays the in-itself of spirit, the other its for-itself. Architecture progresses from abstract forms to more living forms. The dialectic of the column mixes plant life and the regular form of understanding. This life is reproduced by the artisan as animal figures are in the first rough sculptures. Spirit is thus raised above what it reproduces. Animal form becomes "the hieroglyph of another signification, that is, of a thought" (*PE*, II, 220; *PG*, 488; *PM*, 706). Slowly human form is separated from animal form. But the work of art does not contain its meaning within itself; it is unable to express its inner meaning to the outer world; it lacks "language, the element in which is present the very meaning that fulfills it." This language is still too external, as in the statues of Memnon, or too internal, as in the black stone whose pure externality simply states that it hides an infinitely profound meaning.

The internal and the external must be joined in a work which is the daughter of spirit.

These monstrosities in figure, word, and operation are resolved into a spiritual figure, an exterior figure which has gone into itself, an interior figure which by itself exteriorizes itself; and they are resolved by themselves into a thought, which is Dasein begetting itself and preserving its figure in conformity to thought, a transparent Dasein. Spirit is an artist (*PE*, II, 221–22; *PG*, 489; *PM*, 708).

II. Religion in the Form of Art

The few pages of the *Phenomenology* that Hegel devoted to the introduction of religion in the form of art are particularly beautiful and suggestive, despite a certain heaviness of expression. Art-religion is the ethical spirit's self-knowledge, the very spirit we studied under the name of true spirit. This real spirit is no longer the spirit of Oriental despotism or of un-

social tribes still lost in the life of nature, but rather the substantive spirit of a human polis which has surpassed the sav-
agery of nature and which has not yet reached the abstraction
and the torments of subjectivity. It is the moment of "splendid
individuality." The Greek city appears as a self-conscious work,
"a universal, individualized, and concrete spirit." One might say
that nature is immediately the adequate expression of the
spiritual self, whereas the self has not abstracted itself from its
substance. The mores of the Greek city are the work of each one
and of everyone. The populace which lives in this substance is a
free people. This happy equilibrium is that of a humanity which
is perfect in its finitude, but it is an unstable equilibrium, the
youth of world spirit. Before this equilibrium, man had been
crushed by nature and did not discover himself as man; after it,
man will surpass himself and will have within himself a consciousness of his infinite disquiet. Between natural religion and
the Christian religion there thus surges up this art-religion which
is the self-consciousness of spirit as *finite humanity*.

But this self-consciousness on the part of ethical spirit is
already beyond that spirit; it is its apex and at the same time the
beginning of its decline. To know oneself, to come to consciousness of self, is to raise oneself above one's being. The spirit we
studied under the name of true spirit, that is, objective spirit,
is no longer that when it knows itself. Coming to consciousness
destroys the immediate confidence which harmoniously united
the truth of a being with the certainty of a self. It supposes that
the self has already withdrawn itself from its substance and has
entered deeply into its subjectivity. The beauty of ancient Greek
art appears when spirit has raised itself above its reality, when
it has turned back from its objective truth into pure self-
knowledge. Thus this art is no longer ethical being, but rather
the remembering and the interiorization of this being (*Erinnerung*). "This self-consciousness is self-certain spirit which
laments the loss of its world, and which now, starting from the
purity of the self, produces its essence (that is, produces it by
reproducing it) raised above actuality" (*PE*, II, 225; *PG*, 491–92;
PM, 711). Much later, apropos of the history of peoples in
general, Hegel wrote: "Thus it is that national spirit seeks to
grasp itself in its most advanced action. The height of spirit
is to know itself, to arrive not only at intuition, but at the
thought of itself. Every national spirit must accomplish this
action, but this accomplishment is equally its decline and this

decline marks the opening of another stage, of another spirit." [19]

When Greek spirit becomes self-knowledge and reproduces itself in works of art, this remembering is the sign of a higher form. The evolution of art-religion is its passage to abstract subjectivity, to pure concept which in this artistic creation is as yet only the *form* of creative activity. "Such a form is the night to which substance was delivered up and in which substance transformed itself into subject. From this night of pure certainty of oneself, ethical spirit surged forth as the liberated figure of nature and of the immediate Dasein of spirit." This night is the creative activity of the subject who at first disappears in his work and does not yet portray himself as such to himself. "This pure activity, conscious of its inalienable force, wrestles with the essence that has no figure (its pathos). Becoming its master, it makes of this pathos its material, its content; this unity emerges as a work, as universal spirit individualized and portrayed" (*PE*, II, 226; *PG*, 492; *PM*, 712).

In this divine work of art everything which can thus be portrayed objectively will be. Everything except the concept, the absolute certainty of the self within itself. The Greek spirit is spirit which manifests itself externally [*au dehors*], but which knows spirit only as this capacity of being manifested. In Christian religion the revelation is indeed complete, but the revelation is more than objective manifestation: it contains the moment of the negation of this manifestation, the *depths of the night*, whereas the artistic spirit knows only the *life of day*.

The dialectic of art-religion by itself leads us toward the revelation of subjectivity to which, through the knowledge of its substance, it has already raised itself in-itself; this absolute certainty of the self into which substance has resolved itself must finally become the figure in which spirit contemplates itself. But then Greek tragedy, which as yet is only representation, will have become Christian drama, the drama of the life and death of a God played out in actual history. Thus this dialectic goes from the objective and transcendental work of art to subjectivity, from nature to spirit, from thingness to self, from substance to subject. The three moments of this development are the *abstract work of art*, in which ethical spirit appears to itself in the form of pure divine figures; the *living work of art*, in which man becomes the figure of the divine elaborated

19. Hegel's introduction to the *Philosophy of History*.

in festivals and games; and the *spiritual work of art,* in which spirit is present in the *language* of the epic, of tragedy, and of comedy. In its movement, language reproduces the development of substance as it is resolved into pure self-certainty. The epic reproduces the plastic figures of the gods, tragedy continues the living work of art, and, finally, in comedy, man knows himself as the destiny of the gods; he absorbs within himself the entirety of divine substantiveness and is *happy consciousness,* but also *unhappy consciousness* still ignorant of its existence.

The abstract work of art

The work of art is abstract in its two extreme forms: sculpture in the portrayal of the Olympian gods and pure lyricism in the hymns. In Greek architecture and sculpture, spirit portrays itself to itself; the temple is destined to contain the statue of a god. This portrait or representation of the divine is abstract to the extent that it is pure objectivity and that creative spirit has ignored itself in relation to its work. The plastic image of the gods abstracts from the artist's individuality and is enthroned in its serene majesty beyond the disquiet of human events; both its greatness and its limitations consist in that fact. "The figure of the god rejects the poverty of the natural conditions of existence"; this figure is the pure(ly) human figure, which retains in itself only an obscure reminiscence of the reign of the Titans. The animal is lowered to the rank of a symbol, like the eagle of Zeus or the owl of Minerva. It is no longer merely elementary natural powers that are thus portrayed, but lucid spirits of peoples conscious of themselves. The Greek city pays homage to itself in Athena. However, this serenity lacks the activity that gave birth to the work of art; it is beyond its coming to be. "And if the concept, as artist or spectator, is sufficiently disinterested to declare the work of art absolutely animated by itself, and to forget himself, creator or contemplator, we on the contrary must firmly insist on the concept of the spirit which cannot dispense with the moment of being conscious of itself" (*PE,* II, 229; *PG,* 495; *PM,* 715–16).

In Greek philosophy as well, the idea is beyond subjectivity: it does not integrate the development of its conception with its pure and objective essence. Platonism does not incorporate subjective certainty into truth, though the former is the movement by which truth posits itself and establishes itself. Love is poverty, it is beneath [*en deçà*] the thing loved. The aim of Hegelianism, by contrast, is to grasp truth as self-certainty.

> Thus the work of art is not for-itself the whole become alive in actuality; rather it is this *whole* only when it is considered together with its own *coming to be*. The fact common to works of art, namely, that they are engendered by consciousness and produced by human hands, is the moment of the concept existing as concept, and is opposed to the work of art (*PE,* II, 229; *PG,* 495; *PM,* 715).

Once more, we see the very particular signification of Hegel's use of the term "concept" (*Begriff*).

The plastic work of art was abstract because, as objective truth, it was beyond creative individuality. The pure lyricism of the hymn is abstract for the opposite reason. The fluidity of the hymn, which fuses particular consciousnesses with the operation of all consciousnesses, is pure interiority. "The hymn is the spiritual flow which within the multiplicity of self-consciousness is conscious of itself as an operation of everyone equally and as a simple being" (*PE,* II, 231; *PG,* 496; *PM,* 717). The language of the hymn is even more pure than that of the oracle, which expresses only the contingency of a situation and the arbitrariness of a decision which is necessary as decision but not as to content.

The opposition between sculpture and lyricism, which Hegel stresses so strongly, was taken up again by Nietzsche; the contrast between Apollonian and Dionysian art already appears in these passages as it also does in the following ones on the living work of art. In them, Hegel is seeking the unity that mediates exteriority and interiority, and he finds it in the *movement of worship.* Worship culminates in the living unity of the divine and the human, of *essence* and *self-consciousness.* In worship, human self-consciousness draws nearer to the Olympian god who was hovering beyond it, but conversely, in man, the abstract god obtains consciousness of himself. From the fact that men name the gods, said Hölderlin, the gods acquire not existence, but self-consciousness. "The gods willingly reside in the depths of human hearts." The divine does not fulfill itself without man's help, and man discovers himself only by elevating himself to the divine. Thus worship purifies the human self and leads it to participating in beatitude. Worship does not imply in man the deeper consciousness of Christian interiority that will be found in the consciousness of evil or of sin before reconciliation. Thus this purification remains external, just as the reconciliation of essence and self remains superficial.[20] In the form of the sacrifice, man renounces his particularity, and conversely, by that very fact the objective essence disappears. "The animal that is sacrificed is the *sign* of a god; the fruits that are consumed are the living Ceres and Bacchus themselves" (*PE*, II, 235; *PG*, 500; *PM*, 722). The sacrifice of man is thus reciprocally the sacrifice of the gods who give themselves to man. The gods renounce their abstract universality and gain human consciousness, while man renounces his particularity. Yet that is still not authentic sacrifice, the Christian sacrifice in which spirit sacrifices itself as such to spirit, and in which the mystery of bread and wine becomes that of flesh and blood.

The living work of art

The result of worship is the *immediate unity of the human and the divine*. The work of art is now no longer an abstract work; it is a living work. It is man himself who portrays himself to man, *he knows himself to be at one with the divine essence.*[21] The bacchantes and the torchbearers are no longer distant gods, but divinized men. Man has taken the place of the statue, but here only the corporality of the divine is realized: it is exteriority without interiority. On the other hand, interiority appears in unconscious extravaganzas [*Schwärmerei*], when the essence of nature reveals itself to man and participates in his self-conscious life while at the same time communicating to him its depth. In the mysteries of Ceres and Dionysus there is no secret, as is commonly believed, but on the contrary essence has become completely at one with the self: "Thus essence is

20. The comparison between Hellenism and Christianity dominates all of Hegel's early works. We know that this comparison is originally favorable to Hellenism. Only progressively does Hegel elevate Christianity above paganism. At the same time, he arrives at his philosophic conception that "The absolute is subject."

21. In the *Greek people*, Hegel perceived the historical happy people, realizing the immediate unity of the human and the divine. In his early works, he contraposed to the Greek people the *Jewish spirit* which by contrast makes the separation of the two terms greater (cf. unhappy consciousness in the *Phenomenology*).

completely unveiled and manifest for the self." In its metamorphoses, the earth spirit has become the feminine principle of nutrition or the male principle of virile force. "Through the utility of being able to be eaten and drunk, nature attains its highest perfection; in effect in this act nature is the possibility of a higher existence and comes close to the confines of spiritual Dasein" (*PE*, II, 238; *PG*, 503; *PM*, 726).

Unconscious extravaganzas and splendid corporality are assembled in the feast that man gives in his own honor, but this extravaganza lacks self-possession, and this splendid corporality lacks the depth of essence. "Once again, the perfect element, at the heart of which interiority is exterior just as much as exteriority is interior, is language" (*PE*, II, 240–41; *PG*, 505; *PM*, 729). This language is no longer that of the oracle, of the hymn, or of bacchic frenzy; it has become clear to itself and poses the pantheon of representations in an element that is simultaneously transcendent and immanent, that of logos.

The spiritual work of art

We have finally arrived at the spiritual work of art, which, in the element of language, will again take up and reexamine all the previous moments: the Olympian gods in the epic, the living unity of the divine and the human in tragedy, finally the resolution of divine substantiveness in the happy self-certainty of Greek comedy. At that point all substance will have been resolved into the human self. The divine is no longer realized in marble, but rather in the language of a people able to raise itself to universality. It is at this point that the Greeks obtain their most adequate portrayal. The Homeric poems, the tragedy of Aeschylus and Sophocles, and the comedy of Aristophanes together constitute a dialectical development whose general meaning is *the return of the divine into the human*. Human self at first is effaced vis-à-vis the world it reveals in its song, as the artist in the face of his statue. The world of the epic is that of gods and of men; but the bard who is its bearer disappears in the content of his song, which thus appears as a vast syllogism. At the top, one of the extremes is constituted by the Olympian gods who take part in the action without losing any of their unchangeable serenity; at the bottom, the other extreme is the bard, who, as specific subject of this world, engenders and contains it. His pathos is not the power of nature, but *mnēmosynē*, the awakening of consciousness, "the recollection by memory of the essence which previously was immediate. The bard is the organ that disappears into its content; it is not his own self that counts, but his muse, his universal song" (*PG*, II, 243; *PG*, 507; *PM*, 732). At the center, the middle term consists of the heroes (Agamemnon, Achilles, Ulysses) who are specific men like the bard, "but who are merely portrayed, and thus are at the same time universal, like the free extreme of universality, the gods." The movement from *epic* to *comedy* presents the complete inversion of the syllogism.[22] In comedy it is in fact the specific self of the bard that has become the essential, whereas the universality of the divine world is lowered to the private—and thus fleeting—substantiveness of the self. At the center of this movement, tragedy most closely links the divine and the human; the self enters into the movement of language, whereas the divine is organized according to the internal forces of substance.

Apropos of the epic, as one of his commentators has said, Hegel offers us a phenomenology of the Homeric poems.[23] He translated the language of the poet philosophically. The problem is that of the unity of two worlds, the divine and the human. By getting involved in the action, the gods appear to be superior men, whereas men who have been raised to universality by the recollection of memory in their turn become mortal gods. The unity of action, like that of the Greek world as a whole, is not an abstract unity like the unity of the Roman Empire, but a living and supple unity. However, this unity of representation cannot avoid demonstrating its instability, both in the inconsistent plurality of the divine and in the relation of these gods to men. The former, while maintaining their serenity in action, manifest characteristics so magnificent as to be comic, whereas the latter, despite the fact that they are the force of acting individuality, manifest characteristics of a tragic weakness. "The seriousness of these divine powers is thus ridiculously superfluous, since men are in fact the force of acting individuality;

22. Need we repeat that for Hegel, the *syllogism* is essentially the *movement* from the universal to the specific through the mediation of determination? There is no juxtaposition of terms, but the very act of mediation, *infinite relation*.

23. R. Kroner, *Von Kant bis Hegel*, II, 408.

and the effort and labors that individuality expends are an equally useless torment, since it is rather the divine powers that direct everything" (*PE*, II, 244; *PG*, 508; *PM*, 734). Above gods and men alike hovers the abstract unity of the *event*, the movement of time which is stated in the objective rhythm of the poem and in the impersonality of its language. *Destiny does not yet know itself as self.*[24]

In *tragedy*, the abstract necessity, which is that of the concept as yet unconscious of itself, draws closer to content, while the language of the bard ceases to be impersonal and participates in the content. The bard becomes the actor who intervenes directly in the drama. "It is the hero himself who speaks, and the spectacle that is portrayed shows to the listener, who is at the same time the spectator, men who are conscious of themselves as determinate beings and who know, and are able to state, their goal and their rights, the power and will of that being" (*PE*, II, 247; *PG*, 511; *PM*, 736–37). Their language is not that of common life; rather, its elevation and precision express the pathos of the hero. Language separates ethical action from the contingency of circumstance and in its purity presents the "characters" who express themselves in action. Destiny approaches man and becomes the center of gravity of his life at the same time that it elevates life above itself. The terrain of this tragic action is "the language of the epic become conscious of its own dispersion." "It is the common people in general whose wisdom finds expression in the chorus of elders; the people does indeed have its representative in this weakness of the chorus, since it itself constituted the positive and passive material of the individuality of the government that stands face to face with it" (*PE*, II, 248; *PG*, 511; *PM*, 737). We shall not stress the conception of the content of Greek tragedy that Hegel presents here; it is the self-knowledge of the true spirit about which we have spoken at length. The powers that confront each other, each of which has its incarnation in characters who are simultaneously natural and spiritual, are those of divine law and

24. Here, in the *ideal*, religion again takes up the *real* movement which we have already described and which leads from true spirit to the abstract person (cf., in the present work, part V, chapters 1 and 2). Hegel demonstrates the relation between this *representation* and *real spirit* in respect to revealed religion, in the passage from happy consciousness to unhappy consciousness (cf. above, "Revealed Religion").

human law, of the family and the polis. The division of the divine which appears at the center of each of these characters is that of knowledge and nonknowledge, of Apollo and the Erinyes, and their unity is that of ethical substance itself, "Zeus, who is the necessity of their mutual relation." According to Hegel, Greek tragedy begins to realize the unity of the gods called for by the Greek philosophers. It is the concept itself which is divided according to its internal law into knowledge and nonknowledge and which seeks its unity in the reconciliation of *forgetfulness*. But this destiny is self-consciousness, which has not yet found itself. "However, self-consciousness, simple self-certainty, is in fact the negative power, the unity of Zeus, of substantive essence and abstract necessity; it is the spiritual unity to which everything returns" (*PE*, II, 253; *PG*, 517; *PM*, 744). Thus we have seen the decline of true spirit into abstract self-certainty. The substantive world again discovers itself in the self which is the negative power of that world.

This negativity of the self finally manifests itself as such in Greek comedy. Self has elevated itself above the content into which it had been absorbed; it has become *the destiny of the gods and of ethical powers*, and it knows itself as such. The weakness of men and of the gods, in contrast to their claims is the source of the comic. The tragic actor merged with his mask and raised himself above himself; now he states the vanity of these substantive elements and reduces them to what they really are, finite moments which have their signification only in the self. Heroes cease to be heroes and become ordinary men; the actor jettisons his mask and appears on stage in flesh and blood. The divine and the human, which were separated in the epic and still in the tragedy, are now completely unified, but in such a way that only the human and the contingent subsist, and that the self can be ironic about the gods' claims to be ethical powers in their universality. The people, which knows itself as the power of the Greek city, "offers the laughable contrast between its opinion of itself and its immediate Dasein, between its necessity and its contingency, between its universality and its vulgarity" (*PE*, II, 255; *PG*, 519; *PM*, 746). In comedy, the people has lost its divinity and is ironic about itself and about its gods.

In modern comedy the seriousness of Greek comedy is revealed, because man seems to elevate to the absolute what has only a finite value—money, for example—and the laughter is not on the stage itself but rather among the spectators who contemplate the spectacle; in Greek comedy, by contrast, the laughter is the actors'.[25] It is the *self* of the actor that states the vanity of all divine and human powers by demonstrating their continuous dissolution, and also states the vanity of ethical formulas which, reduced to themselves, are nothing more than *clouds*, while the abstract thoughts of the good and the beautiful, when freed from the contingency of their content, can be filled with any appearance whatsoever.

The ethical world has lost its substance, has terminated its movement, and has been completely resolved into the *self certain of itself*. Henceforth it is this certainty which surges forth and which constitutes the essential content of comedy; it is happy consciousness, "the return of everything universal into self-certainty. Consequently this certainty is the complete absence of fear, the complete absence of essence in everything that is alien, a well-being and a relaxation of consciousness such as cannot be found outside this comedy" (*PE*, II, 257; *PG*, 520; *PM*, 748–49).

The principle that expresses this joy can be stated as follows: "Self is absolute essence," but this self must discover its inconsistency; when it claims to attain itself, it finds itself alienated from itself. By itself finite, *it is human, all too human*. The truth of this absolute self-certainty is that it is the opposite of itself; it claims to be happy consciousness, but it must learn that it is unhappy consciousness, the consciousness for which "God himself is dead." Thus it is the arena for a higher form of religion, Christianity. But in this dialectic of Greek comedy, we find a thought which continually reappears in Hegelianism: man is the truth of the divine, but each time that he reduces the divine to himself, each time he loses the movement of transcending himself, he loses himself. Hence the harsh phrase: "God himself is dead."

III. Revealed (or Manifest) Religion

THE TRANSITION FROM HAPPY CONSCIOUSNESS to unhappy consciousness, the end and the general decadence of the ancient world, constitute the historical presuppositions of the Christian religion in which at last spirit will know itself in

25. On *Greek comedy* and *modern comedy*, the latter being the destiny of the former, cf. the Jena article "Naturrecht," pp. 385 ff.

the form of spirit. Religion in the form of art led us from the knowledge of spirit as substance to the knowledge of spirit as subject. In the Eastern religions the absolute appears as the substance in which self-consciousness as such disappears; as a finite being man is only an accident, his life is that of a slave, and universal being has no true relation with the self-knowledge that is awakening in him. This religion is one of fear and trembling; God, if we may call him that, who is already a subject of it, is beyond the finite, he is the *abstract in-itself*. However, art-religion has *humanized* this divine essence; consciousness itself has posed the figure of the divine by its own activity so that at the end of its development substance has completely alienated itself into the self. "All essentiality has been absorbed into the spirit, which in the specificity of its consciousness is perfectly certain of itself. The proposition that expresses this relief [*Leichtsinn*] can be stated thus: the self is absolute essence" (*PE*, II, 258; *PG*, 521; *PM*, 750). But the self in question is only abstract negation, or again, self discovers itself only as finite self, as self deprived of spirit. The joy of the unshakable self-certainty which appears in the audacious and formal affirmation of stoic consciousness must degenerate into the consciousness of the total loss of the divine through the unassuageable disquiet of skeptic consciousness. In reality, this loss is the disappearance of the ethical world, which is now but a memory in the Roman pantheon.

> Confidence in the eternal laws of the gods has become mute, as has confidence in the oracles which were supposed to know the particular. Now the statues are corpses from which the life-giving soul has fled, the hymns are words deserted by faith. The tables of the gods are bare of spiritual food and drink, and the games and festivals no longer restore to consciousness the blissful unity of itself with essence (*PE*, II, 261; *PG*, 523; *PM*, 753).

Destiny has merely preserved this past world in the interiority of memory and the universality of thought; but by that very fact it has made possible *the birth of spirit conscious of itself as spirit* (*PE*, II, 262; *PG*, 525; *PM*, 754).

This birth has a double origin: on the one hand it results from the alienation of substance, whose realization we have seen in art-religion; on the other hand it results from the opposite movement, during which the self alienates itself and rises to essence. Thus essence turns into self-consciousness while self-consciousness turns into essence. The historical presence of Christ, true man and true God, expresses this double movement. In him God, as abstract essence, becomes self-consciousness, no longer through the mediation of producing consciousness but immediately, in accord with a sensuous necessity which reveals that "divine nature and human nature are identical" (*PE*, II, 267; *PG*, 529; *PM*, 760). But in God man also elevates himself to essence and surpasses himself as mere finitude. This is an alienation that is the converse of the preceding one, that of the self which reinstates substance "not so that the consciousness of spirit is led back to its starting point, natural religion, but rather so that this conversion is actualized for and through self-consciousness itself" (*PE*, II, 259; *PG*, 522; *PM*, 751). The alienation of self-certainty is already expressed in unhappy consciousness. The tragic destiny of the self of happy consciousness is to be unable to find itself when it seeks itself. It is beyond itself, and when it thinks it has reached itself, it discovers it has become lost. As self-consciousness, man thus alienates his self-certainty, he makes of it a beyond, an immutable essence. But because of the indivisible unity of being-for-itself, this alienation remains conscious, "so that it is conserved [*aufgehoben*] in this alienation of self and remains the subject of its substance." But unhappy consciousness is only a historical precondition of Christianity; it is the torment of subjectivity which would like to renounce itself and discover again in objectivity the unity of essence and self-consciousness that is its content.

This is the content that the revelation of Christ, his birth, life, death, and resurrection in the community, presents in actuality. By studying unhappy consciousness as such, we have seen only one aspect of the Christian religion; we have had to leave aside the movement of the in-itself or of essence revealing itself to man as unity, a unity in which specific self becomes substantive, while substance becomes self. This unity, let us repeat, is not imagined in being, it is not an interpretation that would allow any doubts to remain concerning the basis of things, it is not an inner meaning "fantastically attributed both to nature and to history, . . . an inner meaning other than that which they offer immediately to consciousness in their manifestation" (*PE*, II, 264; *PG*, 526; *PM*, 756); rather, this unity is an immediate revelation. It is quite true that the concept originated for us by going from sensuous certainty to understanding, but what was for-us must also be for the consciousness of spirit and for its immediate consciousness. Necessity that has been thought through is distinct from immediate necessity, but this distinction disappears in the concept (*PE*, II, 264; *PG*, 526; *PM*, 757).[26] What is thought through as necessary must also appear and manifest itself in experience. "There is nothing that is not in human experience." The moment of historical positivity is contained in the nature of the concept, which is "what alienates itself" and turns itself into Dasein while also remaining concept in its Dasein.

When the real world spirit has arrived at this knowledge of the *unity of human nature and divine nature*, this unity must still become positive for the consciousness of spirit. This positivity is the sensuous presence of Christ: "He who has seen me has seen the Father." "Believing consciousness sees, touches, and hears this divinity"; it sees a human self-consciousness, but at the same time it sees God, for both essence and sensuous Dasein are present in this human self-consciousness. "The lowliest is at the same time the highest; . . . the fact that supreme essence becomes seen, heard, and so on, as a self-consciousness in the element of being is in fact the perfection of its concept, and through this perfection the essence is just as much immediately *there* as it is essence" (*PE*, II, 268; *PG*, 529; *PM*, 760).[27]

What comes toward being in this way, not only for us or in-itself but for its own self, is the concept qua concept. It is given to intuition as the unity of substance and subject, of the sensuous and the spiritual, of the universal and the particular, of the infinite and the finite. In this unity God is known as spirit, "for only in spirit is the man-God unity." Spirit indeed is the knowledge of oneself in one's alienation, it is the essence that is the movement of retaining in its being-other spirit's equality with itself (*PE*, II, 266; *PG*, 528; *PM*, 758). Thus being is not impenetrable immediateness; it is essence, but it is not merely essence qua unchanging equality with itself, its own infinity in opposition to finite human consciousness. Being is essence which is immediate presence and in this presence it is the negation of itself; "thus as self it is both this particular self and universal self." Now this is precisely what revealed religion

26. That is how Hegel expresses the necessary unity of the a posteriori and the a priori.

27. We see why spirit has been completely *revealed* to itself in this religion.

knows: "The hopes and expectations of the preceding world only progressed toward this revelation in order to attain the intuition of what absolute essence is and to discover itself in it. The joy of contemplating itself in absolute essence comes to self-consciousness and captures the entire world, for self-consciousness is spirit" (*PE*, II, 269; *PG*, 530; *PM*, 761).

Consequently the knowledge of Christ—all that is positive in Christianity—is not merely sensuous knowledge, but also speculative knowledge which is given along with this presence and which belongs to a religious community, to a church in which spirit realizes itself as *universal self-consciousness*. "This unity of being and essence, of thought which is immediate Dasein, is the immediate knowledge of this religious consciousness just as it is its thought or its mediate knowledge" (*PE*, II, 268; *PG*, 530; *PM*, 761). Here God is revealed as he is; he is there as he is in-itself, he is there as spirit. Thus Hegel will develop the diverse moments of the speculative knowledge of the Christian community. The unity of the two natures, human and divine, is not in fact a static unity but a development and a dialectic which precisely constitutes spirit as it now appears to itself. The God-man must disappear in time like every "sensuous here" and every historical here, but he is resurrected transformed. Thus specific self alienates itself and rises to divine essence; conversely the abstract essence of God dies and becomes specific self. This unity is expressed in spirit, the universal self-consciousness of the religious community. This concrete spirit is the truth of the dialectic which religious consciousness thinks through or rather portrays to itself. Indeed, the latter is not yet conceptual thought or absolute self-knowledge. Not yet fully possessing a consciousness of itself, it expresses in *the as-yet alien form of a portrait* the spirit that it itself is; it speaks of the relation between essence and self-consciousness as a relation between father and son; it introduces historical events and a contingent succession where these are merely the revelation of an intrinsic necessity. We will rapidly trace this speculative knowledge of the religious community as Hegel presents it here. He distinguishes the reign of the Father, that of the Son, and that of Spirit, "that is, logos, nature and finite self, finally universal self, spirit in the community." Notice that this knowledge of the community in the language of *representation* is the text of which Hegelian philosophy claims to be the authentic translation into the language of *concept*.

Speculative knowledge of the community

How does the revelation which becomes the knowledge and life of the community manifest itself in the sensuous world—as a religion of the Holy Ghost? Hegel rapidly expounds on this question in the *Phenomenology*, but he is only taking up again the early works. In the *Phenomenology*, his thought is much more fully worked out, much more sure of itself, but what had been so striking in the Frankfurt theological studies, the existential relation with the sources of Christianity, with the Gospels, has nearly disappeared. The philosophical interpretation overlays the religious sources.

Absolute religion is a *positive* religion "in the sense that everything that is for consciousness is an objective reality. Everything must come to us from the exterior. Thus the sensuous is a positivity. At first there is nothing positive except what we have before us in immediate intuition." [28] Before it can be raised to the level of thought, revelation must first present itself as "a pure given." Christian religion is thus a revealed religion in a double sense: it is the manifestation of the depth of self-certain spirit which appears to its consciousness, but it is also a given, which is at first alien and which self-consciousness must grasp in order to integrate. One must believe "in spirit," and this transformation of immediate faith into a spiritual faith is the life of the community, which therefore plays an essential role in absolute religion. We have said that a philosophy of the church was possible starting from the *Phenomenology*,[29] although Hegel certainly did not intend the elaboration of such a philosophy. For him, this community is rather the first imperfect form of reason, of universal self-consciousness which elaborates itself in community.

The disciples saw and heard the historical Christ who was still separated from them by the entire abyss of sensuous objectivity. His presence in a here-and-now had to be transformed into a spiritual presence. But this mediation, which is thought,

28. From Hegel's *Lectures on the Philosophy of Religion*.
29. In the notes to our translation of the *Phenomenology* (PE, II, 270). The church may indeed appear as concrete universal self-consciousness which spiritualizes the coming of the Incarnation; but for Hegel, this community is as yet only an imperfect form, as he says in the chapter on absolute knowledge (PE, II, 306; PG, 559; PM, 801–2).

was accomplished for them in the midst of the sensuous world. The past and distance constitute "the imperfect form according to which the immediate mode receives mediation or is posed universally" (*PE*, II, 270; *PG*, 531; *PM*, 763). The disciples must understand the entire signification of the dialectic of the sensuous here with which the *Phenomenology of Spirit* begins. The immediately present God must disappear; he no longer is but he has been, and this having-been must become, in *Erinnerung* (remembrance), the interiority of common memory, a spiritual presence. Only because the consciousness of the disciples has seen and heard him does it become a spiritual consciousness. Spirit is no longer separate from them, it inhabits them: "Where two or three are gathered in my name, there am I in the midst of them." Thus spirit remains the immediate self of actuality but in the form of the universal self-consciousness of the community (*PE*, II, 270; *PG*, 531; *PM*, 763). The "do this in memory of me" indeed signifies the return to the past, but a return at a higher power, for the past has become spirit living in the community, mediated by the history of this community, that is, by its tradition which is not only a repetition, but a continual revelation. "It is not the specific for-itself (Christ) that constitutes the totality of this spirit, but the specific for-itself together with the consciousness of the community [and what it is for this community]" (*PE*, II, 270; *PG*, 531; *PM*, 763). During the course of its history, this community will continually want to reform itself in order to return to its source, to what the God-man said and did. This need for *reform* is not without signification, but it confuses the original immediateness with the demands of the concept.

> Thus what this spirit which reveals itself is, in-and-for-itself, is not brought out into the open because the rich content of its life in the community is, so to speak, unraveled and reduced to the original threads, for example, to the portrayals of the first imperfect community, or even to what the actual man said. Behind this return to the past there is the instinct to proceed to the concept, but this instinct confuses the origin, as the immediate Dasein of the first manifestation, with the simplicity of the concept (*PE*, II, 271; *PG*, 532; *PM*, 764).

Only spiritless memories would result from this impoverishment, and not the thought of the spiritual self which has become the self of the community, the self which has become universal self, "which is universality without in this universality losing its actual reality."

The knowledge of the community is simultaneously its substance and its self-certainty. In it, this knowledge reunites the two moments that were presented in their separation during the itinerary of consciousness: that of the subjectivity of *unhappy consciousness,* which corresponds to the community's self-certainty, and that of the objectivity of the *faith of the world of culture,* which corresponds to its substance.[30] The community possesses a truth which is at the same time certainty. In other words, for the community the truth is not a content that is alien to it; the community is itself this truth, and this truth is its self-knowledge. It is not by accident that we have encountered these two moments in a state of separation. By studying only self-consciousness, we should have come across the moment of self-certainty separated from its truth in-itself; on the other hand, by studying the world of culture, we should have found this truth as the substance of faith, but without the self-certainty which then appears to pure intellection. It is in a *phenomenology* of religion as such that the two moments would be reunited, since religion is the self-consciousness of spiritual substance. However, the religious community is not the highest form of this self-knowledge of spirit. The modality of representation renders consciousness and self-consciousness disparate. Absolute knowledge will overcome this last form of disparity.

The three moments of the knowledge of the community already exist for us in the element of concept when they still exist for the community in the element of representation: hence Hegel's double presentation. He expounds what these moments are in the portrayal of religious consciousness and at the same time what they mean for us. Biblical history begins with the *creation* of the world, but that is "the representational term to designate the concept itself according to its absolute movement" (*PE*, II, 276; *PG*, 536; *PM*, 769). Before the creation of the world, or rather without the world, God is an abstraction of pure thought, and for Hegel the abstraction is not our abstraction, it is at the heart of the absolute, which is negativity. Insofar as this pure thought is in-itself spirit, it is not only eternal and simple essence, it is already otherness and as such it is logos. Religious consciousness portrays God to itself before the creation of the world as Trinity and introduces "the natural relations of father and son in place of the form of the concept"

---

30. See the present work, part V, chapter 3.

(*PE*, II, 274; *PG*, 535; *PM*, 767). For us, this logos is the thought of itself such as it will be seen in the speculative logic. "If these moments are taken in their purity, they are the restless concepts which exist only insofar as they are within themselves their contrary and find peace only in the whole" (*PE*, II, 274; *PG*, 535; *PM*, 767).

But logos does not exist without nature or the world. What representation translates by the term "creation" expresses the movement of the concept. In the element of pure thought, being-other is not really posed; nor is alienation (without which the absolute is not for-itself and is not spirit) as yet complete. Hegelian philosophy does not deduce the world from the logos. Logos and nature mutually require each other. God without the world, or pure thought without nature, is what is separated from itself; it is only a moment contraposed to a being-other. Doubtless this being-other is already in the essence to the extent that this essence is logos, but this otherness is only the concept of otherness; "in this simple intuition of oneself in the other, being-other is thus not posed as such; it is a difference such that in pure thought it is not immediately any difference: a recognition of love in which the two are not opposed in their essence" (*PE*, II, 275; *PG*, 536; *PM*, 769).[31] But spirit is only actual if it actually negates itself; it is self only in this negation or mediation which, as absolute negativity, reestablishes it. Thus in the element of pure thought God is his own becoming-other, his negation as nature. "In the beginning God created the heavens and the earth"; in this element, which properly speaking is that of representation and no longer that of thought, differences acquire a substantive existence; spirit is as if lost and has become external to itself. Nature is not only the other of logos, as logos is the other of nature; there is an essential otherness within nature. When Biblical history speaks of the creation of the world, it means that the world cannot be conceived of in-itself, that it is always *posed* as a moment. Hegel would later say that "nature is, in-itself, in the idea, divine, but since it exists, its being does not correspond to its concept; instead it is a contradiction which is never resolved."[32] God becomes self in the creation, but the world, insofar as it expresses this movement itself, becomes a finite self in-the-world. "How-

31. Cf. the passage in the preface on the torment of the negative (*PE*, I, 18; *PG*, 20; *PM*, 81).
32. *Encyclopaedia*, p. 208.

ever, the world is not only this spirit cast forth into the integrality of existence and its external order; since this spirit is essentially simple self, this self is also present in the world: spirit existing-there [*daseiende*] which is specific self, which is conscious and as other or as world distinguishes itself from itself" (*PE*, II, 276; *PG*, 537; *PM*, 770). According to a Romantic image, spirit comes forth from the depths of nature and is nature first before being itself. This is why the state of nature or of original innocence must necessarily disappear. Religious consciousness speaks of an earthly paradise, and then of disobedience; it is by eating the fruit of the tree of knowledge of good and evil that man lost the innocence that was his when he was lost in creation; but we know that he had to leave this animal innocence in order to become spirit for-itself. "So that it be in fact self and spirit, it must first become an other for itself, just as eternal essence presents itself as the movement of being equal to itself in its being-other" (*PE*, II, 276; *PG*, 537; *PM*, 770). This rending of human consciousness or this otherness which has been introduced into it is the *knowledge of good and evil*. Man, as the field of this opposition, and to the extent that he is for himself the consciousness of this contradiction, takes himself as evil and expels the good beyond himself. Thus he poses his *difference* from and his *equality* with God. Spirit knows itself in-itself as absolute, divine as essence, but for-itself as nonabsolute, as being-in-the-world. This contradiction makes it both self and spirit, but it does not yet know this. Indeed, this contradiction is not only that of finite spirit; absolute spirit is absolute because it always poses this contradiction in-itself and always overcomes it, which in logical terms signifies its negativity, in more concrete terms its being-self or spirit. That is why religious consciousness can expel the origin of evil out beyond man into a fall of angels, but it cannot go so far as to portray evil in God, despite Böhme's attempt to see evil in him as his anger. *Representative* thought, which *portrays*, always grasps the terms of the contradiction in their spiritless *exteriority* and cannot understand that God himself poses his otherness so as to discover himself as self and as spirit (*PE*, II, 279; *PG*, 539; *PM*, 773).[33]

This thought occurs to religious consciousness, but as the

33. The movement by which man, as *consciousness of this contradiction*, poses himself as evil and poses the good, God, outside himself, recalls the movement of *unhappy consciousness*. It is the same dialectic.

event of the Incarnation and as the sacrifice and voluntary death of the God-man. If Dasein is evil in relation to divine *essence,* nevertheless God made himself flesh. Divine essence humiliated itself to Dasein which is alien to it, but in the sacrifice and the death of the mediator, it suppressed that alien Dasein and raised it to itself. At that point, and only then, God *revealed himself as spirit.* That is why his death is not the pure and simple return to the original essence, to the abstract God or to substance which was all that natural religion knew.

> As death, the death of the divine man is abstract negativity . . . but it loses this natural signification in the self-consciousness of the community, . . . which alone understood the resurrection, *the death of death.* . . . Death is no longer what it immediately signifies, the nonbeing of this specific entity; it is transformed into the universality of spirit which lives in its community, and dies and is resurrected in it every day (*PE,* II, 286; *PG,* 545; *PM,* 780).

The death of Christ is thus the position of the spirit of the community, universal self-consciousness. The movement that took place in Christ *must now be executed in the midst of the community* and must become *its own* movement instead of being alien to it. That is the passage into the third element, that of self-consciousness. "Spirit is thus posed in the third element, in universal self-consciousness; it is its own community. The movement of the community, like the movement of self-consciousness, which distinguishes between itself and its portrayal, is the movement of producing what has become in-itself" (*PE,* II, 284; *PG,* 543; *PM,* 778). What has become in-itself is the descent of the abstract and distant God, his reconciliation with human existence, that is, his being posited as spirit; the community in turn must reconcile finite existence with divine essence, by internalizing the death and resurrection of Christ. The relation between these two dialectics is this death of the mediator; what must be understood in all possible meanings is the phrase "God himself is dead."

The death of Christ is not only the death of the God-man, but also the death of the abstract God whose transcendence radically separated human existence from his divine essence. The life and death of Christ mean "that the pure or nonactual spirit of mere thought has become actual" (*PE,* II, 287; *PG,* 546; *PM,* 781). What dies is the abstraction of divine essence "which is not posed as self." As spirit God has become the universal

self-consciousness of the community which, through the mediation of its history, raises its particularity to universality and
makes this universality, within which the particular dies, concrete and moving. *For its own self*, spirit is the reconciliation
which we encountered as the in-itself of religion, and from
which our dialectic issued. "This self-consciousness does not
die in actuality in the same way that we think of the particular
being actually dying, but its particularity dies into its universality, that is, into its knowledge, which is essence reconciling itself with itself." The tragedy of human existence is not
eliminated, as though one were to say "evil is good." For, as
immediateness, this "is" of judgment is found to be without
spirit, whereas what is at stake is the living spirit. The tragic is
in the movement by means of which finite existence raises itself
to universality and dies into this universality, while in this
existence universality becomes for its own self and shows
through in that which dies. As Hegel writes in the preface to the
Phenomenology: "Manifestation is the movement of being born
and dying, a movement which itself neither is born nor dies,
but which is in-itself and constitutes actuality and the movement of the life of truth" (*PE*, I, 40; *PG*, 39; *PM*, 105). The
death of the mediator signifies the death of the sensuous here-
below [*en-deça*] that the disciples vainly tried to retain, as well
as that of the unfathomable *beyond* [*au-dela*] which would irremediably condemn all human existence. Through this death,
substance wholly transforms itself into subject. "God himself is
dead. This harsh phrase is the expression of the simplest and
most intimate self-knowledge, the return of consciousness back
into the depth of the night of I = I, which neither distinguishes
nor knows anything anymore outside itself." [34] But since this
expression is the torment of unhappy consciousness which has
lost the substance of the divine, it is also the alienation of this
specific consciousness and its ascension to concrete spirit which
lives in the community. This community is no longer Christ as
a specific figure, but the Holy Ghost in which the Incarnation
becomes eternal. The Christocentric point of view of the Bible
tends to disappear to make place for this universal Christ which
is the community. "The divine man—or the human God who is
dead—is in-itself universal self-consciousness," and now be-

34. It is the depth of this subjectivity that Hegel expressed as
follows in the Jena *Realphilosophie:* "I is the night of disappearing"
(*SW*, XX, 185), and also "we are nothingness" (*SW*, XX, 80).

comes so for-itself in the knowledge that this community has of spirit, a knowledge that is its own self-knowledge. "This knowledge is thus the spiritualization through which substance has become subject, through which its abstraction and its non-vitality have died, through which it has become actually both simple and universal self-consciousness" (*PE*, II, 287; *PG*, 546; *PM*, 782).

But as yet the religious community is only an imperfect form of absolute knowledge. Even though in this community representation comes back into self-consciousness, this return is not actual for it; it still represents the return to itself in such a way that the reconciliation that the community embodies does not appear to it as *its* work; the community is indeed truth that knows itself, but it is not conscious of producing this truth. Production of truth as a development of the self belongs to absolute knowledge. "Its own reconciliation enters its consciousness as something far off in the future, just as the reconciliation effected by the other is manifest as something far off in the past." *The nostalgia for the past, the fervent expectation of the future* constitute the imperfection of the religious community which casts out away from itself the church triumphal, and awaits its salvation in a beyond which presents itself to it in the form of *temporality*. Specific divine man has the abstract God for his father and actual self-consciousness for his mother; universal divine man, that is, the community, has its own action and its own knowledge for father, but for mother it has eternal love which it only feels but does not contemplate consciously as an immediate actual object (*PE*, II, 290; *PG*, 548; *PM*, 784). The community's reconciliation lies in this love, but love appears nonactual to it. What enters into its consciousness is the world which awaits transfiguration. The world is indeed in-itself reconciled with essence, but this in-itself is not given to consciousness as such, so that the consciousness of the world or actual spirit is, for this community, distinct from its religious consciousness or from spirit in religion. We have seen that this distinction which, like that between consciousness and self-consciousness, was the driving force of the dialectic of religion, still subsists. It is suppressed *in-itself* for the community, but "this in-itself is not realized or has not yet become absolute being-for-itself."

But what does this realization mean for Hegel himself? That actual spirit, the spirit of history, becomes its own self-knowledge, and that this knowledge of itself is presented to its consciousness in history, indeed imply the dialectical reconciliation of finite human existence with essence; but when this reconciliation is grasped as *our work,* this double requirement leads to a divine humanity which temporally poses an eternal truth. Aren't all the difficulties of the Hegelian system brought together in this last relation between the finite and the infinite, the specific and the universal, in the form of time and eternity? The *Phenomenology* presents the temporal conditions of this absolute knowledge of the self. But how can we conceive this absolute knowledge? What community succeeds the imperfect religious community? History presents us only with nations which live and die; in this life and death spirit again finds that it is "that which is equal to itself in its being-other," and takes refuge in the knowledge of itself which becomes its eternal self-knowledge, philosophy. But is philosophy merely a knowledge, or is it at the same time an act? These last questions must be resolved by the chapter on absolute knowledge, but in that chapter they are merely posed. In the works of nineteenth- and twentieth-century philosophers Hegelianism proved unstable as a dialectical synthesis: it opens the way to multiple possible interpretations.[35]

35. Indeed, absolute spirit appears as the self-knowledge of humanity, and this self-knowledge must have actual history as its object—as consciousness. In the religious community, there is still a surpassing (nostalgia for the past or expectation of the future). In philosophy, this self-knowledge is identical to *our* action. We think of *Marx's* formula: "Until now the philosophers have only *interpreted* the world in various ways; the point, however, is to *change* it." But Hegelianism contents itself with the knowledge of the universal in the particular and of the particular in the universal; cf. the passage in Hegel, "Philosophy escapes from the weary strife of passions that agitate the surface of society into the calm region of contemplation" (*Philosophy of History,* p. 457).

PART VII

Conclusion

Phenomenology and Logic: Absolute Knowledge

No CHAPTER OF THE *Phenomenology* is more obscure than the one with which the book ends, "Absolute Knowledge." This obscurity no doubt has multiple causes: the difficulty of the subject matter, Hegel's varied intentions, probably also a hasty composition which is sufficiently explained by the circumstances of the book's publication. Only these external circumstances can explain the fact that Hegel, when he deals with absolute knowledge, that is, speculative philosophy, condensed the entire development of philosophy into a single page, beginning with the medieval church and ending with the philosophy of his time (*PE*, II, 307; *PG*, 560; *PM*, 802–3).[1] The extreme condensation of the passage makes it difficult to interpret. Since the preface of the *Phenomenology* was written after the work with intentions similar to those of the conclusion, we can use it to help us in interpreting this chapter. For Hegel, it is a question of introducing the *Logic*, or speculative philosophy, which is supposed to constitute the second part of the system of science, the first part being the *Phenomenology of Spirit*.[2] What is the originality of this logic, which in a sense is all philosophy? How does the *Phenomenology of Spirit* prepare for it? What is the meaning of this absolute knowledge which

1. In one page, Hegel summarizes the movement of philosophical thought from Descartes to Fichte, via Spinoza and Leibniz, but he doesn't name any philosophers.
2. Cf. part I, "Generalities on the *Phenomenology*," for the difference between the preface and the introduction; for the circumstances of the work's publication, part I, chapter 3, "The Structure of the *Phenomenology*."

raises itself above religion, and how is religion surpassed? Why does this absolute knowledge appear at this era in the history of the world and no other? What role does time play in this knowledge, which in its essence is nontemporal? These are the main questions that Hegel raises in these passages; all are important for comprehending Hegelian philosophy.

However, the main lines of the organization of the chapter on absolute knowledge are fairly clear. We have indicated them in a note to our edition of the *Phenomenology* (PE, II, 293, n. 1). Through the reconsideration of certain previous figures of consciousness, Hegel begins by showing how the self has experienced itself as *identical with being*. This identity between self and being, which has been revealed concretely through the various alienations of the self and through the characters of being-for-consciousness, is the result of the *Phenomenology*, which culminates in the conception of a science which is simultaneously the science of being and the position of the self in being. Being thinks itself as self, and self thinks itself as being. This thought of the self, this ontologic, which is the thought of thought at the same time that it is the thought of all things, constitutes absolute knowledge. In a second paragraph, Hegel summarily indicates the characteristics of this science, which essentially exists in the form of the *concept*, and he examines the historical and philosophical presuppositions of this absolute knowledge. Then, in a last paragraph, Hegel—following his circular method—comes back from this ontological logic to phenomenology, to nature and history. Just as phenomenology is the path leading to speculative philosophy, so too, speculative philosophy leads us back to the experience of consciousness and to its development, to the alienation of spirit in space (nature) and in time (history).

As we can see, the difficulties have to do less with the general movement of the thought than with its details. But these details are essential. It is meaningless to say that a philosopher is an absolute idealist if we cannot see the exact meaning of this idealism. The identity of the "I" (or of the "self," since reflection and identity are better indicated by the term *Selbst* than by the preceding *Ich*) and being is a very general proposition which remains merely verbal if we do not specify its scope and its consequences (for example, the dialectical character of both knowledge and being). Then too, we have encountered the word "concept" (*Begriff*) in too many different meanings not to be suspicious of the interpretation that we might at first give to a proposition such as this one: "Science, that is, philosophy, essentially is in the form of the concept." With Hegel, the reduction of philosophy to logic does not at all lead to formalism or even to the intellectualism (i.e., the idea that he constructs the universe a priori with only his thoughts) for which he has often been reproached. Rather, it leads to a spiritualization of logic. If we want to understand Hegel, it is thus important to interpret exactly this reduction of philosophy to logic. Rather than following Hegel's outline, we think it preferable here to grasp some of his questions in order better to bring out certain characteristics of Hegelian thought and to indicate the difficulties of interpretation that present themselves.

I. CHARACTERISTICS OF THE *Phenomenology*

WE BEGIN BY INSISTING on the distinctive characteristics of the *Phenomenology* as compared with the *Logic*. We will then be in a better position to specify the precise characteristics of this *Logic* and the link between the two works, both of which express the entire Hegelian philosophy, but from two different points of view.

Such as it immediately exists, spirit is consciousness. "The element of immediate Dasein is thus the characteristic by which this part of science (phenomenology) is set off from other parts." In this element consciousness is presented as duality. "The immediate Dasein of spirit, consciousness, possesses two moments: that of knowledge, and that of objectivity which is negative with respect to knowledge" (*PE*, I, 31; *PG*, 32; *PM*, 96). This distinction is characteristic of the entire *phenomenology* or *science of the experience of consciousness*. It is nothing other than the distinction on which every theory of knowledge rests, in particular Kant's transcendental philosophy: it is the distinction between subject and object, knowledge and being, for-itself and in-itself, certainty (*Gewissheit*) and truth (*Wahrheit*). Hegel presents it most often in this last form. Consciousness is consciousness of an object which constitutes the truth of consciousness and which appears to it as alien, as other than itself. But consciousness is also conscious of its own knowledge of this truth. The knowledge that consciousness has is overlaid with a knowledge of its knowledge, with a subjective reflection—that of the self with respect to being or to substance.

The disparity between these two moments is the motive force of phenomenological development; it is the mainspring of what is called "experience." We insisted on this fact at the beginning of this book, when we examined the technique of phenomenological development.[3]

The distinction between knowledge and its truth is "the internal opposition of the concept" (*PE*, II, 311; *PG*, 562; *PM*, 806);[4] it is what disappears at the end of the *Phenomenology*. Broadly interpreted, it means that knowledge is contraposed to being, self to substance. Being appears to consciousness as alien to the self; for its part, the self, with its reflectiveness, is distinct from being. For this reason any philosophy that is limited to an *epistemology* may culminate in the *thing-in-itself*, in an opaque being which is impenetrable for knowledge. Knowledge will always be subjective knowledge, understanding will always be our human understanding, and the basis of things, being, will be unknowable. In certain respects, despite Kant's remarkable statement of the problem ("how are synthetic a priori judgments possible?"), despite his thesis which grounds synthetic judgments and according to which "the possibility of experience is the very possibility of the objects of experience," Kant never went very far beyond the subjectivity of Locke. The natural attitude of human spirit is a naïve realism which then degenerates into a critical skepticism.[5]

But the *Phenomenology* has shown us that the object of knowledge is none other than spiritual substance. This is the spirit that comprehends itself in the universe, the spirit that presents itself to consciousness as its object. That is what the *Phenomenology* has to reveal progressively during the course of its winding and varied itinerary. The knowledge of being was shown to be a knowledge of self, and, inversely, self-knowledge has led back to the knowledge of being; finally, reason, the synthesis of consciousness and self-consciousness, did indeed grasp being as thought and thought as being, but it did so in an immediate fashion. Insofar as this reason was the reason of the

3. Part I, chapter 1, "Meaning and Method of the *Phenomenology*."

4. "The concept which is posed [in the *Logic*] in its simple mediation as thought separates [in the *Phenomenology*] the moments of this mediation and portrays itself to itself as *internal opposition*" (our emphasis).

5. Cf. the particularly remarkable study that Hegel makes of Kantian philosophy in "Glauben und Wissen," pp. 235–62.

Phenomenology, it allowed "the internal opposition of the concept," that between the for-itself and the in-itself, between the subject and the object of knowledge, to subsist in observation and in action. This internal opposition of the concept, in Hegel's words, constitutes consciousness itself, which results from this internal requirement of the self that exists for-itself only in this split. Self exists only by opposing itself; life is self only because it appears to itself as other than itself. "However, spirit becomes object because it is this movement, this becoming an other to itself, that is, becoming the object of its own self and then suppressing [*aufheben*] this being-other" (*PE*, Preface, I, 32; *PG*, 32; *PM*, 96).[6] We know that the entire Hegelian system starts from the intuition that absolute life is absolute only in the movement by means of which life poses itself by contraposing itself to self. It is not Fichte's absolute "yes" elevated above every dialectic (primacy of the thesis); rather, it is this "yes" only through *negativity*, that is, the negation of its negation. Life which discovers itself in the midst of the deepest laceration: therein lies the soul of the dialectic of life. Consciousness expresses this division in the opposition between self and being, an opposition internal to the concept.

But if this opposition is suppressed by demonstrating the *identity of being and self*, do we not fall back into the immobilism of the Eleatics, or into Schelling's absolute, the identity about which Hegel wrote in the preface to his work: "To consider a certain Dasein as it is in the absolute amounts to stating that we may well be able to talk about it now as though about something, but that in the absolute, in A = A, there certainly are no such things because everything is one" (*PE*, I, 16; *PG*, 19; *PM*, 79)? Beyond the phenomenology of consciousness, is there no room for anything except a philosophy of identity, like Schelling's? In his 1801 system, Schelling, going beyond transcendental philosophy and in particular Fichte's philosophy of the I, rejoined Spinoza's ontologism. Intellectual intuition attains "the self-intuition of the absolute," and this intuition can only be that of the identity of this absolute with itself. "The supreme law for the being of reason is the law of identity."[7] Absolute life knows itself, and knowledge is buried in this life, which is therefore the total indifference of the subjective and the objective. Everything

6. In this passage, Hegel defines experience and the necessity for experience: "What there is in this experience is merely spiritual substance as, indeed, *object* of its own self."

7. Schelling, *SW*, IV, 116.

that is, is this absolute identity and not its manifestation. Being and knowledge of being are but one, and the law of identity expresses this unity. But Schelling does not manage to explain the differences presented in existence. "Nothing," he says, "is finite when observed by itself" and since "philosophy considers everything by itself," it runs the risk of rendering incomprehensible the differences which emerge from the absolute and which are presented in experience. "Knowledge cannot content itself with the in-itself or with essence while ignoring form" (*PE*, I, 18; *PG*, 20; *PM*, 81). Nor can differences be grasped as mere quantitative powers, as different degrees of expressions of the same absolute intuition. And yet Hegel takes up Schelling's ontologism in his *Logic*, whereas the *Phenomenology* corresponded to transcendental philosophy or to the theory of knowledge.[8] But opposition, the essential difference, abstraction, and mediation will not be absent from this thought, from the thought that at the same time is the thought of being. We no longer find the internal opposition of the concept, that of knowledge and being, but rather the opposition within content which will be presented in another form. Be that as it may, we still have to show the originality of Hegel's *Logic* by justifying its dialectical character and by insisting on the difference between this dialectic and the one proper to the *Phenomenology*, which rests on the difference between knowledge and being.

Thus the *Phenomenology* rests on a difference which is not that of the *Logic* and which, at the very least, is presented in a distinct form in the two works. In the *Phenomenology*, the movement of spirit to overcome this difference is what is properly called "experience." "For this reason we should say that nothing is known that is not in experience, or to express the same thing in a different way, nothing is known that is not present as felt truth, as the eternal revealed internally, as the sacred in which one believes, or whatever other expression one wants to use" (*PE*, II, 305; *PG*, 558; *PM*, 800). In effect, experience consists in the fact that content in-itself becomes the object of consciousness and links itself to self-certainty, to self-consciousness. Experience is the transformation of the in-itself to the for-itself; it expresses the necessity of "making real and revealing what is at first only interior, that is, of demanding (and link-

8. R. Kroner has conclusively shown that after adopting Schelling's ontologism, Hegel returns to the theory of knowledge in the *Phenomenology* and then once again to *ontology* in the *Logic* (*Von Kant bis Hegel* [Tübingen 1921, 1924], II, 433).

ing it to) the certainty of oneself" (*PE*, II, 305; *PG*, 558; *PM*, 800).

The history of consciousness—the *Phenomenology of Spirit* —is thus the history of its experience, the progressive revelation of spiritual substance to the self. "Consciousness knows and grasps nothing other than what is in its experience; indeed what is in this experience is merely spiritual substance and is, in fact, the object of its own self" (*PE*, I, 32; *PG*, 32; *PM*, 96). In the *Phenomenology*, spirit stages itself as a spectacle for itself; it conquers its own wealth, posits it outside itself as its substance, and then brings it back to itself; "only then, by becoming the property of consciousness, is immediateness presented in its actuality and in its truth." We have already indicated the broad sense that should be given to the term "experience," which in Kant was restricted to the realm of theoretical experience; the passage we quoted above is further evidence for our interpretation. What is at issue here is all human experience: theoretical, practical, esthetic, and religious. Human experience allows the self to discover itself and substance to reveal itself to the self. This experience necessarily takes place in time, for within consciousness "the whole, although not conceived of, precedes its moments" (*PE*, II, 305; *PG*, 558; *PM*, 800).[9] Thus the concept appears to consciousness as an *unfulfilled requirement,* as the self which is still outside itself and in a sort of ex-tasy in relation to self. The point is that the substance which presents itself as the object of consciousness is not yet conceived of, that is, does not pertain to the self; it must be developed in an experience which links it to self-consciousness, to the concept, but then this concept is present as a possible experience. That is why "time is the very concept that is there and that presents itself to consciousness as a vacant intuition." Time is thus the disquiet of consciousness which has not attained itself, which sees its self as outside itself. Time is the teleology immanent in this consciousness; thus it manifests itself as the destiny and the necessity of spirit which has not yet culminated within itself, as the necessity of enriching the participation of self-consciousness in consciousness, of beginning the movement of the immediateness of the in-itself—the form in which substance is in

9. In the concept that knows itself as concept (the *Logic*), the moments thus surge up sooner than the full whole whose coming to be is the movement of these moments. Inversely, in *consciousness*, the whole, although not conceived of, precedes the moments.

consciousness—"or conversely of making real and revealing what at first is only interior" (*PE, II, 305; PG, 558; PM, 800*). The intuited concept is *time* whereas the content to be revealed is the *in-itself*.

However, this spiritual substance which is revealed through experience is not equal to the self of consciousness. But this disparity, which is the common source of their movement, pertains to substance as well as to consciousness. "One can envisage this disparity as their common defect, but in fact it is their soul, it propels them both" (*PE, I, 32; PG, 32; PM, 96–97*). The disparity between consciousness and substance is that between knowledge and its object, a difference which calls for a perpetual self-transcendence in the *Phenomenology*. "But this disparity is also disparity of the substance with itself. What seems to occur outside it, to be an activity directed against it, is its own action: substance is shown to be essentially subject" (*PE, I, 32; PG, 32; PM, 97*).[10] Thus the object of consciousness becomes subject for consciousness. Its revelation consists of manifesting itself to the self as it is in-itself. Yet it is essentially spirit, and it must therefore manifest itself to consciousness, which finally discovers in its object what it itself is. Thus in the *Phenomenology* we have seen the immediate being of the beginning of the book present itself as a *thing*, as *force*, as *life*, and finally as *spirit*. This spirit in turn, "the *I* that is a *we* and the *we* that is an *I*," has become for consciousness spirit certain of itself, infinite spirit which through its reconciliation with finite spirit is the spiritual subject, absolute spirit. Absolute spirit finally appeared in religion and manifested itself completely in manifest or revealed religion. Religious consciousness grasped in its object what it is within itself; it discovered itself. However, this object still has the form of an object; it is beyond the self. It does indeed contain all speculative truth, but it contains it as a content contraposed to the self. The proof of this lies in the nostalgia of Christian consciousness, which feels reconciliation but projects it into a far-off time "Its own reconciliation enters its consciousness as something far off in the future, just as the reconciliation effected by the other self is manifest as something far off in the past." This *future* of religious consciousness is also the sign

10. Hegel adds: "Then the spirit as it is is an object to itself . . . the separation of knowledge and truth is overcome [*aufgehoben*]." That is indeed the result of the *Phenomenology*, as we have shown even with respect to the dialectic of religion.

that it has remained a representational consciousness, that truth is indeed for-it, but that it is *not itself this truth,* and that the separation of knowledge from truth has not yet been overcome; it is overcome in faith but not in knowledge. "Divine universal man, the community, has not arrived at the knowledge of spirit as itself, and of itself as spirit. Its knowledge is not absolute knowledge."

II. THE *Logic* OR SPECULATIVE PHILOSOPHY

THE ABSOLUTE KNOWLEDGE that results from the fact that substance has presented itself objectively as subject, and that the subject, the self, has become equal to its own substance, is the last figure of consciousness. In this last figure, the element of existence of the spirit is no longer the Dasein of consciousness, but the concept, universal self-consciousness. Spirit now reflects itself into itself in this element; it becomes the thought of itself, or logos. What does this speculative logic mean and how should it be characterized in relation to the *Phenomenology?* Here we cannot imagine giving even a sketch of Hegel's *Logic*—one of the richest and deepest works of the entire philosophical literature. To do so would markedly go beyond the scope we have set for ourselves; and yet since this *Logic* is mentioned at several points in the *Phenomenology,* our task would not truly be accomplished if we did not show the signification of this philosophic *Logic,* as it is derived from passages in the *Phenomenology.*

We know that in this *Logic*—divided into "Objective Logic" and "Subjective Logic"—Hegel starts from the poorest and most abstract categories to raise himself progressively to the richest and most concrete ones. He starts from *being,* passes through *essence,* which is the negation of immediate being, and arrives at the *concept* which is nothing other than the self positing itself as identical to itself in its being-other. The last section on the concept concerns subjective logic as opposed to the logic of being and of essence, which was objective logic. The distinction we have just mentioned brings us back in certain respects to the distinction between self and being which seemed specific to epistemology. This is because Hegel's speculative *Logic* claims to reconcile Schelling's dogmatism, the ontology of the system of identity, with Kant's criticism. In the *Phenomenology,* Hegel

is spirit—it is a dialectic and not merely an identity. This absolute reason is like Fichte's *Tathandlung;* it is the self that posits itself in each category and at the same time surpasses the finitude that is specific to limitation and to the abstraction of this particular moment of absolute thought. It might be said that this *infinite* thought of self is at the same time *finite* thought, thought which reflects itself, and that it is infinite thought only because it is simultaneously finite thought, or again (which amounts to the same thing), that the dialectical character of Hegelian logos reconciles Kant's *intuitive understanding* with *discursive understanding.*

Understanding (*Verstand*), as it is presented to us in the preface to the *Phenomenology*, is

> the activity of dividing, [it] is the greatest and most astonishing power that exists, or rather absolute power. The circle which rests closed in on itself and which, as substance, grasps and includes all its moments is the immediate relation which therefore arouses no astonishment. But that the accidental as such, separated from its environs, which are linked and are actual only in their connection to something other, obtains its own Dasein and a distinct freedom, shows the prodigious power of the negative, the energy of thought, of the pure I (*PE,* I, 29; *PG,* 29; *PM,* 93).

That is surely the first time that a philosopher referred to understanding as "the most astonishing power that exists." Now this understanding is not only ours, it is also the understanding of things, of being, of the absolute, or whatever one wants to call it. The power to divide, which constitutes the finitude of every determination, is not excluded from the absolute, which is thus simultaneously finite and infinite. Hegel's allusion to death in the passage following the one we have just quoted recalls to us the image that dominates his entire system, that of an absolute which is not alien to death itself, of a God who knows death and survives himself in death. "Spirit is this power only by being able to look the negative in the face and by being able to stay close to it. This staying power is the magical power which converts the negative into being . . . it is identical to what we have called the 'subject.' "

The system of categories, speculative logic, is therefore not only our thought; it is also the absolute's thought of itself, the spirit which poses itself as logos. Here absolute reason overcomes the opposition between intellectual intuition and discursive understanding, and reconciles them into itself. "But the truth of reason is spirit, spirit that is higher than understanding or reason (when separated); it is reason that possesses understanding or rational understanding (*verständige Vernunft oder vernünftiger Verstand*)." [13]

The reason that is spirit is the absolute's self-knowledge; it is *universal self-consciousness* and as such it is that truth that is a life unto itself, a subject. "Thus the true is the bacchic ecstasy in which no member is sober; and since this delirium immediately dissolves into itself every moment that tends to become separated from the whole, this delirium is also translucid and simple repose" (*PE,* I, 40; *PG,* 39; *PM,* 105). The true that is subject—and not merely substance—indeed reconciles into itself ontology and the Fichtean theory of the I. It is simultaneously the logos of being and *Tathandlung,* the self-positing of the I; for being is basically identical to self. It is the self that poses itself in every determinateness and, abstracting itself from self, through this negativity that characterizes it, contraposes itself to itself. Hence the unique character of Hegelian logic: it is both analytic and synthetic, it unites the thought of identity with that of contradiction. *Because* the self contradicts itself, negates itself, it can be identical to itself. The role of contradiction and negation in Hegelian logic follows from the conception according to which being is self and every identity has meaning only because it is the identity of self in a certain content. Thus this identity is of itself contradictory, for the self can pose itself only by negating itself.

> By virtue of this simplicity or this equality with itself, substance manifests itself as firm and permanent. But this self-equality is also negativity, and that is why this stable Dasein passes over into its own disintegration. Determinateness at first appears as such only because it is related to something *other,* and its movement appears to be imposed on it by an alien power. But this very simplicity of thought precisely implies that determinateness has its being-other within itself and that it is self-movement (*Selbstbewegung*); in fact this simplicity of thought is thought propelling itself and differentiating itself, it is interiority itself, the pure concept. Thus understanding is a development and as development it is rationality (*PE,* I, 49; *PG,* 46–47; *PM,* 115).

As a moment of logos, finitude is the abstract or *discrete* characteristic of categories, their mutual separation; but their infinity, their concrete becoming, is the suppression [*Aufhebung*] of this

13. *Logic,* p. 7.

state of abstraction, the *continuity* of the categories, and their totality or unity. This totality or unity would only be an idea in Kant's sense of the term if it did not develop, that is, progress to the point of distinct moments, thereby suppressing its finitude as *mere* idea or *postulate*.

III. DIFFERENCE BETWEEN THE *Phenomenology* AND THE *Logic;* THEIR MUTUAL CORRESPONDENCE

THUS WE FIND IN *absolute knowledge,* just as in the *Phenomenology,* difference and mediation, but we find them in another form. Since opposition between knowledge and being, between certainty and truth, has been overcome, every moment is presented as a pure determination, and its movement is the result of its determinate and hence finite character. "In this science the moments of the movement of spirit are no longer presented as determinate figures of consciousness, but since the difference of consciousness is turned back into the self, these moments are presented as determinate concepts and as their organic movement grounded in itself" (*PE,* II, 310; *PG,* 562; *PM,* 805). And yet the *same content,* the *same determinations* are offered both in the *Phenomenology,* in the guise of *figures* of consciousness, and in the *Logic,* in the guise of determinate *concepts.* There is a perfect correlation between the *Phenomenology of Spirit* and the *Logic.* But in one case the dialectic is based on the difference between knowledge and truth "and is the movement during which this difference eliminates [*aufheben*] itself." In the other case, "the pure figure of the moment freed from its (phenomenal) manifestation in consciousness, that is, the pure concept, and its progression depend only on its pure determination" (*PE,* II, 310; *PG,* 562; *PM,* 806).[14] In the *Phenomenology,* experience—which is dialectical—appears as an oscillation between a truth which is alien to certainty and a subjective certainty which lacks truth. In the *Logic,* experience as such is surpassed; it is truth itself that develops in-and-for-itself, but self-certainty is *immanent* in this truth and "this simple mediation, this unity, constitutes the concept." The form of the concept unites in an immediate unity the objective form of the truth

14. For example, we can compare the dialectic of sensuous certainty with that of being, of Dasein, etc.

and that of the self that knows (*PE*, II, 310; *PG*, 562; *PM* 805).[15] This unity is the presupposition of the *Logic* or speculative philosophy; it is the result of the *Phenomenology*. But nothing is known that does not exist in experience, and consequently the experience of phenomenal consciousness contains in its fashion the entire content of the logos. To every abstract *moment* of science there corresponds a *figure* of phenomenal spirit in general. Spirit being-there is no richer than science, but neither is it poorer in its content. To comprehend the pure concepts of science in the form of figures of consciousness (for example, apropos of perception, understanding, and observation) constitutes that aspect of their reality according to which their essence, the concept—which in science is posed in its simple mediation, as thought—separates the moments of this mediation and portrays itself according to internal opposition. This simple mediation is undone and the concept that opposes itself within itself becomes knowledge *and* being, certainty *and* truth. We can attempt to go still further in the correspondence between the *Logic* and the *Phenomenology*. (It is here that we feel the entire problem of the Hegelian system in general lies.) The *Phenomenology* is not a phenomenalism, a description of finite experience, or rather it is not merely this description; it includes a "for-us," an aspect which pertains only to speculative philosophy, and in this respect it is more than a theory of knowledge. Kant had already far surpassed phenomenalism with his conception of *transcendental* logic, but in the *Phenomenology*, Hegel surpasses Kantian criticism by as much again. He presents a *speculative theory of experience*; the philosopher who says "we" in the *Phenomenology*, and sets himself apart from consciousness enmeshed in experience, perceives the speculative necessity for the progression of consciousness, a necessity not seen by the naïve consciousness. The *Phenomenology* deals with the problem of experience according to the speculative method.[16] Reciprocally, the *Logic* or speculative philosophy is not without its phenomenological aspect; it is a speculative logic and *also* a theory of knowledge, but the roles are, so to speak, reversed. The theory of knowledge appears in the foreground of the *Phenomenology*,

---

15. One might compare what we have termed the "phenomenological genesis of the concept" (part II) with objective logic (being, essence), which is an ontological genesis of the concept.

16. Cf. part I, chapter 1: "Meaning and Method of the *Phenomenology*."

whereas speculative thought is "behind the back of conscious-ness" (*PE*, I, 77; *PG*, 74; *PM*, 144).[17] In the *Logic*, speculative thought is in the foreground, whereas the theory of knowledge is only "for-us," that is, for thinking spirit which reflects the movement of categories. This reflection accompanies this move-ment, although it *plays no role in it,* and only at the end of the *Logic* does identity appear between this thinking spirit and the actions of thought that lead from being to essence, from being to nothingness, from being to becoming, and so on.

Again, we may say that in the *Logic* the identity of being and self is implicit or presupposed at the beginning and progres-sively becomes explicit, whereas in the *Phenomenology* this identity is the problem which must be resolved (but which spec-ulative thought has already resolved in-itself). All the objections to the Hegelian system bear on this passage from the implicit to the explicit, from potentiality to action, as well as on this problem that is "already resolved." The *Phenomenology* is ac-cused of containing something beyond the description of experi-ence, which then makes possible its genesis and the *Logic* is ac-cused of supposing at the beginning what is shown only at the end. In other words, it is the mode of Hegelian thought itself that is in question, *the circularity of the thought or the finality of the self.* "The true is its own becoming, it is the circle which at its beginning presupposes and has its own end as its purpose and which is actual only by means of its developed actualization and by means of its end" (*PE*, I, 18; *PG*, 20; *PM*, 81). "What we have said can also be expressed this way: reason is action in ac-cordance with a goal. . . . The result is what the beginning is, because the beginning is the goal" (*PE*, I, 20; *PG*, 22; *PM*, 83).

Logic is *also* a theory of knowledge because it is truly a "self-knowledge," which Schelling's absolute identity was not. It is the self that poses itself as being, determinate being, quantity, measure, and so on, but self knows that explicitly only at the end of the *Logic* in a new reflection which embraces the general movement of the moments of the logos. It is this "new reflec-tion" which is *for-us* in the *Logic* and which is not yet explicit in the moment we have considered. At this point it would be use-ful to give an example of this *phenomenological* character of Hegelian *Logic;* perhaps the correspondence between the *Phe-*

17. "But this very necessity or the *birth* of the new object . . . is what for us takes place so to speak behind the back of conscious-ness."

nomenology and the *Logic* will become clearer. Let us consider the point of departure of the *Logic* and the famous opposition between being and nothingness. This corresponds to the starting point of the *Phenomenology*, but whereas, in the *Phenomenology*, immediately given being is opposed by the no less immediate knowledge of that being, and whereas a disparity comes to light that is the germ of the opposition between realism and idealism, in the *Logic* being is given as pure category, the object of thought which does not have to be confronted with knowledge. Being and the consciousness that thinks being are immediately, *in-itself*, identical. As such, this being has only one determination: it excludes nothingness from itself and it is by itself the contrary of itself, nothingness. Indeed, at the start being occupies the entire field of the conceivable, but its contrary, nothingness—which is the nothingness of being—also demands for itself this same extension. Being and nothingness contradict each other because they are these determinations and not others. But if we reflect on this first dialectic, we see that it is possible only because the *self has posed itself as being.* The judgment "being is nothingness" is not made by being itself, but by thinking spirit which is immanent in this first determination and which will not be made explicit until the end of the *Logic*, when being itself will be completely explicit and will have become *concept for-itself.* It is because *being is the concept of being* that it is this movement and this dialectic, and that fact is *for-us* in the first chapter of the *Logic.* Thought does not think itself here as thought; it thinks itself as being, and yet implicitly it already thinks itself, and this appears in the judgment "being is nothingness." We subsequently see that the opposition between knowledge and being which was specific to the *Phenomenology* reappears implicitly—for us—in this opposition between being and nothingness. Being, being-in-itself as immediate determination, would be opaque, massive, impenetrable to knowledge. Besides, how can we say that this—purely positive—being is in-itself, since that would introduce a sort of relation with itself, or distance from itself, which pertains to the category of essence (identity, difference, and so on) and is not applicable to the immediateness affirmed by this first moment? Even if being is intended, thought is completely excluded by this being, and without being thought is nothingness; it is a thought that thinks . . . nothing. Conversely, this being that is excluded from any thought falls back into nothingness. In fact, the exclusion cannot be maintained since *thought thinks being;* and for this reason this purely *positive* determination, which absolutely excludes thought, is that which is purely *negative.* Thus thought and being are recovered *for us* in the famous opposition between being and nothingness as well as in their identity. But that is due to the fact that it is the *self that has posited itself as being* and that this positing is not tenable; it engenders a dialectic. The self is absolute *negativity* and this negativity shows through in its *positing* itself as being. If the self is being, that is because being as such negates itself, and if being is the self, that is because it is in-itself this negation of itself. But once again, all this is for-us at the beginning of the *Logic;* it is to us that being *appears* as a positing of self, and thus as a contradiction. As far as being itself is concerned, it is merely nothingness.

There is yet another way of manifesting this *immanence of self in the determinations of logic.* We might say that it is because being is not only being, but nothingness as well, that the *question of being is possible.* The problem of being is the problem of the *positing* of being. In the question, "Why being rather than nothing?", thought rises above being. Seeming to confront two opposite possibilities, repeating Hamlet's "To be or not to be, that is the question," thought, the thought that asks the question, seems to transcend these two possibilities. But being replies that the question itself is possible only because being is already presupposed. In the question "Why isn't it nothingness that *is?*" the verb "to be" reappears; when nothingness is posited hypothetically in place of being, it becomes being. But how can being reply, if not by its own positing of *itself?* "I am that which is, I am still *I* in my contrary." This answer reveals only the power of thought, of the self in being. In this reply, being is revealed to us as thought, *as itself.* It no longer is the immediate being from which logic began; it is already essence, self-identity, "being is being," which implies a contradiction, and by the fact of this contradiction it is more than essence, it is the concept, that which is itself in the contrary of itself.

Thus it is indeed because the content of the *Logic* is the self which thinks itself and which opposes itself in each of its moments, that this content is propelled forward and *explicitly* uncovers the *implicit* identity of self and being. In the *Logic,* the I *has completely alienated itself into content,* and this alienation or negativity of content is the source of the development of the categories. That is what Hegel expresses in the section on absolute knowledge when he writes:

In line with the freedom of its being, content is the self that alienates itself, or the immediate unity of the knowledge of oneself. The pure movement of this alienation, considered in content, constitutes the necessity of content itself. In its diversity, content as determinate content is in relation; it is not in-itself, and its disquiet consists of suppressing itself dialectically, that is, it is negativity. Thus necessity or diversity are equally free being and self, and within this form of self, in which Dasein is immediately thought, content is concept (*PE*, II, 309–10; *PG*, 562; *PM*, 805).

What Hegel calls here "the freedom of the being of content" results from the complete alienation of the self, which has disappeared into content instead of abstractly turning back on itself; what he calls "necessity" (or "diversity") is the movement of content which stems from the fact that the self has posed itself in content and thus has opposed itself to itself. That is why this content is an abstraction in-itself and why it negates itself, *necessarily* becoming other. But this becoming, which is rationality, is nothing other than the movement of the self. Science is thus the conception of the self itself, its thought of itself.[18]

IV. DEMONSTRATION OF THE IDENTITY OF SELF AND BEING

THE *Phenomenology* SETS OUT to establish this identity of self and being from which the *Logic* starts and which is a paradox for the common consciousness, "an attempt to walk on one's head" (*PE*, I, 24; *PG*, 25; *PM*, 87). It culminates in the element of existence that Hegel terms the "concept" and in which alone—as if in ether—science can develop for its own self. We will examine in succession, using the passages of the *Phenomenology* on absolute knowledge, how the *Phenomenology*

18. We can understand the dialectic logos, nature, spirit in the same way. The logos is the whole, the self, which poses itself as *thought of itself;* but this thought which is *only* thought contradicts itself by posing itself (just as being which is essence contradicts itself as immediate being and consequently becomes concept). Logos is therefore itself and the contrary of itself; that is why it is *nature* by this negation of itself. But logos negates itself because it is more than logos, because it is spirit; and it is through this negation of itself, nature, that *spirit is real.*

proved this identity, how this element of existence of science is characterized, and how it could appear temporally (*how can the self-consciousness of the absolute at the same time be a self-consciousness of humanity?*)

Concerning the first point, at the beginning of the section on absolute knowledge, Hegel again takes up certain figures of consciousness to show how the object of consciousness as object, or if one prefers the object of consciousness as form of objectivity, has been surpassed along the way. The truth of the object is the self; consciousness of the other (first section of the *Phenomenology*, consciousness) has been shown to be a self-consciousness (second section of the *Phenomenology*). But this demonstration is insufficient. If being leads to self as its truth, then conversely the self must have discovered itself as possessing the characteristics of being and of objectivity. By alienating itself, the self posits "thingness," and remains close to itself in this alienation. Thus the demonstration must consist in seeking those figures of consciousness in which the self has alienated and posited itself with the different determinations appropriate to objective being. "In this alienation self-consciousness poses itself as object, or by virtue of the indivisible unity of being-for-itself, poses the object as itself" (*PE*, II, 294; *PG*, 549; *PM*, 789).

Now, what are the different determinatenesses of objective being as manifested by the first experiences of consciousness? These determinatenesses are not presented to us in their pure conceptual form, as will be the case in the *Logic;* instead, *we* gather them ourselves by considering the different figures of consciousness. The object is first revealed as an *immediate being*, a thing in general (sensuous certainty); then as a *relation*, a determinate being which is just as much for-itself as it is for-others, that is, the thing with its multiple properties (perception); and finally as *essence* and universal (force, the law or the interior of the phenomenal world, which corresponds to understanding). In its totality, the object is presented as the movement from the immediate universal (or specific) to the concrete specific (or universal) by traversing particularity, that is, mediation and determination. "The entire object is the syllogism or the movement from the universal, traversing determination, toward specificity, as well as the converse movement from specificity, traversing specificity as suppressed [*aufgehoben*], or determination, toward the universal" (*PE*, II, 294; *PG*, 550; *PM*, 790).

This totality is only for-us. For consciousness, it was a new object, for example life at the moment of self-consciousness. Self-consciousness must have alienated itself according to each of these determinations and have presented itself to itself as "thingness" according to the three dimensions of this thingness. Self had to alienate itself and become an immediate thing, a pure being without signification; it had to become a system of relations like the thing of perception; and then finally it had to become a universal that was still objective, an interior like the "force" of understanding. By recollecting the entire previous experience, we should rediscover these successive alienations, which not only prove that being has been resolved into self, but that *self has posed itself in being.* Given the indivisible character of the self, this alienation of self, which only shows that self itself poses thingness, constitutes the strength of the demonstration as well as that of the converse proposition, that which unveils the truth of the thing to be the self.

I. The self as immediate being has alienated itself. In its observation of nature, the self indeed discovered itself as a thing in general. It observed the world, and what it was unconsiously seeking in this world was itself. Thus it discovers itself, but it discovers itself as absolutely alien to itself, as a pure thing, an existence without meaning. When we say "the soul is," or "the self is," we don't yet quite know exactly what we are saying. But when we contemplate a skull and find in it the being of the self, we understand for the first time the absurd signification (the infinite judgment) of the verb "to be," applied to the self. Self has retrogressed into mere nature, "into the facticity of Dasein," as we would say today. "As regards the object, insofar as it is immediate, an indifferent being, we have seen observing reason seek itself and find itself in this indifferent thing" (*PE*, II, 295; *PG*, 551; *PM*, 791).[19] Its action, for the self is pure action (*Tat*), has appeared to it as just as exterior as the immediate being of the dialectic of sensuous certainty. Hence the infinite judgment, which is absurd for representational consciousness, but so profound for spiritual consciousness (which right away inverts its meaning), that *the being of the I is a thing* and *precisely an im-*

19. The figure of consciousness to which Hegel alludes is that which ends the chapter on the observation of nature and human individuality, *phrenology* (*PE*, I, 272; *PG*, 241; *PM*, 355). Cf. our part IV, chapter 3: The consciousness of self as thing is individuality as the only originary nature.

mediate and sensuous thing. Self is just as much posed in this complete exteriority to itself, in this alien being, as it is in mere being-for-itself.

2. Self has alienated itself as determinateness and as relation. In the world of *utility*, which is the expression of the truth of the Enlightenment, the thing is suppressed; it only has meaning in relation, "only through the I and its reference to the I" (*PE*, II, 296; *PG*, 551; *PM*, 791–92).[20] Self posed itself in the fabric of exterior relations, which allow being-for-itself to subsist for a moment only then to dissolve it in its relations to others. The perpetual movement of utility expressed the self, just as through perception the dialectic of things and their properties expressed itself. The "cultivated I, through its alienation," produced "the thing as its own self"; thus it rediscovers itself in this social universe, in the perpetual alternation of its being-for-itself and its being-for-others. The thing and the self here have the characteristic of *useableness* which modern philosophy since pragmatism has often described. One should notice in passing the concrete character of the demonstration of the identity of self and being that Hegel gives; it can clarify the scope and the meaning of this demonstration for us.

3. Self has alienated itself as essence or interiority. "The thing must be known as self, not only insofar as the immediateness of its being or its determinateness is concerned, but also as essence or interior. This last is what is given in moral self-consciousness" (*PE*, II, 296; *PG*, 551; *PM*, 792).[21] For understanding, the objective thing was a universal, an interior of the phenomenal world in contraposition to its manifestation. The same was true for moral self-consciousness as Kant conceived it. "Moral self-consciousness knows its own knowledge as absolute essentiality or knows being uniquely as pure will or pure knowledge; it *is* only this will and this knowledge." In this world view, the suprasensuous is the self as pure knowledge and pure will indivisibly. Here self has alienated itself; it is pure knowing will, but this will is still, insofar as it is pure, an interior, a beyond in opposition to sensuous Dasein in time and space, just as the force of understanding was contraposed to its phenomenon.

20. The figure of consciousness to which Hegel refers is that of the *world of utility* (PE, II, 121; PG, 407; PM, 589).

21. For the opposition between essence and manifestation in understanding, see *PE*, I, 118; *PG*, 110; *PM*, 200. On pure will and knowledge beyond immediate Dasein, see the moral world view (*PE*, II, 142 ff.; *PG*, 423 ff.; *PM*, 611 ff.).

However, in neither case does this opposition stand up: for understanding just as for moral self-consciousness, there is a perpetual passage from interior to exterior, from the suprasensuous to the sensuous. "Insofar as moral consciousness unshackles the Dasein of self in its portrayal of the world, to that extent it gathers it up into itself." That is why, just as understanding became the unity of this transition or living self-consciousness, so too moral consciousness becomes the *Gewissen* "which knows that its Dasein as such is this pure self-certainty." If self-consciousness alienates itself now, it is into an element of existence such that it is for self-consciousness simultaneously *objective* and *subjective,* that it is simultaneously *being* and *self-certainty.* "The objective element in which it exposes itself as acting is none other than the pure knowledge that the self has of itself" (*PE, II,* 297; *PG,* 552; *PM,* 792–93).[22]

V. The Element of Existence of Science: Universal Self-Consciousness

Thus the self has alienated and posed itself in all the dimensions of being: at least that is what we, philosophers, retrospectively discover through the recollection of figures of consciousness, which is our job. But the last figure, that of *Gewissen,* must contain all the others in a condensed form. It offers us precisely this element of existence, this ether, in which absolute knowledge becomes possible. Spirit certain of itself has for its truth, for its objective element, the very self-certainty that it is inside itself. This self-knowledge is mediated only by the universality of self-consciousnesses, by universal recognition. It is expressed by language, which is authentically the prefiguration of the logos of the *Logic.* We should say explicitly that this element of existence is the *universal self-consciousness being-there in "the universal divine man."* It is in such an element that the self-consciousness of the absolute will be possible. This last figure indeed presents in a condensed way what we have termed the "three dimensions of being." The knowledge of consciousness certain of itself (*Gewissen*) is *immediately there as a being.* It

22. Hegel's demonstration leads to showing that the universe of the self is both objective and subjective, that this distinction is transcended in the self's observation.

contraposes itself to itself and enters into *relation* and *determination* because it is simultaneously universal and specific and because acting consciousness necessarily poses this duality at the heart of this element. In the same way, what is opposed to itself is a knowledge, qua determinate Dasein or relation; it is a knowledge of the purely specific self on the one hand, of knowledge as universal on the other. "Then it is established here that the third moment, the universality of essence, is valid for each of the two opposites only as knowledge, and they together similarly suppress this empty opposition which still remains and are the knowledge of the I = I, this specific self which is immediately pure knowledge or universal" (*PE*, II, 298; *PG*, 552–53; *PM*, 793).

The reconciliation of finite spirit and infinite spirit expressed in this last passage is absolute knowledge itself, a knowledge which is simultaneously the knowledge that the absolute has of itself and that of this finite spirit which raises itself to universal self-consciousness.[23] This encounter between a nontemporal infinite spirit and temporal humanity in the I = I, an encounter which alone makes spirit absolute, is the central problem of the *Phenomenology of Spirit*. It contains the problem of the relation between religion and philosophy, since religion also presents this reconciliation, albeit in the form of the in-itself. In religion, this reconciliation is the object of *a faith;* in philosophy it is *an act,* an act that is simultaneously a knowledge, which is why in philosophy this reconciliation has become *in-and-for-itself.* In addition, it contains the problem of the link between the *Phenomenology* and the *Logic* in the following form: How can a knowledge which of itself is atemporal, an absolute knowledge, have temporal conditions in the existence and development of a humanity? There is not in Hegelianism a clear solution to these problems, and it is on these points that the great Hegelian synthesis will tend to come apart in the hands of Hegel's disciples. Our task here can only consist in explaining as clearly as we are able the passages in which Hegel raises these different problems and—somewhat symbolically—resolves them.

In the *Phenomenology,* "absolute knowledge" seems to be for Hegel not merely the construction of a speculative logic, a new system of philosophy which is to be added on to the previous ones and complete them, but the inauguration of a new period

23. What logos thinks is the identity of thought thinking with thought thought, of logos with the thought of the philosopher.

in the history of the world spirit. Humanity has come to a consciousness of itself; it has become capable of bearing and generating its own destiny. This idea—which was expressed by certain Romantics as that of a new religion—is basically common to the thinkers of the Enlightenment and to some Romantic poets. In the preface to the *Phenomenology* Hegel expresses the sentiment of an entire generation which had lived through the French Revolution and the Napoleonic epic and which had gorged itself on Germany's philosophic discoveries. "Besides, it is not difficult to see that our time is a time of birth and of transition to a new period. Spirit has broken with the preceding world, with its Dasein and its representation; it is on the verge of burying that world in the past and it is laboring over its own transformation" (*PE*, I, 12; *PG*, 15; *PM*, 75).

For Hegel, absolute knowledge, philosophy, seems destined to play the role that was formerly played by religion. In his early works, there is hardly any possibility of anything other than religion that would allow a people to conceive its reconciliation with its destiny in history. But starting with his arrival at Jena, Hegel attributed equal importance to philosophy. It is philosophy that allows absolute reason to come to consciousness of itself, and in each great system of philosophy, as if in a work of art, "reason has been presented in a form perfect unto itself." "The history of philosophy is thus the history of pure and eternal reason which presents itself in infinitely diverse forms." [24] In the *Phenomenology*, Hegel is less under Schelling's influence, and he no longer compares philosophy to an independent work of art. He no longer says that in philosophy there are "neither precursors nor successors," but speaks of a development that he compares to an organic genesis. "The bud disappears in the blossoming of the flower, and we could say that the bud is refuted by the flower" These forms are not merely distinct; in addition, each one suppresses the other because they are mutually incompatible. "But at the same time their fluid nature makes them moments of an organic unity in which they not only reject each other, but in which each is as necessary as the other, and this equal necessity alone constitutes the life of the whole" (*PE*, I, 6; *PG*, 10; *PM*, 68). It is the province of philosophy to resolve the contradictions of a culture and to reconcile

24. In "Differenz," pp. 172 and 201. It is in this work that Hegel views philosophy as a *phenomenon* of culture, as capable of thinking through and resolving the oppositions of a *culture*.

the rigid determinatenesses in which understanding has fixed the moments of spiritual life. The element of existence of philosophy, as Hegel conceives it in the *Phenomenology,* is the concept, and it is this element of existence that the *Phenomenology* proposes to reveal as the result of human experience. We have already indicated some of the characteristics of this element. The concept is the subject that is simultaneously specific and universal, self-consciousness that is *this specific* self-consciousness and at the same time is *universal.* What is exposed in this element is an objective element and at the same time acting self; that is why the perfection of this element can only be attained by traversing a long history. Specific consciousness, closed in on itself, had to become the milieu of "universal recognition"; in other words, the individual had to become aware that his being depended on recognition by others (as the master by the slave) and by all others, that is, by all of history. It is through the mediation of history and of previous knowledge that this element shapes itself. Thus the thing (*Ding*) of perception became the common deed at the human level (*die Sache selbst*), and this common deed has finally become the self-conscious subject which is subject only in the action through which it reconciles within itself essence or abstract universal with the finitude of its self-consciousness.[25] In the concept—a living contradiction because it is the unity of the infinite and the finite —human and temporal self-consciousness transcends itself; it becomes self-consciousness of absolute spirit, which does not mean that it contemplates this spirit, but rather that it *generates* it. Since it is the dialectical unity of the finite and the infinite, the concept is also the unity of knowledge and action. "It is the knowledge of the action of the self by itself . . . the knowledge of this subject as substance and of substance as this knowledge of the action of the subject" (*PE,* II, 302; *PG,* 556; *PM,* 797). When Marx later wrote "The philosophers have only *interpreted* the world in various ways; the point, however, is to *change* it," he was not too unfaithful to Hegelian thought. To be sure, he broke the equilibrium of the Hegelian synthesis, and tipped the balance toward the side of action. But although Hegel claimed to attain an action that would be self-knowledge and a self-knowledge that would be action, doesn't the philosopher's specu-

25. Cf. the essential chapter on the thing itself (*PE,* I, 324 ff.; *PG,* 285 ff.; *PM,* 417 ff.). In the logic, the unity of being and thought is the "thing itself," *die Sache selbst.* Cf. commentary on this chapter, part IV, chapter 5.

lative thought itself indicate a preference for knowledge? "Philosophy always comes too late, like the owl of Minerva"; it is more a knowledge than a will, and if we still give the name "action" to the conception of self that absolute knowledge is, does that not involve a certain abuse of language? We should most of all say that the meaning of this action in Hegelian philosophy always seems to be to lead to a deeper self-knowledge, as though the supreme goal were this very knowledge. "The access to the goal, absolute knowledge, or spirit knowing itself as spirit, passes through the recollection of spirits as they are in themselves and as they bring about the organization of their (spiritual) kingdom" (*PE*, II, 312; *PG*, 564; *PM*, 808).

However, in the element of the concept, this absolute knowledge appears as the very action of the subject that thinks it. The self-knowledge that is "logos" is not a passive contemplation, for we ourselves are the reason that comprehends itself and poses itself, we are the object that knows itself and produces itself in this self-knowledge. "Spirit manifesting itself to consciousness in this element, or what amounts to the same thing, *produced* by it in such an element, is science" (*PE*, II, 303; *PG*, 556; *PM*, 798). The concept is "the generation of self." Thus infinite reason knows itself in human self-consciousness and is infinite only in this finite knowledge of itself; conversely, human self-consciousness only attains itself in this self-knowledge and this actual reconciliation. Spirit is absolute only when it becomes so, and it only becomes absolute in the action by which it transcends itself as finite spirit.

This reconciliation is indeed portrayed by religion, *but in the form of the in-itself*; it appears to religious consciousness as a content which is still alien to it instead of being its own work. "Thus what in religion was content or the form of the portrayal of an other, that very thing here is precisely the action of the self" (*PE*, II, 302; *PG*, 556; *PM*, 797). In the element of the concept, by contrast, it is this specific subject, this finite self, that raises itself to universal self and brings about the reconciliation, which no longer appears as the effect of an alien self. This moment of the return of consciousness into self-consciousness has in some respects been presented in religion, with regard to the spirit of community. The religious community interiorizes the content, which is the life, death, and resurrection of Christ; it is in this community that spirit lives, dies, and is resurrected. Qua community and tradition, the religious community exists as a continual revelation of speculative truth, and this truth has become its own self. That is why it is a prefiguration of the element of concept, in which speculative truth no longer appears as alien to the self that poses it. If we look back at these passages by Hegel on the religious community, we can say that it would have been possible to elaborate a philosophy of the church on the basis of the *Phenomenology of Spirit*, but Hegel no more ends up with a philosophy of the church than he does with an abstract philosophy of humanity such as that of the Enlightenment. Absolute knowledge, as a moment of world history, which reconciles this temporal moment with a truth which in-itself is atemporal, is presented to us in a form so vague as to open the path to diverse interpretations; we are unable to indicate exactly which interpretation constitutes the authentic heritage of Hegelianism.

If religion portrayed speculative truth in the form of a content still external to self-consciousness, the beautiful soul offered the form of the *concept for-itself*. Indeed, it was not "the intuition of the divine," but the "self-intuition of the divine" (*PE*, II, 299; *PG*, 554; *PM*, 795): it was the figure of self-certain spirit, *absolute subject*. As a figure of consciousness, it was still imperfect, as it remained enclosed within its subjectivity and lacked content. But it is only "in unity with its alienation that the concept exists in its truth." When the beautiful soul renounces its stubborn obstinacy, it becomes spirit that acts, it "abandons its eternal essence, is there in a determinate way, *or acts*" (*PE*, II, 300; *PG*, 554; *PM*, 795). This action, taken up again in the concept, raised above its finitude by the self which has inscribed itself in it and surpassed it by translating it, becomes absolute concept, which, in its *extension* as well as in its *temporal development*, is also in its *depth* (*PE*, II, 312; *PG*, 564; *PM*, 808).

This reconciliation which in religion was *in-itself* becomes *for* consciousness and finally becomes consciousness' *own* action. It is at that precise moment that the self, which "alone actualizes the life of absolute spirit," becomes for its own self this absolute spirit that it already was in-itself. "Now, what happens in-itself in the first instance is at the same time for consciousness, and is thus at the same time reproduced; it is for consciousness and it is its being-for-itself or its own action" (*PE*, II, 301; *PG*, 555; *PM*, 796). Universal self-consciousness *exists* and comprehends itself in this specific and historical self-consciousness, which actualizes this absolute life and in its turn recognizes itself in this universality: I = I.

VI. RETURN FROM SPECULATIVE PHILOSOPHY TO PHENOMENOLOGY, NATURE, AND HISTORY

THE PASSAGES FROM HEGEL do not allow us to delineate further the concrete signification of this universal self-consciousness. In the last pages of his work, after summarily indicating that the primitive religious community, the medieval church, and then modern philosophy prepared the ground for the speculative knowledge that absolute knowledge is, he shows how this philosophy allows for a return to the *Phenomenology*, to the philosophy of nature and of history (which in the last pages seems to occupy, along with the *Phenomenology*, the place that will be occupied by the philosophy of spirit in the *Encyclopaedia*). Absolute knowledge can only appear when the actual history of the world spirit has led it to consciousness of itself.

> But insofar as the Dasein of this concept is concerned, science does not manifest itself in time and in actuality until the spirit arrives at this consciousness about itself. As spirit that knows what it is, it does not exist [earlier *or*] in *any other way*; it *exists only after* the fulfillment of the labor by which, having overcome its imperfect figuration, it creates for its consciousness the figure of its essence, and in this way equalizes its self-consciousness with its consciousness (*PE*, II, 303; *PG;* 557; *PM,* 799; emphasis mine).

Science—the self-thought of logos—which, as we have seen, is the unity of self and being, "also contains the necessity of alienating from itself the form of the pure concept" (*PE*, II, 311; *PG,* 563; *PM,* 806). It thus contains the passage of the concept (as concept) into consciousness (as the division between knowledge and being), then the passage of the logos into nature and into history, its alienation in the form of nature and history. Thus in summary is delineated the entire future organization of the Hegelian system with its divisions: logos, nature, spirit. We would merely like to emphasize an important point concerning the transition from one of these terms to another. Hegel has frequently been criticized for passing arbitrarily from logos to nature, and it has been said that this deduction of nature from logos is unintelligible. How can thought which is only pure thought generate nature? But it seems to us that to ask this is to ask the wrong question, and that this criticism does not apply to the Hegelian system. Logos and nature mutually presuppose each other; one cannot be posed without the other. It is absurd to imagine a causality of any kind in logos which would produce nature. "The very word 'creation,'" Hegel says, "is a word pertaining to representation," and the philosopher adheres to this representational language when he speaks of a reign of pure thought prior to the creation of nature and of a finite spirit. This terminology gives rise to misunderstandings. In the same way, one cannot say that Hegel deduces nature from logos, unless we change the usual meaning of the word "deduction." This is the place to explain the paradox that we mentioned and according to which Hegel reduces philosophy to logic and at the same time surpasses this reduction. Logos does not exist without nature nor nature without logos, just as being is not without nothingness nor nothingness without being. Both of them are the whole, for both are themselves and more than themselves, and it is in that respect that they are spirit.[26] Logos is the whole which negates itself as nature, it is the abstraction of pure thought which poses itself as pure thought and in this posing of itself excludes nature. Now, we have already said that this abstraction—which is negativity itself—was not the work of a simple human understanding, but that it was at the very heart of the absolute. The absolute exists only in this negativity (which insofar as it is pure, that is, insofar as it proceeds to the point of the negation of negation, is the self). So if the absolute poses itself as logos, it is because it negates itself as nature, but by the same token it opposes itself to nature; by excluding nature from itself it presupposes it and bears it within itself, just as nature on its side is the whole which negates itself as logos and thus opposes itself and presupposes this logos. That is why "nature is a hidden spirit"; in-itself it is logos, but a logos which is in nature in the form of having become alien to itself. One might perhaps say that these formulas are unintelligible. In this case what is unintelligible is what Hegel names the "concept," which is "what remains itself in its being-other," the identity which at the same time is a contradiction and which is a contradiction because it is an identity, an equality of that which is differentiated. The Hegelian concept is like "this ensemble of all ensembles" which

26. Logos is the *immediate* (and hence simple and abstract) unity of being and self; this immediate unity is only such because it is opposed to what negates it, to necessary mediation, to *nature;* and in this mediation, unity will rediscover itself as concrete unity, as *spirit.*

contains itself. It is the universal which remains itself in its particularization and which discovers itself in this part of itself. We must not think of nature and logos as two *species* within a genus that subsumes them, in such a way that the negation of logos, far from yielding nature, would simply yield nonlogos and would be shown to be incapable of the creative virtue that Hegel confers on speculative negation. The logos is spirit, it is the whole, the universal, but as logos it abstracts itself from itself. It is this negation of itself as nature which poses logos and which has a creative force only because it is an internal negation, a negation of self, in other words, because it is the *movement of negativity that constitutes the subject.* That is also why logos is more than itself and contains nature in-itself, why it is all of philosophy, and why we cannot however say that Hegel reduces philosophy to the formalism of the *Logic.* The whole (what Hegel calls the "universal") is always immanent in each of its determinate-nesses (which he calls the "particular"), but it is the whole and not an alien understanding that determines itself by negating itself and reconstitutes itself through the negation of negation which is self or *authentic specificity.* Thus there is no reason to speak of a causality of logos which would engender nature, "for if there were only pure thoughts, there would be no thought," nor to speak of a deduction of nature in the sense of an analytic deduction, or even of a mathematical deduction in which, according to Hegel, the abstraction of the proof is the work of comprehending spirit instead of being the very movement of the thing (*die Sache selbst*).[27] Thus there is a certain dualism in Hegelian philosophy, and indeed we must grant it, for if that were not the case, this system would not know "the seriousness, the torment, the patience, and the labor of the negative" (*PE*, I, 18; *PG*, 20; *PM*, 81). But this dualism is not the juxtaposition of two substances, logos and nature, for example; it is the work of the self which poses itself, and, insofar as it poses itself in a determination, opposes itself to itself. But precisely because it is always self that poses itself in a determinateness, it surpasses this determinateness, and as negation congruent to itself, as negation of negation, it is the self itself at the heart of this determinateness. Thus the dialectic of logos and nature is the perpetual self-positing of their living unity, which is spirit. The

27. Cf. the passage on mathematical thought as opposed to philosophical thought in the preface to the *Phenomenology* (*PE*, I, 36 ff., *PG*, 35 ff., *PM*, 100 ff.).

absolute, as Hegel had already said in his first philosophical work, is the *identity of identity and nonidentity*. Spirit—or the absolute—is therefore not only identity, but also contradiction (that between nature and logos), and the identity of this identity with this contradiction. In addition, these logical forms merely translate into a thought, a thought which reunites the ideal of *analysis* (dear to rationalist philosophers) and *synthesis* (dear to empiricist philosophers)—a profound intuition concerning the life of the spirit, to which we have continually returned during the course of this book.

Thus if we pose logos, the thought *immediately* identical to being, we are led to rediscover the opposition from which the *Phenomenology* begins, that between knowledge and being, through a first alienation of the knowledge of self.

> Indeed the spirit that knows itself, precisely because it grasps its concept, is immediate equality with itself, and in its difference (the internal difference which is contained in the concept) this equality is the certainty *of* the immediate or sensuous consciousness, the beginning from which we started; the movement of detaching itself from the form of its self is the highest freedom and the assurance of its self-knowledge (*PE*, II, 311; *PG*, 563; *PM*, 806).[28]

Logos leads us back to consciousness, for the truth which at the same time is self-certainty includes this alienation of self—this becoming other than self—through which spirit discovers itself as alien to itself in the relation of consciousness between object and subject, between *truth* and *certainty*.

But in this relation the *alienation is not complete*. "This alienation is still imperfect; it expresses the *relation* of self-certainty to the object which, precisely because it (the object) is in relation, has not yet gained its full freedom" (*PE*, II, 311; *PG*, 563; *PM*, 806). Knowledge alienates itself from itself and this alienation is termed "nature" and "history." In nature, spirit alienated itself from self by becoming a being dispersed in space; it is spirit that has lost itself, and nature is nothing other than this eternal alienation of its own subsistence and the movement that restores the subject. But we know that this movement is, so to speak, frozen in being—an immediate development—

28. For the commentary on the passage from this *immediate knowledge of self* to the knowledge *of* the immediate, see part II, chapter 1, above.

and that nature which has the form of subsistence "has no history."[29]

"The other side of the development of spirit, history, is the development that actualizes itself in knowledge [is the development that knows, that mediates itself]" (*PE*, II, 311; *PG*, 563; *PM*, 807). This is no longer an immediate development of spirit as nature; it is the mediation by means of which spirit which has alienated itself—in the form of a free contingent event—alienates its own alienation and conquers itself. History makes manifest the way in which "the negative is the negative of itself." In actual history, spirit rises to consciousness of itself as spirit. Because it had lost itself, to take up Hegel's image, it can find itself again, and it is only by finding itself again—in this result—that it makes itself what it is. Concerning this development, Hegel recapitulates what he said in the introduction to the *Phenomenology of Spirit*. In each moment of history, the spirit must penetrate the richness of its substance, where it is entirely present under a certain aspect, just as the Leibnizian monad reflected the absolute from its point of view. Every figure of world spirit is born from the preceding one and bears it within itself; it is the negation of that figure, but a *creative negation* which possesses this virtue because it is always the whole that negates itself as having clothed itself in a certain determinate form, having existed there in a particular way. This negated Dasein is internalized in a new substance of world spirit, and spirit arrives at a deeper knowledge of itself. It is this self-knowledge that is its supreme goal, a knowledge "which is the revelation of the depths" and in which spirit remains close to itself in its depth, at the heart of this extension; "and this revelation is its temporal incarnation, the time during which this alienation alienates itself into itself, and thus in its extension is also in its depth, in the self" (*PE*, II, 312; *PG*, 564; *PM*, 808).

The sequence of these spirits which succeed each other in time is *history*. Seen from the viewpoint of their conceptual organization it is the science of phenomenal knowledge (*phenomenology*). The unity of these two aspects, which Hegel distinguishes from "phenomenology" properly speaking, yields a

29. Cf. part IV, chapter 2. The presentation of his future system that Hegel gives here is not quite the same as the one he carried out in the *Encyclopaedia*, perhaps because the *Phenomenology* will then only have a specific place in it and will no longer constitute the *whole of the system* from a certain point of view.

philosophy of history, conceived history, and this history, far from being a digression, something separate from absolute spirit, an itinerary in God which would not concern God himself, "on the contrary constitutes actuality, the truth and the certainty of [absolute spirit's] throne, without which [spirit] would be a lifeless solitude" (*PE*, II, 313; *PG*, 564; *PM*, 808).

Glossary

act, action	acte, action, opération	Handlung, Tat
actuality, actual reality	effectivité	Wirklichkeit
actualize, realize	réaliser	verwirklichen
aim at, intend	viser	meinen
alien	étranger	fremd
alienation	aliénation	Entäusserung
(to) become aware	prendre conscience	
becoming, develop-ment	le devenir	das Werden
being-other	l'être-autre	Anderssein
cognizance (becoming cognizant, taking cognizance)	prendre connaissance	
contingent	contingent	zufällig
Dasein	l'être-là	Dasein
deed, work	oeuvre	Werke
determinate	déterminé	bestimmt
determinateness, determination	détermination	Bestimmheit
development (see "becoming")		
disparate	inégal	ungleich
displacement	déplacement	Verstellung
disquiet	inquiétude	Unruhe
end point	terme	
entity	l'Un	das Eins
estrangement	extranéation	Entfremdung
the existent	l'existant	das Seiendes
for-itself	pour soi	für sich
formation, education	formation	Bildung
goal	but	Zweck
the here	l'ici	das Hier

the I	*le moi*	*das Ich*
immediate	*immédiat*	*unvermittelt*
individual	*individu*	*Individuum*
individuality	*individualité*	*Individualität*
in-itself	*en-soi*	*an sich*
intellection	*intéllection*	*Einsicht*
intend (see "aim at")		
intuition	*intuition*	*die Anschauung*
knowledge	*connaissance, savoir*	*kennen, wissen*
laceration	*déchirement*	*Zerrissenheit*
mediate	*médiate*	*vermittelt*
meaning	*sens*	*der Sinn*
the now	*le maintenant*	*das Jetzt*
originary	*originaire*	*ursprüngliche*
the other	*l'Autre*	*das Andere*
particular	*particulier*	*eigen*
portrayal, representation	*représentation*	*Vorstellung*
pose, posit	*poser*	*setzen*
reactivity	*irritabilité*	*Irritabilität*
realize (see "actualize")		
reflection	*réflection*	*Reflexion*
representation (see "portrayal")		
the self	*le Soi*	*das Selbst*
sensuous	*sensible*	*sinnlich*
sensuousness	*sensibilité*	*Sinnlichkeit*
signification	*signification*	*die Bedeutung*
specific	*singulier*	*einzelne*
specificity	*singularité*	*Einzelheit*
sublimation, suppression	*suppression*	*Aufhebung*
think through	*penser*	*denken*
the this	*le ceci*	*das Diese*
transcend, go beyond	*dépasser*	*aufheben*
universal	*universel*	*Allgemein*
way of the world	*cours du monde*	*Weltlauf*
world view	*vision du monde*	*Weltanschauung*
work (see "deed")		